the AMAZING SPIDER-MAN

THE VULTURE

Stan Lee, Roger Stern, Louise Simonson, J.M. DeMatteis & Peter David
WRITERS

Steve Ditko, John Romita Sr., Don Heck, John Romita Jr., Greg LaRocque, Sal Buscema & Scot Eaton
PENCILERS

Steve Ditko, Mike Esposito, Pablo Marcos, Bob Layton, Frank Giacoia, Jim Mooney, Sal Buscema & John Dell
INKERS

Glynis Wein, Bob Sharen, George Roussos & Matt Milla
COLORISTS

Artie Simek, Sam Rosen, Joe Rosen, Phil Felix, Rick Parker & VC's Cory Petit with John Duffy
LETTERERS

Mark Gruenwald, Eliot R. Brown, Keith Williams, Eric Fein & Michael O'Connor
ASSISTANT EDITORS

Stan Lee, Tom DeFalco, Jim Owsley, Danny Fingeroth & Axel Alonso
EDITORS

Sal Buscema & Veronica Gandini
FRONT COVER ARTISTS

John Romita Sr.
BACK COVER ARTIST

COLLECTION EDITOR *Mark D. Beazley* · ASSISTANT EDITOR *Caitlin O'Connell*
ASSOCIATE MANAGING EDITOR *Kateri Woody* · ASSOCIATE MANAGER, DIGITAL ASSETS *Joe Hochstein*
MASTERWORKS EDITOR *Cory Sedlmeier* · SENIOR EDITOR, SPECIAL PROJECTS *Jennifer Grünwald*
VP PRODUCTION & SPECIAL PROJECTS *Jeff Youngquist* · RESEARCH & LAYOUT *Jeph York*
PRODUCTION *ColorTek & Ryan Devall* · BOOK DESIGNER *Jay Bowen*
SVP PRINT, SALES & MARKETING *David Gabriel*

EDITOR IN CHIEF *Axel Alonso* · CHIEF CREATIVE OFFICER *Joe Quesada*
PRESIDENT *Dan Buckley* · EXECUTIVE PRODUCER *Alan Fine*

SPECIAL THANKS TO **GARY HENDERSON**
SPIDER-MAN CREATED BY **STAN LEE & STEVE DITKO**

SPIDER-MAN VS. THE VULTURE. Contains material originally published in magazine form as AMAZING SPIDER-MAN #2, #7, #63-64, #224 and #240-241; WEB OF SPIDER-MAN #3; SPECTACULAR SPIDER-MAN #186-188; and FRIENDLY NEIGHBORHOOD SPIDER-MAN #14-16. First printing 2017. ISBN# 978-1-302-90706-8. Published by MARVEL WORLDWIDE, INC., a subsidiary of MARVEL ENTERTAINMENT, LLC. OFFICE OF PUBLICATION: 135 West 50th Street, New York, NY 10020. **Printed in the U.S.A.** DAN BUCKLEY, President, Marvel Entertainment; JOE QUESADA, Chief Creative Officer; TOM BREVOORT, SVP of Publishing; DAVID BOGART, SVP of Business Affairs & Operations, Publishing & Partnership; C.B. CEBULSKI, VP of Brand Management & Development, Asia; DAVID GABRIEL, SVP of Sales & Marketing, Publishing; JEFF YOUNGQUIST, VP of Production & Special Projects; DAN CARR, Executive Director of Publishing Technology; ALEX MORALES, Director of Publishing Operations; SUSAN CRESPI, Production Manager; STAN LEE, Chairman Emeritus. For information regarding advertising in Marvel Comics or on Marvel.com, please contact Vit DeBellis, Integrated Sales Manager, at vdebellis@marvel.com. For Marvel subscription inquiries, please call 888-511-5480. **Manufactured between 3/24/2017 and 4/25/2017 by LSC COMMUNICATIONS INC., SALEM, VA, USA.**

10 9 8 7 6 5 4 3 2 1

We're going to take a terrifying little trip through time in search of one Adrian Toomes, better known to Marvelites and the fearful citizenry of New York City as the Vulture. He was the second costumed foe to face the fledgling Spider-Man way back in 1962, following the Chameleon in *Amazing Spider-Man #1*. Aside from the uniquely Ditkoesque design of the outfit, the Vulture has one very distinguishing physical characteristic: He's old. Being a super villain is usually a young, or, at the very least, a middle-aged man's game. But our Adrian must be well into his sixties—and that was when he was introduced. Now, even though Medicare would pick up the tab if Vulchy's wings failed him and he fell out of the sky, you might think that a gent of his age would simply sit back, relax and collect his Social Security checks. Nope. As we see in his very first appearance, Toomes is determined to rob every bank or jewelry store in Manhattan. And he's got just the nest to return to for a man with his moniker: an abandoned silo in a rural section of Staten Island, moments from the city as the crow—I mean as the Vulture—flies.

Drawn in the inimitable Steve Ditko style, Adrian Toomes is an aged, bald-headed old coot with every line and crease in a face that bespeaks many decades of life. There's something genuinely chilling about seeing this beak-nosed baddie glide through the concrete canyons of New York, on his next mission of larceny. And in pitched battle with the young web-spinner, this human bird of prey gives Spidey everything he could handle, even though there is probably a 40-year age difference between the two. Think about that the next time you yell at a senior citizen to get out of the way.

Apparently, the Vulture's first outing went over big time, because he flew in again to prey on the unsuspecting city in issue seven. Stan's caption on page one said Marvel was swamped with reader requests to see the flying felon again. Lee and Ditko were only too happy to oblige with another polished gem. This one featured a doozy of a climax set in the *Daily Bugle/Now Magazine* offices as the Vulture attempts to steal the newspaper's payroll over the pathetic protests of Publisher J. Jonah Jameson. And even as Spider-Man rescues Jonah and captures the Vulture, Jameson's hatred for the web-slinger is so great that he still blames our hero for wrecking his offices, until he gets his mouth webbed shut. Some guys just get no respect— and I don't mean jolly Jonah.

When everyone's favorite aerial antagonist made his next return, it was illustrated by one of the few men who could replace the departed Steve Ditko, and that was John

Romita Sr. Romita brought his own distinctive look to this title and sales only continued to rise during the Jazzy One's reign. The splash page in issue 63 alone is worth the price of the comic. It's a suitable-for-framing profile shot of the Vulture, poised on a building ledge above the rain-soaked city. It just screams atmosphere. I remember, after buying that issue, just gazing at that page for what seemed like an hour, feeling the coiled power in that silhouetted figure. The fine-feathered fiend had come back from the brink of death and decided to take down Blackie Drago, the man who assumed the Vulture identity and betrayed Toomes when it seemed he was done for. But there is only one man worthy to wear the wings, and Drago finds that out fast enough. And to emphasize that point, despite Spider-Man's best efforts, it's the hero who's on the ground at the story's end and the Vulture who escapes scot-free. Who says the good guys always get their man?

Despite the impact the Vulture made in *Amazing Spider-Man*, for many years, the dirty bird was a bit of a cipher. He was hard to get a handle on if you were looking for some deep motivating factor in his criminal enterprise. He seemed to have no motive beyond sweeping into the local bank and making off with a big bag of cash until the web-spinner arrived on the scene and took him down. Of course, there was always the revenge-on-Spidey urge, but that was a common element among the criminal class. We knew almost nothing about Toomes' background. Who was he? Where did he get the knowledge to build the sophisticated device that powered the costume? His avian alter ego appeared out of nowhere like an actual vulture in issue two to pick the city clean. Each time he showed up subsequently, we found out nothing beyond his surface desire to get rich quick. That certainly didn't hamper anyone's enjoyment of those heralded issues. It's just a point of curiosity how long it took to get his backstory.

All that changed with an awesome two-part tale beginning in *Amazing Spider-Man #240*. Spidey scribe Roger Stern and penciler John Romita Jr., son of the much-lauded Sr., took on the task. At long last we learned why Adrian Toomes assumed the Vulture identity and its significance. Further, we discovered why an old man with no apparent strength-enhancing paraphernalia could go toe-to-claw with a man who has the proportionate strength of a spider. Roger tied it all up very neatly and logically, as is his wont. I'm not going to spoil the origin's surprises for you, but be prepared to see the Vulture through a different lens after these two landmark issues. And don't miss that cover on *#241* with a truly iconic pose of the Vulture. Wow!

After a fine *Web Of Spider-Man* story, we round out this scintillating volume with a pair of three-part powerhouses. In *Spectacular Spider-Man*, scribe Marc DeMatteis crafted an emotional tale that drew Adrian Toomes deeply into the orbit of one Peter Parker. That's right, I said Peter Parker. Things started to get personal between the two and the feathers really flew. I've had the privilege of working with Marc on Spider-Man for several years in the past. He has a knack for getting inside characters' heads like few other scripters can. It's really his specialty. Something I noticed when I served as his editor: Mr. DeMatteis tends to take both hero and villain through their respective dark nights of the soul. The "Funeral Arrangements" storyline is a wrenching journey that examines the seminal topics of life and death in a manner that will leave you emotionally drained. But you'll love every page of it.

I was also favored to work with artist Sal Buscema on *Spider-Man*. Sal is a true gentleman and an absolute pleasure to work with. And no disrespect to any of the superb inkers who've embellished Sal's pencils through the years, but his art reaches new levels when he inks himself as he has here. The layouts take on a higher aspect of sophistication and power, moving the story forward inexorably. And the facial expressions convey so much visual impact, truly enhancing whatever words are in the accompanying balloons. This second Buscema brother really comes into his own here and you Spiderophiles are the lucky beneficiaries.

Not to be outdone, writer Peter David and penciler Scot Eaton finish off this collection in fine style with a triple-header that unexpectedly finds the vituperative Vulture in a role you could never possibly guess: The designated agent of the United States government. His assignment is to hunt and capture—Spider-Man?! If you've been

reading these classics in order of publication, this one is well worth the wait. You'll be utterly stunned at the circumstances that form the scaffolding of "Unmasked." And the slick penciling of Eaton dovetails perfectly with this incredibly offbeat tale.

Rereading all these issues featuring everybody's favorite flying felon has been such a treat for me. They span a more-than-40-year period in which Adrian Toomes has been a constant threat to your friendly neighborhood Spider-Man. And along the way, I went from wide-eyed Spidey reader to longtime Marvel editor, albeit one who never lost his love for this masterfully conceived super villain from the Lee/Ditko dream machine. As you peruse these stories, you'll note how Toomes becomes an increasingly fascinating addition to Spidey's rogues' gallery, as the layers of his background and personality are laid bare. It almost reads like a good novel rather than a series of separate issues.

Now listen to the sinister sound of those flapping wings as a menacing shadow falls over an anxious city. The Vulture is on the prowl! So keep looking over your shoulder, Believer, because no one is safe from his predations. Not even you.

Enjoy

Ralph Macchio

Ralph Macchio

RALPH MACCHIO SPENT OVER 35 YEARS AT MARVEL, STARTING AS AN ASSISTANT EDITOR AND LATER WRITING *AVENGERS, THOR* AND MANY OTHERS. AS EDITOR, HE OVERSAW BOOKS ACROSS THE MARVEL LINE, INCLUDING SHEPHERDING THE ULTIMATE LINE INTO EXISTENCE, AND EDITING ALL OF STEPHEN KING'S MARVEL ADAPTATIONS.

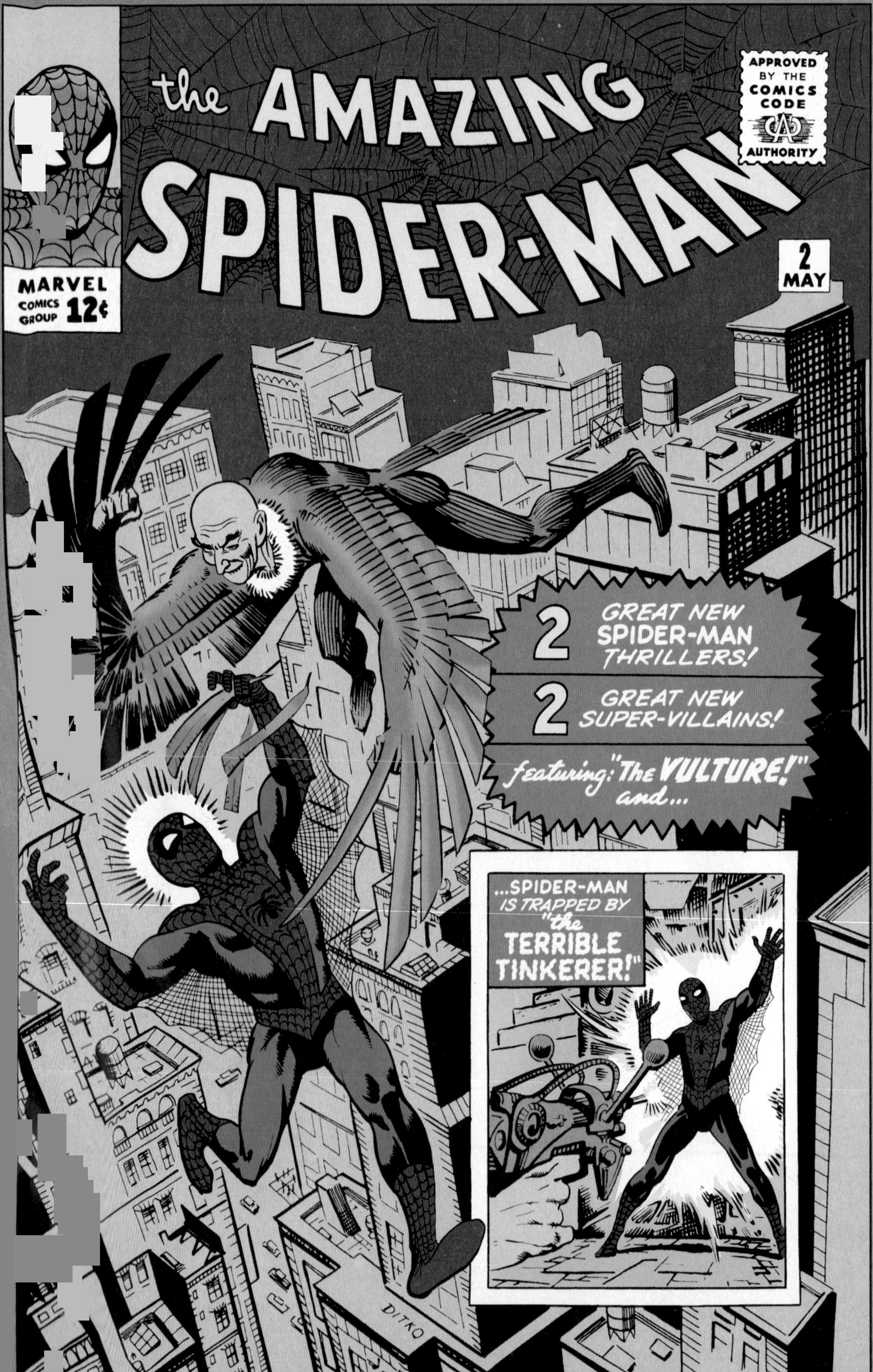

the AMAZING SPIDER-MAN
APPROVED BY THE COMICS CODE AUTHORITY
MARVEL COMICS GROUP 12¢
2 MAY
2 GREAT NEW SPIDER-MAN THRILLERS!
2 GREAT NEW SUPER-VILLAINS!
featuring: "The VULTURE!" and...
...SPIDER-MAN IS TRAPPED BY "the TERRIBLE TINKERER!"
DITKO

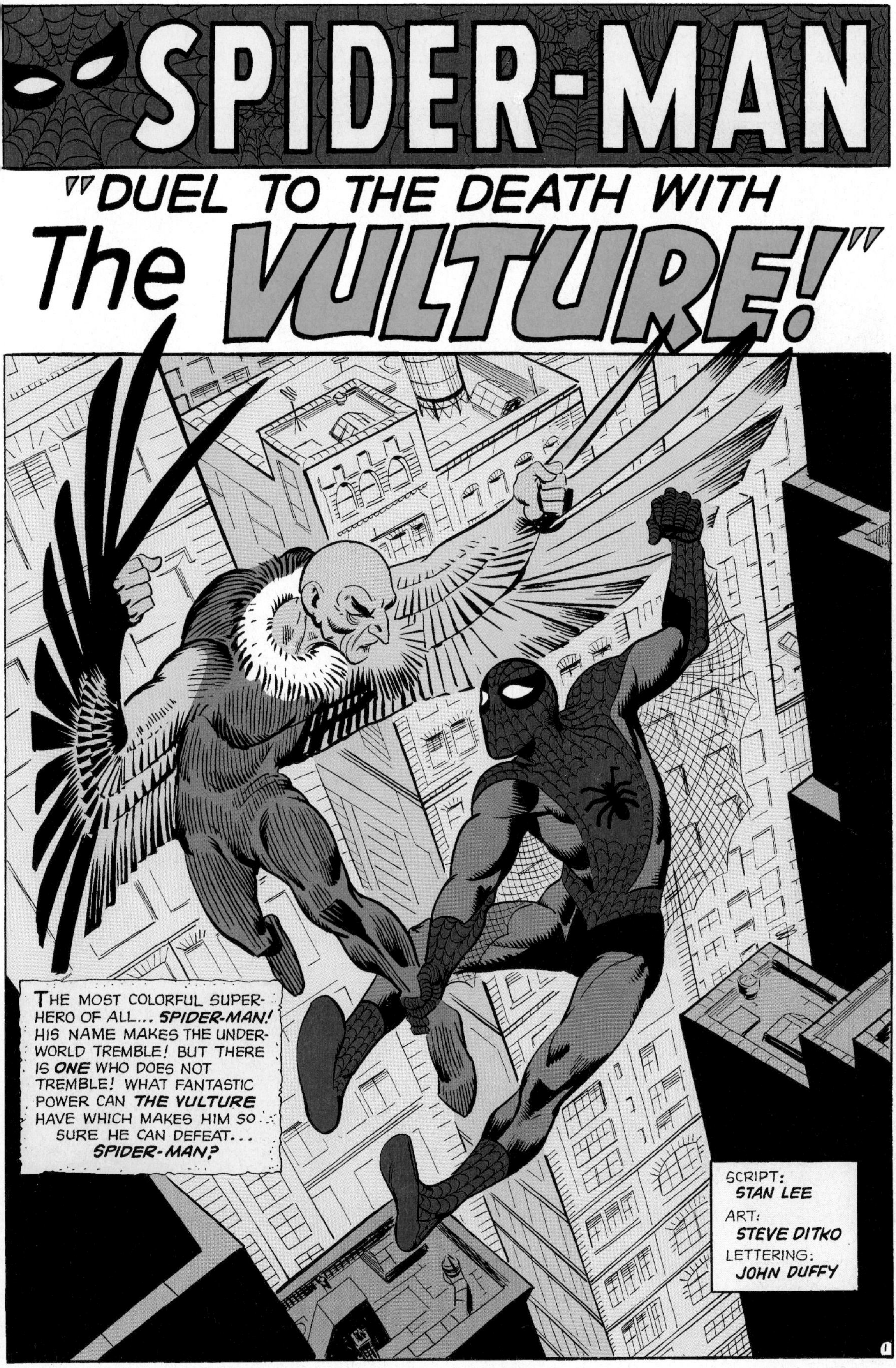
SPIDER-MAN
"DUEL TO THE DEATH WITH The VULTURE!"
THE MOST COLORFUL SUPER-HERO OF ALL... SPIDER-MAN! HIS NAME MAKES THE UNDER-WORLD TREMBLE! BUT THERE IS ONE WHO DOES NOT TREMBLE! WHAT FANTASTIC POWER CAN THE VULTURE HAVE WHICH MAKES HIM SO SURE HE CAN DEFEAT... SPIDER-MAN?
SCRIPT: STAN LEE
ART: STEVE DITKO
LETTERING: JOHN DUFFY

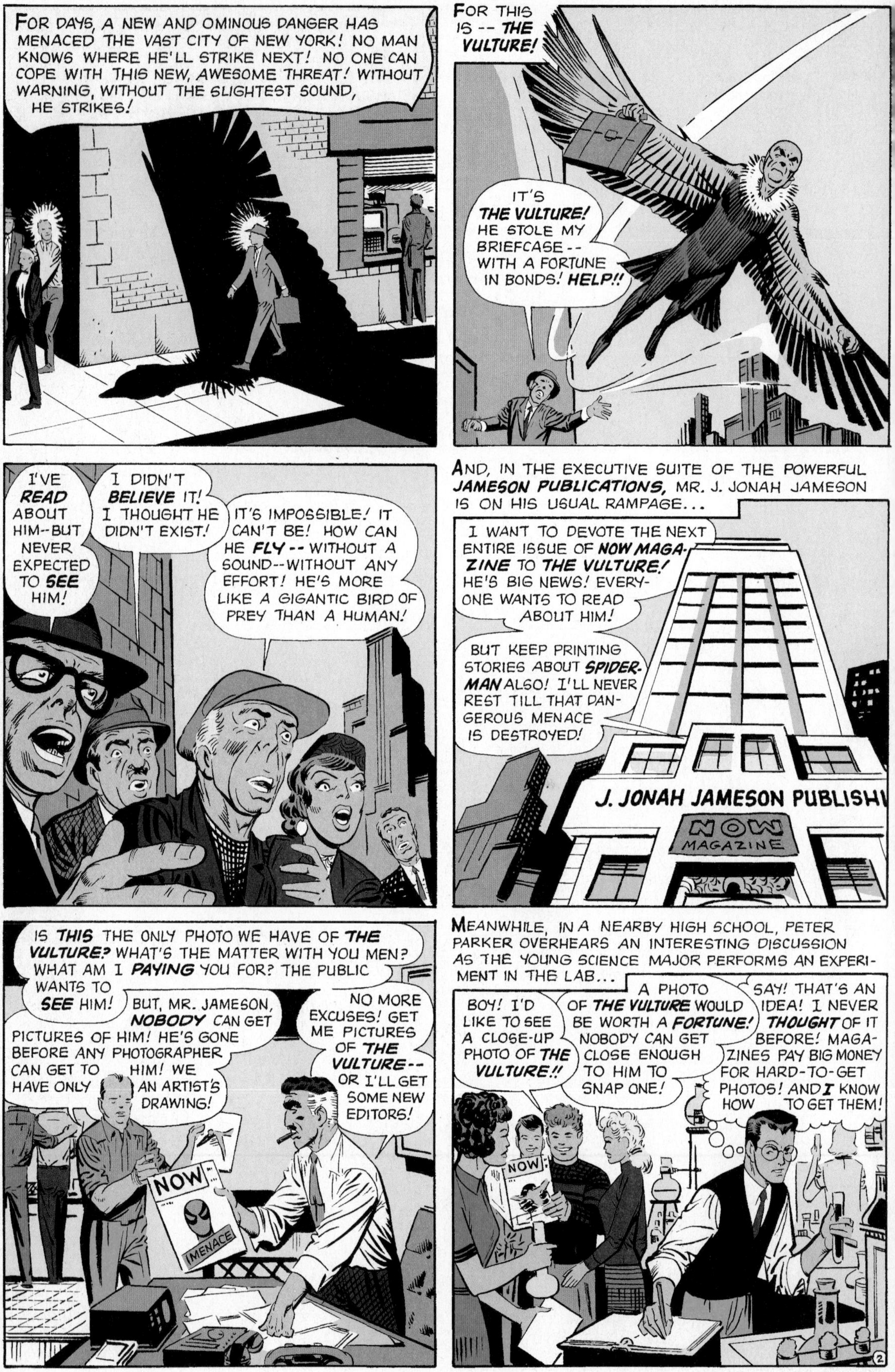
FOR DAYS, A NEW AND OMINOUS DANGER HAS MENACED THE VAST CITY OF NEW YORK! NO MAN KNOWS WHERE HE'LL STRIKE NEXT! NO ONE CAN COPE WITH THIS NEW, AWESOME THREAT! WITHOUT WARNING, WITHOUT THE SLIGHTEST SOUND, HE STRIKES!
FOR THIS IS -- THE VULTURE!
IT'S THE VULTURE! HE STOLE MY BRIEFCASE -- WITH A FORTUNE IN BONDS! HELP!!
I'VE READ ABOUT HIM--BUT NEVER EXPECTED TO SEE HIM!
I DIDN'T BELIEVE IT! I THOUGHT HE DIDN'T EXIST!
IT'S IMPOSSIBLE! IT CAN'T BE! HOW CAN HE FLY -- WITHOUT A SOUND--WITHOUT ANY EFFORT! HE'S MORE LIKE A GIGANTIC BIRD OF PREY THAN A HUMAN!
AND, IN THE EXECUTIVE SUITE OF THE POWERFUL JAMESON PUBLICATIONS, MR. J. JONAH JAMESON IS ON HIS USUAL RAMPAGE...
I WANT TO DEVOTE THE NEXT ENTIRE ISSUE OF NOW MAGAZINE TO THE VULTURE! HE'S BIG NEWS! EVERYONE WANTS TO READ ABOUT HIM!
BUT KEEP PRINTING STORIES ABOUT SPIDER-MAN ALSO! I'LL NEVER REST TILL THAT DANGEROUS MENACE IS DESTROYED!
J. JONAH JAMESON PUBLISH
NOW MAGAZINE
IS THIS THE ONLY PHOTO WE HAVE OF THE VULTURE? WHAT'S THE MATTER WITH YOU MEN? WHAT AM I PAYING YOU FOR? THE PUBLIC WANTS TO SEE HIM!
BUT, MR. JAMESON, NOBODY CAN GET PICTURES OF HIM! HE'S GONE BEFORE ANY PHOTOGRAPHER CAN GET TO HIM! WE HAVE ONLY AN ARTIST'S DRAWING!
NO MORE EXCUSES! GET ME PICTURES OF THE VULTURE -- OR I'LL GET SOME NEW EDITORS!
NOW
MENACE
MEANWHILE, IN A NEARBY HIGH SCHOOL, PETER PARKER OVERHEARS AN INTERESTING DISCUSSION AS THE YOUNG SCIENCE MAJOR PERFORMS AN EXPERIMENT IN THE LAB...
BOY! I'D LIKE TO SEE A CLOSE-UP PHOTO OF THE VULTURE!!
A PHOTO OF THE VULTURE WOULD BE WORTH A FORTUNE! NOBODY CAN GET CLOSE ENOUGH TO HIM TO SNAP ONE!
SAY! THAT'S AN IDEA! I NEVER THOUGHT OF IT BEFORE! MAGAZINES PAY BIG MONEY FOR HARD-TO-GET PHOTOS! AND I KNOW HOW TO GET THEM!
NOW

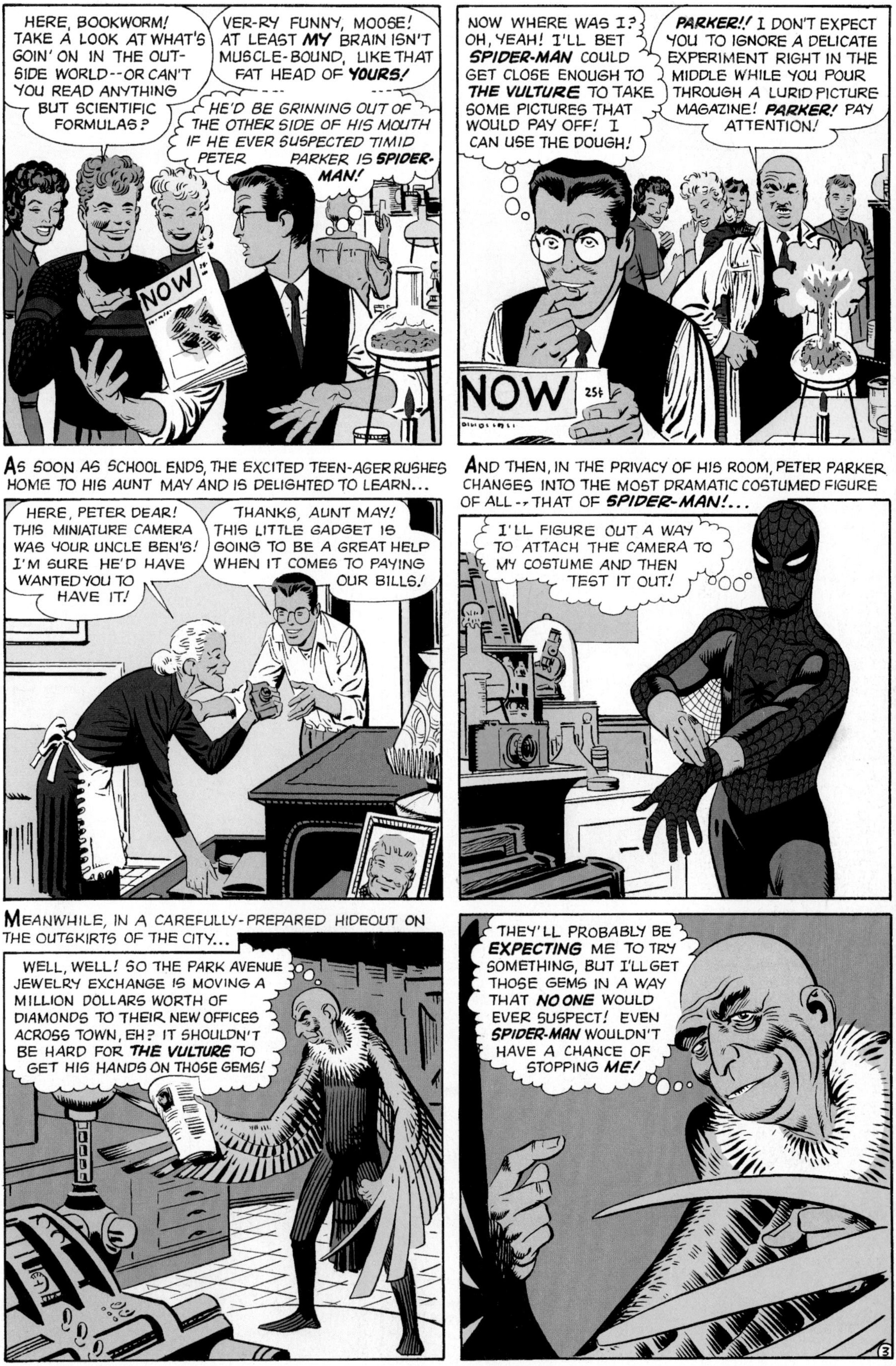
HERE, BOOKWORM! TAKE A LOOK AT WHAT'S GOIN' ON IN THE OUT-SIDE WORLD--OR CAN'T YOU READ ANYTHING BUT SCIENTIFIC FORMULAS?
VER-RY FUNNY, MOOSE! AT LEAST MY BRAIN ISN'T MUSCLE-BOUND, LIKE THAT FAT HEAD OF YOURS!
HE'D BE GRINNING OUT OF THE OTHER SIDE OF HIS MOUTH IF HE EVER SUSPECTED TIMID PETER PARKER IS SPIDER-MAN!
NOW
NOW WHERE WAS I? OH, YEAH! I'LL BET SPIDER-MAN COULD GET CLOSE ENOUGH TO THE VULTURE TO TAKE SOME PICTURES THAT WOULD PAY OFF! I CAN USE THE DOUGH!
PARKER!! I DON'T EXPECT YOU TO IGNORE A DELICATE EXPERIMENT RIGHT IN THE MIDDLE WHILE YOU POUR THROUGH A LURID PICTURE MAGAZINE! PARKER! PAY ATTENTION!
NOW
25¢
AS SOON AS SCHOOL ENDS, THE EXCITED TEEN-AGER RUSHES HOME TO HIS AUNT MAY AND IS DELIGHTED TO LEARN...
HERE, PETER DEAR! THIS MINIATURE CAMERA WAS YOUR UNCLE BEN'S! I'M SURE HE'D HAVE WANTED YOU TO HAVE IT!
THANKS, AUNT MAY! THIS LITTLE GADGET IS GOING TO BE A GREAT HELP WHEN IT COMES TO PAYING OUR BILLS!
AND THEN, IN THE PRIVACY OF HIS ROOM, PETER PARKER CHANGES INTO THE MOST DRAMATIC COSTUMED FIGURE OF ALL--THAT OF SPIDER-MAN!...
I'LL FIGURE OUT A WAY TO ATTACH THE CAMERA TO MY COSTUME AND THEN TEST IT OUT!
MEANWHILE, IN A CAREFULLY-PREPARED HIDEOUT ON THE OUTSKIRTS OF THE CITY...
WELL, WELL! SO THE PARK AVENUE JEWELRY EXCHANGE IS MOVING A MILLION DOLLARS WORTH OF DIAMONDS TO THEIR NEW OFFICES ACROSS TOWN, EH? IT SHOULDN'T BE HARD FOR THE VULTURE TO GET HIS HANDS ON THOSE GEMS!
THEY'LL PROBABLY BE EXPECTING ME TO TRY SOMETHING, BUT I'LL GET THOSE GEMS IN A WAY THAT NO ONE WOULD EVER SUSPECT! EVEN SPIDER-MAN WOULDN'T HAVE A CHANCE OF STOPPING ME!
3

AFTER MAKING CERTAIN HE IS NOT OBSERVED, *THE VULTURE* DARTS FROM HIS HIDING PLACE ATOP AN ABANDONED SILO IN STATEN ISLAND, JUST A FEW SECONDS FROM THE HEART OF MANHATTEN...

NOW FOR THE FIRST PART OF MY INGENIOUS PLAN!

SECONDS LATER, ATOP AN APARTMENT HOUSE WHERE HE HAD BEEN CHECKING HIS CAMERA, *SPIDER-MAN'S* AMAZING SPIDER SENSES PICK UP A STRANGE SENSATION...

SOMETHING COMING THROUGH THE AIR--BUT MAKING NO SOUND!... CAN'T BE A PLANE...

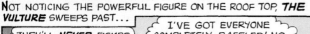

NOT NOTICING THE POWERFUL FIGURE ON THE ROOF TOP, *THE VULTURE* SWEEPS PAST...

THEY'LL *NEVER* FIGURE OUT HOW I'M GOING TO STEAL THOSE DIAMONDS!

I'VE GOT EVERYONE COMPLETELY BAFFLED! NO ONE HAS YET DISCOVERED HOW I MANAGE TO *FLY* WITH THESE ARTIFICIAL WINGS!

WHAT LUCK!... IT'S *THE VULTURE!*

I'LL TOSS SOME MESSAGES WHERE THEY'LL DO THE MOST GOOD!

THE FIRST ONE IS FOR THE *JAMESON PUBLISHING COMPANY* BUILDING!

J.J.

MY NEXT MESSAGE IS FOR THE RADIO NETWORK! NOTHING I LIKE BETTER THAN TAUNTING MY ENEMIES!

C RADIO

AND, FINALLY, ONE FOR THE POLICE CHIEF HIMSELF! I'LL BE GONE BEFORE THEY HAVE A CHANCE TO READ THEM!

THE VULTURE HAS NEVER FAILED TO CARRY OUT A THREAT YET!

BUT WE *MUST* GO AHEAD WITH THE TRANSFER OF THE DIAMONDS! WE CAN'T LET THE CITY THINK THAT ONE CRIMINAL CAN MAKE US CHANGE OUR PLANS!

I SHALL STEAL THE DIAMOND SHIPMENT FROM UNDER YOUR NOSES!
The Vulture

8

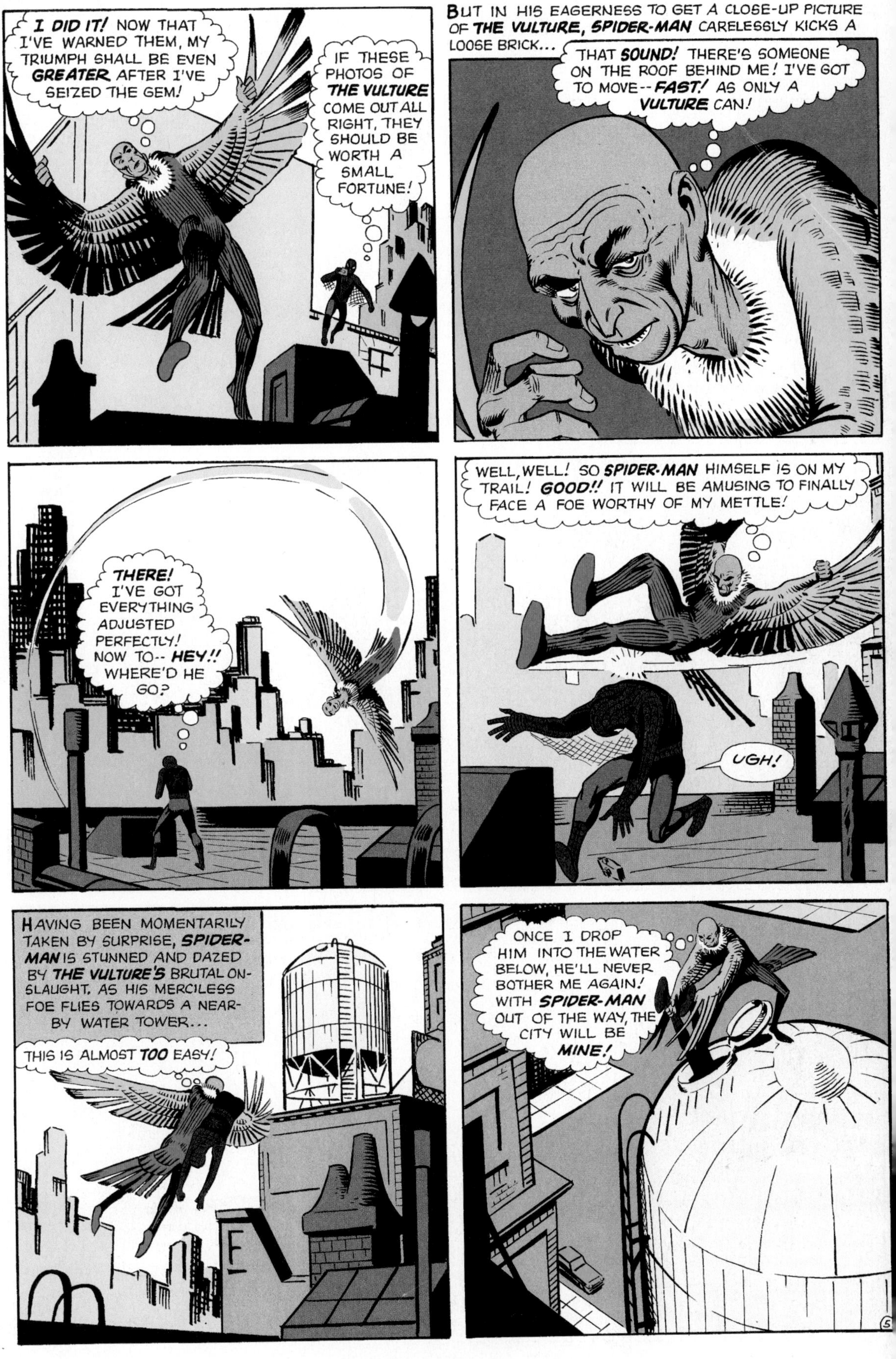
I DID IT! NOW THAT I'VE WARNED THEM, MY TRIUMPH SHALL BE EVEN GREATER AFTER I'VE SEIZED THE GEM!
IF THESE PHOTOS OF THE VULTURE COME OUT ALL RIGHT, THEY SHOULD BE WORTH A SMALL FORTUNE!
BUT IN HIS EAGERNESS TO GET A CLOSE-UP PICTURE OF THE VULTURE, SPIDER-MAN CARELESSLY KICKS A LOOSE BRICK...
THAT SOUND! THERE'S SOMEONE ON THE ROOF BEHIND ME! I'VE GOT TO MOVE--FAST! AS ONLY A VULTURE CAN!
THERE! I'VE GOT EVERYTHING ADJUSTED PERFECTLY! NOW TO-- HEY!! WHERE'D HE GO?
WELL, WELL! SO SPIDER-MAN HIMSELF IS ON MY TRAIL! GOOD!! IT WILL BE AMUSING TO FINALLY FACE A FOE WORTHY OF MY METTLE!
UGH!
HAVING BEEN MOMENTARILY TAKEN BY SURPRISE, SPIDER-MAN IS STUNNED AND DAZED BY THE VULTURE'S BRUTAL ON-SLAUGHT. AS HIS MERCILESS FOE FLIES TOWARDS A NEAR-BY WATER TOWER...
THIS IS ALMOST TOO EASY!
ONCE I DROP HIM INTO THE WATER BELOW, HE'LL NEVER BOTHER ME AGAIN! WITH SPIDER-MAN OUT OF THE WAY, THE CITY WILL BE MINE!
5

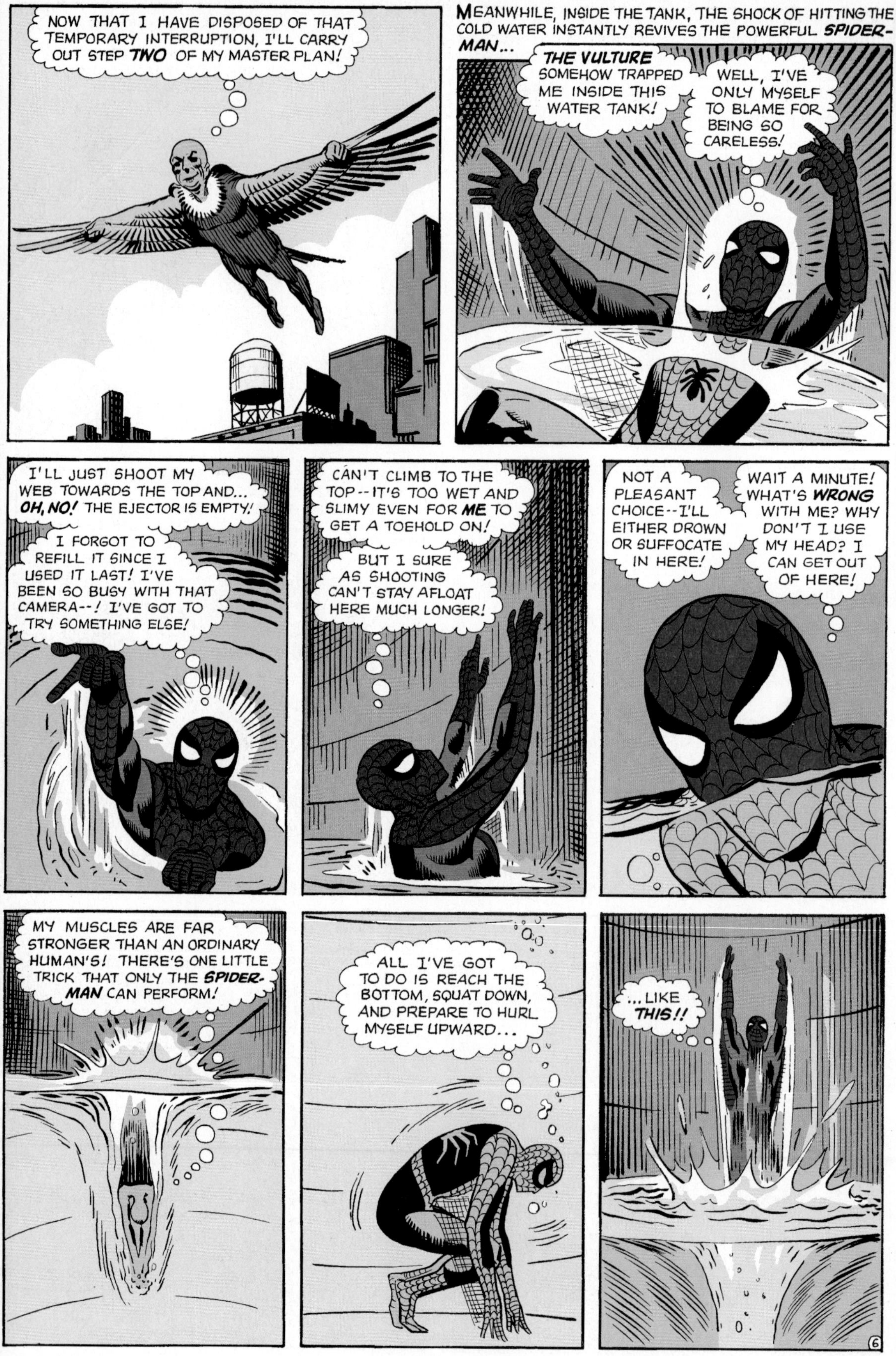
NOW THAT I HAVE DISPOSED OF THAT TEMPORARY INTERRUPTION, I'LL CARRY OUT STEP TWO OF MY MASTER PLAN!
MEANWHILE, INSIDE THE TANK, THE SHOCK OF HITTING THE COLD WATER INSTANTLY REVIVES THE POWERFUL SPIDER-MAN...
THE VULTURE SOMEHOW TRAPPED ME INSIDE THIS WATER TANK!
WELL, I'VE ONLY MYSELF TO BLAME FOR BEING SO CARELESS!
I'LL JUST SHOOT MY WEB TOWARDS THE TOP AND... OH, NO! THE EJECTOR IS EMPTY!
I FORGOT TO REFILL IT SINCE I USED IT LAST! I'VE BEEN SO BUSY WITH THAT CAMERA--! I'VE GOT TO TRY SOMETHING ELSE!
CAN'T CLIMB TO THE TOP--IT'S TOO WET AND SLIMY EVEN FOR ME TO GET A TOEHOLD ON!
BUT I SURE AS SHOOTING CAN'T STAY AFLOAT HERE MUCH LONGER!
NOT A PLEASANT CHOICE--I'LL EITHER DROWN OR SUFFOCATE IN HERE!
WAIT A MINUTE! WHAT'S WRONG WITH ME? WHY DON'T I USE MY HEAD? I CAN GET OUT OF HERE!
MY MUSCLES ARE FAR STRONGER THAN AN ORDINARY HUMAN'S! THERE'S ONE LITTLE TRICK THAT ONLY THE SPIDER-MAN CAN PERFORM!
ALL I'VE GOT TO DO IS REACH THE BOTTOM, SQUAT DOWN, AND PREPARE TO HURL MYSELF UPWARD...
...LIKE THIS!!
6

DID IT!!

I MAY NOT BE ABLE TO FLY LIKE *THE VULTURE*-- BUT MY SPIDER STRENGTH HASN'T LET ME DOWN *YET!*

MY LUCK'S STILL HOLDING OUT-- HERE'S MY CAMERA!

SURE IS UNBELIEVABLE HOW *THE VULTURE* MANAGES TO FLY SO SWIFTLY! I'D SURE LIKE TO FIGURE OUT HOW HE *DOES* IT!

LATER, IN HIS ROOM AGAIN...

THE PICTURES CAME OUT FINE! NOW, WHOM DO I SELL THEM TO? JONAH JAMESON, THE PUBLISHER OF *NOW* MAGAZINE HATES *SPIDER-MAN!* I'D GET A KICK OUT OF MAKING *HIM* PAY GOOD DOUGH FOR MY PICTURES WITHOUT KNOW-ING *I'M* THE PHOTOGRAPHER!

NOW 25¢
SPIDER-MAN MUST BE CAUGHT!

ORIGINALLY, I DESIGNED MY *SPIDER-MAN* COSTUME JUST TO GIVE ME SOME COLOR, SO THAT I COULD MAKE MONEY AS AN ENTERTAINER! BUT, IF...

...I'M REALLY GOING TO BE A SECRET ADVEN-TURER, I'VE GOT TO MAKE SOME CHANGES! FIRST, I'LL ADD AN EXTRA WEB-FLUID CAPSULE, SO I ALWAYS HAVE ENOUGH SPIDER-WEBBING ON HAND!

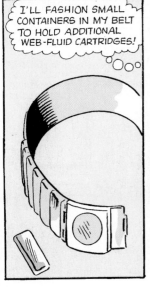

I'LL FASHION SMALL CONTAINERS IN MY BELT TO HOLD ADDITIONAL WEB-FLUID CARTRIDGES!

THEN, WHEN I GET PAID FOR MY PICTURES, I'LL BUY A SPECIAL MINIATURE CAMERA TO SECRETLY ATTACH TO THE BELT BUCKLE!

THERE! THE WHOLE CONTRAPTION FITS UNDER MY SHIRT, WHERE IT'S OUT OF SIGHT, AND DOESN'T INTERFERE WITH MY MOVEMENTS!

AND NOW, I'VE GOT A HUNCH I KNOW THE SECRET OF *THE VULTURE'S* POWER OF FLIGHT! I'LL JUST WORK ON A LITTLE DEVICE WHICH MAY COME IN HANDY NEXT TIME WE MEET!

⑦

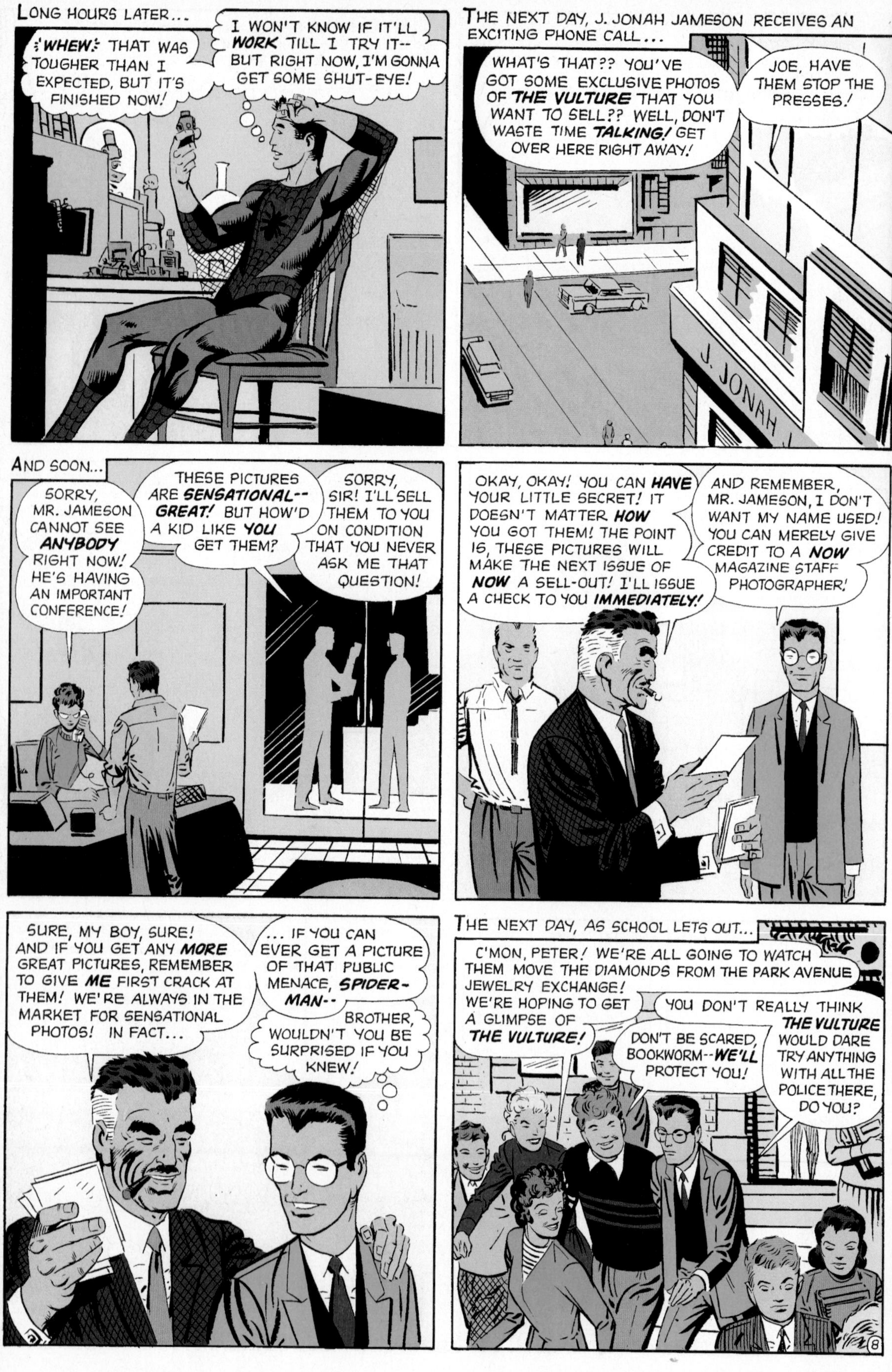
LONG HOURS LATER...
WHEW! THAT WAS TOUGHER THAN I EXPECTED, BUT IT'S FINISHED NOW!
I WON'T KNOW IF IT'LL WORK TILL I TRY IT-- BUT RIGHT NOW, I'M GONNA GET SOME SHUT-EYE!
THE NEXT DAY, J. JONAH JAMESON RECEIVES AN EXCITING PHONE CALL...
WHAT'S THAT?? YOU'VE GOT SOME EXCLUSIVE PHOTOS OF THE VULTURE THAT YOU WANT TO SELL?? WELL, DON'T WASTE TIME TALKING! GET OVER HERE RIGHT AWAY!
JOE, HAVE THEM STOP THE PRESSES!
J. JONAH J
AND SOON...
SORRY, MR. JAMESON CANNOT SEE ANYBODY RIGHT NOW! HE'S HAVING AN IMPORTANT CONFERENCE!
THESE PICTURES ARE SENSATIONAL-- GREAT! BUT HOW'D A KID LIKE YOU GET THEM?
SORRY, SIR! I'LL SELL THEM TO YOU ON CONDITION THAT YOU NEVER ASK ME THAT QUESTION!
OKAY, OKAY! YOU CAN HAVE YOUR LITTLE SECRET! IT DOESN'T MATTER HOW YOU GOT THEM! THE POINT IS, THESE PICTURES WILL MAKE THE NEXT ISSUE OF NOW A SELL-OUT! I'LL ISSUE A CHECK TO YOU IMMEDIATELY!
AND REMEMBER, MR. JAMESON, I DON'T WANT MY NAME USED! YOU CAN MERELY GIVE CREDIT TO A NOW MAGAZINE STAFF PHOTOGRAPHER!
SURE, MY BOY, SURE! AND IF YOU GET ANY MORE GREAT PICTURES, REMEMBER TO GIVE ME FIRST CRACK AT THEM! WE'RE ALWAYS IN THE MARKET FOR SENSATIONAL PHOTOS! IN FACT...
... IF YOU CAN EVER GET A PICTURE OF THAT PUBLIC MENACE, SPIDER-MAN--
BROTHER, WOULDN'T YOU BE SURPRISED IF YOU KNEW!
THE NEXT DAY, AS SCHOOL LETS OUT...
C'MON, PETER! WE'RE ALL GOING TO WATCH THEM MOVE THE DIAMONDS FROM THE PARK AVENUE JEWELRY EXCHANGE! WE'RE HOPING TO GET A GLIMPSE OF THE VULTURE!
YOU DON'T REALLY THINK THE VULTURE WOULD DARE TRY ANYTHING WITH ALL THE POLICE THERE, DO YOU?
DON'T BE SCARED, BOOKWORM--WE'LL PROTECT YOU!
8

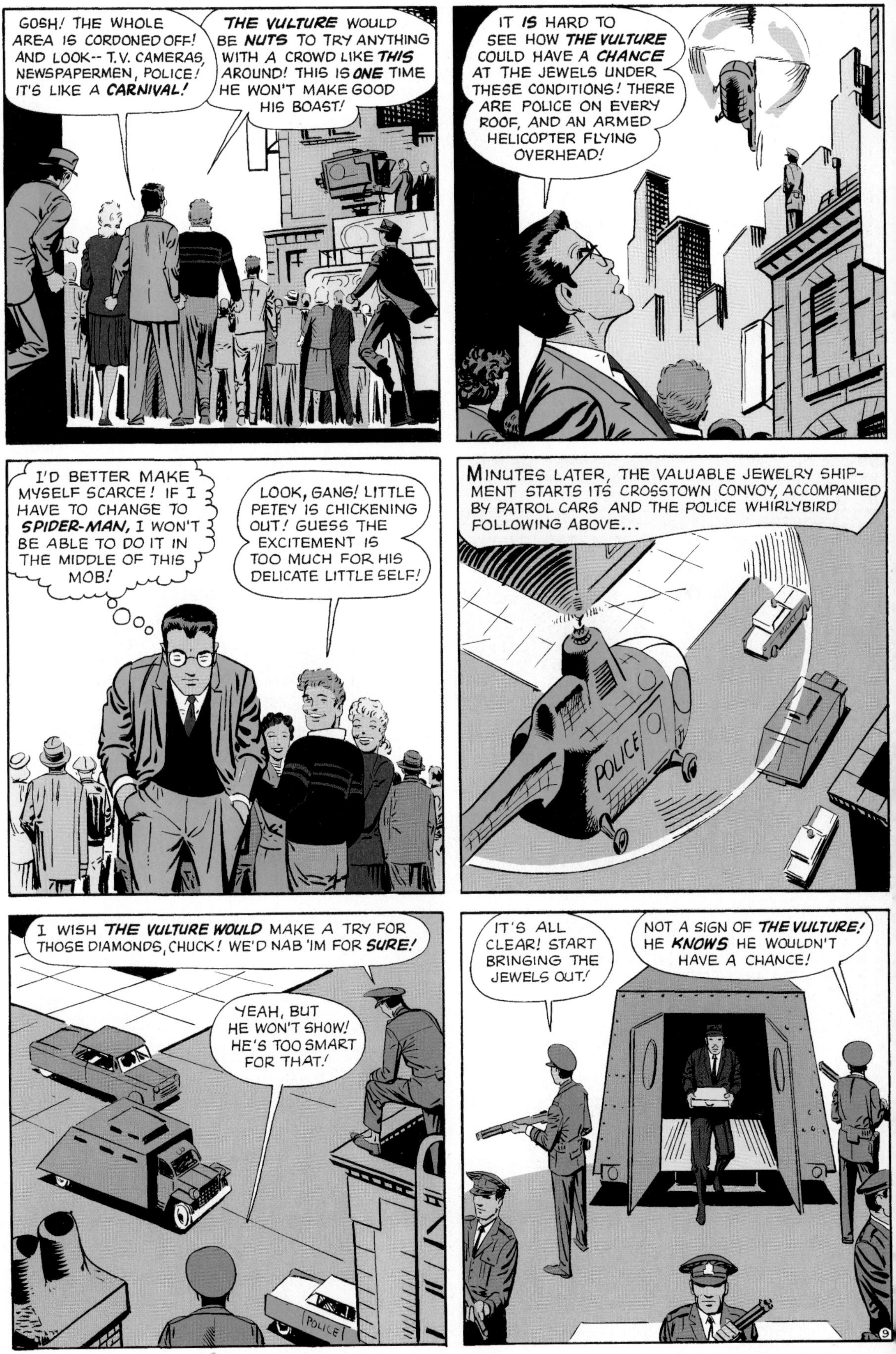
GOSH! THE WHOLE AREA IS CORDONED OFF! AND LOOK-- T.V. CAMERAS, NEWSPAPERMEN, POLICE! IT'S LIKE A CARNIVAL!
THE VULTURE WOULD BE NUTS TO TRY ANYTHING WITH A CROWD LIKE THIS AROUND! THIS IS ONE TIME HE WON'T MAKE GOOD HIS BOAST!
IT IS HARD TO SEE HOW THE VULTURE COULD HAVE A CHANCE AT THE JEWELS UNDER THESE CONDITIONS! THERE ARE POLICE ON EVERY ROOF, AND AN ARMED HELICOPTER FLYING OVERHEAD!
I'D BETTER MAKE MYSELF SCARCE! IF I HAVE TO CHANGE TO SPIDER-MAN, I WON'T BE ABLE TO DO IT IN THE MIDDLE OF THIS MOB!
LOOK, GANG! LITTLE PETEY IS CHICKENING OUT! GUESS THE EXCITEMENT IS TOO MUCH FOR HIS DELICATE LITTLE SELF!
MINUTES LATER, THE VALUABLE JEWELRY SHIPMENT STARTS ITS CROSSTOWN CONVOY, ACCOMPANIED BY PATROL CARS AND THE POLICE WHIRLYBIRD FOLLOWING ABOVE...
POLICE
I WISH THE VULTURE WOULD MAKE A TRY FOR THOSE DIAMONDS, CHUCK! WE'D NAB 'IM FOR SURE!
YEAH, BUT HE WON'T SHOW! HE'S TOO SMART FOR THAT!
POLICE
IT'S ALL CLEAR! START BRINGING THE JEWELS OUT!
NOT A SIGN OF THE VULTURE! HE KNOWS HE WOULDN'T HAVE A CHANCE!
9

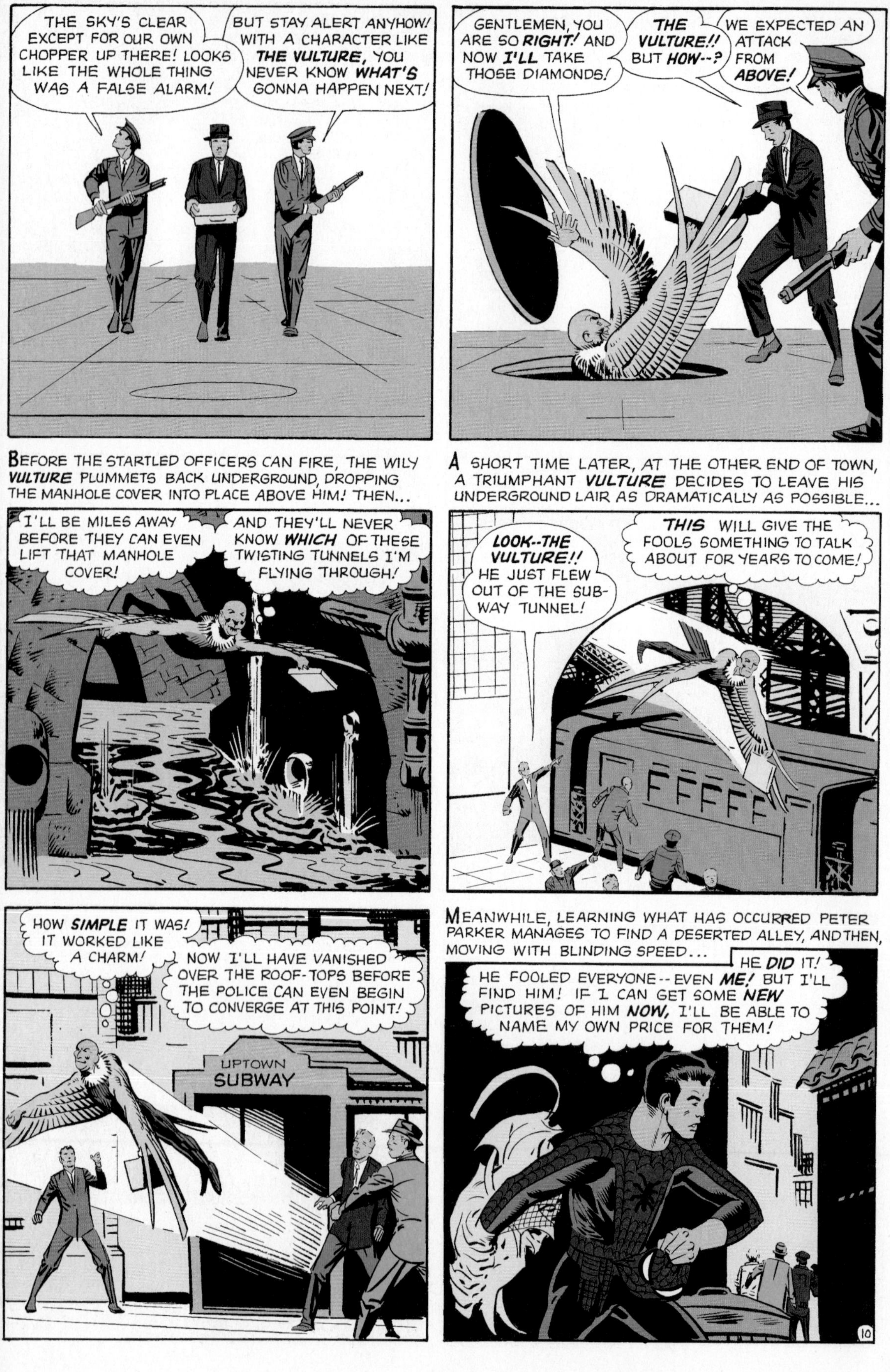
THE SKY'S CLEAR EXCEPT FOR OUR OWN CHOPPER UP THERE! LOOKS LIKE THE WHOLE THING WAS A FALSE ALARM!
BUT STAY ALERT ANYHOW! WITH A CHARACTER LIKE THE VULTURE, YOU NEVER KNOW WHAT'S GONNA HAPPEN NEXT!
GENTLEMEN, YOU ARE SO RIGHT! AND NOW I'LL TAKE THOSE DIAMONDS!
THE VULTURE!! BUT HOW--?
WE EXPECTED AN ATTACK FROM ABOVE!
BEFORE THE STARTLED OFFICERS CAN FIRE, THE WILY VULTURE PLUMMETS BACK UNDERGROUND, DROPPING THE MANHOLE COVER INTO PLACE ABOVE HIM! THEN...
I'LL BE MILES AWAY BEFORE THEY CAN EVEN LIFT THAT MANHOLE COVER!
AND THEY'LL NEVER KNOW WHICH OF THESE TWISTING TUNNELS I'M FLYING THROUGH!
A SHORT TIME LATER, AT THE OTHER END OF TOWN, A TRIUMPHANT VULTURE DECIDES TO LEAVE HIS UNDERGROUND LAIR AS DRAMATICALLY AS POSSIBLE...
THIS WILL GIVE THE FOOLS SOMETHING TO TALK ABOUT FOR YEARS TO COME!
LOOK--THE VULTURE!! HE JUST FLEW OUT OF THE SUB-WAY TUNNEL!
HOW SIMPLE IT WAS! IT WORKED LIKE A CHARM!
NOW I'LL HAVE VANISHED OVER THE ROOF-TOPS BEFORE THE POLICE CAN EVEN BEGIN TO CONVERGE AT THIS POINT!
UPTOWN SUBWAY
MEANWHILE, LEARNING WHAT HAS OCCURRED PETER PARKER MANAGES TO FIND A DESERTED ALLEY, AND THEN, MOVING WITH BLINDING SPEED...
HE DID IT! HE FOOLED EVERYONE -- EVEN ME! BUT I'LL FIND HIM! IF I CAN GET SOME NEW PICTURES OF HIM NOW, I'LL BE ABLE TO NAME MY OWN PRICE FOR THEM!
10

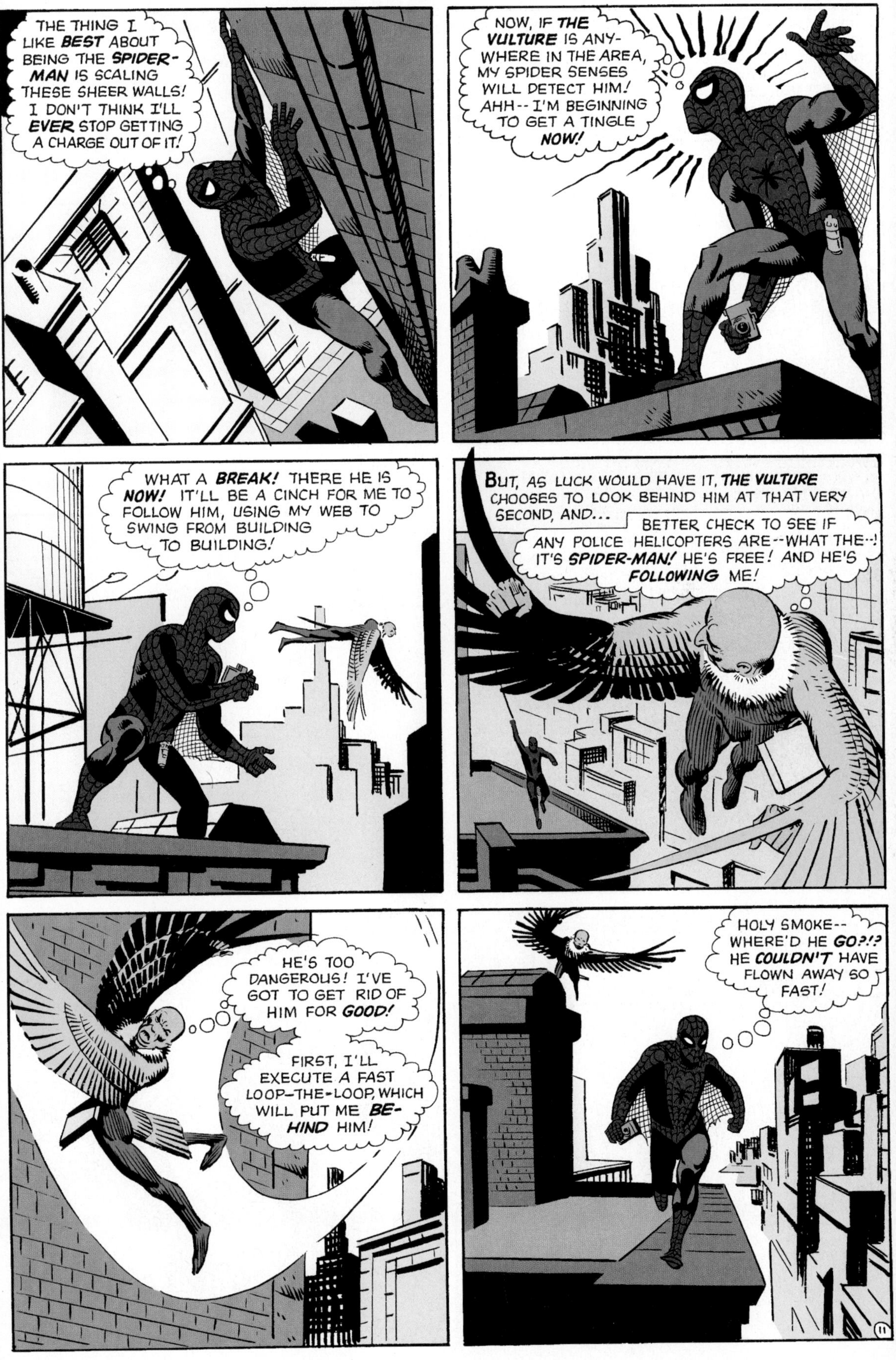
THE THING I LIKE BEST ABOUT BEING THE SPIDER-MAN IS SCALING THESE SHEER WALLS! I DON'T THINK I'LL EVER STOP GETTING A CHARGE OUT OF IT!
NOW, IF THE VULTURE IS ANYWHERE IN THE AREA, MY SPIDER SENSES WILL DETECT HIM! AHH -- I'M BEGINNING TO GET A TINGLE NOW!
WHAT A BREAK! THERE HE IS NOW! IT'LL BE A CINCH FOR ME TO FOLLOW HIM, USING MY WEB TO SWING FROM BUILDING TO BUILDING!
BUT, AS LUCK WOULD HAVE IT, THE VULTURE CHOOSES TO LOOK BEHIND HIM AT THAT VERY SECOND, AND...
BETTER CHECK TO SEE IF ANY POLICE HELICOPTERS ARE -- WHAT THE--! IT'S SPIDER-MAN! HE'S FREE! AND HE'S FOLLOWING ME!
HE'S TOO DANGEROUS! I'VE GOT TO GET RID OF HIM FOR GOOD!
FIRST, I'LL EXECUTE A FAST LOOP-THE-LOOP, WHICH WILL PUT ME BEHIND HIM!
HOLY SMOKE-- WHERE'D HE GO?!? HE COULDN'T HAVE FLOWN AWAY SO FAST!
11

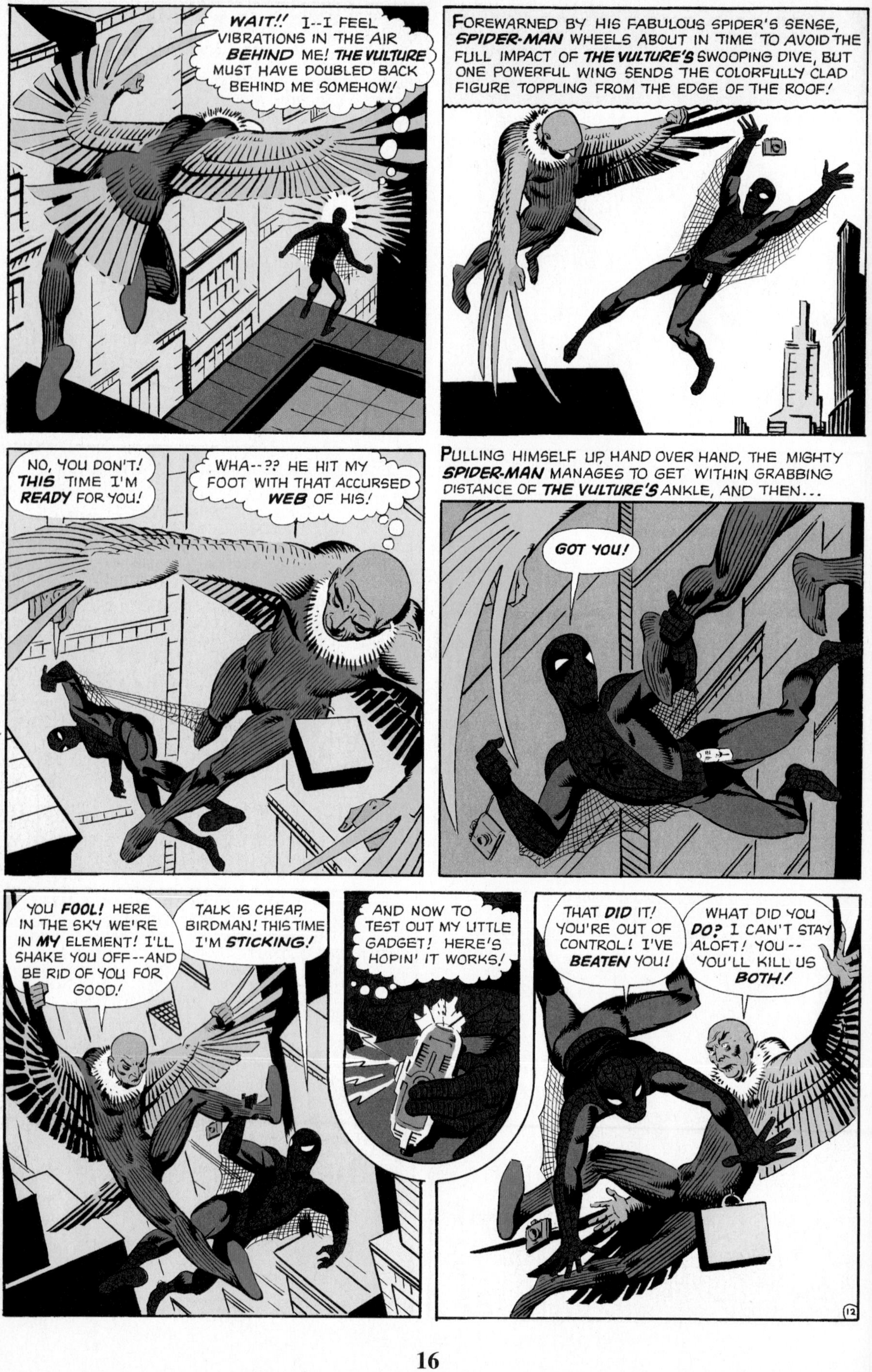
WAIT!! I--I FEEL VIBRATIONS IN THE AIR BEHIND ME! THE VULTURE MUST HAVE DOUBLED BACK BEHIND ME SOMEHOW!
FOREWARNED BY HIS FABULOUS SPIDER'S SENSE, SPIDER-MAN WHEELS ABOUT IN TIME TO AVOID THE FULL IMPACT OF THE VULTURE'S SWOOPING DIVE, BUT ONE POWERFUL WING SENDS THE COLORFULLY CLAD FIGURE TOPPLING FROM THE EDGE OF THE ROOF!
NO, YOU DON'T! THIS TIME I'M READY FOR YOU!
WHA--?? HE HIT MY FOOT WITH THAT ACCURSED WEB OF HIS!
PULLING HIMSELF UP, HAND OVER HAND, THE MIGHTY SPIDER-MAN MANAGES TO GET WITHIN GRABBING DISTANCE OF THE VULTURE'S ANKLE, AND THEN...
GOT YOU!
YOU FOOL! HERE IN THE SKY WE'RE IN MY ELEMENT! I'LL SHAKE YOU OFF--AND BE RID OF YOU FOR GOOD!
TALK IS CHEAP, BIRDMAN! THIS TIME I'M STICKING!
AND NOW TO TEST OUT MY LITTLE GADGET! HERE'S HOPIN' IT WORKS!
THAT DID IT! YOU'RE OUT OF CONTROL! I'VE BEATEN YOU!
WHAT DID YOU DO? I CAN'T STAY ALOFT! YOU--YOU'LL KILL US BOTH!
12

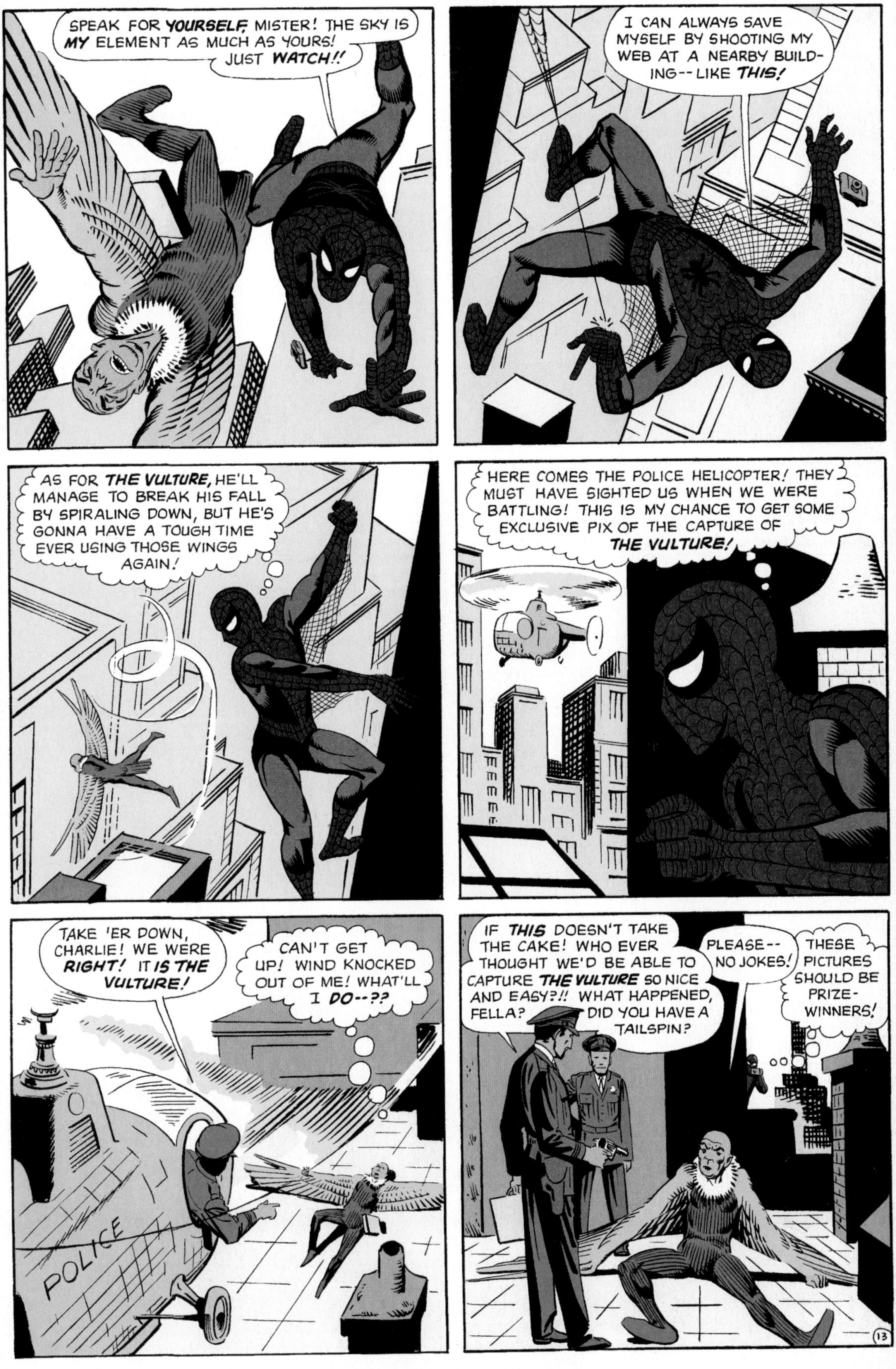
SPEAK FOR YOURSELF, MISTER! THE SKY IS MY ELEMENT AS MUCH AS YOURS! JUST WATCH!!
I CAN ALWAYS SAVE MYSELF BY SHOOTING MY WEB AT A NEARBY BUILDING-- LIKE THIS!
AS FOR THE VULTURE, HE'LL MANAGE TO BREAK HIS FALL BY SPIRALING DOWN, BUT HE'S GONNA HAVE A TOUGH TIME EVER USING THOSE WINGS AGAIN!
HERE COMES THE POLICE HELICOPTER! THEY MUST HAVE SIGHTED US WHEN WE WERE BATTLING! THIS IS MY CHANCE TO GET SOME EXCLUSIVE PIX OF THE CAPTURE OF THE VULTURE!
TAKE 'ER DOWN, CHARLIE! WE WERE RIGHT! IT IS THE VULTURE!
CAN'T GET UP! WIND KNOCKED OUT OF ME! WHAT'LL I DO--??
POLICE
IF THIS DOESN'T TAKE THE CAKE! WHO EVER THOUGHT WE'D BE ABLE TO CAPTURE THE VULTURE SO NICE AND EASY?!! WHAT HAPPENED, FELLA? DID YOU HAVE A TAILSPIN?
PLEASE-- NO JOKES!
THESE PICTURES SHOULD BE PRIZE-WINNERS!
13

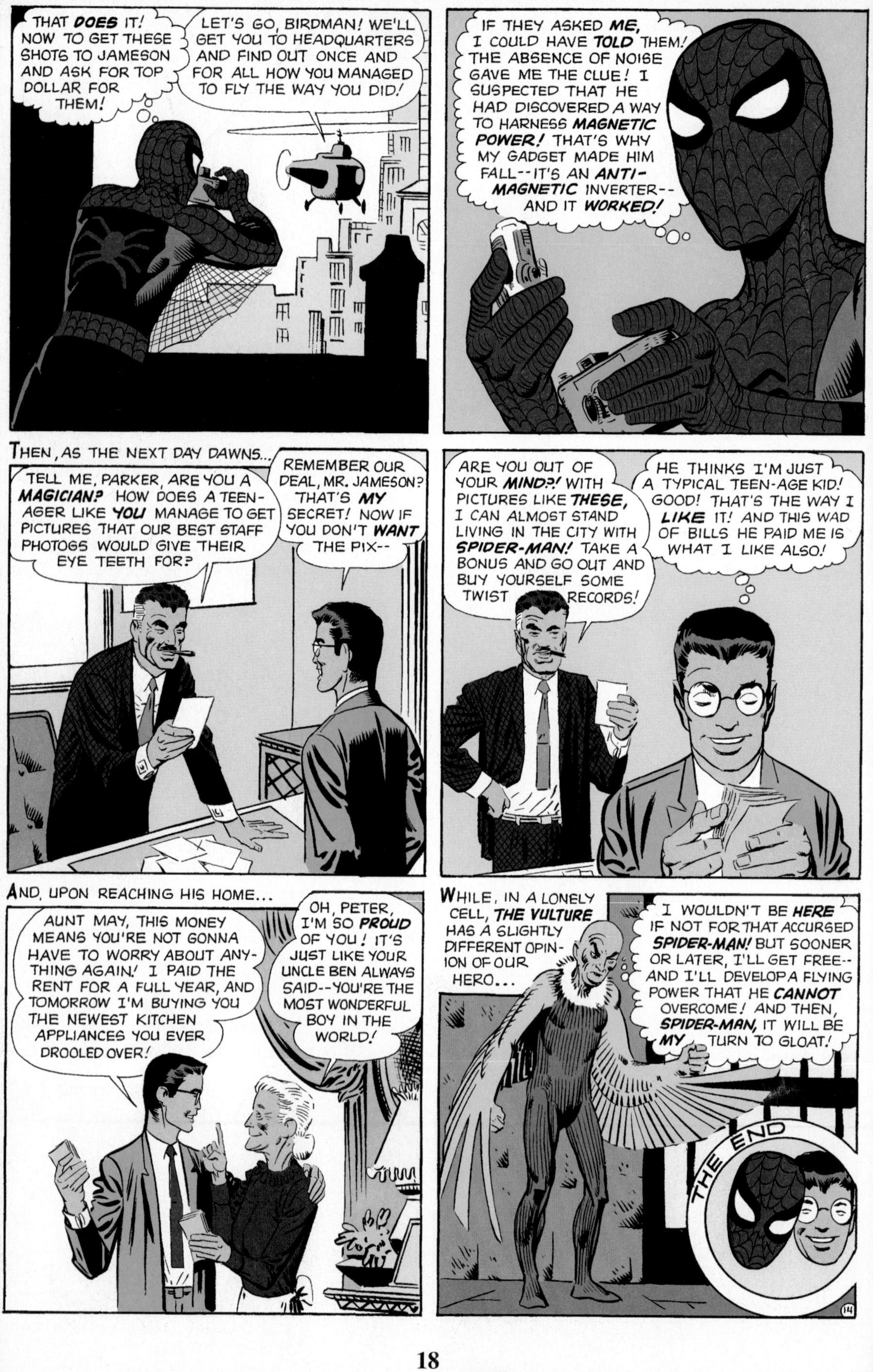
THAT DOES IT! NOW TO GET THESE SHOTS TO JAMESON AND ASK FOR TOP DOLLAR FOR THEM!
LET'S GO, BIRDMAN! WE'LL GET YOU TO HEADQUARTERS AND FIND OUT ONCE AND FOR ALL HOW YOU MANAGED TO FLY THE WAY YOU DID!
IF THEY ASKED ME, I COULD HAVE TOLD THEM! THE ABSENCE OF NOISE GAVE ME THE CLUE! I SUSPECTED THAT HE HAD DISCOVERED A WAY TO HARNESS MAGNETIC POWER! THAT'S WHY MY GADGET MADE HIM FALL--IT'S AN ANTI-MAGNETIC INVERTER--AND IT WORKED!
THEN, AS THE NEXT DAY DAWNS...
TELL ME, PARKER, ARE YOU A MAGICIAN? HOW DOES A TEEN-AGER LIKE YOU MANAGE TO GET PICTURES THAT OUR BEST STAFF PHOTOGS WOULD GIVE THEIR EYE TEETH FOR?
REMEMBER OUR DEAL, MR. JAMESON? THAT'S MY SECRET! NOW IF YOU DON'T WANT THE PIX--
ARE YOU OUT OF YOUR MIND?! WITH PICTURES LIKE THESE, I CAN ALMOST STAND LIVING IN THE CITY WITH SPIDER-MAN! TAKE A BONUS AND GO OUT AND BUY YOURSELF SOME TWIST RECORDS!
HE THINKS I'M JUST A TYPICAL TEEN-AGE KID! GOOD! THAT'S THE WAY I LIKE IT! AND THIS WAD OF BILLS HE PAID ME IS WHAT I LIKE ALSO!
AND, UPON REACHING HIS HOME...
AUNT MAY, THIS MONEY MEANS YOU'RE NOT GONNA HAVE TO WORRY ABOUT ANY-THING AGAIN! I PAID THE RENT FOR A FULL YEAR, AND TOMORROW I'M BUYING YOU THE NEWEST KITCHEN APPLIANCES YOU EVER DROOLED OVER!
OH, PETER, I'M SO PROUD OF YOU! IT'S JUST LIKE YOUR UNCLE BEN ALWAYS SAID--YOU'RE THE MOST WONDERFUL BOY IN THE WORLD!
WHILE, IN A LONELY CELL, THE VULTURE HAS A SLIGHTLY DIFFERENT OPIN-ION OF OUR HERO...
I WOULDN'T BE HERE IF NOT FOR THAT ACCURSED SPIDER-MAN! BUT SOONER OR LATER, I'LL GET FREE--AND I'LL DEVELOP A FLYING POWER THAT HE CANNOT OVERCOME! AND THEN, SPIDER-MAN, IT WILL BE MY TURN TO GLOAT!
THE END
14

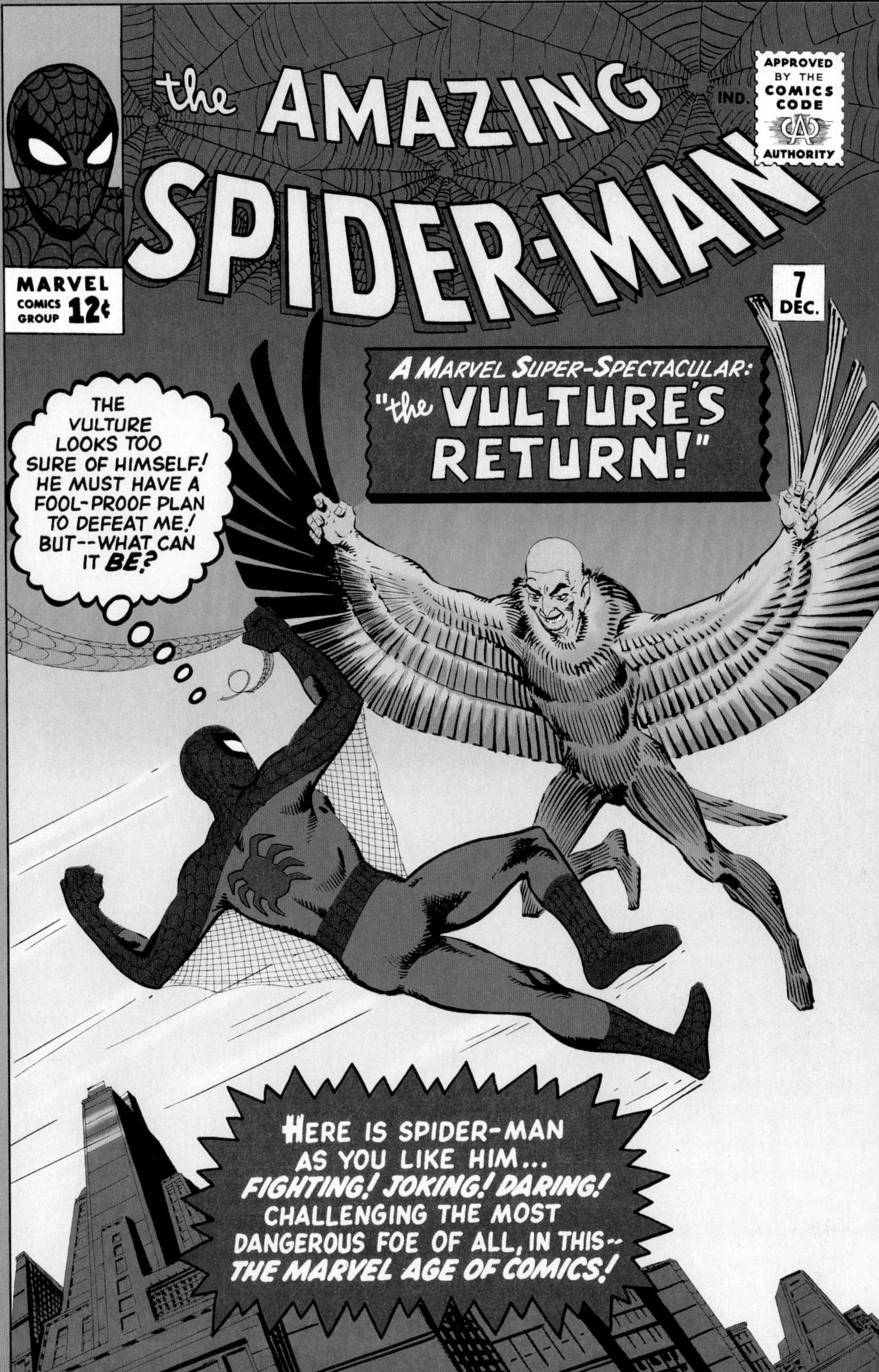
APPROVED BY THE COMICS CODE AUTHORITY
the AMAZING SPIDER-MAN
IND.
MARVEL COMICS GROUP 12¢
7 DEC.
A MARVEL SUPER-SPECTACULAR: "the VULTURE'S RETURN!"
THE VULTURE LOOKS TOO SURE OF HIMSELF! HE MUST HAVE A FOOL-PROOF PLAN TO DEFEAT ME! BUT--WHAT CAN IT BE?
HERE IS SPIDER-MAN AS YOU LIKE HIM... FIGHTING! JOKING! DARING! CHALLENGING THE MOST DANGEROUS FOE OF ALL, IN THIS-- THE MARVEL AGE OF COMICS!

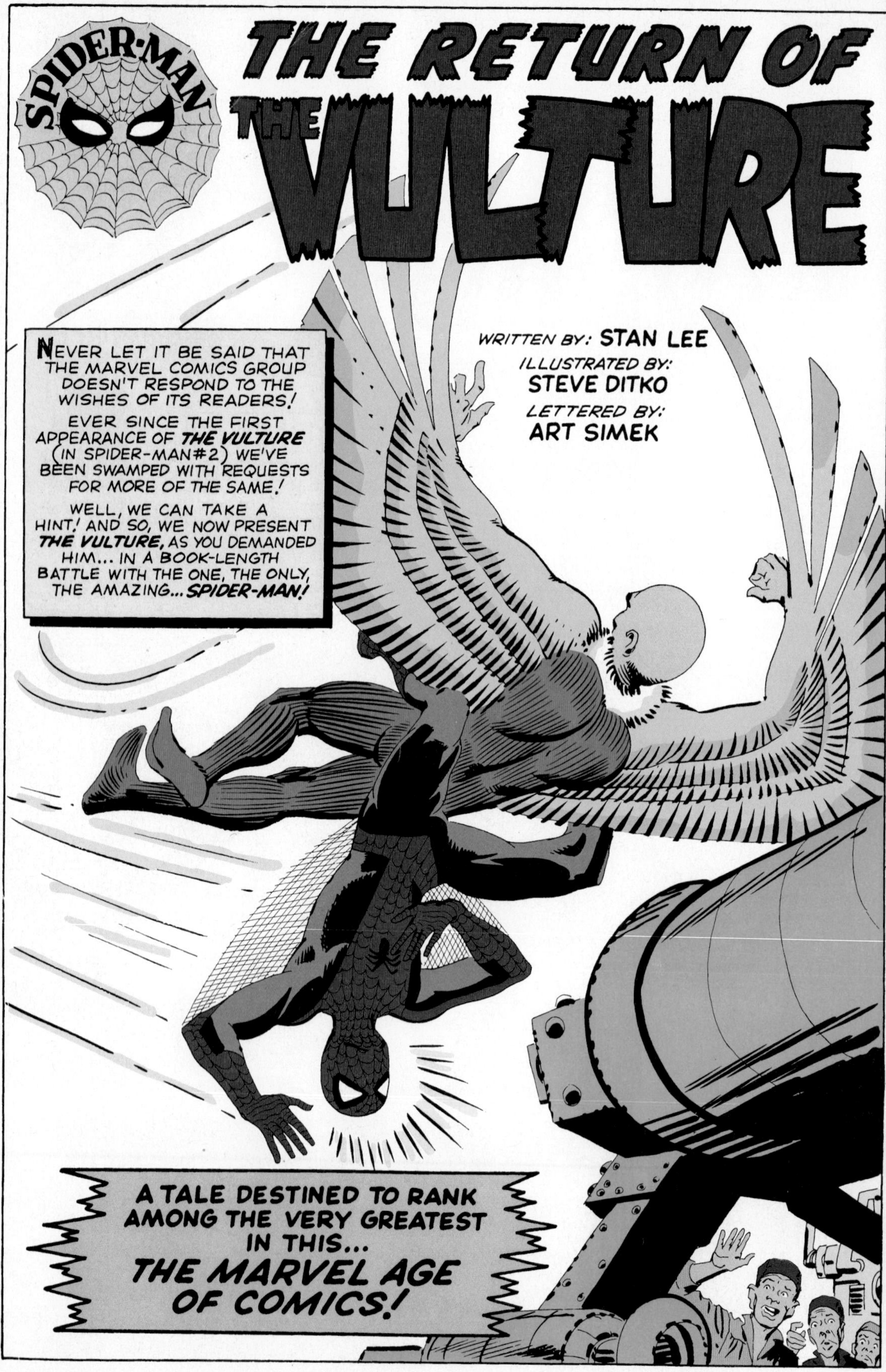
SPIDER-MAN
THE RETURN OF THE VULTURE
NEVER LET IT BE SAID THAT THE MARVEL COMICS GROUP DOESN'T RESPOND TO THE WISHES OF ITS READERS! EVER SINCE THE FIRST APPEARANCE OF THE VULTURE (IN SPIDER-MAN #2) WE'VE BEEN SWAMPED WITH REQUESTS FOR MORE OF THE SAME! WELL, WE CAN TAKE A HINT! AND SO, WE NOW PRESENT THE VULTURE, AS YOU DEMANDED HIM... IN A BOOK-LENGTH BATTLE WITH THE ONE, THE ONLY, THE AMAZING... SPIDER-MAN!
WRITTEN BY: STAN LEE
ILLUSTRATED BY: STEVE DITKO
LETTERED BY: ART SIMEK
A TALE DESTINED TO RANK AMONG THE VERY GREATEST IN THIS... THE MARVEL AGE OF COMICS!

FOR THOSE OF YOU WHO MISSED **SPIDER-MAN #2,** IT CONCERNED HIS SPECTACULAR BATTLE WITH ONE OF THE MOST DANGEROUS VILLAINS OF ALL TIME...THE AWESOME FLYING **VULTURE!** NO MAN KNEW THE SECRET BEHIND THE VULTURE'S ABILITY TO FLY...UNTIL SPIDER-MAN DEDUCED THAT HIS WINGS WERE OPERATED BY A UNIQUE FORM OF **MAGNETIC POWER...**

...AND SO, SPIDER-MAN CREATED A POWERFUL **ANTI-MAGNETIC INVERTER** WHICH HE USED AGAINST THE VULTURE IN THEIR FINAL BATTLE...

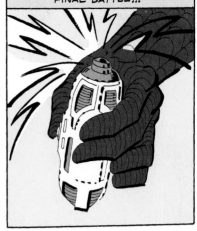

WITH HIS MAGNETIC POWER NULLIFIED, DUE TO **SPIDER-MAN'S** INVERTER, THE VULTURE WAS FORCED TO SPIRAL TO THE GROUND, INTO THE WAITING ARMS OF THE POLICE! AND SO ENDED THAT EPIC BATTLE!

THE VULTURE WILL NEVER THREATEN ANYONE AGAIN!

FOR MONTHS IT SEEMS THAT SPIDER-MAN'S PREDICTION IS CORRECT, AS THE IMPRISONED VULTURE BECOMES A MODEL INMATE OF STATE PRISON...

THE VULTURE IS THE BEST BEHAVED PRISONER IN THE PLACE!

THAT'S WHY THE WARDEN MADE HIM A TRUSTEE AND LETS HIM USE THE MACHINE SHOP!

THE GULLIBLE FOOLS! THEY DON'T SUSPECT THAT I'M PUTTING TOGETHER **ANOTHER** FLYING DEVICE FOR MYSELF--RIGHT UNDER THEIR NOSES!

I'VE TAKEN ALL THE PARTS I NEED! TONIGHT I'LL MAKE MY FINAL TEST IN MY CELL!

AND, AFTER BED CHECK...

IT WORKS! NOT AS POWERFUL AS MY **ORIGINAL** FLYING DEVICE...

...BUT GOOD ENOUGH TO GET ME OVER THE WALL--**TO FREEDOM!**

2

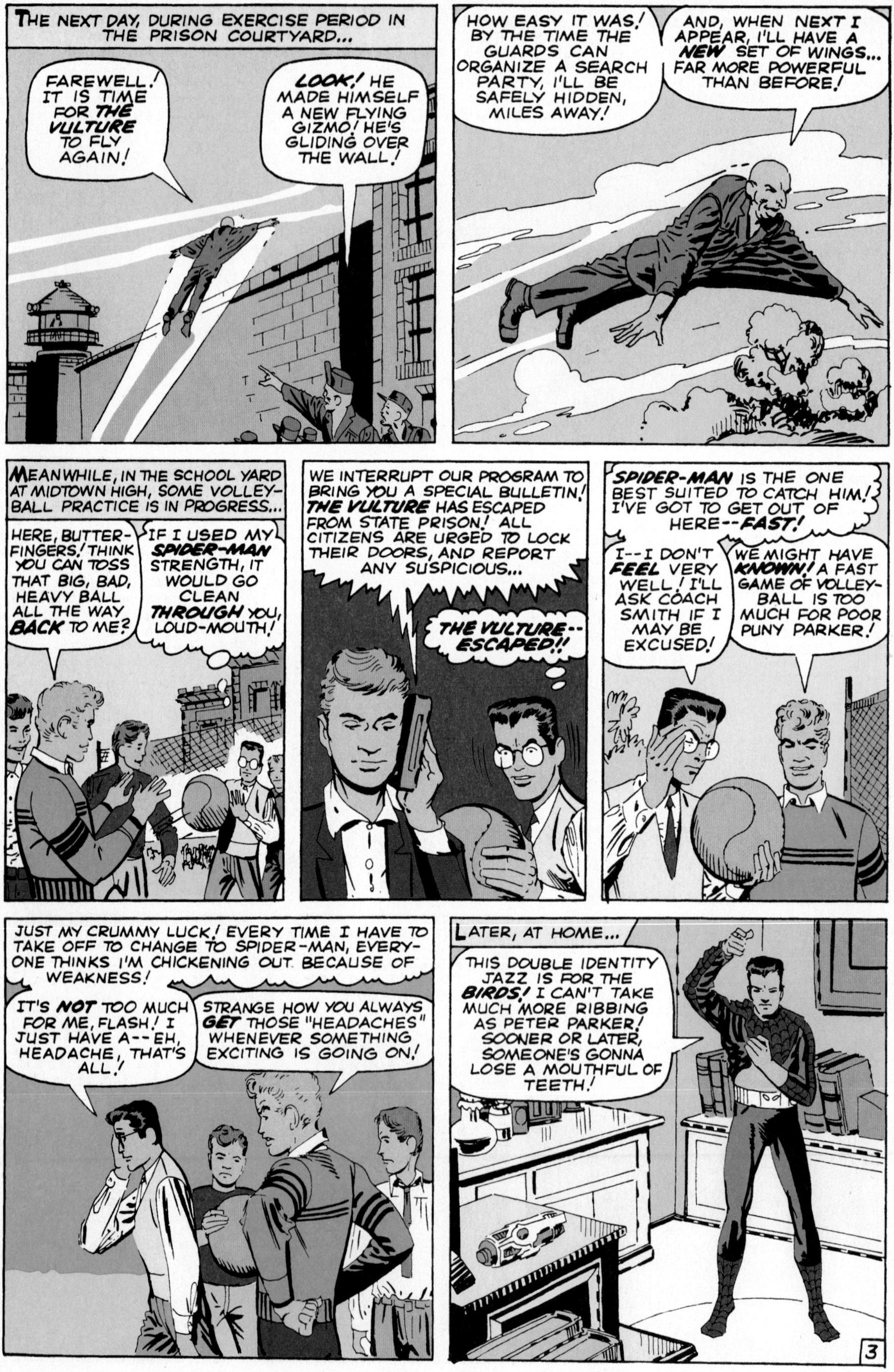
THE NEXT DAY, DURING EXERCISE PERIOD IN THE PRISON COURTYARD...
FAREWELL! IT IS TIME FOR THE VULTURE TO FLY AGAIN!
LOOK! HE MADE HIMSELF A NEW FLYING GIZMO! HE'S GLIDING OVER THE WALL!
HOW EASY IT WAS! BY THE TIME THE GUARDS CAN ORGANIZE A SEARCH PARTY, I'LL BE SAFELY HIDDEN, MILES AWAY!
AND, WHEN NEXT I APPEAR, I'LL HAVE A NEW SET OF WINGS... FAR MORE POWERFUL THAN BEFORE!
MEANWHILE, IN THE SCHOOL YARD AT MIDTOWN HIGH, SOME VOLLEY-BALL PRACTICE IS IN PROGRESS...
HERE, BUTTER-FINGERS! THINK YOU CAN TOSS THAT BIG, BAD, HEAVY BALL ALL THE WAY BACK TO ME?
IF I USED MY SPIDER-MAN STRENGTH, IT WOULD GO CLEAN THROUGH YOU, LOUD-MOUTH!
WE INTERRUPT OUR PROGRAM TO BRING YOU A SPECIAL BULLETIN! THE VULTURE HAS ESCAPED FROM STATE PRISON! ALL CITIZENS ARE URGED TO LOCK THEIR DOORS, AND REPORT ANY SUSPICIOUS...
THE VULTURE--ESCAPED!!
SPIDER-MAN IS THE ONE BEST SUITED TO CATCH HIM! I'VE GOT TO GET OUT OF HERE--FAST!
I--I DON'T FEEL VERY WELL! I'LL ASK COACH SMITH IF I MAY BE EXCUSED!
WE MIGHT HAVE KNOWN! A FAST GAME OF VOLLEY-BALL IS TOO MUCH FOR POOR PUNY PARKER!
JUST MY CRUMMY LUCK! EVERY TIME I HAVE TO TAKE OFF TO CHANGE TO SPIDER-MAN, EVERY-ONE THINKS I'M CHICKENING OUT BECAUSE OF WEAKNESS!
IT'S NOT TOO MUCH FOR ME, FLASH! I JUST HAVE A--EH, HEADACHE, THAT'S ALL!
STRANGE HOW YOU ALWAYS GET THOSE "HEADACHES" WHENEVER SOMETHING EXCITING IS GOING ON!
LATER, AT HOME...
THIS DOUBLE IDENTITY JAZZ IS FOR THE BIRDS! I CAN'T TAKE MUCH MORE RIBBING AS PETER PARKER! SOONER OR LATER, SOMEONE'S GONNA LOSE A MOUTHFUL OF TEETH!
3

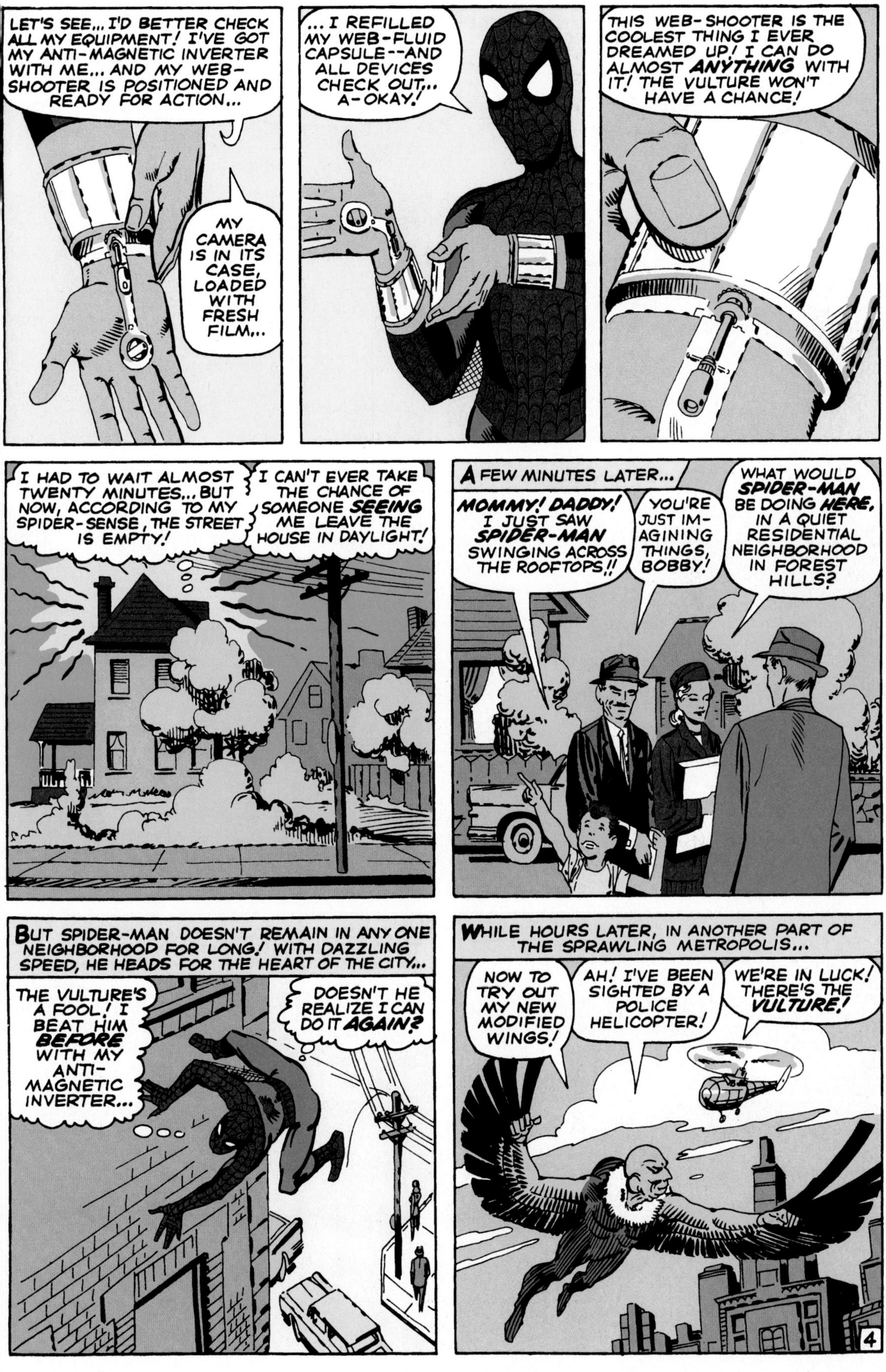
LET'S SEE... I'D BETTER CHECK ALL MY EQUIPMENT! I'VE GOT MY ANTI-MAGNETIC INVERTER WITH ME... AND MY WEB-SHOOTER IS POSITIONED AND READY FOR ACTION...
MY CAMERA IS IN ITS CASE, LOADED WITH FRESH FILM...
...I REFILLED MY WEB-FLUID CAPSULE--AND ALL DEVICES CHECK OUT... A-OKAY!
THIS WEB-SHOOTER IS THE COOLEST THING I EVER DREAMED UP! I CAN DO ALMOST ANYTHING WITH IT! THE VULTURE WON'T HAVE A CHANCE!
I HAD TO WAIT ALMOST TWENTY MINUTES... BUT NOW, ACCORDING TO MY SPIDER-SENSE, THE STREET IS EMPTY!
I CAN'T EVER TAKE THE CHANCE OF SOMEONE SEEING ME LEAVE THE HOUSE IN DAYLIGHT!
A FEW MINUTES LATER...
MOMMY! DADDY! I JUST SAW SPIDER-MAN SWINGING ACROSS THE ROOFTOPS!!
YOU'RE JUST IMAGINING THINGS, BOBBY!
WHAT WOULD SPIDER-MAN BE DOING HERE, IN A QUIET RESIDENTIAL NEIGHBORHOOD IN FOREST HILLS?
BUT SPIDER-MAN DOESN'T REMAIN IN ANY ONE NEIGHBORHOOD FOR LONG! WITH DAZZLING SPEED, HE HEADS FOR THE HEART OF THE CITY...
THE VULTURE'S A FOOL! I BEAT HIM BEFORE WITH MY ANTI-MAGNETIC INVERTER...
DOESN'T HE REALIZE I CAN DO IT AGAIN?
WHILE HOURS LATER, IN ANOTHER PART OF THE SPRAWLING METROPOLIS...
NOW TO TRY OUT MY NEW MODIFIED WINGS!
AH! I'VE BEEN SIGHTED BY A POLICE HELICOPTER!
WE'RE IN LUCK! THERE'S THE VULTURE!
4

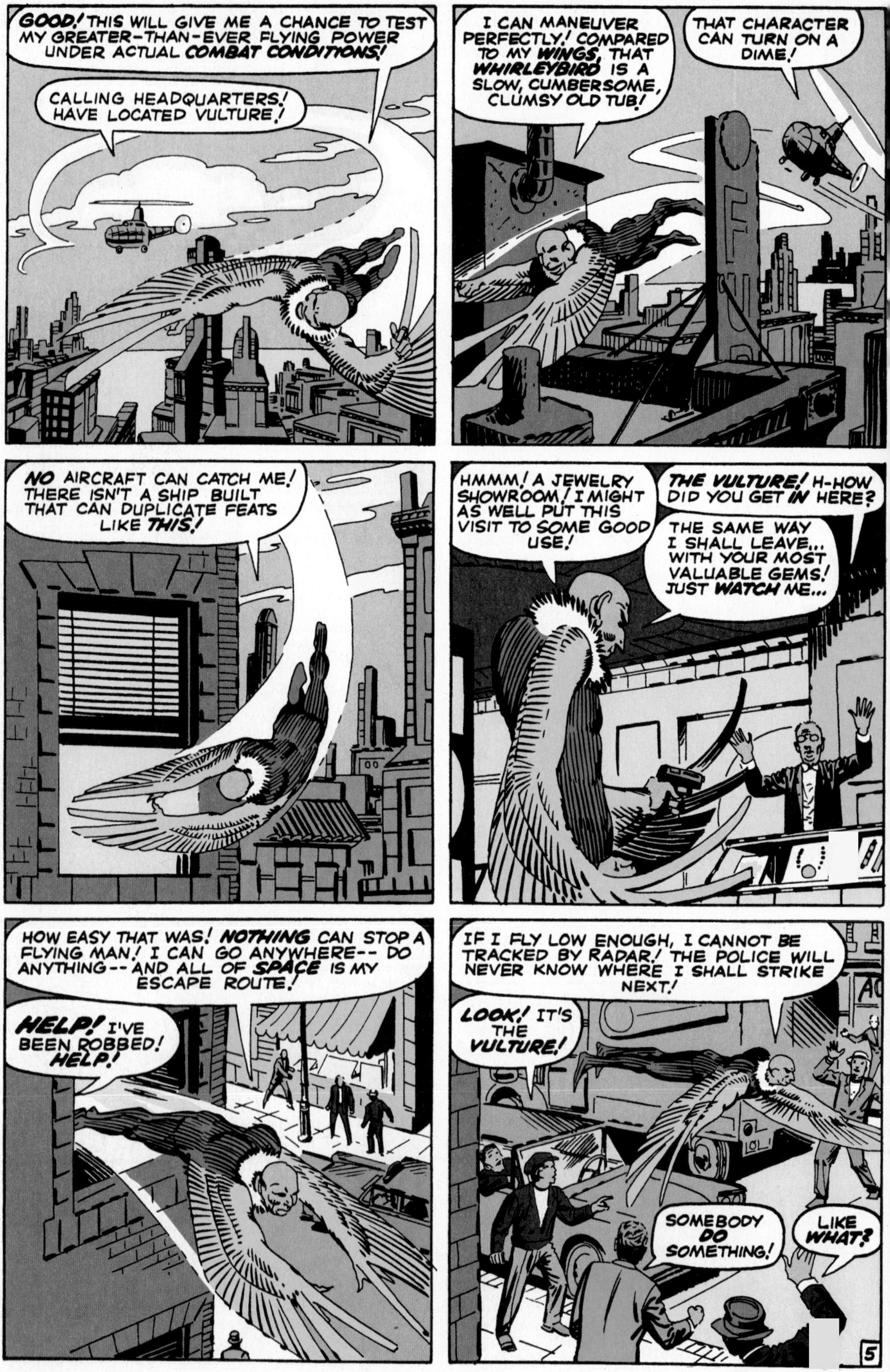
GOOD! THIS WILL GIVE ME A CHANCE TO TEST MY GREATER-THAN-EVER FLYING POWER UNDER ACTUAL COMBAT CONDITIONS!
CALLING HEADQUARTERS! HAVE LOCATED VULTURE!
I CAN MANEUVER PERFECTLY! COMPARED TO MY WINGS, THAT WHIRLEYBIRD IS A SLOW, CUMBERSOME, CLUMSY OLD TUB!
THAT CHARACTER CAN TURN ON A DIME!
NO AIRCRAFT CAN CATCH ME! THERE ISN'T A SHIP BUILT THAT CAN DUPLICATE FEATS LIKE THIS!
HMMM! A JEWELRY SHOWROOM! I MIGHT AS WELL PUT THIS VISIT TO SOME GOOD USE!
THE VULTURE! H-HOW DID YOU GET IN HERE?
THE SAME WAY I SHALL LEAVE... WITH YOUR MOST VALUABLE GEMS! JUST WATCH ME...
HOW EASY THAT WAS! NOTHING CAN STOP A FLYING MAN! I CAN GO ANYWHERE-- DO ANYTHING-- AND ALL OF SPACE IS MY ESCAPE ROUTE!
HELP! I'VE BEEN ROBBED! HELP!
IF I FLY LOW ENOUGH, I CANNOT BE TRACKED BY RADAR! THE POLICE WILL NEVER KNOW WHERE I SHALL STRIKE NEXT!
LOOK! IT'S THE VULTURE!
SOMEBODY DO SOMETHING!
LIKE WHAT?
5

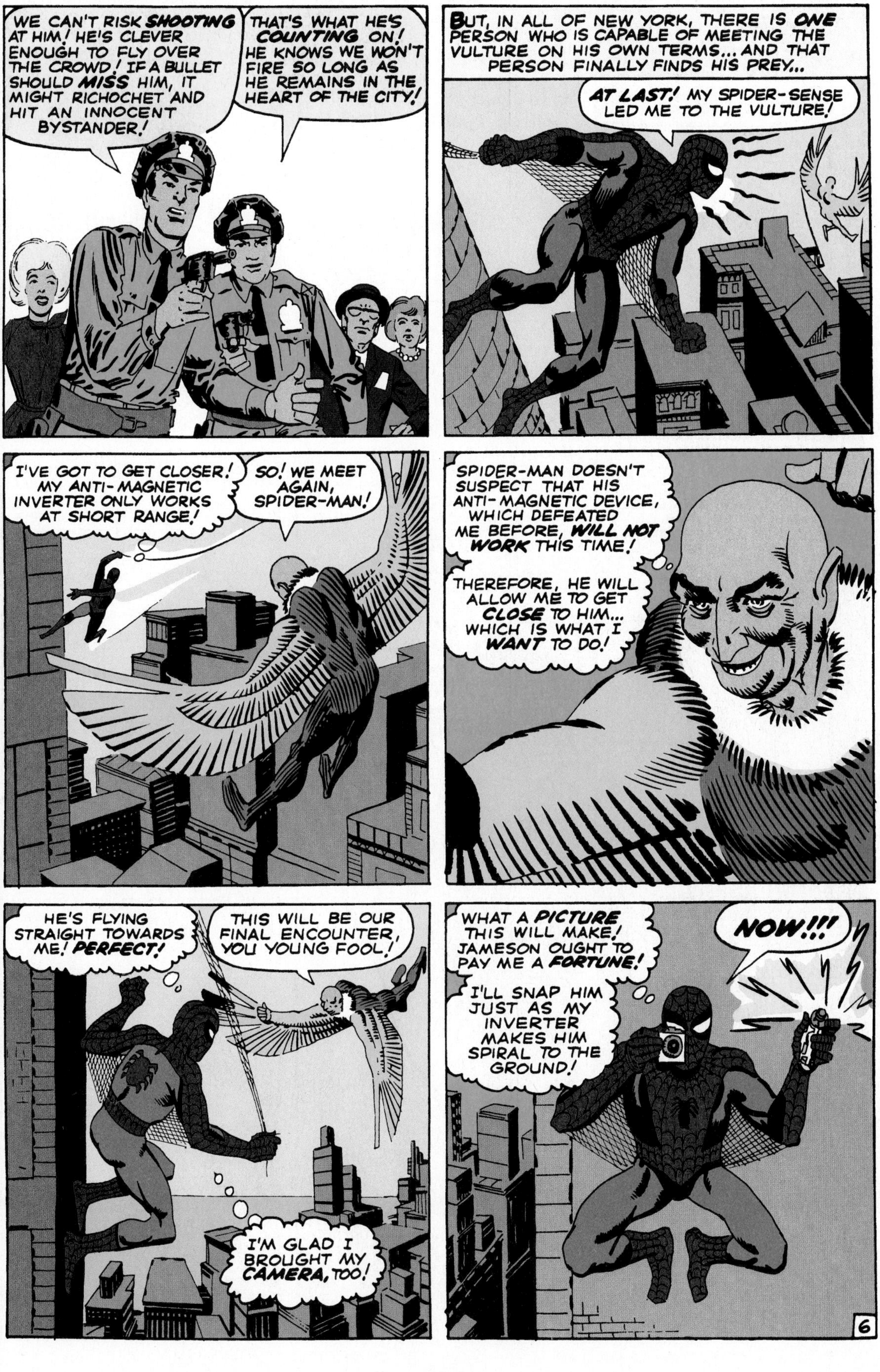

WE CAN'T RISK SHOOTING AT HIM! HE'S CLEVER ENOUGH TO FLY OVER THE CROWD! IF A BULLET SHOULD MISS HIM, IT MIGHT RICHOCHET AND HIT AN INNOCENT BYSTANDER!
THAT'S WHAT HE'S COUNTING ON! HE KNOWS WE WON'T FIRE SO LONG AS HE REMAINS IN THE HEART OF THE CITY!
BUT, IN ALL OF NEW YORK, THERE IS ONE PERSON WHO IS CAPABLE OF MEETING THE VULTURE ON HIS OWN TERMS... AND THAT PERSON FINALLY FINDS HIS PREY...
AT LAST! MY SPIDER-SENSE LED ME TO THE VULTURE!
I'VE GOT TO GET CLOSER! MY ANTI-MAGNETIC INVERTER ONLY WORKS AT SHORT RANGE!
SO! WE MEET AGAIN, SPIDER-MAN!
SPIDER-MAN DOESN'T SUSPECT THAT HIS ANTI-MAGNETIC DEVICE, WHICH DEFEATED ME BEFORE, WILL NOT WORK THIS TIME!
THEREFORE, HE WILL ALLOW ME TO GET CLOSE TO HIM... WHICH IS WHAT I WANT TO DO!
HE'S FLYING STRAIGHT TOWARDS ME! PERFECT!
THIS WILL BE OUR FINAL ENCOUNTER, YOU YOUNG FOOL!
I'M GLAD I BROUGHT MY CAMERA, TOO!
WHAT A PICTURE THIS WILL MAKE! JAMESON OUGHT TO PAY ME A FORTUNE!
NOW!!!
I'LL SNAP HIM JUST AS MY INVERTER MAKES HIM SPIRAL TO THE GROUND!
6

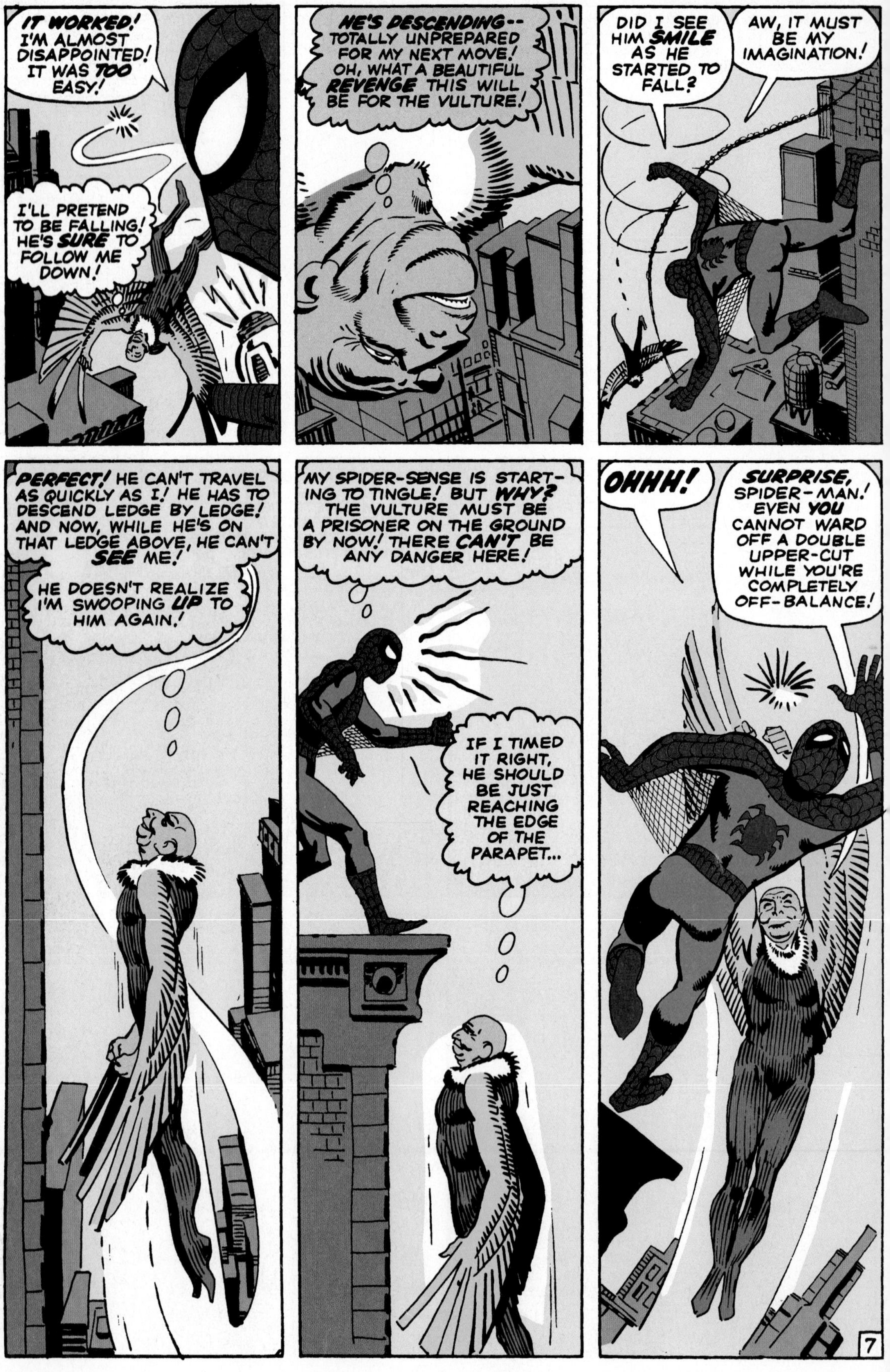
IT WORKED! I'M ALMOST DISAPPOINTED! IT WAS TOO EASY!
I'LL PRETEND TO BE FALLING! HE'S SURE TO FOLLOW ME DOWN!
HE'S DESCENDING-- TOTALLY UNPREPARED FOR MY NEXT MOVE! OH, WHAT A BEAUTIFUL REVENGE THIS WILL BE FOR THE VULTURE!
DID I SEE HIM SMILE AS HE STARTED TO FALL?
AW, IT MUST BE MY IMAGINATION!
PERFECT! HE CAN'T TRAVEL AS QUICKLY AS I! HE HAS TO DESCEND LEDGE BY LEDGE! AND NOW, WHILE HE'S ON THAT LEDGE ABOVE, HE CAN'T SEE ME!
HE DOESN'T REALIZE I'M SWOOPING UP TO HIM AGAIN!
MY SPIDER-SENSE IS STARTING TO TINGLE! BUT WHY? THE VULTURE MUST BE A PRISONER ON THE GROUND BY NOW! THERE CAN'T BE ANY DANGER HERE!
IF I TIMED IT RIGHT, HE SHOULD BE JUST REACHING THE EDGE OF THE PARAPET...
OHHH!
SURPRISE, SPIDER-MAN! EVEN YOU CANNOT WARD OFF A DOUBLE UPPER-CUT WHILE YOU'RE COMPLETELY OFF-BALANCE!
7

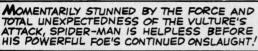

MOMENTARILY STUNNED BY THE FORCE AND TOTAL UNEXPECTEDNESS OF THE VULTURE'S ATTACK, SPIDER-MAN IS HELPLESS BEFORE HIS POWERFUL FOE'S CONTINUED ONSLAUGHT!

THIS TIME THE VICTORY IS MINE!

LOOK! UP THERE... ABOVE THE ROOFTOPS! IT'S THE VULTURE... BATTLING WITH SPIDER-MAN!

THANK HEAVEN SPIDER-MAN FOUND HIM! HE'S THE ONLY ONE WHO CAN DEFEAT THE VULTURE SINGLE-HANDED!

GUESS AGAIN, LADY! THE VULTURE IS CLOBBERING HIM!

YOU NEVER SUSPECTED I HAD IMPROVED MY WINGS SO THAT THEY COULD CHANGE MAGNETIC POLES INSTANTLY, NULLIFYING YOUR USELESS INVERTER!

SO THAT'S WHY... -OOOF-!

HAPPY LANDINGS, SPIDER-MAN!

GOT TO SHOOT MY WEB--FAST-- CATCH ON TO BUILDING--BREAK MY FALL--

MISSED!!

MUST TRY AGAIN! FALLING TOO FAST... TOO FAR...

CAN'T DO IT! IT FELL SHORT! ...NO TIME FOR ANOTHER TRY--!!

8

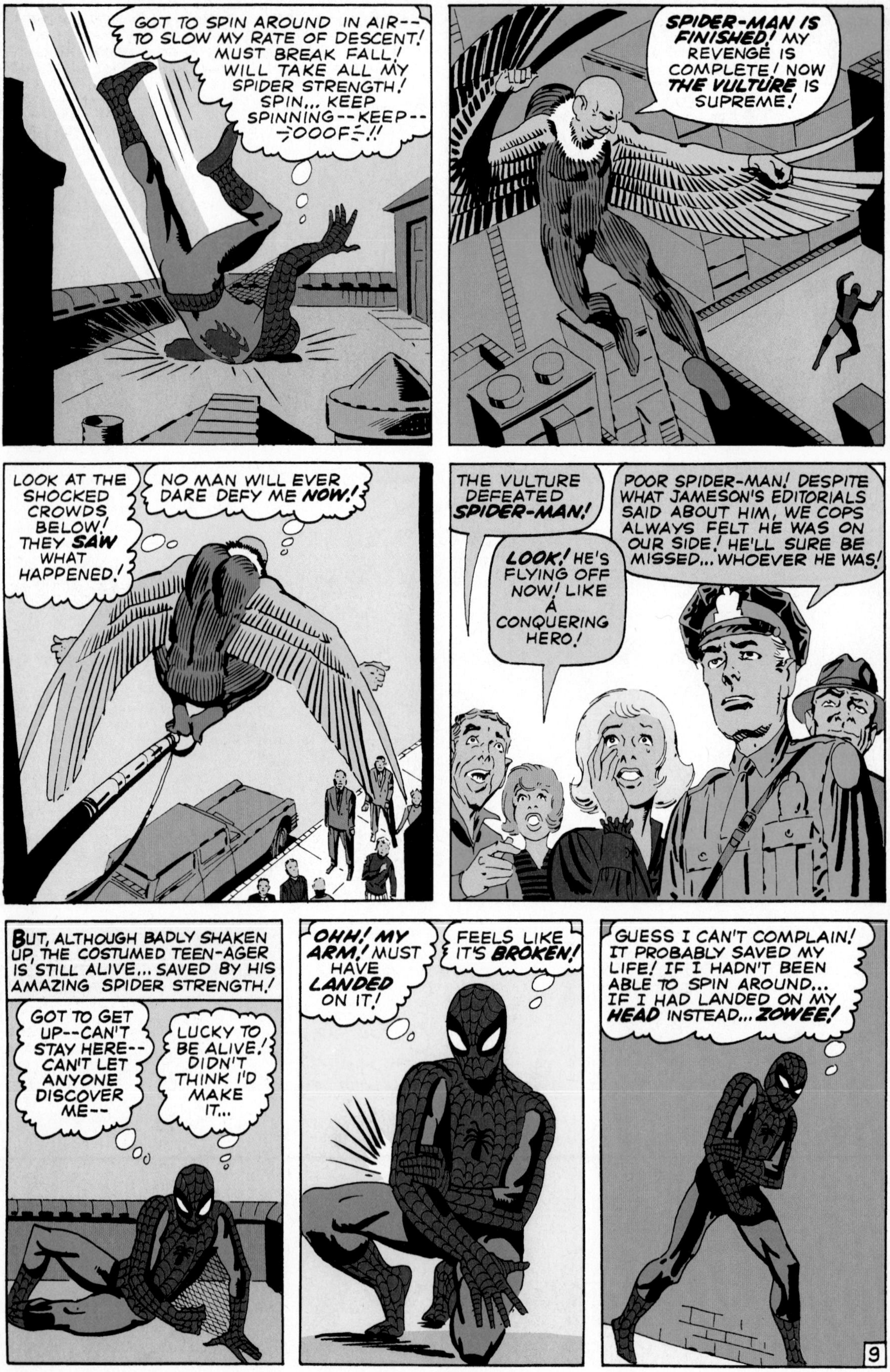
GOT TO SPIN AROUND IN AIR--TO SLOW MY RATE OF DESCENT! MUST BREAK FALL! WILL TAKE ALL MY SPIDER STRENGTH! SPIN... KEEP SPINNING--KEEP--OOOF!!
SPIDER-MAN IS FINISHED! MY REVENGE IS COMPLETE! NOW THE VULTURE IS SUPREME!
LOOK AT THE SHOCKED CROWDS BELOW! THEY SAW WHAT HAPPENED!
NO MAN WILL EVER DARE DEFY ME NOW!
THE VULTURE DEFEATED SPIDER-MAN!
POOR SPIDER-MAN! DESPITE WHAT JAMESON'S EDITORIALS SAID ABOUT HIM, WE COPS ALWAYS FELT HE WAS ON OUR SIDE! HE'LL SURE BE MISSED... WHOEVER HE WAS!
LOOK! HE'S FLYING OFF NOW! LIKE A CONQUERING HERO!
BUT, ALTHOUGH BADLY SHAKEN UP, THE COSTUMED TEEN-AGER IS STILL ALIVE... SAVED BY HIS AMAZING SPIDER STRENGTH!
GOT TO GET UP--CAN'T STAY HERE--CAN'T LET ANYONE DISCOVER ME--
LUCKY TO BE ALIVE! DIDN'T THINK I'D MAKE IT...
OHH! MY ARM! MUST HAVE LANDED ON IT!
FEELS LIKE IT'S BROKEN!
GUESS I CAN'T COMPLAIN! IT PROBABLY SAVED MY LIFE! IF I HADN'T BEEN ABLE TO SPIN AROUND... IF I HAD LANDED ON MY HEAD INSTEAD... ZOWEE!
9

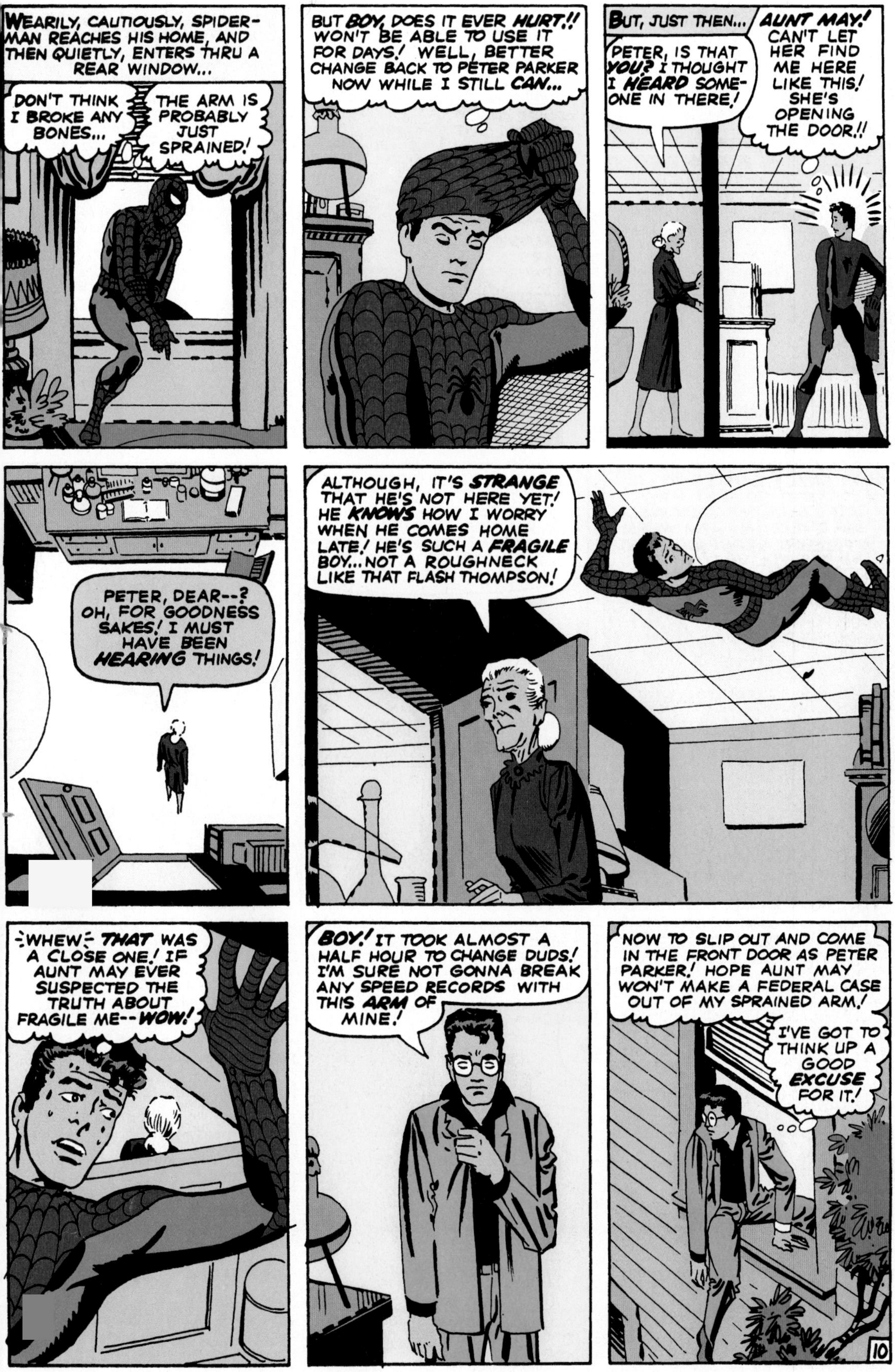
WEARILY, CAUTIOUSLY, SPIDER-MAN REACHES HIS HOME, AND THEN QUIETLY, ENTERS THRU A REAR WINDOW...
DON'T THINK I BROKE ANY BONES...
THE ARM IS PROBABLY JUST SPRAINED!
BUT BOY, DOES IT EVER HURT!! WON'T BE ABLE TO USE IT FOR DAYS! WELL, BETTER CHANGE BACK TO PETER PARKER NOW WHILE I STILL CAN...
BUT, JUST THEN...
PETER, IS THAT YOU? I THOUGHT I HEARD SOME-ONE IN THERE!
AUNT MAY! CAN'T LET HER FIND ME HERE LIKE THIS! SHE'S OPENING THE DOOR!!
PETER, DEAR--? OH, FOR GOODNESS SAKES! I MUST HAVE BEEN HEARING THINGS!
ALTHOUGH, IT'S STRANGE THAT HE'S NOT HERE YET! HE KNOWS HOW I WORRY WHEN HE COMES HOME LATE! HE'S SUCH A FRAGILE BOY...NOT A ROUGHNECK LIKE THAT FLASH THOMPSON!
-WHEW- THAT WAS A CLOSE ONE! IF AUNT MAY EVER SUSPECTED THE TRUTH ABOUT FRAGILE ME--WOW!
BOY! IT TOOK ALMOST A HALF HOUR TO CHANGE DUDS! I'M SURE NOT GONNA BREAK ANY SPEED RECORDS WITH THIS ARM OF MINE!
NOW TO SLIP OUT AND COME IN THE FRONT DOOR AS PETER PARKER! HOPE AUNT MAY WON'T MAKE A FEDERAL CASE OUT OF MY SPRAINED ARM!
I'VE GOT TO THINK UP A GOOD EXCUSE FOR IT!
10

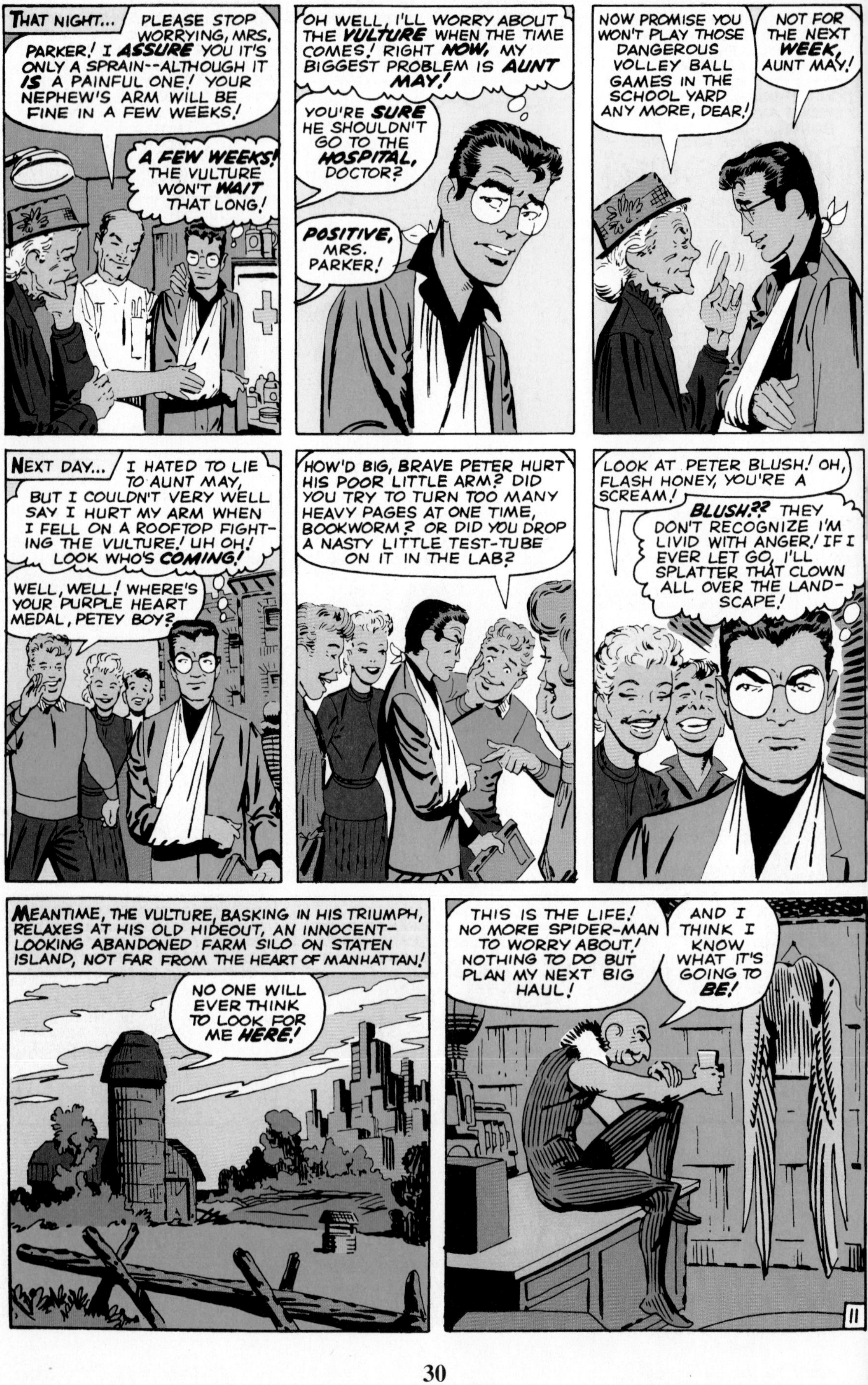

THAT NIGHT...
PLEASE STOP WORRYING, MRS. PARKER! I ASSURE YOU IT'S ONLY A SPRAIN--ALTHOUGH IT IS A PAINFUL ONE! YOUR NEPHEW'S ARM WILL BE FINE IN A FEW WEEKS!
A FEW WEEKS! THE VULTURE WON'T WAIT THAT LONG!
OH WELL, I'LL WORRY ABOUT THE VULTURE WHEN THE TIME COMES! RIGHT NOW, MY BIGGEST PROBLEM IS AUNT MAY!
YOU'RE SURE HE SHOULDN'T GO TO THE HOSPITAL, DOCTOR?
POSITIVE, MRS. PARKER!
NOW PROMISE YOU WON'T PLAY THOSE DANGEROUS VOLLEY BALL GAMES IN THE SCHOOL YARD ANY MORE, DEAR!
NOT FOR THE NEXT WEEK, AUNT MAY!
NEXT DAY...
I HATED TO LIE TO AUNT MAY, BUT I COULDN'T VERY WELL SAY I HURT MY ARM WHEN I FELL ON A ROOFTOP FIGHTING THE VULTURE! UH OH! LOOK WHO'S COMING!
WELL, WELL! WHERE'S YOUR PURPLE HEART MEDAL, PETEY BOY?
HOW'D BIG, BRAVE PETER HURT HIS POOR LITTLE ARM? DID YOU TRY TO TURN TOO MANY HEAVY PAGES AT ONE TIME, BOOKWORM? OR DID YOU DROP A NASTY LITTLE TEST-TUBE ON IT IN THE LAB?
LOOK AT PETER BLUSH! OH, FLASH HONEY, YOU'RE A SCREAM!
BLUSH?? THEY DON'T RECOGNIZE I'M LIVID WITH ANGER! IF I EVER LET GO, I'LL SPLATTER THAT CLOWN ALL OVER THE LANDSCAPE!
MEANTIME, THE VULTURE, BASKING IN HIS TRIUMPH, RELAXES AT HIS OLD HIDEOUT, AN INNOCENT-LOOKING ABANDONED FARM SILO ON STATEN ISLAND, NOT FAR FROM THE HEART OF MANHATTAN!
NO ONE WILL EVER THINK TO LOOK FOR ME HERE!
THIS IS THE LIFE! NO MORE SPIDER-MAN TO WORRY ABOUT! NOTHING TO DO BUT PLAN MY NEXT BIG HAUL!
AND I THINK I KNOW WHAT IT'S GOING TO BE!
11

ONE OF THE BIGGEST PAYROLLS IN NEW YORK IS AT THE OFFICE OF *J. JONAH JAMESON!* HE PUBLISHES THE "DAILY BUGLE" AND "NOW" MAGAZINE! HE MUST EMPLOY *HUNDREDS* OF WORKERS!

AND *THAT* MEANS HUNDREDS OF NICE, FAT, JUICY *PAY ENVELOPES*, JUST WAITING FOR THE VULTURE TO FLY IN AND GRAB THEM!

IT'S THE END OF THE WEEK NOW, SO ALL THE DOUGH MUST BE IN THE SAFE, READY FOR PAY DAY! ONLY, IT'S GONNA BE *MY* PAY DAY THIS TIME!

AND, AT THE OFFICES OF THE DAILY BUGLE, WE FIND YOUNG PETER PARKER, TALKING TO J. JONAH JAMESON'S SECRETARY...

OH, PETER, *NOBODY* COULD SPRAIN HIS ARM PLAYING VOLLEY BALL!

WHAT *REALLY* HAPPENED?

OKAY, I'LL TELL YOU THE *TRUTH*...

IT HAPPENED IN THE AIR, WHILE I WAS FIGHTING THE VULTURE FOR DEAR LIFE!

OH, WELL! ASK A SILLY QUESTION

SO LET'S STICK TO THE VOLLEY BALL STORY! OKAY?

MISS BRANT! SEND PARKER IN NOW!

I'LL *ADMIT* THAT'S A FINE PICTURE OF THE VULTURE, PARKER, BUT I CAN'T PAY MORE THAN TEN DOLLARS FOR IT! AFTER ALL, HE'S BEEN SEEN ALL OVER TOWN! *LOTS* OF PEOPLE HAVE SNAPPED HIM! I WANT SOMETHING *DIFFERENT!*

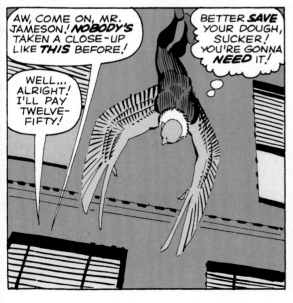

AW, COME ON, MR. JAMESON! *NOBODY'S* TAKEN A CLOSE-UP LIKE *THIS* BEFORE!

BETTER *SAVE* YOUR DOUGH, SUCKER! YOU'RE GONNA *NEED* IT!

WELL... ALRIGHT! I'LL PAY TWELVE-FIFTY!

GREETINGS, JAMESON! IF YOU'LL PAY FOR A MERE *PHOTO* OF ME, WHAT WILL YOU GIVE FOR THE VULTURE IN THE *FLESH??!*

HOLY COW! IT'S HIM!

THE VULTURE!!

12

31

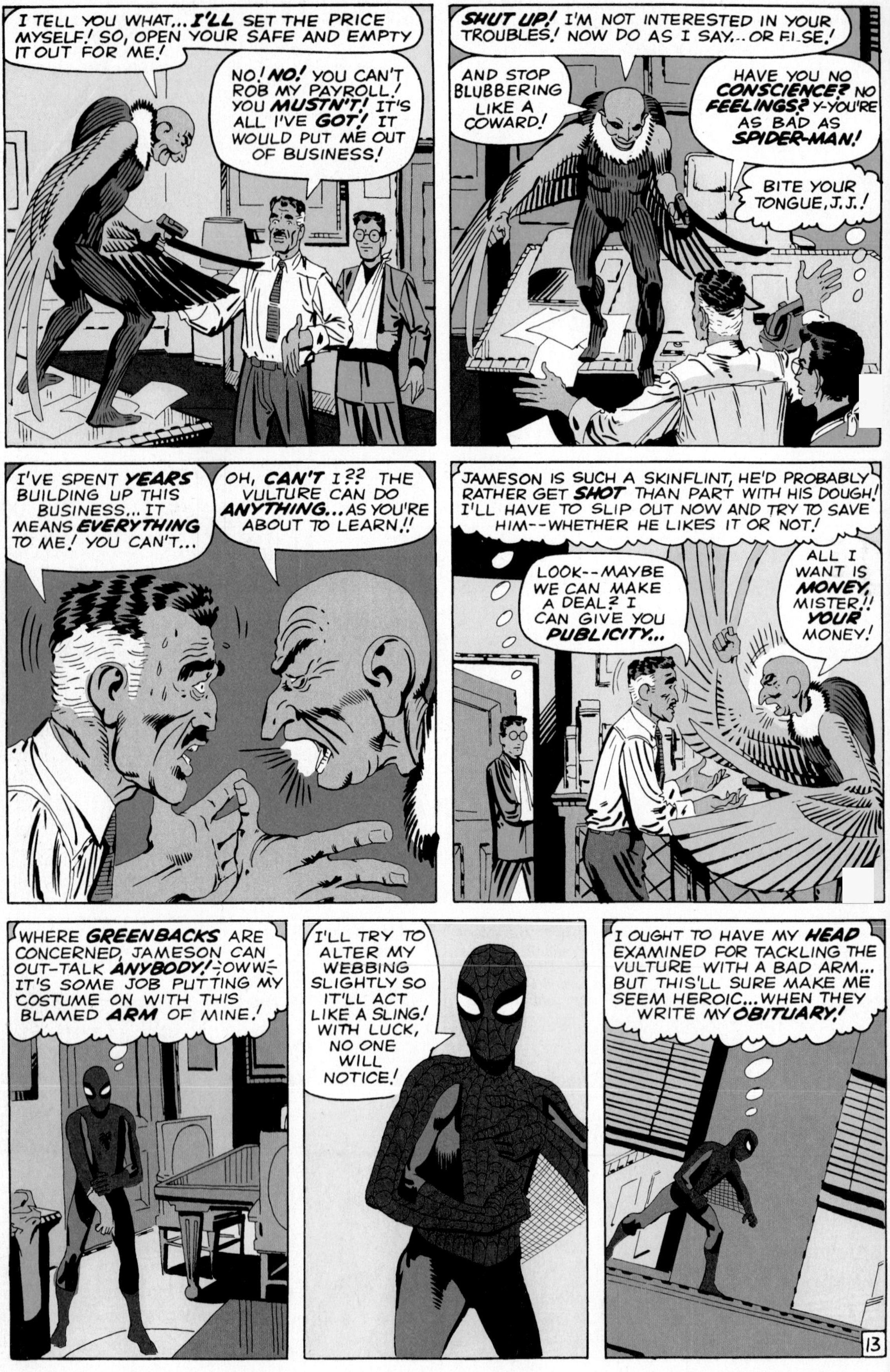
I TELL YOU WHAT... I'LL SET THE PRICE MYSELF! SO, OPEN YOUR SAFE AND EMPTY IT OUT FOR ME!
NO! NO! YOU CAN'T ROB MY PAYROLL! YOU MUSTN'T! IT'S ALL I'VE GOT! IT WOULD PUT ME OUT OF BUSINESS!
SHUT UP! I'M NOT INTERESTED IN YOUR TROUBLES! NOW DO AS I SAY... OR ELSE!
AND STOP BLUBBERING LIKE A COWARD!
HAVE YOU NO CONSCIENCE? NO FEELINGS? Y-YOU'RE AS BAD AS SPIDER-MAN!
BITE YOUR TONGUE, J.J.!
I'VE SPENT YEARS BUILDING UP THIS BUSINESS... IT MEANS EVERYTHING TO ME! YOU CAN'T...
OH, CAN'T I?? THE VULTURE CAN DO ANYTHING... AS YOU'RE ABOUT TO LEARN!!
JAMESON IS SUCH A SKINFLINT, HE'D PROBABLY RATHER GET SHOT THAN PART WITH HIS DOUGH! I'LL HAVE TO SLIP OUT NOW AND TRY TO SAVE HIM--WHETHER HE LIKES IT OR NOT!
LOOK--MAYBE WE CAN MAKE A DEAL? I CAN GIVE YOU PUBLICITY...
ALL I WANT IS MONEY, MISTER!! YOUR MONEY!
WHERE GREENBACKS ARE CONCERNED, JAMESON CAN OUT-TALK ANYBODY! -OWW- IT'S SOME JOB PUTTING MY COSTUME ON WITH THIS BLAMED ARM OF MINE!
I'LL TRY TO ALTER MY WEBBING SLIGHTLY SO IT'LL ACT LIKE A SLING! WITH LUCK, NO ONE WILL NOTICE!
I OUGHT TO HAVE MY HEAD EXAMINED FOR TACKLING THE VULTURE WITH A BAD ARM... BUT THIS'LL SURE MAKE ME SEEM HEROIC... WHEN THEY WRITE MY OBITUARY!
13

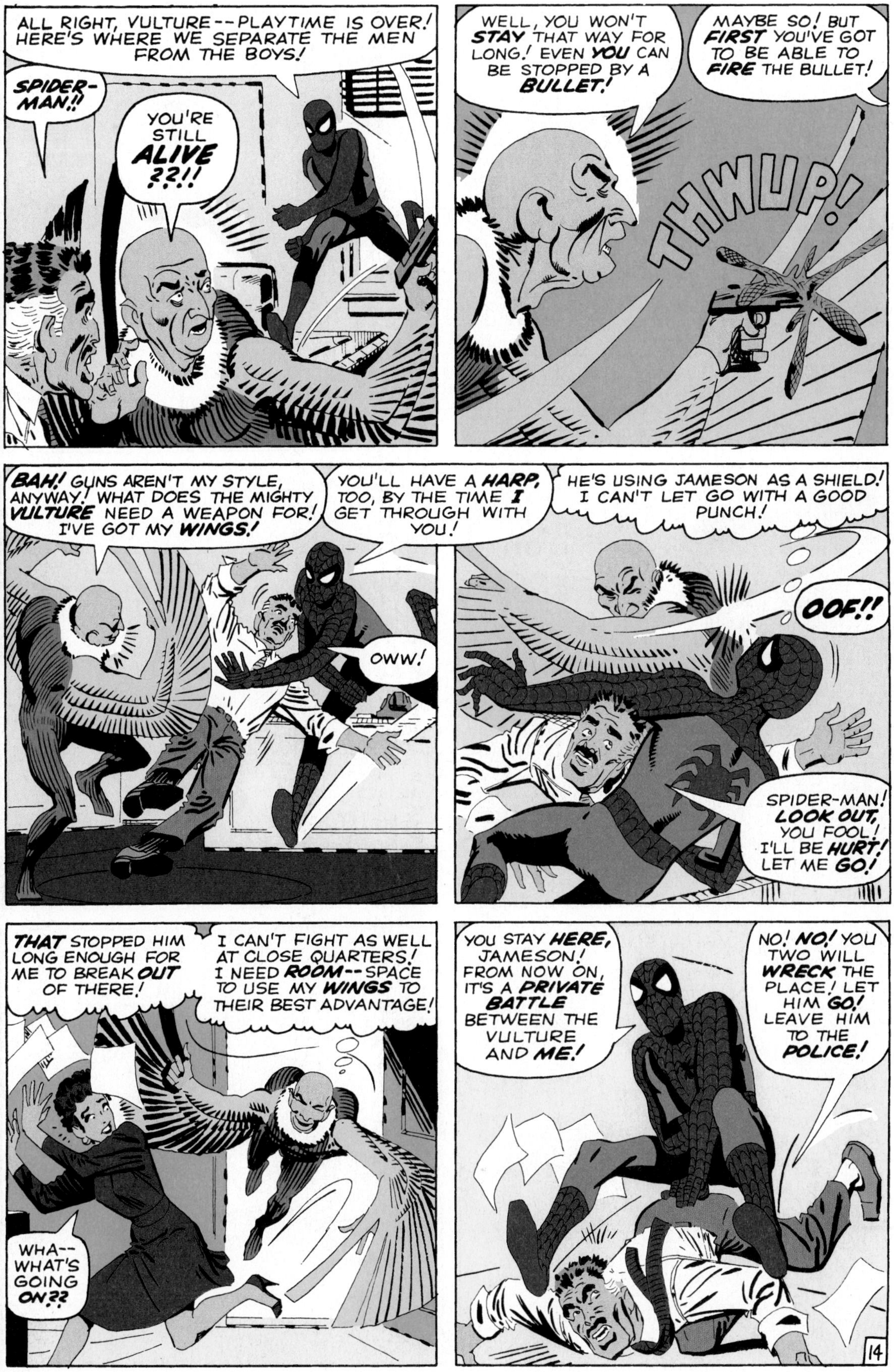
ALL RIGHT, VULTURE--PLAYTIME IS OVER! HERE'S WHERE WE SEPARATE THE MEN FROM THE BOYS!
SPIDER-MAN!!
YOU'RE STILL ALIVE ??!!
WELL, YOU WON'T STAY THAT WAY FOR LONG! EVEN YOU CAN BE STOPPED BY A BULLET!
MAYBE SO! BUT FIRST YOU'VE GOT TO BE ABLE TO FIRE THE BULLET!
THWUP!
BAH! GUNS AREN'T MY STYLE, ANYWAY! WHAT DOES THE MIGHTY VULTURE NEED A WEAPON FOR! I'VE GOT MY WINGS!
YOU'LL HAVE A HARP, TOO, BY THE TIME I GET THROUGH WITH YOU!
OWW!
HE'S USING JAMESON AS A SHIELD! I CAN'T LET GO WITH A GOOD PUNCH!
OOF!!
SPIDER-MAN! LOOK OUT, YOU FOOL! I'LL BE HURT! LET ME GO!
THAT STOPPED HIM LONG ENOUGH FOR ME TO BREAK OUT OF THERE!
I CAN'T FIGHT AS WELL AT CLOSE QUARTERS! I NEED ROOM--SPACE TO USE MY WINGS TO THEIR BEST ADVANTAGE!
WHA-- WHAT'S GOING ON??
YOU STAY HERE, JAMESON! FROM NOW ON, IT'S A PRIVATE BATTLE BETWEEN THE VULTURE AND ME!
NO! NO! YOU TWO WILL WRECK THE PLACE! LET HIM GO! LEAVE HIM TO THE POLICE!
14

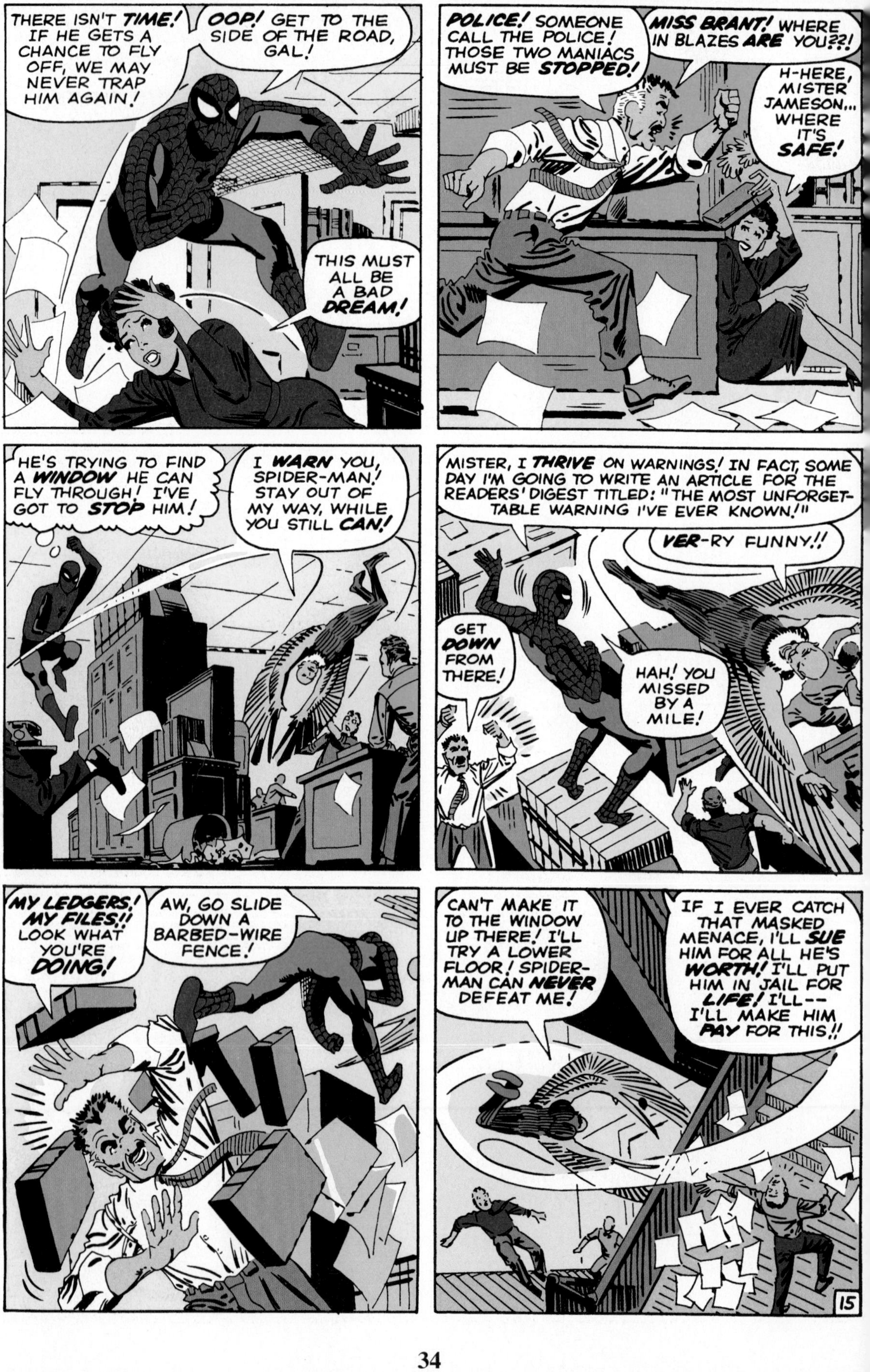
THERE ISN'T TIME! IF HE GETS A CHANCE TO FLY OFF, WE MAY NEVER TRAP HIM AGAIN!
OOP! GET TO THE SIDE OF THE ROAD, GAL!
THIS MUST ALL BE A BAD DREAM!
POLICE! SOMEONE CALL THE POLICE! THOSE TWO MANIACS MUST BE STOPPED!
MISS BRANT! WHERE IN BLAZES ARE YOU??!
H-HERE, MISTER JAMESON... WHERE IT'S SAFE!
HE'S TRYING TO FIND A WINDOW HE CAN FLY THROUGH! I'VE GOT TO STOP HIM!
I WARN YOU, SPIDER-MAN! STAY OUT OF MY WAY, WHILE YOU STILL CAN!
MISTER, I THRIVE ON WARNINGS! IN FACT, SOME DAY I'M GOING TO WRITE AN ARTICLE FOR THE READERS' DIGEST TITLED: "THE MOST UNFORGET-TABLE WARNING I'VE EVER KNOWN!"
VER-RY FUNNY!!
GET DOWN FROM THERE!
HAH! YOU MISSED BY A MILE!
MY LEDGERS! MY FILES!! LOOK WHAT YOU'RE DOING!
AW, GO SLIDE DOWN A BARBED-WIRE FENCE!
CAN'T MAKE IT TO THE WINDOW UP THERE! I'LL TRY A LOWER FLOOR! SPIDER-MAN CAN NEVER DEFEAT ME!
IF I EVER CATCH THAT MASKED MENACE, I'LL SUE HIM FOR ALL HE'S WORTH! I'LL PUT HIM IN JAIL FOR LIFE! I'LL-- I'LL MAKE HIM PAY FOR THIS!!
15

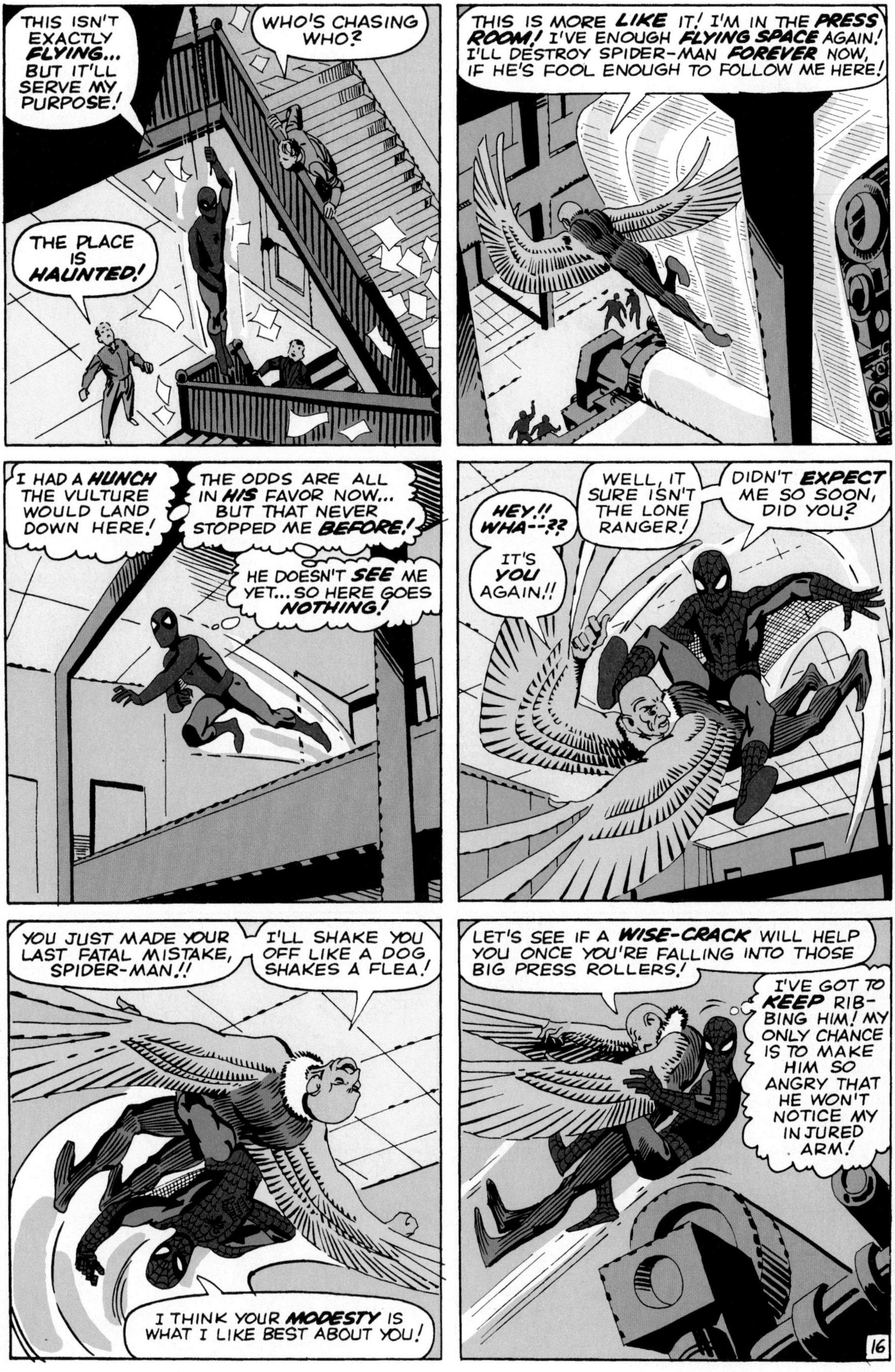
THIS ISN'T EXACTLY FLYING... BUT IT'LL SERVE MY PURPOSE!
WHO'S CHASING WHO?
THE PLACE IS HAUNTED!
THIS IS MORE LIKE IT! I'M IN THE PRESS ROOM! I'VE ENOUGH FLYING SPACE AGAIN! I'LL DESTROY SPIDER-MAN FOREVER NOW, IF HE'S FOOL ENOUGH TO FOLLOW ME HERE!
I HAD A HUNCH THE VULTURE WOULD LAND DOWN HERE!
THE ODDS ARE ALL IN HIS FAVOR NOW... BUT THAT NEVER STOPPED ME BEFORE!
HE DOESN'T SEE ME YET... SO HERE GOES NOTHING!
HEY!! WHA--??
IT'S YOU AGAIN!!
WELL, IT SURE ISN'T THE LONE RANGER!
DIDN'T EXPECT ME SO SOON, DID YOU?
YOU JUST MADE YOUR LAST FATAL MISTAKE, SPIDER-MAN!!
I'LL SHAKE YOU OFF LIKE A DOG SHAKES A FLEA!
I THINK YOUR MODESTY IS WHAT I LIKE BEST ABOUT YOU!
LET'S SEE IF A WISE-CRACK WILL HELP YOU ONCE YOU'RE FALLING INTO THOSE BIG PRESS ROLLERS!
I'VE GOT TO KEEP RIB-BING HIM! MY ONLY CHANCE IS TO MAKE HIM SO ANGRY THAT HE WON'T NOTICE MY INJURED ARM!
16

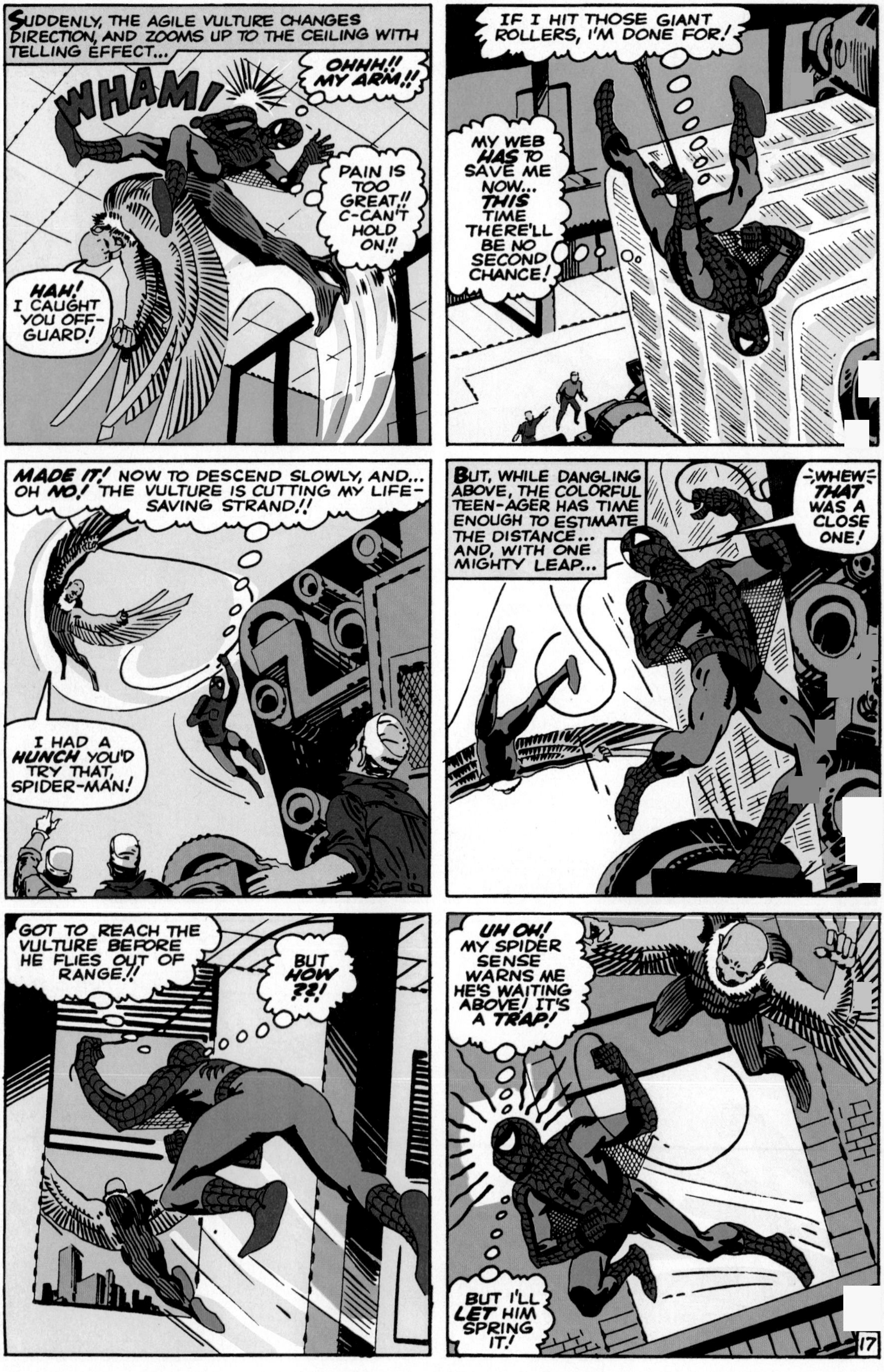
SUDDENLY, THE AGILE VULTURE CHANGES DIRECTION, AND ZOOMS UP TO THE CEILING WITH TELLING EFFECT...
WHAM!
OHHH!! MY ARM!!
PAIN IS TOO GREAT!! C-CAN'T HOLD ON!!
HAH! I CAUGHT YOU OFF-GUARD!
IF I HIT THOSE GIANT ROLLERS, I'M DONE FOR!
MY WEB HAS TO SAVE ME NOW... THIS TIME THERE'LL BE NO SECOND CHANCE!
MADE IT! NOW TO DESCEND SLOWLY, AND... OH NO! THE VULTURE IS CUTTING MY LIFE-SAVING STRAND!!
I HAD A HUNCH YOU'D TRY THAT, SPIDER-MAN!
BUT, WHILE DANGLING ABOVE, THE COLORFUL TEEN-AGER HAS TIME ENOUGH TO ESTIMATE THE DISTANCE... AND, WITH ONE MIGHTY LEAP...
WHEW THAT WAS A CLOSE ONE!
GOT TO REACH THE VULTURE BEFORE HE FLIES OUT OF RANGE!!
BUT HOW ??!
UH OH! MY SPIDER SENSE WARNS ME HE'S WAITING ABOVE! IT'S A TRAP!
BUT I'LL LET HIM SPRING IT!
17

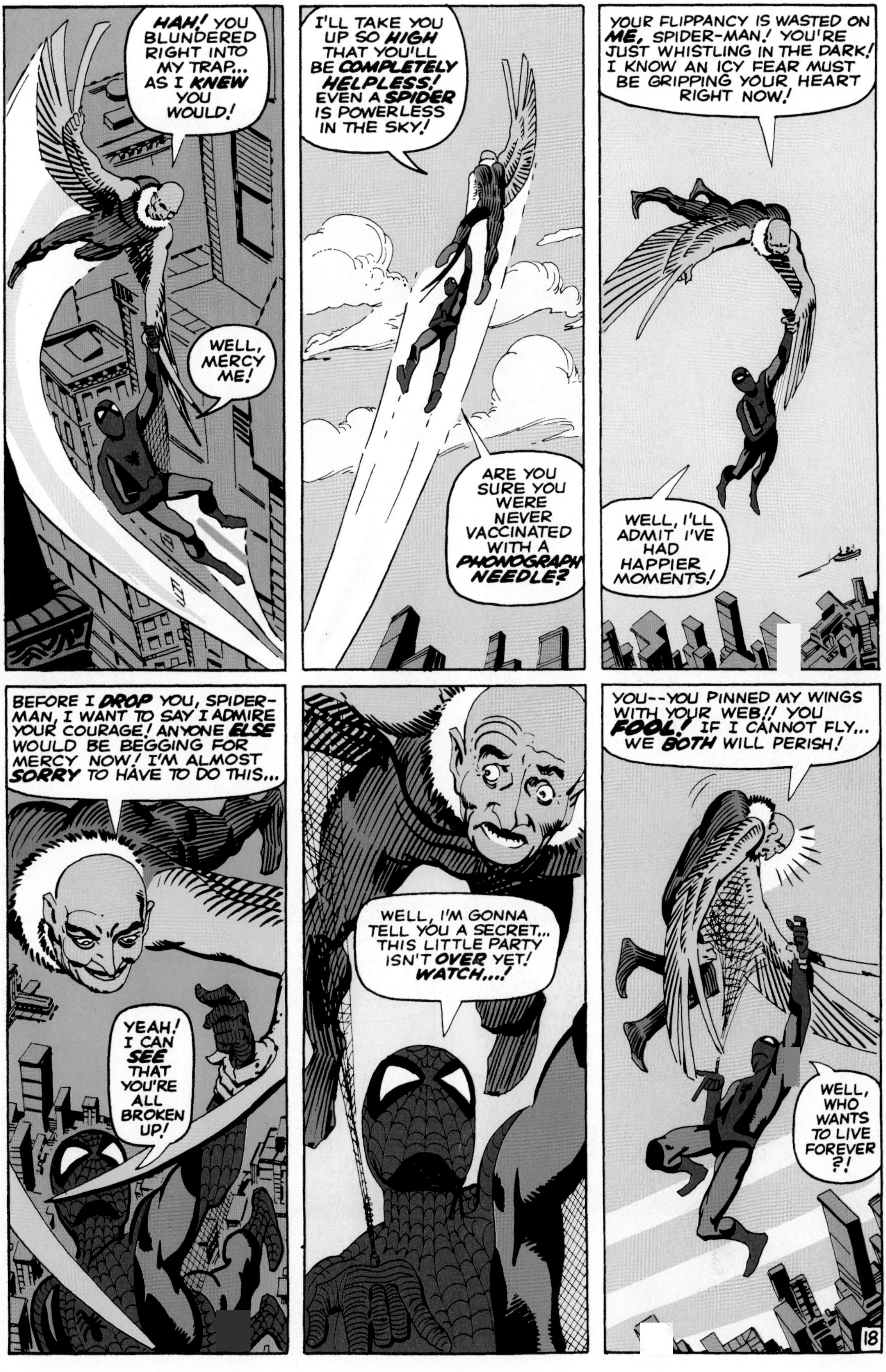
HAH! YOU BLUNDERED RIGHT INTO MY TRAP... AS I KNEW YOU WOULD!
WELL, MERCY ME!
I'LL TAKE YOU UP SO HIGH THAT YOU'LL BE COMPLETELY HELPLESS! EVEN A SPIDER IS POWERLESS IN THE SKY!
ARE YOU SURE YOU WERE NEVER VACCINATED WITH A PHONOGRAPH NEEDLE?
YOUR FLIPPANCY IS WASTED ON ME, SPIDER-MAN! YOU'RE JUST WHISTLING IN THE DARK! I KNOW AN ICY FEAR MUST BE GRIPPING YOUR HEART RIGHT NOW!
WELL, I'LL ADMIT I'VE HAD HAPPIER MOMENTS!
BEFORE I DROP YOU, SPIDER-MAN, I WANT TO SAY I ADMIRE YOUR COURAGE! ANYONE ELSE WOULD BE BEGGING FOR MERCY NOW! I'M ALMOST SORRY TO HAVE TO DO THIS...
YEAH! I CAN SEE THAT YOU'RE ALL BROKEN UP!
WELL, I'M GONNA TELL YOU A SECRET... THIS LITTLE PARTY ISN'T OVER YET! WATCH...!
YOU--YOU PINNED MY WINGS WITH YOUR WEB!! YOU FOOL! IF I CANNOT FLY... WE BOTH WILL PERISH!
WELL, WHO WANTS TO LIVE FOREVER?!
18

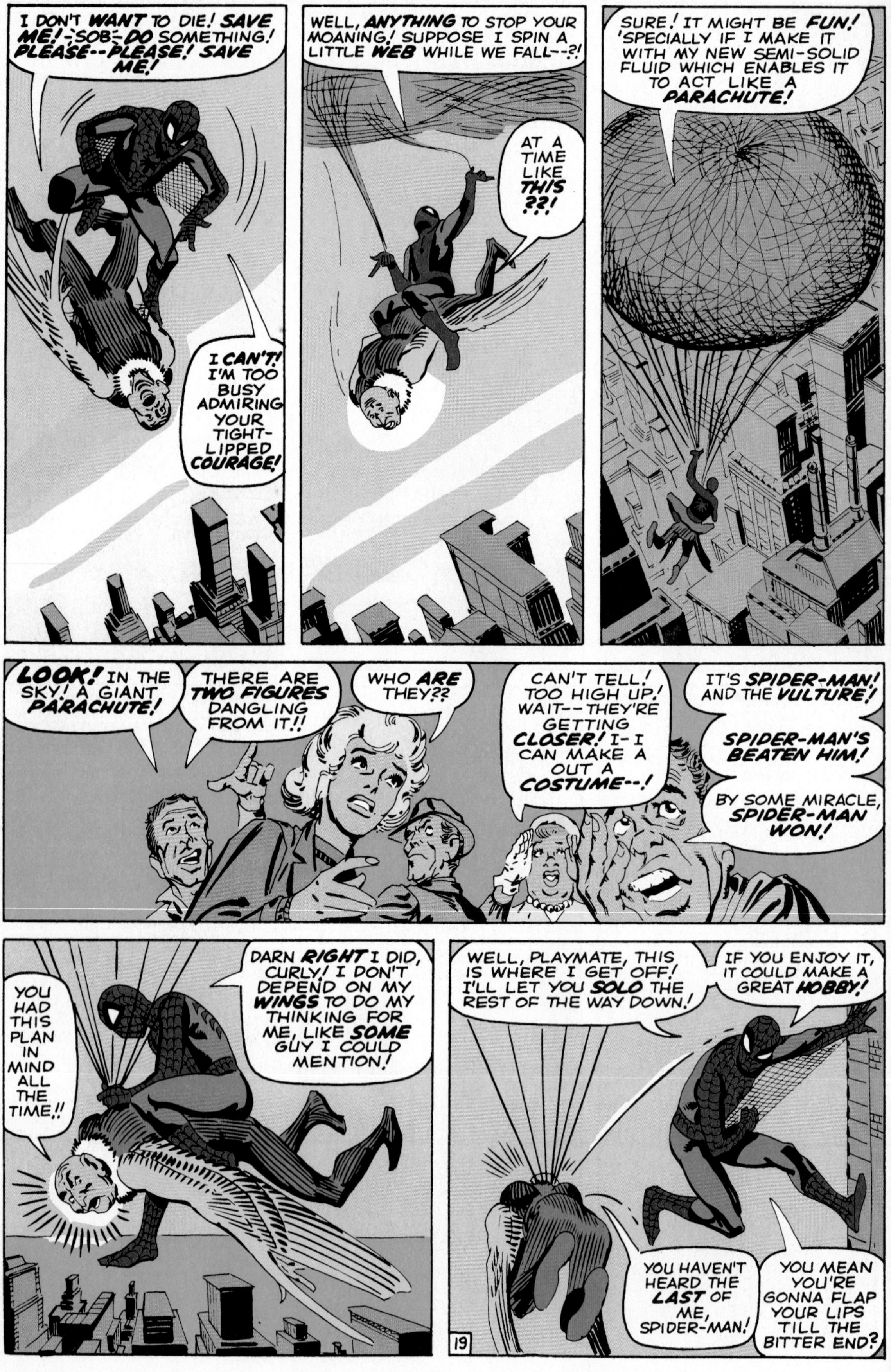
I DON'T WANT TO DIE! SAVE ME! -SOB- DO SOMETHING! PLEASE--PLEASE! SAVE ME!
I CAN'T! I'M TOO BUSY ADMIRING YOUR TIGHT-LIPPED COURAGE!
WELL, ANYTHING TO STOP YOUR MOANING! SUPPOSE I SPIN A LITTLE WEB WHILE WE FALL--?!
AT A TIME LIKE THIS ??!
SURE! IT MIGHT BE FUN! 'SPECIALLY IF I MAKE IT WITH MY NEW SEMI-SOLID FLUID WHICH ENABLES IT TO ACT LIKE A PARACHUTE!
LOOK! IN THE SKY! A GIANT PARACHUTE!
THERE ARE TWO FIGURES DANGLING FROM IT!!
WHO ARE THEY??
CAN'T TELL! TOO HIGH UP! WAIT--THEY'RE GETTING CLOSER! I-I CAN MAKE A OUT A COSTUME--!
IT'S SPIDER-MAN! AND THE VULTURE!
SPIDER-MAN'S BEATEN HIM!
BY SOME MIRACLE, SPIDER-MAN WON!
YOU HAD THIS PLAN IN MIND ALL THE TIME!!
DARN RIGHT I DID, CURLY! I DON'T DEPEND ON MY WINGS TO DO MY THINKING FOR ME, LIKE SOME GUY I COULD MENTION!
WELL, PLAYMATE, THIS IS WHERE I GET OFF! I'LL LET YOU SOLO THE REST OF THE WAY DOWN!
IF YOU ENJOY IT, IT COULD MAKE A GREAT HOBBY!
YOU HAVEN'T HEARD THE LAST OF ME, SPIDER-MAN!
YOU MEAN YOU'RE GONNA FLAP YOUR LIPS TILL THE BITTER END?
19

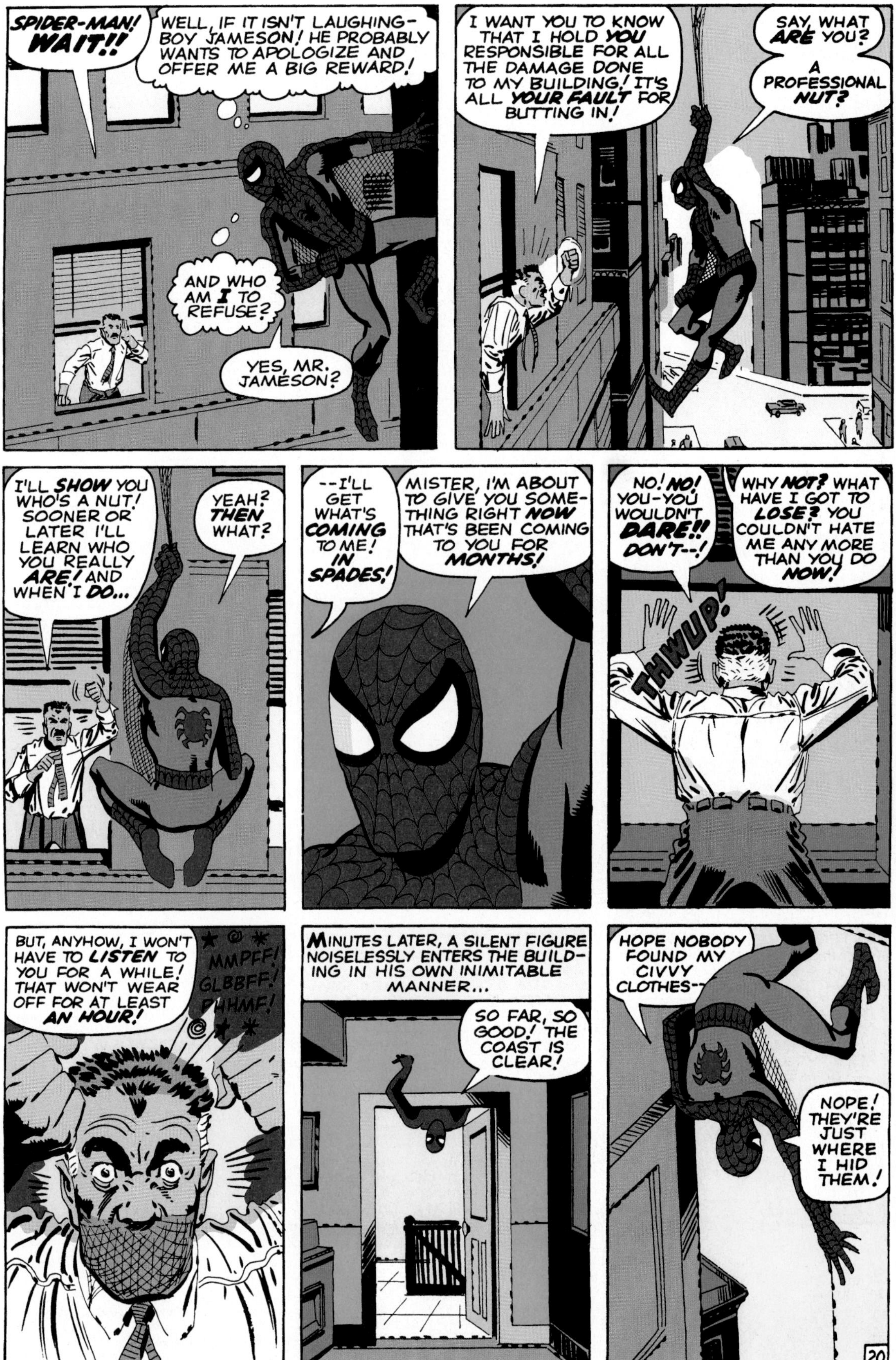
SPIDER-MAN! WAIT!!
WELL, IF IT ISN'T LAUGHING-BOY JAMESON! HE PROBABLY WANTS TO APOLOGIZE AND OFFER ME A BIG REWARD!
AND WHO AM I TO REFUSE?
YES, MR. JAMESON?
I WANT YOU TO KNOW THAT I HOLD YOU RESPONSIBLE FOR ALL THE DAMAGE DONE TO MY BUILDING! IT'S ALL YOUR FAULT FOR BUTTING IN!
SAY, WHAT ARE YOU? A PROFESSIONAL NUT?
I'LL SHOW YOU WHO'S A NUT! SOONER OR LATER I'LL LEARN WHO YOU REALLY ARE! AND WHEN I DO...
YEAH? THEN WHAT?
--I'LL GET WHAT'S COMING TO ME! IN SPADES!
MISTER, I'M ABOUT TO GIVE YOU SOMETHING RIGHT NOW THAT'S BEEN COMING TO YOU FOR MONTHS!
NO! NO! YOU-YOU WOULDN'T DARE!! DON'T--!
WHY NOT? WHAT HAVE I GOT TO LOSE? YOU COULDN'T HATE ME ANY MORE THAN YOU DO NOW!
THWUP!
BUT, ANYHOW, I WON'T HAVE TO LISTEN TO YOU FOR A WHILE! THAT WON'T WEAR OFF FOR AT LEAST AN HOUR!
MMPFF! GLBBFF! PHHMF!
MINUTES LATER, A SILENT FIGURE NOISELESSLY ENTERS THE BUILDING IN HIS OWN INIMITABLE MANNER...
SO FAR, SO GOOD! THE COAST IS CLEAR!
HOPE NOBODY FOUND MY CIVVY CLOTHES--
NOPE! THEY'RE JUST WHERE I HID THEM!
20

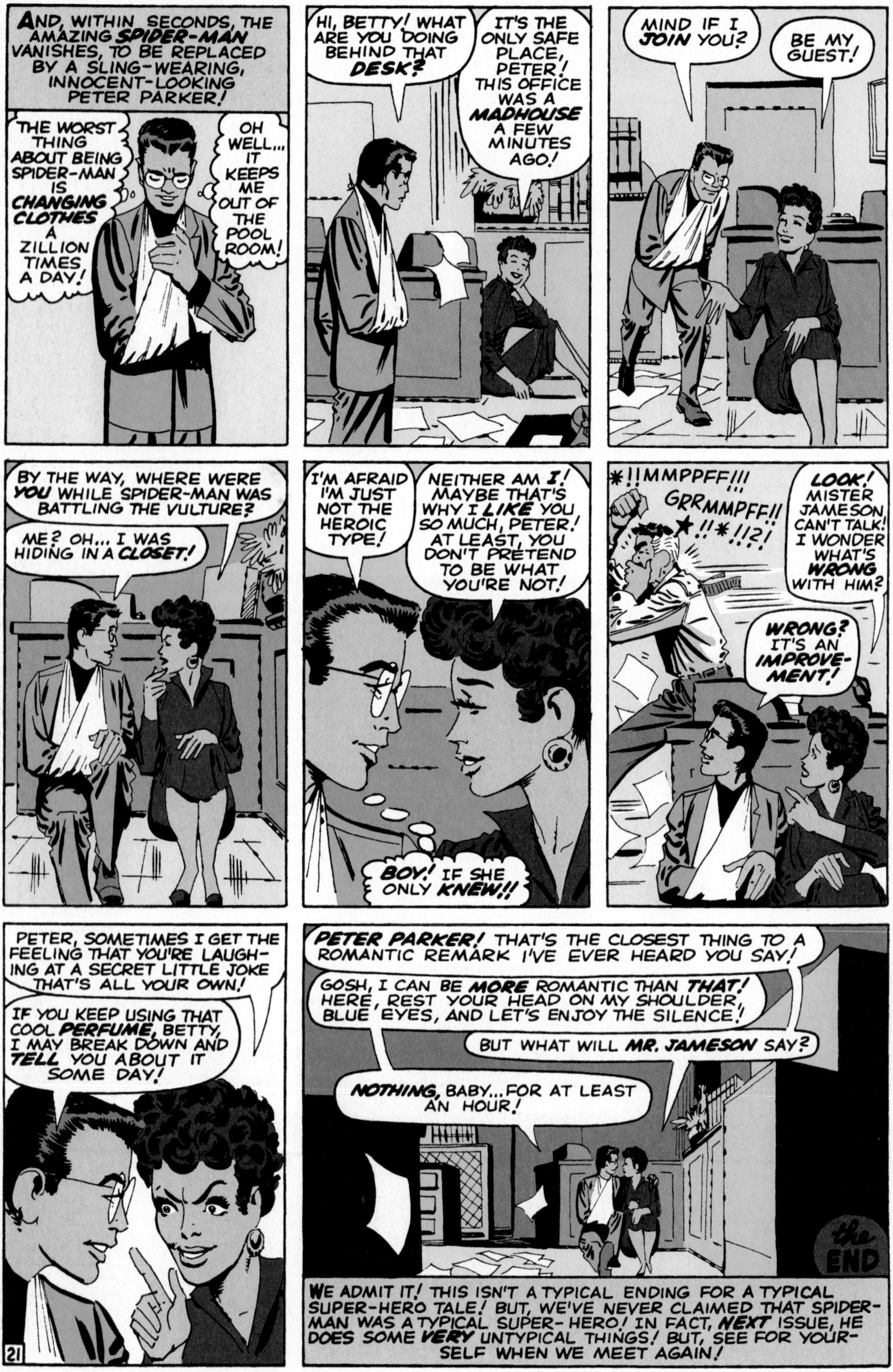
AND, WITHIN SECONDS, THE AMAZING SPIDER-MAN VANISHES, TO BE REPLACED BY A SLING-WEARING, INNOCENT-LOOKING PETER PARKER!
THE WORST THING ABOUT BEING SPIDER-MAN IS CHANGING CLOTHES A ZILLION TIMES A DAY!
OH WELL... IT KEEPS ME OUT OF THE POOL ROOM!
HI, BETTY! WHAT ARE YOU DOING BEHIND THAT DESK?
IT'S THE ONLY SAFE PLACE, PETER! THIS OFFICE WAS A MADHOUSE A FEW MINUTES AGO!
MIND IF I JOIN YOU?
BE MY GUEST!
BY THE WAY, WHERE WERE YOU WHILE SPIDER-MAN WAS BATTLING THE VULTURE?
ME? OH... I WAS HIDING IN A CLOSET!
I'M AFRAID I'M JUST NOT THE HEROIC TYPE!
NEITHER AM I! MAYBE THAT'S WHY I LIKE YOU SO MUCH, PETER! AT LEAST, YOU DON'T PRETEND TO BE WHAT YOU'RE NOT!
BOY! IF SHE ONLY KNEW!!
*!!MMPPFF!!!
GRRMMPFF!!
!!*!!?!
LOOK! MISTER JAMESON CAN'T TALK! I WONDER WHAT'S WRONG WITH HIM?
WRONG? IT'S AN IMPROVEMENT!
PETER, SOMETIMES I GET THE FEELING THAT YOU'RE LAUGHING AT A SECRET LITTLE JOKE THAT'S ALL YOUR OWN!
IF YOU KEEP USING THAT COOL PERFUME, BETTY, I MAY BREAK DOWN AND TELL YOU ABOUT IT SOME DAY!
21
PETER PARKER! THAT'S THE CLOSEST THING TO A ROMANTIC REMARK I'VE EVER HEARD YOU SAY!
GOSH, I CAN BE MORE ROMANTIC THAN THAT! HERE, REST YOUR HEAD ON MY SHOULDER, BLUE EYES, AND LET'S ENJOY THE SILENCE!
BUT WHAT WILL MR. JAMESON SAY?
NOTHING, BABY... FOR AT LEAST AN HOUR!
the END
WE ADMIT IT! THIS ISN'T A TYPICAL ENDING FOR A TYPICAL SUPER-HERO TALE! BUT, WE'VE NEVER CLAIMED THAT SPIDER-MAN WAS A TYPICAL SUPER-HERO! IN FACT, NEXT ISSUE, HE DOES SOME VERY UNTYPICAL THINGS! BUT, SEE FOR YOURSELF WHEN WE MEET AGAIN!

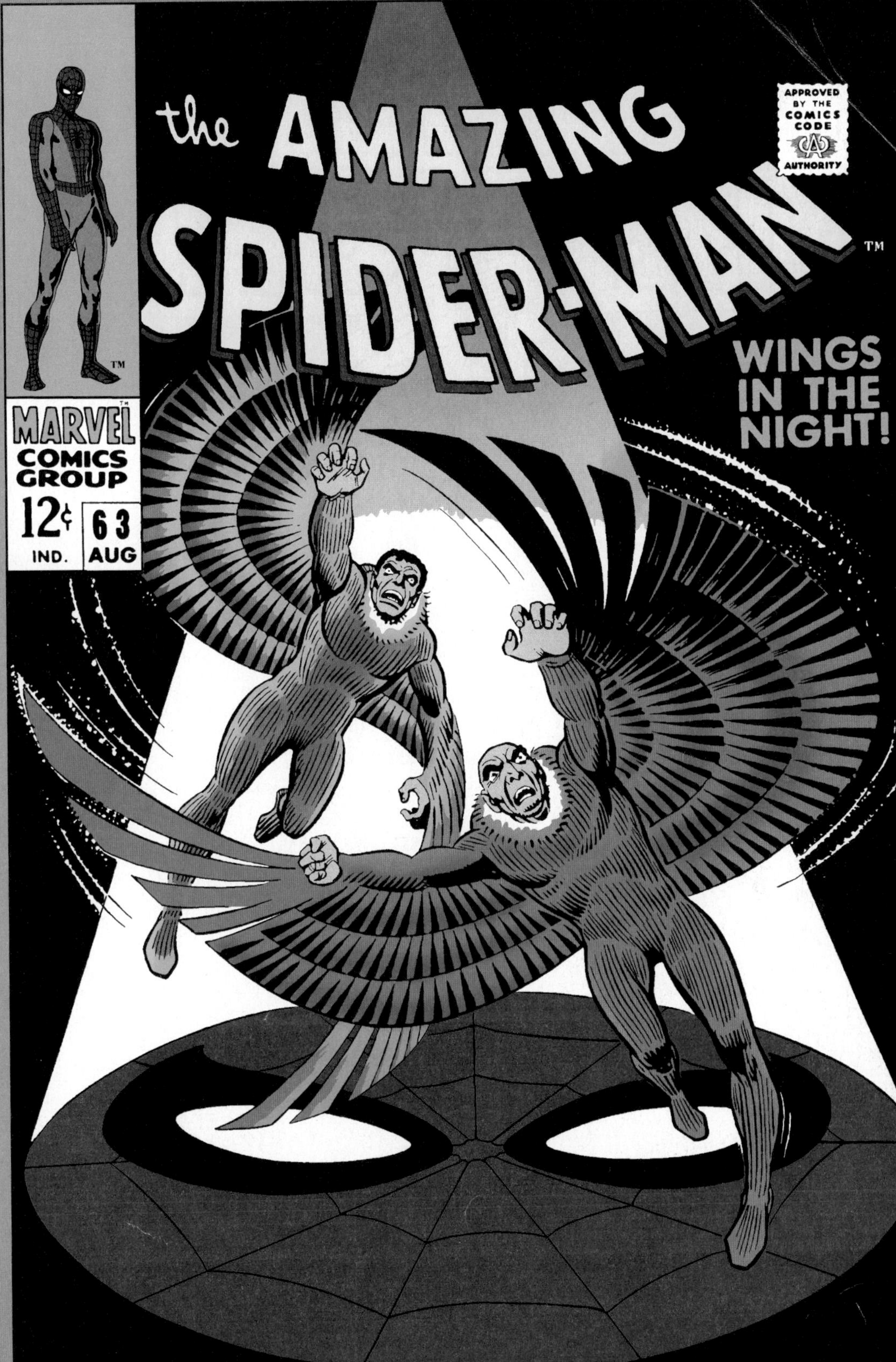

MARVEL COMICS GROUP
12¢
IND.
63
AUG
APPROVED BY THE COMICS CODE AUTHORITY
the AMAZING SPIDER-MAN™
WINGS IN THE NIGHT!

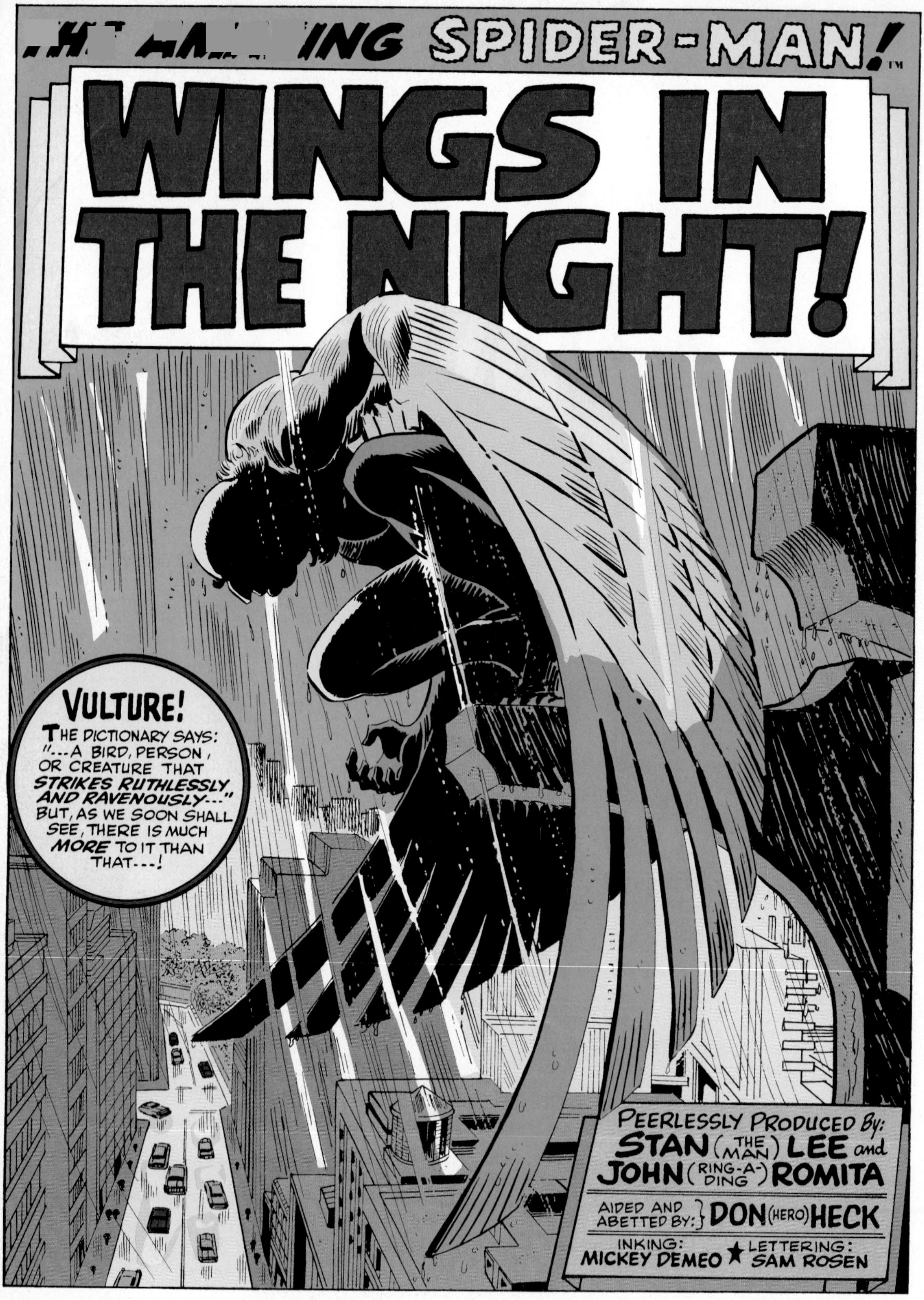
SPIDER-MAN!
WINGS IN THE NIGHT!
VULTURE! THE DICTIONARY SAYS: "...A BIRD, PERSON, OR CREATURE THAT STRIKES RUTHLESSLY AND RAVENOUSLY..." BUT, AS WE SOON SHALL SEE, THERE IS MUCH MORE TO IT THAN THAT...!
PEERLESSLY PRODUCED BY: STAN (THE MAN) LEE and JOHN (RING-A-DING) ROMITA
AIDED AND ABETTED BY: DON (HERO) HECK
INKING: MICKEY DEMEO ★ LETTERING: SAM ROSEN

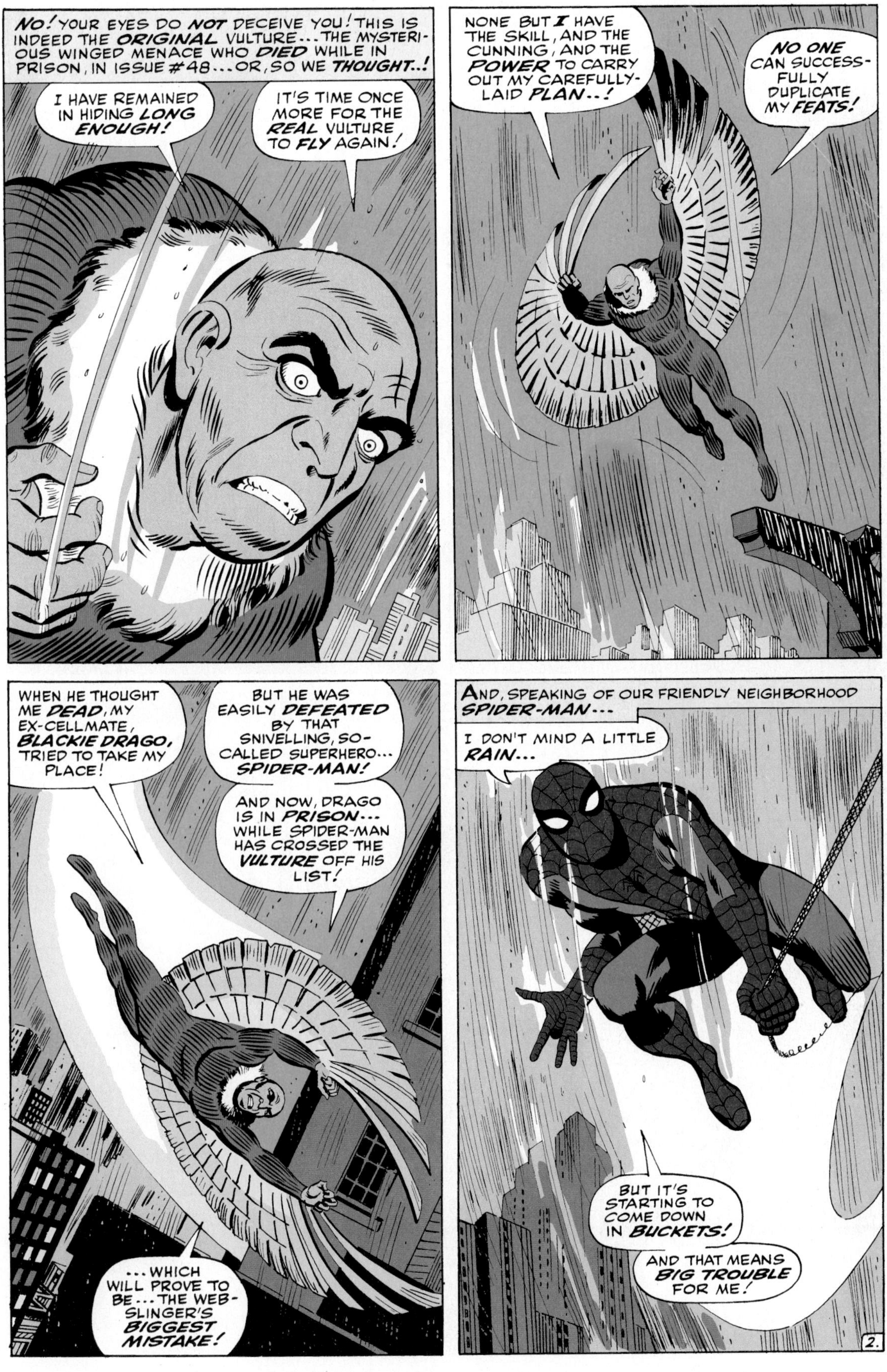
NO! YOUR EYES DO NOT DECEIVE YOU! THIS IS INDEED THE ORIGINAL VULTURE... THE MYSTERIOUS WINGED MENACE WHO DIED WHILE IN PRISON, IN ISSUE #48... OR, SO WE THOUGHT..!
I HAVE REMAINED IN HIDING LONG ENOUGH!
IT'S TIME ONCE MORE FOR THE REAL VULTURE TO FLY AGAIN!
NONE BUT I HAVE THE SKILL, AND THE CUNNING, AND THE POWER TO CARRY OUT MY CAREFULLY-LAID PLAN..!
NO ONE CAN SUCCESSFULLY DUPLICATE MY FEATS!
WHEN HE THOUGHT ME DEAD, MY EX-CELLMATE, BLACKIE DRAGO, TRIED TO TAKE MY PLACE!
BUT HE WAS EASILY DEFEATED BY THAT SNIVELLING, SO-CALLED SUPERHERO... SPIDER-MAN!
AND NOW, DRAGO IS IN PRISON... WHILE SPIDER-MAN HAS CROSSED THE VULTURE OFF HIS LIST!
...WHICH WILL PROVE TO BE... THE WEB-SLINGER'S BIGGEST MISTAKE!
AND, SPEAKING OF OUR FRIENDLY NEIGHBORHOOD SPIDER-MAN...
I DON'T MIND A LITTLE RAIN...
BUT IT'S STARTING TO COME DOWN IN BUCKETS!
AND THAT MEANS BIG TROUBLE FOR ME!
2.

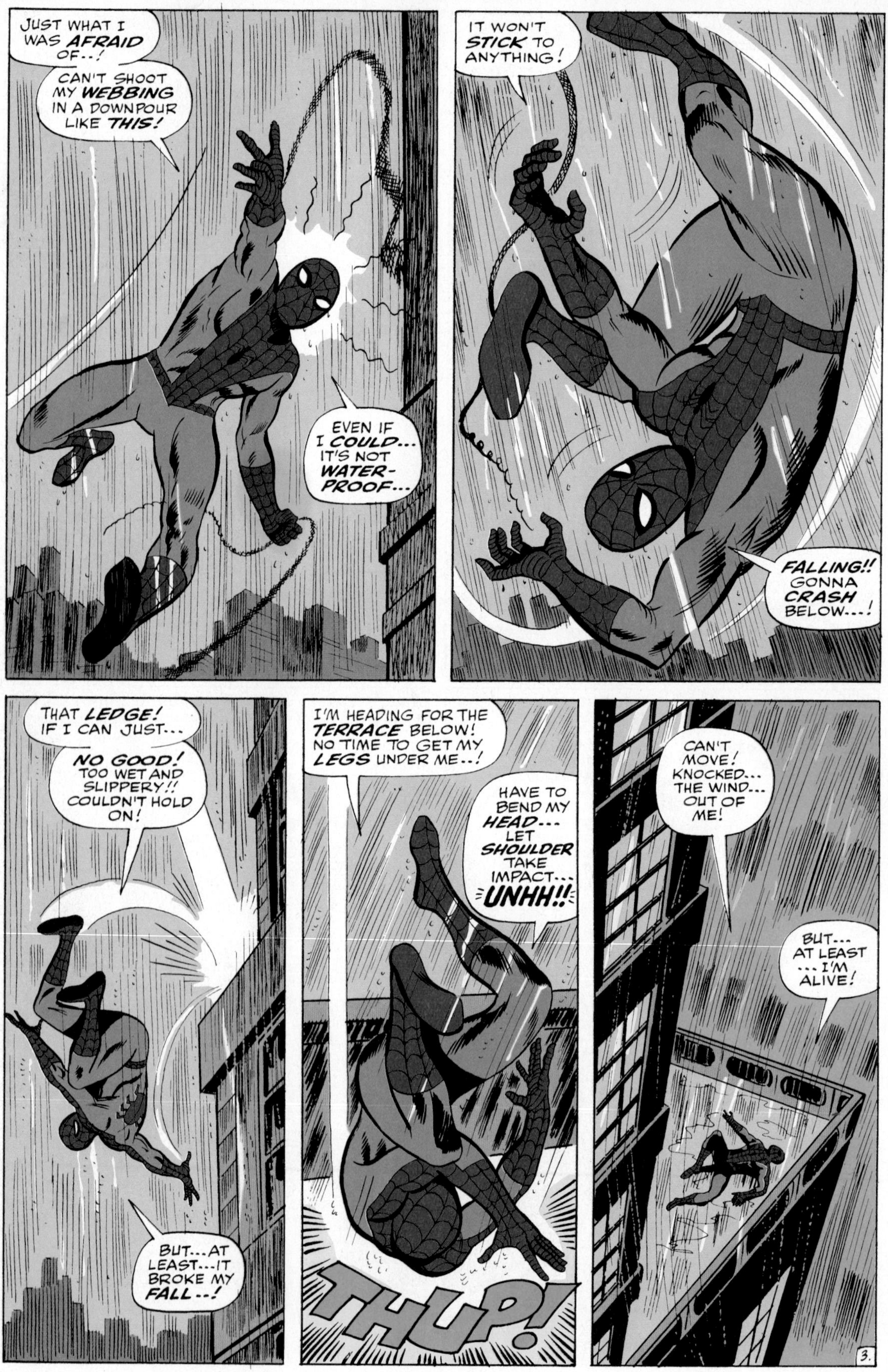
JUST WHAT I WAS AFRAID OF--!
CAN'T SHOOT MY WEBBING IN A DOWNPOUR LIKE THIS!
EVEN IF I COULD... IT'S NOT WATER-PROOF...
IT WON'T STICK TO ANYTHING!
FALLING!! GONNA CRASH BELOW...!
THAT LEDGE! IF I CAN JUST...
NO GOOD! TOO WET AND SLIPPERY!! COULDN'T HOLD ON!
BUT...AT LEAST...IT BROKE MY FALL--!
I'M HEADING FOR THE TERRACE BELOW! NO TIME TO GET MY LEGS UNDER ME--!
HAVE TO BEND MY HEAD... LET SHOULDER TAKE IMPACT... UNHH!!
THUD!
CAN'T MOVE! KNOCKED... THE WIND... OUT OF ME!
BUT... AT LEAST ... I'M ALIVE!
3.

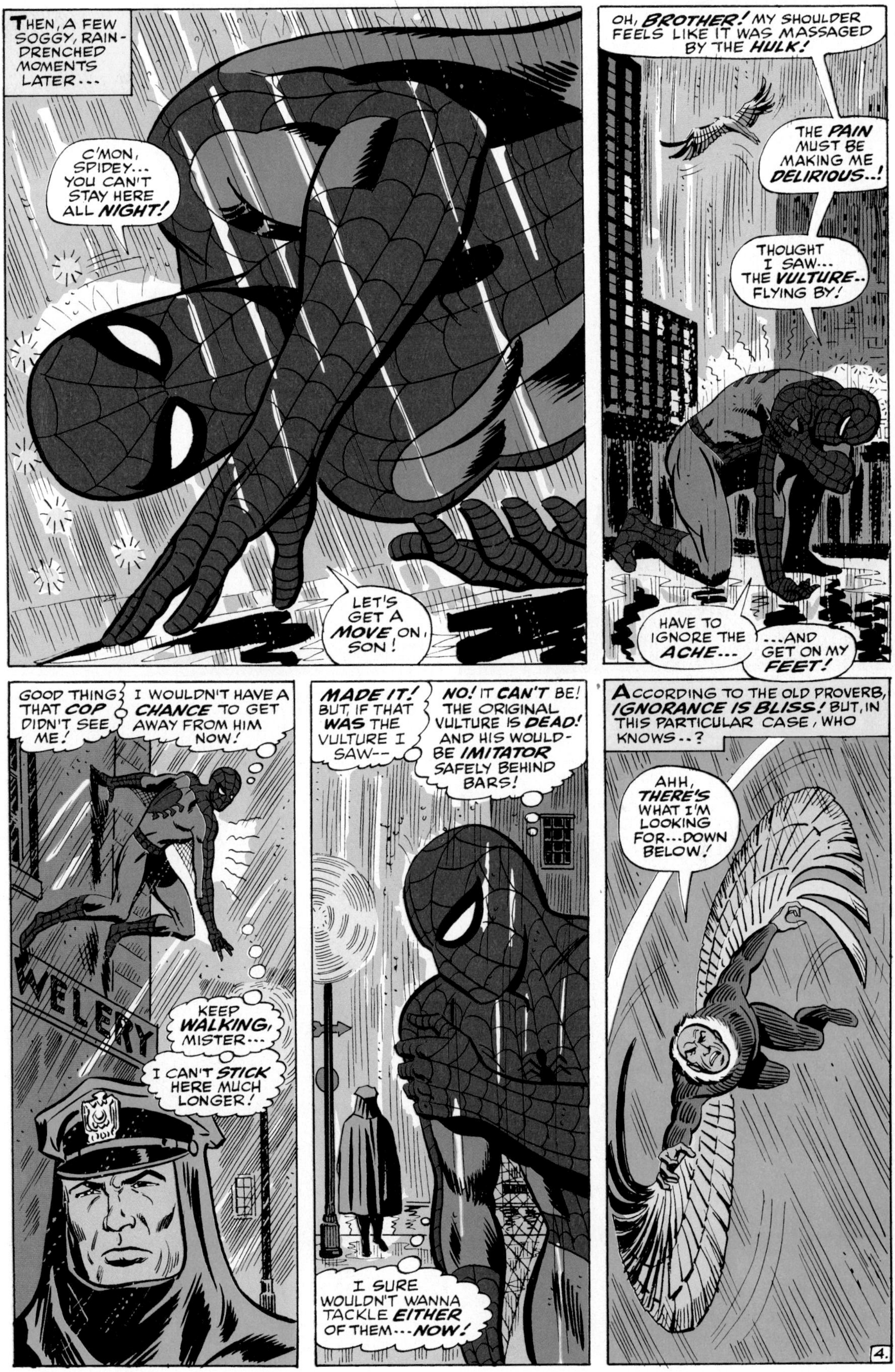
THEN, A FEW SOGGY, RAIN-DRENCHED MOMENTS LATER...
C'MON, SPIDEY... YOU CAN'T STAY HERE ALL NIGHT!
LET'S GET A MOVE ON, SON!
OH, BROTHER! MY SHOULDER FEELS LIKE IT WAS MASSAGED BY THE HULK!
THE PAIN MUST BE MAKING ME DELIRIOUS..!
THOUGHT I SAW... THE VULTURE.. FLYING BY!
HAVE TO IGNORE THE ACHE...
...AND GET ON MY FEET!
GOOD THING THAT COP DIDN'T SEE ME!
I WOULDN'T HAVE A CHANCE TO GET AWAY FROM HIM NOW!
KEEP WALKING, MISTER...
I CAN'T STICK HERE MUCH LONGER!
WELERY
MADE IT! BUT, IF THAT WAS THE VULTURE I SAW--
NO! IT CAN'T BE! THE ORIGINAL VULTURE IS DEAD! AND HIS WOULD-BE IMITATOR SAFELY BEHIND BARS!
I SURE WOULDN'T WANNA TACKLE EITHER OF THEM...NOW!
ACCORDING TO THE OLD PROVERB, IGNORANCE IS BLISS! BUT, IN THIS PARTICULAR CASE, WHO KNOWS..?
AHH, THERE'S WHAT I'M LOOKING FOR...DOWN BELOW!
4.

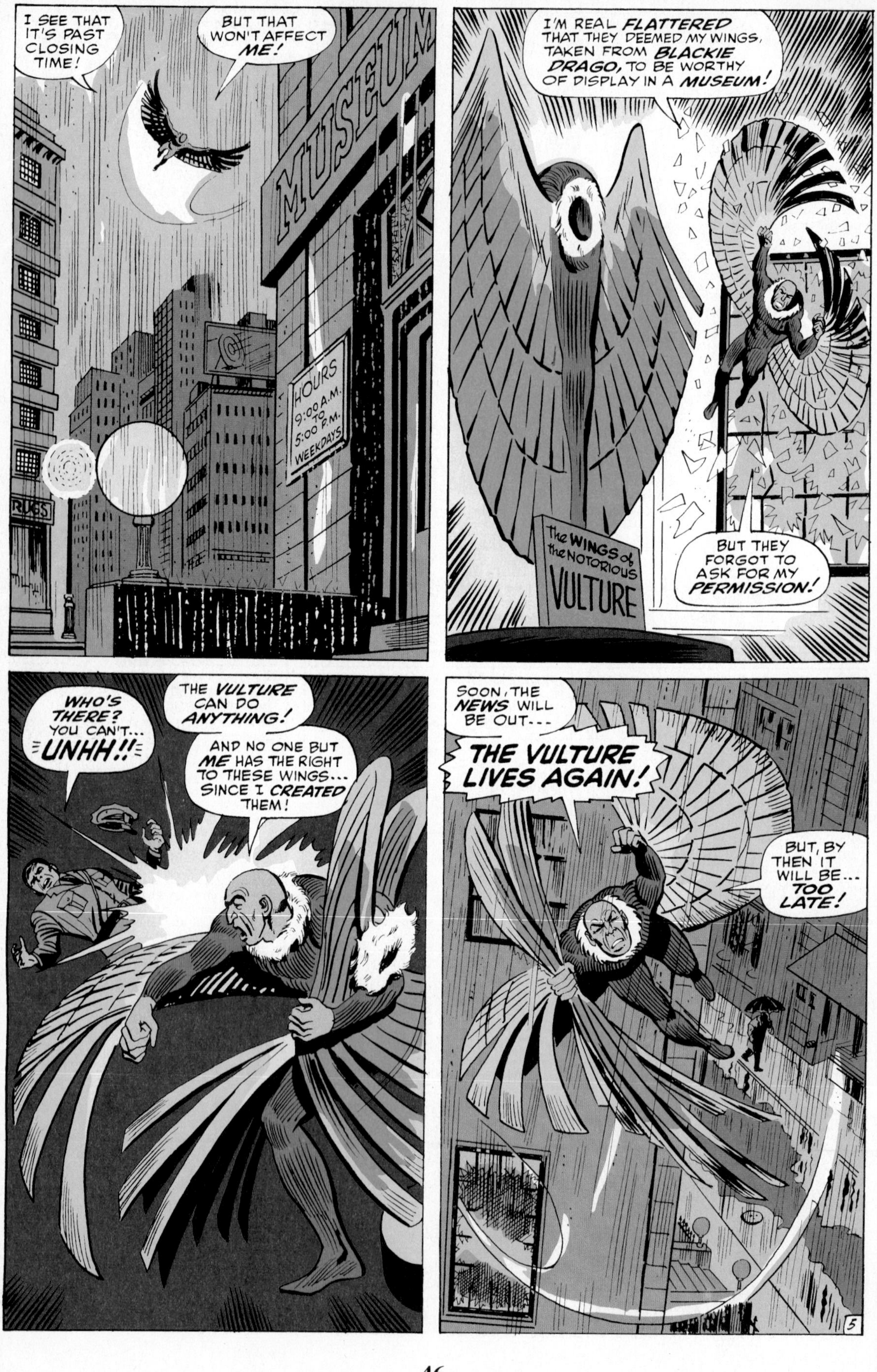
I SEE THAT IT'S PAST CLOSING TIME!
BUT THAT WON'T AFFECT ME!
MUSEUM
HOURS 9:00 A.M. TO 5:00 P.M. WEEKDAYS
I'M REAL FLATTERED THAT THEY DEEMED MY WINGS, TAKEN FROM BLACKIE DRAGO, TO BE WORTHY OF DISPLAY IN A MUSEUM!
The WINGS of the NOTORIOUS VULTURE
BUT THEY FORGOT TO ASK FOR MY PERMISSION!
WHO'S THERE? YOU CAN'T... UNHH!!
THE VULTURE CAN DO ANYTHING!
AND NO ONE BUT ME HAS THE RIGHT TO THESE WINGS... SINCE I CREATED THEM!
SOON, THE NEWS WILL BE OUT---
THE VULTURE LIVES AGAIN!
BUT, BY THEN IT WILL BE... TOO LATE!
5

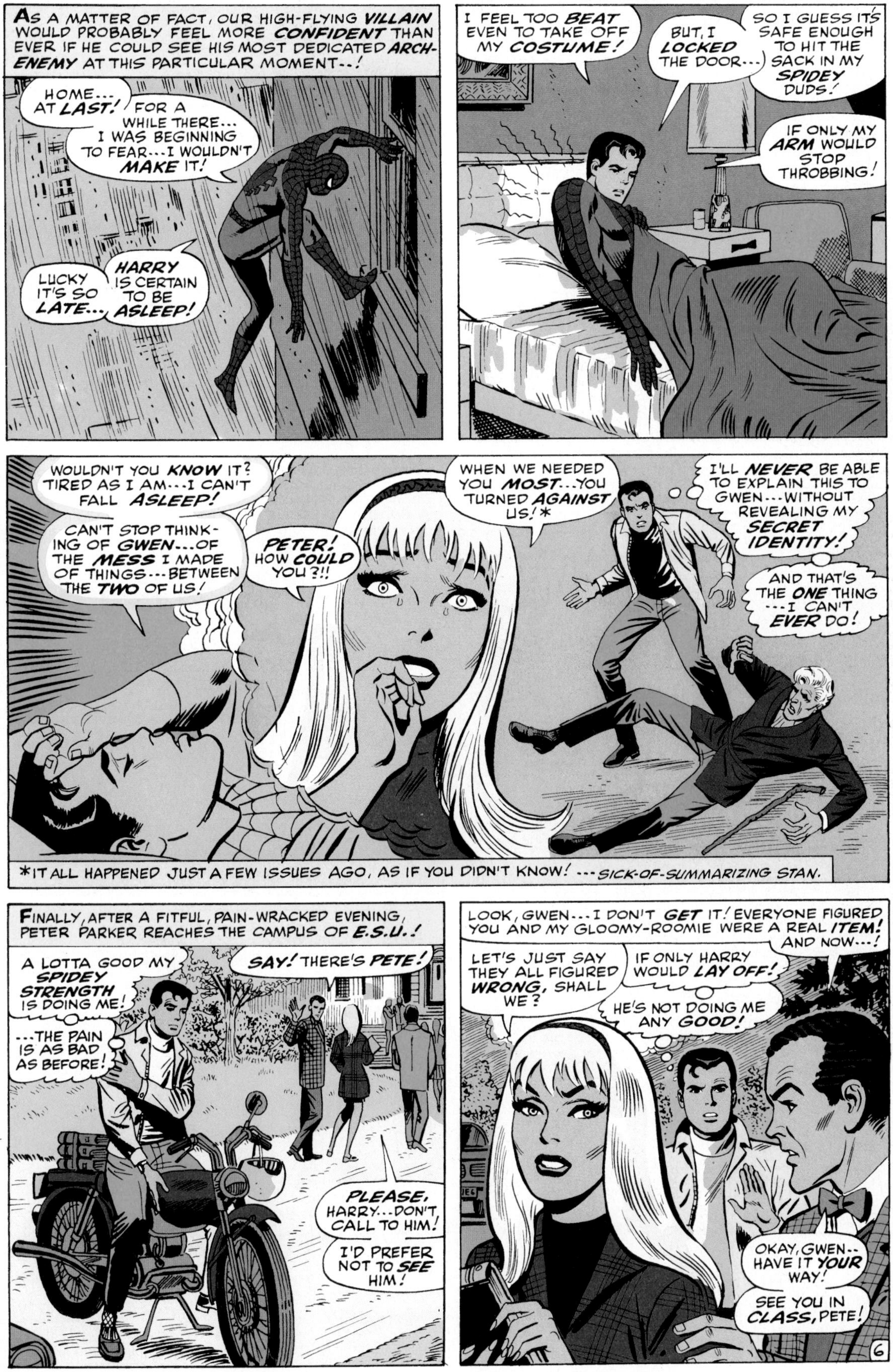
AS A MATTER OF FACT, OUR HIGH-FLYING VILLAIN WOULD PROBABLY FEEL MORE CONFIDENT THAN EVER IF HE COULD SEE HIS MOST DEDICATED ARCH-ENEMY AT THIS PARTICULAR MOMENT--!
HOME... AT LAST!
FOR A WHILE THERE... I WAS BEGINNING TO FEAR---I WOULDN'T MAKE IT!
LUCKY IT'S SO LATE...
HARRY IS CERTAIN TO BE ASLEEP!
I FEEL TOO BEAT EVEN TO TAKE OFF MY COSTUME!
BUT, I LOCKED THE DOOR...
SO I GUESS IT'S SAFE ENOUGH TO HIT THE SACK IN MY SPIDEY DUDS!
IF ONLY MY ARM WOULD STOP THROBBING!
WOULDN'T YOU KNOW IT? TIRED AS I AM---I CAN'T FALL ASLEEP!
CAN'T STOP THINK-ING OF GWEN---OF THE MESS I MADE OF THINGS---BETWEEN THE TWO OF US!
PETER! HOW COULD YOU?!!
WHEN WE NEEDED YOU MOST...YOU TURNED AGAINST US!*
I'LL NEVER BE ABLE TO EXPLAIN THIS TO GWEN---WITHOUT REVEALING MY SECRET IDENTITY!
AND THAT'S THE ONE THING ---I CAN'T EVER DO!
*IT ALL HAPPENED JUST A FEW ISSUES AGO, AS IF YOU DIDN'T KNOW! ---SICK-OF-SUMMARIZING STAN.
FINALLY, AFTER A FITFUL, PAIN-WRACKED EVENING, PETER PARKER REACHES THE CAMPUS OF E.S.U.!
A LOTTA GOOD MY SPIDEY STRENGTH IS DOING ME!
---THE PAIN IS AS BAD AS BEFORE!
SAY! THERE'S PETE!
PLEASE, HARRY...DON'T CALL TO HIM!
I'D PREFER NOT TO SEE HIM!
LOOK, GWEN---I DON'T GET IT! EVERYONE FIGURED YOU AND MY GLOOMY-ROOMIE WERE A REAL ITEM! AND NOW---!
LET'S JUST SAY THEY ALL FIGURED WRONG, SHALL WE?
IF ONLY HARRY WOULD LAY OFF!
HE'S NOT DOING ME ANY GOOD!
OKAY, GWEN-- HAVE IT YOUR WAY!
SEE YOU IN CLASS, PETE!
6

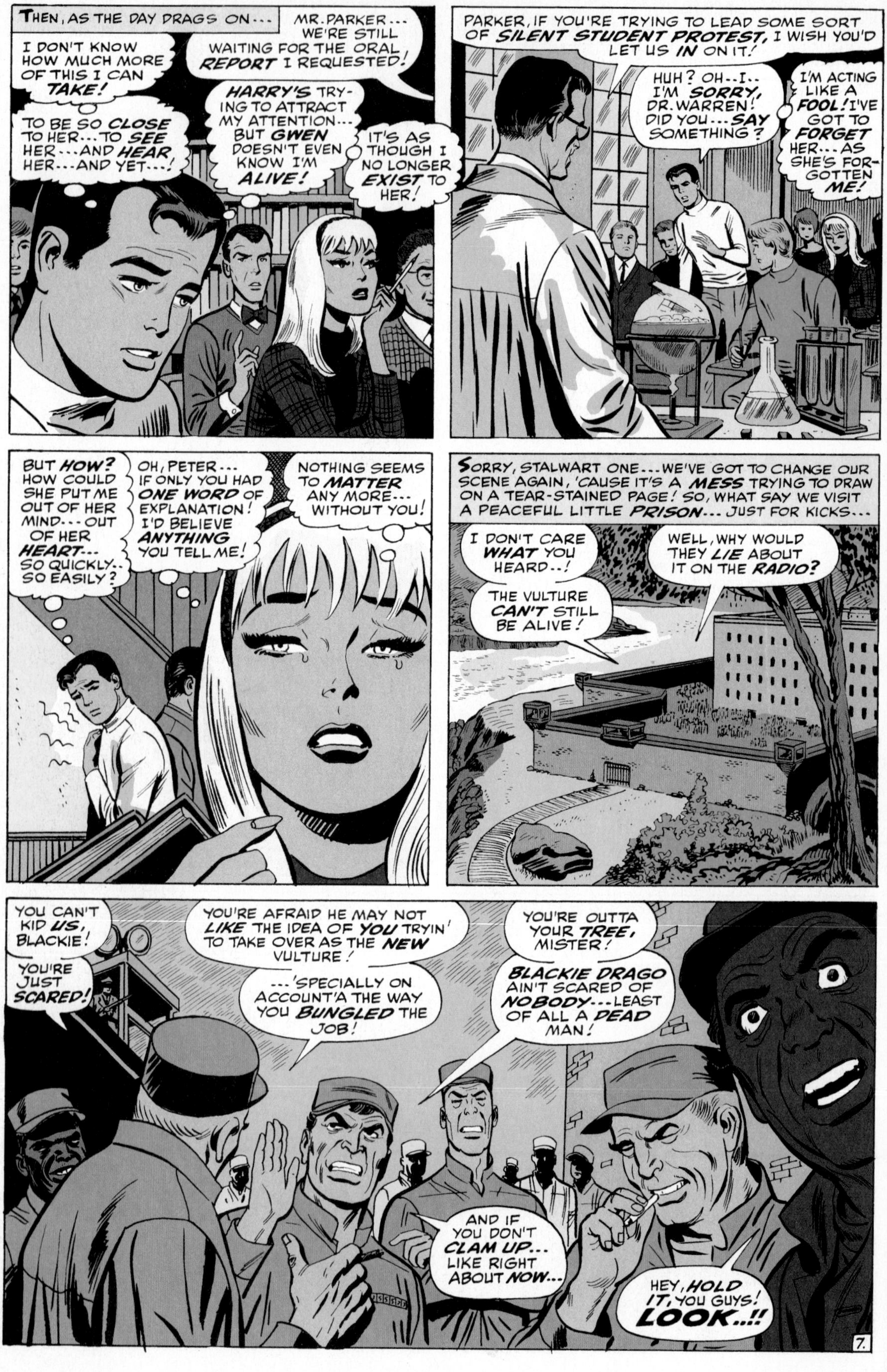
THEN, AS THE DAY DRAGS ON...
MR. PARKER... WE'RE STILL WAITING FOR THE ORAL REPORT I REQUESTED!
I DON'T KNOW HOW MUCH MORE OF THIS I CAN TAKE!
TO BE SO CLOSE TO HER... TO SEE HER... AND HEAR HER... AND YET...!
HARRY'S TRYING TO ATTRACT MY ATTENTION... BUT GWEN DOESN'T EVEN KNOW I'M ALIVE!
IT'S AS THOUGH I NO LONGER EXIST TO HER!
PARKER, IF YOU'RE TRYING TO LEAD SOME SORT OF SILENT STUDENT PROTEST, I WISH YOU'D LET US IN ON IT!
HUH? OH--I-- I'M SORRY, DR. WARREN! DID YOU... SAY SOMETHING?
I'M ACTING LIKE A FOOL! I'VE GOT TO FORGET HER... AS SHE'S FORGOTTEN ME!
BUT HOW? HOW COULD SHE PUT ME OUT OF HER MIND... OUT OF HER HEART... SO QUICKLY.. SO EASILY?
OH, PETER... IF ONLY YOU HAD ONE WORD OF EXPLANATION! I'D BELIEVE ANYTHING YOU TELL ME!
NOTHING SEEMS TO MATTER ANY MORE... WITHOUT YOU!
SORRY, STALWART ONE... WE'VE GOT TO CHANGE OUR SCENE AGAIN, 'CAUSE IT'S A MESS TRYING TO DRAW ON A TEAR-STAINED PAGE! SO, WHAT SAY WE VISIT A PEACEFUL LITTLE PRISON... JUST FOR KICKS...
I DON'T CARE WHAT YOU HEARD--!
THE VULTURE CAN'T STILL BE ALIVE!
WELL, WHY WOULD THEY LIE ABOUT IT ON THE RADIO?
YOU CAN'T KID US, BLACKIE!
YOU'RE JUST SCARED!
YOU'RE AFRAID HE MAY NOT LIKE THE IDEA OF YOU TRYIN' TO TAKE OVER AS THE NEW VULTURE!
...'SPECIALLY ON ACCOUNT'A THE WAY YOU BUNGLED THE JOB!
YOU'RE OUTTA YOUR TREE, MISTER!
BLACKIE DRAGO AIN'T SCARED OF NOBODY... LEAST OF ALL A DEAD MAN!
AND IF YOU DON'T CLAM UP... LIKE RIGHT ABOUT NOW...
HEY, HOLD IT, YOU GUYS! LOOK..!!
7.

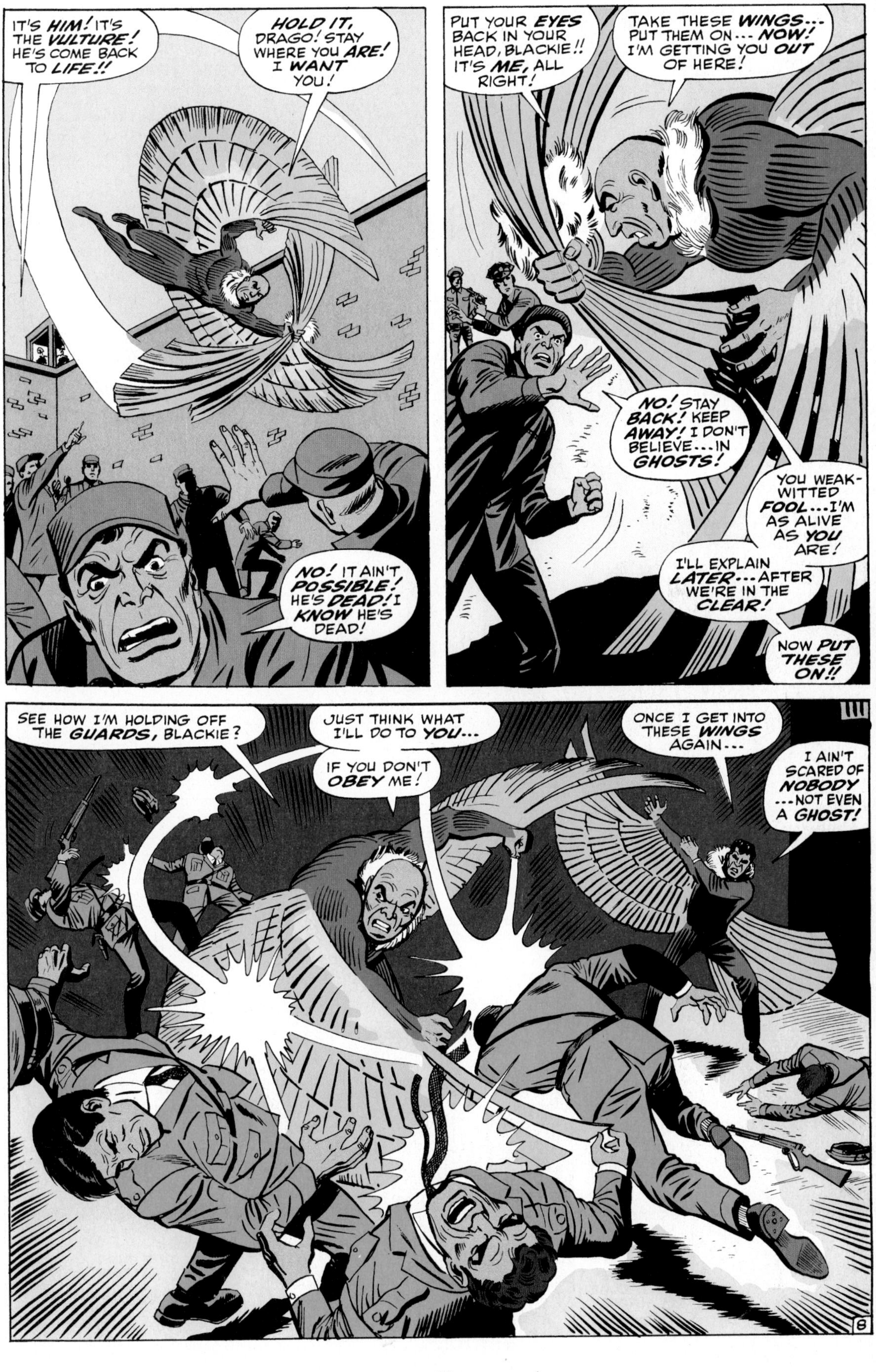
IT'S HIM! IT'S THE VULTURE! HE'S COME BACK TO LIFE!!
HOLD IT, DRAGO! STAY WHERE YOU ARE! I WANT YOU!
NO! IT AIN'T POSSIBLE! HE'S DEAD! I KNOW HE'S DEAD!
PUT YOUR EYES BACK IN YOUR HEAD, BLACKIE!! IT'S ME, ALL RIGHT!
TAKE THESE WINGS... PUT THEM ON... NOW! I'M GETTING YOU OUT OF HERE!
NO! STAY BACK! KEEP AWAY! I DON'T BELIEVE... IN GHOSTS!
YOU WEAK-WITTED FOOL... I'M AS ALIVE AS YOU ARE!
I'LL EXPLAIN LATER... AFTER WE'RE IN THE CLEAR!
NOW PUT THESE ON!!
SEE HOW I'M HOLDING OFF THE GUARDS, BLACKIE?
JUST THINK WHAT I'LL DO TO YOU...
IF YOU DON'T OBEY ME!
ONCE I GET INTO THESE WINGS AGAIN...
I AIN'T SCARED OF NOBODY ...NOT EVEN A GHOST!
8

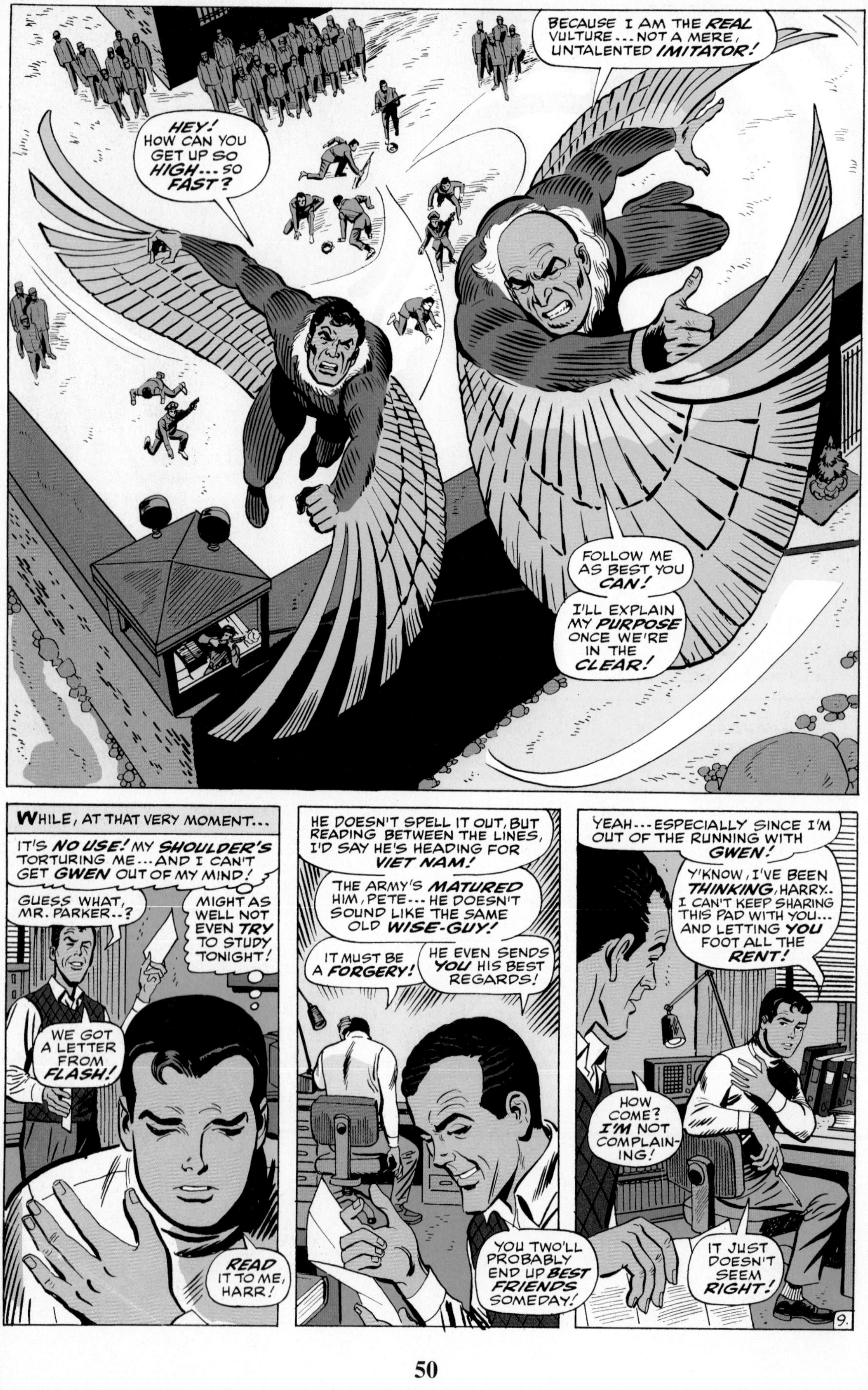
BECAUSE I AM THE REAL VULTURE... NOT A MERE, UNTALENTED IMITATOR!
HEY! HOW CAN YOU GET UP SO HIGH... SO FAST?
FOLLOW ME AS BEST YOU CAN!
I'LL EXPLAIN MY PURPOSE ONCE WE'RE IN THE CLEAR!
WHILE, AT THAT VERY MOMENT...
IT'S NO USE! MY SHOULDER'S TORTURING ME... AND I CAN'T GET GWEN OUT OF MY MIND!
GUESS WHAT, MR. PARKER..?
MIGHT AS WELL NOT EVEN TRY TO STUDY TONIGHT!
WE GOT A LETTER FROM FLASH!
READ IT TO ME, HARR!
HE DOESN'T SPELL IT OUT, BUT READING BETWEEN THE LINES, I'D SAY HE'S HEADING FOR VIET NAM!
THE ARMY'S MATURED HIM, PETE... HE DOESN'T SOUND LIKE THE SAME OLD WISE-GUY!
IT MUST BE A FORGERY!
HE EVEN SENDS YOU HIS BEST REGARDS!
YOU TWO'LL PROBABLY END UP BEST FRIENDS SOMEDAY!
YEAH... ESPECIALLY SINCE I'M OUT OF THE RUNNING WITH GWEN!
Y'KNOW, I'VE BEEN THINKING, HARRY.. I CAN'T KEEP SHARING THIS PAD WITH YOU... AND LETTING YOU FOOT ALL THE RENT!
HOW COME? I'M NOT COMPLAINING!
IT JUST DOESN'T SEEM RIGHT!
9.

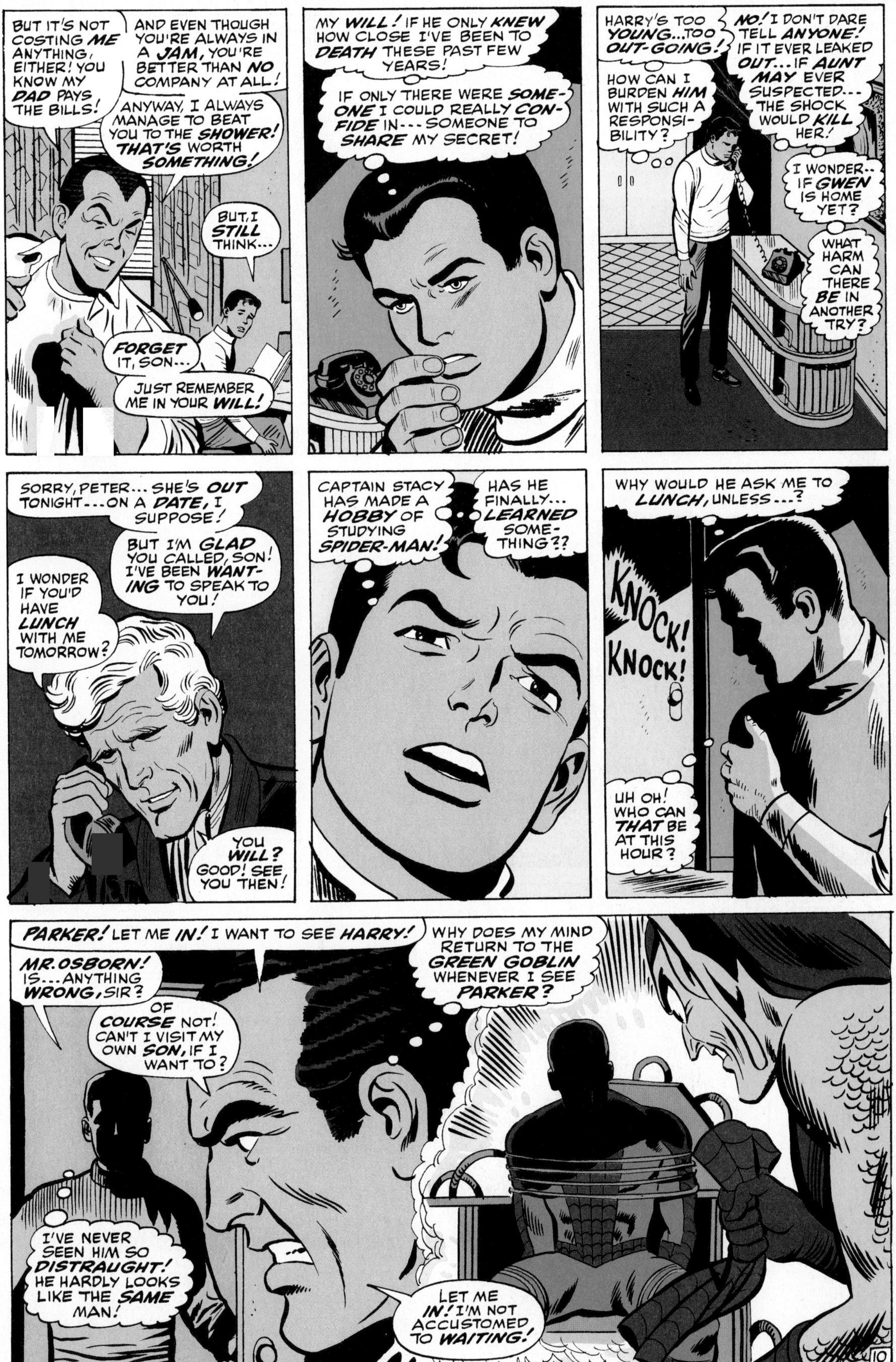

BUT IT'S NOT COSTING ME ANYTHING, EITHER! YOU KNOW MY DAD PAYS THE BILLS!
AND EVEN THOUGH YOU'RE ALWAYS IN A JAM, YOU'RE BETTER THAN NO COMPANY AT ALL!
ANYWAY, I ALWAYS MANAGE TO BEAT YOU TO THE SHOWER! THAT'S WORTH SOMETHING!
BUT, I STILL THINK...
FORGET IT, SON...
JUST REMEMBER ME IN YOUR WILL!
MY WILL! IF HE ONLY KNEW HOW CLOSE I'VE BEEN TO DEATH THESE PAST FEW YEARS!
IF ONLY THERE WERE SOME-ONE I COULD REALLY CON-FIDE IN--- SOMEONE TO SHARE MY SECRET!
HARRY'S TOO YOUNG...TOO OUT-GOING!
HOW CAN I BURDEN HIM WITH SUCH A RESPONSI-BILITY?
NO! I DON'T DARE TELL ANYONE! IF IT EVER LEAKED OUT...IF AUNT MAY EVER SUSPECTED--- THE SHOCK WOULD KILL HER!
I WONDER-- IF GWEN IS HOME YET?
WHAT HARM CAN THERE BE IN ANOTHER TRY?
SORRY, PETER... SHE'S OUT TONIGHT---ON A DATE, I SUPPOSE!
BUT I'M GLAD YOU CALLED, SON! I'VE BEEN WANT-ING TO SPEAK TO YOU!
I WONDER IF YOU'D HAVE LUNCH WITH ME TOMORROW?
YOU WILL? GOOD! SEE YOU THEN!
CAPTAIN STACY HAS MADE A HOBBY OF STUDYING SPIDER-MAN!
HAS HE FINALLY... LEARNED SOME-THING??
WHY WOULD HE ASK ME TO LUNCH, UNLESS ...?
KNOCK! KNOCK!
UH OH! WHO CAN THAT BE AT THIS HOUR?
PARKER! LET ME IN! I WANT TO SEE HARRY!
MR. OSBORN! IS...ANYTHING WRONG, SIR?
OF COURSE NOT! CAN'T I VISIT MY OWN SON, IF I WANT TO?
WHY DOES MY MIND RETURN TO THE GREEN GOBLIN WHENEVER I SEE PARKER?
I'VE NEVER SEEN HIM SO DISTRAUGHT! HE HARDLY LOOKS LIKE THE SAME MAN!
LET ME IN! I'M NOT ACCUSTOMED TO WAITING!
10

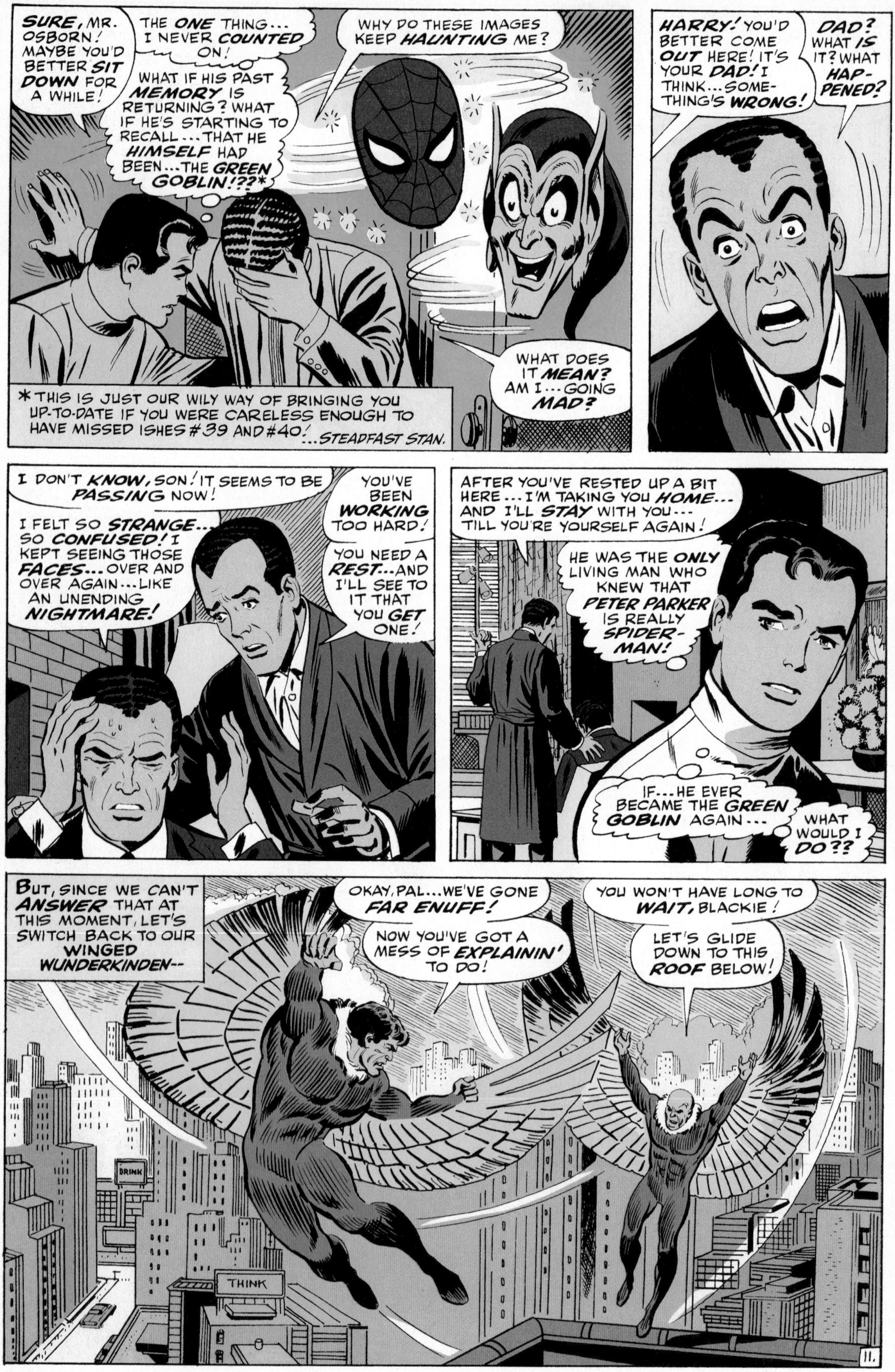
SURE, MR. OSBORN! MAYBE YOU'D BETTER SIT DOWN FOR A WHILE!
THE ONE THING... I NEVER COUNTED ON!
WHAT IF HIS PAST MEMORY IS RETURNING? WHAT IF HE'S STARTING TO RECALL... THAT HE HIMSELF HAD BEEN... THE GREEN GOBLIN!??*
WHY DO THESE IMAGES KEEP HAUNTING ME?
WHAT DOES IT MEAN? AM I... GOING MAD?
* THIS IS JUST OUR WILY WAY OF BRINGING YOU UP-TO-DATE IF YOU WERE CARELESS ENOUGH TO HAVE MISSED ISHES #39 AND #40! ...STEADFAST STAN.
HARRY! YOU'D BETTER COME OUT HERE! IT'S YOUR DAD! I THINK... SOME-THING'S WRONG!
DAD? WHAT IS IT? WHAT HAP-PENED?
I DON'T KNOW, SON! IT SEEMS TO BE PASSING NOW!
I FELT SO STRANGE... SO CONFUSED! I KEPT SEEING THOSE FACES... OVER AND OVER AGAIN... LIKE AN UNENDING NIGHTMARE!
YOU'VE BEEN WORKING TOO HARD!
YOU NEED A REST... AND I'LL SEE TO IT THAT YOU GET ONE!
AFTER YOU'VE RESTED UP A BIT HERE... I'M TAKING YOU HOME... AND I'LL STAY WITH YOU... TILL YOU'RE YOURSELF AGAIN!
HE WAS THE ONLY LIVING MAN WHO KNEW THAT PETER PARKER IS REALLY SPIDER-MAN!
IF... HE EVER BECAME THE GREEN GOBLIN AGAIN...
WHAT WOULD I DO??
BUT, SINCE WE CAN'T ANSWER THAT AT THIS MOMENT, LET'S SWITCH BACK TO OUR WINGED WUNDERKINDEN--
OKAY, PAL... WE'VE GONE FAR ENUFF!
NOW YOU'VE GOT A MESS OF EXPLAININ' TO DO!
YOU WON'T HAVE LONG TO WAIT, BLACKIE!
LET'S GLIDE DOWN TO THIS ROOF BELOW!
DRINK
THINK
11.

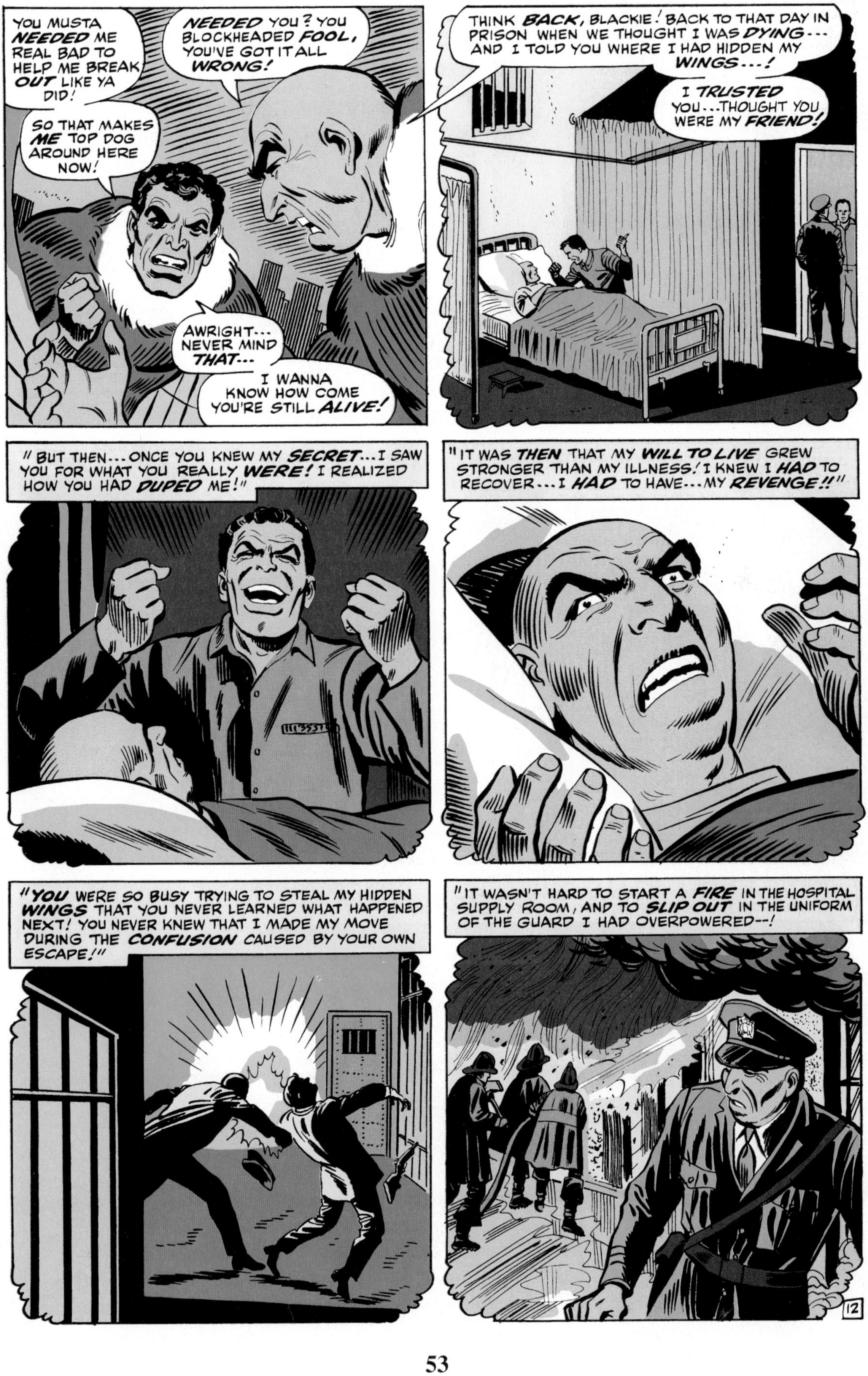

YOU MUSTA NEEDED ME REAL BAD TO HELP ME BREAK OUT LIKE YA DID!
SO THAT MAKES ME TOP DOG AROUND HERE NOW!
NEEDED YOU? YOU BLOCKHEADED FOOL, YOU'VE GOT IT ALL WRONG!
AWRIGHT--- NEVER MIND THAT---
I WANNA KNOW HOW COME YOU'RE STILL ALIVE!
THINK BACK, BLACKIE! BACK TO THAT DAY IN PRISON WHEN WE THOUGHT I WAS DYING--- AND I TOLD YOU WHERE I HAD HIDDEN MY WINGS---!
I TRUSTED YOU---THOUGHT YOU WERE MY FRIEND!
"BUT THEN---ONCE YOU KNEW MY SECRET---I SAW YOU FOR WHAT YOU REALLY WERE! I REALIZED HOW YOU HAD DUPED ME!"
"IT WAS THEN THAT MY WILL TO LIVE GREW STRONGER THAN MY ILLNESS! I KNEW I HAD TO RECOVER---I HAD TO HAVE---MY REVENGE!!"
"YOU WERE SO BUSY TRYING TO STEAL MY HIDDEN WINGS THAT YOU NEVER LEARNED WHAT HAPPENED NEXT! YOU NEVER KNEW THAT I MADE MY MOVE DURING THE CONFUSION CAUSED BY YOUR OWN ESCAPE!"
"IT WASN'T HARD TO START A FIRE IN THE HOSPITAL SUPPLY ROOM, AND TO SLIP OUT IN THE UNIFORM OF THE GUARD I HAD OVERPOWERED--!
12

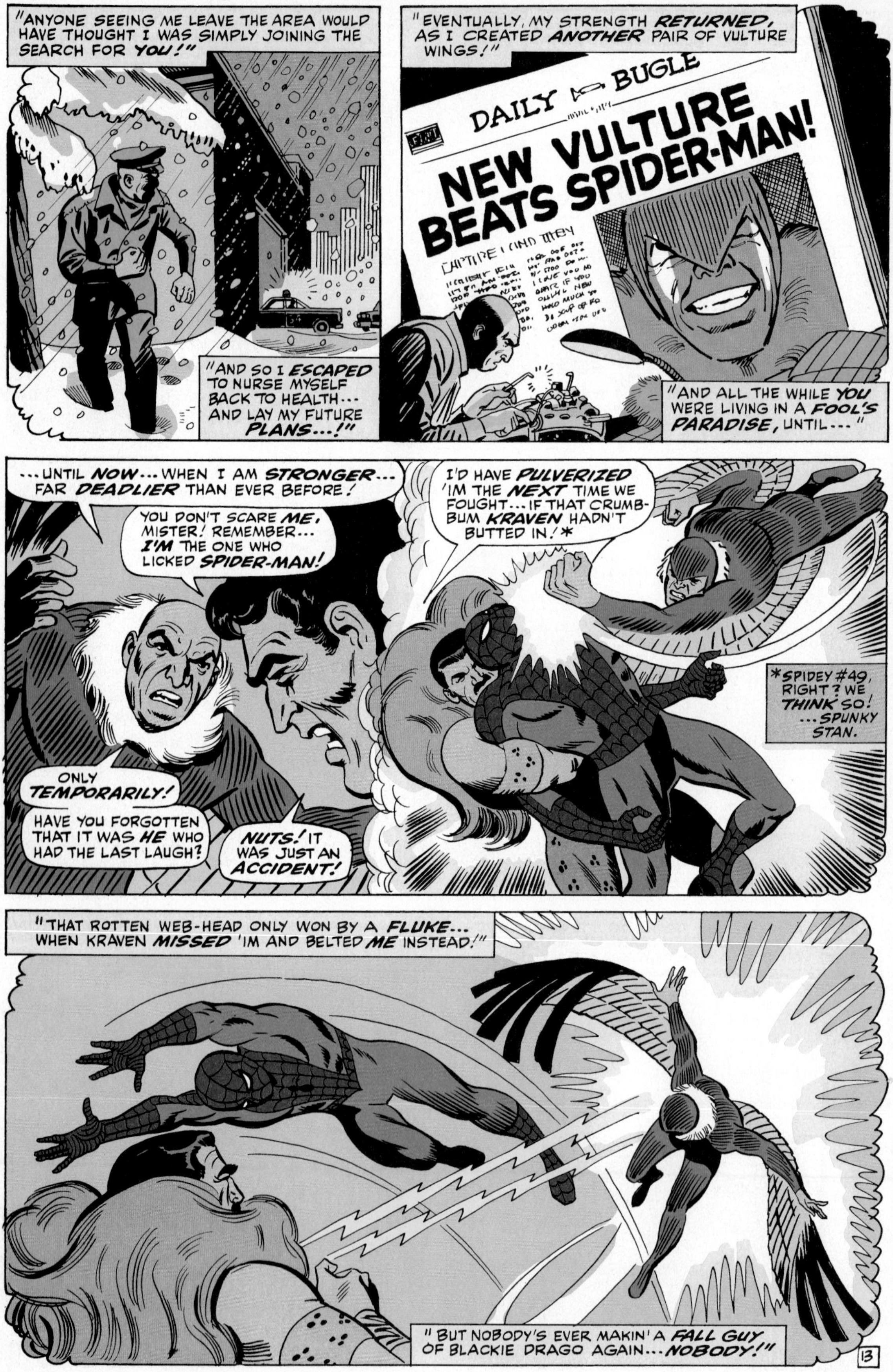
"ANYONE SEEING ME LEAVE THE AREA WOULD HAVE THOUGHT I WAS SIMPLY JOINING THE SEARCH FOR YOU!"
"AND SO I ESCAPED TO NURSE MYSELF BACK TO HEALTH... AND LAY MY FUTURE PLANS...!"
"EVENTUALLY, MY STRENGTH RETURNED, AS I CREATED ANOTHER PAIR OF VULTURE WINGS!"
DAILY BUGLE
NEW VULTURE BEATS SPIDER-MAN!
"AND ALL THE WHILE YOU WERE LIVING IN A FOOL'S PARADISE, UNTIL..."
...UNTIL NOW... WHEN I AM STRONGER... FAR DEADLIER THAN EVER BEFORE!
YOU DON'T SCARE ME, MISTER! REMEMBER... I'M THE ONE WHO LICKED SPIDER-MAN!
I'D HAVE PULVERIZED 'IM THE NEXT TIME WE FOUGHT... IF THAT CRUMB-BUM KRAVEN HADN'T BUTTED IN!*
*SPIDEY #49, RIGHT? WE THINK SO! ...SPUNKY STAN.
ONLY TEMPORARILY!
HAVE YOU FORGOTTEN THAT IT WAS HE WHO HAD THE LAST LAUGH?
NUTS! IT WAS JUST AN ACCIDENT!
"THAT ROTTEN WEB-HEAD ONLY WON BY A FLUKE... WHEN KRAVEN MISSED 'IM AND BELTED ME INSTEAD!"
"BUT NOBODY'S EVER MAKIN' A FALL GUY OF BLACKIE DRAGO AGAIN... NOBODY!"
13

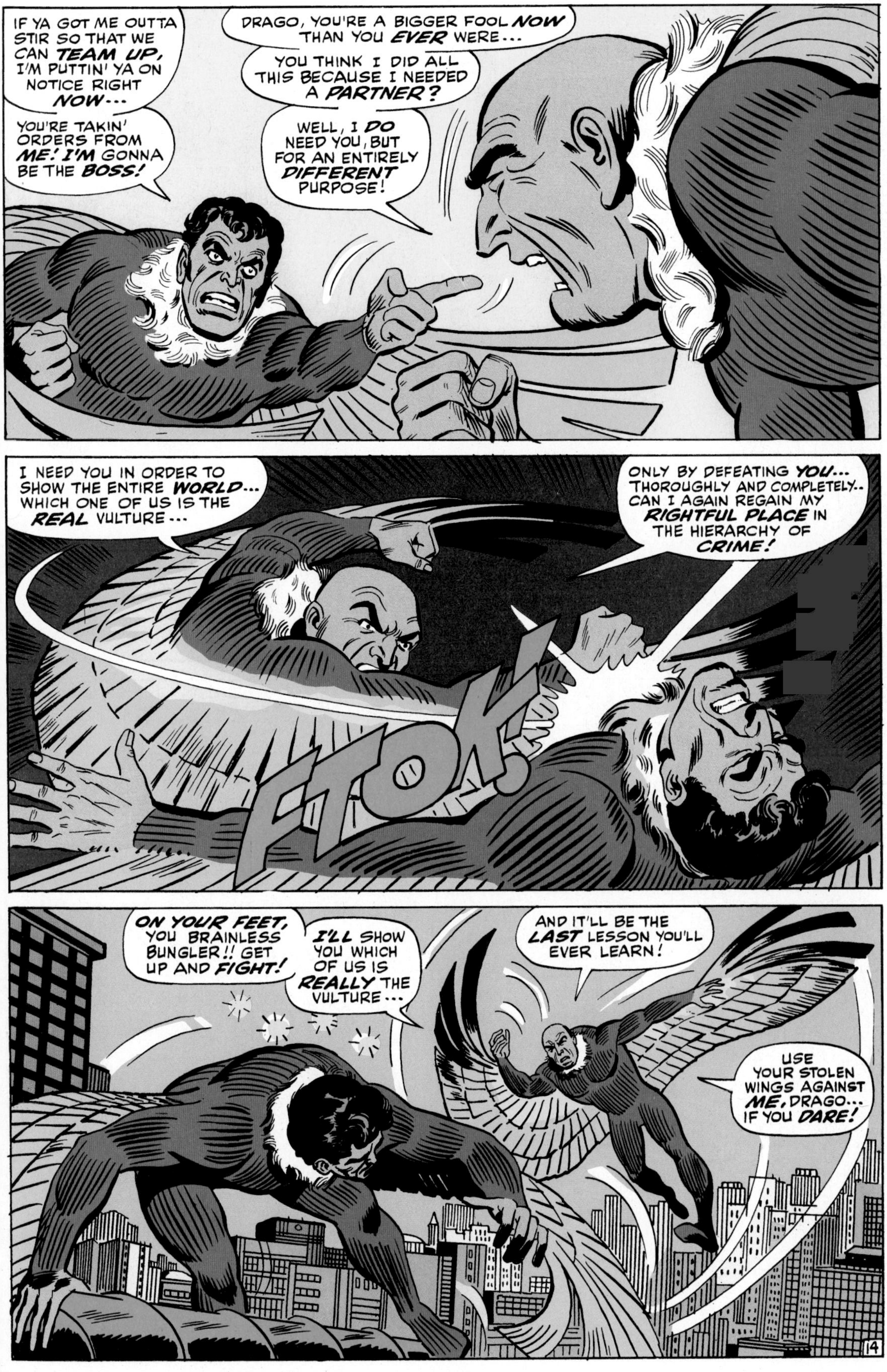

IF YA GOT ME OUTTA STIR SO THAT WE CAN TEAM UP, I'M PUTTIN' YA ON NOTICE RIGHT NOW...
YOU'RE TAKIN' ORDERS FROM ME! I'M GONNA BE THE BOSS!
DRAGO, YOU'RE A BIGGER FOOL NOW THAN YOU EVER WERE...
YOU THINK I DID ALL THIS BECAUSE I NEEDED A PARTNER?
WELL, I DO NEED YOU, BUT FOR AN ENTIRELY DIFFERENT PURPOSE!
I NEED YOU IN ORDER TO SHOW THE ENTIRE WORLD... WHICH ONE OF US IS THE REAL VULTURE...
ONLY BY DEFEATING YOU... THOROUGHLY AND COMPLETELY.. CAN I AGAIN REGAIN MY RIGHTFUL PLACE IN THE HIERARCHY OF CRIME!
FTOK!
ON YOUR FEET, YOU BRAINLESS BUNGLER!! GET UP AND FIGHT!
I'LL SHOW YOU WHICH OF US IS REALLY THE VULTURE...
AND IT'LL BE THE LAST LESSON YOU'LL EVER LEARN!
USE YOUR STOLEN WINGS AGAINST ME, DRAGO... IF YOU DARE!
14

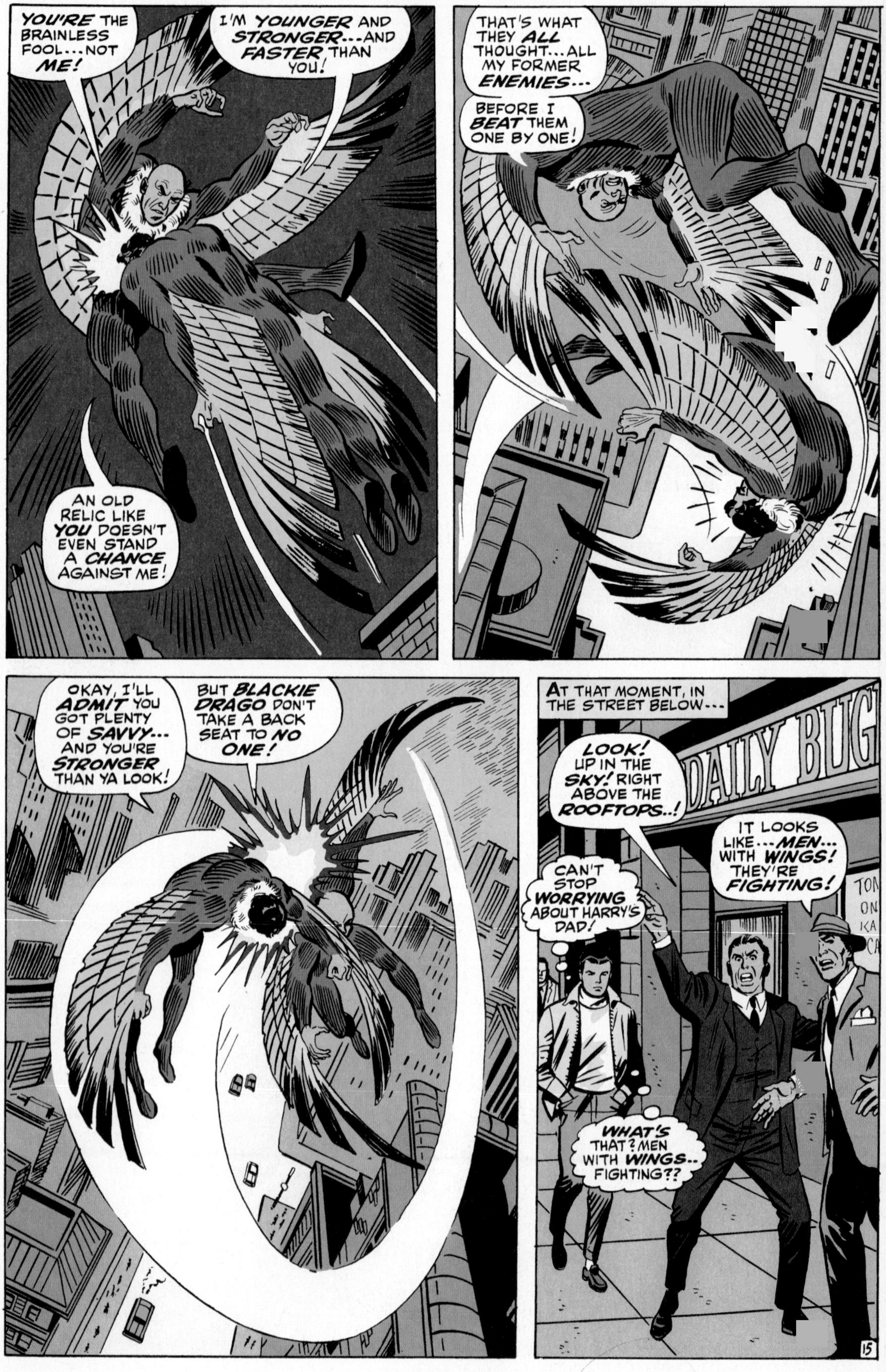

YOU'RE THE BRAINLESS FOOL... NOT ME!
I'M YOUNGER AND STRONGER... AND FASTER THAN YOU!
AN OLD RELIC LIKE YOU DOESN'T EVEN STAND A CHANCE AGAINST ME!
THAT'S WHAT THEY ALL THOUGHT... ALL MY FORMER ENEMIES...
BEFORE I BEAT THEM ONE BY ONE!
OKAY, I'LL ADMIT YOU GOT PLENTY OF SAVVY... AND YOU'RE STRONGER THAN YA LOOK!
BUT BLACKIE DRAGO DON'T TAKE A BACK SEAT TO NO ONE!
AT THAT MOMENT, IN THE STREET BELOW...
DAILY BUG
LOOK! UP IN THE SKY! RIGHT ABOVE THE ROOFTOPS..!
IT LOOKS LIKE... MEN... WITH WINGS! THEY'RE FIGHTING!
CAN'T STOP WORRYING ABOUT HARRY'S DAD!
WHAT'S THAT? MEN WITH WINGS.. FIGHTING??
15

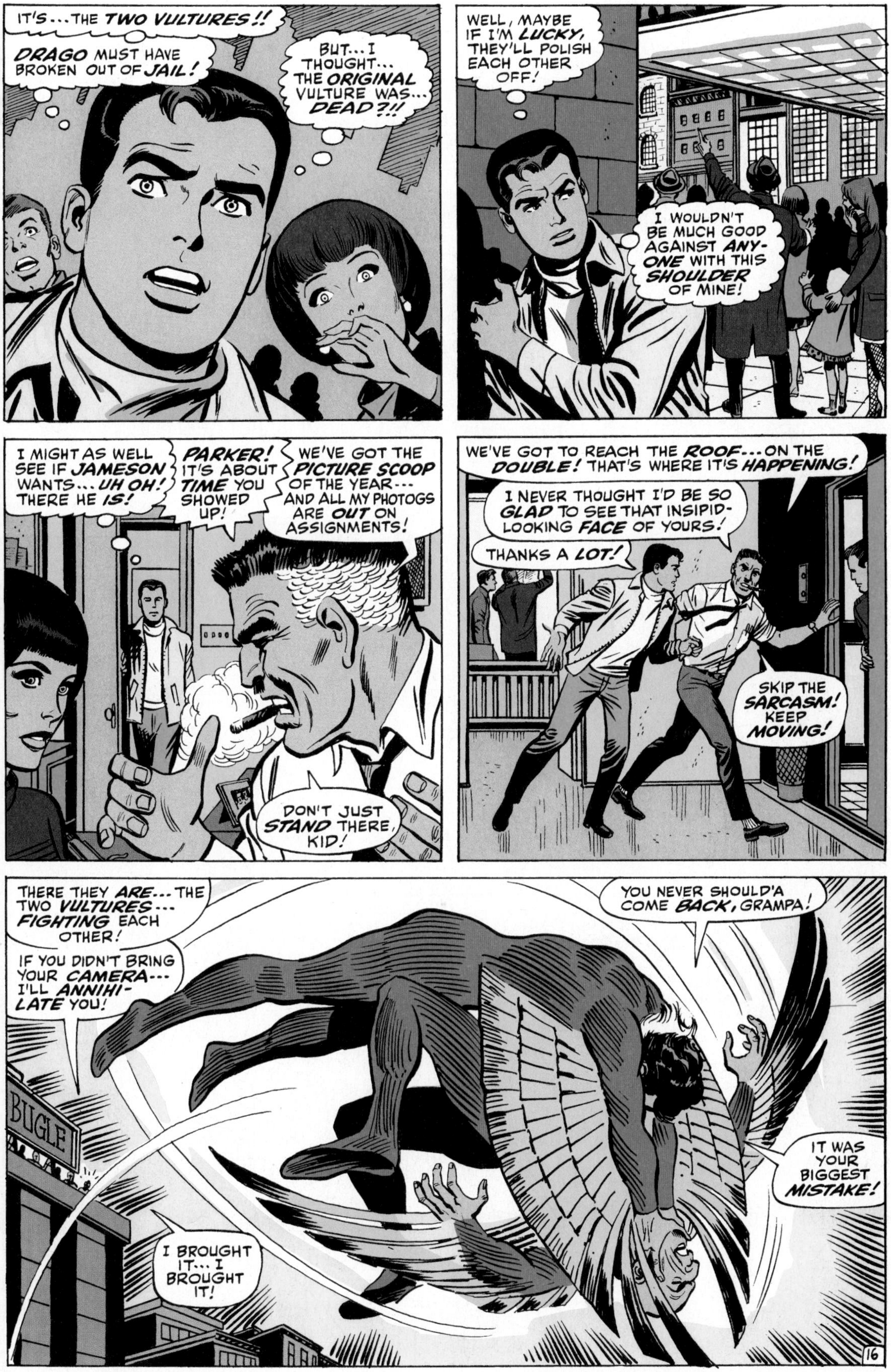
IT'S... THE TWO VULTURES!!
DRAGO MUST HAVE BROKEN OUT OF JAIL!
BUT... I THOUGHT... THE ORIGINAL VULTURE WAS... DEAD?!!
WELL, MAYBE IF I'M LUCKY, THEY'LL POLISH EACH OTHER OFF!
I WOULDN'T BE MUCH GOOD AGAINST ANY-ONE WITH THIS SHOULDER OF MINE!
I MIGHT AS WELL SEE IF JAMESON WANTS... UH OH! THERE HE IS!
PARKER! IT'S ABOUT TIME YOU SHOWED UP!
WE'VE GOT THE PICTURE SCOOP OF THE YEAR--- AND ALL MY PHOTOGS ARE OUT ON ASSIGNMENTS!
DON'T JUST STAND THERE, KID!
WE'VE GOT TO REACH THE ROOF... ON THE DOUBLE! THAT'S WHERE IT'S HAPPENING!
I NEVER THOUGHT I'D BE SO GLAD TO SEE THAT INSIPID-LOOKING FACE OF YOURS!
THANKS A LOT!
SKIP THE SARCASM! KEEP MOVING!
THERE THEY ARE--- THE TWO VULTURES--- FIGHTING EACH OTHER!
IF YOU DIDN'T BRING YOUR CAMERA--- I'LL ANNIHI-LATE YOU!
I BROUGHT IT... I BROUGHT IT!
YOU NEVER SHOULD'A COME BACK, GRAMPA!
IT WAS YOUR BIGGEST MISTAKE!
BUGLE
16

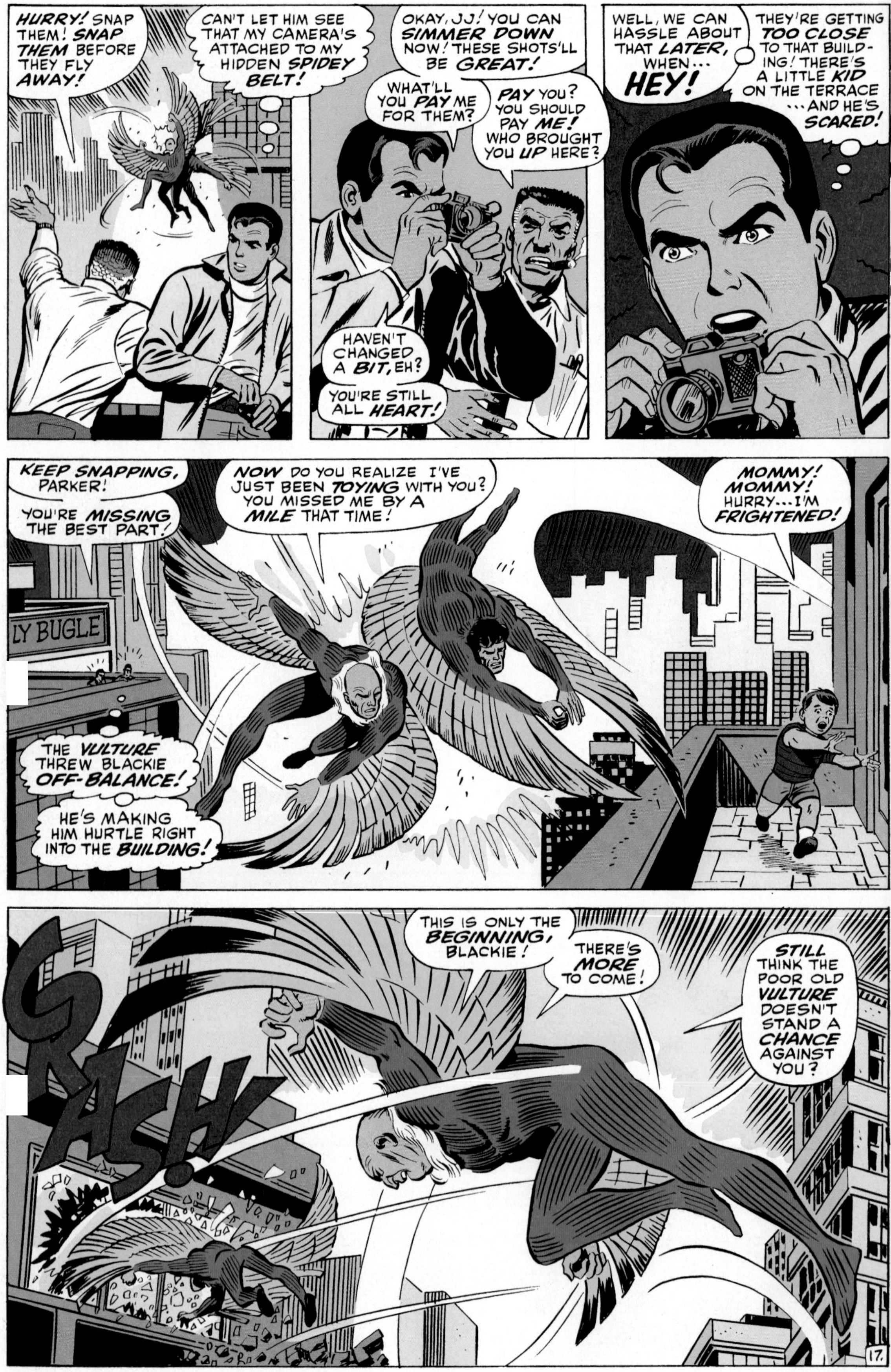
HURRY! SNAP THEM! SNAP THEM BEFORE THEY FLY AWAY!
CAN'T LET HIM SEE THAT MY CAMERA'S ATTACHED TO MY HIDDEN SPIDEY BELT!
OKAY, JJ! YOU CAN SIMMER DOWN NOW! THESE SHOTS'LL BE GREAT!
WHAT'LL YOU PAY ME FOR THEM?
PAY YOU? YOU SHOULD PAY ME! WHO BROUGHT YOU UP HERE?
HAVEN'T CHANGED A BIT, EH?
YOU'RE STILL ALL HEART!
WELL, WE CAN HASSLE ABOUT THAT LATER, WHEN... HEY!
THEY'RE GETTING TOO CLOSE TO THAT BUILDING! THERE'S A LITTLE KID ON THE TERRACE ...AND HE'S SCARED!
KEEP SNAPPING, PARKER!
YOU'RE MISSING THE BEST PART!
NOW DO YOU REALIZE I'VE JUST BEEN TOYING WITH YOU? YOU MISSED ME BY A MILE THAT TIME!
MOMMY! MOMMY! HURRY...I'M FRIGHTENED!
LY BUGLE
THE VULTURE THREW BLACKIE OFF-BALANCE!
HE'S MAKING HIM HURTLE RIGHT INTO THE BUILDING!
CRASH!
THIS IS ONLY THE BEGINNING, BLACKIE!
THERE'S MORE TO COME!
STILL THINK THE POOR OLD VULTURE DOESN'T STAND A CHANCE AGAINST YOU?
17.

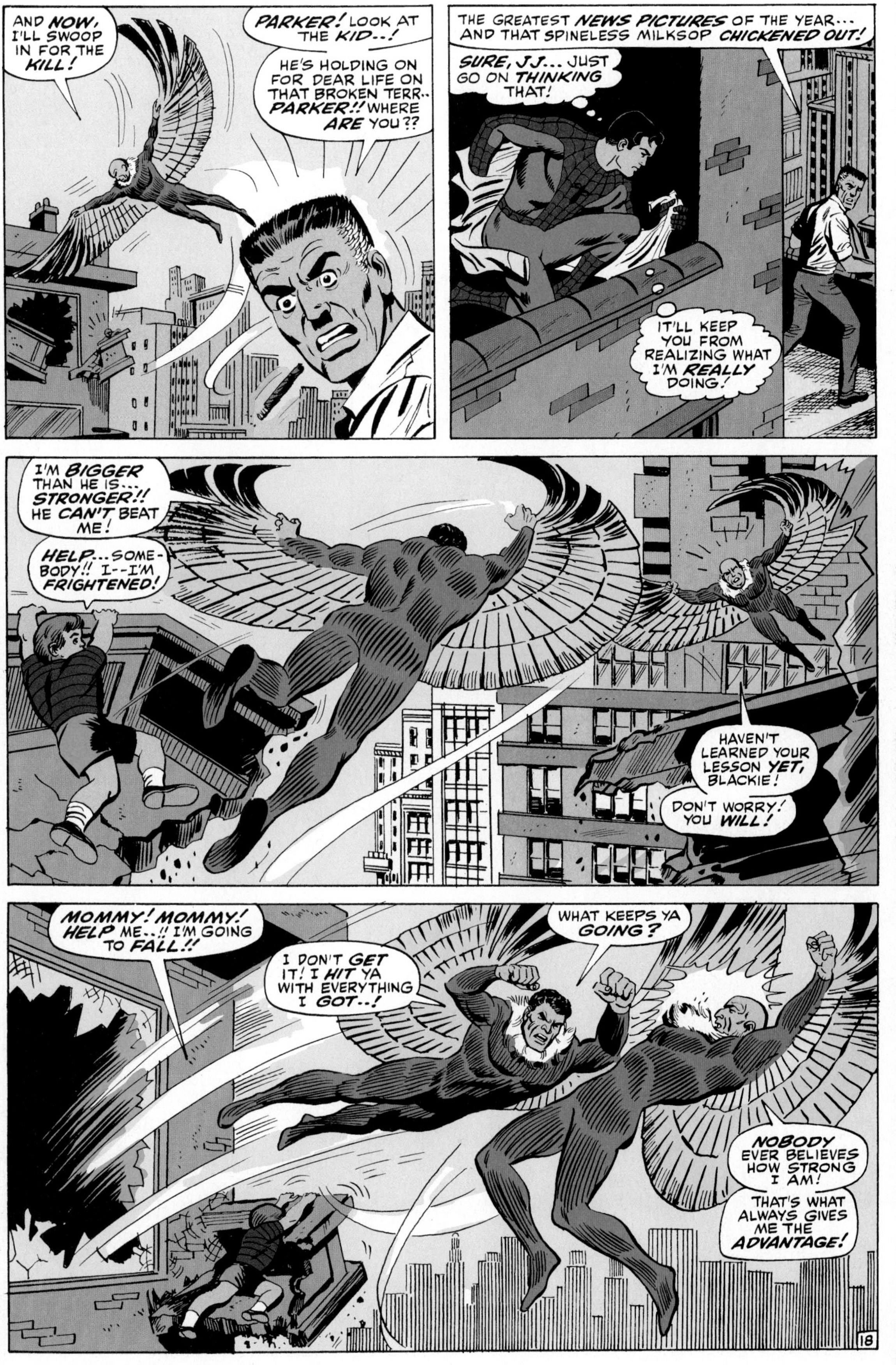
AND NOW, I'LL SWOOP IN FOR THE KILL!
PARKER! LOOK AT THE KID--!
HE'S HOLDING ON FOR DEAR LIFE ON THAT BROKEN TERR.. PARKER!! WHERE ARE YOU??
THE GREATEST NEWS PICTURES OF THE YEAR... AND THAT SPINELESS MILKSOP CHICKENED OUT!
SURE, JJ... JUST GO ON THINKING THAT!
IT'LL KEEP YOU FROM REALIZING WHAT I'M REALLY DOING!
I'M BIGGER THAN HE IS... STRONGER!! HE CAN'T BEAT ME!
HELP...SOME-BODY!! I--I'M FRIGHTENED!
HAVEN'T LEARNED YOUR LESSON YET, BLACKIE!
DON'T WORRY! YOU WILL!
MOMMY! MOMMY! HELP ME..!! I'M GOING TO FALL!!
I DON'T GET IT! I HIT YA WITH EVERYTHING I GOT..!
WHAT KEEPS YA GOING?
NOBODY EVER BELIEVES HOW STRONG I AM!
THAT'S WHAT ALWAYS GIVES ME THE ADVANTAGE!
18

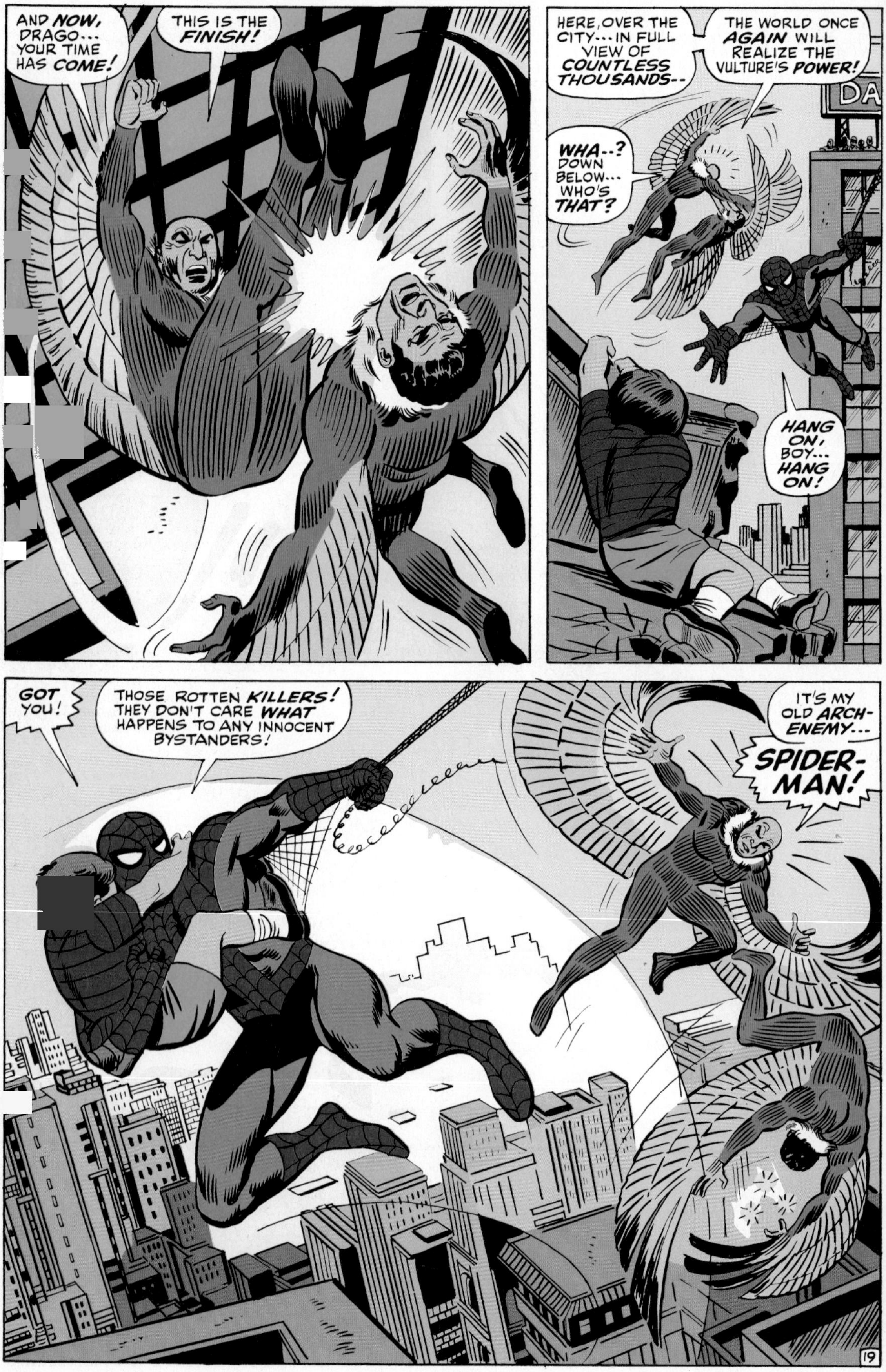
AND NOW, DRAGO... YOUR TIME HAS COME!
THIS IS THE FINISH!
HERE, OVER THE CITY... IN FULL VIEW OF COUNTLESS THOUSANDS--
THE WORLD ONCE AGAIN WILL REALIZE THE VULTURE'S POWER!
WHA--? DOWN BELOW... WHO'S THAT?
HANG ON, BOY... HANG ON!
GOT YOU!
THOSE ROTTEN KILLERS! THEY DON'T CARE WHAT HAPPENS TO ANY INNOCENT BYSTANDERS!
IT'S MY OLD ARCH-ENEMY...
SPIDER-MAN!
19

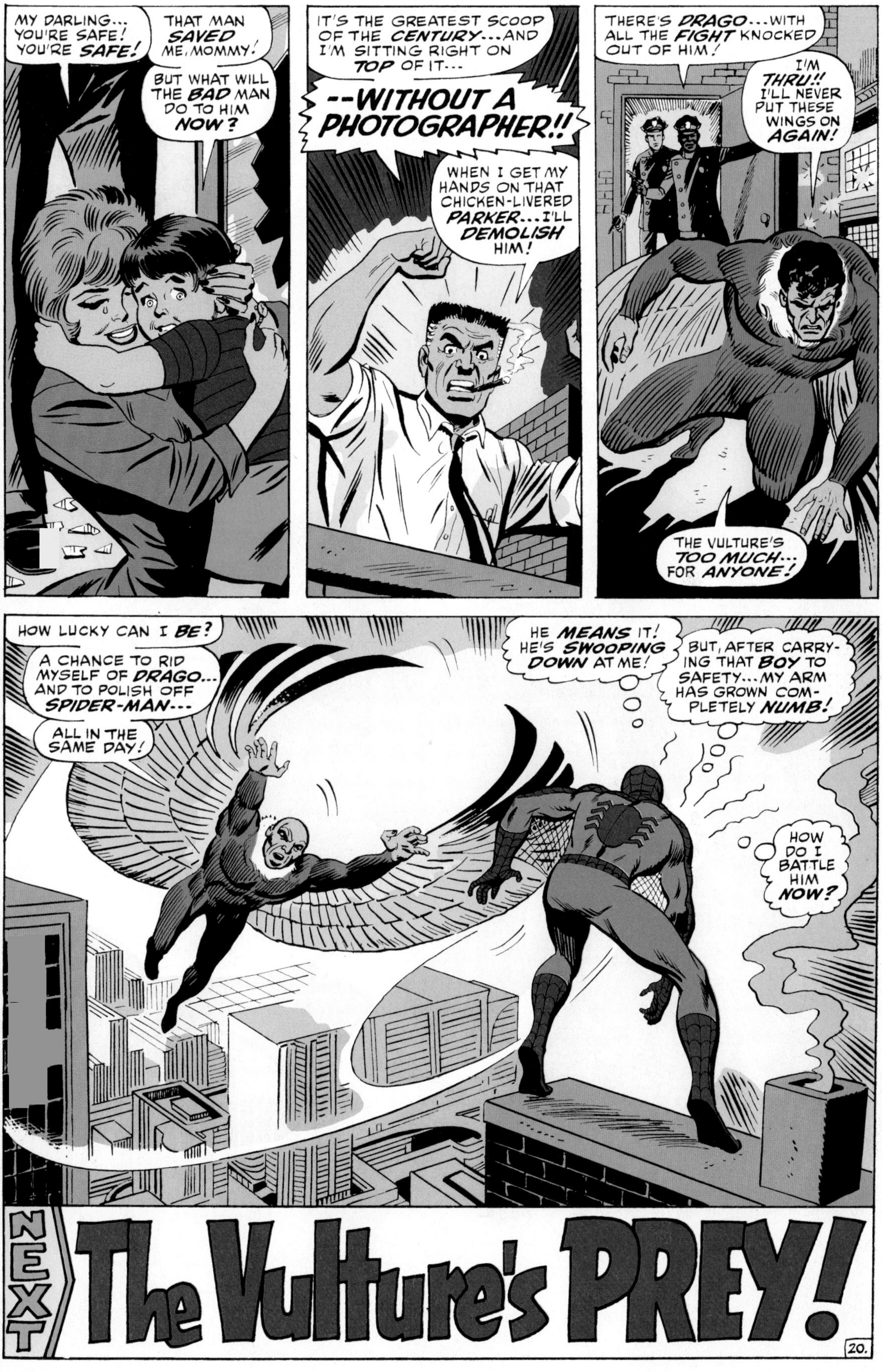
MY DARLING... YOU'RE SAFE! YOU'RE SAFE!
THAT MAN SAVED ME, MOMMY!
BUT WHAT WILL THE BAD MAN DO TO HIM NOW?
IT'S THE GREATEST SCOOP OF THE CENTURY... AND I'M SITTING RIGHT ON TOP OF IT---
--WITHOUT A PHOTOGRAPHER!!
WHEN I GET MY HANDS ON THAT CHICKEN-LIVERED PARKER... I'LL DEMOLISH HIM!
THERE'S DRAGO... WITH ALL THE FIGHT KNOCKED OUT OF HIM!
I'M THRU!! I'LL NEVER PUT THESE WINGS ON AGAIN!
THE VULTURE'S TOO MUCH... FOR ANYONE!
HOW LUCKY CAN I BE?
A CHANCE TO RID MYSELF OF DRAGO... AND TO POLISH OFF SPIDER-MAN---
ALL IN THE SAME DAY!
HE MEANS IT! HE'S SWOOPING DOWN AT ME!
BUT, AFTER CARRYING THAT BOY TO SAFETY... MY ARM HAS GROWN COMPLETELY NUMB!
HOW DO I BATTLE HIM NOW?
NEXT
The Vulture's PREY!
20.

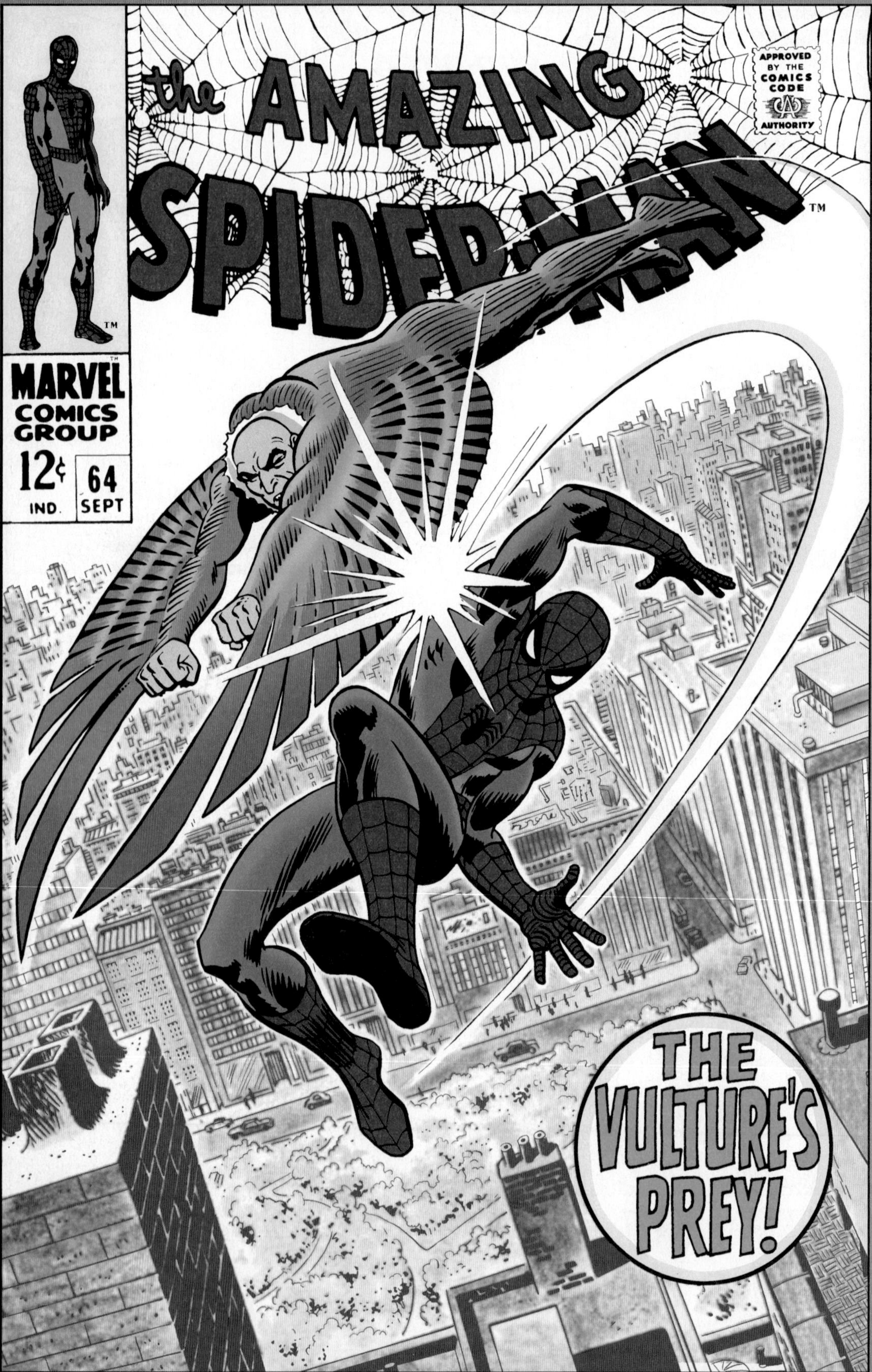
the AMAZING
SPIDER-MAN™
APPROVED BY THE COMICS CODE AUTHORITY
MARVEL COMICS GROUP
12¢ IND.
64 SEPT
THE VULTURE'S PREY!

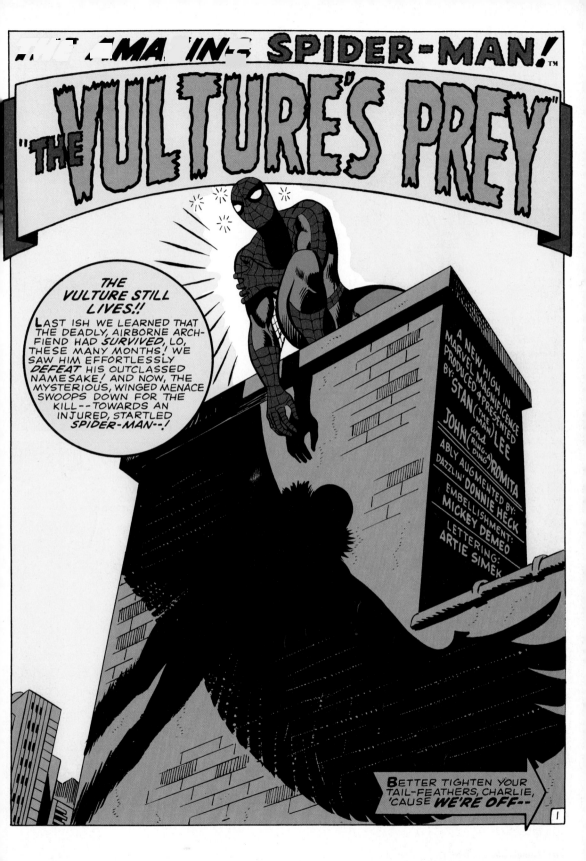

THE AMAZING SPIDER-MAN!

"THE VULTURE'S PREY"

THE VULTURE STILL LIVES!! LAST ISH WE LEARNED THAT THE DEADLY, AIRBORNE ARCH-FIEND HAD SURVIVED, LO, THESE MANY MONTHS! WE SAW HIM EFFORTLESSLY DEFEAT HIS OUTCLASSED NAMESAKE! AND NOW, THE MYSTERIOUS, WINGED MENACE SWOOPS DOWN FOR THE KILL--TOWARDS AN INJURED, STARTLED SPIDER-MAN--!

A NEW HIGH IN MARVEL MAGNIFICENCE PRODUCED & PRESENTED BY: STAN (THE MAN) LEE and JOHN (RING-A-DING) ROMITA ABLY AUGMENTED BY: DAZZLIN' DONNIE HECK EMBELLISHMENT: MICKEY DEMEO LETTERING: ARTIE SIMEK

BETTER TIGHTEN YOUR TAIL-FEATHERS, CHARLIE, 'CAUSE WE'RE OFF--

1

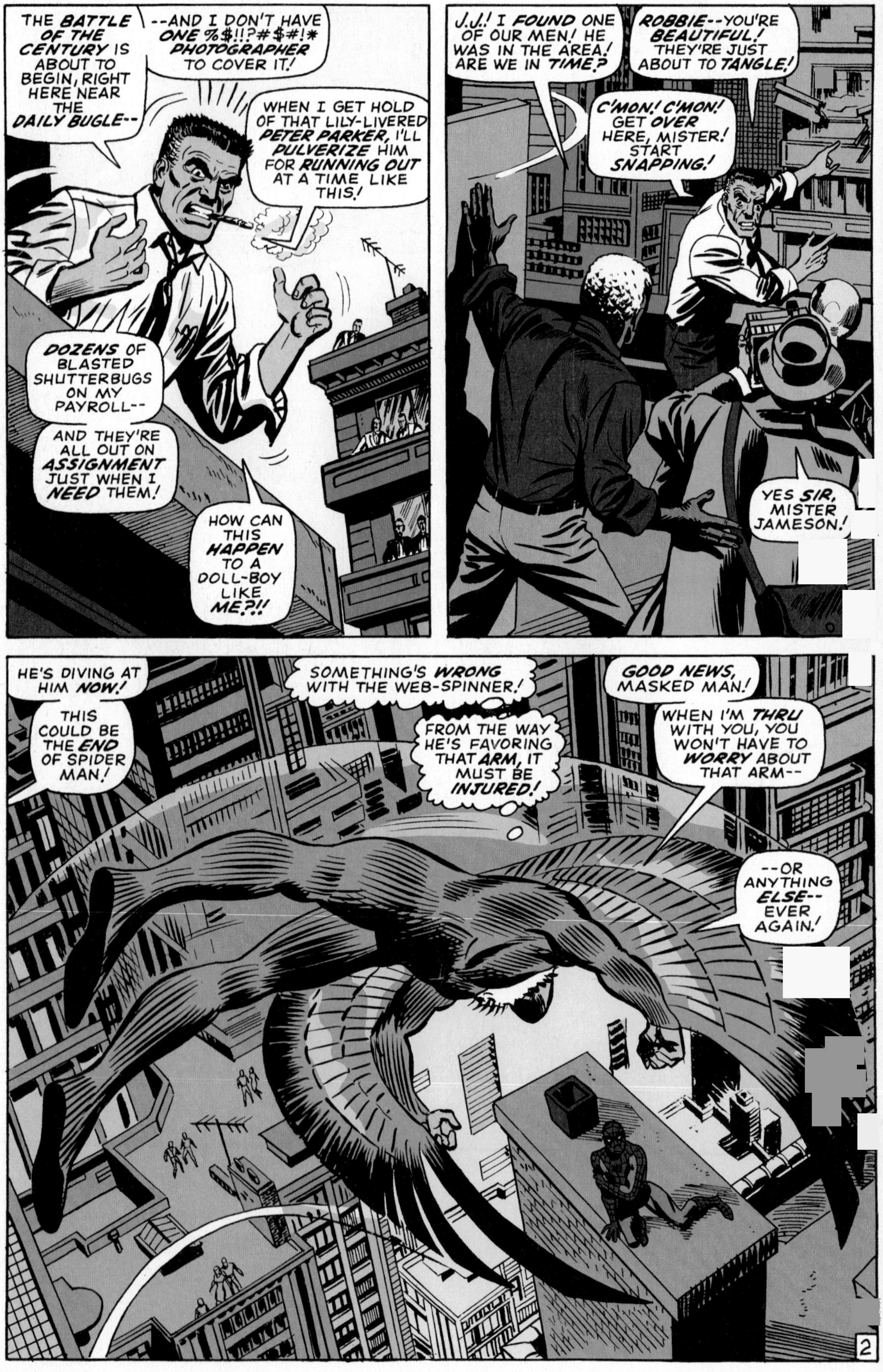
THE BATTLE OF THE CENTURY IS ABOUT TO BEGIN, RIGHT HERE NEAR THE DAILY BUGLE--
--AND I DON'T HAVE ONE %$!!?#$#!* PHOTOGRAPHER TO COVER IT!
WHEN I GET HOLD OF THAT LILY-LIVERED PETER PARKER, I'LL PULVERIZE HIM FOR RUNNING OUT AT A TIME LIKE THIS!
DOZENS OF BLASTED SHUTTERBUGS ON MY PAYROLL--
AND THEY'RE ALL OUT ON ASSIGNMENT JUST WHEN I NEED THEM!
HOW CAN THIS HAPPEN TO A DOLL-BOY LIKE ME?!!
J.J.! I FOUND ONE OF OUR MEN! HE WAS IN THE AREA! ARE WE IN TIME?
ROBBIE--YOU'RE BEAUTIFUL! THEY'RE JUST ABOUT TO TANGLE!
C'MON! C'MON! GET OVER HERE, MISTER! START SNAPPING!
YES SIR, MISTER JAMESON!
HE'S DIVING AT HIM NOW!
THIS COULD BE THE END OF SPIDER MAN!
SOMETHING'S WRONG WITH THE WEB-SPINNER!
FROM THE WAY HE'S FAVORING THAT ARM, IT MUST BE INJURED!
GOOD NEWS, MASKED MAN!
WHEN I'M THRU WITH YOU, YOU WON'T HAVE TO WORRY ABOUT THAT ARM--
--OR ANYTHING ELSE-- EVER AGAIN!
2

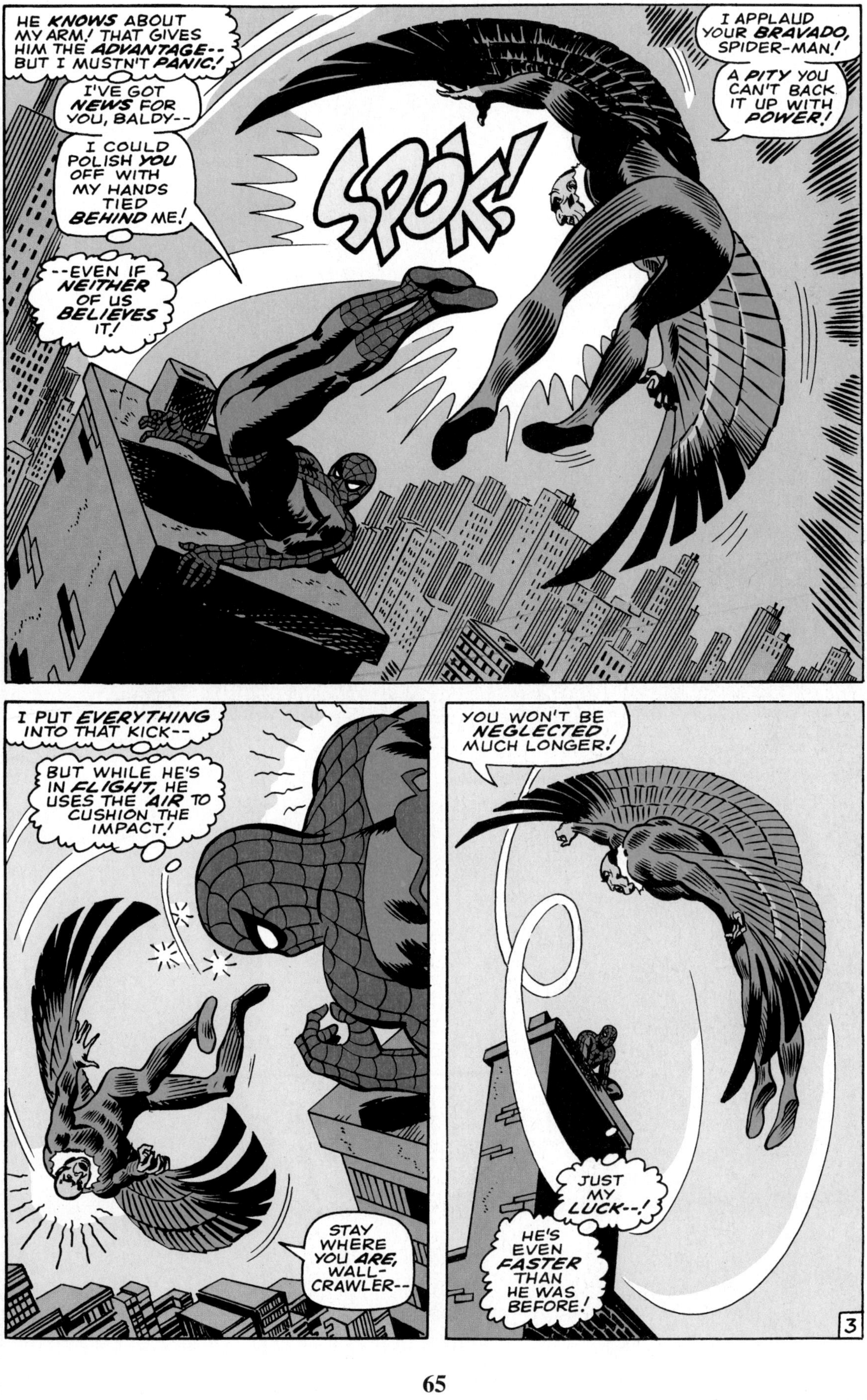
HE KNOWS ABOUT MY ARM! THAT GIVES HIM THE ADVANTAGE-- BUT I MUSTN'T PANIC!
I'VE GOT NEWS FOR YOU, BALDY--
I COULD POLISH YOU OFF WITH MY HANDS TIED BEHIND ME!
--EVEN IF NEITHER OF US BELIEVES IT!
SPOK!
I APPLAUD YOUR BRAVADO, SPIDER-MAN!
A PITY YOU CAN'T BACK IT UP WITH POWER!
I PUT EVERYTHING INTO THAT KICK--
BUT WHILE HE'S IN FLIGHT, HE USES THE AIR TO CUSHION THE IMPACT!
STAY WHERE YOU ARE, WALL-CRAWLER--
YOU WON'T BE NEGLECTED MUCH LONGER!
JUST MY LUCK--!
HE'S EVEN FASTER THAN HE WAS BEFORE!
3

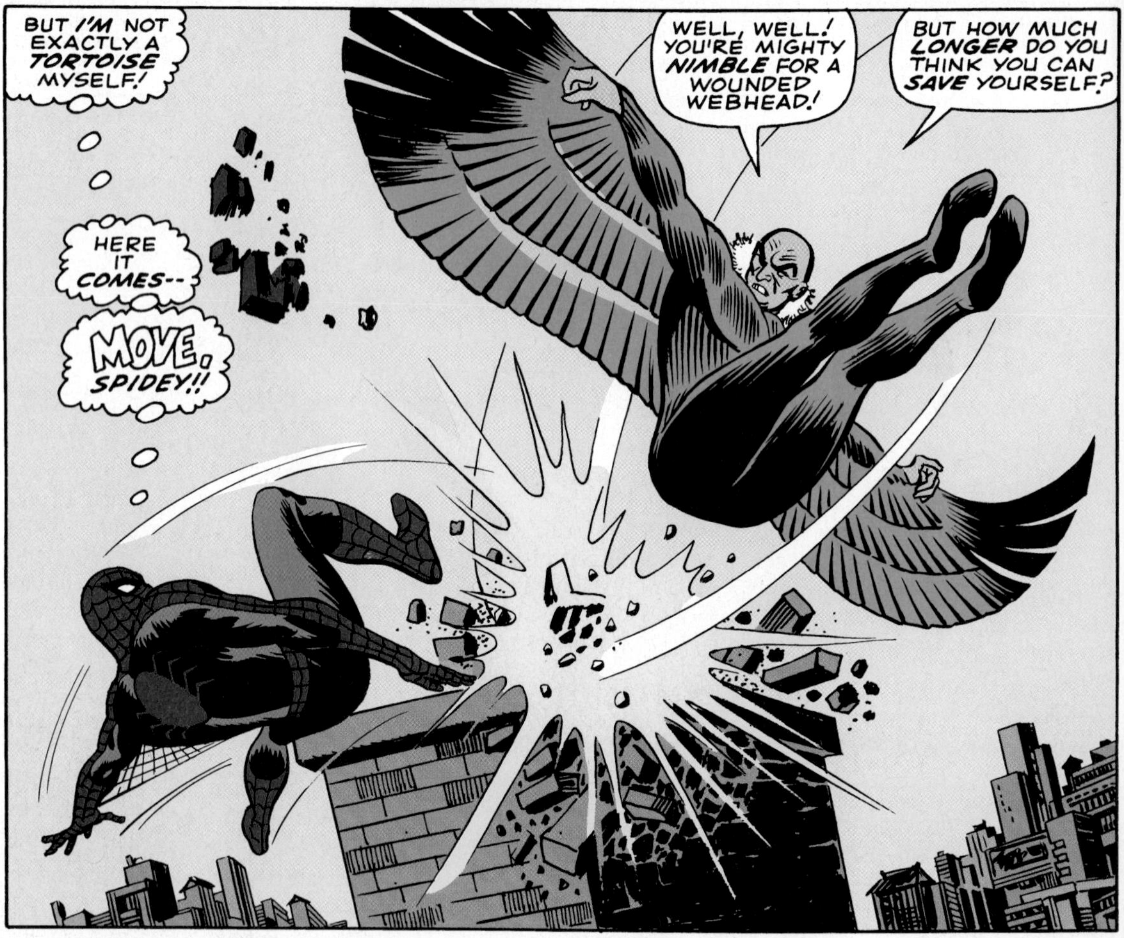
BUT I'M NOT EXACTLY A TORTOISE MYSELF!
HERE IT COMES--
MOVE, SPIDEY!!
WELL, WELL! YOU'RE MIGHTY NIMBLE FOR A WOUNDED WEBHEAD!
BUT HOW MUCH LONGER DO YOU THINK YOU CAN SAVE YOURSELF?

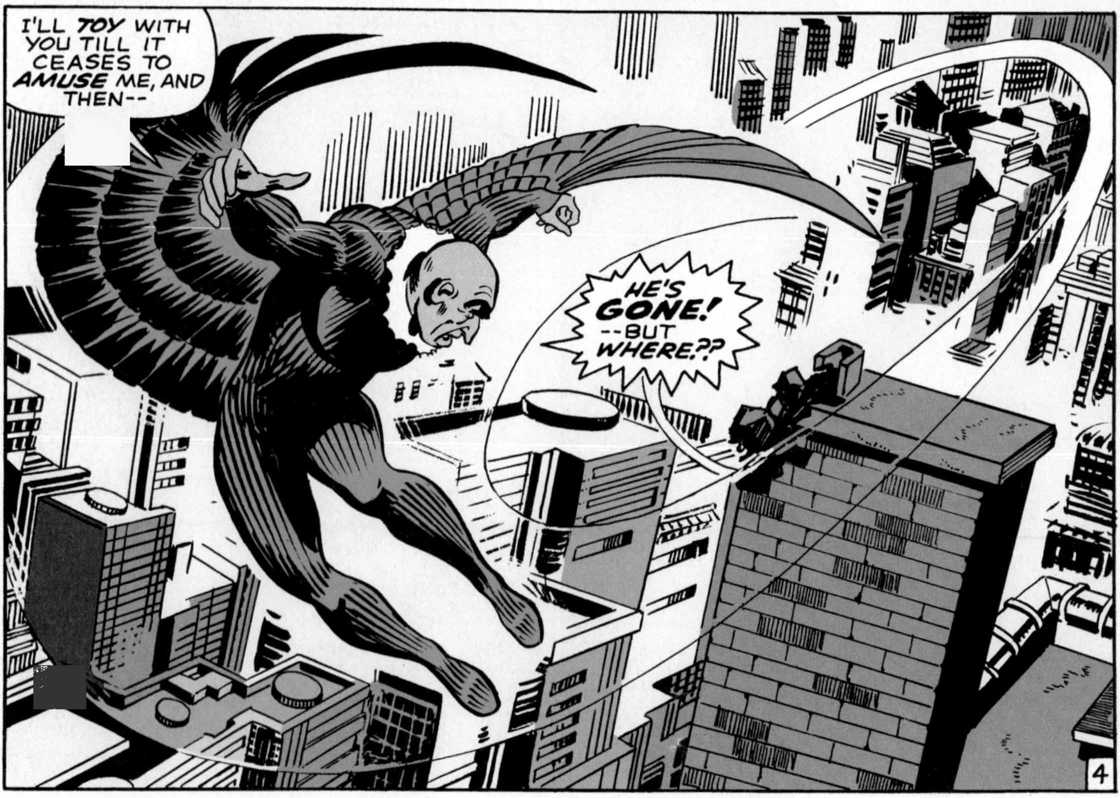
I'LL TOY WITH YOU TILL IT CEASES TO AMUSE ME, AND THEN--
HE'S GONE! --BUT WHERE??
4

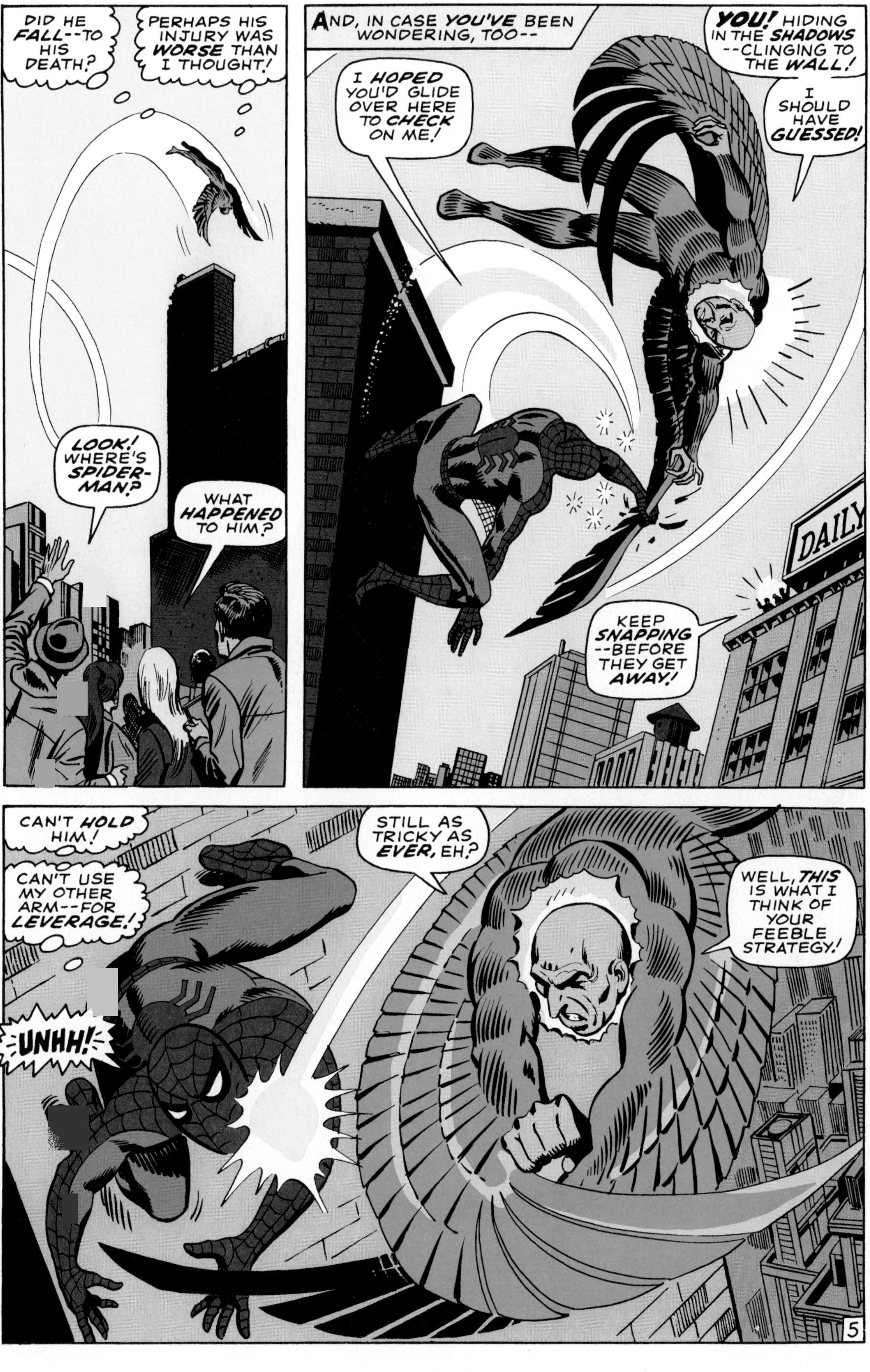
DID HE FALL--TO HIS DEATH?
PERHAPS HIS INJURY WAS WORSE THAN I THOUGHT!
LOOK! WHERE'S SPIDER-MAN?
WHAT HAPPENED TO HIM?
AND, IN CASE YOU'VE BEEN WONDERING, TOO--
YOU! HIDING IN THE SHADOWS --CLINGING TO THE WALL!
I SHOULD HAVE GUESSED!
I HOPED YOU'D GLIDE OVER HERE TO CHECK ON ME!
DAILY
KEEP SNAPPING --BEFORE THEY GET AWAY!
CAN'T HOLD HIM!
CAN'T USE MY OTHER ARM--FOR LEVERAGE!
STILL AS TRICKY AS EVER, EH?
WELL, THIS IS WHAT I THINK OF YOUR FEEBLE STRATEGY!
UNHH!
5

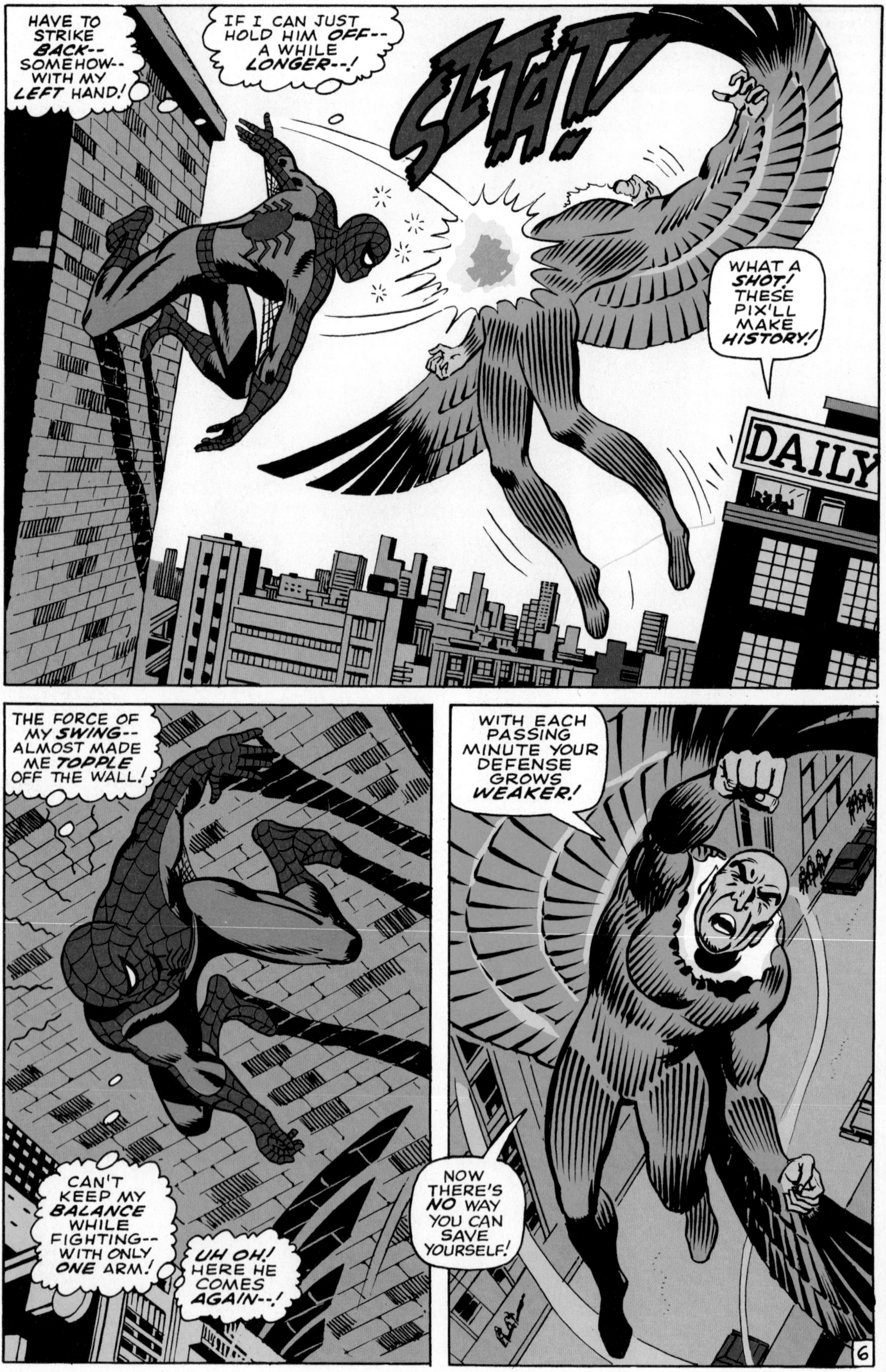
HAVE TO STRIKE BACK-- SOMEHOW-- WITH MY LEFT HAND!
IF I CAN JUST HOLD HIM OFF-- A WHILE LONGER--!
SLTAT!!
WHAT A SHOT! THESE PIX'LL MAKE HISTORY!
DAILY
THE FORCE OF MY SWING-- ALMOST MADE ME TOPPLE OFF THE WALL!
CAN'T KEEP MY BALANCE WHILE FIGHTING-- WITH ONLY ONE ARM!
UH OH! HERE HE COMES AGAIN--!
WITH EACH PASSING MINUTE YOUR DEFENSE GROWS WEAKER!
NOW THERE'S NO WAY YOU CAN SAVE YOURSELF!
6

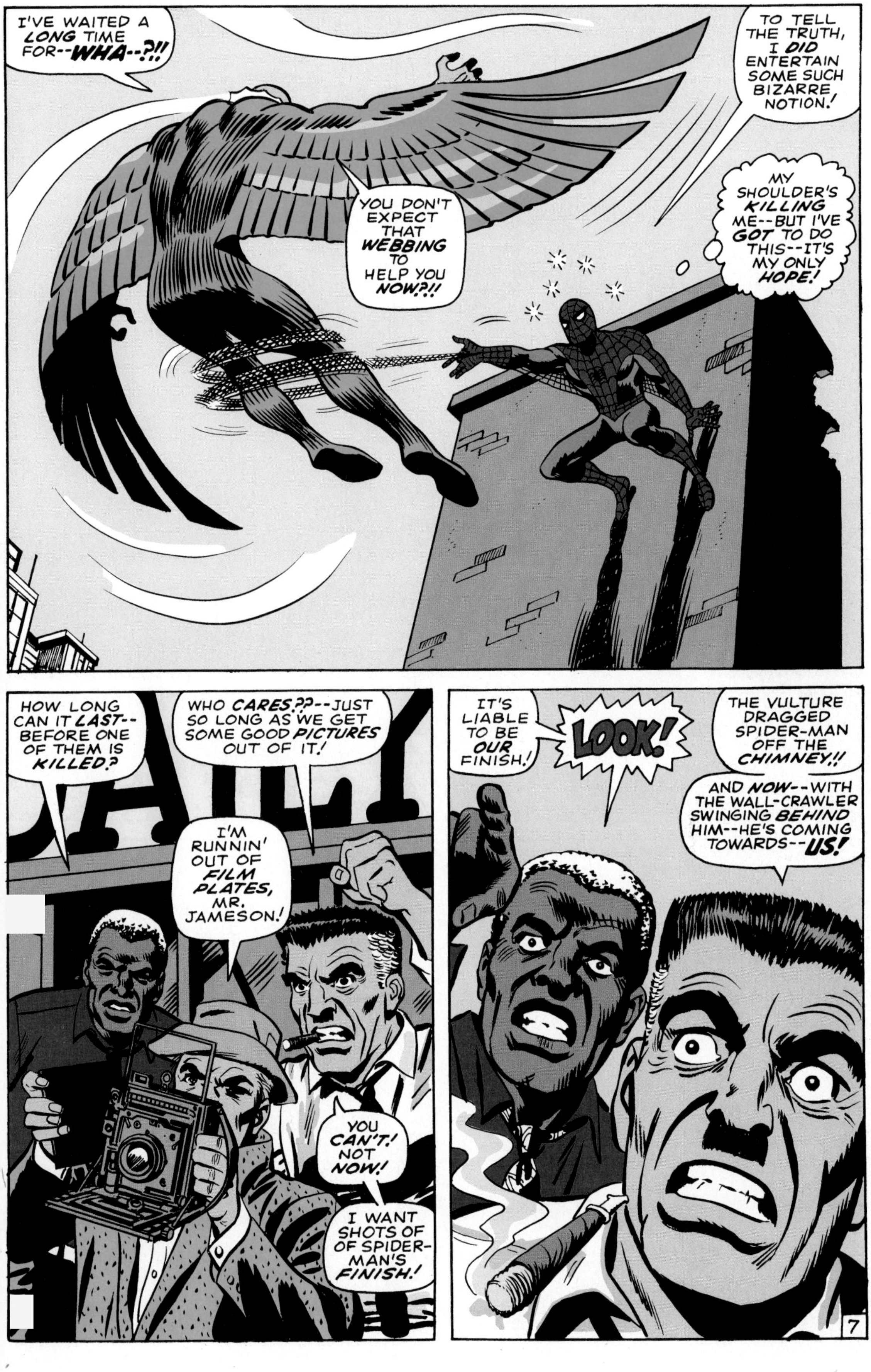
I'VE WAITED A LONG TIME FOR--WHA--?!!
TO TELL THE TRUTH, I DID ENTERTAIN SOME SUCH BIZARRE NOTION!
YOU DON'T EXPECT THAT WEBBING TO HELP YOU NOW?!!
MY SHOULDER'S KILLING ME--BUT I'VE GOT TO DO THIS--IT'S MY ONLY HOPE!
HOW LONG CAN IT LAST--BEFORE ONE OF THEM IS KILLED?
WHO CARES??--JUST SO LONG AS WE GET SOME GOOD PICTURES OUT OF IT!
I'M RUNNIN' OUT OF FILM PLATES, MR. JAMESON!
YOU CAN'T! NOT NOW!
I WANT SHOTS OF OF SPIDER-MAN'S FINISH!
IT'S LIABLE TO BE OUR FINISH!
LOOK!
THE VULTURE DRAGGED SPIDER-MAN OFF THE CHIMNEY!!
AND NOW--WITH THE WALL-CRAWLER SWINGING BEHIND HIM--HE'S COMING TOWARDS--US!
7

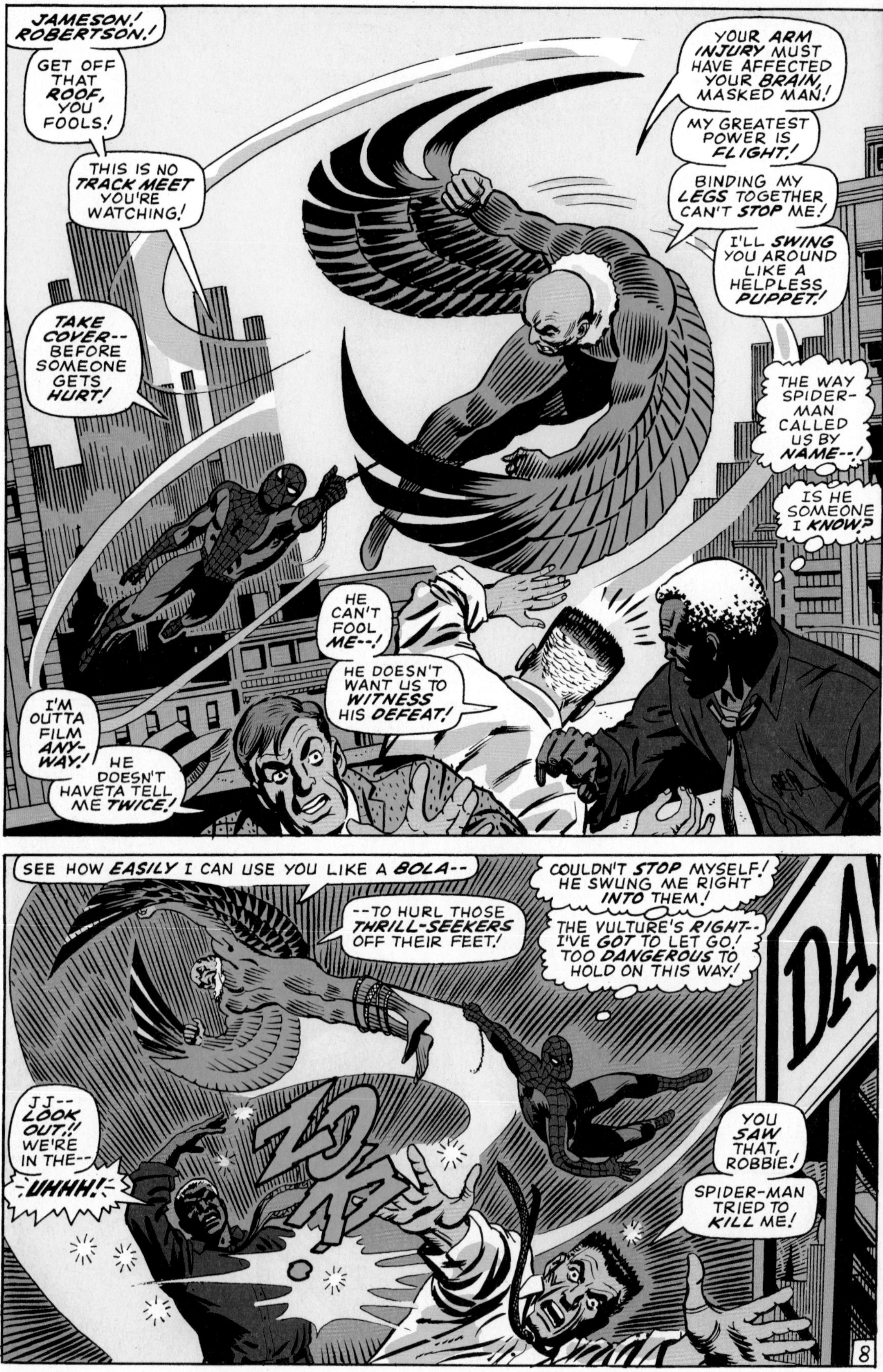

JAMESON! ROBERTSON!
GET OFF THAT ROOF, YOU FOOLS!
THIS IS NO TRACK MEET YOU'RE WATCHING!
TAKE COVER-- BEFORE SOMEONE GETS HURT!
YOUR ARM INJURY MUST HAVE AFFECTED YOUR BRAIN, MASKED MAN!
MY GREATEST POWER IS FLIGHT!
BINDING MY LEGS TOGETHER CAN'T STOP ME!
I'LL SWING YOU AROUND LIKE A HELPLESS PUPPET!
THE WAY SPIDER-MAN CALLED US BY NAME--!
IS HE SOMEONE I KNOW?
HE CAN'T FOOL ME--!
HE DOESN'T WANT US TO WITNESS HIS DEFEAT!
I'M OUTTA FILM ANY-WAY!
HE DOESN'T HAVETA TELL ME TWICE!
SEE HOW EASILY I CAN USE YOU LIKE A BOLA--
--TO HURL THOSE THRILL-SEEKERS OFF THEIR FEET!
COULDN'T STOP MYSELF! HE SWUNG ME RIGHT INTO THEM!
THE VULTURE'S RIGHT-- I'VE GOT TO LET GO! TOO DANGEROUS TO HOLD ON THIS WAY!
DA
JJ-- LOOK OUT!! WE'RE IN THE--
UHHH!
ZOK
YOU SAW THAT, ROBBIE!
SPIDER-MAN TRIED TO KILL ME!
8

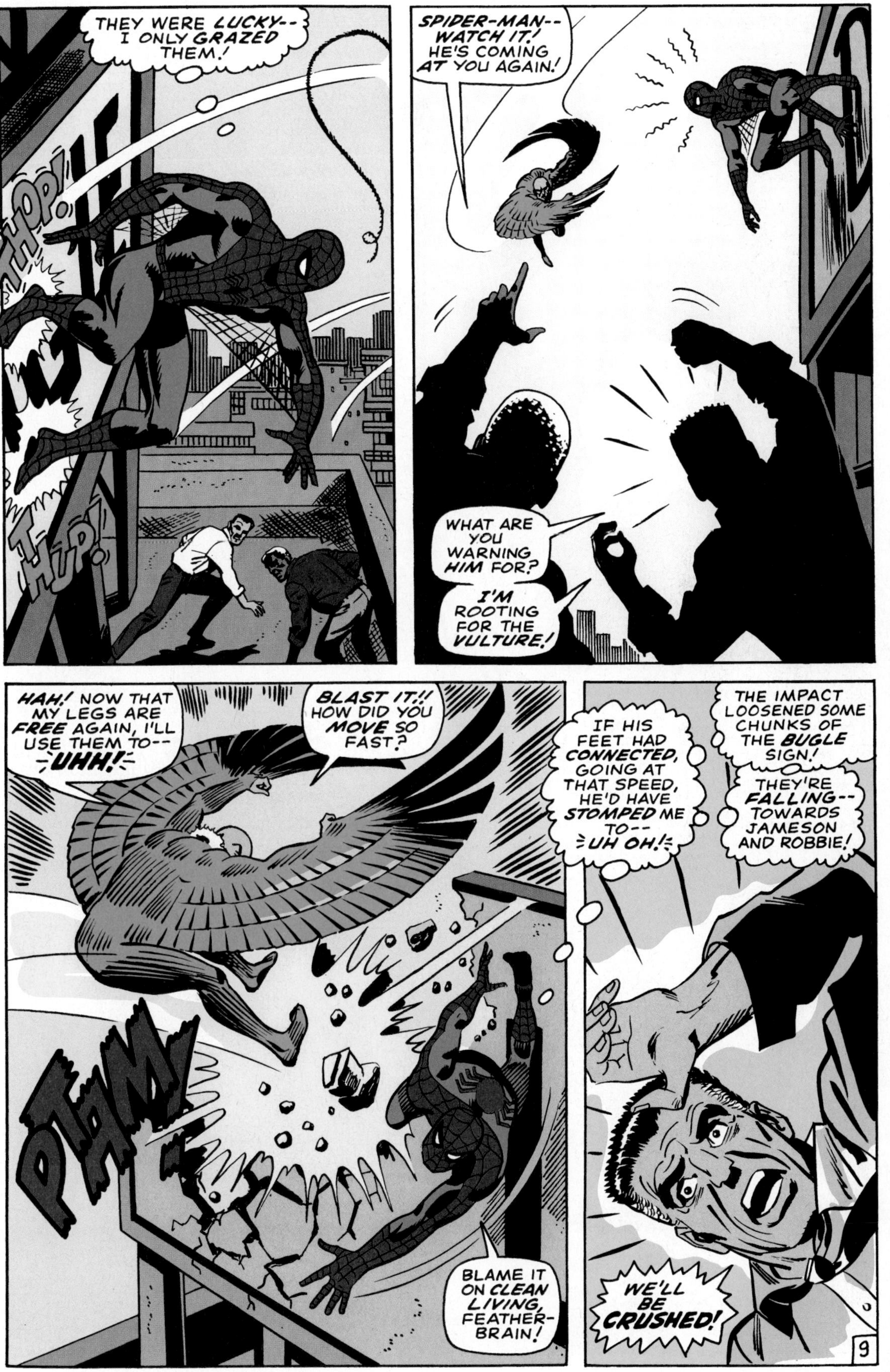

THEY WERE LUCKY-- I ONLY GRAZED THEM!
THP!
THUP!
SPIDER-MAN-- WATCH IT! HE'S COMING AT YOU AGAIN!
WHAT ARE YOU WARNING HIM FOR?
I'M ROOTING FOR THE VULTURE!
HAH! NOW THAT MY LEGS ARE FREE AGAIN, I'LL USE THEM TO-- -UHH!-
BLAST IT!! HOW DID YOU MOVE SO FAST?
PTHAM!
BLAME IT ON CLEAN LIVING, FEATHER-BRAIN!
IF HIS FEET HAD CONNECTED, GOING AT THAT SPEED, HE'D HAVE STOMPED ME TO-- -UH OH!-
THE IMPACT LOOSENED SOME CHUNKS OF THE BUGLE SIGN!
THEY'RE FALLING-- TOWARDS JAMESON AND ROBBIE!
WE'LL BE CRUSHED!
9

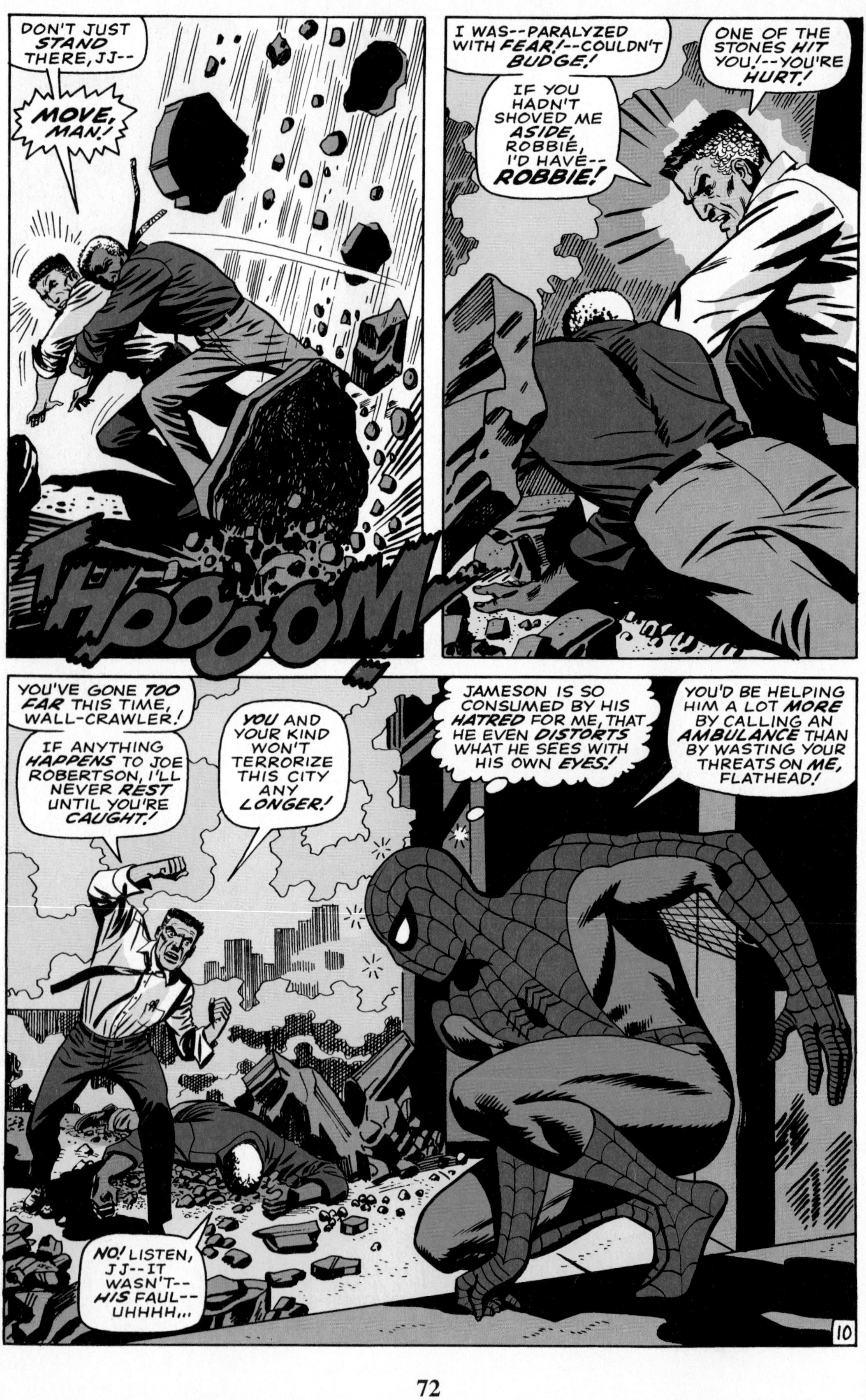
DON'T JUST STAND THERE, JJ--
MOVE, MAN!
THOOOOM
I WAS--PARALYZED WITH FEAR!--COULDN'T BUDGE!
IF YOU HADN'T SHOVED ME ASIDE, ROBBIE, I'D HAVE-- ROBBIE!
ONE OF THE STONES HIT YOU!--YOU'RE HURT!
YOU'VE GONE TOO FAR THIS TIME, WALL-CRAWLER!
IF ANYTHING HAPPENS TO JOE ROBERTSON, I'LL NEVER REST UNTIL YOU'RE CAUGHT!
YOU AND YOUR KIND WON'T TERRORIZE THIS CITY ANY LONGER!
JAMESON IS SO CONSUMED BY HIS HATRED FOR ME, THAT HE EVEN DISTORTS WHAT HE SEES WITH HIS OWN EYES!
YOU'D BE HELPING HIM A LOT MORE BY CALLING AN AMBULANCE THAN BY WASTING YOUR THREATS ON ME, FLATHEAD!
NO! LISTEN, JJ--IT WASN'T--HIS FAUL--UHHHH...
10

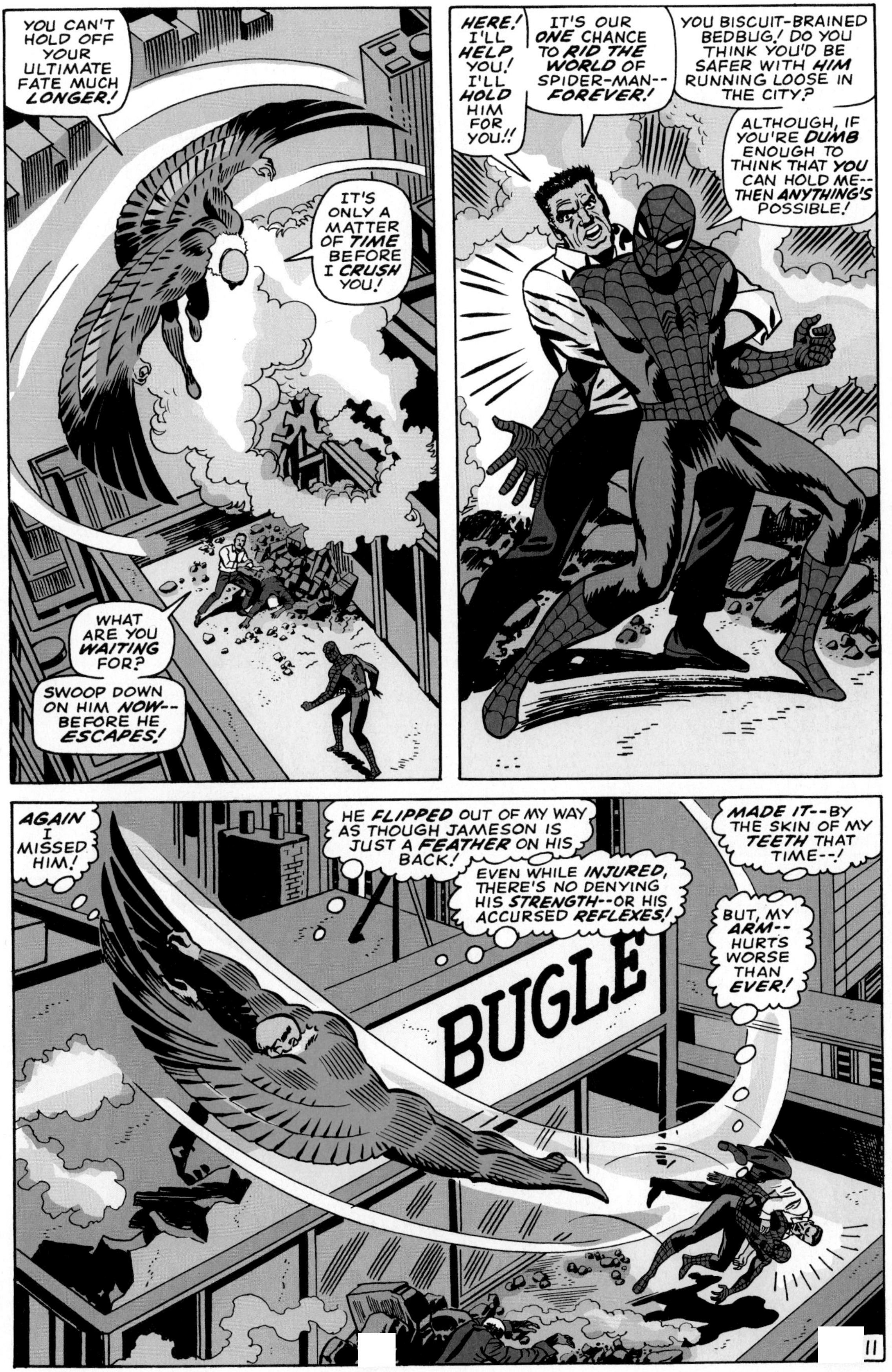

YOU CAN'T HOLD OFF YOUR ULTIMATE FATE MUCH LONGER!
IT'S ONLY A MATTER OF TIME BEFORE I CRUSH YOU!
WHAT ARE YOU WAITING FOR?
SWOOP DOWN ON HIM NOW-- BEFORE HE ESCAPES!
HERE! I'LL HELP YOU! I'LL HOLD HIM FOR YOU!!
IT'S OUR ONE CHANCE TO RID THE WORLD OF SPIDER-MAN-- FOREVER!
YOU BISCUIT-BRAINED BEDBUG! DO YOU THINK YOU'D BE SAFER WITH HIM RUNNING LOOSE IN THE CITY?
ALTHOUGH, IF YOU'RE DUMB ENOUGH TO THINK THAT YOU CAN HOLD ME-- THEN ANYTHING'S POSSIBLE!
AGAIN I MISSED HIM!
HE FLIPPED OUT OF MY WAY AS THOUGH JAMESON IS JUST A FEATHER ON HIS BACK!
EVEN WHILE INJURED, THERE'S NO DENYING HIS STRENGTH--OR HIS ACCURSED REFLEXES!
MADE IT--BY THE SKIN OF MY TEETH THAT TIME--!
BUT, MY ARM-- HURTS WORSE THAN EVER!
BUGLE
11

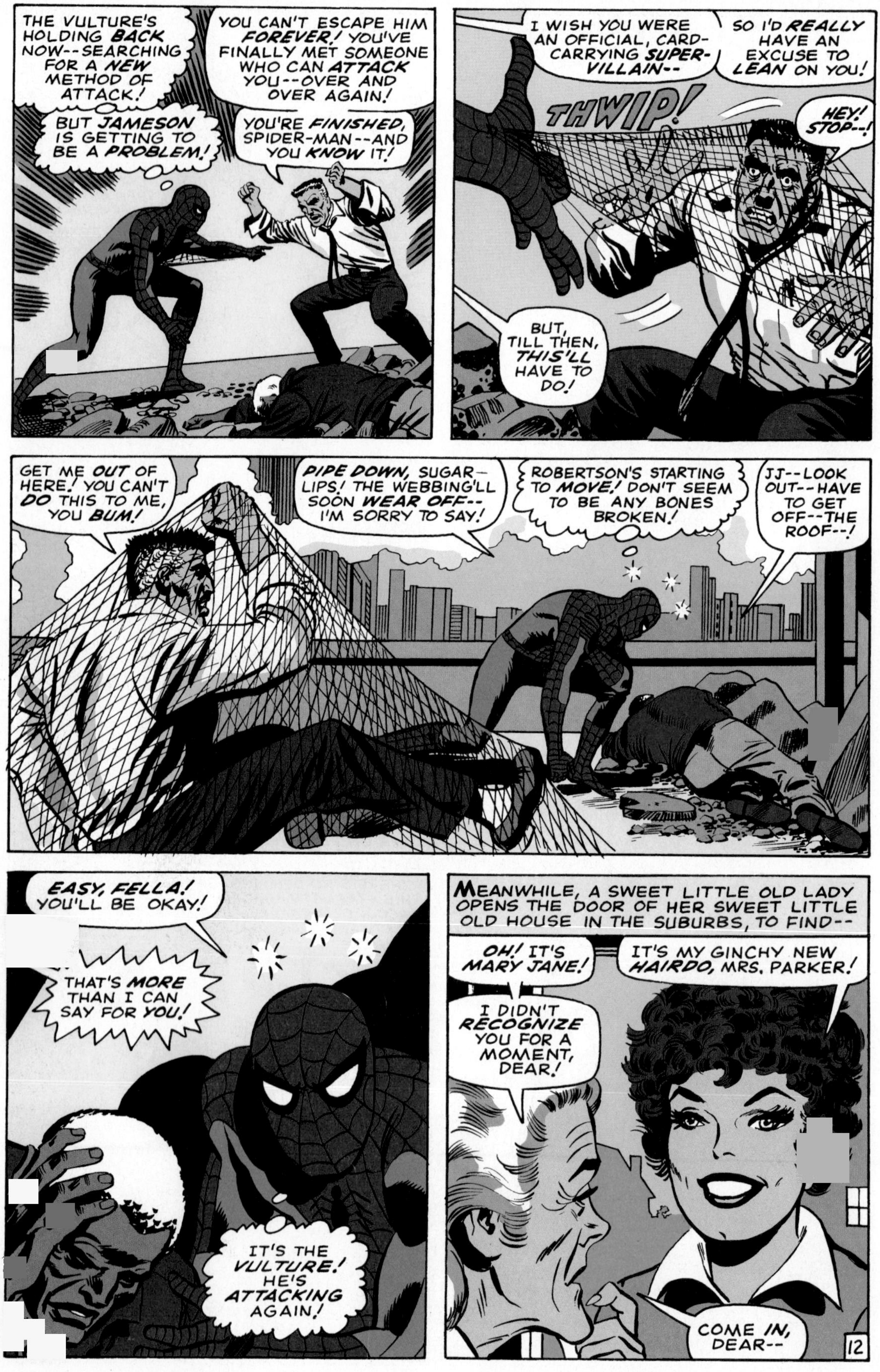
THE VULTURE'S HOLDING BACK NOW--SEARCHING FOR A NEW METHOD OF ATTACK!
BUT JAMESON IS GETTING TO BE A PROBLEM!
YOU CAN'T ESCAPE HIM FOREVER! YOU'VE FINALLY MET SOMEONE WHO CAN ATTACK YOU--OVER AND OVER AGAIN!
YOU'RE FINISHED, SPIDER-MAN--AND YOU KNOW IT!
I WISH YOU WERE AN OFFICIAL, CARD-CARRYING SUPER-VILLAIN--
SO I'D REALLY HAVE AN EXCUSE TO LEAN ON YOU!
THWIP!
HEY! STOP--!
BUT, TILL THEN, THIS'LL HAVE TO DO!
GET ME OUT OF HERE! YOU CAN'T DO THIS TO ME, YOU BUM!
PIPE DOWN, SUGAR-LIPS! THE WEBBING'LL SOON WEAR OFF-- I'M SORRY TO SAY!
ROBERTSON'S STARTING TO MOVE! DON'T SEEM TO BE ANY BONES BROKEN!
JJ--LOOK OUT--HAVE TO GET OFF--THE ROOF--!
EASY, FELLA! YOU'LL BE OKAY!
THAT'S MORE THAN I CAN SAY FOR YOU!
IT'S THE VULTURE! HE'S ATTACKING AGAIN!
MEANWHILE, A SWEET LITTLE OLD LADY OPENS THE DOOR OF HER SWEET LITTLE OLD HOUSE IN THE SUBURBS, TO FIND--
OH! IT'S MARY JANE!
I DIDN'T RECOGNIZE YOU FOR A MOMENT, DEAR!
IT'S MY GINCHY NEW HAIRDO, MRS. PARKER!
COME IN, DEAR--
12

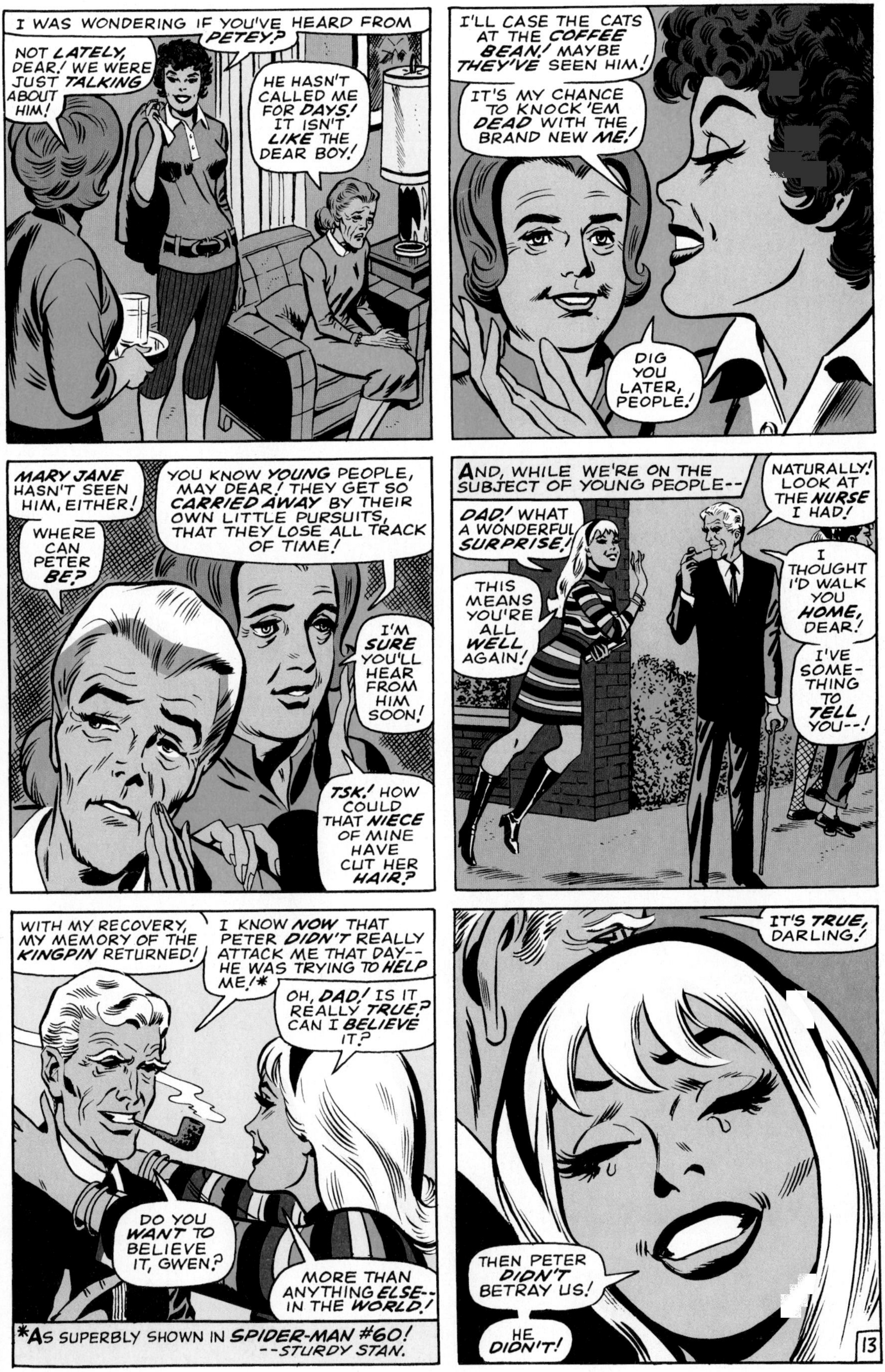

I WAS WONDERING IF YOU'VE HEARD FROM PETEY?
NOT LATELY, DEAR! WE WERE JUST TALKING ABOUT HIM!
HE HASN'T CALLED ME FOR DAYS! IT ISN'T LIKE THE DEAR BOY!
I'LL CASE THE CATS AT THE COFFEE BEAN! MAYBE THEY'VE SEEN HIM!
IT'S MY CHANCE TO KNOCK 'EM DEAD WITH THE BRAND NEW ME!
DIG YOU LATER, PEOPLE!
MARY JANE HASN'T SEEN HIM, EITHER!
WHERE CAN PETER BE?
YOU KNOW YOUNG PEOPLE, MAY DEAR! THEY GET SO CARRIED AWAY BY THEIR OWN LITTLE PURSUITS, THAT THEY LOSE ALL TRACK OF TIME!
I'M SURE YOU'LL HEAR FROM HIM SOON!
TSK! HOW COULD THAT NIECE OF MINE HAVE CUT HER HAIR?
AND, WHILE WE'RE ON THE SUBJECT OF YOUNG PEOPLE--
DAD! WHAT A WONDERFUL SURPRISE!
THIS MEANS YOU'RE ALL WELL AGAIN!
NATURALLY! LOOK AT THE NURSE I HAD!
I THOUGHT I'D WALK YOU HOME, DEAR!
I'VE SOME-THING TO TELL YOU--!
WITH MY RECOVERY, MY MEMORY OF THE KINGPIN RETURNED!
I KNOW NOW THAT PETER DIDN'T REALLY ATTACK ME THAT DAY--HE WAS TRYING TO HELP ME!*
OH, DAD! IS IT REALLY TRUE? CAN I BELIEVE IT?
DO YOU WANT TO BELIEVE IT, GWEN?
MORE THAN ANYTHING ELSE--IN THE WORLD!
*AS SUPERBLY SHOWN IN SPIDER-MAN #60! --STURDY STAN.
IT'S TRUE, DARLING!
THEN PETER DIDN'T BETRAY US!
HE DIDN'T!
13

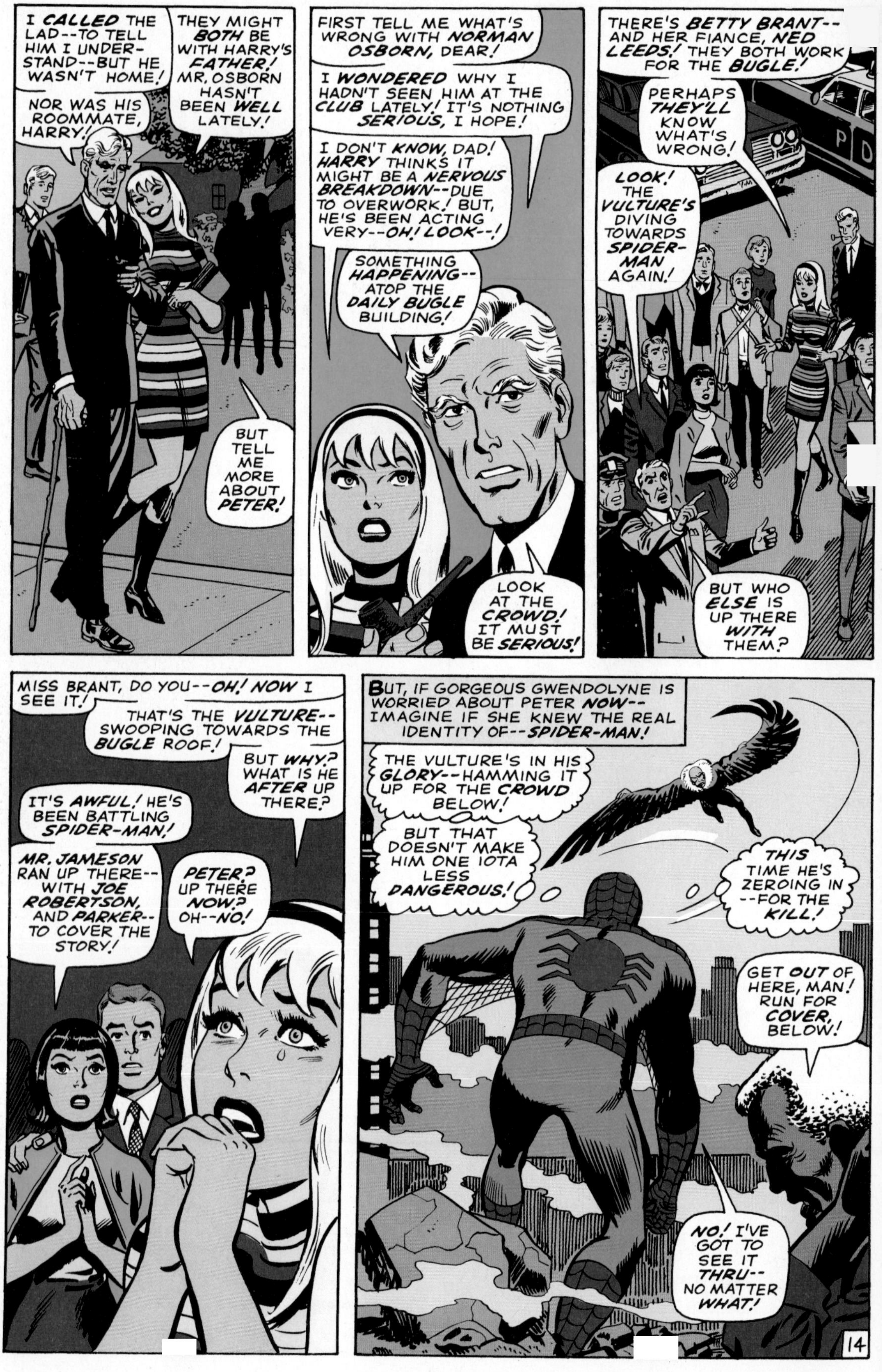

I CALLED THE LAD--TO TELL HIM I UNDERSTAND--BUT HE WASN'T HOME!
NOR WAS HIS ROOMMATE, HARRY!
THEY MIGHT BOTH BE WITH HARRY'S FATHER! MR. OSBORN HASN'T BEEN WELL LATELY!
BUT TELL ME MORE ABOUT PETER!
FIRST TELL ME WHAT'S WRONG WITH NORMAN OSBORN, DEAR!
I WONDERED WHY I HADN'T SEEN HIM AT THE CLUB LATELY! IT'S NOTHING SERIOUS, I HOPE!
I DON'T KNOW, DAD! HARRY THINKS IT MIGHT BE A NERVOUS BREAKDOWN--DUE TO OVERWORK! BUT, HE'S BEEN ACTING VERY--OH! LOOK--!
SOMETHING HAPPENING--ATOP THE DAILY BUGLE BUILDING!
LOOK AT THE CROWD! IT MUST BE SERIOUS!
THERE'S BETTY BRANT--AND HER FIANCE, NED LEEDS! THEY BOTH WORK FOR THE BUGLE!
PERHAPS THEY'LL KNOW WHAT'S WRONG!
LOOK! THE VULTURE'S DIVING TOWARDS SPIDER-MAN AGAIN!
BUT WHO ELSE IS UP THERE WITH THEM?
MISS BRANT, DO YOU--OH! NOW I SEE IT!
THAT'S THE VULTURE--SWOOPING TOWARDS THE BUGLE ROOF!
BUT WHY? WHAT IS HE AFTER UP THERE?
IT'S AWFUL! HE'S BEEN BATTLING SPIDER-MAN!
MR. JAMESON RAN UP THERE--WITH JOE ROBERTSON, AND PARKER--TO COVER THE STORY!
PETER? UP THERE NOW? OH--NO!
BUT, IF GORGEOUS GWENDOLYNE IS WORRIED ABOUT PETER NOW--IMAGINE IF SHE KNEW THE REAL IDENTITY OF--SPIDER-MAN!
THE VULTURE'S IN HIS GLORY--HAMMING IT UP FOR THE CROWD BELOW!
BUT THAT DOESN'T MAKE HIM ONE IOTA LESS DANGEROUS!
THIS TIME HE'S ZEROING IN--FOR THE KILL!
GET OUT OF HERE, MAN! RUN FOR COVER, BELOW!
NO! I'VE GOT TO SEE IT THRU--NO MATTER WHAT!
14

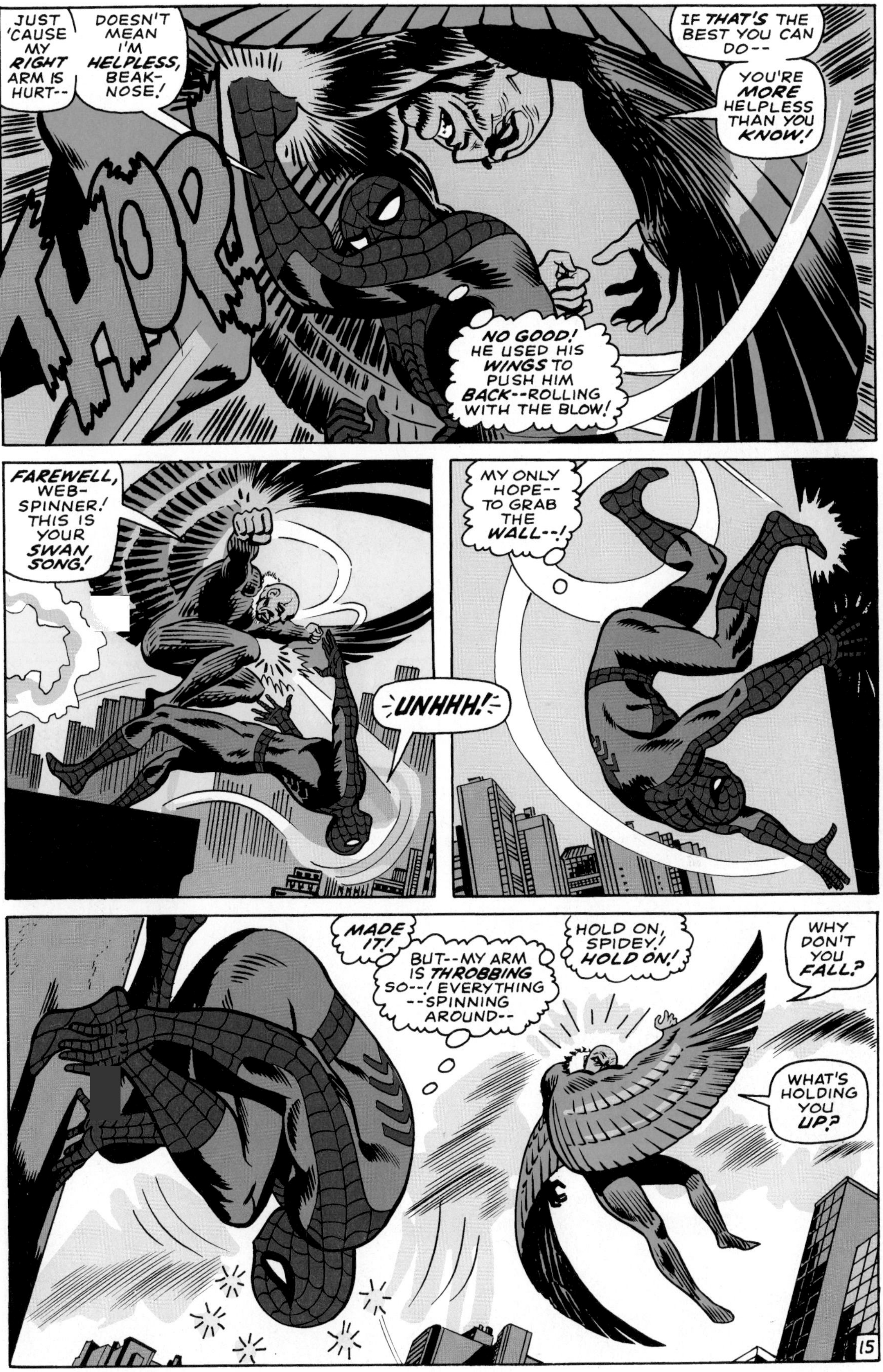

JUST 'CAUSE MY RIGHT ARM IS HURT--
DOESN'T MEAN I'M HELPLESS, BEAK-NOSE!
THOP
IF THAT'S THE BEST YOU CAN DO--
YOU'RE MORE HELPLESS THAN YOU KNOW!
NO GOOD! HE USED HIS WINGS TO PUSH HIM BACK--ROLLING WITH THE BLOW!
FAREWELL, WEB-SPINNER! THIS IS YOUR SWAN SONG!
UNHHH!
MY ONLY HOPE-- TO GRAB THE WALL--!
MADE IT!
BUT--MY ARM IS THROBBING SO--! EVERYTHING --SPINNING AROUND--
HOLD ON, SPIDEY! HOLD ON!
WHY DON'T YOU FALL?
WHAT'S HOLDING YOU UP?
15

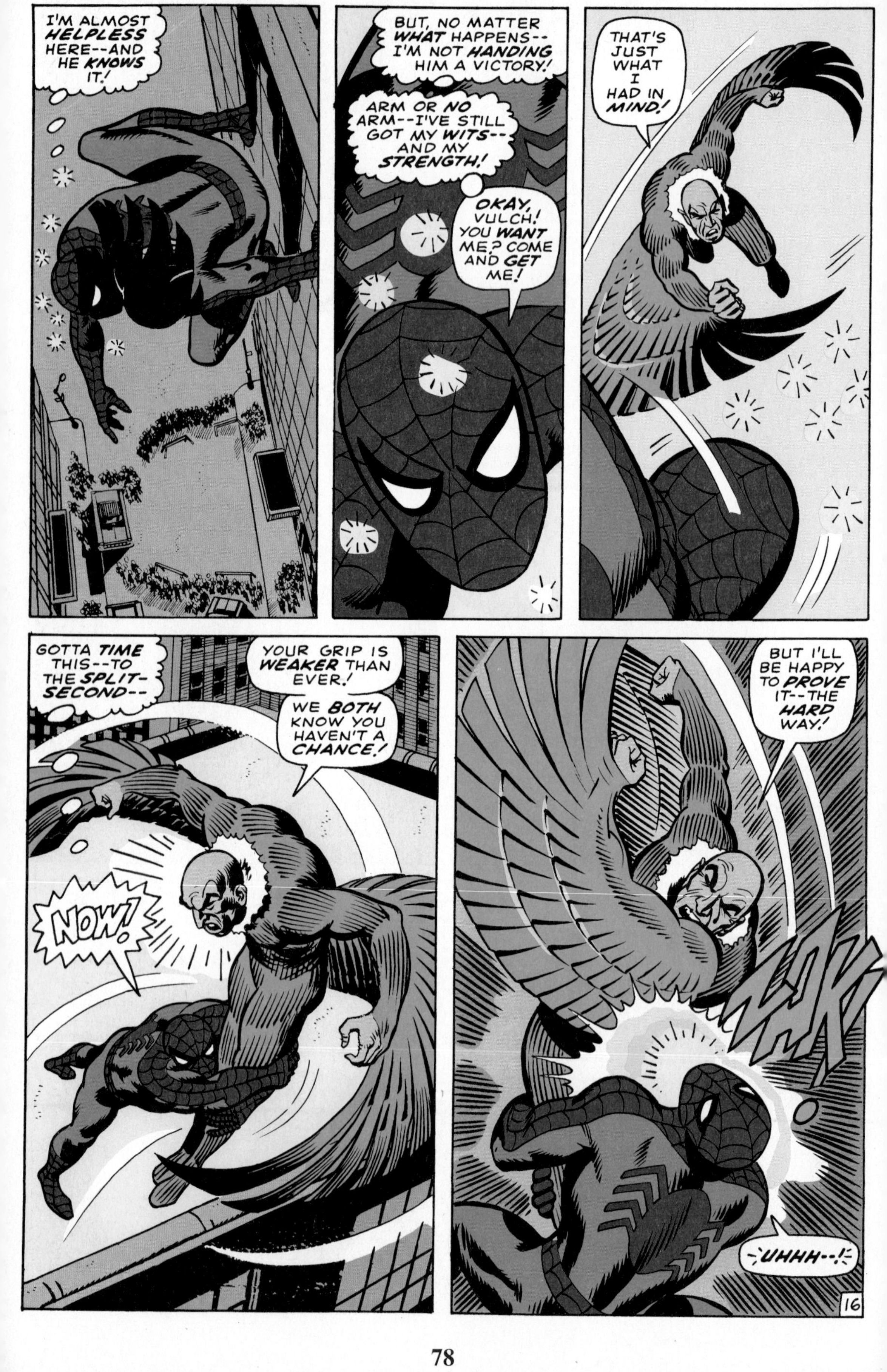
I'M ALMOST HELPLESS HERE--AND HE KNOWS IT!
BUT, NO MATTER WHAT HAPPENS--I'M NOT HANDING HIM A VICTORY!
ARM OR NO ARM--I'VE STILL GOT MY WITS--AND MY STRENGTH!
OKAY, VULCH! YOU WANT ME? COME AND GET ME!
THAT'S JUST WHAT I HAD IN MIND!
GOTTA TIME THIS--TO THE SPLIT-SECOND--
YOUR GRIP IS WEAKER THAN EVER!
WE BOTH KNOW YOU HAVEN'T A CHANCE!
NOW!
BUT I'LL BE HAPPY TO PROVE IT--THE HARD WAY!
UHHH--!
16

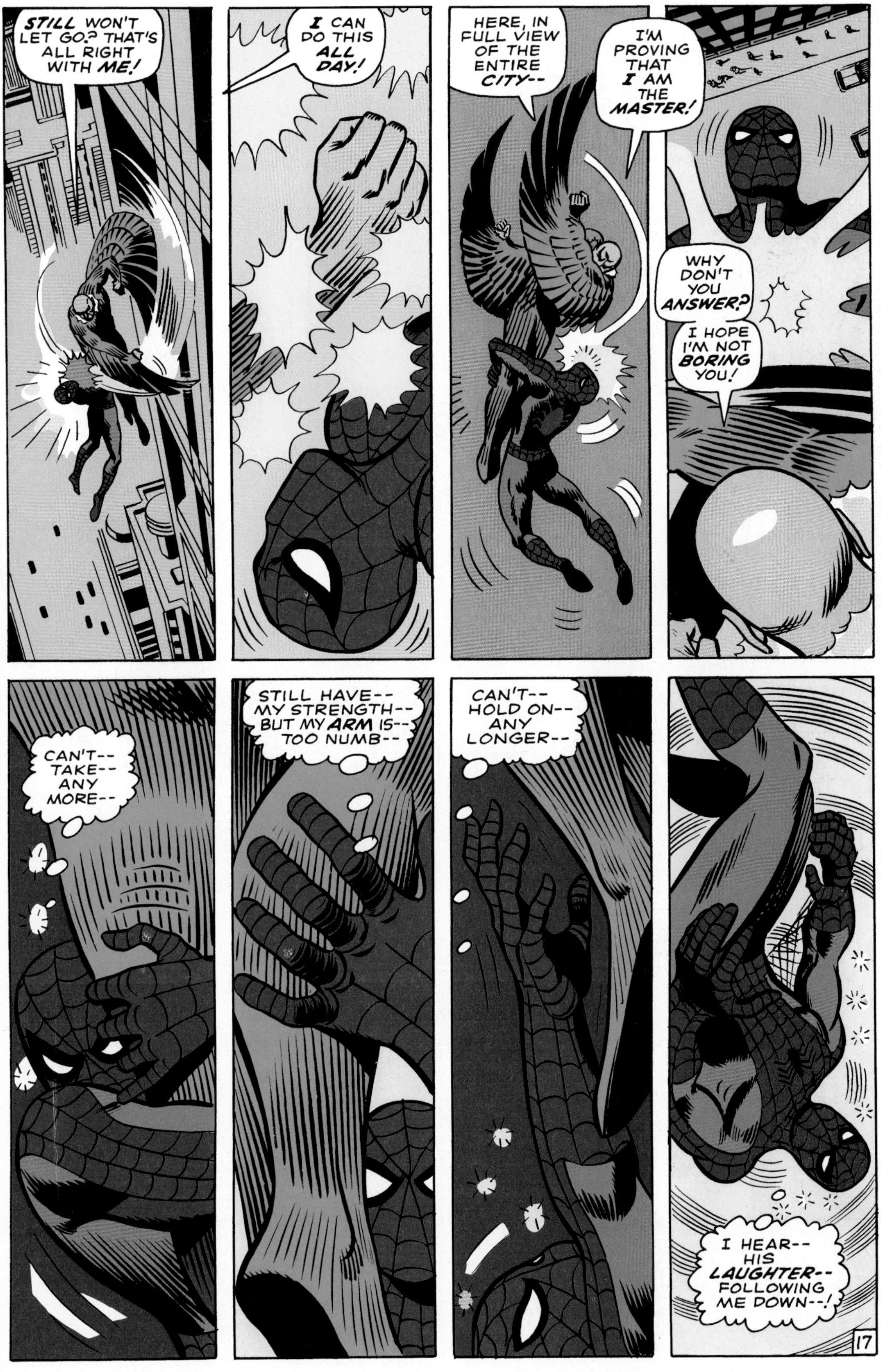
STILL WON'T LET GO? THAT'S ALL RIGHT WITH ME!
I CAN DO THIS ALL DAY!
HERE, IN FULL VIEW OF THE ENTIRE CITY--
I'M PROVING THAT I AM THE MASTER!
WHY DON'T YOU ANSWER?
I HOPE I'M NOT BORING YOU!
CAN'T-- TAKE-- ANY MORE--
STILL HAVE-- MY STRENGTH-- BUT MY ARM IS-- TOO NUMB--
CAN'T-- HOLD ON-- ANY LONGER--
I HEAR-- HIS LAUGHTER-- FOLLOWING ME DOWN--!
17

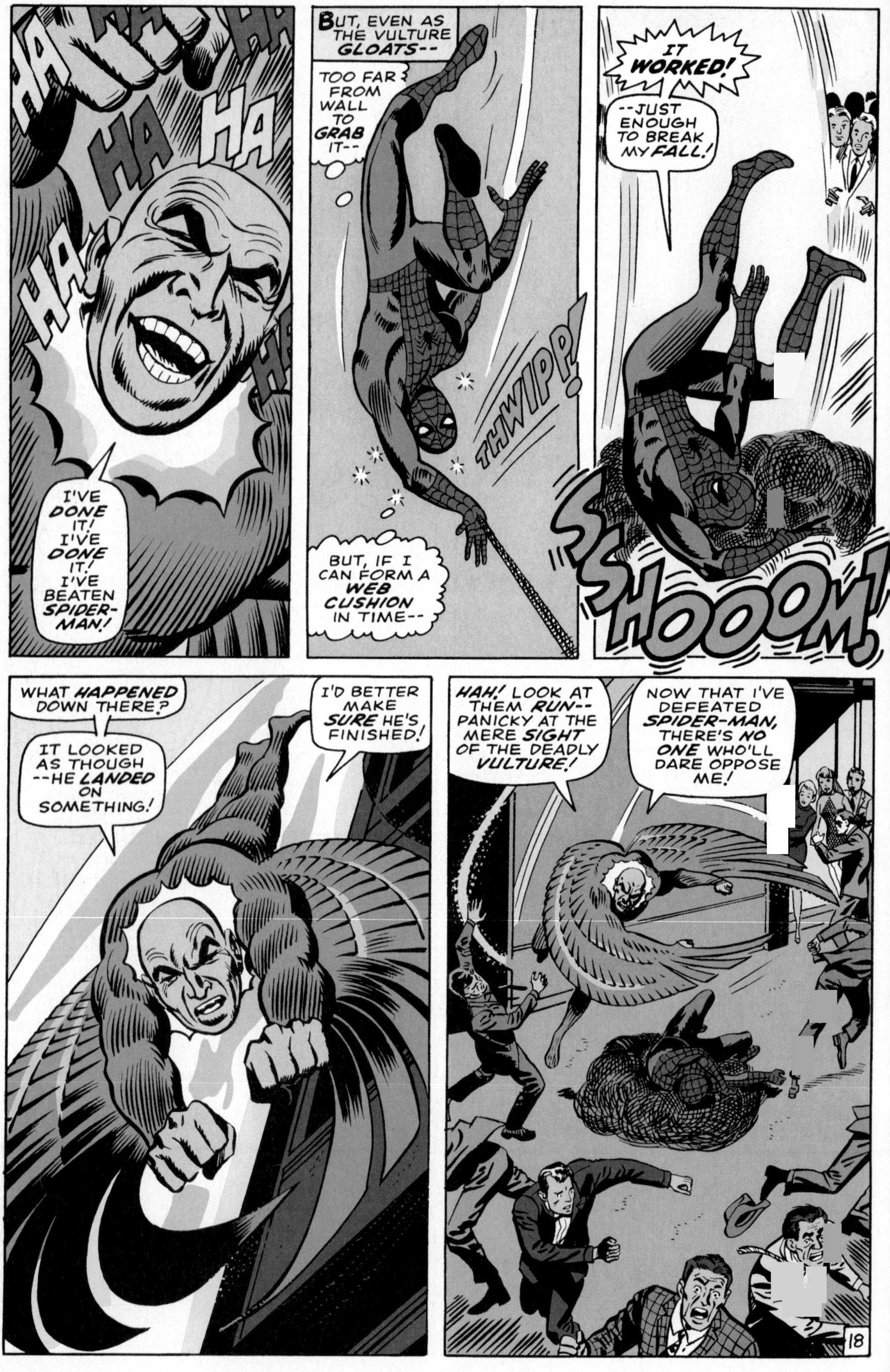
HA HA HA HA
HA HA
HA
HA
I'VE DONE IT! I'VE DONE IT! I'VE BEATEN SPIDER-MAN!
BUT, EVEN AS THE VULTURE GLOATS--
TOO FAR FROM WALL TO GRAB IT--
THWIPP!
BUT, IF I CAN FORM A WEB CUSHION IN TIME--
IT WORKED!
--JUST ENOUGH TO BREAK MY FALL!
SSHOOOM!
WHAT HAPPENED DOWN THERE?
IT LOOKED AS THOUGH --HE LANDED ON SOMETHING!
I'D BETTER MAKE SURE HE'S FINISHED!
HAH! LOOK AT THEM RUN-- PANICKY AT THE MERE SIGHT OF THE DEADLY VULTURE!
NOW THAT I'VE DEFEATED SPIDER-MAN, THERE'S NO ONE WHO'LL DARE OPPOSE ME!
18

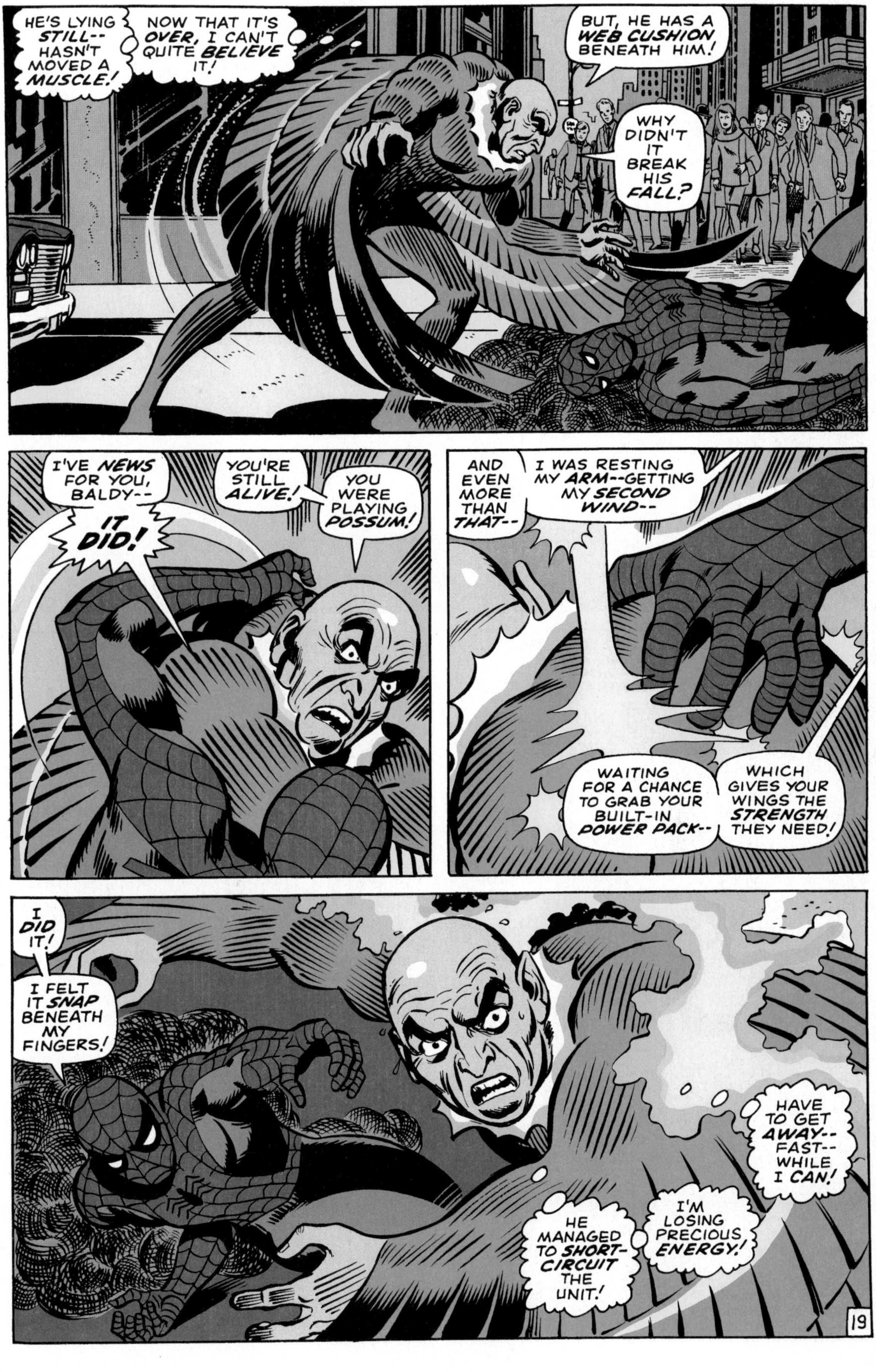
HE'S LYING STILL-- HASN'T MOVED A MUSCLE!
NOW THAT IT'S OVER, I CAN'T QUITE BELIEVE IT!
BUT, HE HAS A WEB CUSHION BENEATH HIM!
WHY DIDN'T IT BREAK HIS FALL?
I'VE NEWS FOR YOU, BALDY--
IT DID!
YOU'RE STILL ALIVE!
YOU WERE PLAYING POSSUM!
AND EVEN MORE THAN THAT--
I WAS RESTING MY ARM--GETTING MY SECOND WIND--
WAITING FOR A CHANCE TO GRAB YOUR BUILT-IN POWER PACK--
WHICH GIVES YOUR WINGS THE STRENGTH THEY NEED!
I DID IT!
I FELT IT SNAP BENEATH MY FINGERS!
HAVE TO GET AWAY--FAST--WHILE I CAN!
HE MANAGED TO SHORT-CIRCUIT THE UNIT!
I'M LOSING PRECIOUS ENERGY!
19

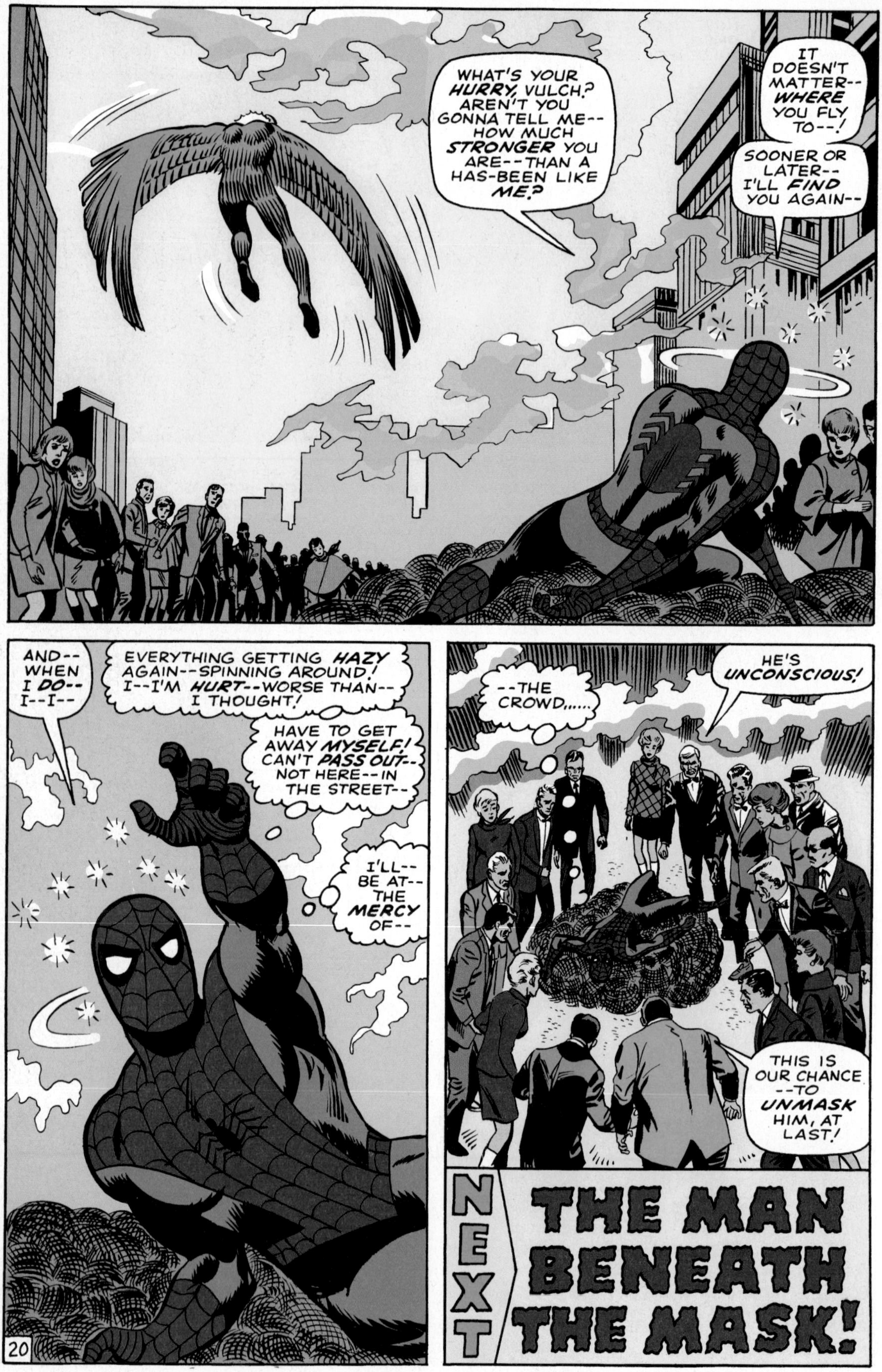
WHAT'S YOUR HURRY, VULCH? AREN'T YOU GONNA TELL ME-- HOW MUCH STRONGER YOU ARE--THAN A HAS-BEEN LIKE ME?
IT DOESN'T MATTER-- WHERE YOU FLY TO--!
SOONER OR LATER-- I'LL FIND YOU AGAIN--
AND-- WHEN I DO-- I--I--
EVERYTHING GETTING HAZY AGAIN--SPINNING AROUND! I--I'M HURT--WORSE THAN-- I THOUGHT!
HAVE TO GET AWAY MYSELF! CAN'T PASS OUT-- NOT HERE--IN THE STREET--
I'LL-- BE AT-- THE MERCY OF--
20
--THE CROWD......
HE'S UNCONSCIOUS!
THIS IS OUR CHANCE --TO UNMASK HIM, AT LAST!
NEXT
THE MAN BENEATH THE MASK!

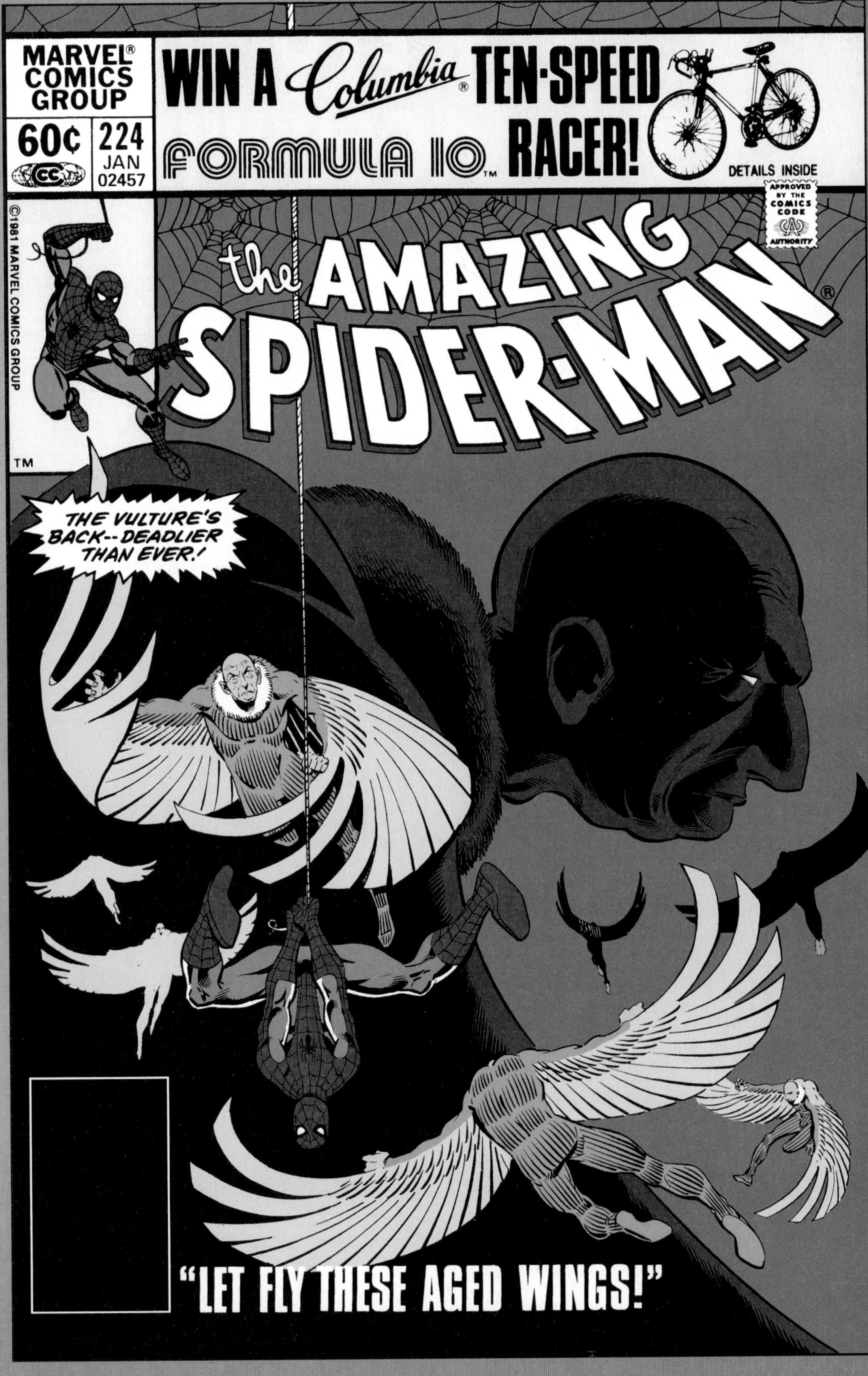

MARVEL® COMICS GROUP
60¢
224
JAN
02457
WIN A Columbia® TEN-SPEED
FORMULA 10™ RACER!
DETAILS INSIDE
APPROVED BY THE COMICS CODE AUTHORITY
©1981 MARVEL COMICS GROUP
the AMAZING SPIDER-MAN®
TM
THE VULTURE'S BACK--DEADLIER THAN EVER!
"LET FLY THESE AGED WINGS!"

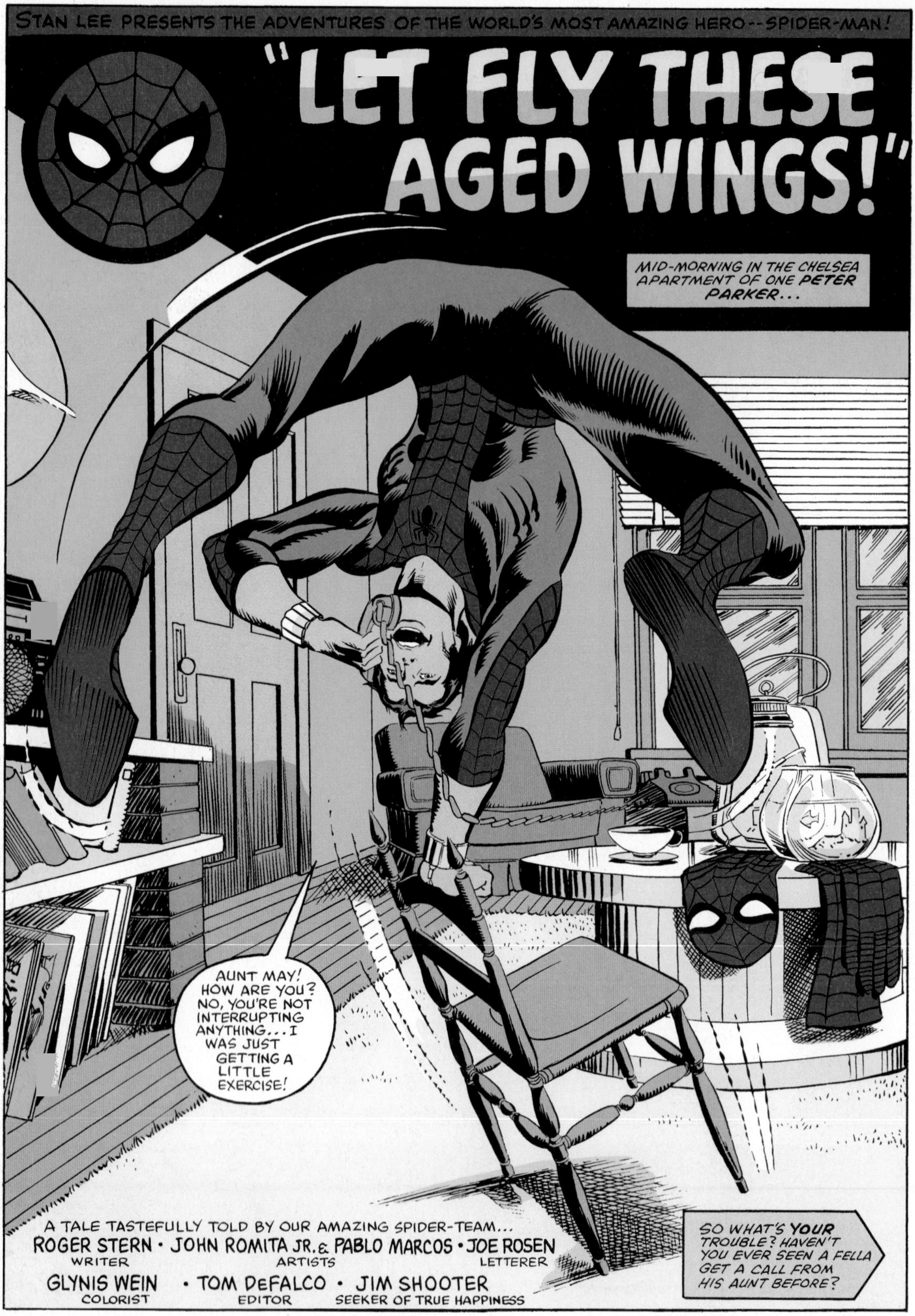
STAN LEE PRESENTS THE ADVENTURES OF THE WORLD'S MOST AMAZING HERO--SPIDER-MAN!
"LET FLY THESE AGED WINGS!"
MID-MORNING IN THE CHELSEA APARTMENT OF ONE PETER PARKER...
AUNT MAY! HOW ARE YOU? NO, YOU'RE NOT INTERRUPTING ANYTHING... I WAS JUST GETTING A LITTLE EXERCISE!
A TALE TASTEFULLY TOLD BY OUR AMAZING SPIDER-TEAM...
ROGER STERN · JOHN ROMITA JR. & PABLO MARCOS · JOE ROSEN
WRITER ARTISTS LETTERER
GLYNIS WEIN · TOM DeFALCO · JIM SHOOTER
COLORIST EDITOR SEEKER OF TRUE HAPPINESS
SO WHAT'S YOUR TROUBLE? HAVEN'T YOU EVER SEEN A FELLA GET A CALL FROM HIS AUNT BEFORE?

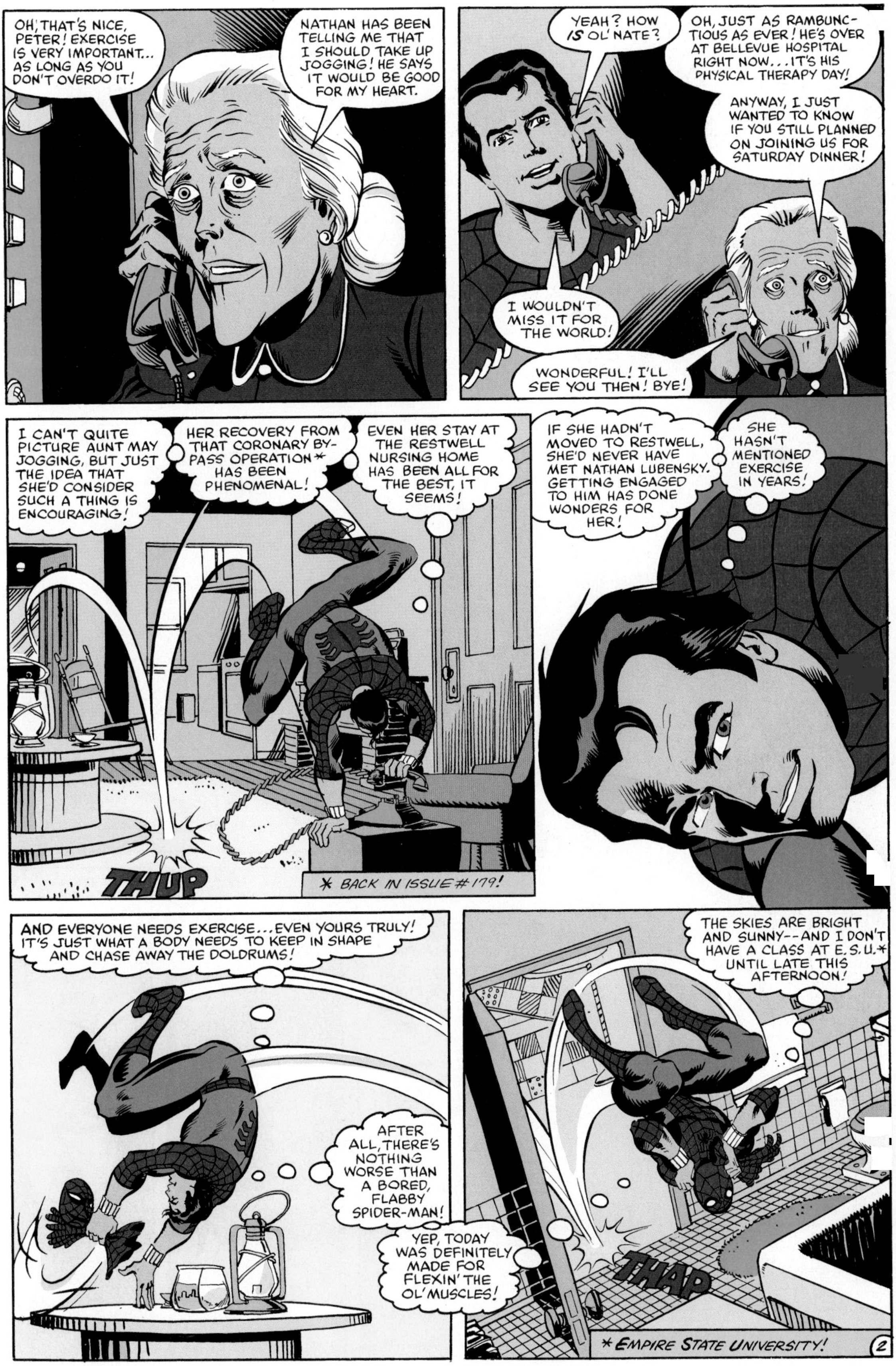

OH, THAT'S NICE, PETER! EXERCISE IS VERY IMPORTANT... AS LONG AS YOU DON'T OVERDO IT!
NATHAN HAS BEEN TELLING ME THAT I SHOULD TAKE UP JOGGING! HE SAYS IT WOULD BE GOOD FOR MY HEART.
YEAH? HOW IS OL' NATE?
OH, JUST AS RAMBUNCTIOUS AS EVER! HE'S OVER AT BELLEVUE HOSPITAL RIGHT NOW...IT'S HIS PHYSICAL THERAPY DAY!
ANYWAY, I JUST WANTED TO KNOW IF YOU STILL PLANNED ON JOINING US FOR SATURDAY DINNER!
I WOULDN'T MISS IT FOR THE WORLD!
WONDERFUL! I'LL SEE YOU THEN! BYE!
I CAN'T QUITE PICTURE AUNT MAY JOGGING, BUT JUST THE IDEA THAT SHE'D CONSIDER SUCH A THING IS ENCOURAGING!
HER RECOVERY FROM THAT CORONARY BY-PASS OPERATION* HAS BEEN PHENOMENAL!
EVEN HER STAY AT THE RESTWELL NURSING HOME HAS BEEN ALL FOR THE BEST, IT SEEMS!
THUP
* BACK IN ISSUE #179!
IF SHE HADN'T MOVED TO RESTWELL, SHE'D NEVER HAVE MET NATHAN LUBENSKY. GETTING ENGAGED TO HIM HAS DONE WONDERS FOR HER!
SHE HASN'T MENTIONED EXERCISE IN YEARS!
AND EVERYONE NEEDS EXERCISE...EVEN YOURS TRULY! IT'S JUST WHAT A BODY NEEDS TO KEEP IN SHAPE AND CHASE AWAY THE DOLDRUMS!
AFTER ALL, THERE'S NOTHING WORSE THAN A BORED, FLABBY SPIDER-MAN!
YEP, TODAY WAS DEFINITELY MADE FOR FLEXIN' THE OL' MUSCLES!
THE SKIES ARE BRIGHT AND SUNNY--AND I DON'T HAVE A CLASS AT E.S.U.* UNTIL LATE THIS AFTERNOON!
THAP
* EMPIRE STATE UNIVERSITY!
2

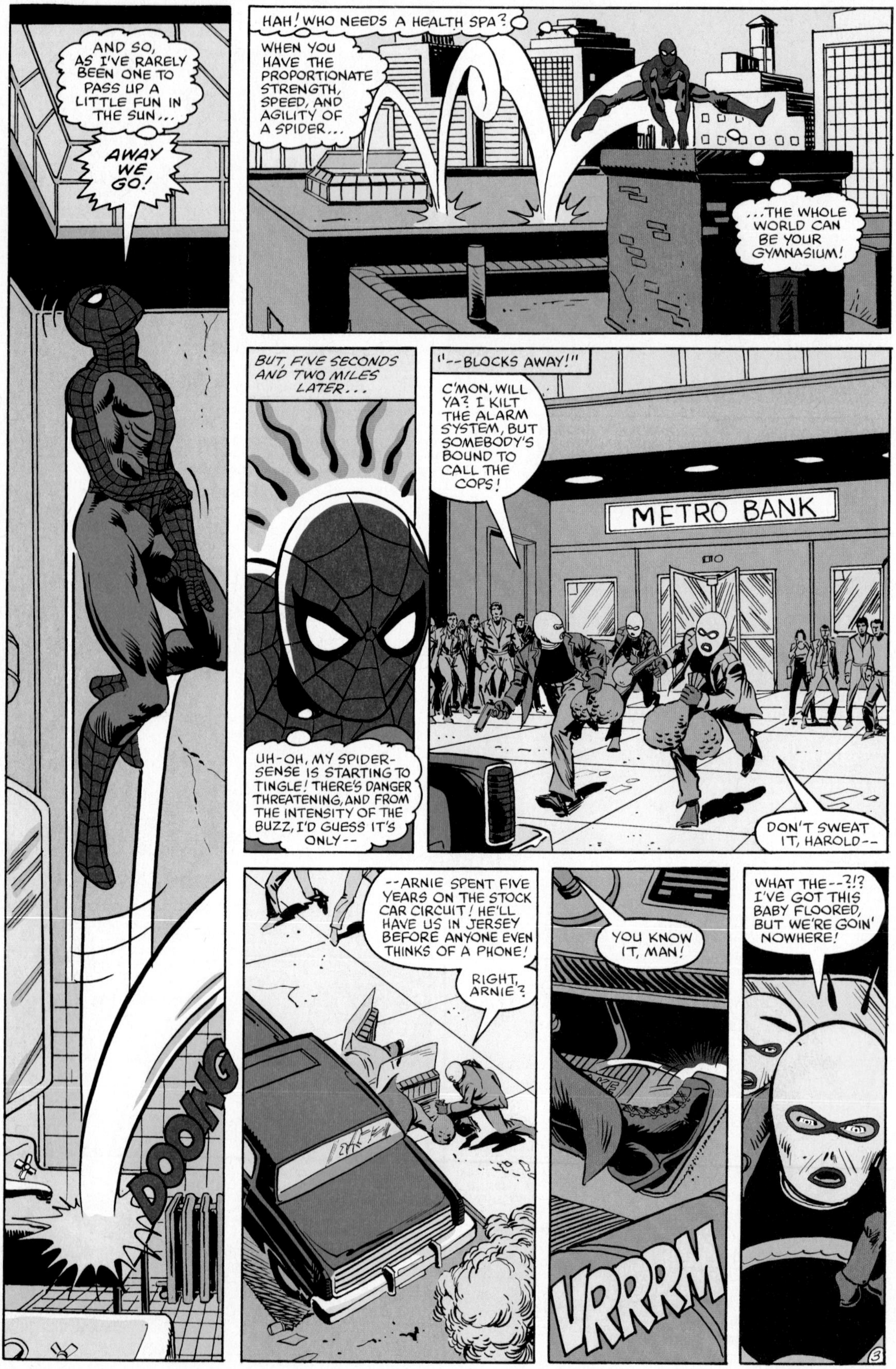
AND SO, AS I'VE RARELY BEEN ONE TO PASS UP A LITTLE FUN IN THE SUN...
AWAY WE GO!
HAH! WHO NEEDS A HEALTH SPA?
WHEN YOU HAVE THE PROPORTIONATE STRENGTH, SPEED, AND AGILITY OF A SPIDER...
...THE WHOLE WORLD CAN BE YOUR GYMNASIUM!
DOOING
BUT, FIVE SECONDS AND TWO MILES LATER...
UH-OH, MY SPIDER-SENSE IS STARTING TO TINGLE! THERE'S DANGER THREATENING, AND FROM THE INTENSITY OF THE BUZZ, I'D GUESS IT'S ONLY--
"--BLOCKS AWAY!"
C'MON, WILL YA? I KILT THE ALARM SYSTEM, BUT SOMEBODY'S BOUND TO CALL THE COPS!
METRO BANK
DON'T SWEAT IT, HAROLD--
--ARNIE SPENT FIVE YEARS ON THE STOCK CAR CIRCUIT! HE'LL HAVE US IN JERSEY BEFORE ANYONE EVEN THINKS OF A PHONE!
RIGHT, ARNIE?
YOU KNOW IT, MAN!
VRRRM
WHAT THE--?!? I'VE GOT THIS BABY FLOORED, BUT WE'RE GOIN' NOWHERE!
3

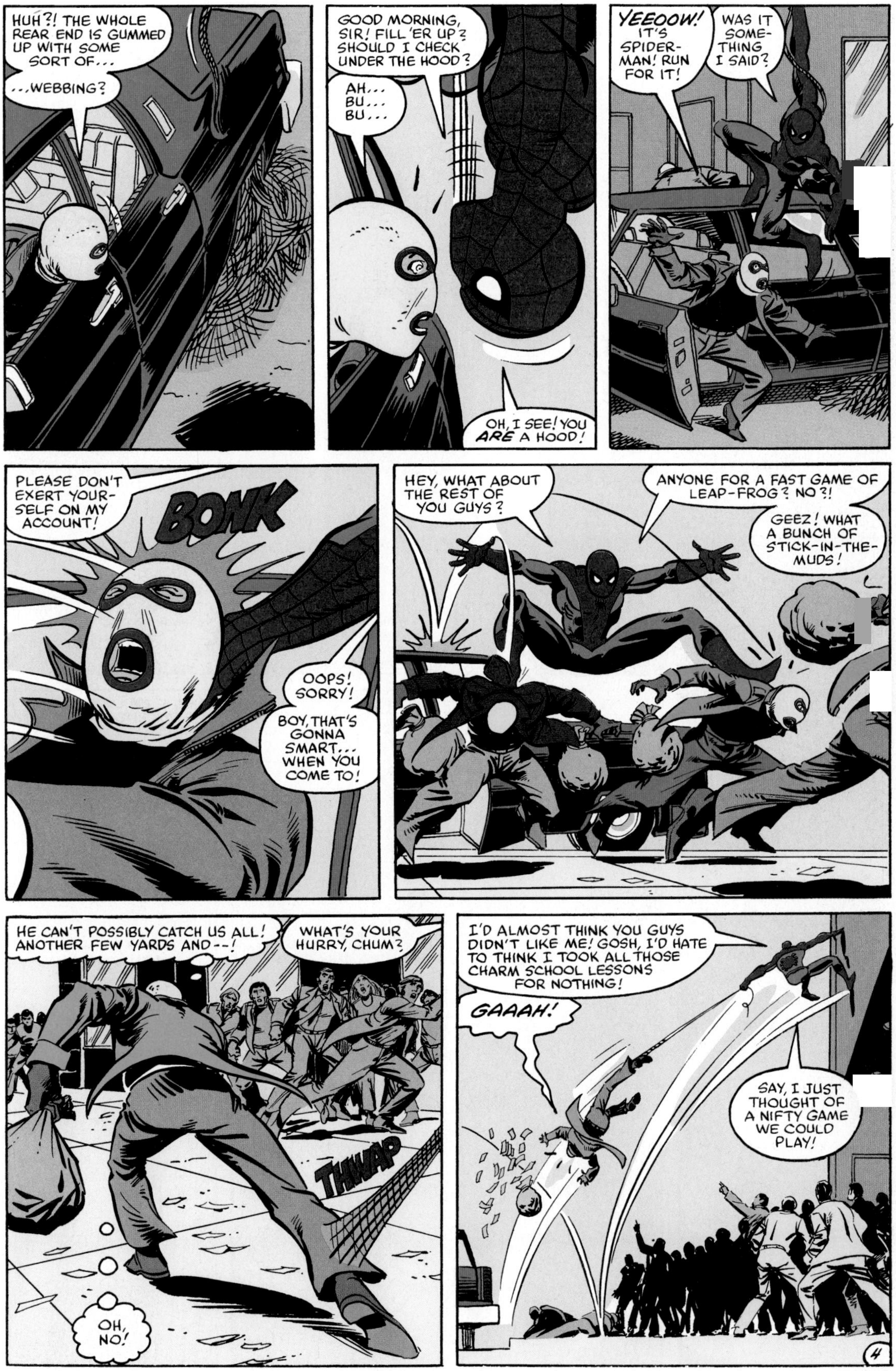
HUH?! THE WHOLE REAR END IS GUMMED UP WITH SOME SORT OF...
...WEBBING?
GOOD MORNING, SIR! FILL 'ER UP? SHOULD I CHECK UNDER THE HOOD?
AH... BU... BU...
OH, I SEE! YOU ARE A HOOD!
YEEOOW! IT'S SPIDER-MAN! RUN FOR IT!
WAS IT SOME-THING I SAID?
PLEASE DON'T EXERT YOUR-SELF ON MY ACCOUNT!
BONK
OOPS! SORRY!
BOY, THAT'S GONNA SMART... WHEN YOU COME TO!
HEY, WHAT ABOUT THE REST OF YOU GUYS?
ANYONE FOR A FAST GAME OF LEAP-FROG? NO?!
GEEZ! WHAT A BUNCH OF STICK-IN-THE-MUDS!
HE CAN'T POSSIBLY CATCH US ALL! ANOTHER FEW YARDS AND--!
WHAT'S YOUR HURRY, CHUM?
THWAP
OH, NO!
I'D ALMOST THINK YOU GUYS DIDN'T LIKE ME! GOSH, I'D HATE TO THINK I TOOK ALL THOSE CHARM SCHOOL LESSONS FOR NOTHING!
GAAAH!
SAY, I JUST THOUGHT OF A NIFTY GAME WE COULD PLAY!
4

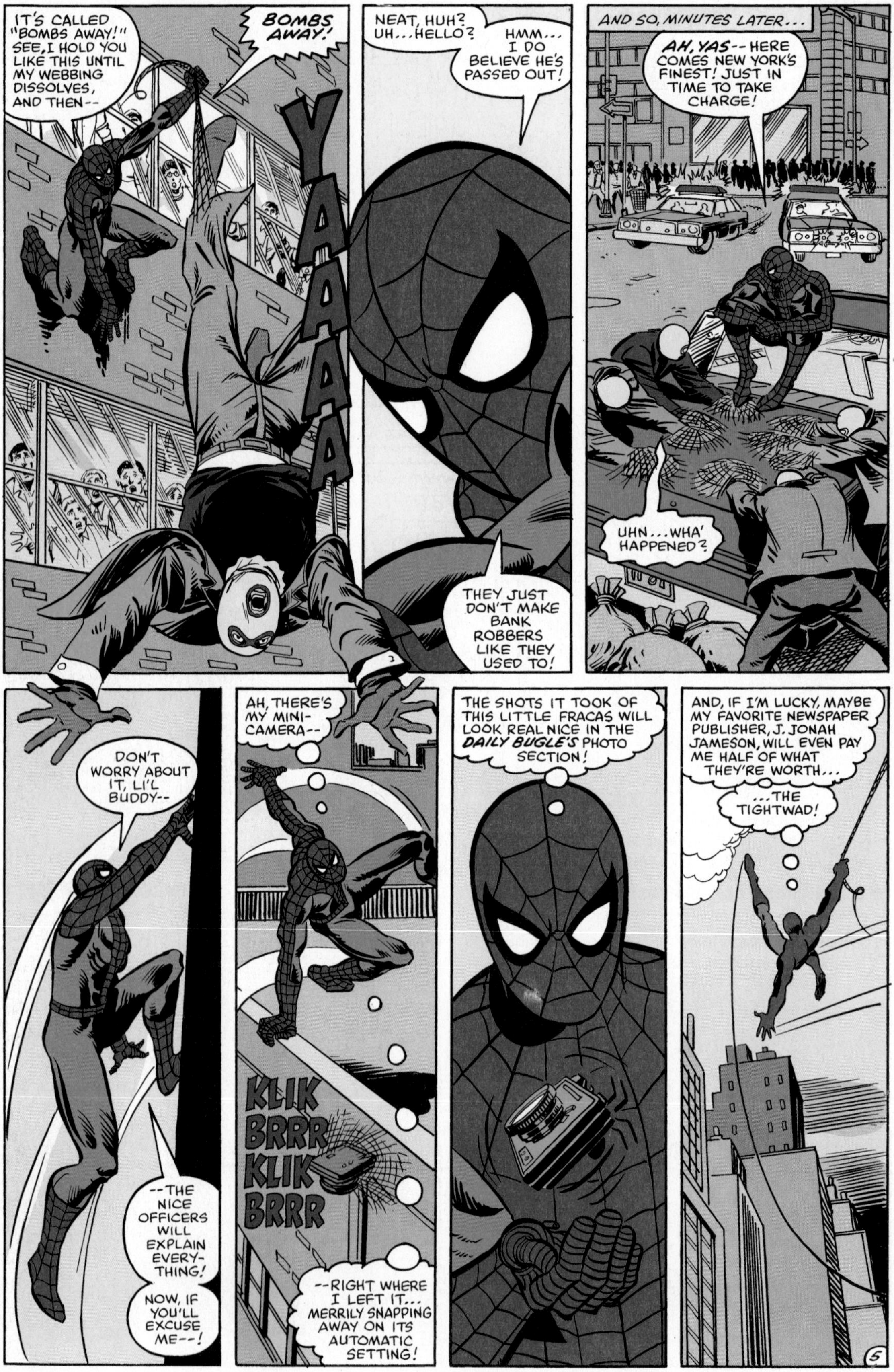
IT'S CALLED "BOMBS AWAY!" SEE, I HOLD YOU LIKE THIS UNTIL MY WEBBING DISSOLVES, AND THEN--
BOMBS AWAY!
YAAAAA
NEAT, HUH? UH...HELLO?
HMM... I DO BELIEVE HE'S PASSED OUT!
THEY JUST DON'T MAKE BANK ROBBERS LIKE THEY USED TO!
AND SO, MINUTES LATER...
AH, YAS-- HERE COMES NEW YORK'S FINEST! JUST IN TIME TO TAKE CHARGE!
UHN...WHA' HAPPENED?
DON'T WORRY ABOUT IT, LI'L BUDDY--
--THE NICE OFFICERS WILL EXPLAIN EVERY-THING!
NOW, IF YOU'LL EXCUSE ME--!
AH, THERE'S MY MINI-CAMERA--
KLIK BRRR KLIK BRRR
--RIGHT WHERE I LEFT IT... MERRILY SNAPPING AWAY ON ITS AUTOMATIC SETTING!
THE SHOTS IT TOOK OF THIS LITTLE FRACAS WILL LOOK REAL NICE IN THE DAILY BUGLE'S PHOTO SECTION!
AND, IF I'M LUCKY, MAYBE MY FAVORITE NEWSPAPER PUBLISHER, J. JONAH JAMESON, WILL EVEN PAY ME HALF OF WHAT THEY'RE WORTH...
...THE TIGHTWAD!
5

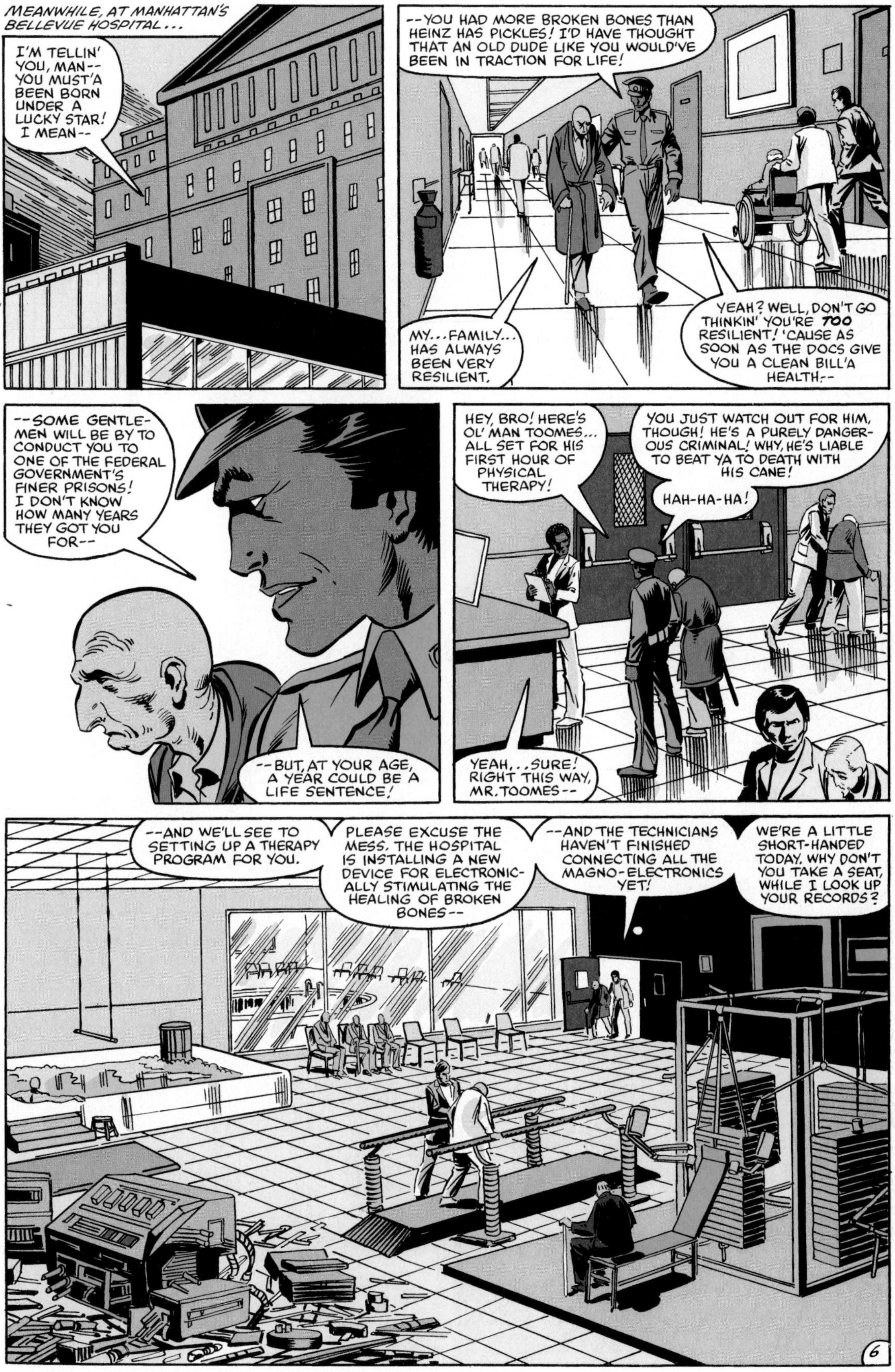
MEANWHILE, AT MANHATTAN'S BELLEVUE HOSPITAL...
I'M TELLIN' YOU, MAN-- YOU MUST'A BEEN BORN UNDER A LUCKY STAR! I MEAN--
--YOU HAD MORE BROKEN BONES THAN HEINZ HAS PICKLES! I'D HAVE THOUGHT THAT AN OLD DUDE LIKE YOU WOULD'VE BEEN IN TRACTION FOR LIFE!
MY... FAMILY... HAS ALWAYS BEEN VERY RESILIENT.
YEAH? WELL, DON'T GO THINKIN' YOU'RE TOO RESILIENT! 'CAUSE AS SOON AS THE DOCS GIVE YOU A CLEAN BILL'A HEALTH--
--SOME GENTLEMEN WILL BE BY TO CONDUCT YOU TO ONE OF THE FEDERAL GOVERNMENT'S FINER PRISONS! I DON'T KNOW HOW MANY YEARS THEY GOT YOU FOR--
--BUT, AT YOUR AGE, A YEAR COULD BE A LIFE SENTENCE!
HEY, BRO! HERE'S OL' MAN TOOMES... ALL SET FOR HIS FIRST HOUR OF PHYSICAL THERAPY!
YOU JUST WATCH OUT FOR HIM, THOUGH! HE'S A PURELY DANGEROUS CRIMINAL! WHY, HE'S LIABLE TO BEAT YA TO DEATH WITH HIS CANE!
HAH-HA-HA!
YEAH,.. SURE! RIGHT THIS WAY, MR. TOOMES--
--AND WE'LL SEE TO SETTING UP A THERAPY PROGRAM FOR YOU.
PLEASE EXCUSE THE MESS. THE HOSPITAL IS INSTALLING A NEW DEVICE FOR ELECTRONICALLY STIMULATING THE HEALING OF BROKEN BONES--
--AND THE TECHNICIANS HAVEN'T FINISHED CONNECTING ALL THE MAGNO-ELECTRONICS YET!
WE'RE A LITTLE SHORT-HANDED TODAY. WHY DON'T YOU TAKE A SEAT, WHILE I LOOK UP YOUR RECORDS?
6

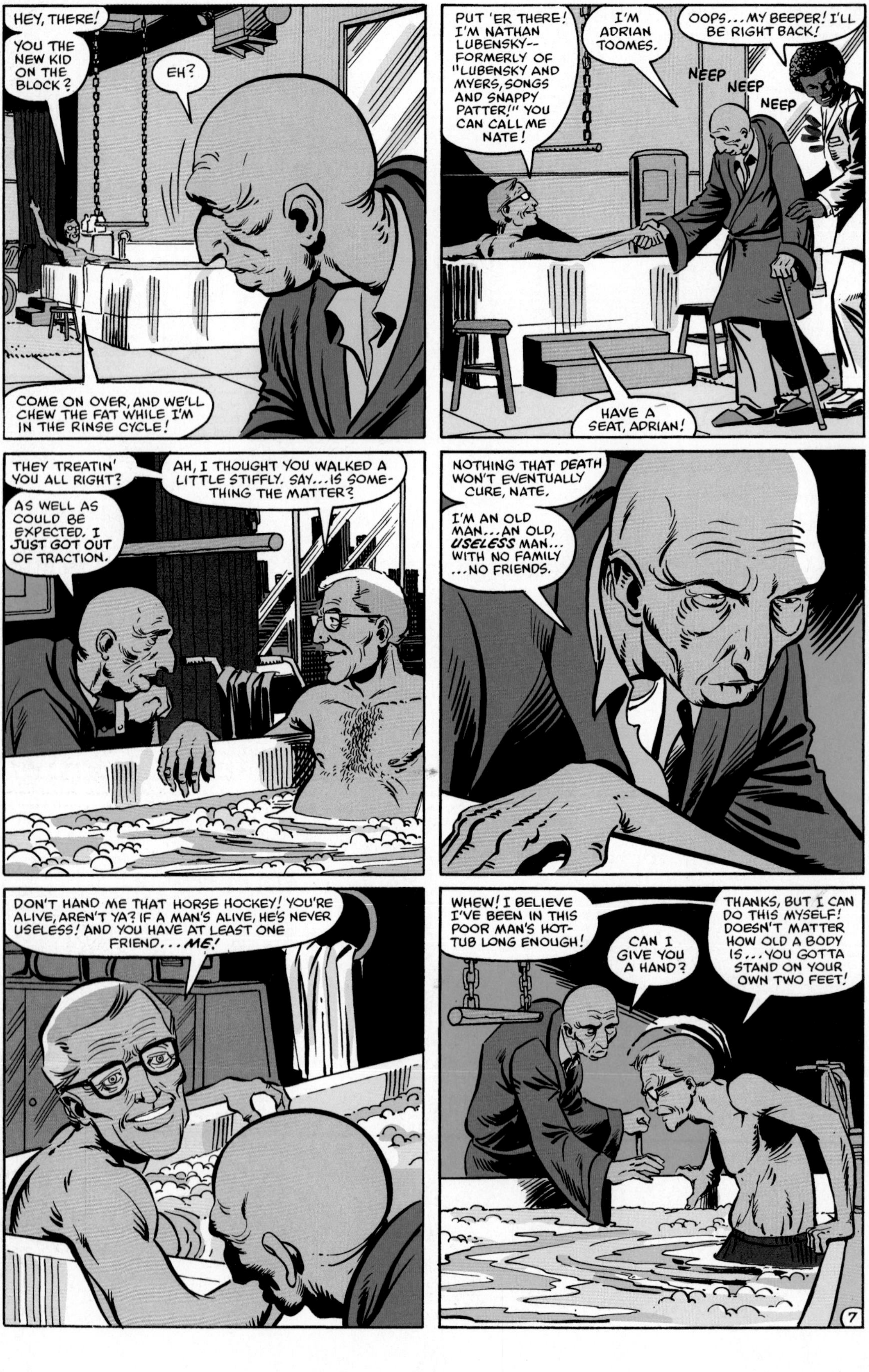
HEY, THERE!
YOU THE NEW KID ON THE BLOCK?
EH?
COME ON OVER, AND WE'LL CHEW THE FAT WHILE I'M IN THE RINSE CYCLE!
PUT 'ER THERE! I'M NATHAN LUBENSKY-- FORMERLY OF "LUBENSKY AND MYERS, SONGS AND SNAPPY PATTER!" YOU CAN CALL ME NATE!
I'M ADRIAN TOOMES.
OOPS... MY BEEPER! I'LL BE RIGHT BACK!
NEEP NEEP NEEP
HAVE A SEAT, ADRIAN!
THEY TREATIN' YOU ALL RIGHT?
AS WELL AS COULD BE EXPECTED. I JUST GOT OUT OF TRACTION.
AH, I THOUGHT YOU WALKED A LITTLE STIFFLY. SAY... IS SOMETHING THE MATTER?
NOTHING THAT DEATH WON'T EVENTUALLY CURE, NATE.
I'M AN OLD MAN... AN OLD, USELESS MAN... WITH NO FAMILY ...NO FRIENDS.
DON'T HAND ME THAT HORSE HOCKEY! YOU'RE ALIVE, AREN'T YA? IF A MAN'S ALIVE, HE'S NEVER USELESS! AND YOU HAVE AT LEAST ONE FRIEND... ME!
WHEW! I BELIEVE I'VE BEEN IN THIS POOR MAN'S HOT-TUB LONG ENOUGH!
CAN I GIVE YOU A HAND?
THANKS, BUT I CAN DO THIS MYSELF! DOESN'T MATTER HOW OLD A BODY IS... YOU GOTTA STAND ON YOUR OWN TWO FEET!
7

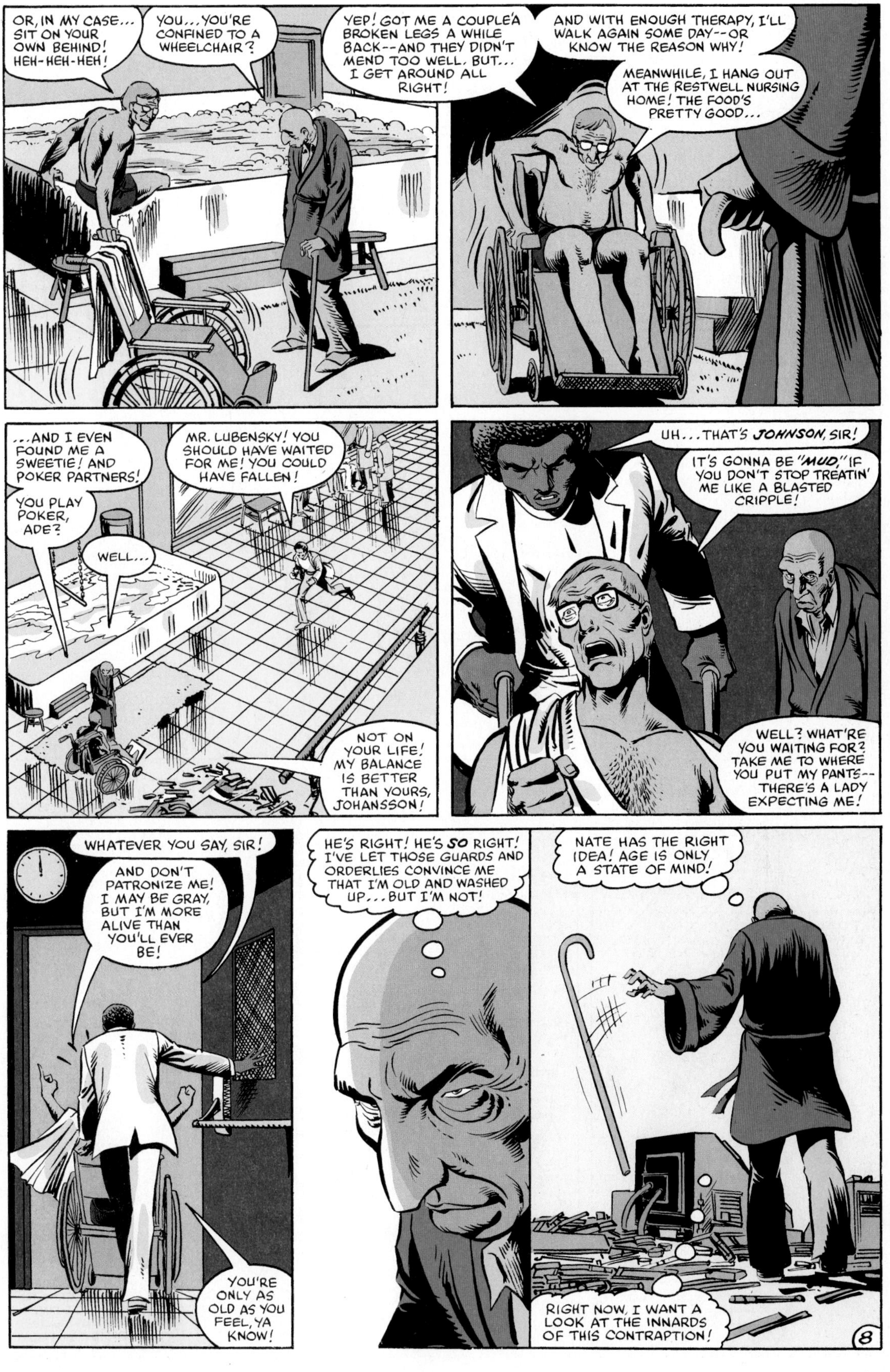
OR, IN MY CASE... SIT ON YOUR OWN BEHIND! HEH-HEH-HEH!
YOU...YOU'RE CONFINED TO A WHEELCHAIR?
YEP! GOT ME A COUPLE'A BROKEN LEGS A WHILE BACK--AND THEY DIDN'T MEND TOO WELL. BUT... I GET AROUND ALL RIGHT!
AND WITH ENOUGH THERAPY, I'LL WALK AGAIN SOME DAY--OR KNOW THE REASON WHY!
MEANWHILE, I HANG OUT AT THE RESTWELL NURSING HOME! THE FOOD'S PRETTY GOOD...
...AND I EVEN FOUND ME A SWEETIE! AND POKER PARTNERS!
YOU PLAY POKER, ADE?
WELL...
MR. LUBENSKY! YOU SHOULD HAVE WAITED FOR ME! YOU COULD HAVE FALLEN!
NOT ON YOUR LIFE! MY BALANCE IS BETTER THAN YOURS, JOHANSSON!
UH...THAT'S JOHNSON, SIR!
IT'S GONNA BE "MUD," IF YOU DON'T STOP TREATIN' ME LIKE A BLASTED CRIPPLE!
WELL? WHAT'RE YOU WAITING FOR? TAKE ME TO WHERE YOU PUT MY PANTS--THERE'S A LADY EXPECTING ME!
WHATEVER YOU SAY, SIR!
AND DON'T PATRONIZE ME! I MAY BE GRAY, BUT I'M MORE ALIVE THAN YOU'LL EVER BE!
YOU'RE ONLY AS OLD AS YOU FEEL, YA KNOW!
HE'S RIGHT! HE'S SO RIGHT! I'VE LET THOSE GUARDS AND ORDERLIES CONVINCE ME THAT I'M OLD AND WASHED UP...BUT I'M NOT!
NATE HAS THE RIGHT IDEA! AGE IS ONLY A STATE OF MIND!
RIGHT NOW, I WANT A LOOK AT THE INNARDS OF THIS CONTRAPTION!
8

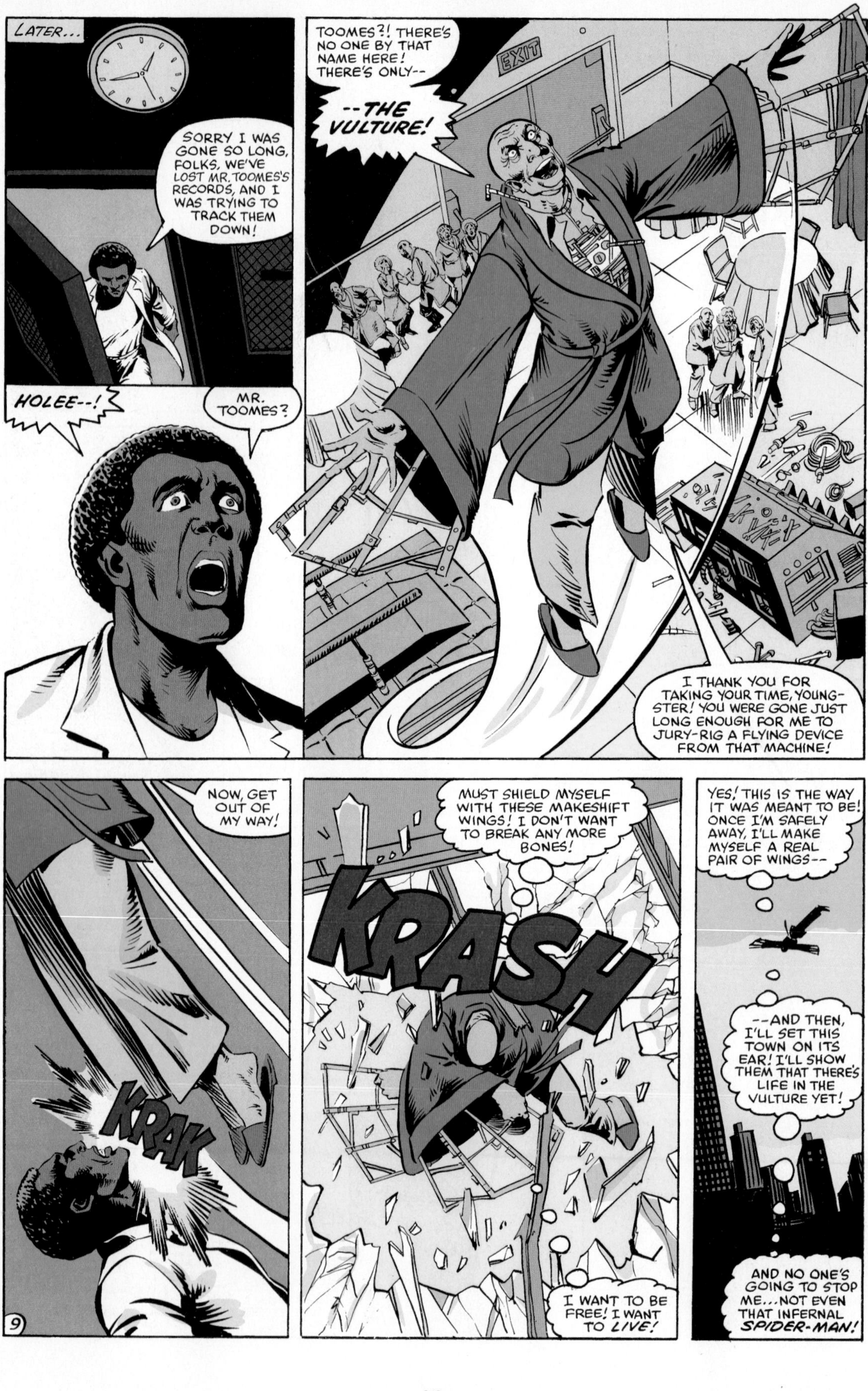
LATER...
SORRY I WAS GONE SO LONG, FOLKS, WE'VE LOST MR. TOOMES'S RECORDS, AND I WAS TRYING TO TRACK THEM DOWN!
HOLEE--!
MR. TOOMES?
TOOMES?! THERE'S NO ONE BY THAT NAME HERE! THERE'S ONLY--
--THE VULTURE!
EXIT
I THANK YOU FOR TAKING YOUR TIME, YOUNGSTER! YOU WERE GONE JUST LONG ENOUGH FOR ME TO JURY-RIG A FLYING DEVICE FROM THAT MACHINE!
NOW, GET OUT OF MY WAY!
KRAK
9
MUST SHIELD MYSELF WITH THESE MAKESHIFT WINGS! I DON'T WANT TO BREAK ANY MORE BONES!
KRASH
I WANT TO BE FREE! I WANT TO LIVE!
YES! THIS IS THE WAY IT WAS MEANT TO BE! ONCE I'M SAFELY AWAY, I'LL MAKE MYSELF A REAL PAIR OF WINGS--
--AND THEN, I'LL SET THIS TOWN ON ITS EAR! I'LL SHOW THEM THAT THERE'S LIFE IN THE VULTURE YET!
AND NO ONE'S GOING TO STOP ME...NOT EVEN THAT INFERNAL SPIDER-MAN!

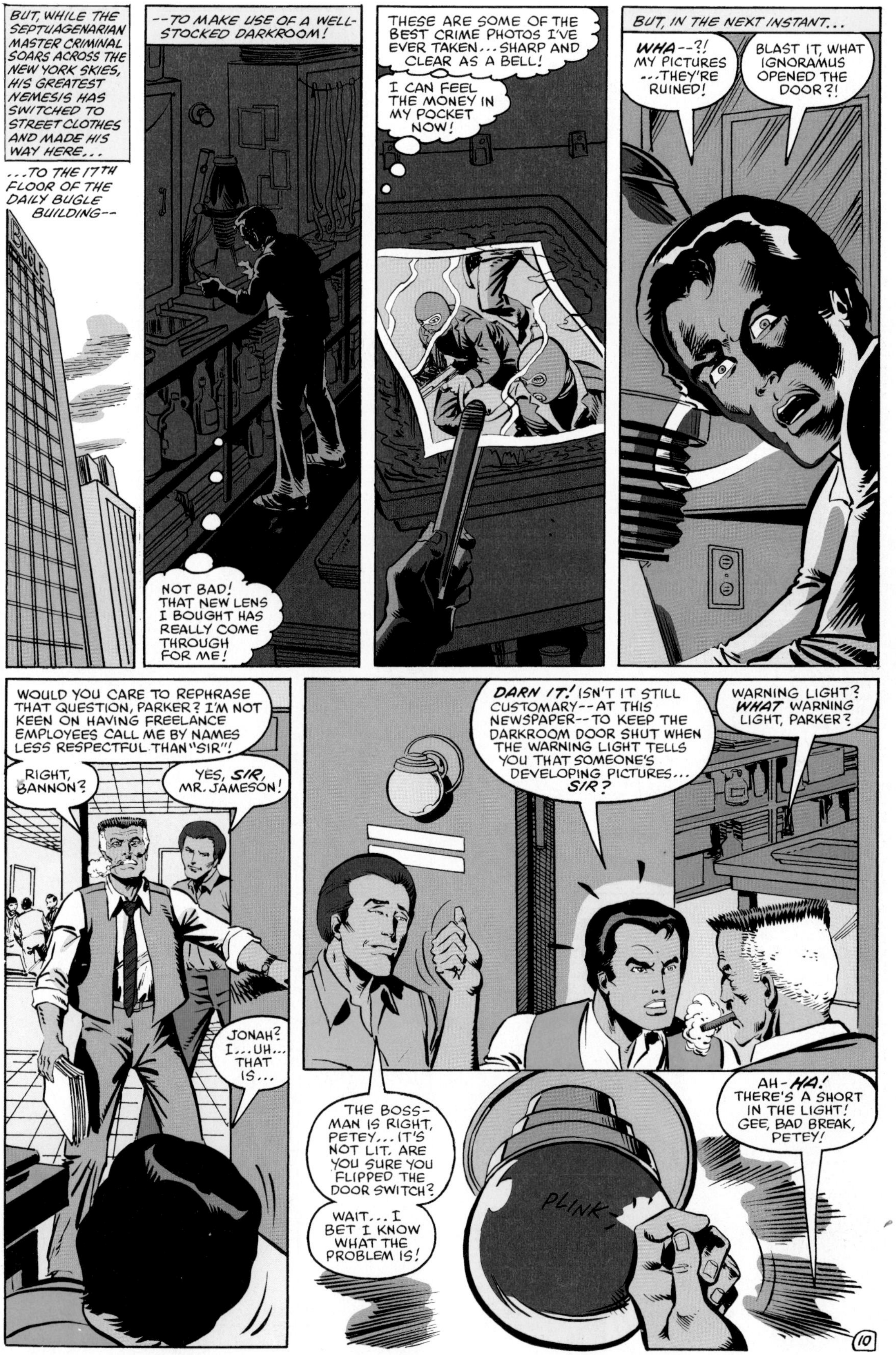
BUT, WHILE THE SEPTUAGENARIAN MASTER CRIMINAL SOARS ACROSS THE NEW YORK SKIES, HIS GREATEST NEMESIS HAS SWITCHED TO STREET CLOTHES AND MADE HIS WAY HERE...
...TO THE 17TH FLOOR OF THE DAILY BUGLE BUILDING--
BUGLE
--TO MAKE USE OF A WELL-STOCKED DARKROOM!
NOT BAD! THAT NEW LENS I BOUGHT HAS REALLY COME THROUGH FOR ME!
THESE ARE SOME OF THE BEST CRIME PHOTOS I'VE EVER TAKEN... SHARP AND CLEAR AS A BELL!
I CAN FEEL THE MONEY IN MY POCKET NOW!
BUT, IN THE NEXT INSTANT...
WHA--?! MY PICTURES ...THEY'RE RUINED!
BLAST IT, WHAT IGNORAMUS OPENED THE DOOR?!
WOULD YOU CARE TO REPHRASE THAT QUESTION, PARKER? I'M NOT KEEN ON HAVING FREELANCE EMPLOYEES CALL ME BY NAMES LESS RESPECTFUL THAN "SIR"!
RIGHT, BANNON?
YES, SIR, MR. JAMESON!
JONAH? I...UH... THAT IS...
DARN IT! ISN'T IT STILL CUSTOMARY--AT THIS NEWSPAPER--TO KEEP THE DARKROOM DOOR SHUT WHEN THE WARNING LIGHT TELLS YOU THAT SOMEONE'S DEVELOPING PICTURES... SIR?
WARNING LIGHT? WHAT WARNING LIGHT, PARKER?
THE BOSS-MAN IS RIGHT, PETEY... IT'S NOT LIT. ARE YOU SURE YOU FLIPPED THE DOOR SWITCH?
WAIT... I BET I KNOW WHAT THE PROBLEM IS!
PLINK
AH-HA! THERE'S A SHORT IN THE LIGHT! GEE, BAD BREAK, PETEY!
10

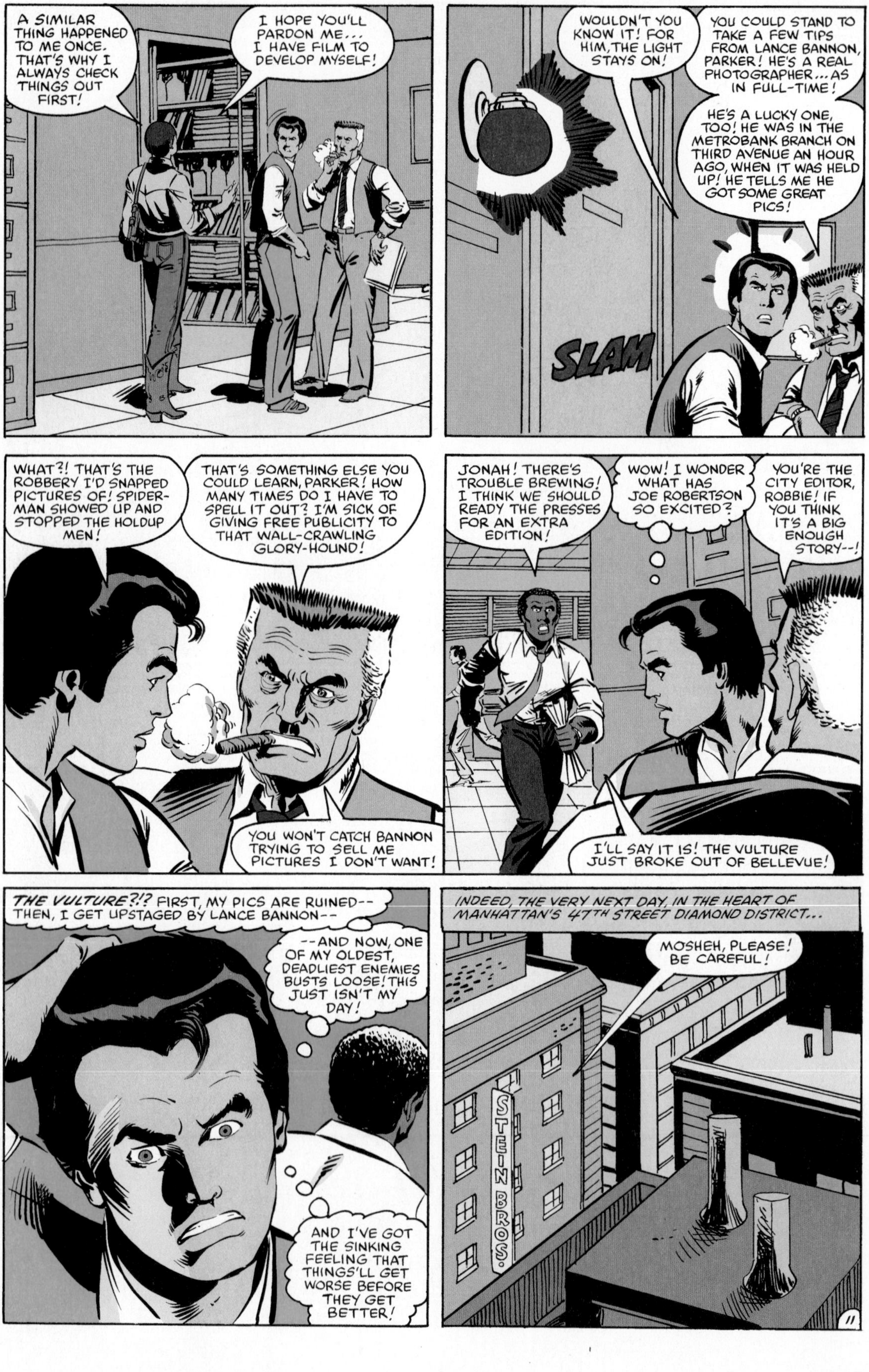
A SIMILAR THING HAPPENED TO ME ONCE. THAT'S WHY I ALWAYS CHECK THINGS OUT FIRST!
I HOPE YOU'LL PARDON ME... I HAVE FILM TO DEVELOP MYSELF!
WOULDN'T YOU KNOW IT! FOR HIM, THE LIGHT STAYS ON!
YOU COULD STAND TO TAKE A FEW TIPS FROM LANCE BANNON, PARKER! HE'S A REAL PHOTOGRAPHER... AS IN FULL-TIME!
HE'S A LUCKY ONE, TOO! HE WAS IN THE METROBANK BRANCH ON THIRD AVENUE AN HOUR AGO, WHEN IT WAS HELD UP! HE TELLS ME HE GOT SOME GREAT PICS!
SLAM
WHAT?! THAT'S THE ROBBERY I'D SNAPPED PICTURES OF! SPIDER-MAN SHOWED UP AND STOPPED THE HOLDUP MEN!
THAT'S SOMETHING ELSE YOU COULD LEARN, PARKER! HOW MANY TIMES DO I HAVE TO SPELL IT OUT? I'M SICK OF GIVING FREE PUBLICITY TO THAT WALL-CRAWLING GLORY-HOUND!
YOU WON'T CATCH BANNON TRYING TO SELL ME PICTURES I DON'T WANT!
JONAH! THERE'S TROUBLE BREWING! I THINK WE SHOULD READY THE PRESSES FOR AN EXTRA EDITION!
WOW! I WONDER WHAT HAS JOE ROBERTSON SO EXCITED?
YOU'RE THE CITY EDITOR, ROBBIE! IF YOU THINK IT'S A BIG ENOUGH STORY--!
I'LL SAY IT IS! THE VULTURE JUST BROKE OUT OF BELLEVUE!
THE VULTURE?!? FIRST, MY PICS ARE RUINED-- THEN, I GET UPSTAGED BY LANCE BANNON--
--AND NOW, ONE OF MY OLDEST, DEADLIEST ENEMIES BUSTS LOOSE! THIS JUST ISN'T MY DAY!
AND I'VE GOT THE SINKING FEELING THAT THINGS'LL GET WORSE BEFORE THEY GET BETTER!
INDEED, THE VERY NEXT DAY, IN THE HEART OF MANHATTAN'S 47TH STREET DIAMOND DISTRICT...
MOSHEH, PLEASE! BE CAREFUL!
STEIN BROS.
11

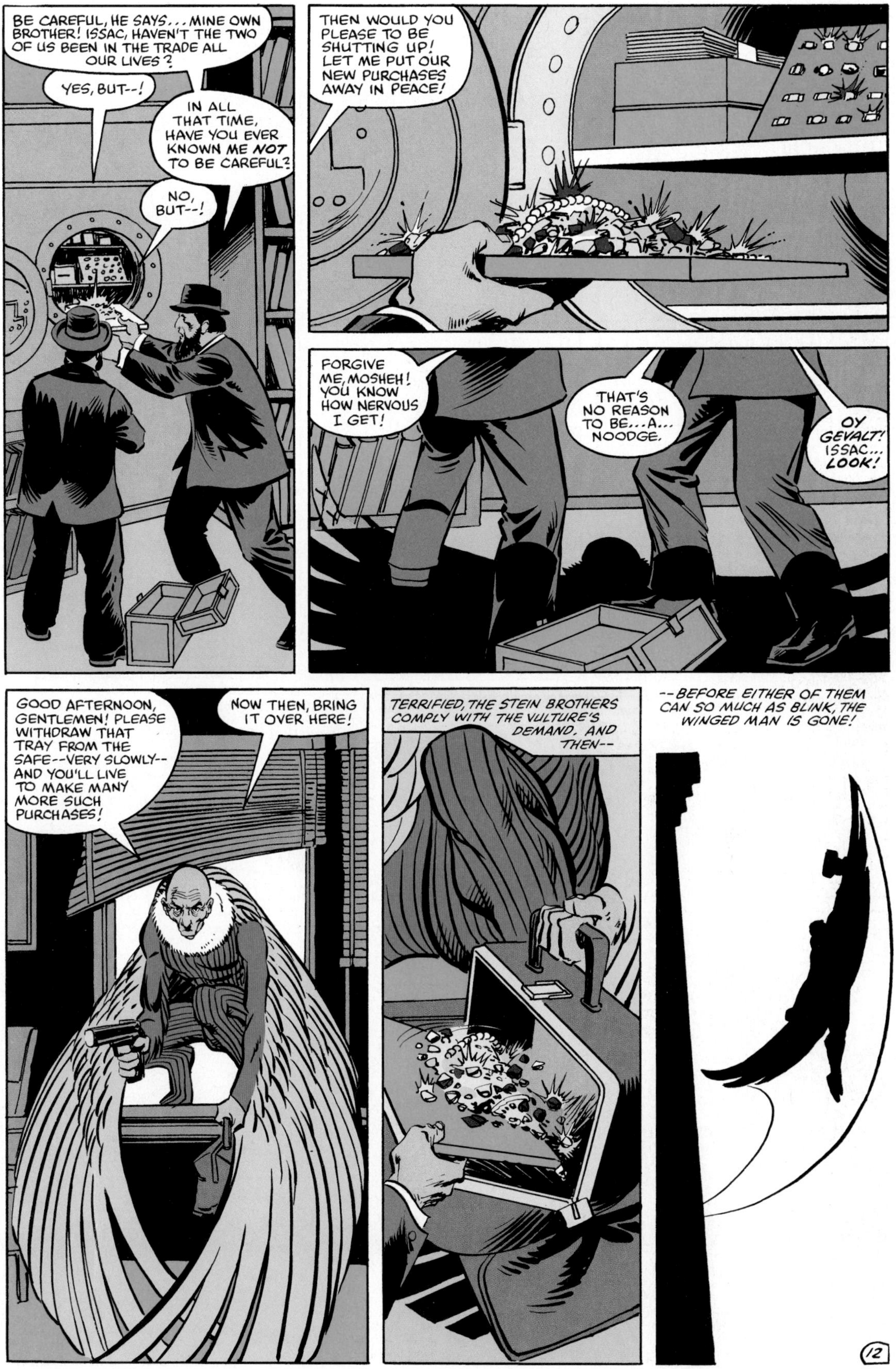
BE CAREFUL, HE SAYS... MINE OWN BROTHER! ISSAC, HAVEN'T THE TWO OF US BEEN IN THE TRADE ALL OUR LIVES?
YES, BUT--!
IN ALL THAT TIME, HAVE YOU EVER KNOWN ME NOT TO BE CAREFUL?
NO, BUT--!
THEN WOULD YOU PLEASE TO BE SHUTTING UP! LET ME PUT OUR NEW PURCHASES AWAY IN PEACE!
FORGIVE ME, MOSHEH! YOU KNOW HOW NERVOUS I GET!
THAT'S NO REASON TO BE...A... NOODGE.
OY GEVALT! ISSAC... LOOK!
GOOD AFTERNOON, GENTLEMEN! PLEASE WITHDRAW THAT TRAY FROM THE SAFE--VERY SLOWLY--AND YOU'LL LIVE TO MAKE MANY MORE SUCH PURCHASES!
NOW THEN, BRING IT OVER HERE!
TERRIFIED, THE STEIN BROTHERS COMPLY WITH THE VULTURE'S DEMAND. AND THEN--
--BEFORE EITHER OF THEM CAN SO MUCH AS BLINK, THE WINGED MAN IS GONE!
12

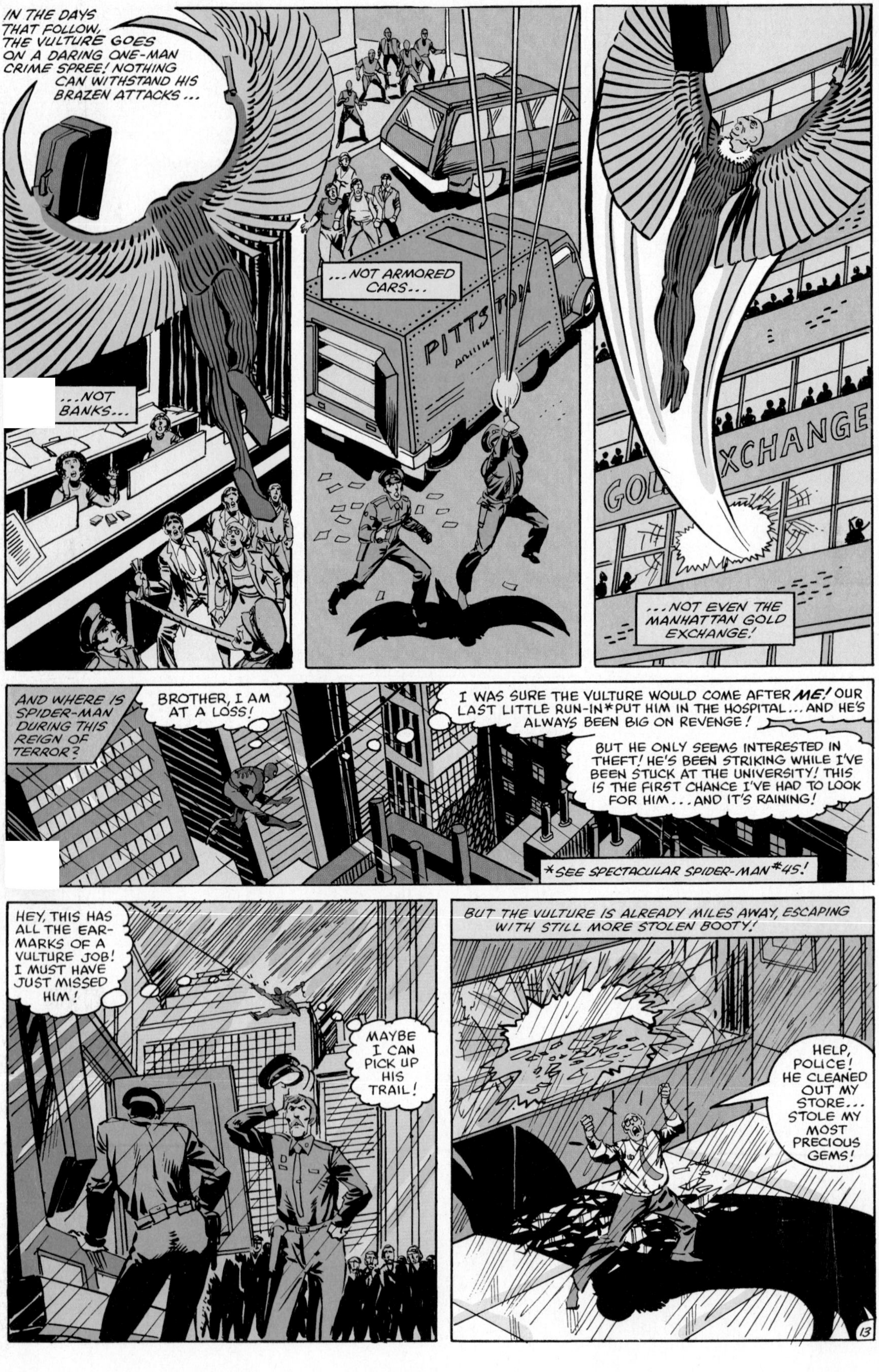
IN THE DAYS THAT FOLLOW, THE VULTURE GOES ON A DARING ONE-MAN CRIME SPREE! NOTHING CAN WITHSTAND HIS BRAZEN ATTACKS ...
...NOT BANKS...
...NOT ARMORED CARS...
PITTSTON
...NOT EVEN THE MANHATTAN GOLD EXCHANGE!
GOL XCHANGE
AND WHERE IS SPIDER-MAN DURING THIS REIGN OF TERROR?
BROTHER, I AM AT A LOSS!
I WAS SURE THE VULTURE WOULD COME AFTER ME! OUR LAST LITTLE RUN-IN* PUT HIM IN THE HOSPITAL... AND HE'S ALWAYS BEEN BIG ON REVENGE!
BUT HE ONLY SEEMS INTERESTED IN THEFT! HE'S BEEN STRIKING WHILE I'VE BEEN STUCK AT THE UNIVERSITY! THIS IS THE FIRST CHANCE I'VE HAD TO LOOK FOR HIM... AND IT'S RAINING!
*SEE SPECTACULAR SPIDER-MAN #45!
HEY, THIS HAS ALL THE EAR-MARKS OF A VULTURE JOB! I MUST HAVE JUST MISSED HIM!
MAYBE I CAN PICK UP HIS TRAIL!
BUT THE VULTURE IS ALREADY MILES AWAY, ESCAPING WITH STILL MORE STOLEN BOOTY!
HELP, POLICE! HE CLEANED OUT MY STORE... STOLE MY MOST PRECIOUS GEMS!
13

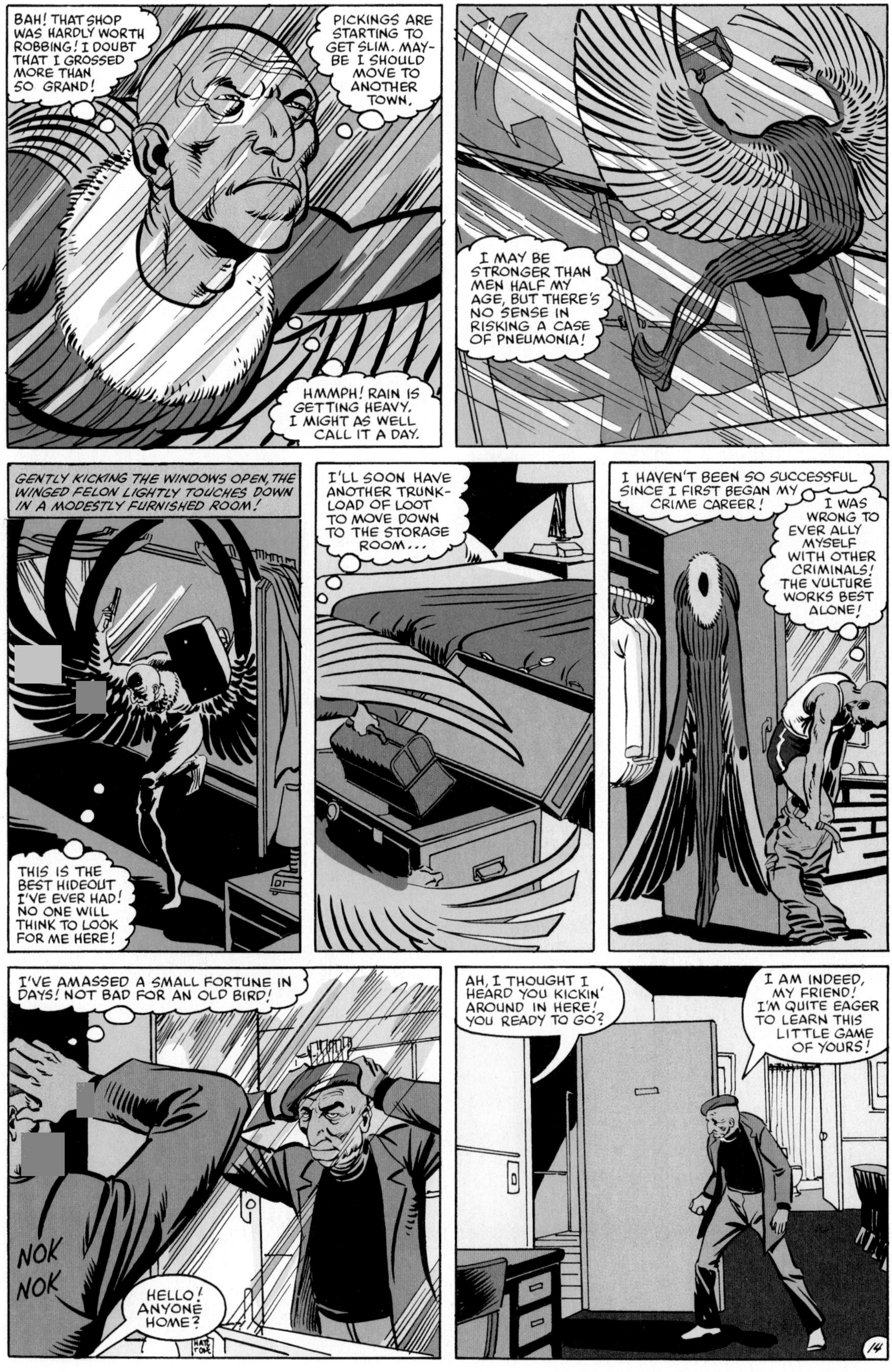
BAH! THAT SHOP WAS HARDLY WORTH ROBBING! I DOUBT THAT I GROSSED MORE THAN 50 GRAND!
PICKINGS ARE STARTING TO GET SLIM. MAYBE I SHOULD MOVE TO ANOTHER TOWN.
HMMPH! RAIN IS GETTING HEAVY. I MIGHT AS WELL CALL IT A DAY.
I MAY BE STRONGER THAN MEN HALF MY AGE, BUT THERE'S NO SENSE IN RISKING A CASE OF PNEUMONIA!
GENTLY KICKING THE WINDOWS OPEN, THE WINGED FELON LIGHTLY TOUCHES DOWN IN A MODESTLY FURNISHED ROOM!
THIS IS THE BEST HIDEOUT I'VE EVER HAD! NO ONE WILL THINK TO LOOK FOR ME HERE!
I'LL SOON HAVE ANOTHER TRUNK-LOAD OF LOOT TO MOVE DOWN TO THE STORAGE ROOM...
I HAVEN'T BEEN SO SUCCESSFUL SINCE I FIRST BEGAN MY CRIME CAREER!
I WAS WRONG TO EVER ALLY MYSELF WITH OTHER CRIMINALS! THE VULTURE WORKS BEST ALONE!
I'VE AMASSED A SMALL FORTUNE IN DAYS! NOT BAD FOR AN OLD BIRD!
NOK NOK
HELLO! ANYONE HOME?
AH, I THOUGHT I HEARD YOU KICKIN' AROUND IN HERE! YOU READY TO GO?
I AM INDEED, MY FRIEND! I'M QUITE EAGER TO LEARN THIS LITTLE GAME OF YOURS!
14

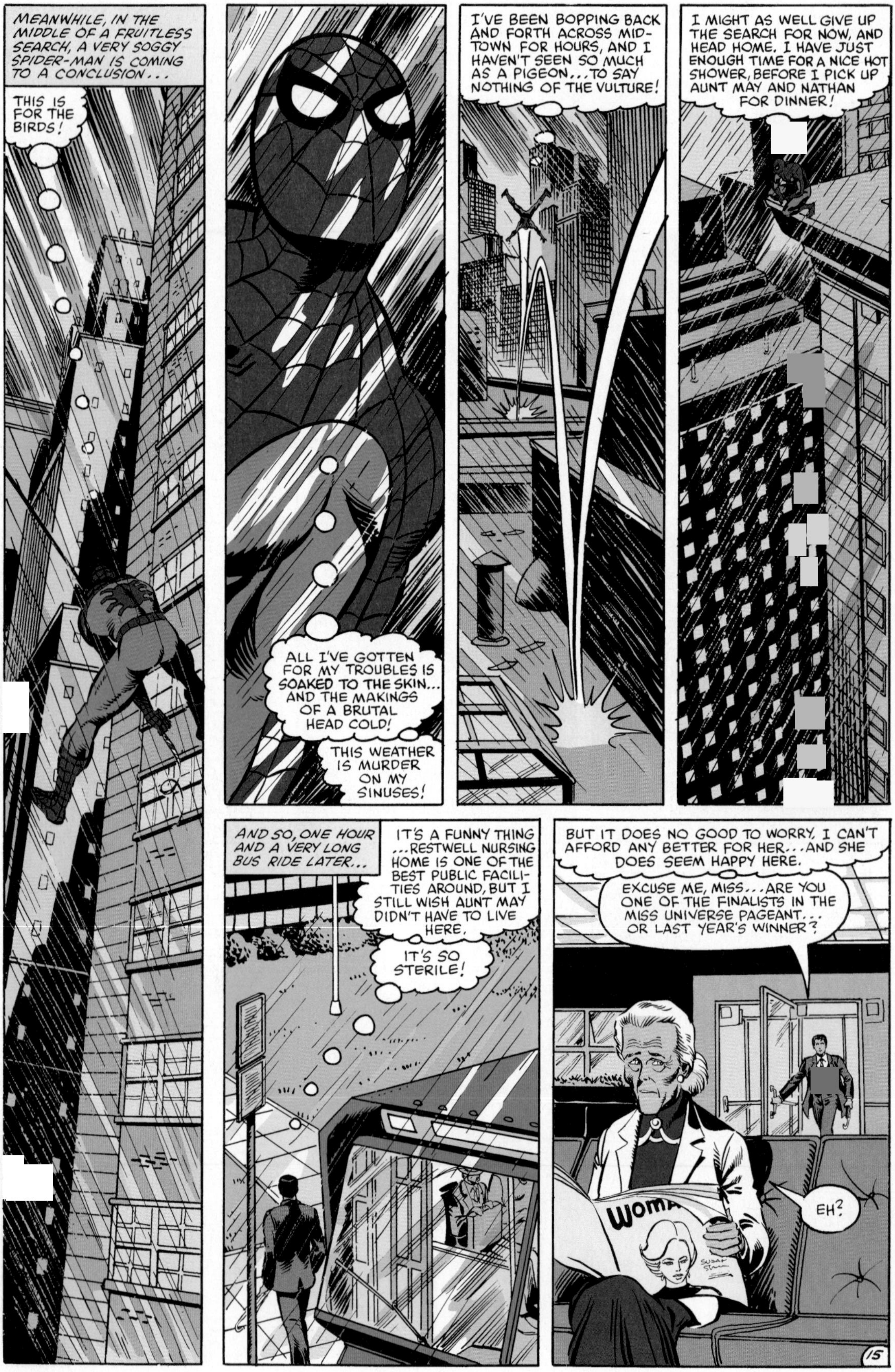
MEANWHILE, IN THE MIDDLE OF A FRUITLESS SEARCH, A VERY SOGGY SPIDER-MAN IS COMING TO A CONCLUSION...
THIS IS FOR THE BIRDS!
ALL I'VE GOTTEN FOR MY TROUBLES IS SOAKED TO THE SKIN... AND THE MAKINGS OF A BRUTAL HEAD COLD!
THIS WEATHER IS MURDER ON MY SINUSES!
I'VE BEEN BOPPING BACK AND FORTH ACROSS MID-TOWN FOR HOURS, AND I HAVEN'T SEEN SO MUCH AS A PIGEON... TO SAY NOTHING OF THE VULTURE!
I MIGHT AS WELL GIVE UP THE SEARCH FOR NOW, AND HEAD HOME. I HAVE JUST ENOUGH TIME FOR A NICE HOT SHOWER, BEFORE I PICK UP AUNT MAY AND NATHAN FOR DINNER!
AND SO, ONE HOUR AND A VERY LONG BUS RIDE LATER...
IT'S A FUNNY THING ...RESTWELL NURSING HOME IS ONE OF THE BEST PUBLIC FACILITIES AROUND, BUT I STILL WISH AUNT MAY DIDN'T HAVE TO LIVE HERE.
IT'S SO STERILE!
BUT IT DOES NO GOOD TO WORRY. I CAN'T AFFORD ANY BETTER FOR HER... AND SHE DOES SEEM HAPPY HERE.
EXCUSE ME, MISS... ARE YOU ONE OF THE FINALISTS IN THE MISS UNIVERSE PAGEANT... OR LAST YEAR'S WINNER?
EH?
15

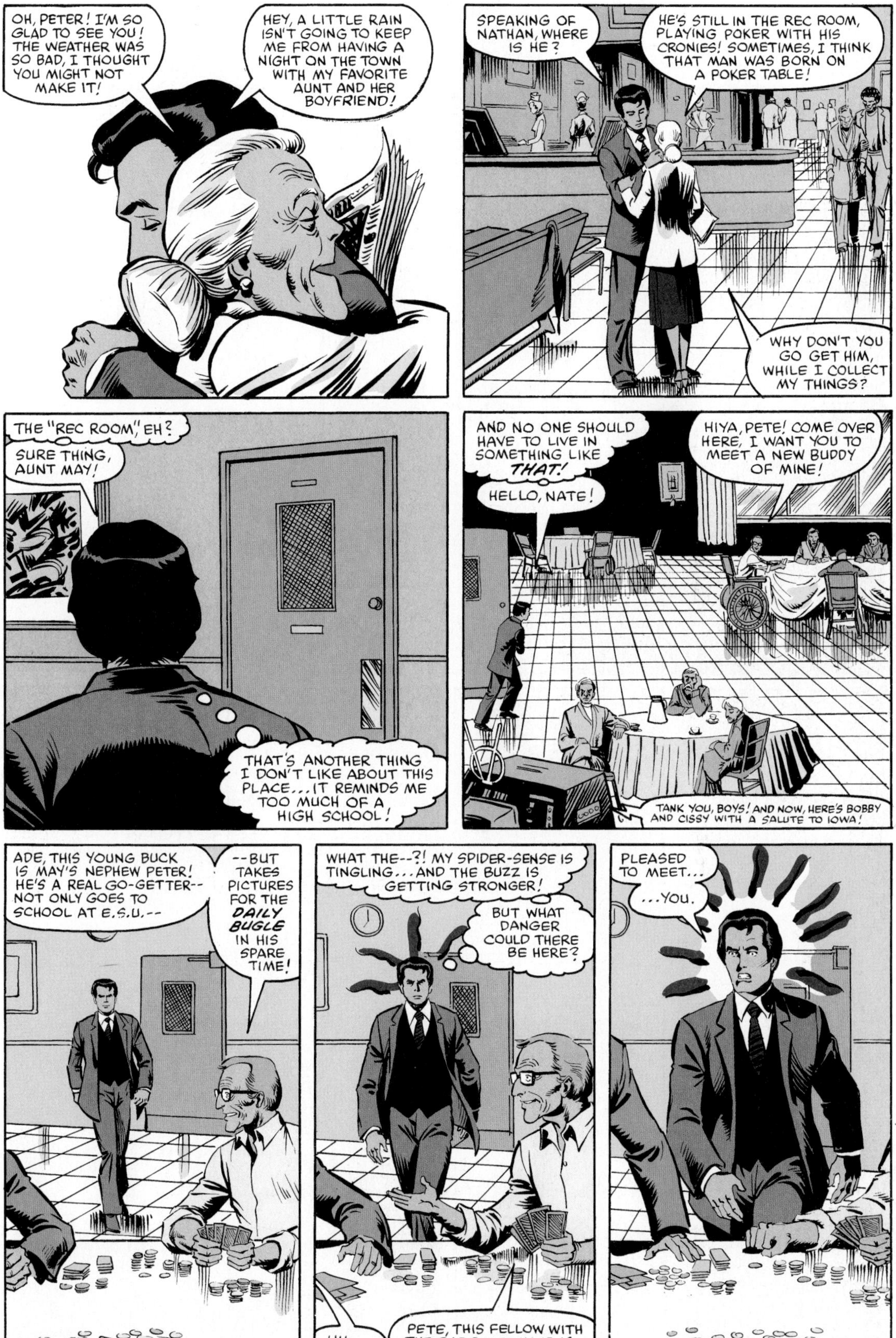
OH, PETER! I'M SO GLAD TO SEE YOU! THE WEATHER WAS SO BAD, I THOUGHT YOU MIGHT NOT MAKE IT!
HEY, A LITTLE RAIN ISN'T GOING TO KEEP ME FROM HAVING A NIGHT ON THE TOWN WITH MY FAVORITE AUNT AND HER BOYFRIEND!
SPEAKING OF NATHAN, WHERE IS HE?
HE'S STILL IN THE REC ROOM, PLAYING POKER WITH HIS CRONIES! SOMETIMES, I THINK THAT MAN WAS BORN ON A POKER TABLE!
WHY DON'T YOU GO GET HIM, WHILE I COLLECT MY THINGS?
THE "REC ROOM", EH?
SURE THING, AUNT MAY!
THAT'S ANOTHER THING I DON'T LIKE ABOUT THIS PLACE... IT REMINDS ME TOO MUCH OF A HIGH SCHOOL!
AND NO ONE SHOULD HAVE TO LIVE IN SOMETHING LIKE THAT!
HELLO, NATE!
HIYA, PETE! COME OVER HERE, I WANT YOU TO MEET A NEW BUDDY OF MINE!
TANK YOU, BOYS! AND NOW, HERE'S BOBBY AND CISSY WITH A SALUTE TO IOWA!
ADE, THIS YOUNG BUCK IS MAY'S NEPHEW PETER! HE'S A REAL GO-GETTER-- NOT ONLY GOES TO SCHOOL AT E.S.U.--
--BUT TAKES PICTURES FOR THE DAILY BUGLE IN HIS SPARE TIME!
WHAT THE--?! MY SPIDER-SENSE IS TINGLING... AND THE BUZZ IS GETTING STRONGER!
BUT WHAT DANGER COULD THERE BE HERE?
UH... I FOLD.
PETE, THIS FELLOW WITH THE BAD POKER HAND IS ADRIAN TOOMES!
PLEASED TO MEET...
...YOU.
16

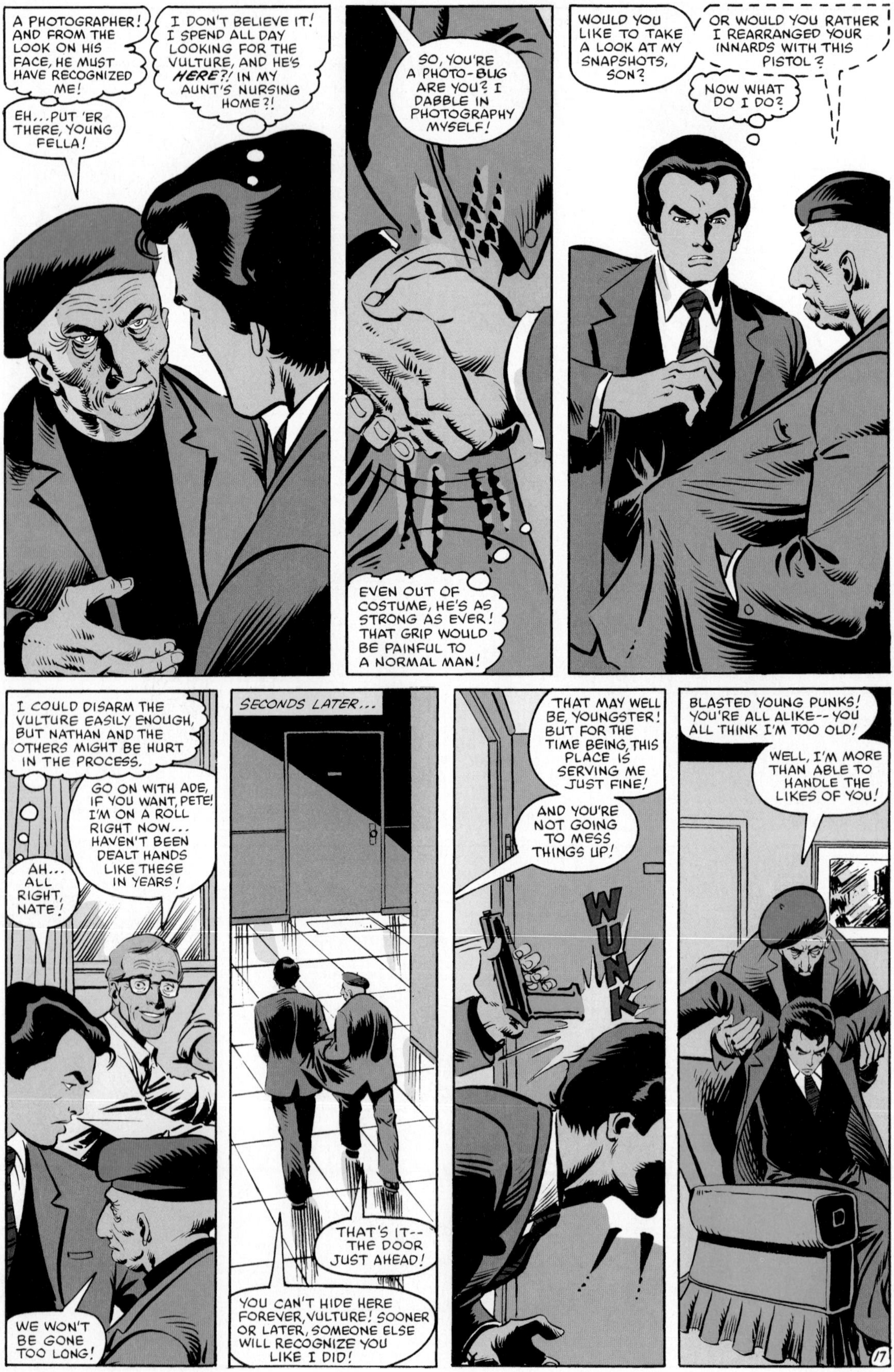
A PHOTOGRAPHER! AND FROM THE LOOK ON HIS FACE, HE MUST HAVE RECOGNIZED ME!
I DON'T BELIEVE IT! I SPEND ALL DAY LOOKING FOR THE VULTURE, AND HE'S HERE?! IN MY AUNT'S NURSING HOME?!
EH...PUT 'ER THERE, YOUNG FELLA!
SO, YOU'RE A PHOTO-BUG ARE YOU? I DABBLE IN PHOTOGRAPHY MYSELF!
EVEN OUT OF COSTUME, HE'S AS STRONG AS EVER! THAT GRIP WOULD BE PAINFUL TO A NORMAL MAN!
WOULD YOU LIKE TO TAKE A LOOK AT MY SNAPSHOTS, SON?
OR WOULD YOU RATHER I REARRANGED YOUR INNARDS WITH THIS PISTOL?
NOW WHAT DO I DO?
I COULD DISARM THE VULTURE EASILY ENOUGH, BUT NATHAN AND THE OTHERS MIGHT BE HURT IN THE PROCESS.
GO ON WITH ADE, IF YOU WANT, PETE! I'M ON A ROLL RIGHT NOW... HAVEN'T BEEN DEALT HANDS LIKE THESE IN YEARS!
AH... ALL RIGHT, NATE!
WE WON'T BE GONE TOO LONG!
SECONDS LATER...
THAT'S IT-- THE DOOR JUST AHEAD!
YOU CAN'T HIDE HERE FOREVER, VULTURE! SOONER OR LATER, SOMEONE ELSE WILL RECOGNIZE YOU LIKE I DID!
THAT MAY WELL BE, YOUNGSTER! BUT FOR THE TIME BEING, THIS PLACE IS SERVING ME JUST FINE!
AND YOU'RE NOT GOING TO MESS THINGS UP!
WUNK
BLASTED YOUNG PUNKS! YOU'RE ALL ALIKE-- YOU ALL THINK I'M TOO OLD!
WELL, I'M MORE THAN ABLE TO HANDLE THE LIKES OF YOU!
17

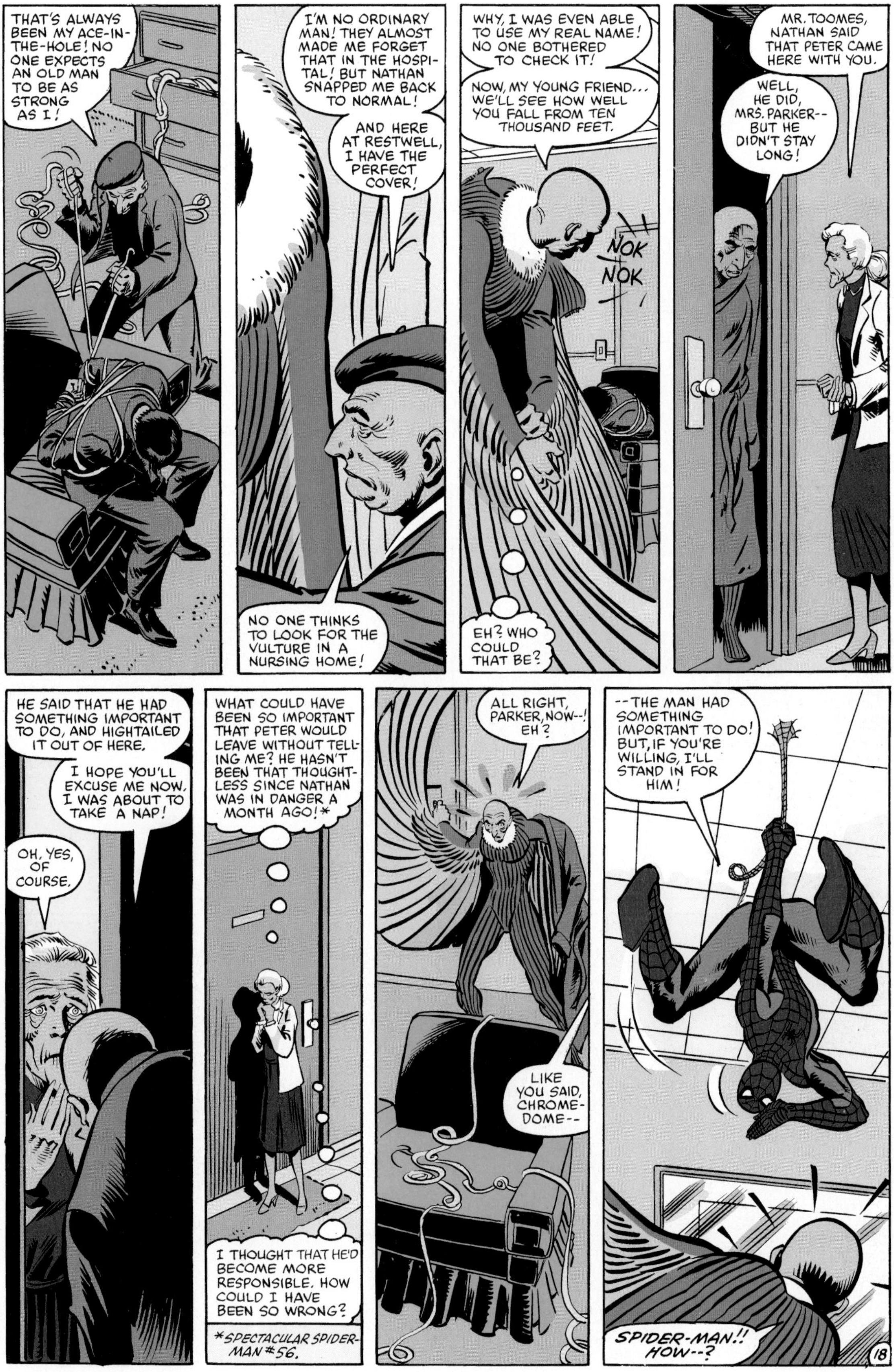
THAT'S ALWAYS BEEN MY ACE-IN-THE-HOLE! NO ONE EXPECTS AN OLD MAN TO BE AS STRONG AS I!
I'M NO ORDINARY MAN! THEY ALMOST MADE ME FORGET THAT IN THE HOSPITAL! BUT NATHAN SNAPPED ME BACK TO NORMAL!
AND HERE AT RESTWELL, I HAVE THE PERFECT COVER!
NO ONE THINKS TO LOOK FOR THE VULTURE IN A NURSING HOME!
WHY, I WAS EVEN ABLE TO USE MY REAL NAME! NO ONE BOTHERED TO CHECK IT!
NOW, MY YOUNG FRIEND... WE'LL SEE HOW WELL YOU FALL FROM TEN THOUSAND FEET.
NOK NOK
EH? WHO COULD THAT BE?
MR. TOOMES, NATHAN SAID THAT PETER CAME HERE WITH YOU.
WELL, HE DID, MRS. PARKER-- BUT HE DIDN'T STAY LONG!
HE SAID THAT HE HAD SOMETHING IMPORTANT TO DO, AND HIGHTAILED IT OUT OF HERE.
I HOPE YOU'LL EXCUSE ME NOW. I WAS ABOUT TO TAKE A NAP!
OH, YES, OF COURSE.
WHAT COULD HAVE BEEN SO IMPORTANT THAT PETER WOULD LEAVE WITHOUT TELLING ME? HE HASN'T BEEN THAT THOUGHTLESS SINCE NATHAN WAS IN DANGER A MONTH AGO!*
I THOUGHT THAT HE'D BECOME MORE RESPONSIBLE. HOW COULD I HAVE BEEN SO WRONG?
*SPECTACULAR SPIDER-MAN #56.
ALL RIGHT, PARKER, NOW--! EH?
LIKE YOU SAID, CHROME-DOME--
--THE MAN HAD SOMETHING IMPORTANT TO DO! BUT, IF YOU'RE WILLING, I'LL STAND IN FOR HIM!
SPIDER-MAN!! HOW--?
18

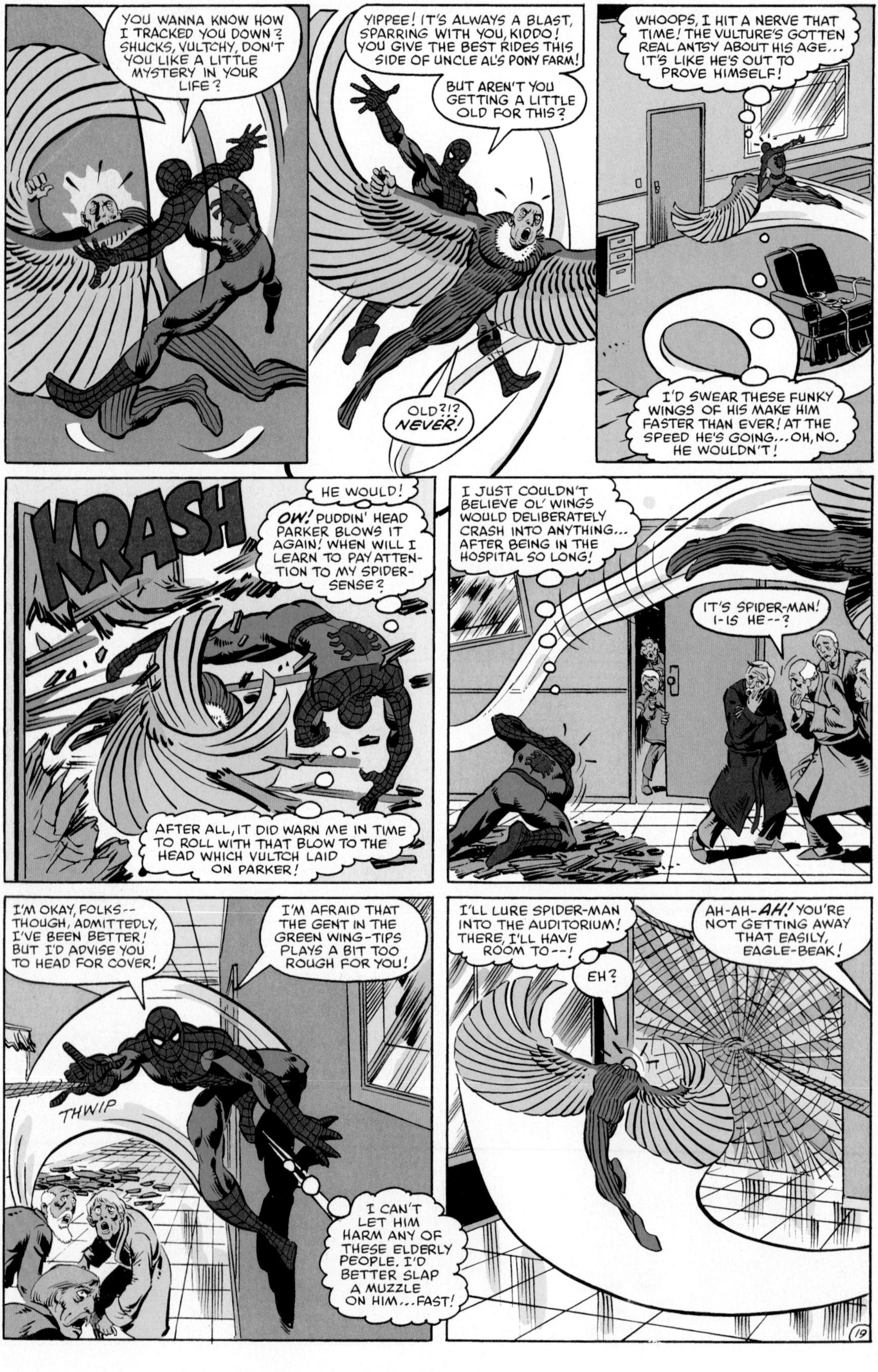
YOU WANNA KNOW HOW I TRACKED YOU DOWN? SHUCKS, VULTCHY, DON'T YOU LIKE A LITTLE MYSTERY IN YOUR LIFE?
YIPPEE! IT'S ALWAYS A BLAST, SPARRING WITH YOU, KIDDO! YOU GIVE THE BEST RIDES THIS SIDE OF UNCLE AL'S PONY FARM!
BUT AREN'T YOU GETTING A LITTLE OLD FOR THIS?
OLD?!? NEVER!
WHOOPS, I HIT A NERVE THAT TIME! THE VULTURE'S GOTTEN REAL ANTSY ABOUT HIS AGE... IT'S LIKE HE'S OUT TO PROVE HIMSELF!
I'D SWEAR THESE FUNKY WINGS OF HIS MAKE HIM FASTER THAN EVER! AT THE SPEED HE'S GOING... OH, NO. HE WOULDN'T!
HE WOULD!
KRASH
OW! PUDDIN' HEAD PARKER BLOWS IT AGAIN! WHEN WILL I LEARN TO PAY ATTENTION TO MY SPIDER-SENSE?
AFTER ALL, IT DID WARN ME IN TIME TO ROLL WITH THAT BLOW TO THE HEAD WHICH VULTCH LAID ON PARKER!
I JUST COULDN'T BELIEVE OL' WINGS WOULD DELIBERATELY CRASH INTO ANYTHING... AFTER BEING IN THE HOSPITAL SO LONG!
IT'S SPIDER-MAN! I-IS HE--?
I'M OKAY, FOLKS-- THOUGH, ADMITTEDLY, I'VE BEEN BETTER! BUT I'D ADVISE YOU TO HEAD FOR COVER!
I'M AFRAID THAT THE GENT IN THE GREEN WING-TIPS PLAYS A BIT TOO ROUGH FOR YOU!
THWIP
I CAN'T LET HIM HARM ANY OF THESE ELDERLY PEOPLE. I'D BETTER SLAP A MUZZLE ON HIM... FAST!
I'LL LURE SPIDER-MAN INTO THE AUDITORIUM! THERE, I'LL HAVE ROOM TO--!
EH?
AH-AH-AH! YOU'RE NOT GETTING AWAY THAT EASILY, EAGLE-BEAK!
19

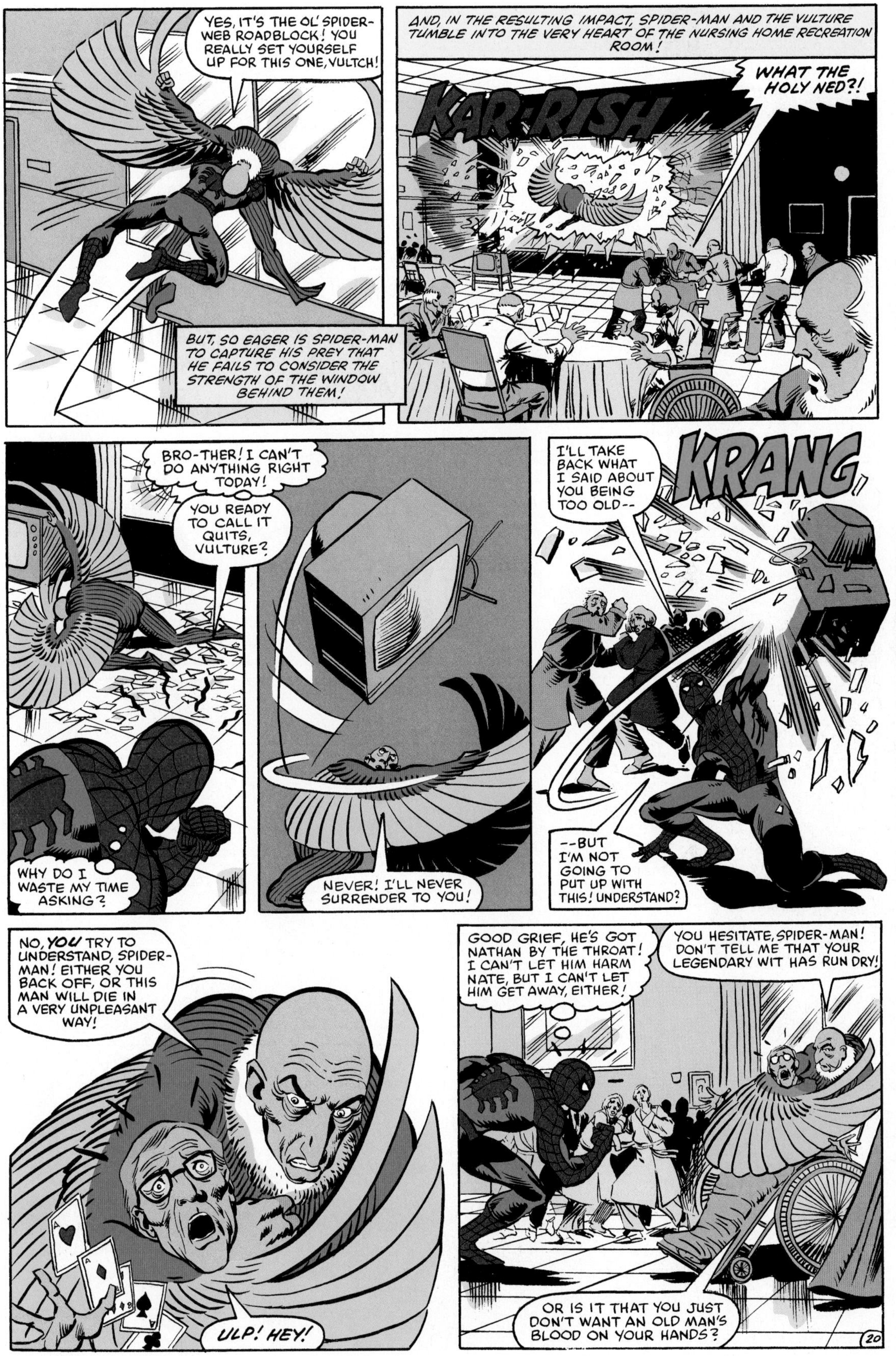
YES, IT'S THE OL' SPIDER-WEB ROADBLOCK! YOU REALLY SET YOURSELF UP FOR THIS ONE, VULTCH!
BUT, SO EAGER IS SPIDER-MAN TO CAPTURE HIS PREY THAT HE FAILS TO CONSIDER THE STRENGTH OF THE WINDOW BEHIND THEM!
AND, IN THE RESULTING IMPACT, SPIDER-MAN AND THE VULTURE TUMBLE INTO THE VERY HEART OF THE NURSING HOME RECREATION ROOM!
KAR-RISH
WHAT THE HOLY NED?!
BRO-THER! I CAN'T DO ANYTHING RIGHT TODAY!
YOU READY TO CALL IT QUITS, VULTURE?
WHY DO I WASTE MY TIME ASKING?
NEVER! I'LL NEVER SURRENDER TO YOU!
KRANG
I'LL TAKE BACK WHAT I SAID ABOUT YOU BEING TOO OLD--
--BUT I'M NOT GOING TO PUT UP WITH THIS! UNDERSTAND?
NO, YOU TRY TO UNDERSTAND, SPIDER-MAN! EITHER YOU BACK OFF, OR THIS MAN WILL DIE IN A VERY UNPLEASANT WAY!
ULP! HEY!
GOOD GRIEF, HE'S GOT NATHAN BY THE THROAT! I CAN'T LET HIM HARM NATE, BUT I CAN'T LET HIM GET AWAY, EITHER!
YOU HESITATE, SPIDER-MAN! DON'T TELL ME THAT YOUR LEGENDARY WIT HAS RUN DRY!
OR IS IT THAT YOU JUST DON'T WANT AN OLD MAN'S BLOOD ON YOUR HANDS?
20

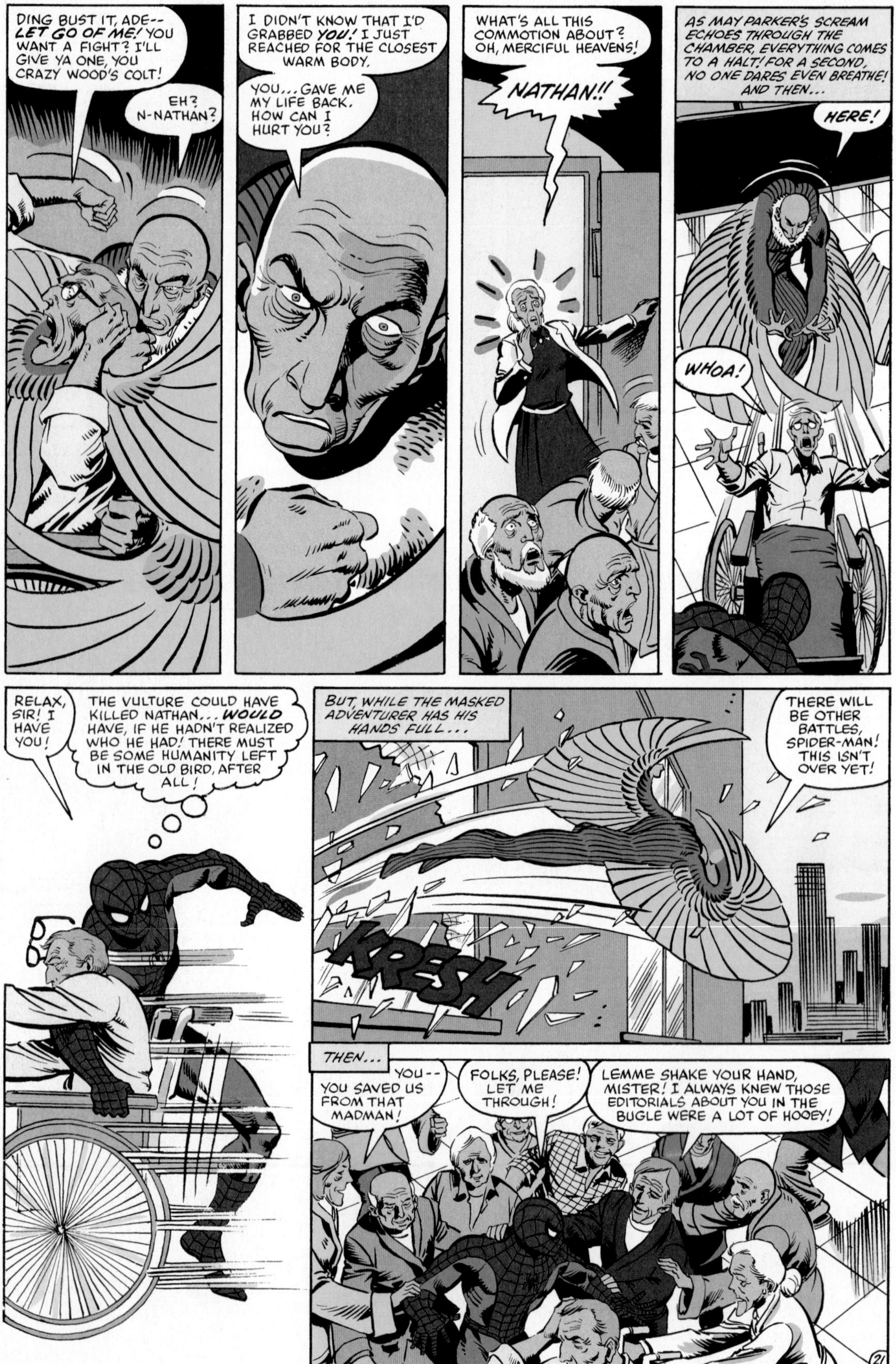
DING BUST IT, ADE-- LET GO OF ME! YOU WANT A FIGHT? I'LL GIVE YA ONE, YOU CRAZY WOOD'S COLT!
EH? N-NATHAN?
I DIDN'T KNOW THAT I'D GRABBED YOU! I JUST REACHED FOR THE CLOSEST WARM BODY.
YOU... GAVE ME MY LIFE BACK. HOW CAN I HURT YOU?
WHAT'S ALL THIS COMMOTION ABOUT? OH, MERCIFUL HEAVENS!
NATHAN!!
AS MAY PARKER'S SCREAM ECHOES THROUGH THE CHAMBER, EVERYTHING COMES TO A HALT! FOR A SECOND, NO ONE DARES EVEN BREATHE! AND THEN...
HERE!
WHOA!
RELAX, SIR! I HAVE YOU!
THE VULTURE COULD HAVE KILLED NATHAN... WOULD HAVE, IF HE HADN'T REALIZED WHO HE HAD! THERE MUST BE SOME HUMANITY LEFT IN THE OLD BIRD, AFTER ALL!
BUT, WHILE THE MASKED ADVENTURER HAS HIS HANDS FULL...
THERE WILL BE OTHER BATTLES, SPIDER-MAN! THIS ISN'T OVER YET!
KRESH
THEN...
YOU-- YOU SAVED US FROM THAT MADMAN!
FOLKS, PLEASE! LET ME THROUGH!
LEMME SHAKE YOUR HAND, MISTER! I ALWAYS KNEW THOSE EDITORIALS ABOUT YOU IN THE BUGLE WERE A LOT OF HOOEY!
21

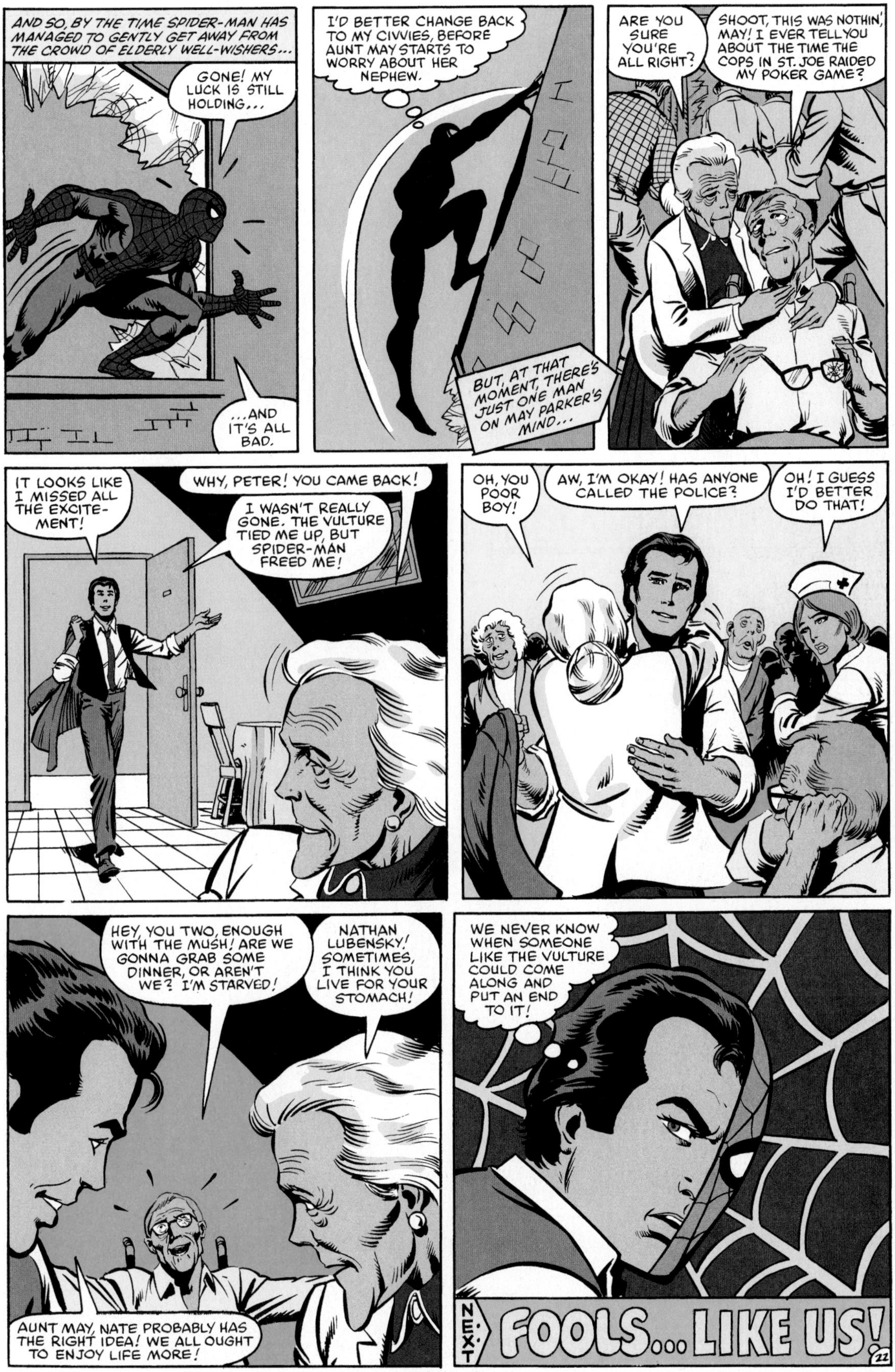
AND SO, BY THE TIME SPIDER-MAN HAS MANAGED TO GENTLY GET AWAY FROM THE CROWD OF ELDERLY WELL-WISHERS...
GONE! MY LUCK IS STILL HOLDING...
...AND IT'S ALL BAD.
I'D BETTER CHANGE BACK TO MY CIVVIES, BEFORE AUNT MAY STARTS TO WORRY ABOUT HER NEPHEW.
BUT, AT THAT MOMENT, THERE'S JUST ONE MAN ON MAY PARKER'S MIND...
ARE YOU SURE YOU'RE ALL RIGHT?
SHOOT, THIS WAS NOTHIN', MAY! I EVER TELL YOU ABOUT THE TIME THE COPS IN ST. JOE RAIDED MY POKER GAME?
IT LOOKS LIKE I MISSED ALL THE EXCITEMENT!
WHY, PETER! YOU CAME BACK!
I WASN'T REALLY GONE. THE VULTURE TIED ME UP, BUT SPIDER-MAN FREED ME!
OH, YOU POOR BOY!
AW, I'M OKAY! HAS ANYONE CALLED THE POLICE?
OH! I GUESS I'D BETTER DO THAT!
HEY, YOU TWO, ENOUGH WITH THE MUSH! ARE WE GONNA GRAB SOME DINNER, OR AREN'T WE? I'M STARVED!
NATHAN LUBENSKY! SOMETIMES, I THINK YOU LIVE FOR YOUR STOMACH!
AUNT MAY, NATE PROBABLY HAS THE RIGHT IDEA! WE ALL OUGHT TO ENJOY LIFE MORE!
WE NEVER KNOW WHEN SOMEONE LIKE THE VULTURE COULD COME ALONG AND PUT AN END TO IT!
NEXT
FOOLS... LIKE US!
22

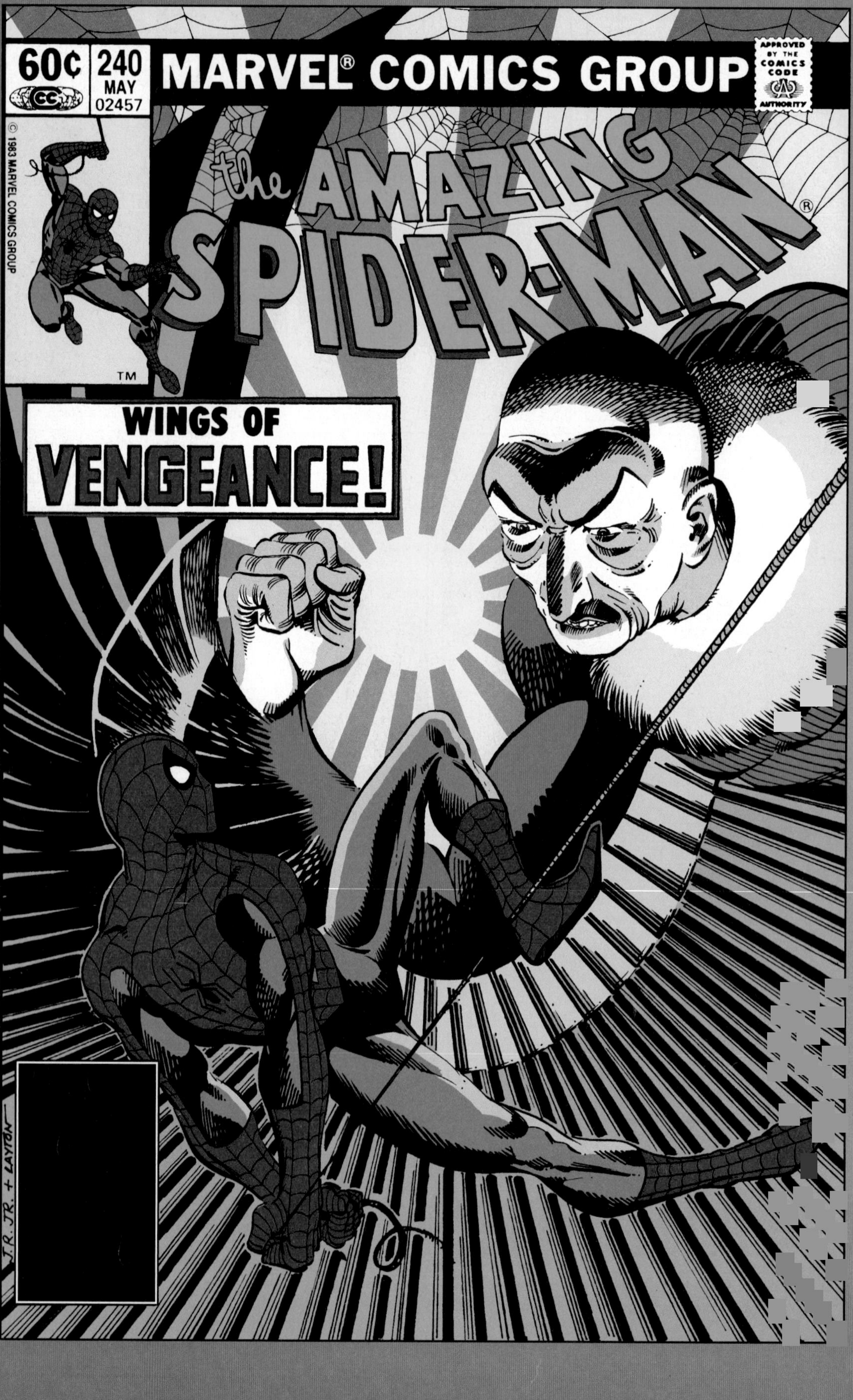
60¢
240
MAY
02457
MARVEL® COMICS GROUP
APPROVED BY THE COMICS CODE AUTHORITY
© 1983 MARVEL COMICS GROUP
the AMAZING SPIDER-MAN®
TM
WINGS OF VENGEANCE!
J.R. JR. + LAYTON

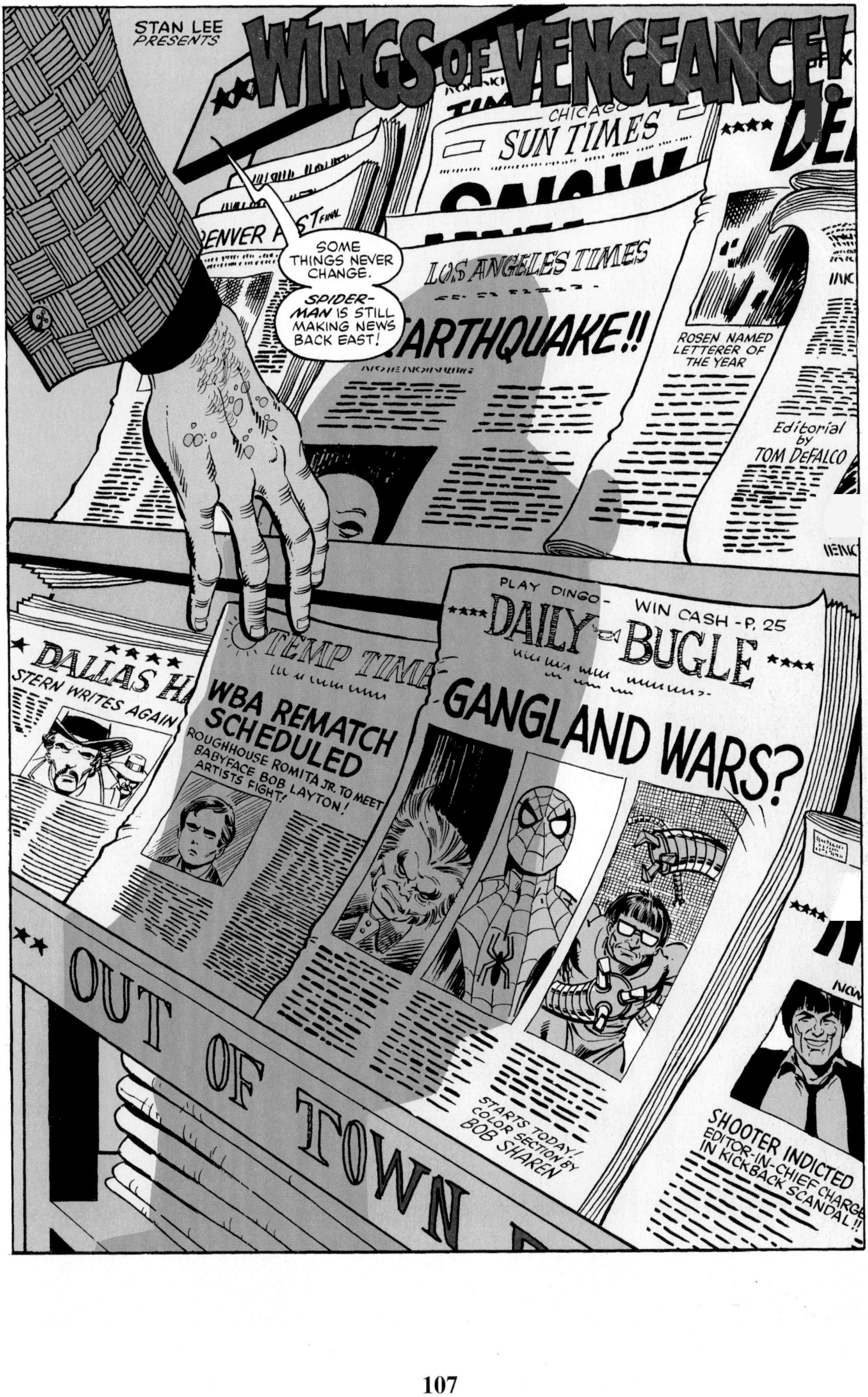
STAN LEE PRESENTS
WINGS OF VENGEANCE!
CHICAGO SUN TIMES
DENVER POST FINAL
SOME THINGS NEVER CHANGE.
SPIDER-MAN IS STILL MAKING NEWS BACK EAST!
LOS ANGELES TIMES
EARTHQUAKE!!
ROSEN NAMED LETTERER OF THE YEAR
Editorial by TOM DeFALCO
PLAY DINGO- WIN CASH -P. 25
DAILY BUGLE
GANGLAND WARS?
TEMP TIMES
WBA REMATCH SCHEDULED
ROUGHHOUSE ROMITA JR. TO MEET BABYFACE BOB LAYTON! ARTISTS FIGHT!
STERN WRITES AGAIN
STARTS TODAY! COLOR SECTION BY BOB SHAREN
SHOOTER INDICTED
EDITOR-IN-CHIEF CHARGED IN KICKBACK SCANDAL!!
OUT OF TOWN

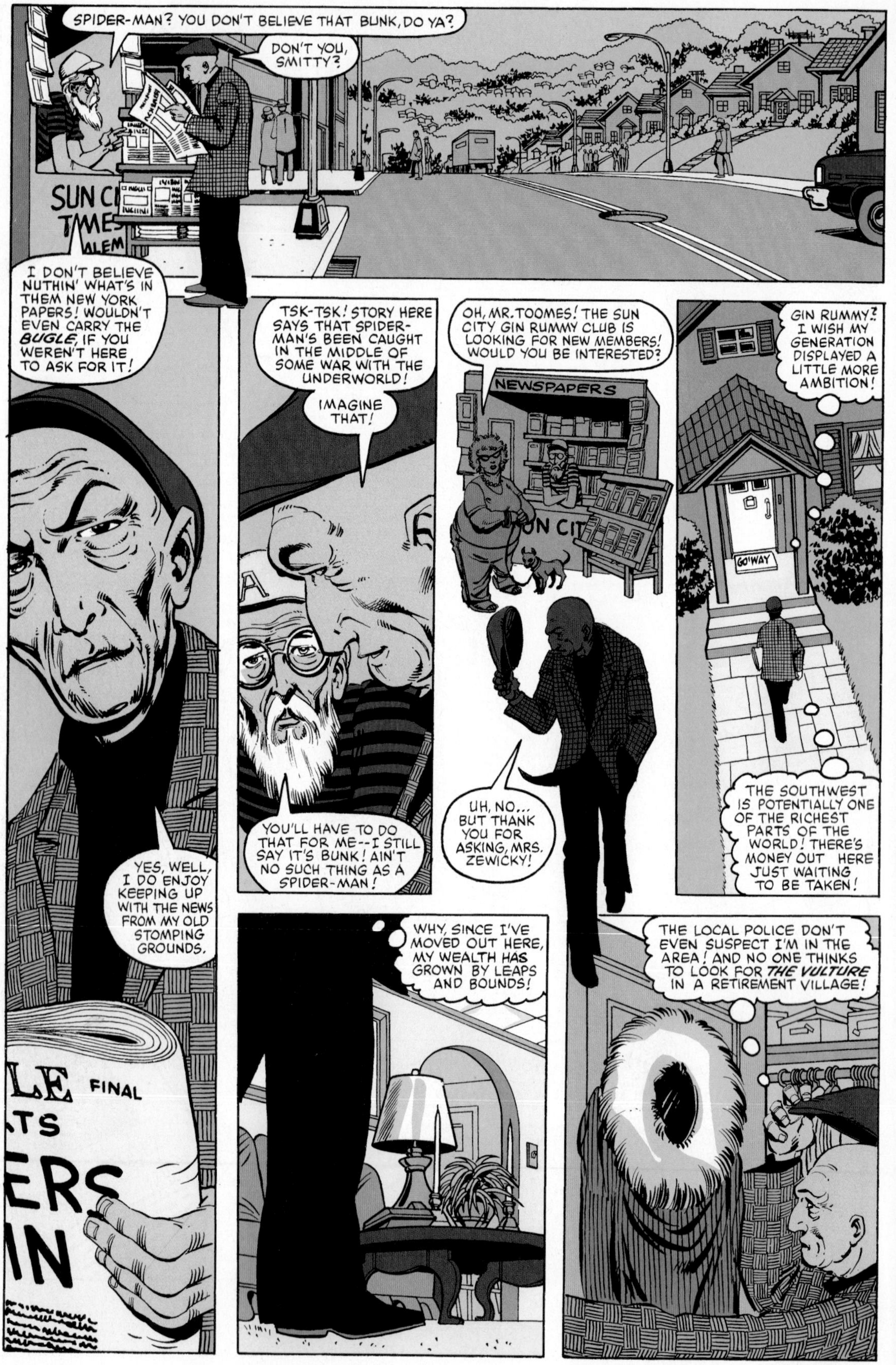
SPIDER-MAN? YOU DON'T BELIEVE THAT BUNK, DO YA?
DON'T YOU, SMITTY?
I DON'T BELIEVE NUTHIN' WHAT'S IN THEM NEW YORK PAPERS! WOULDN'T EVEN CARRY THE *BUGLE*, IF YOU WEREN'T HERE TO ASK FOR IT!
YES, WELL, I DO ENJOY KEEPING UP WITH THE NEWS FROM MY OLD STOMPING GROUNDS.
FINAL
TSK-TSK! STORY HERE SAYS THAT SPIDER-MAN'S BEEN CAUGHT IN THE MIDDLE OF SOME WAR WITH THE UNDERWORLD!
IMAGINE THAT!
YOU'LL HAVE TO DO THAT FOR ME--I STILL SAY IT'S BUNK! AIN'T NO SUCH THING AS A SPIDER-MAN!
OH, MR. TOOMES! THE SUN CITY GIN RUMMY CLUB IS LOOKING FOR NEW MEMBERS! WOULD YOU BE INTERESTED?
NEWSPAPERS
UH, NO... BUT THANK YOU FOR ASKING, MRS. ZEWICKY!
GIN RUMMY? I WISH MY GENERATION DISPLAYED A LITTLE MORE AMBITION!
GO'WAY
THE SOUTHWEST IS POTENTIALLY ONE OF THE RICHEST PARTS OF THE WORLD! THERE'S MONEY OUT HERE JUST WAITING TO BE TAKEN!
WHY, SINCE I'VE MOVED OUT HERE, MY WEALTH HAS GROWN BY LEAPS AND BOUNDS!
THE LOCAL POLICE DON'T EVEN SUSPECT I'M IN THE AREA! AND NO ONE THINKS TO LOOK FOR *THE VULTURE* IN A RETIREMENT VILLAGE!

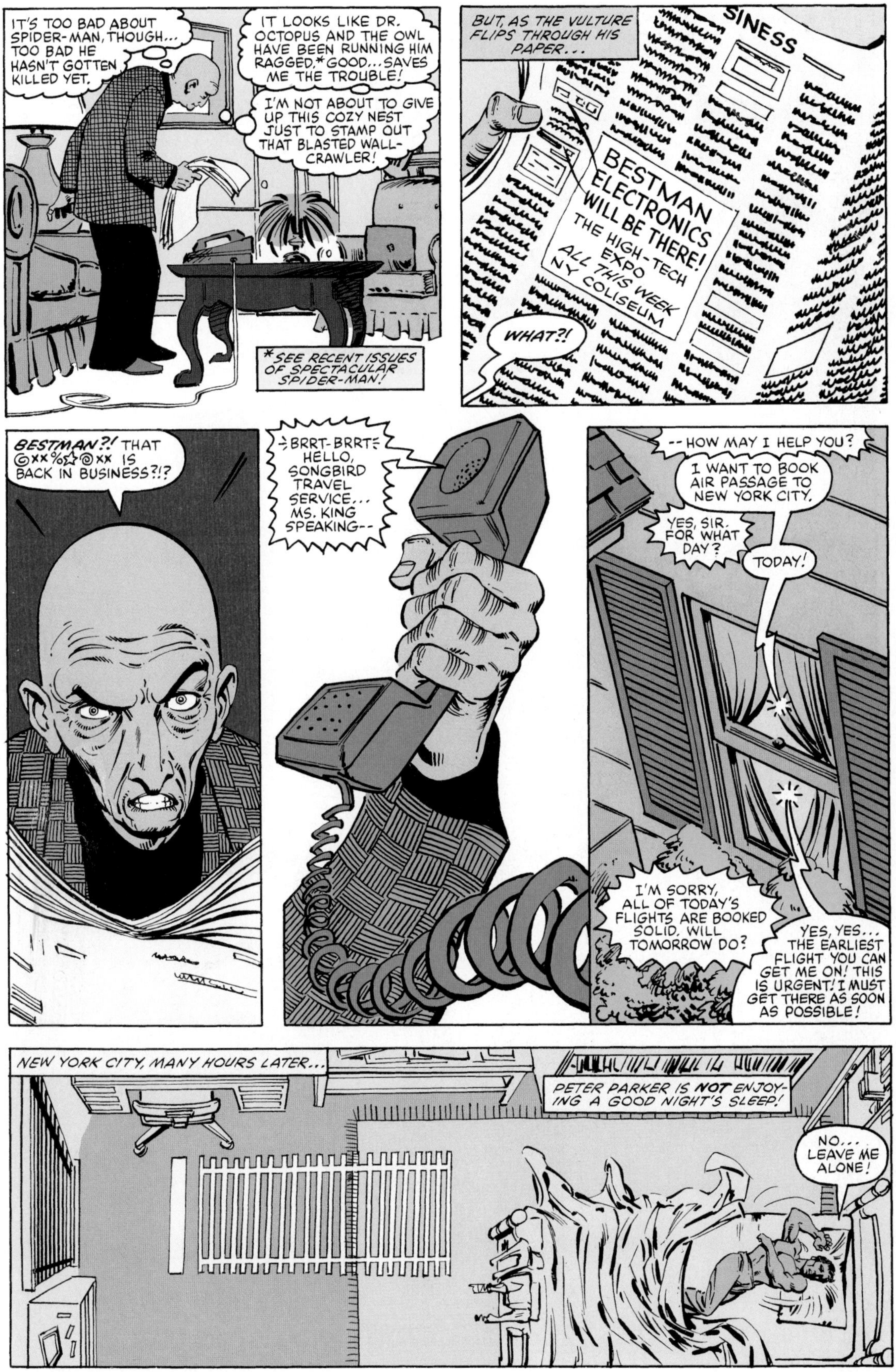
IT'S TOO BAD ABOUT SPIDER-MAN, THOUGH... TOO BAD HE HASN'T GOTTEN KILLED YET.
IT LOOKS LIKE DR. OCTOPUS AND THE OWL HAVE BEEN RUNNING HIM RAGGED,* GOOD... SAVES ME THE TROUBLE!
I'M NOT ABOUT TO GIVE UP THIS COZY NEST JUST TO STAMP OUT THAT BLASTED WALL-CRAWLER!
*SEE RECENT ISSUES OF SPECTACULAR SPIDER-MAN!
BUT, AS THE VULTURE FLIPS THROUGH HIS PAPER...
SINESS
BESTMAN ELECTRONICS WILL BE THERE!
THE HIGH-TECH EXPO
ALL THIS WEEK
NY COLISEUM
WHAT?!
BESTMAN?! THAT ©××%☆@×× IS BACK IN BUSINESS?!?
BRRT-BRRT HELLO, SONGBIRD TRAVEL SERVICE... MS. KING SPEAKING--
--HOW MAY I HELP YOU?
I WANT TO BOOK AIR PASSAGE TO NEW YORK CITY.
YES, SIR. FOR WHAT DAY?
TODAY!
I'M SORRY, ALL OF TODAY'S FLIGHTS ARE BOOKED SOLID. WILL TOMORROW DO?
YES, YES... THE EARLIEST FLIGHT YOU CAN GET ME ON! THIS IS URGENT! I MUST GET THERE AS SOON AS POSSIBLE!
NEW YORK CITY, MANY HOURS LATER...
PETER PARKER IS NOT ENJOYING A GOOD NIGHT'S SLEEP!
NO... LEAVE ME ALONE!

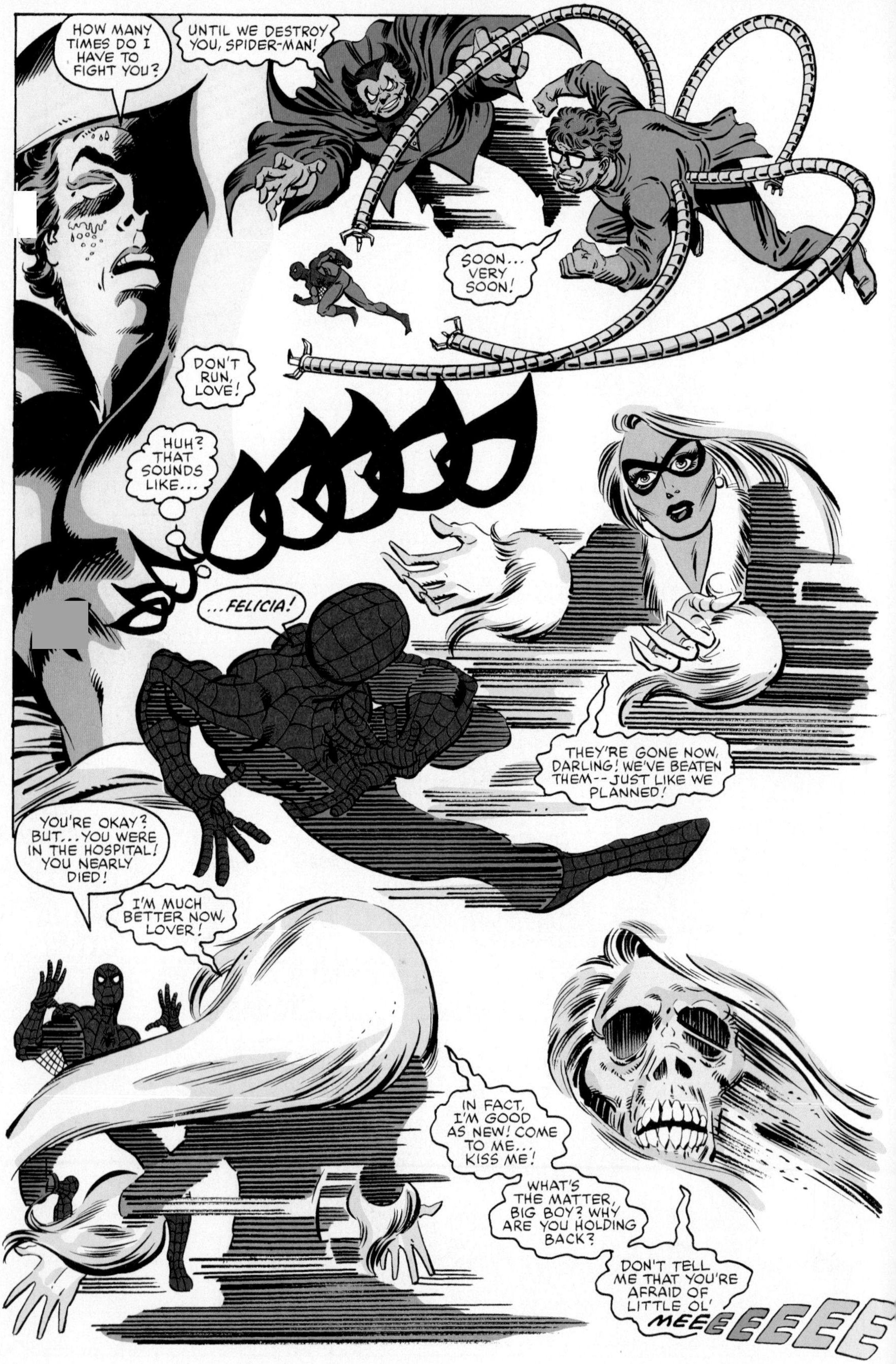
HOW MANY TIMES DO I HAVE TO FIGHT YOU?
UNTIL WE DESTROY YOU, SPIDER-MAN!
SOON... VERY SOON!
DON'T RUN, LOVE!
HUH? THAT SOUNDS LIKE...
...FELICIA!
THEY'RE GONE NOW, DARLING! WE'VE BEATEN THEM--JUST LIKE WE PLANNED!
YOU'RE OKAY? BUT... YOU WERE IN THE HOSPITAL! YOU NEARLY DIED!
I'M MUCH BETTER NOW, LOVER!
IN FACT, I'M GOOD AS NEW! COME TO ME... KISS ME!
WHAT'S THE MATTER, BIG BOY? WHY ARE YOU HOLDING BACK?
DON'T TELL ME THAT YOU'RE AFRAID OF LITTLE OL' MEEEEEEEE

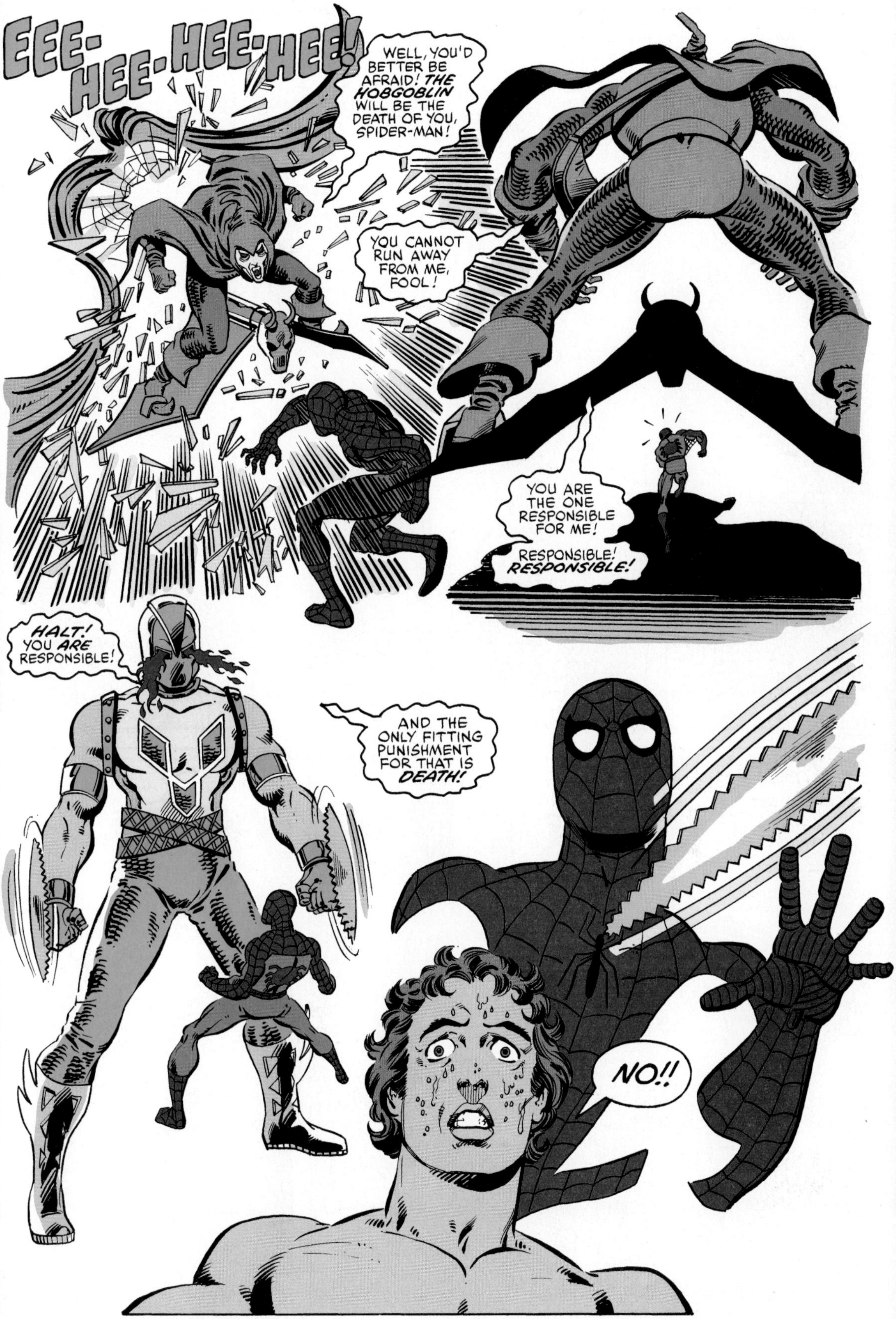
EEE-HEE-HEE-HEE!
WELL, YOU'D BETTER BE AFRAID! THE HOBGOBLIN WILL BE THE DEATH OF YOU, SPIDER-MAN!
YOU CANNOT RUN AWAY FROM ME, FOOL!
YOU ARE THE ONE RESPONSIBLE FOR ME!
RESPONSIBLE! RESPONSIBLE!
HALT! YOU ARE RESPONSIBLE!
AND THE ONLY FITTING PUNISHMENT FOR THAT IS DEATH!
NO!!

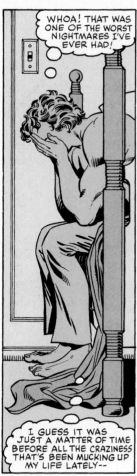

WHOA! THAT WAS ONE OF THE WORST NIGHTMARES I'VE EVER HAD!

I GUESS IT WAS JUST A MATTER OF TIME BEFORE ALL THE CRAZINESS THAT'S BEEN MUCKING UP MY LIFE LATELY--

--SPILLED OVER INTO MY DREAMS! I COULD ALMOST FEEL THOSE WHIRLING WRIST BLADES OF THE *GLADIATOR!* ≥BRRR!≤

I'LL NEVER GET BACK TO SLEEP NOW ...MIGHT AS WELL GET UP!

KLIK

OH, DANDY! MY LIGHTS ARE EVEN MORE BURNT OUT THAN I AM!

THIS'LL TEACH ME NOT TO BUY THOSE BARGAIN-BRAND BULBS!

I MUST BE GOING THROUGH ONE A MONTH! OH, WELL...

...AT LEAST IT'S NO HASSLE CHANGING THEM!

MAYBE THIS IS ALL THAT BEING SPIDER-MAN IS GOOD FOR-- CHANGING LIGHT BULBS! I SURE HAVEN'T BEEN ANY GREAT SHAKES IN THE HERO BIZ LATELY!

DOC OCK GOT AWAY FROM ME... THIS NEW HOBGOBLIN CREEP GOT AWAY FROM ME!

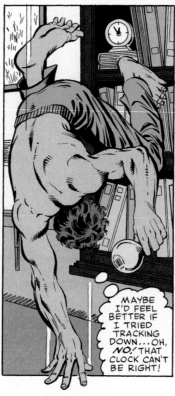

MAYBE I'D FEEL BETTER IF I TRIED TRACKING DOWN...OH, *NO!* THAT CLOCK CAN'T BE RIGHT!

IT IS. I'VE SLEPT THE WHOLE MORNING AWAY!

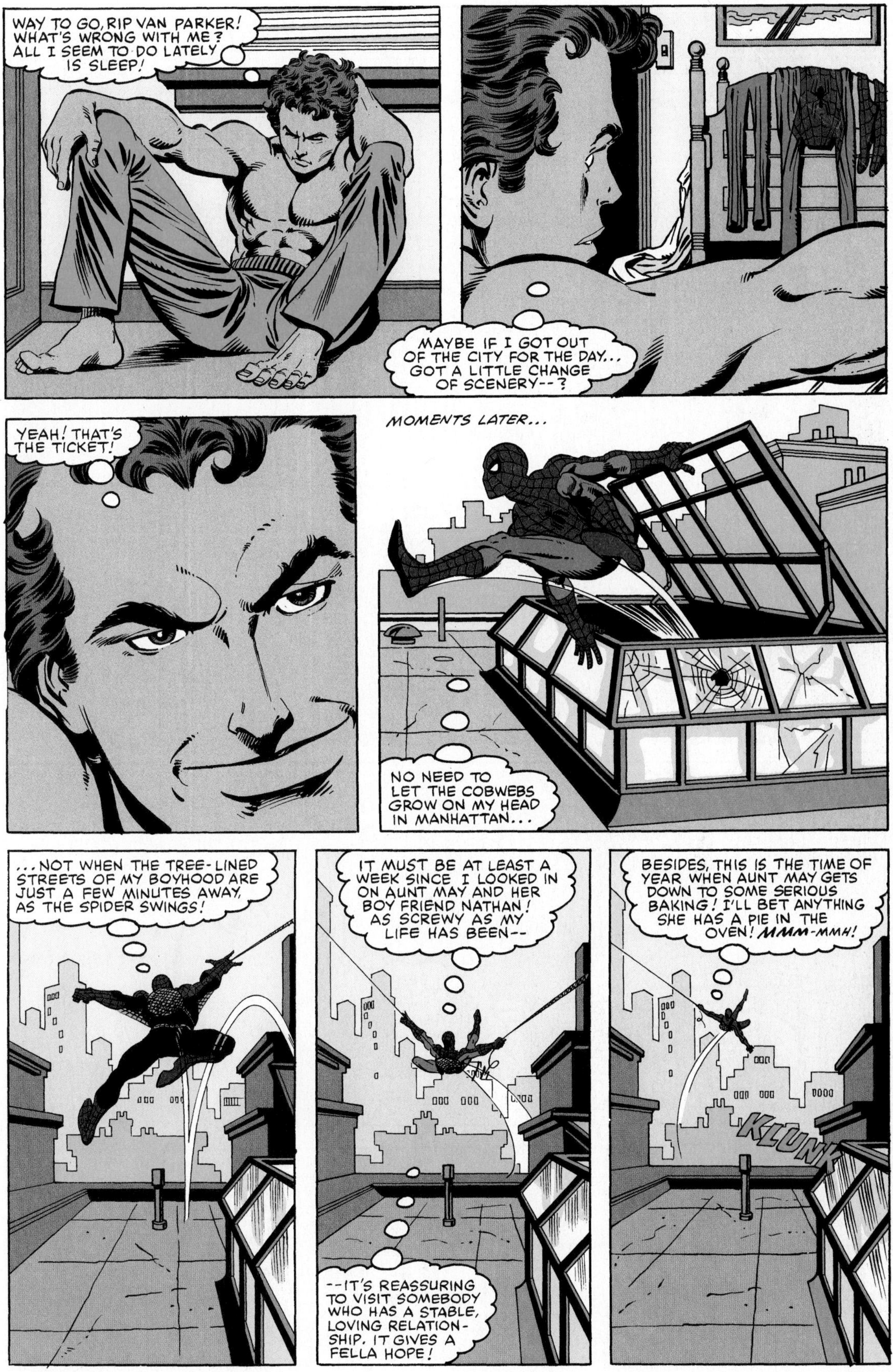
WAY TO GO, RIP VAN PARKER! WHAT'S WRONG WITH ME? ALL I SEEM TO DO LATELY IS SLEEP!
MAYBE IF I GOT OUT OF THE CITY FOR THE DAY... GOT A LITTLE CHANGE OF SCENERY--?
YEAH! THAT'S THE TICKET!
MOMENTS LATER...
NO NEED TO LET THE COBWEBS GROW ON MY HEAD IN MANHATTAN...
...NOT WHEN THE TREE-LINED STREETS OF MY BOYHOOD ARE JUST A FEW MINUTES AWAY, AS THE SPIDER SWINGS!
IT MUST BE AT LEAST A WEEK SINCE I LOOKED IN ON AUNT MAY AND HER BOY FRIEND NATHAN! AS SCREWY AS MY LIFE HAS BEEN--
--IT'S REASSURING TO VISIT SOMEBODY WHO HAS A STABLE, LOVING RELATION-SHIP. IT GIVES A FELLA HOPE!
BESIDES, THIS IS THE TIME OF YEAR WHEN AUNT MAY GETS DOWN TO SOME SERIOUS BAKING! I'LL BET ANYTHING SHE HAS A PIE IN THE OVEN! MMM-MMH!
KLUNK

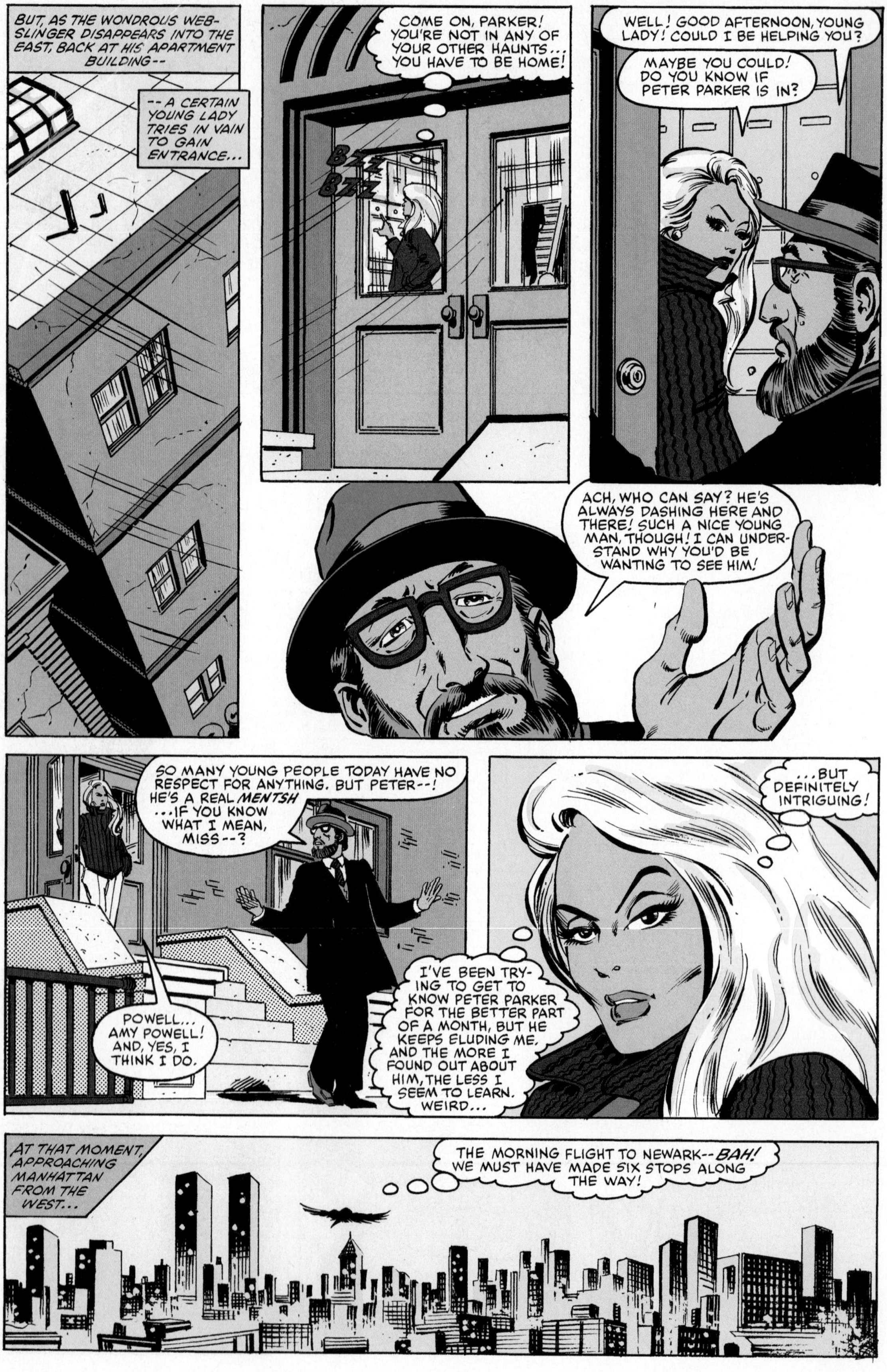
BUT, AS THE WONDROUS WEB-SLINGER DISAPPEARS INTO THE EAST, BACK AT HIS APARTMENT BUILDING--
--A CERTAIN YOUNG LADY TRIES IN VAIN TO GAIN ENTRANCE...
COME ON, PARKER! YOU'RE NOT IN ANY OF YOUR OTHER HAUNTS... YOU HAVE TO BE HOME!
BZZ BZZ
WELL! GOOD AFTERNOON, YOUNG LADY! COULD I BE HELPING YOU?
MAYBE YOU COULD! DO YOU KNOW IF PETER PARKER IS IN?
ACH, WHO CAN SAY? HE'S ALWAYS DASHING HERE AND THERE! SUCH A NICE YOUNG MAN, THOUGH! I CAN UNDERSTAND WHY YOU'D BE WANTING TO SEE HIM!
SO MANY YOUNG PEOPLE TODAY HAVE NO RESPECT FOR ANYTHING. BUT PETER--! HE'S A REAL MENTSH ...IF YOU KNOW WHAT I MEAN, MISS--?
POWELL... AMY POWELL! AND, YES, I THINK I DO.
I'VE BEEN TRYING TO GET TO KNOW PETER PARKER FOR THE BETTER PART OF A MONTH, BUT HE KEEPS ELUDING ME. AND THE MORE I FOUND OUT ABOUT HIM, THE LESS I SEEM TO LEARN. WEIRD...
...BUT DEFINITELY INTRIGUING!
AT THAT MOMENT, APPROACHING MANHATTAN FROM THE WEST...
THE MORNING FLIGHT TO NEWARK--BAH! WE MUST HAVE MADE SIX STOPS ALONG THE WAY!

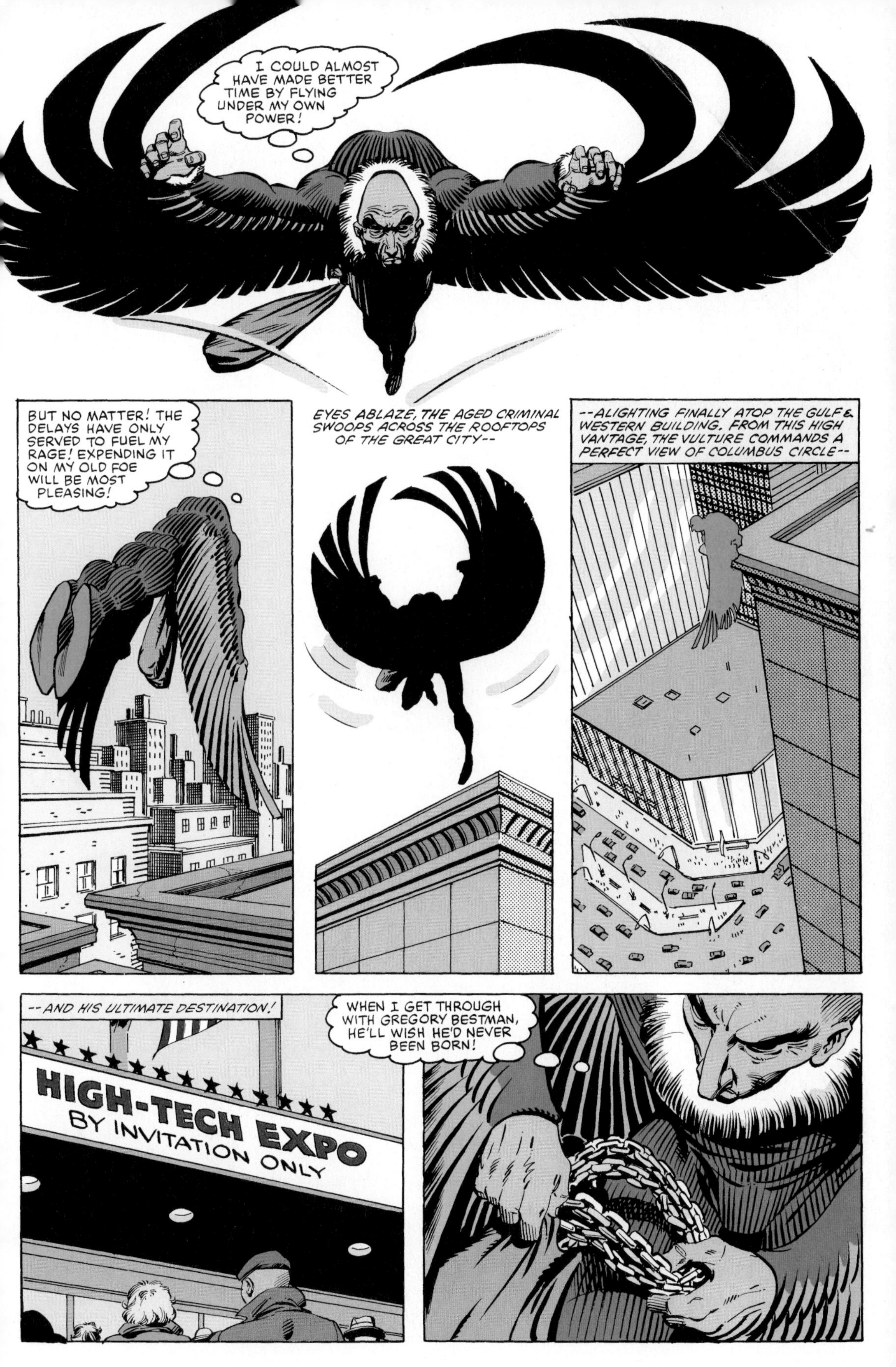
I COULD ALMOST HAVE MADE BETTER TIME BY FLYING UNDER MY OWN POWER!
BUT NO MATTER! THE DELAYS HAVE ONLY SERVED TO FUEL MY RAGE! EXPENDING IT ON MY OLD FOE WILL BE MOST PLEASING!
EYES ABLAZE, THE AGED CRIMINAL SWOOPS ACROSS THE ROOFTOPS OF THE GREAT CITY--
--ALIGHTING FINALLY ATOP THE GULF & WESTERN BUILDING. FROM THIS HIGH VANTAGE, THE VULTURE COMMANDS A PERFECT VIEW OF COLUMBUS CIRCLE--
--AND HIS ULTIMATE DESTINATION!
HIGH-TECH EXPO
BY INVITATION ONLY
WHEN I GET THROUGH WITH GREGORY BESTMAN, HE'LL WISH HE'D NEVER BEEN BORN!

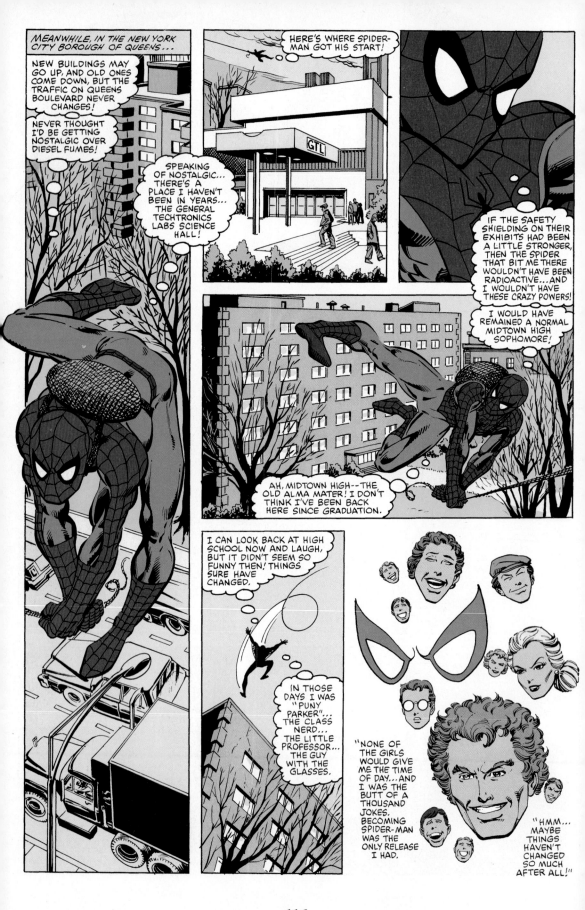

MEANWHILE, IN THE NEW YORK CITY BOROUGH OF QUEENS...

NEW BUILDINGS MAY GO UP, AND OLD ONES COME DOWN, BUT THE TRAFFIC ON QUEENS BOULEVARD NEVER CHANGES!

NEVER THOUGHT I'D BE GETTING NOSTALGIC OVER DIESEL FUMES!

SPEAKING OF NOSTALGIC... THERE'S A PLACE I HAVEN'T BEEN IN YEARS... THE GENERAL TECHTRONICS LABS SCIENCE HALL!

HERE'S WHERE SPIDER-MAN GOT HIS START!

IF THE SAFETY SHIELDING ON THEIR EXHIBITS HAD BEEN A LITTLE STRONGER, THEN THE SPIDER THAT BIT ME THERE WOULDN'T HAVE BEEN RADIOACTIVE...AND I WOULDN'T HAVE THESE CRAZY POWERS!

I WOULD HAVE REMAINED A NORMAL MIDTOWN HIGH SOPHOMORE!

AH, MIDTOWN HIGH--THE OLD ALMA MATER! I DON'T THINK I'VE BEEN BACK HERE SINCE GRADUATION.

I CAN LOOK BACK AT HIGH SCHOOL NOW AND LAUGH, BUT IT DIDN'T SEEM SO FUNNY THEN! THINGS SURE HAVE CHANGED.

IN THOSE DAYS I WAS "PUNY PARKER"... THE CLASS NERD... THE LITTLE PROFESSOR... THE GUY WITH THE GLASSES.

"NONE OF THE GIRLS WOULD GIVE ME THE TIME OF DAY...AND I WAS THE BUTT OF A THOUSAND JOKES. BECOMING SPIDER-MAN WAS THE ONLY RELEASE I HAD.

"HMM... MAYBE THINGS HAVEN'T CHANGED SO MUCH AFTER ALL!"

116

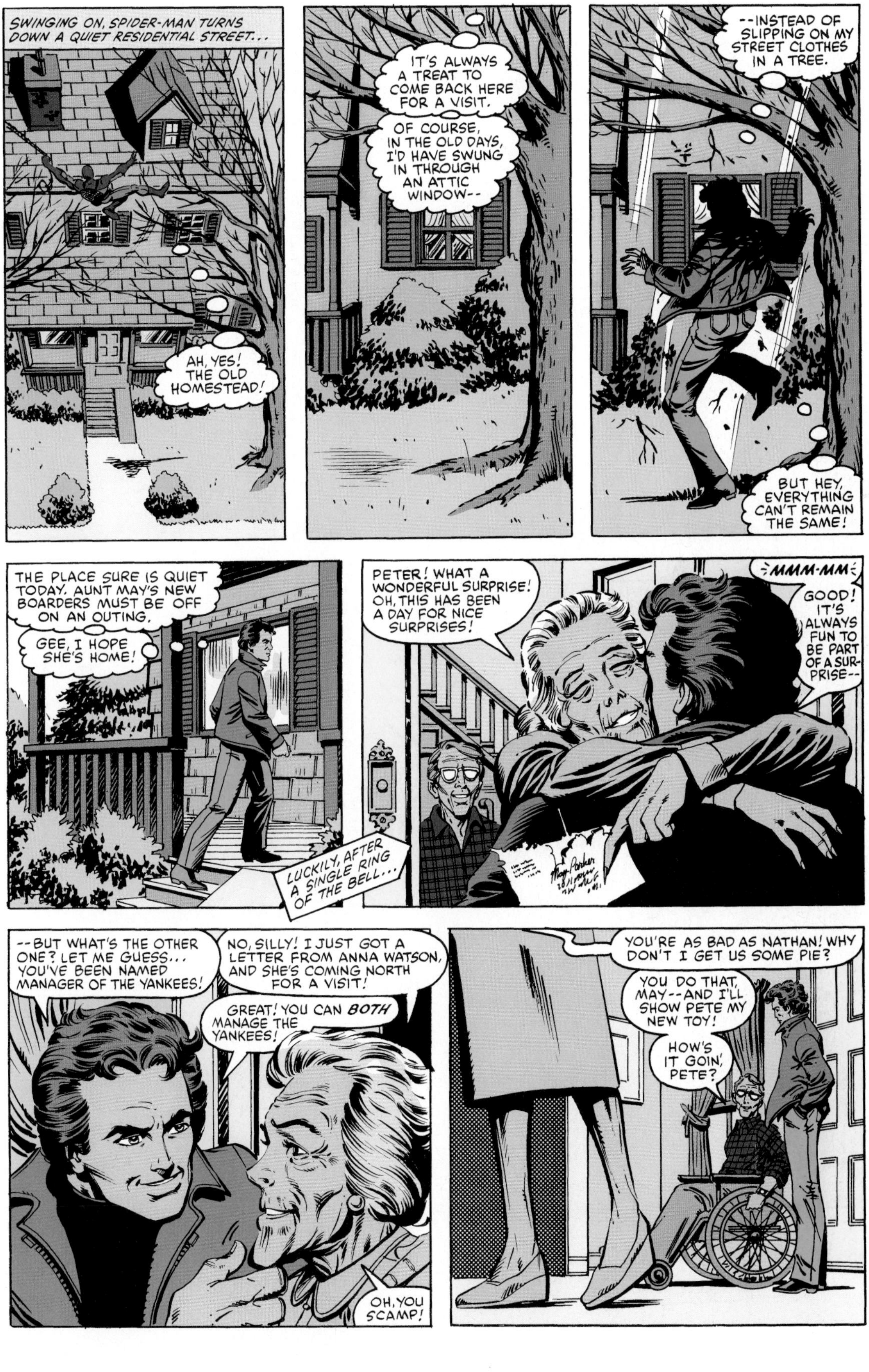

SWINGING ON, SPIDER-MAN TURNS DOWN A QUIET RESIDENTIAL STREET...
AH, YES! THE OLD HOMESTEAD!
IT'S ALWAYS A TREAT TO COME BACK HERE FOR A VISIT.
OF COURSE, IN THE OLD DAYS, I'D HAVE SWUNG IN THROUGH AN ATTIC WINDOW--
--INSTEAD OF SLIPPING ON MY STREET CLOTHES IN A TREE.
BUT HEY, EVERYTHING CAN'T REMAIN THE SAME!
THE PLACE SURE IS QUIET TODAY. AUNT MAY'S NEW BOARDERS MUST BE OFF ON AN OUTING.
GEE, I HOPE SHE'S HOME!
LUCKILY, AFTER A SINGLE RING OF THE BELL...
PETER! WHAT A WONDERFUL SURPRISE! OH, THIS HAS BEEN A DAY FOR NICE SURPRISES!
MMM-MM
GOOD! IT'S ALWAYS FUN TO BE PART OF A SURPRISE--
--BUT WHAT'S THE OTHER ONE? LET ME GUESS... YOU'VE BEEN NAMED MANAGER OF THE YANKEES!
NO, SILLY! I JUST GOT A LETTER FROM ANNA WATSON, AND SHE'S COMING NORTH FOR A VISIT!
GREAT! YOU CAN BOTH MANAGE THE YANKEES!
OH, YOU SCAMP!
YOU'RE AS BAD AS NATHAN! WHY DON'T I GET US SOME PIE?
YOU DO THAT, MAY--AND I'LL SHOW PETE MY NEW TOY!
HOW'S IT GOIN', PETE?

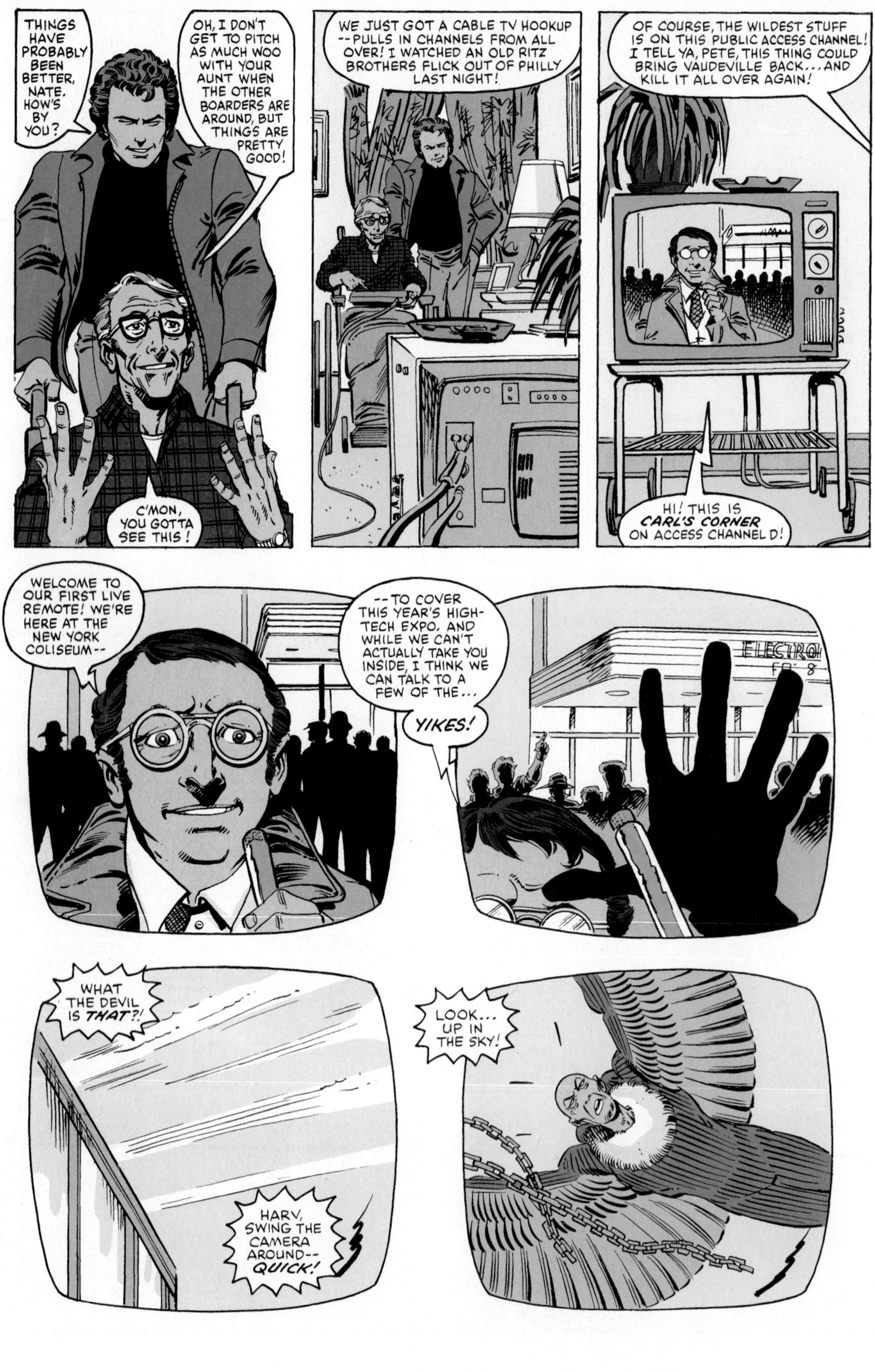
THINGS HAVE PROBABLY BEEN BETTER, NATE. HOW'S BY YOU?
OH, I DON'T GET TO PITCH AS MUCH WOO WITH YOUR AUNT WHEN THE OTHER BOARDERS ARE AROUND, BUT THINGS ARE PRETTY GOOD!
C'MON, YOU GOTTA SEE THIS!
WE JUST GOT A CABLE TV HOOKUP --PULLS IN CHANNELS FROM ALL OVER! I WATCHED AN OLD RITZ BROTHERS FLICK OUT OF PHILLY LAST NIGHT!
OF COURSE, THE WILDEST STUFF IS ON THIS PUBLIC ACCESS CHANNEL! I TELL YA, PETE, THIS THING COULD BRING VAUDEVILLE BACK... AND KILL IT ALL OVER AGAIN!
HI! THIS IS CARL'S CORNER ON ACCESS CHANNEL D!
WELCOME TO OUR FIRST LIVE REMOTE! WE'RE HERE AT THE NEW YORK COLISEUM--
--TO COVER THIS YEAR'S HIGH-TECH EXPO. AND WHILE WE CAN'T ACTUALLY TAKE YOU INSIDE, I THINK WE CAN TALK TO A FEW OF THE...
YIKES!
WHAT THE DEVIL IS THAT?!
HARV, SWING THE CAMERA AROUND-- QUICK!
LOOK... UP IN THE SKY!

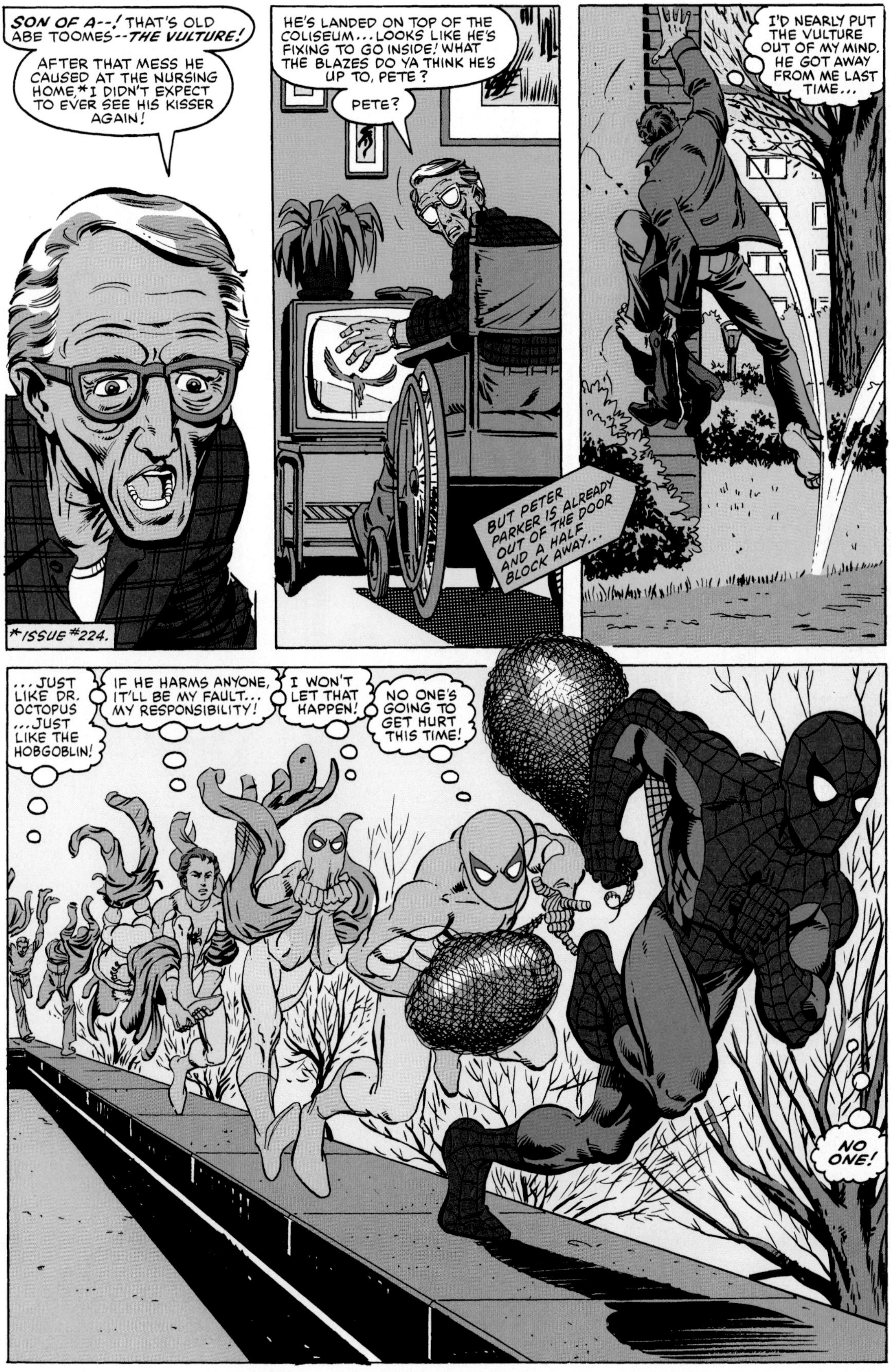
SON OF A--! THAT'S OLD ABE TOOMES--THE VULTURE!
AFTER THAT MESS HE CAUSED AT THE NURSING HOME,* I DIDN'T EXPECT TO EVER SEE HIS KISSER AGAIN!
*ISSUE #224.
HE'S LANDED ON TOP OF THE COLISEUM... LOOKS LIKE HE'S FIXING TO GO INSIDE! WHAT THE BLAZES DO YA THINK HE'S UP TO, PETE?
PETE?
I'D NEARLY PUT THE VULTURE OUT OF MY MIND. HE GOT AWAY FROM ME LAST TIME...
BUT PETER PARKER IS ALREADY OUT OF THE DOOR AND A HALF BLOCK AWAY...
...JUST LIKE DR. OCTOPUS ...JUST LIKE THE HOBGOBLIN!
IF HE HARMS ANYONE, IT'LL BE MY FAULT... MY RESPONSIBILITY!
I WON'T LET THAT HAPPEN!
NO ONE'S GOING TO GET HURT THIS TIME!
NO ONE!

COLUMBUS CIRCLE IS ALREADY JAMMED WITH EMERGENCY VEHICLES, AS SPIDER-MAN STASHES HIS WEBBED-UP STREET CLOTHES ON A NEARBY ROOFTOP AND DROPS IN...

HE'S CHAIN-LOCKED ALL THE EXITS! I WANT MARKSMEN DEPLOYED THERE, THERE, AND...

SPIDER-MAN?!?

SORRY TO CRASH YOUR PARTY, LT. KEATING--

--BUT I FIGURED THAT YOU AND YOUR BOYS COULD USE A HAND.

WELL, YOU FIGURED WRONG! THIS IS A POLICE MATTER! YOU STICK YOUR NOSE IN AND, SO HELP ME--!

KEATING, FOR ONCE IN YOUR LIFE, SHUT UP AND LISTEN!

THE VULTURE CAN BE A VERY DESPERATE CHARACTER! IF YOUR BOYS STORM THE COLISEUM, HE MIGHT JUST DECIDE TO KILL EVERYONE WHO'S IN THERE! YOU KNOW THAT!

BUT IF I GO IN, CHANCES ARE THAT HE'LL COME AFTER ME. HE HATES MY GUTS... EVEN MORE THAN YOU DO!

SO WHAT'S IT GONNA BE...YOUR WAY, OR MINE?

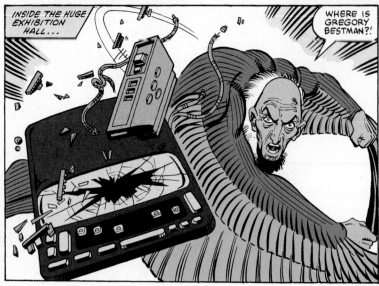

INSIDE THE HUGE EXHIBITION HALL...

WHERE IS GREGORY BESTMAN?!

120

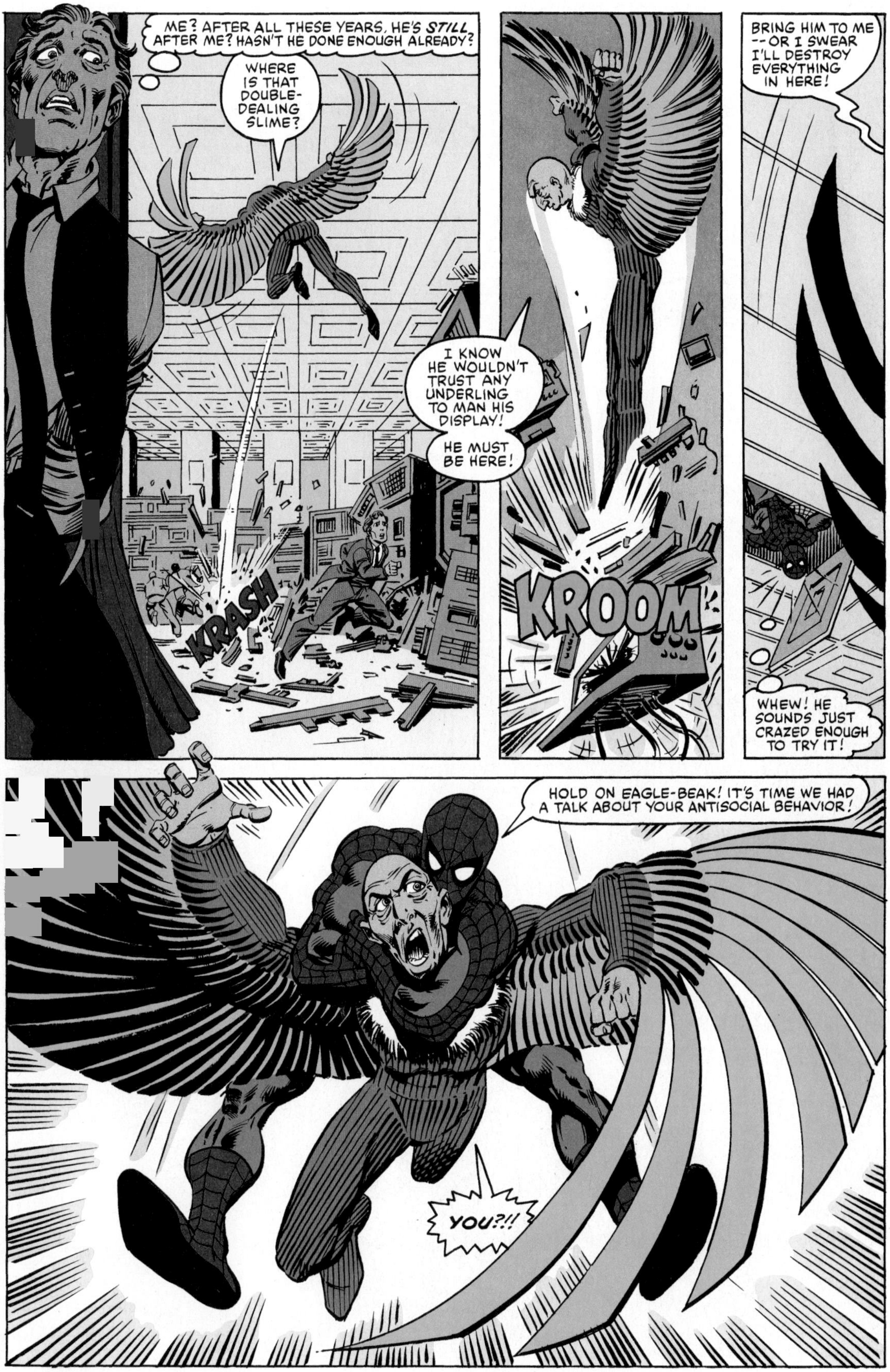
ME? AFTER ALL THESE YEARS, HE'S STILL AFTER ME? HASN'T HE DONE ENOUGH ALREADY?
WHERE IS THAT DOUBLE-DEALING SLIME?
KRASH
I KNOW HE WOULDN'T TRUST ANY UNDERLING TO MAN HIS DISPLAY!
HE MUST BE HERE!
KROOM
BRING HIM TO ME --OR I SWEAR I'LL DESTROY EVERYTHING IN HERE!
WHEW! HE SOUNDS JUST CRAZED ENOUGH TO TRY IT!
HOLD ON EAGLE-BEAK! IT'S TIME WE HAD A TALK ABOUT YOUR ANTISOCIAL BEHAVIOR!
YOU?!!

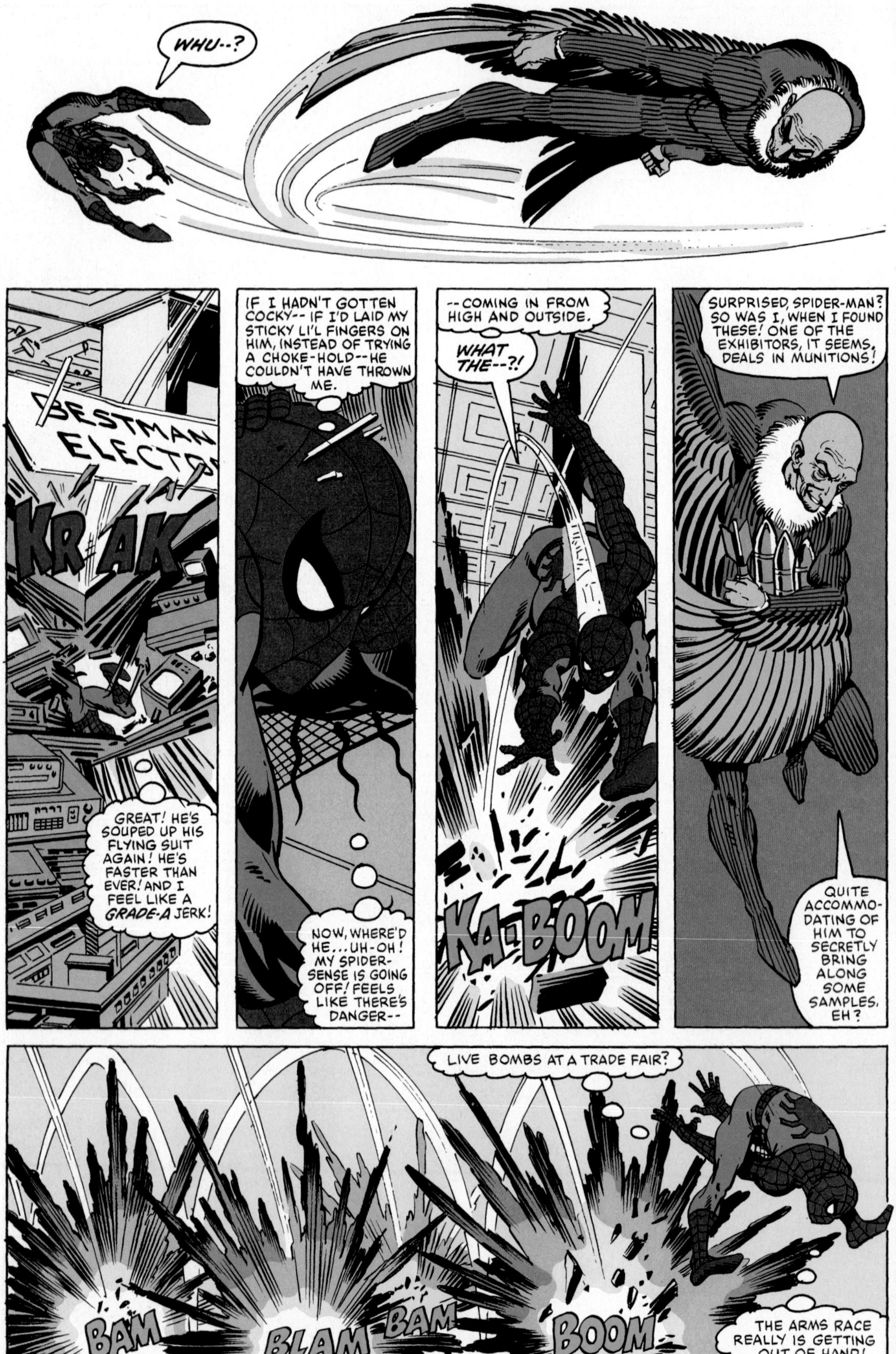
WHU--?
BESTMAN ELECTR
KRAK
GREAT! HE'S SOUPED UP HIS FLYING SUIT AGAIN! HE'S FASTER THAN EVER! AND I FEEL LIKE A GRADE-A JERK!
IF I HADN'T GOTTEN COCKY-- IF I'D LAID MY STICKY LI'L FINGERS ON HIM, INSTEAD OF TRYING A CHOKE-HOLD--HE COULDN'T HAVE THROWN ME.
NOW, WHERE'D HE... UH-OH! MY SPIDER-SENSE IS GOING OFF! FEELS LIKE THERE'S DANGER--
--COMING IN FROM HIGH AND OUTSIDE.
WHAT THE--?!
KA-BOOM
SURPRISED, SPIDER-MAN? SO WAS I, WHEN I FOUND THESE! ONE OF THE EXHIBITORS, IT SEEMS, DEALS IN MUNITIONS!
QUITE ACCOMMODATING OF HIM TO SECRETLY BRING ALONG SOME SAMPLES, EH?
LIVE BOMBS AT A TRADE FAIR?
BAM
BLAM
BAM
BOOM
THE ARMS RACE REALLY IS GETTING OUT OF HAND!

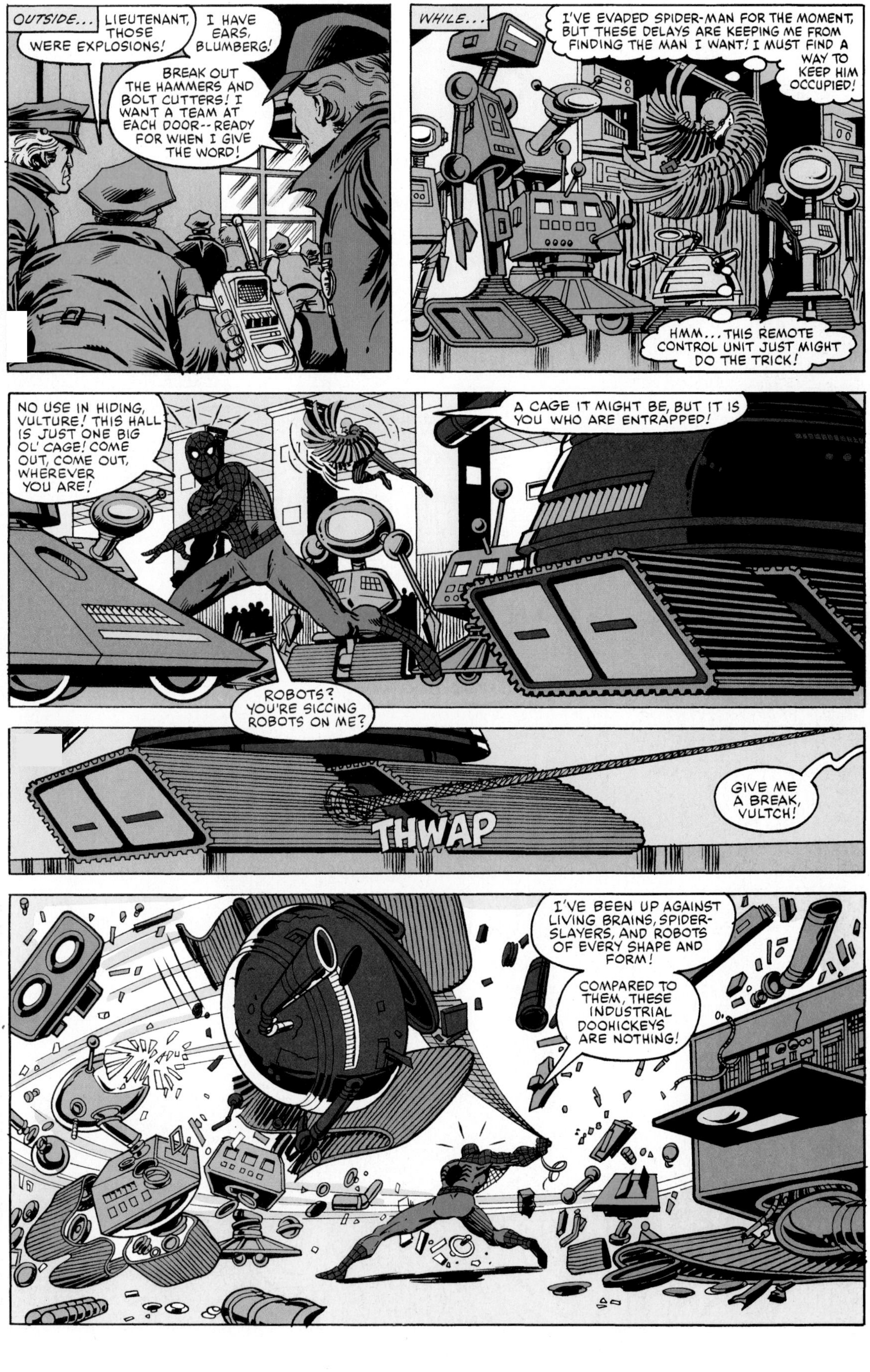

OUTSIDE...
LIEUTENANT, THOSE WERE EXPLOSIONS!
I HAVE EARS, BLUMBERG!
BREAK OUT THE HAMMERS AND BOLT CUTTERS! I WANT A TEAM AT EACH DOOR--READY FOR WHEN I GIVE THE WORD!
WHILE...
I'VE EVADED SPIDER-MAN FOR THE MOMENT, BUT THESE DELAYS ARE KEEPING ME FROM FINDING THE MAN I WANT! I MUST FIND A WAY TO KEEP HIM OCCUPIED!
HMM... THIS REMOTE CONTROL UNIT JUST MIGHT DO THE TRICK!
NO USE IN HIDING, VULTURE! THIS HALL IS JUST ONE BIG OL' CAGE! COME OUT, COME OUT, WHEREVER YOU ARE!
A CAGE IT MIGHT BE, BUT IT IS YOU WHO ARE ENTRAPPED!
ROBOTS? YOU'RE SICCING ROBOTS ON ME?
THWAP
GIVE ME A BREAK, VULTCH!
I'VE BEEN UP AGAINST LIVING BRAINS, SPIDER-SLAYERS, AND ROBOTS OF EVERY SHAPE AND FORM!
COMPARED TO THEM, THESE INDUSTRIAL DOOHICKEYS ARE NOTHING!

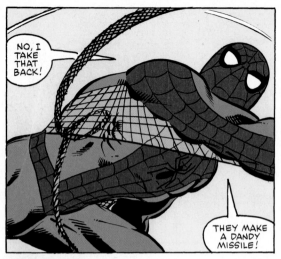

NO, I TAKE THAT BACK!

THEY MAKE A DANDY MISSILE!

BLAST HIS HIDE!

KRANG

HE'S STILL PRACTICALLY UNBEATABLE! I'LL NEVER FIND BESTMAN NOW! I MUST RETREAT TO PLAN ANEW!

AH! THIS POWER SYSTEM SHOULD GIVE ME THE DIVERSION I NEED FOR MY GET-AWAY!

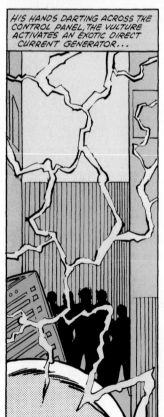

HIS HANDS DARTING ACROSS THE CONTROL PANEL, THE VULTURE ACTIVATES AN EXOTIC DIRECT CURRENT GENERATOR...

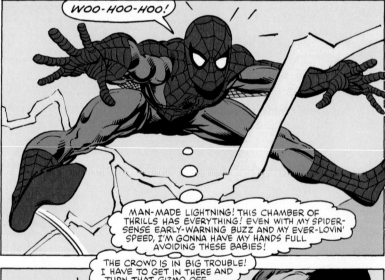

WOO-HOO-HOO!

MAN-MADE LIGHTNING! THIS CHAMBER OF THRILLS HAS EVERYTHING! EVEN WITH MY SPIDER-SENSE EARLY-WARNING BUZZ AND MY EVER-LOVIN' SPEED, I'M GONNA HAVE MY HANDS FULL AVOIDING THESE BABIES!

THE CROWD IS IN BIG TROUBLE! I HAVE TO GET IN THERE AND TURN THAT GIZMO OFF SOMEHOW!

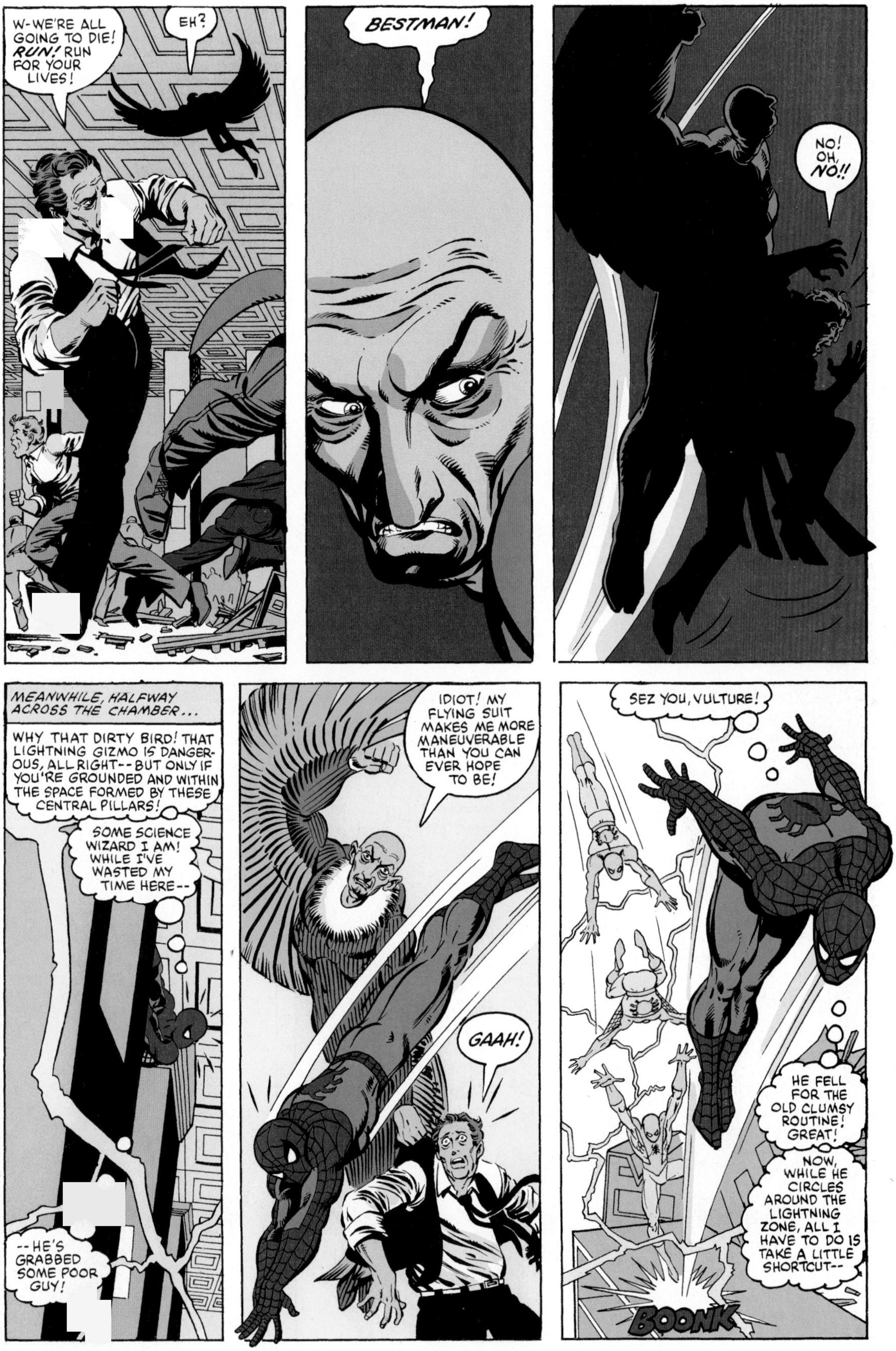
W-WE'RE ALL GOING TO DIE! RUN! RUN FOR YOUR LIVES!
EH?
BESTMAN!
NO! OH, NO!!
MEANWHILE, HALFWAY ACROSS THE CHAMBER...
WHY THAT DIRTY BIRD! THAT LIGHTNING GIZMO IS DANGEROUS, ALL RIGHT--BUT ONLY IF YOU'RE GROUNDED AND WITHIN THE SPACE FORMED BY THESE CENTRAL PILLARS!
SOME SCIENCE WIZARD I AM! WHILE I'VE WASTED MY TIME HERE--
--HE'S GRABBED SOME POOR GUY!
IDIOT! MY FLYING SUIT MAKES ME MORE MANEUVERABLE THAN YOU CAN EVER HOPE TO BE!
GAAH!
SEZ YOU, VULTURE!
HE FELL FOR THE OLD CLUMSY ROUTINE! GREAT!
NOW, WHILE HE CIRCLES AROUND THE LIGHTNING ZONE, ALL I HAVE TO DO IS TAKE A LITTLE SHORTCUT--
BOONK

--FLIP UP INTO THE SHADOWS, AND WAIT FOR HIM BY THE MAIN VENT!

THIS IS WHERE HE CAME IN, AND IT'S THE ONLY WAY OUT FOR HIM AND HIS CAPTIVE!

BUT, AT THE VERY INSTANT SPIDER-MAN MAKES CONTACT WITH THE CEILING, THE LIGHTNING MACHINE CUTS LOOSE WITH YET ANOTHER RANDOM BOLT!

STREAKING OUT AT JUST UNDER THE SPEED OF LIGHT--

--THE BOLT MAKES CONTACT WITH THE METAL CEILING GRID UPON WHICH SPIDER-MAN FINDS HIMSELF GROUNDED!

YAAAH!

A NORMAL MAN WOULD HAVE BEEN SHOCKED SENSELESS ...OR KILLED.

BUT, AS SPIDER-MAN DROPS, HE STUBBORNLY CLINGS TO CONSCIOUSNESS.

MUST... STOP VULTURE...

TWISTING, TURNING IN MIDAIR, THE GROGGY MASKED MAN MAKES A DESPERATE GRAB...

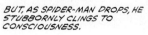

126

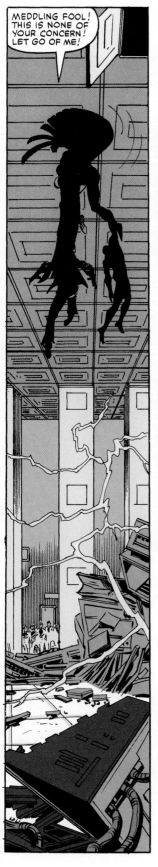

MEDDLING FOOL! THIS IS NONE OF YOUR CONCERN! LET GO OF ME!

YOU HEAR? LET GO!

KRAK

W-WHAT'RE YOU--? NO! NO! DON'T TOUCH ME!!

WHAK WHAK

HEY, DON'T! YOU... STUPID...

...JERK! I'M... TRYING TO HELP!

NO USE...HE'S... HYSTERICALLL

127

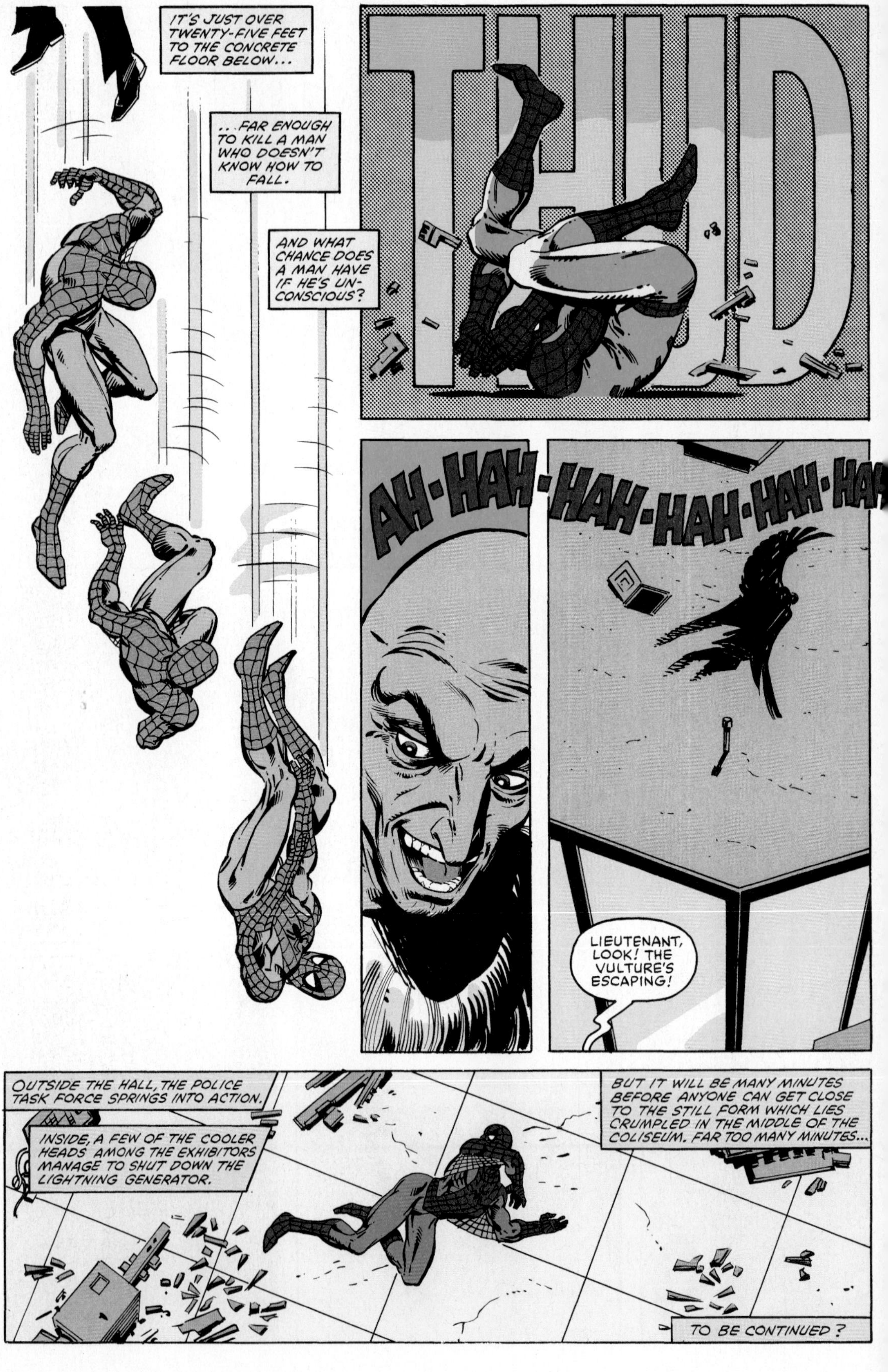
IT'S JUST OVER TWENTY-FIVE FEET TO THE CONCRETE FLOOR BELOW...
...FAR ENOUGH TO KILL A MAN WHO DOESN'T KNOW HOW TO FALL.
AND WHAT CHANCE DOES A MAN HAVE IF HE'S UNCONSCIOUS?
THUD
AH-HAH-HAH-HAH-HAH-HAH
LIEUTENANT, LOOK! THE VULTURE'S ESCAPING!
OUTSIDE THE HALL, THE POLICE TASK FORCE SPRINGS INTO ACTION.
INSIDE, A FEW OF THE COOLER HEADS AMONG THE EXHIBITORS MANAGE TO SHUT DOWN THE LIGHTNING GENERATOR.
BUT IT WILL BE MANY MINUTES BEFORE ANYONE CAN GET CLOSE TO THE STILL FORM WHICH LIES CRUMPLED IN THE MIDDLE OF THE COLISEUM. FAR TOO MANY MINUTES...
TO BE CONTINUED?

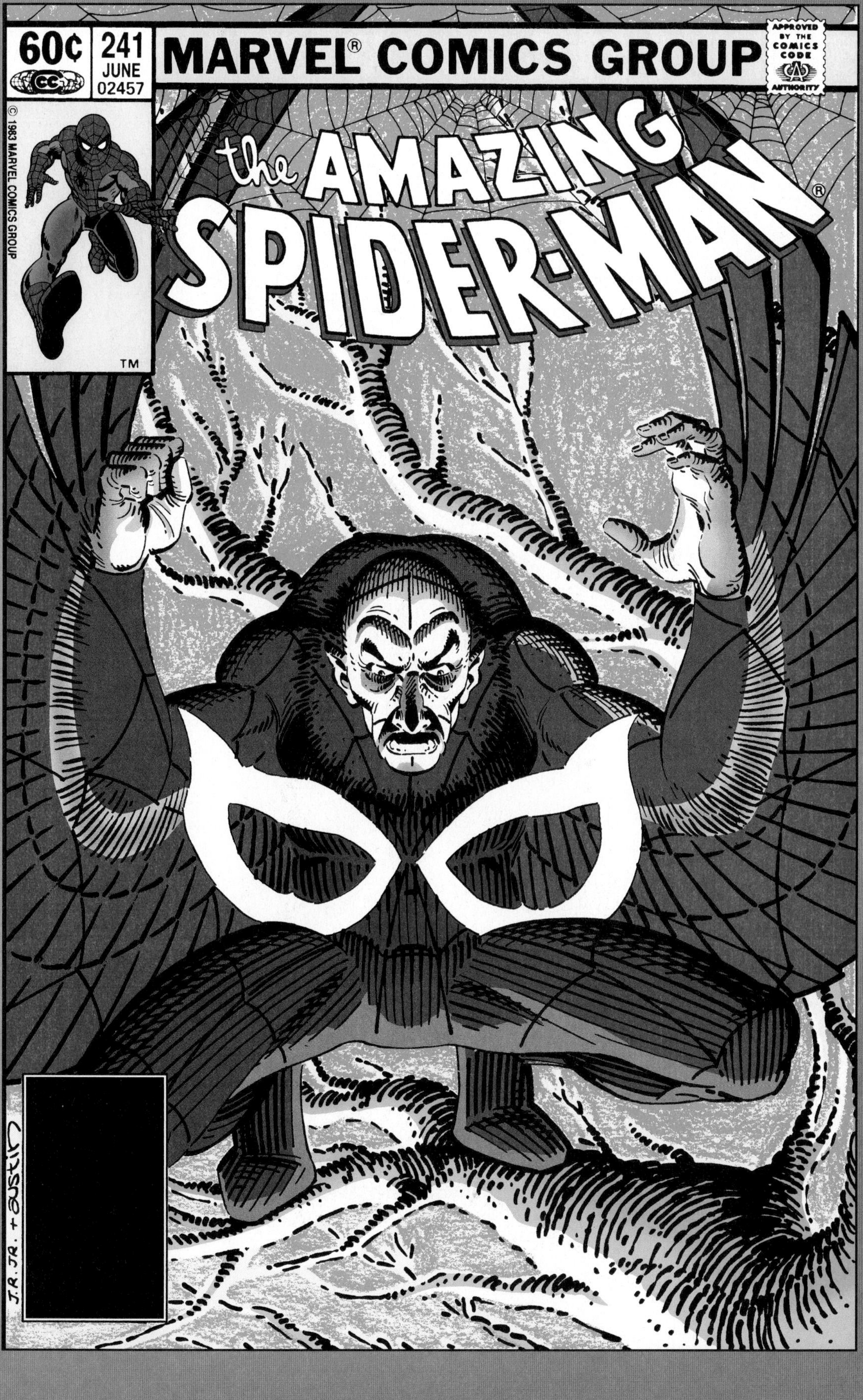
60¢
241
JUNE
02457
MARVEL® COMICS GROUP
APPROVED BY THE COMICS CODE AUTHORITY
© 1983 MARVEL COMICS GROUP
the AMAZING SPIDER-MAN®
TM
J.R. JR. + austin

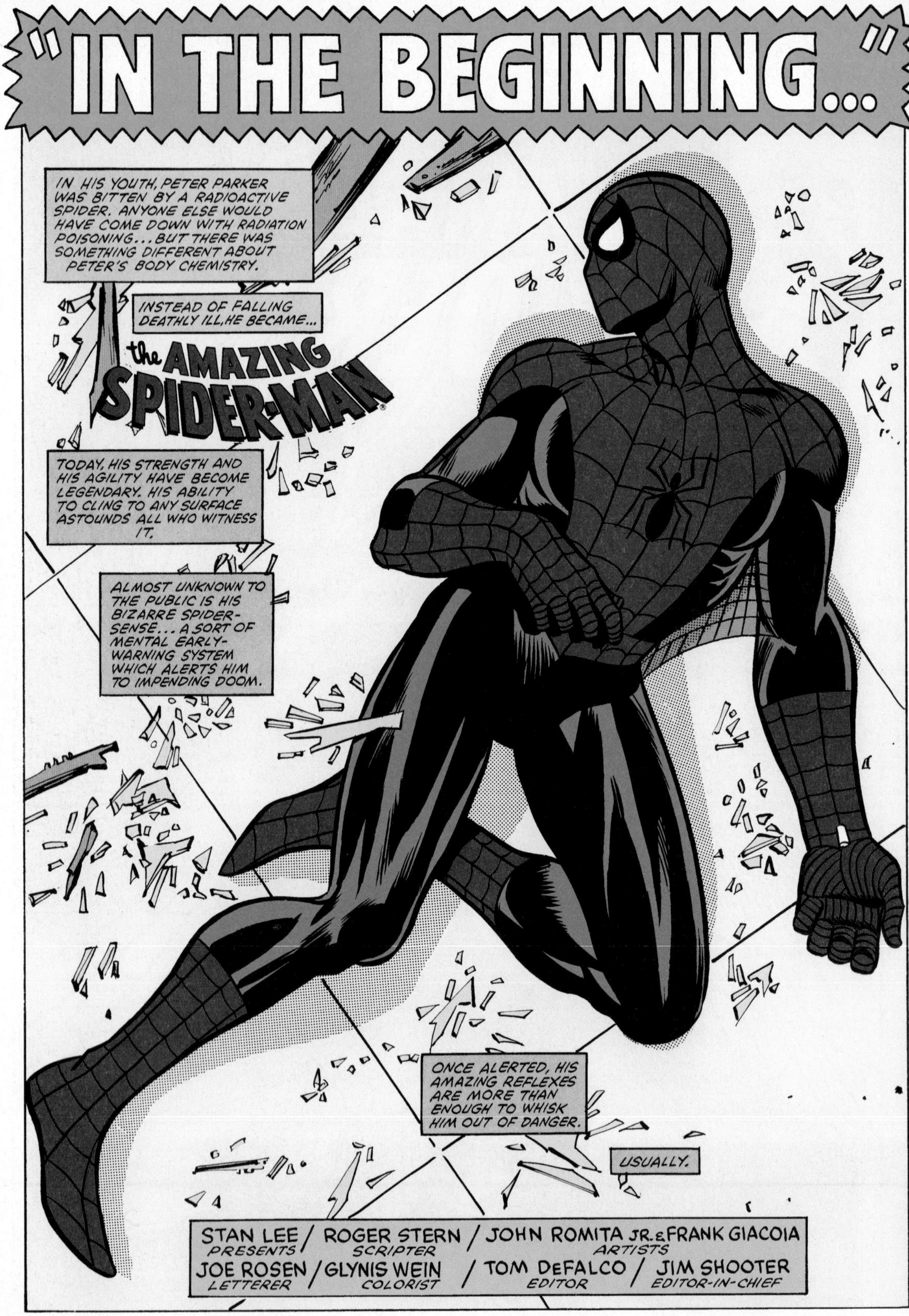
"IN THE BEGINNING..."
IN HIS YOUTH, PETER PARKER WAS BITTEN BY A RADIOACTIVE SPIDER. ANYONE ELSE WOULD HAVE COME DOWN WITH RADIATION POISONING... BUT THERE WAS SOMETHING DIFFERENT ABOUT PETER'S BODY CHEMISTRY.
INSTEAD OF FALLING DEATHLY ILL, HE BECAME...
the AMAZING SPIDER-MAN®
TODAY, HIS STRENGTH AND HIS AGILITY HAVE BECOME LEGENDARY. HIS ABILITY TO CLING TO ANY SURFACE ASTOUNDS ALL WHO WITNESS IT.
ALMOST UNKNOWN TO THE PUBLIC IS HIS BIZARRE SPIDER-SENSE... A SORT OF MENTAL EARLY-WARNING SYSTEM WHICH ALERTS HIM TO IMPENDING DOOM.
ONCE ALERTED, HIS AMAZING REFLEXES ARE MORE THAN ENOUGH TO WHISK HIM OUT OF DANGER.
USUALLY.
STAN LEE / PRESENTS / ROGER STERN / SCRIPTER / JOHN ROMITA JR. & FRANK GIACOIA / ARTISTS
JOE ROSEN / LETTERER / GLYNIS WEIN / COLORIST / TOM DeFALCO / EDITOR / JIM SHOOTER / EDITOR-IN-CHIEF

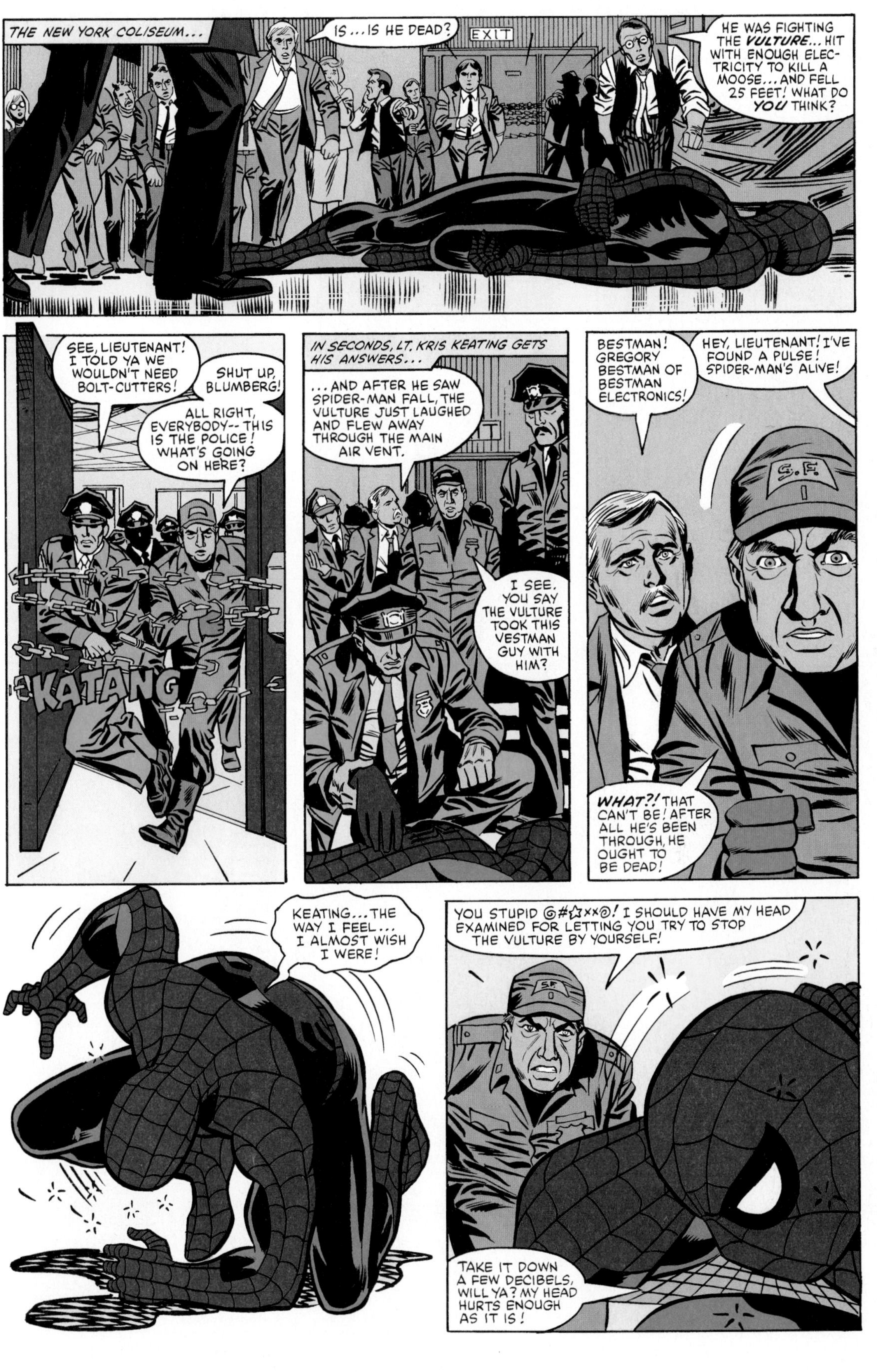
THE NEW YORK COLISEUM...
IS... IS HE DEAD?
EXIT
HE WAS FIGHTING THE VULTURE... HIT WITH ENOUGH ELECTRICITY TO KILL A MOOSE... AND FELL 25 FEET! WHAT DO YOU THINK?
SEE, LIEUTENANT! I TOLD YA WE WOULDN'T NEED BOLT-CUTTERS!
SHUT UP, BLUMBERG!
ALL RIGHT, EVERYBODY-- THIS IS THE POLICE! WHAT'S GOING ON HERE?
KATANG
IN SECONDS, LT. KRIS KEATING GETS HIS ANSWERS...
...AND AFTER HE SAW SPIDER-MAN FALL, THE VULTURE JUST LAUGHED AND FLEW AWAY THROUGH THE MAIN AIR VENT.
I SEE. YOU SAY THE VULTURE TOOK THIS VESTMAN GUY WITH HIM?
BESTMAN! GREGORY BESTMAN OF BESTMAN ELECTRONICS!
HEY, LIEUTENANT! I'VE FOUND A PULSE! SPIDER-MAN'S ALIVE!
S.F.
WHAT?! THAT CAN'T BE! AFTER ALL HE'S BEEN THROUGH, HE OUGHT TO BE DEAD!
KEATING... THE WAY I FEEL... I ALMOST WISH I WERE!
YOU STUPID @#☆××@! I SHOULD HAVE MY HEAD EXAMINED FOR LETTING YOU TRY TO STOP THE VULTURE BY YOURSELF!
S.F.
TAKE IT DOWN A FEW DECIBELS, WILL YA? MY HEAD HURTS ENOUGH AS IT IS!

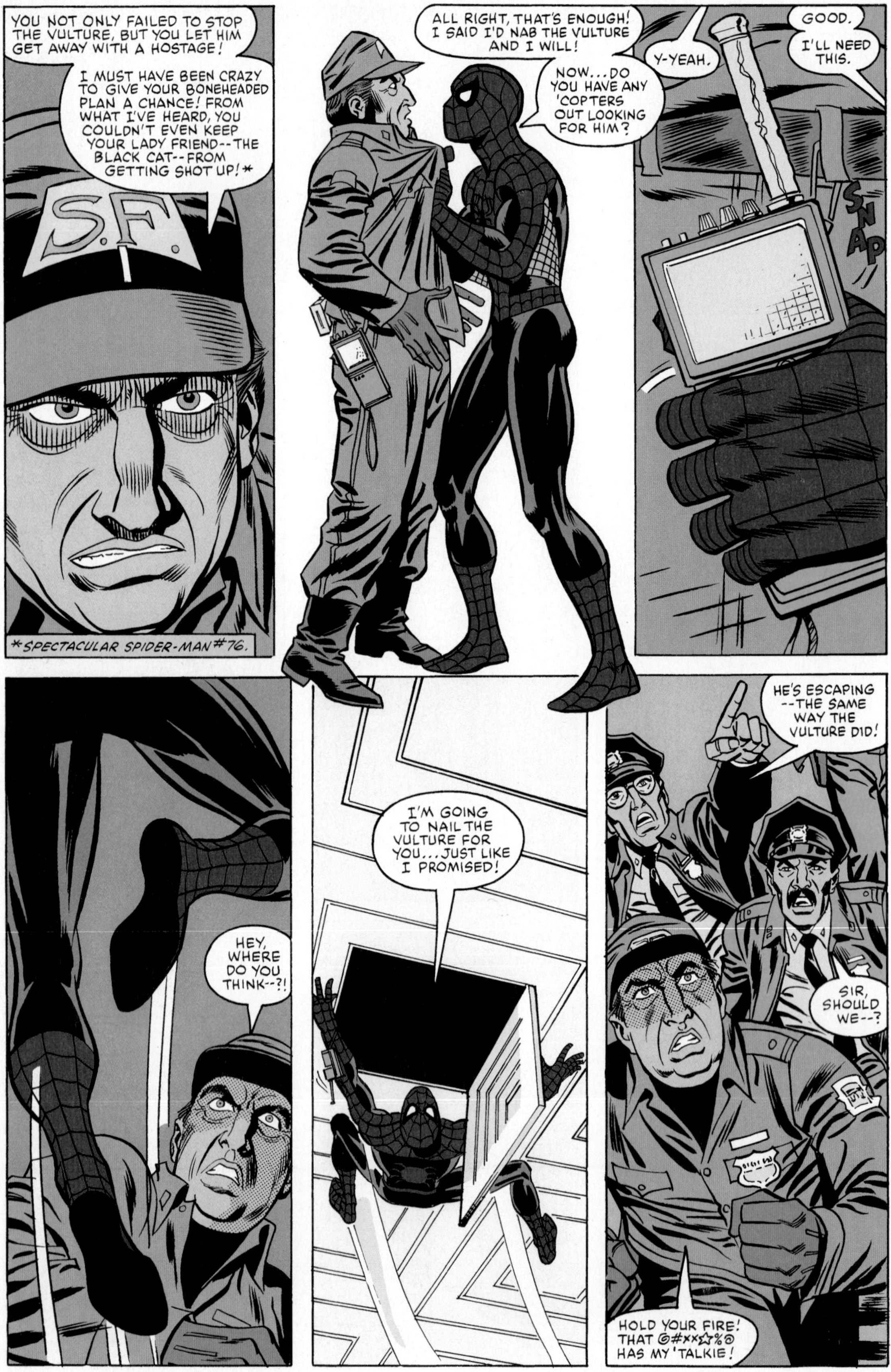

YOU NOT ONLY FAILED TO STOP THE VULTURE, BUT YOU LET HIM GET AWAY WITH A HOSTAGE!
I MUST HAVE BEEN CRAZY TO GIVE YOUR BONEHEADED PLAN A CHANCE! FROM WHAT I'VE HEARD, YOU COULDN'T EVEN KEEP YOUR LADY FRIEND--THE BLACK CAT--FROM GETTING SHOT UP!*
S.F.
*SPECTACULAR SPIDER-MAN #76.
ALL RIGHT, THAT'S ENOUGH! I SAID I'D NAB THE VULTURE AND I WILL!
NOW...DO YOU HAVE ANY 'COPTERS OUT LOOKING FOR HIM?
Y-YEAH.
GOOD.
I'LL NEED THIS.
SNAP
HEY, WHERE DO YOU THINK--?!
I'M GOING TO NAIL THE VULTURE FOR YOU...JUST LIKE I PROMISED!
HE'S ESCAPING --THE SAME WAY THE VULTURE DID!
SIR, SHOULD WE--?
HOLD YOUR FIRE! THAT @#xx☆%@ HAS MY 'TALKIE!

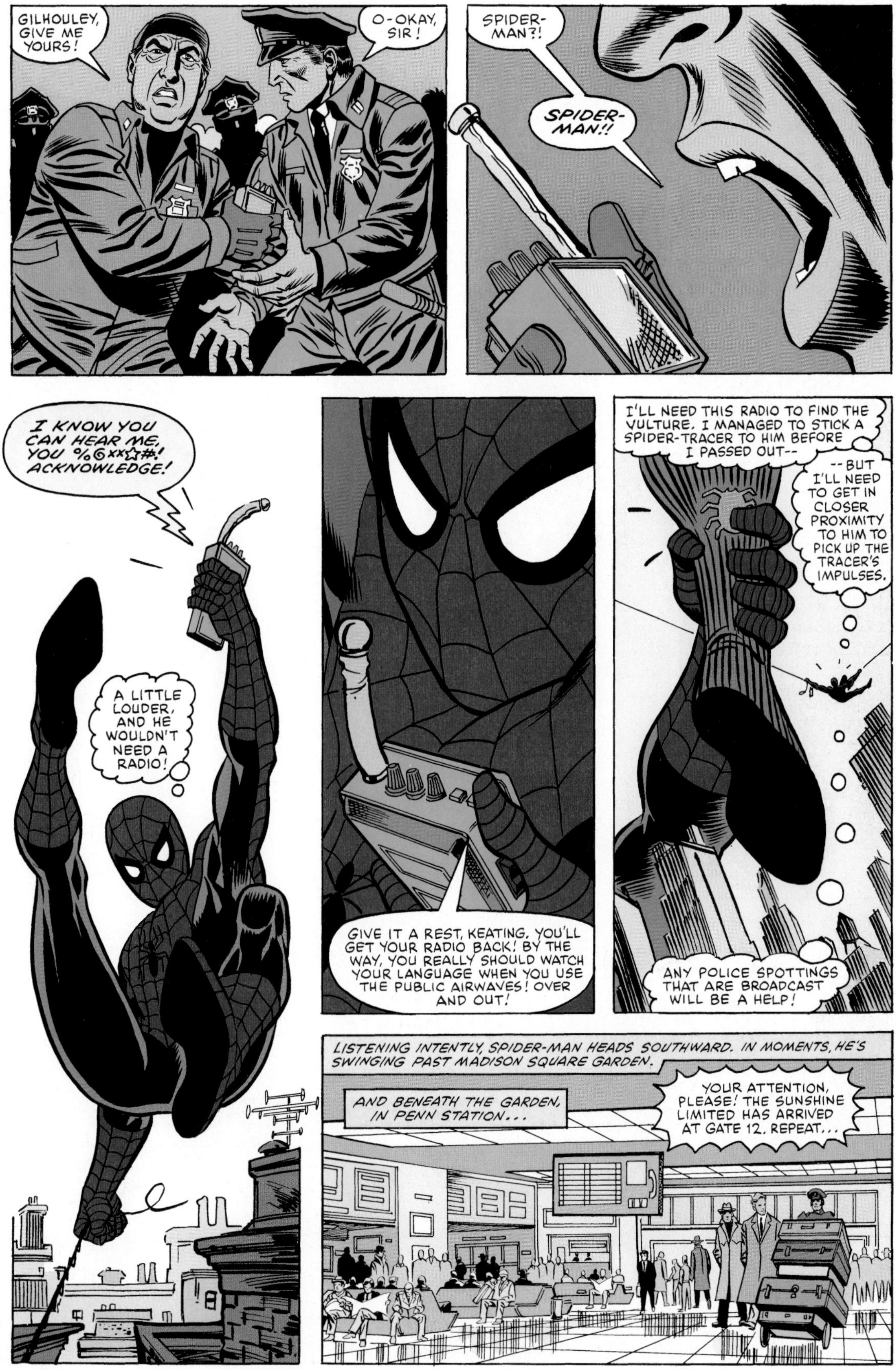
GILHOULEY, GIVE ME YOURS!
O-OKAY, SIR!
SPIDER-MAN?!
SPIDER-MAN!!
I KNOW YOU CAN HEAR ME, YOU %@xx☆#! ACKNOWLEDGE!
A LITTLE LOUDER, AND HE WOULDN'T NEED A RADIO!
GIVE IT A REST, KEATING. YOU'LL GET YOUR RADIO BACK! BY THE WAY, YOU REALLY SHOULD WATCH YOUR LANGUAGE WHEN YOU USE THE PUBLIC AIRWAVES! OVER AND OUT!
I'LL NEED THIS RADIO TO FIND THE VULTURE. I MANAGED TO STICK A SPIDER-TRACER TO HIM BEFORE I PASSED OUT--
--BUT I'LL NEED TO GET IN CLOSER PROXIMITY TO HIM TO PICK UP THE TRACER'S IMPULSES.
ANY POLICE SPOTTINGS THAT ARE BROADCAST WILL BE A HELP!
LISTENING INTENTLY, SPIDER-MAN HEADS SOUTHWARD. IN MOMENTS, HE'S SWINGING PAST MADISON SQUARE GARDEN.
AND BENEATH THE GARDEN, IN PENN STATION...
YOUR ATTENTION, PLEASE! THE SUNSHINE LIMITED HAS ARRIVED AT GATE 12. REPEAT...

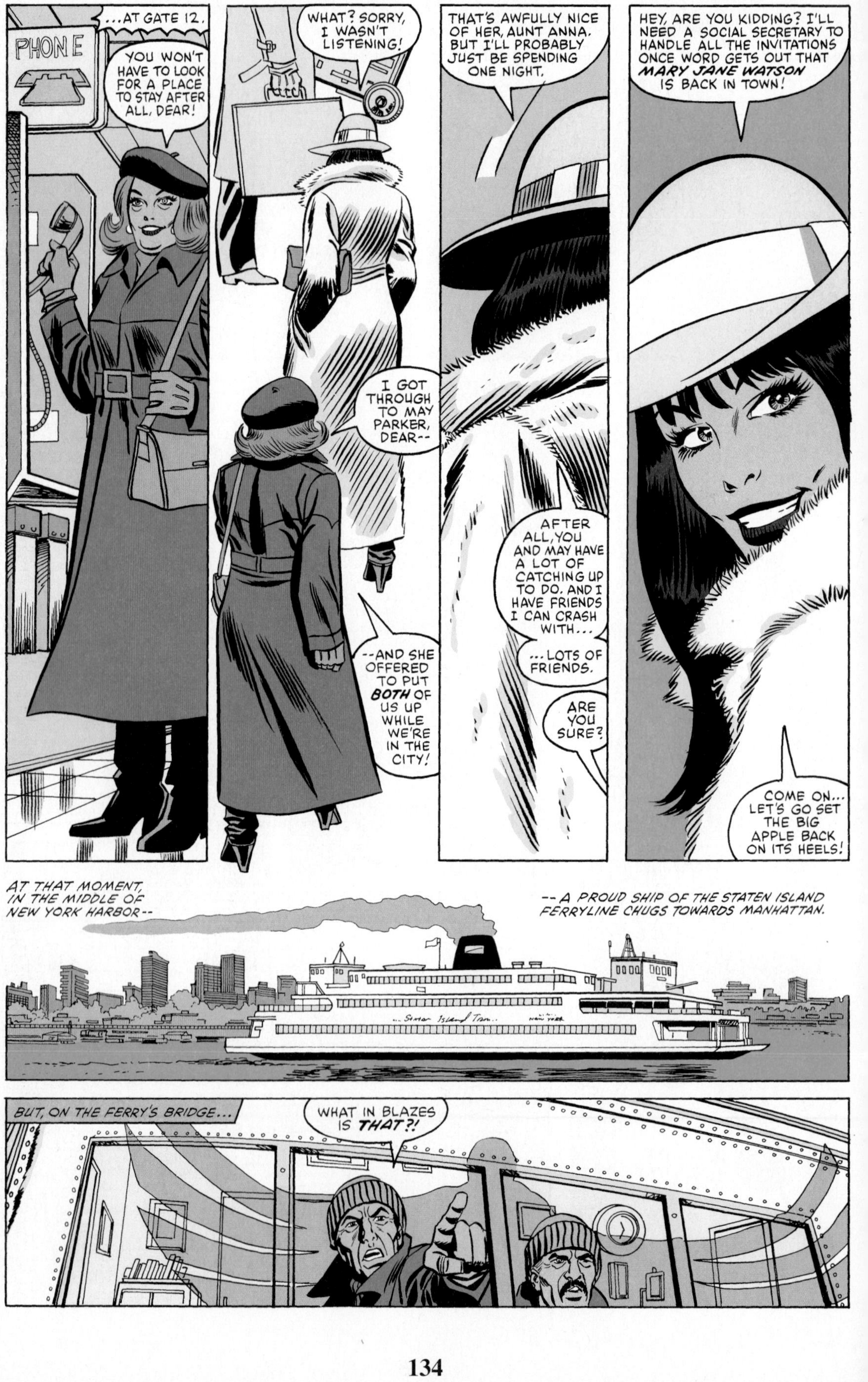
...AT GATE 12.
YOU WON'T HAVE TO LOOK FOR A PLACE TO STAY AFTER ALL, DEAR!
PHONE
WHAT? SORRY, I WASN'T LISTENING!
I GOT THROUGH TO MAY PARKER, DEAR--
--AND SHE OFFERED TO PUT BOTH OF US UP WHILE WE'RE IN THE CITY!
THAT'S AWFULLY NICE OF HER, AUNT ANNA. BUT I'LL PROBABLY JUST BE SPENDING ONE NIGHT.
AFTER ALL, YOU AND MAY HAVE A LOT OF CATCHING UP TO DO. AND I HAVE FRIENDS I CAN CRASH WITH...
...LOTS OF FRIENDS.
ARE YOU SURE?
HEY, ARE YOU KIDDING? I'LL NEED A SOCIAL SECRETARY TO HANDLE ALL THE INVITATIONS ONCE WORD GETS OUT THAT MARY JANE WATSON IS BACK IN TOWN!
COME ON... LET'S GO SET THE BIG APPLE BACK ON ITS HEELS!
AT THAT MOMENT, IN THE MIDDLE OF NEW YORK HARBOR--
--A PROUD SHIP OF THE STATEN ISLAND FERRYLINE CHUGS TOWARDS MANHATTAN.
BUT, ON THE FERRY'S BRIDGE...
WHAT IN BLAZES IS THAT?!

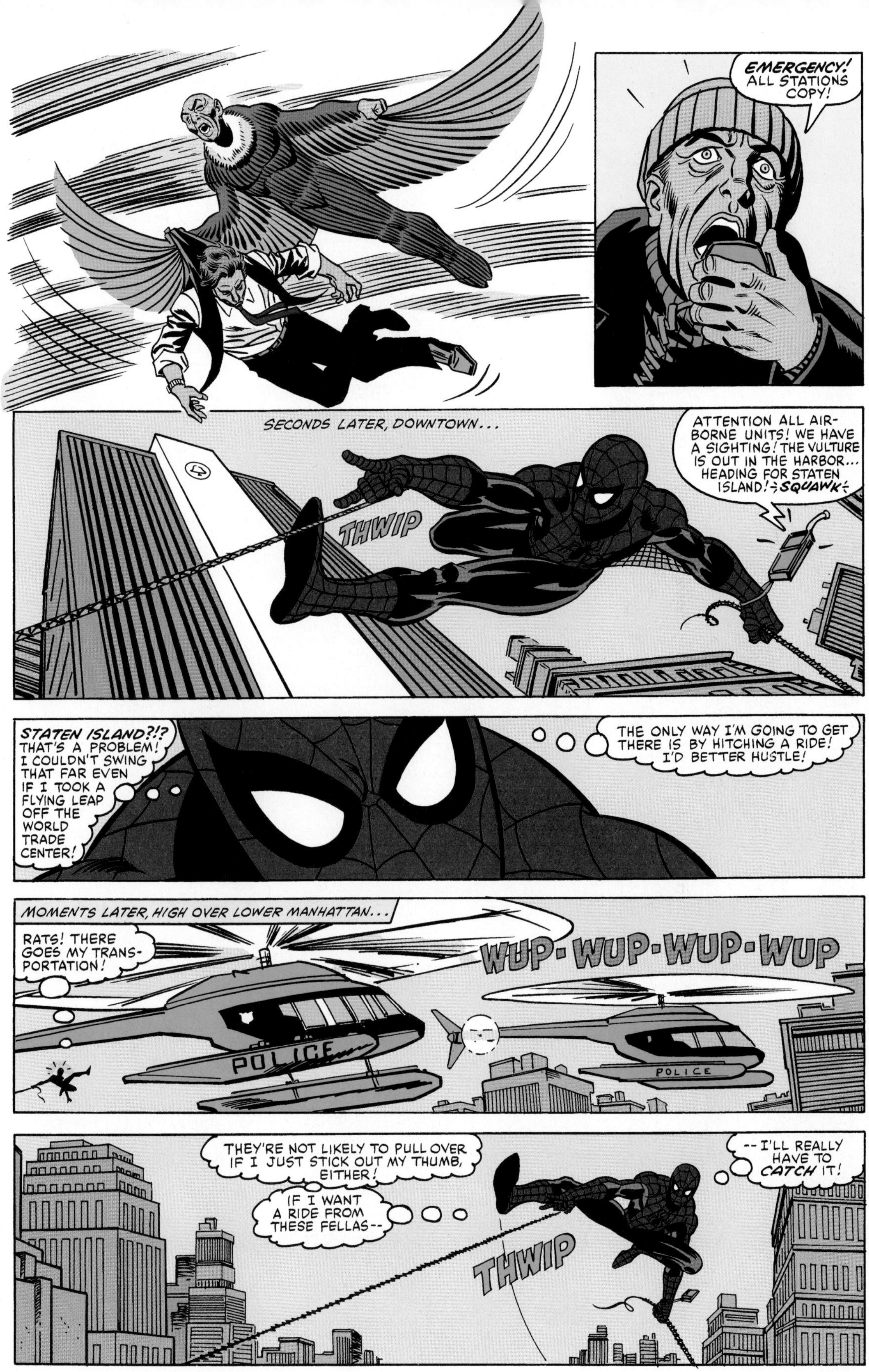
EMERGENCY! ALL STATIONS COPY!
SECONDS LATER, DOWNTOWN...
ATTENTION ALL AIRBORNE UNITS! WE HAVE A SIGHTING! THE VULTURE IS OUT IN THE HARBOR... HEADING FOR STATEN ISLAND! ⚡SQUAWK⚡
THWIP
STATEN ISLAND?!? THAT'S A PROBLEM! I COULDN'T SWING THAT FAR EVEN IF I TOOK A FLYING LEAP OFF THE WORLD TRADE CENTER!
THE ONLY WAY I'M GOING TO GET THERE IS BY HITCHING A RIDE! I'D BETTER HUSTLE!
MOMENTS LATER, HIGH OVER LOWER MANHATTAN...
RATS! THERE GOES MY TRANSPORTATION!
WUP-WUP-WUP-WUP
POLICE
POLICE
THEY'RE NOT LIKELY TO PULL OVER IF I JUST STICK OUT MY THUMB, EITHER!
IF I WANT A RIDE FROM THESE FELLAS--
--I'LL REALLY HAVE TO CATCH IT!
THWIP

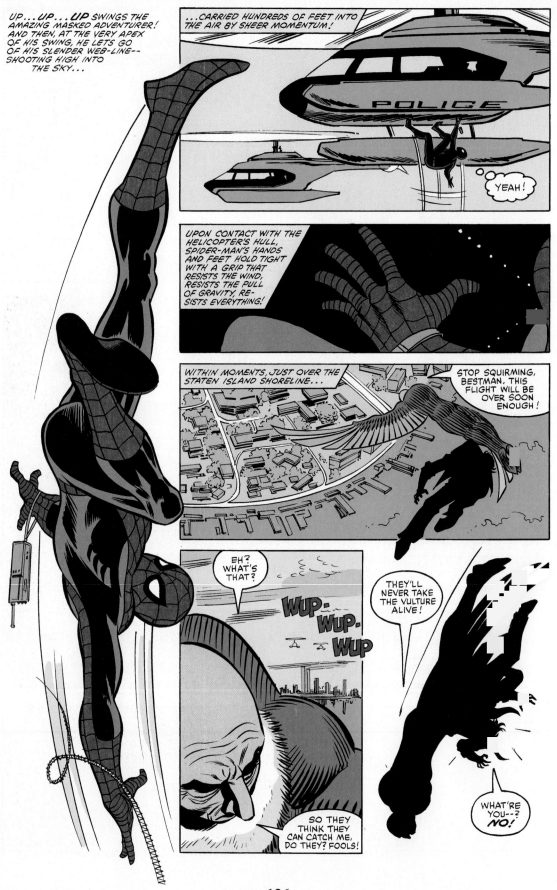

UP...*UP*...*UP* SWINGS THE AMAZING MASKED ADVENTURER! AND THEN, AT THE VERY APEX OF HIS SWING, HE LETS GO OF HIS SLENDER WEB-LINE-- SHOOTING HIGH INTO THE SKY...

...CARRIED HUNDREDS OF FEET INTO THE AIR BY SHEER MOMENTUM!

POLICE

YEAH!

UPON CONTACT WITH THE HELICOPTER'S HULL, SPIDER-MAN'S HANDS AND FEET HOLD TIGHT WITH A GRIP THAT RESISTS THE WIND, RESISTS THE PULL OF GRAVITY, RE- SISTS EVERYTHING!

WITHIN MOMENTS, JUST OVER THE STATEN ISLAND SHORELINE...

STOP SQUIRMING, BESTMAN, THIS FLIGHT WILL BE OVER SOON ENOUGH!

EH? WHAT'S THAT?

WUP- WUP- WUP

THEY'LL NEVER TAKE THE VULTURE ALIVE!

SO THEY THINK THEY CAN CATCH ME, DO THEY? FOOLS!

WHAT'RE YOU--? *NO!*

136

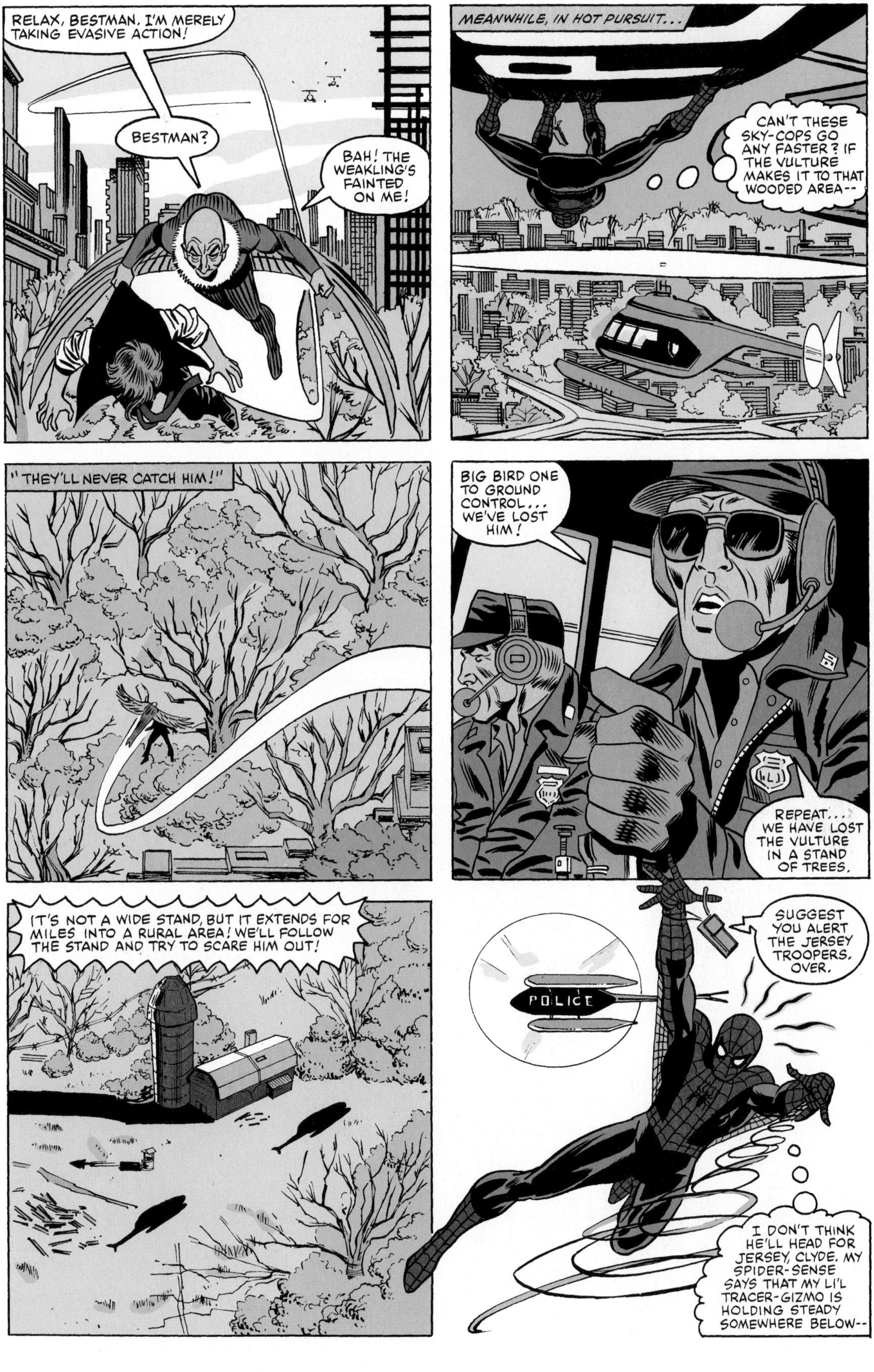
RELAX, BESTMAN. I'M MERELY TAKING EVASIVE ACTION!
BESTMAN?
BAH! THE WEAKLING'S FAINTED ON ME!
MEANWHILE, IN HOT PURSUIT...
CAN'T THESE SKY-COPS GO ANY FASTER? IF THE VULTURE MAKES IT TO THAT WOODED AREA--
"THEY'LL NEVER CATCH HIM!"
BIG BIRD ONE TO GROUND CONTROL... WE'VE LOST HIM!
REPEAT... WE HAVE LOST THE VULTURE IN A STAND OF TREES.
IT'S NOT A WIDE STAND, BUT IT EXTENDS FOR MILES INTO A RURAL AREA! WE'LL FOLLOW THE STAND AND TRY TO SCARE HIM OUT!
POLICE
SUGGEST YOU ALERT THE JERSEY TROOPERS. OVER.
I DON'T THINK HE'LL HEAD FOR JERSEY, CLYDE. MY SPIDER-SENSE SAYS THAT MY LI'L TRACER-GIZMO IS HOLDING STEADY SOMEWHERE BELOW--

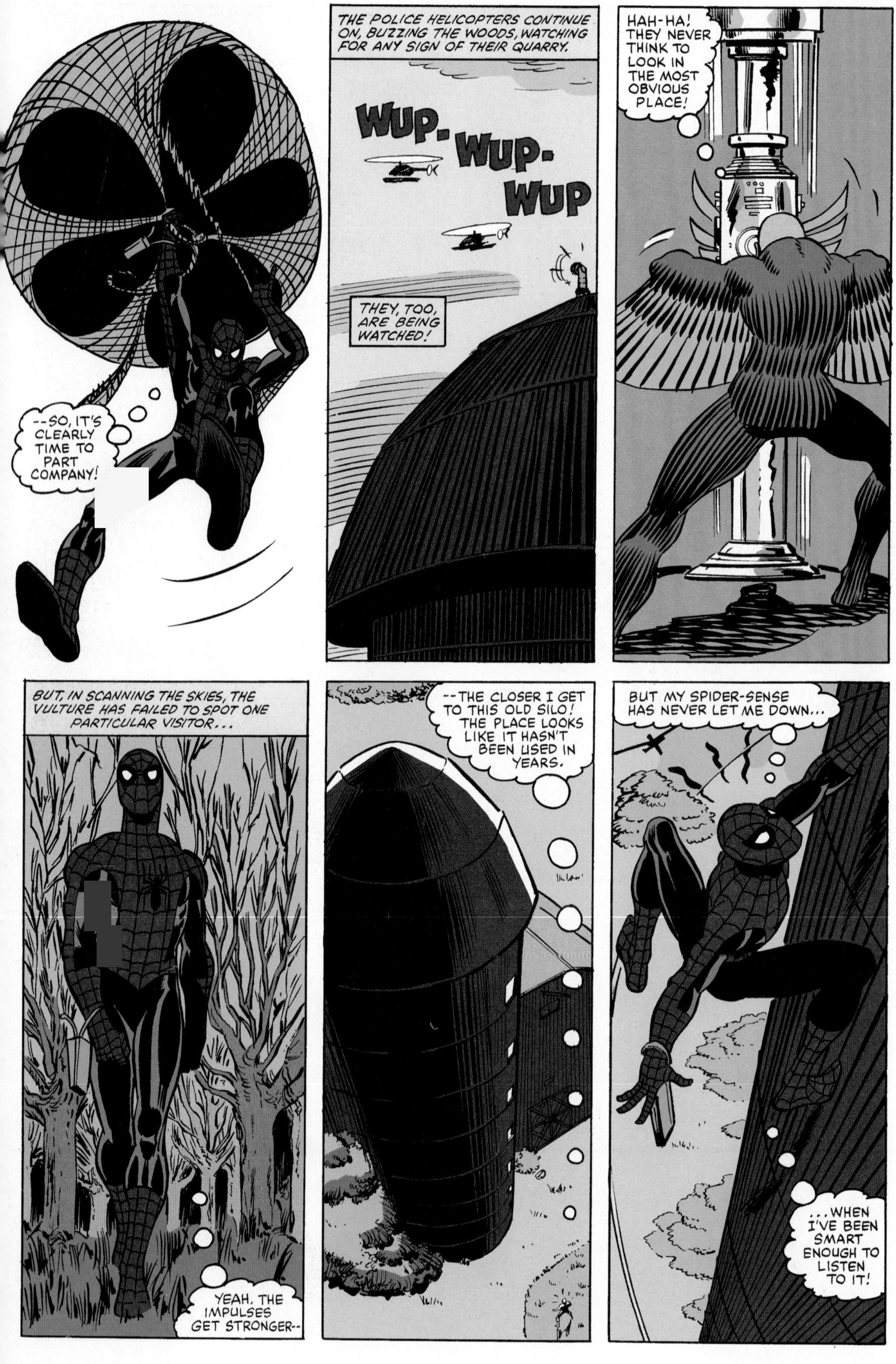
--SO, IT'S CLEARLY TIME TO PART COMPANY!
THE POLICE HELICOPTERS CONTINUE ON, BUZZING THE WOODS, WATCHING FOR ANY SIGN OF THEIR QUARRY.
WUP-WUP-WUP
THEY, TOO, ARE BEING WATCHED!
HAH-HA! THEY NEVER THINK TO LOOK IN THE MOST OBVIOUS PLACE!
BUT, IN SCANNING THE SKIES, THE VULTURE HAS FAILED TO SPOT ONE PARTICULAR VISITOR...
YEAH. THE IMPULSES GET STRONGER--
--THE CLOSER I GET TO THIS OLD SILO! THE PLACE LOOKS LIKE IT HASN'T BEEN USED IN YEARS.
BUT MY SPIDER-SENSE HAS NEVER LET ME DOWN...
...WHEN I'VE BEEN SMART ENOUGH TO LISTEN TO IT!

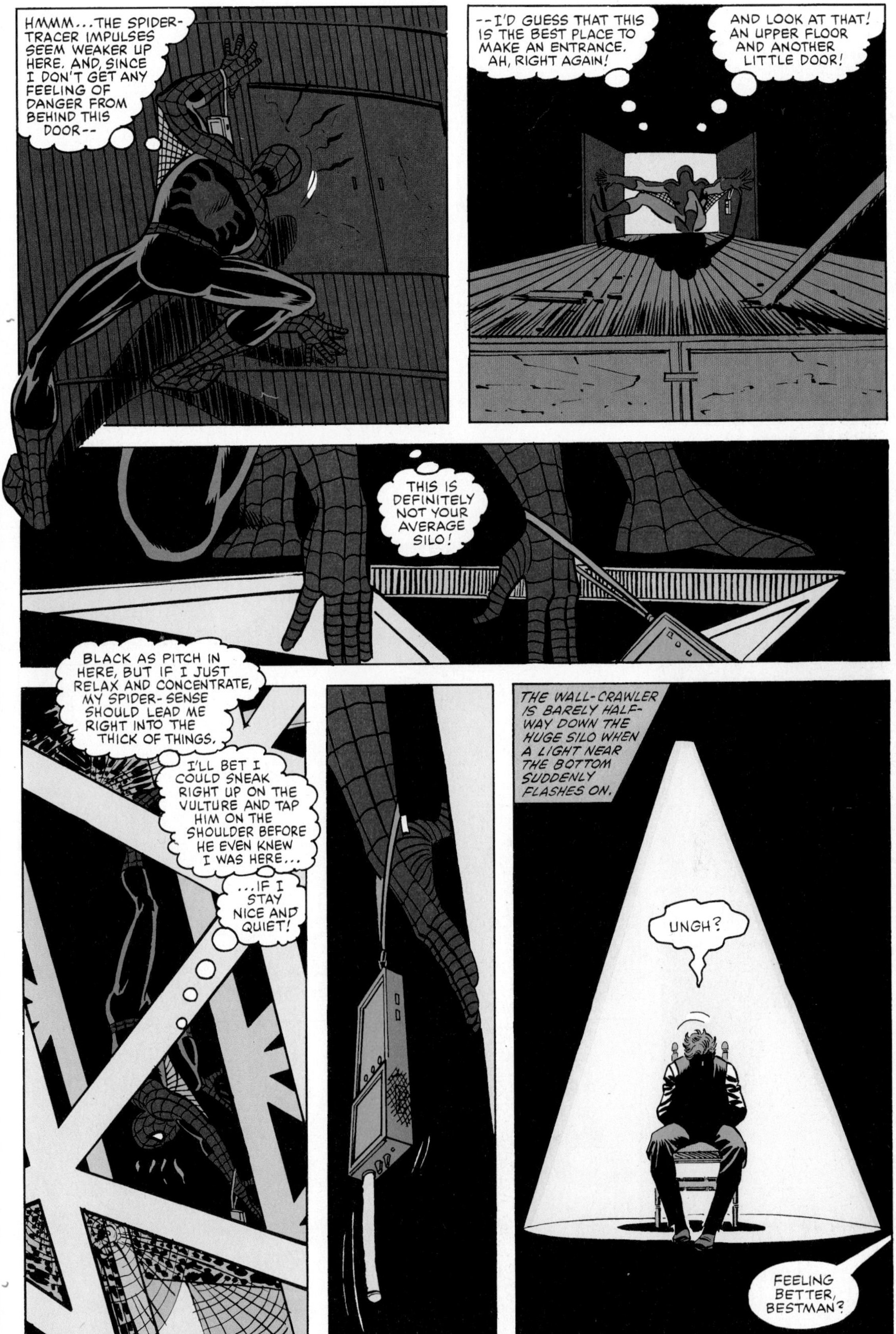
HMMM...THE SPIDER-TRACER IMPULSES SEEM WEAKER UP HERE. AND, SINCE I DON'T GET ANY FEELING OF DANGER FROM BEHIND THIS DOOR--
--I'D GUESS THAT THIS IS THE BEST PLACE TO MAKE AN ENTRANCE. AH, RIGHT AGAIN!
AND LOOK AT THAT! AN UPPER FLOOR AND ANOTHER LITTLE DOOR!
THIS IS DEFINITELY NOT YOUR AVERAGE SILO!
BLACK AS PITCH IN HERE, BUT IF I JUST RELAX AND CONCENTRATE, MY SPIDER-SENSE SHOULD LEAD ME RIGHT INTO THE THICK OF THINGS.
I'LL BET I COULD SNEAK RIGHT UP ON THE VULTURE AND TAP HIM ON THE SHOULDER BEFORE HE EVEN KNEW I WAS HERE...
...IF I STAY NICE AND QUIET!
THE WALL-CRAWLER IS BARELY HALF-WAY DOWN THE HUGE SILO WHEN A LIGHT NEAR THE BOTTOM SUDDENLY FLASHES ON.
UNGH?
FEELING BETTER, BESTMAN?

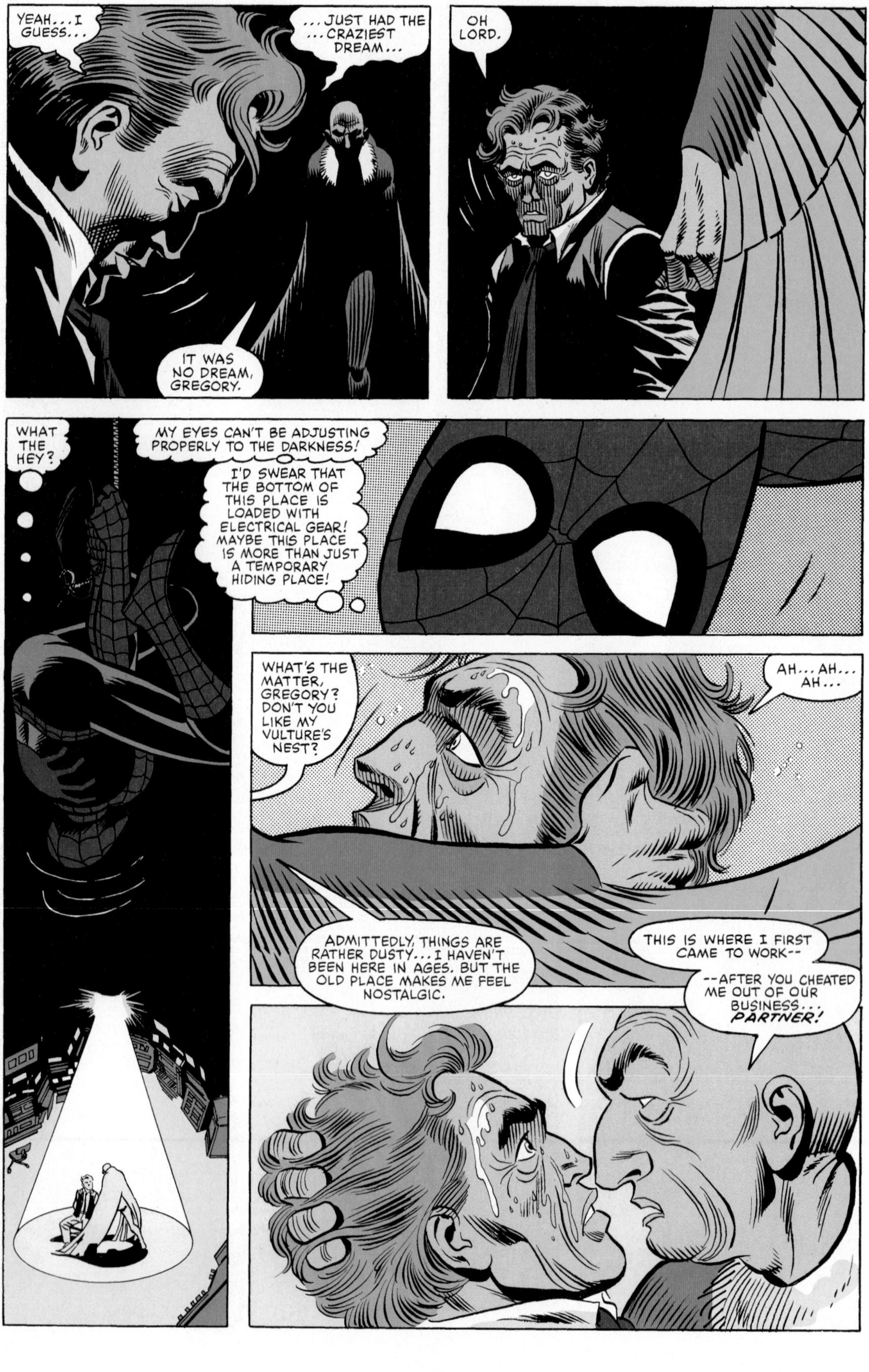
YEAH...I GUESS...
...JUST HAD THE ...CRAZIEST DREAM...
IT WAS NO DREAM, GREGORY.
OH LORD.
WHAT THE HEY?
MY EYES CAN'T BE ADJUSTING PROPERLY TO THE DARKNESS!
I'D SWEAR THAT THE BOTTOM OF THIS PLACE IS LOADED WITH ELECTRICAL GEAR! MAYBE THIS PLACE IS MORE THAN JUST A TEMPORARY HIDING PLACE!
WHAT'S THE MATTER, GREGORY? DON'T YOU LIKE MY VULTURE'S NEST?
AH...AH... AH...
ADMITTEDLY, THINGS ARE RATHER DUSTY...I HAVEN'T BEEN HERE IN AGES. BUT THE OLD PLACE MAKES ME FEEL NOSTALGIC.
THIS IS WHERE I FIRST CAME TO WORK--
--AFTER YOU CHEATED ME OUT OF OUR BUSINESS... PARTNER!

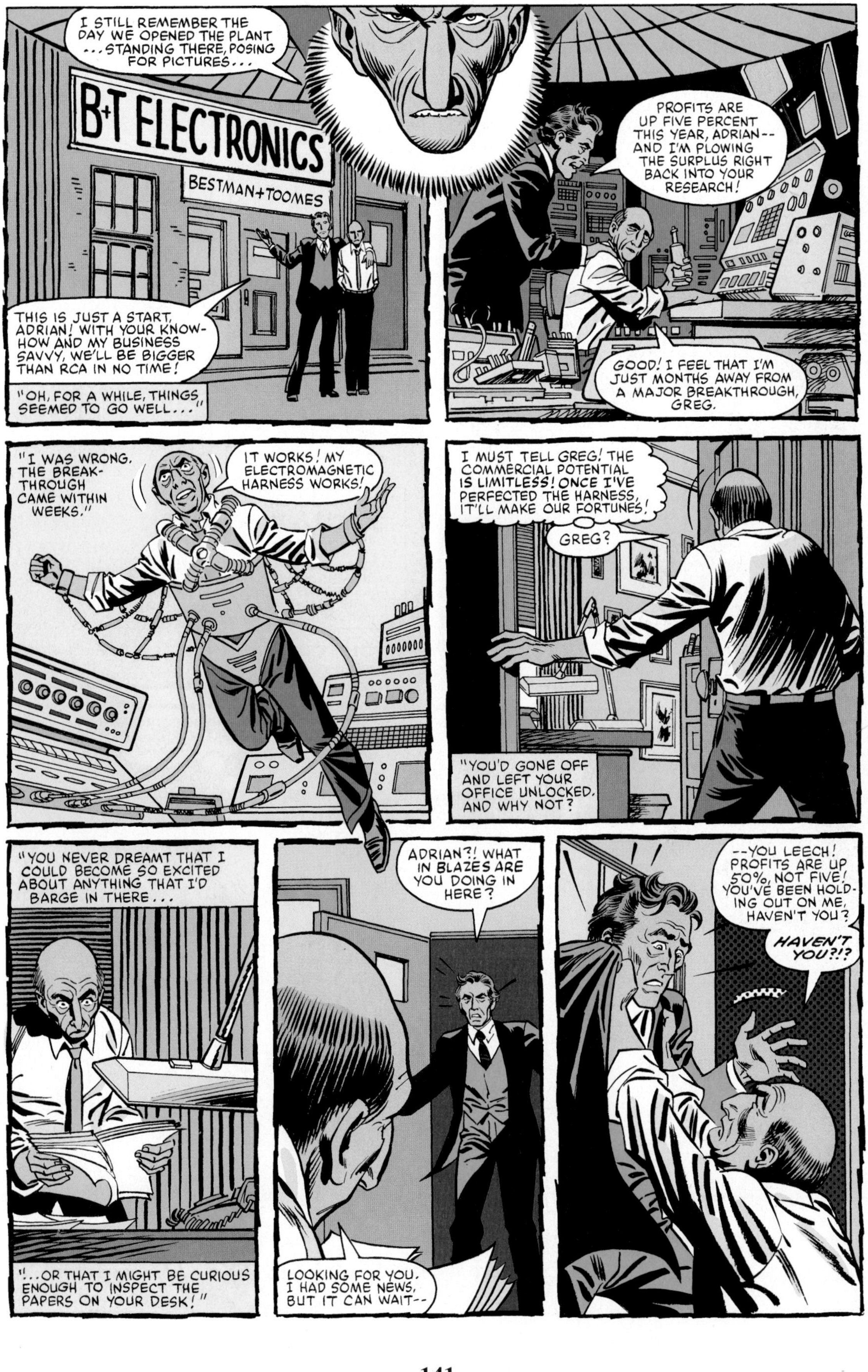
I STILL REMEMBER THE DAY WE OPENED THE PLANT . . . STANDING THERE, POSING FOR PICTURES . . .
B+T ELECTRONICS
BESTMAN+TOOMES
THIS IS JUST A START, ADRIAN! WITH YOUR KNOW-HOW AND MY BUSINESS SAVVY, WE'LL BE BIGGER THAN RCA IN NO TIME!
"OH, FOR A WHILE, THINGS SEEMED TO GO WELL . . ."
PROFITS ARE UP FIVE PERCENT THIS YEAR, ADRIAN-- AND I'M PLOWING THE SURPLUS RIGHT BACK INTO YOUR RESEARCH!
GOOD! I FEEL THAT I'M JUST MONTHS AWAY FROM A MAJOR BREAKTHROUGH, GREG.
"I WAS WRONG. THE BREAK-THROUGH CAME WITHIN WEEKS."
IT WORKS! MY ELECTROMAGNETIC HARNESS WORKS!
I MUST TELL GREG! THE COMMERCIAL POTENTIAL IS LIMITLESS! ONCE I'VE PERFECTED THE HARNESS, IT'LL MAKE OUR FORTUNES!
GREG?
"YOU'D GONE OFF AND LEFT YOUR OFFICE UNLOCKED. AND WHY NOT?
"YOU NEVER DREAMT THAT I COULD BECOME SO EXCITED ABOUT ANYTHING THAT I'D BARGE IN THERE . . .
". . . OR THAT I MIGHT BE CURIOUS ENOUGH TO INSPECT THE PAPERS ON YOUR DESK!"
ADRIAN?! WHAT IN BLAZES ARE YOU DOING IN HERE?
LOOKING FOR YOU. I HAD SOME NEWS, BUT IT CAN WAIT--
--YOU LEECH! PROFITS ARE UP 50%, NOT FIVE! YOU'VE BEEN HOLDING OUT ON ME, HAVEN'T YOU?
HAVEN'T YOU?!?

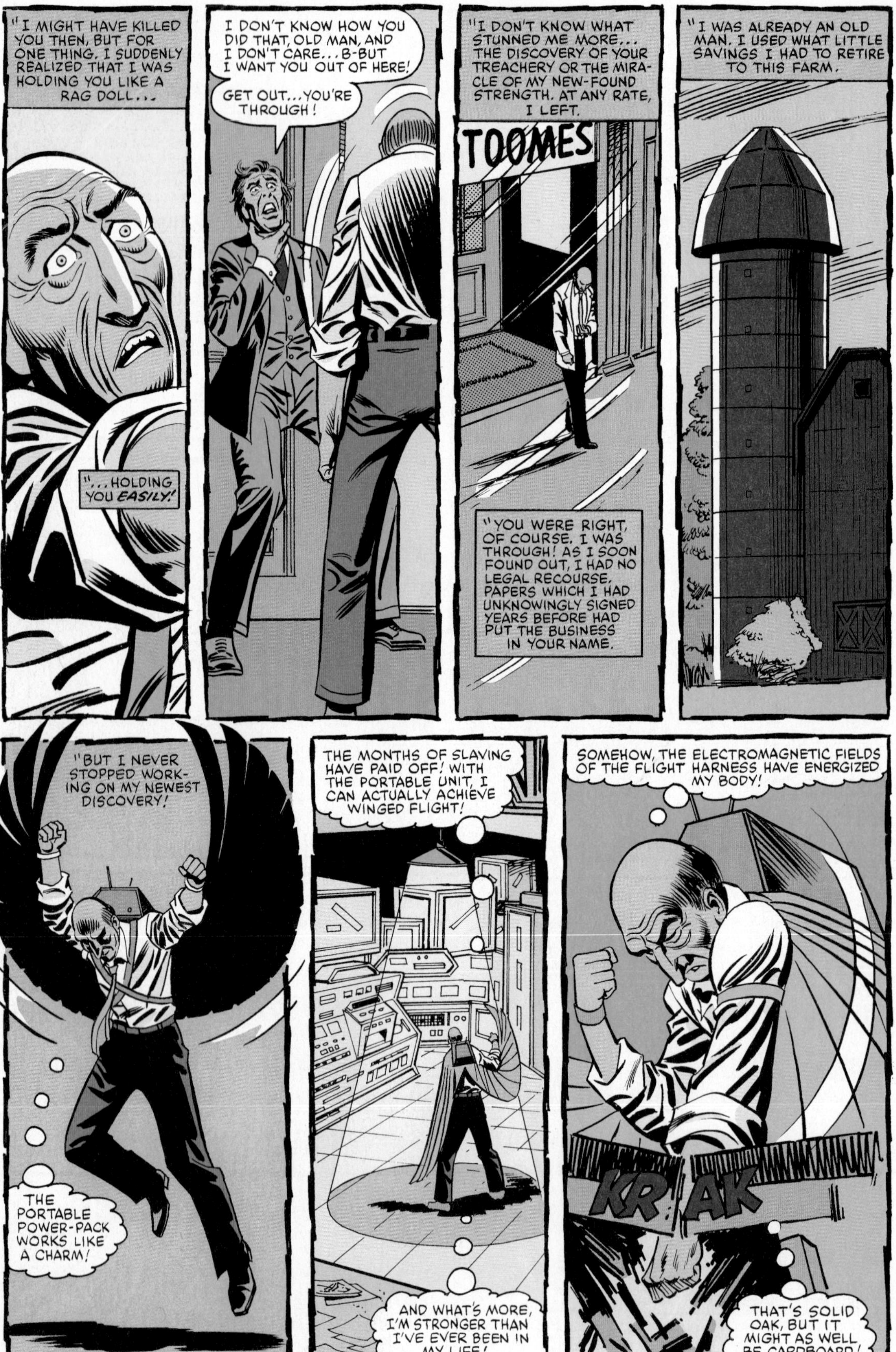
"I MIGHT HAVE KILLED YOU THEN, BUT FOR ONE THING. I SUDDENLY REALIZED THAT I WAS HOLDING YOU LIKE A RAG DOLL...
"...HOLDING YOU EASILY!
I DON'T KNOW HOW YOU DID THAT, OLD MAN, AND I DON'T CARE... B-BUT I WANT YOU OUT OF HERE!
GET OUT...YOU'RE THROUGH!
"I DON'T KNOW WHAT STUNNED ME MORE... THE DISCOVERY OF YOUR TREACHERY OR THE MIRACLE OF MY NEW-FOUND STRENGTH. AT ANY RATE, I LEFT.
TOOMES
"YOU WERE RIGHT, OF COURSE. I WAS THROUGH! AS I SOON FOUND OUT, I HAD NO LEGAL RECOURSE. PAPERS WHICH I HAD UNKNOWINGLY SIGNED YEARS BEFORE HAD PUT THE BUSINESS IN YOUR NAME.
"I WAS ALREADY AN OLD MAN. I USED WHAT LITTLE SAVINGS I HAD TO RETIRE TO THIS FARM.
"BUT I NEVER STOPPED WORKING ON MY NEWEST DISCOVERY!
THE PORTABLE POWER-PACK WORKS LIKE A CHARM!
THE MONTHS OF SLAVING HAVE PAID OFF! WITH THE PORTABLE UNIT, I CAN ACTUALLY ACHIEVE WINGED FLIGHT!
AND WHAT'S MORE, I'M STRONGER THAN I'VE EVER BEEN IN MY LIFE!
SOMEHOW, THE ELECTROMAGNETIC FIELDS OF THE FLIGHT HARNESS HAVE ENERGIZED MY BODY!
KRAK
THAT'S SOLID OAK, BUT IT MIGHT AS WELL BE CARDBOARD!

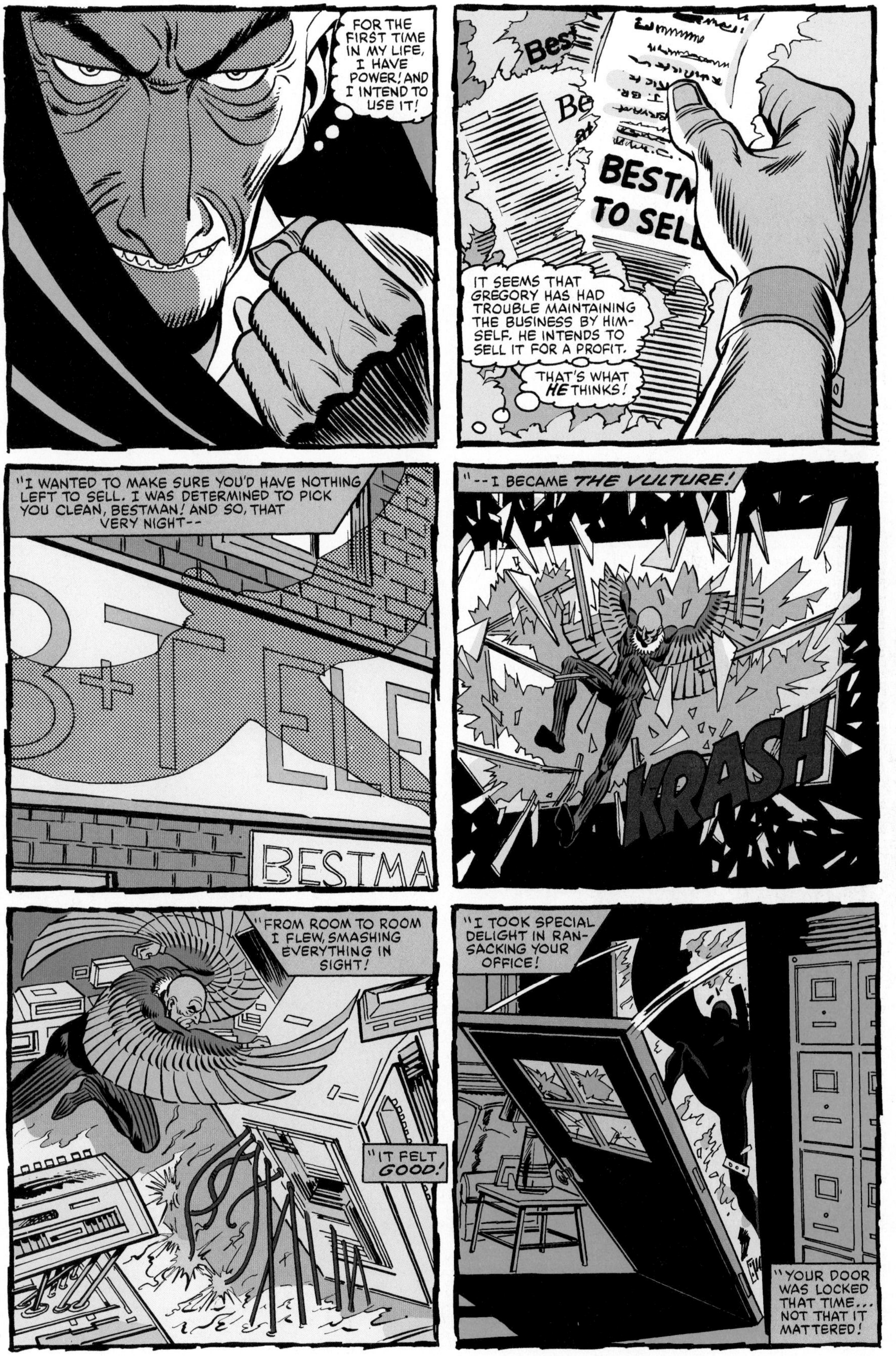
FOR THE FIRST TIME IN MY LIFE, I HAVE POWER! AND I INTEND TO USE IT!
BESTM
TO SELL
IT SEEMS THAT GREGORY HAS HAD TROUBLE MAINTAINING THE BUSINESS BY HIM-SELF. HE INTENDS TO SELL IT FOR A PROFIT.
THAT'S WHAT HE THINKS!
"I WANTED TO MAKE SURE YOU'D HAVE NOTHING LEFT TO SELL. I WAS DETERMINED TO PICK YOU CLEAN, BESTMAN! AND SO, THAT VERY NIGHT--
BESTMA
"--I BECAME THE VULTURE!
KRASH
"FROM ROOM TO ROOM I FLEW, SMASHING EVERYTHING IN SIGHT!
"IT FELT GOOD!
"I TOOK SPECIAL DELIGHT IN RAN-SACKING YOUR OFFICE!
"YOUR DOOR WAS LOCKED THAT TIME... NOT THAT IT MATTERED!

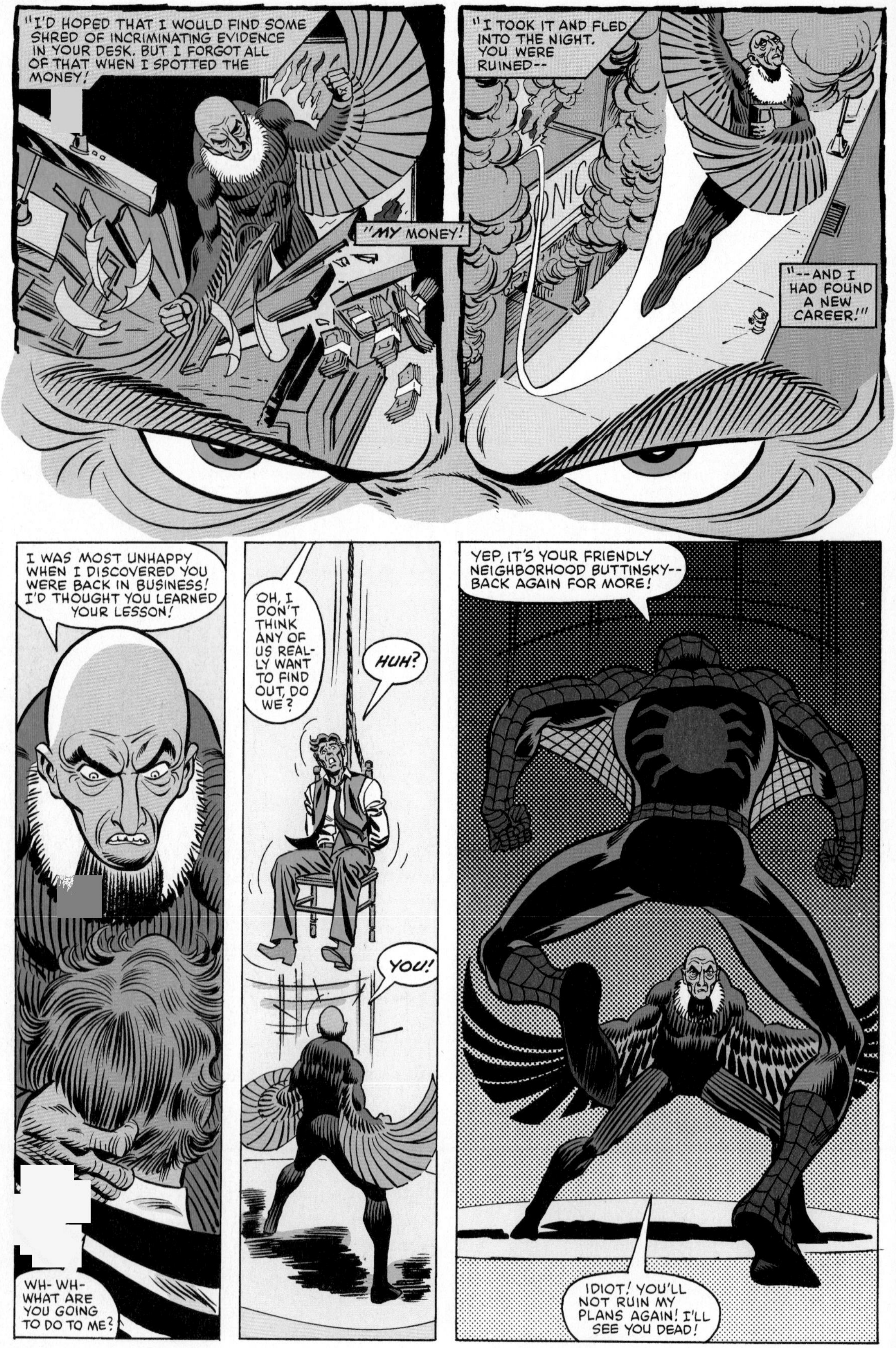
"I'D HOPED THAT I WOULD FIND SOME SHRED OF INCRIMINATING EVIDENCE IN YOUR DESK. BUT I FORGOT ALL OF THAT WHEN I SPOTTED THE MONEY!
"MY MONEY!
"I TOOK IT AND FLED INTO THE NIGHT. YOU WERE RUINED--
"--AND I HAD FOUND A NEW CAREER!"
I WAS MOST UNHAPPY WHEN I DISCOVERED YOU WERE BACK IN BUSINESS! I'D THOUGHT YOU LEARNED YOUR LESSON!
WH- WH- WHAT ARE YOU GOING TO DO TO ME?
OH, I DON'T THINK ANY OF US REALLY WANT TO FIND OUT, DO WE?
HUH?
YOU!
YEP, IT'S YOUR FRIENDLY NEIGHBORHOOD BUTTINSKY-- BACK AGAIN FOR MORE!
IDIOT! YOU'LL NOT RUIN MY PLANS AGAIN! I'LL SEE YOU DEAD!

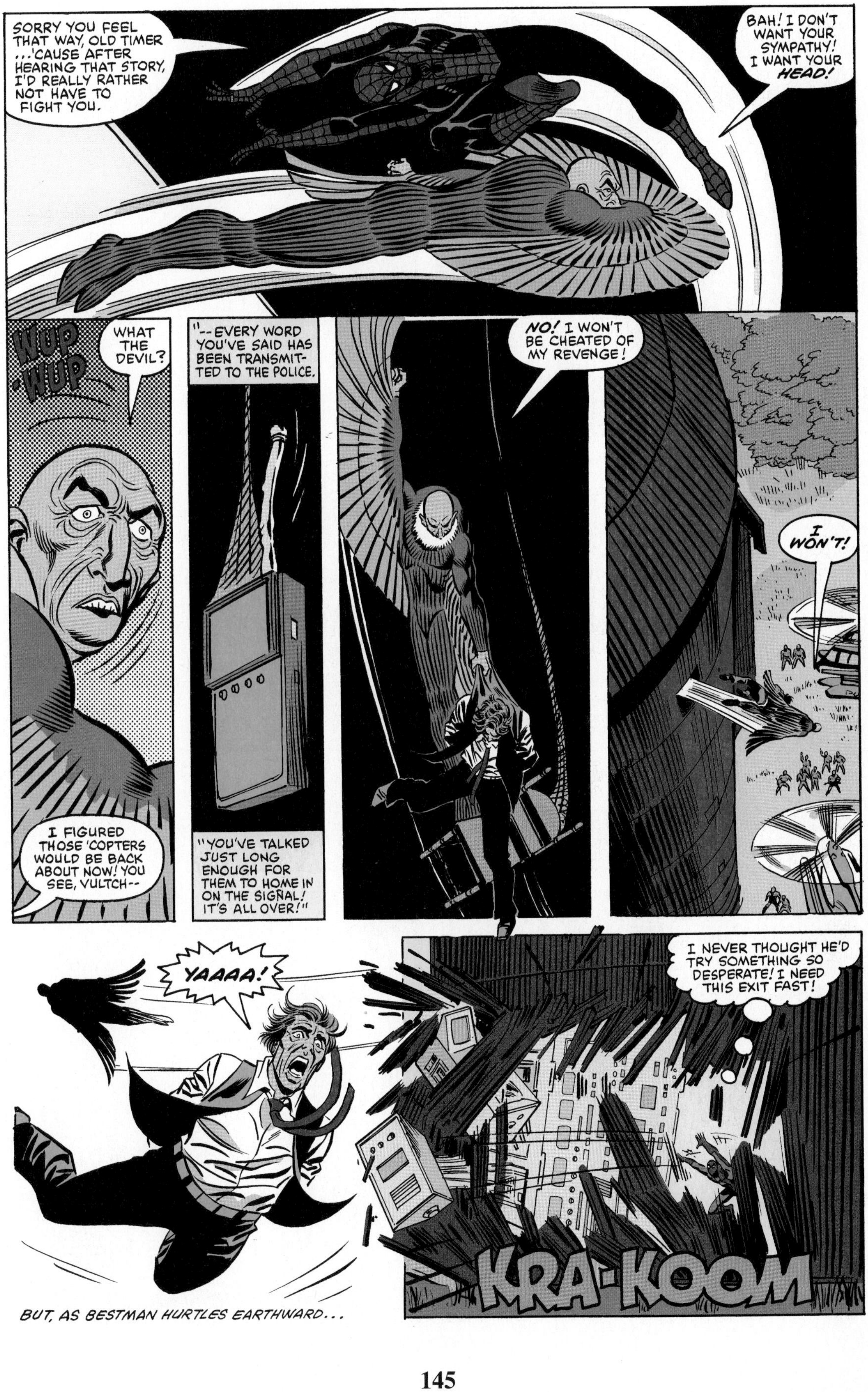
SORRY YOU FEEL THAT WAY, OLD TIMER ...'CAUSE AFTER HEARING THAT STORY, I'D REALLY RATHER NOT HAVE TO FIGHT YOU.
BAH! I DON'T WANT YOUR SYMPATHY! I WANT YOUR HEAD!
WUP WUP
WHAT THE DEVIL?
I FIGURED THOSE 'COPTERS WOULD BE BACK ABOUT NOW! YOU SEE, VULTCH--
"--EVERY WORD YOU'VE SAID HAS BEEN TRANSMITTED TO THE POLICE.
"YOU'VE TALKED JUST LONG ENOUGH FOR THEM TO HOME IN ON THE SIGNAL! IT'S ALL OVER!"
NO! I WON'T BE CHEATED OF MY REVENGE!
I WON'T!
YAAAA!
I NEVER THOUGHT HE'D TRY SOMETHING SO DESPERATE! I NEED THIS EXIT FAST!
KRA-KOOM
BUT, AS BESTMAN HURTLES EARTHWARD...

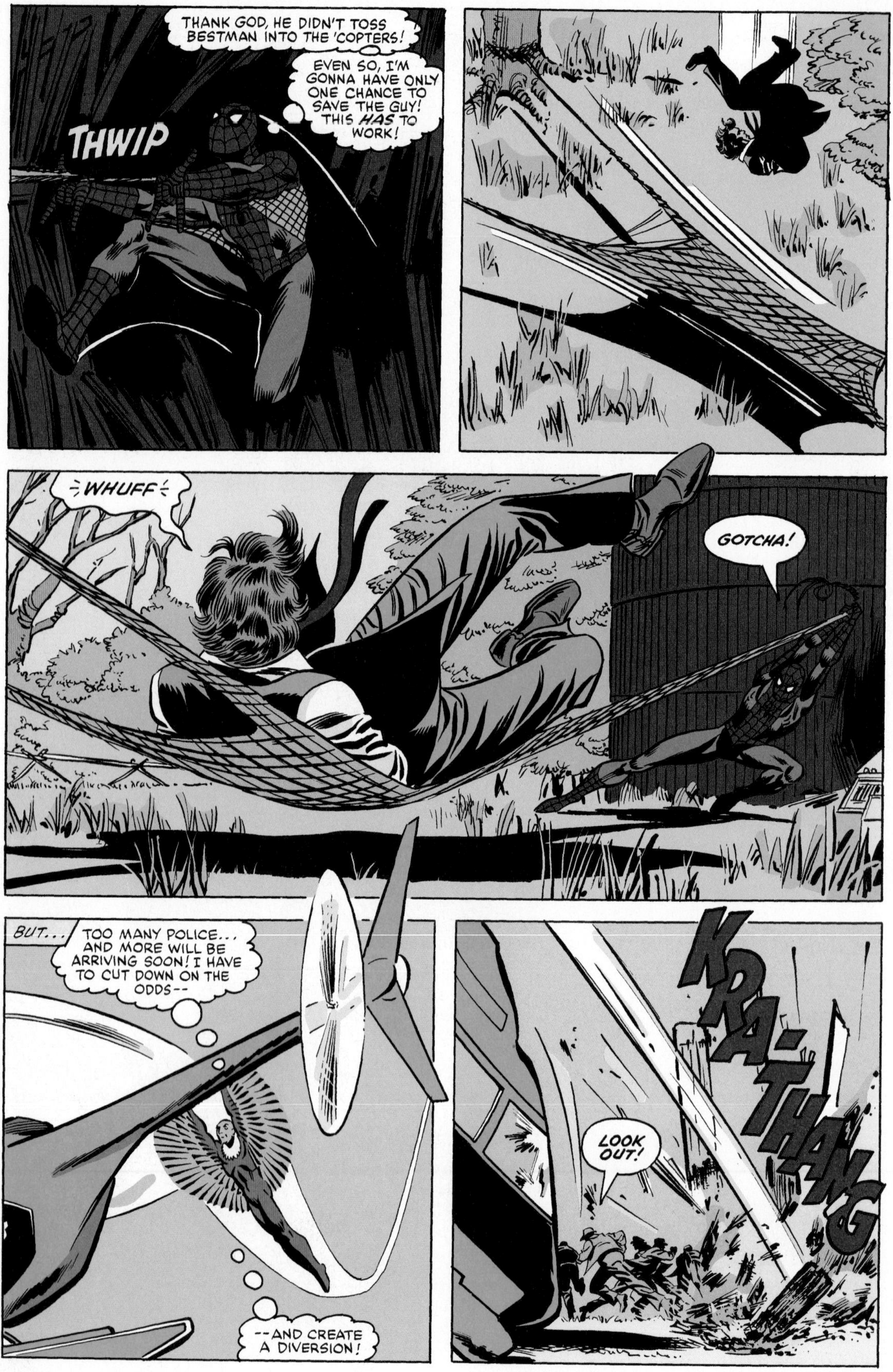

THANK GOD, HE DIDN'T TOSS BESTMAN INTO THE 'COPTERS!
EVEN SO, I'M GONNA HAVE ONLY ONE CHANCE TO SAVE THE GUY! THIS HAS TO WORK!
THWIP
WHUFF
GOTCHA!
BUT...
TOO MANY POLICE... AND MORE WILL BE ARRIVING SOON! I HAVE TO CUT DOWN ON THE ODDS--
--AND CREATE A DIVERSION!
KRA-THANG
LOOK OUT!

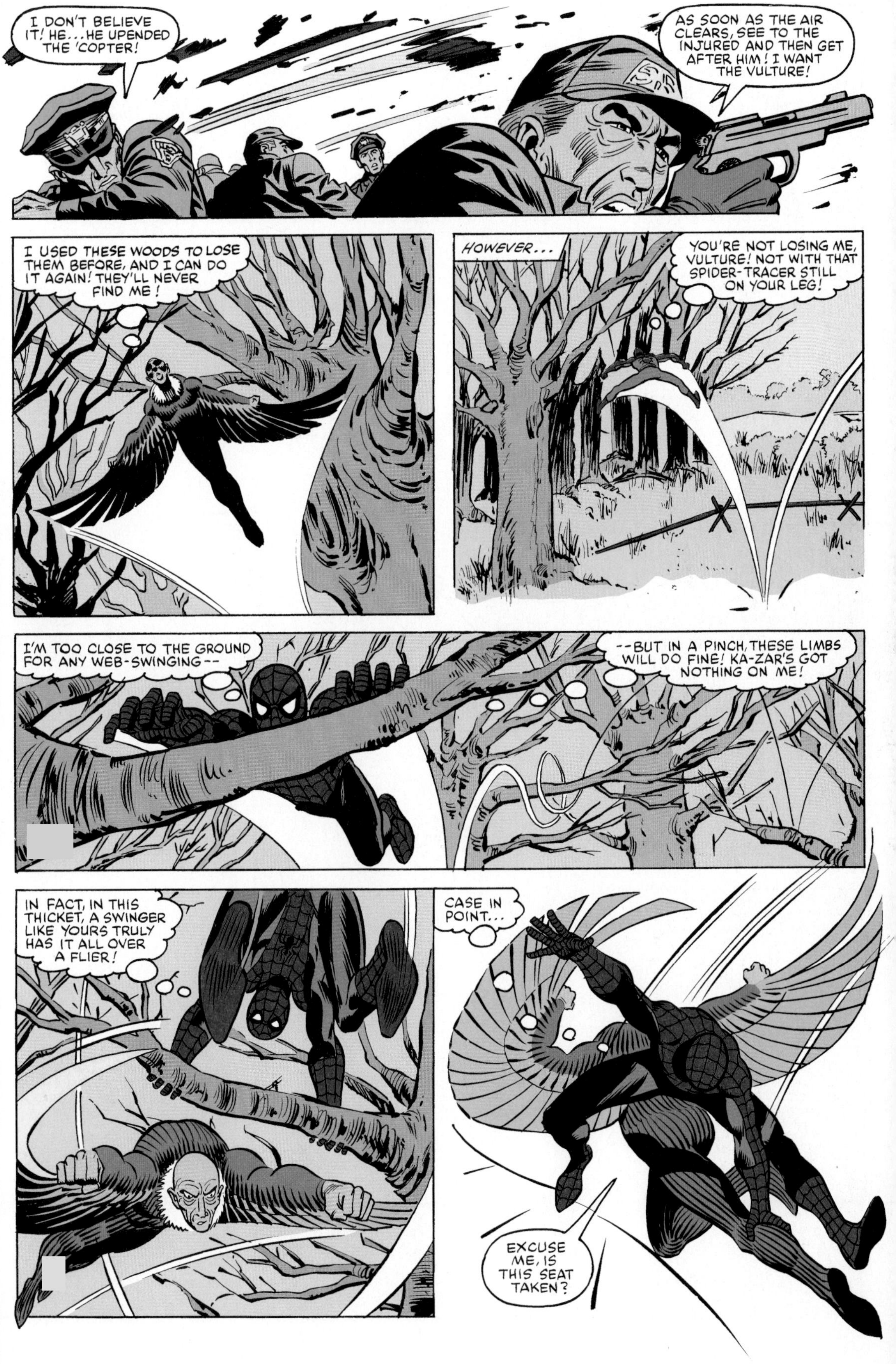
I DON'T BELIEVE IT! HE...HE UPENDED THE 'COPTER!
AS SOON AS THE AIR CLEARS, SEE TO THE INJURED AND THEN GET AFTER HIM! I WANT THE VULTURE!
I USED THESE WOODS TO LOSE THEM BEFORE, AND I CAN DO IT AGAIN! THEY'LL NEVER FIND ME!
HOWEVER...
YOU'RE NOT LOSING ME, VULTURE! NOT WITH THAT SPIDER-TRACER STILL ON YOUR LEG!
I'M TOO CLOSE TO THE GROUND FOR ANY WEB-SWINGING--
--BUT IN A PINCH, THESE LIMBS WILL DO FINE! KA-ZAR'S GOT NOTHING ON ME!
IN FACT, IN THIS THICKET, A SWINGER LIKE YOURS TRULY HAS IT ALL OVER A FLIER!
CASE IN POINT...
EXCUSE ME, IS THIS SEAT TAKEN?

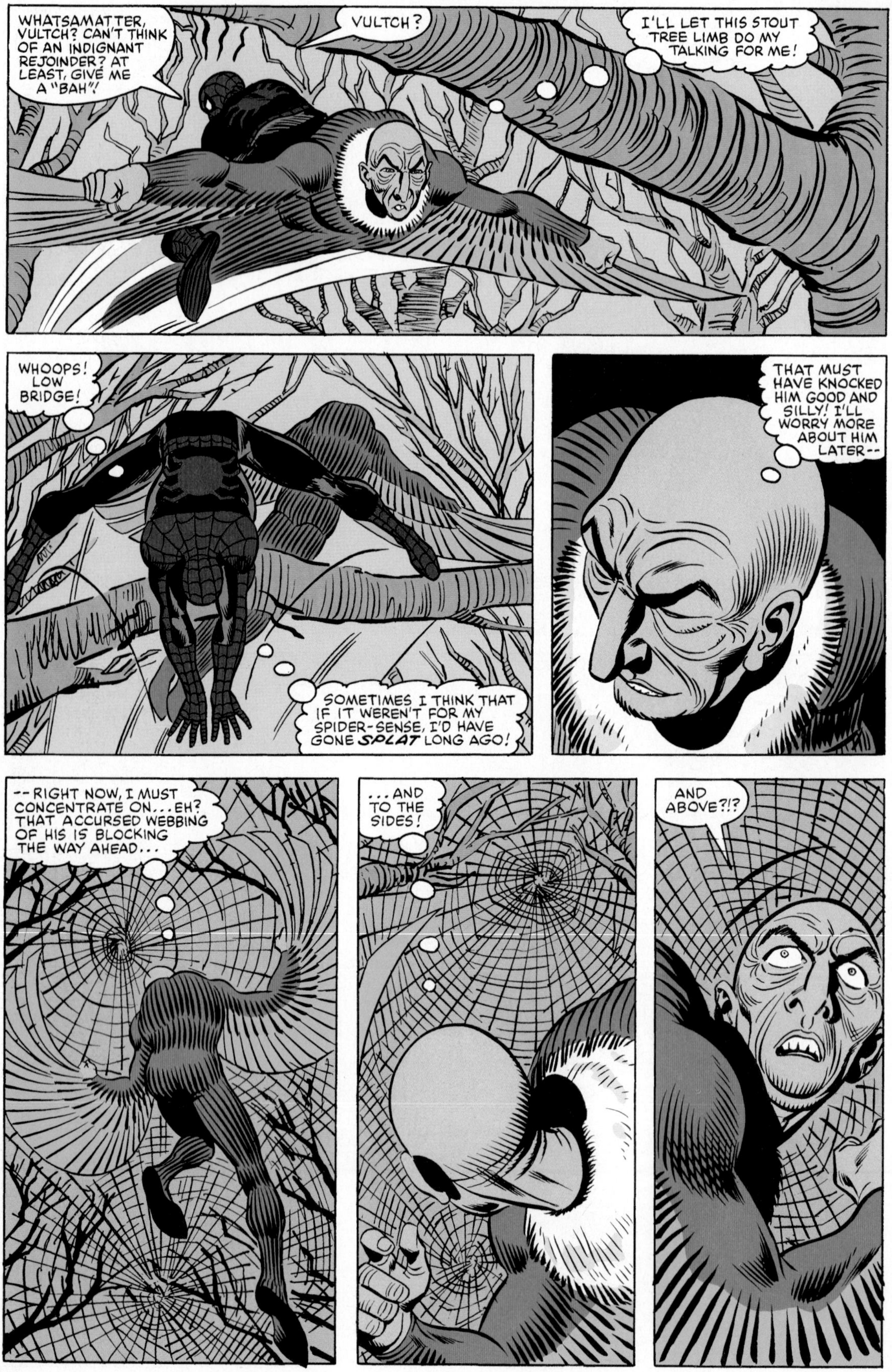
WHATSAMATTER, VULTCH? CAN'T THINK OF AN INDIGNANT REJOINDER? AT LEAST, GIVE ME A "BAH"!
VULTCH?
I'LL LET THIS STOUT TREE LIMB DO MY TALKING FOR ME!
WHOOPS! LOW BRIDGE!
SOMETIMES I THINK THAT IF IT WEREN'T FOR MY SPIDER-SENSE, I'D HAVE GONE SPLAT LONG AGO!
THAT MUST HAVE KNOCKED HIM GOOD AND SILLY! I'LL WORRY MORE ABOUT HIM LATER--
--RIGHT NOW, I MUST CONCENTRATE ON...EH? THAT ACCURSED WEBBING OF HIS IS BLOCKING THE WAY AHEAD...
...AND TO THE SIDES!
AND ABOVE?!?

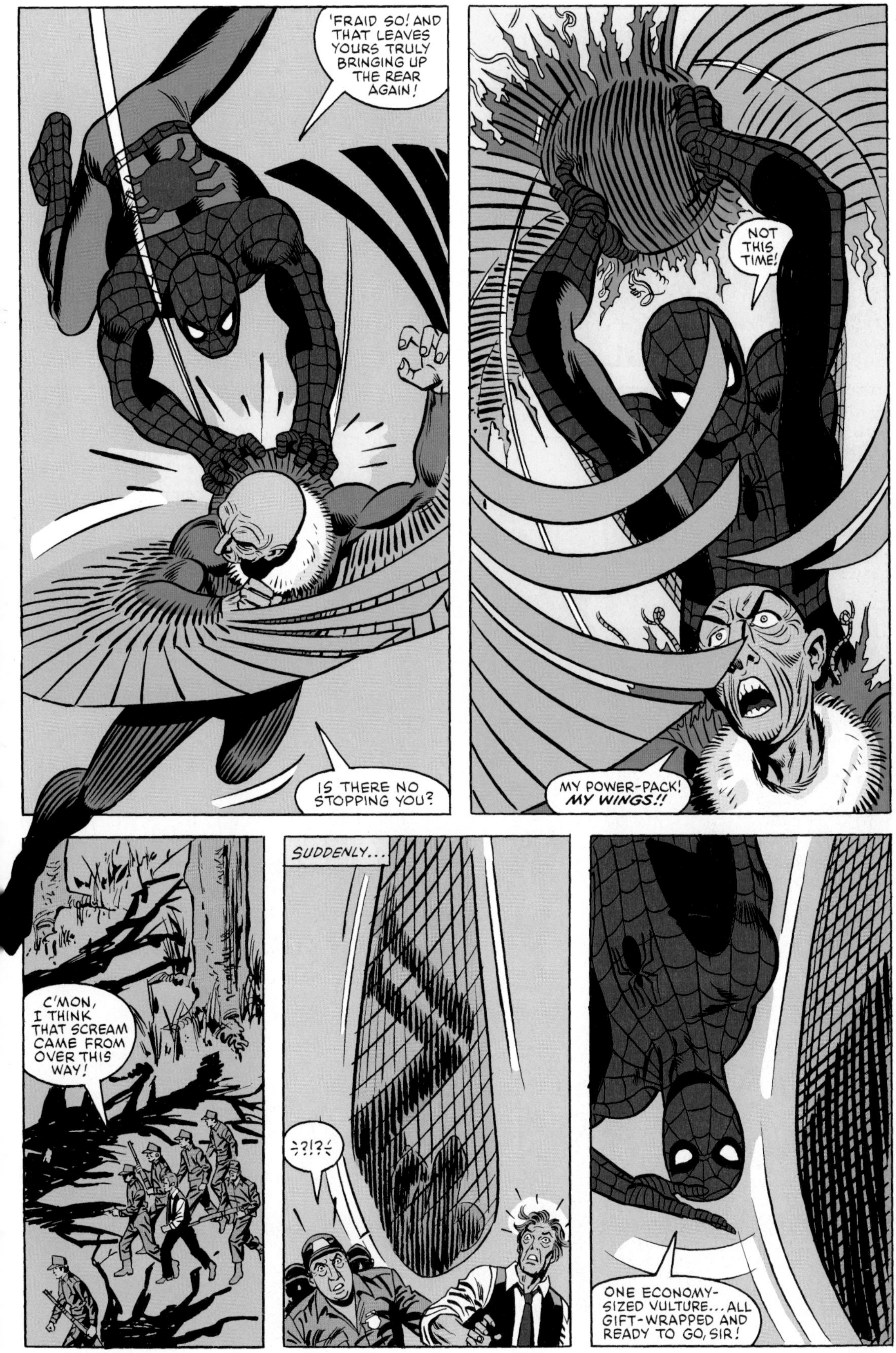
'FRAID SO! AND THAT LEAVES YOURS TRULY BRINGING UP THE REAR AGAIN!
IS THERE NO STOPPING YOU?
NOT THIS TIME!
MY POWER-PACK! **MY WINGS!!**
C'MON, I THINK THAT SCREAM CAME FROM OVER THIS WAY!
SUDDENLY...
?!?!
ONE ECONOMY-SIZED VULTURE... ALL GIFT-WRAPPED AND READY TO GO, SIR!

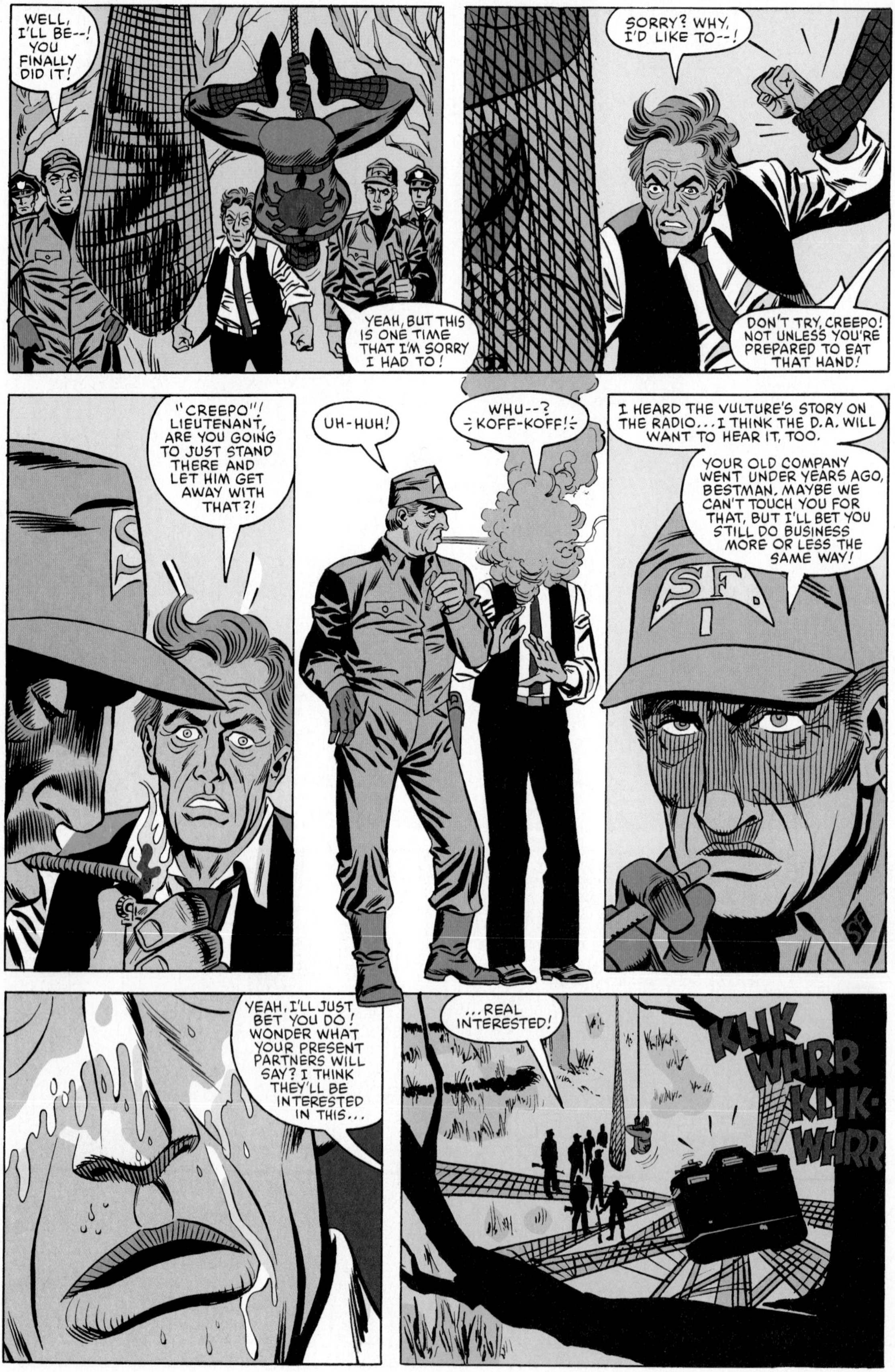

WELL, I'LL BE--! YOU FINALLY DID IT!
YEAH, BUT THIS IS ONE TIME THAT I'M SORRY I HAD TO!
SORRY? WHY, I'D LIKE TO--!
DON'T TRY, CREEPO! NOT UNLESS YOU'RE PREPARED TO EAT THAT HAND!
"CREEPO"! LIEUTENANT, ARE YOU GOING TO JUST STAND THERE AND LET HIM GET AWAY WITH THAT?!
UH-HUH!
WHU--? KOFF-KOFF!
I HEARD THE VULTURE'S STORY ON THE RADIO... I THINK THE D.A. WILL WANT TO HEAR IT, TOO.
YOUR OLD COMPANY WENT UNDER YEARS AGO, BESTMAN. MAYBE WE CAN'T TOUCH YOU FOR THAT, BUT I'LL BET YOU STILL DO BUSINESS MORE OR LESS THE SAME WAY!
YEAH, I'LL JUST BET YOU DO! WONDER WHAT YOUR PRESENT PARTNERS WILL SAY? I THINK THEY'LL BE INTERESTED IN THIS...
...REAL INTERESTED!
KLIK WHRR KLIK-WHRR

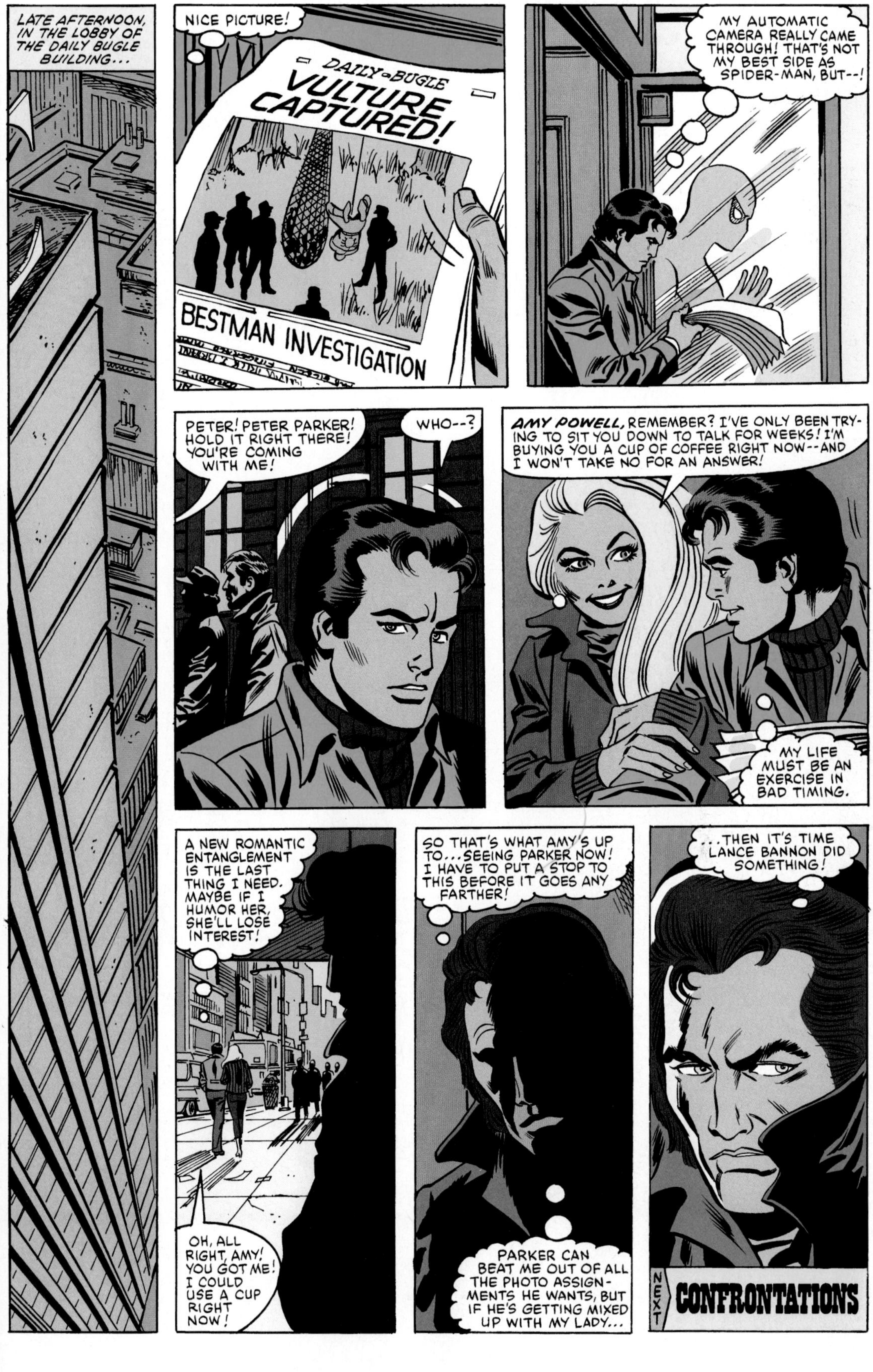
LATE AFTERNOON, IN THE LOBBY OF THE DAILY BUGLE BUILDING...
NICE PICTURE!
DAILY BUGLE
VULTURE CAPTURED!
BESTMAN INVESTIGATION
MY AUTOMATIC CAMERA REALLY CAME THROUGH! THAT'S NOT MY BEST SIDE AS SPIDER-MAN, BUT--!
PETER! PETER PARKER! HOLD IT RIGHT THERE! YOU'RE COMING WITH ME!
WHO--?
AMY POWELL, REMEMBER? I'VE ONLY BEEN TRYING TO SIT YOU DOWN TO TALK FOR WEEKS! I'M BUYING YOU A CUP OF COFFEE RIGHT NOW--AND I WON'T TAKE NO FOR AN ANSWER!
MY LIFE MUST BE AN EXERCISE IN BAD TIMING.
A NEW ROMANTIC ENTANGLEMENT IS THE LAST THING I NEED. MAYBE IF I HUMOR HER, SHE'LL LOSE INTEREST!
OH, ALL RIGHT, AMY! YOU GOT ME! I COULD USE A CUP RIGHT NOW!
SO THAT'S WHAT AMY'S UP TO... SEEING PARKER NOW! I HAVE TO PUT A STOP TO THIS BEFORE IT GOES ANY FARTHER!
PARKER CAN BEAT ME OUT OF ALL THE PHOTO ASSIGNMENTS HE WANTS, BUT IF HE'S GETTING MIXED UP WITH MY LADY...
...THEN IT'S TIME LANCE BANNON DID SOMETHING!
NEXT
CONFRONTATIONS

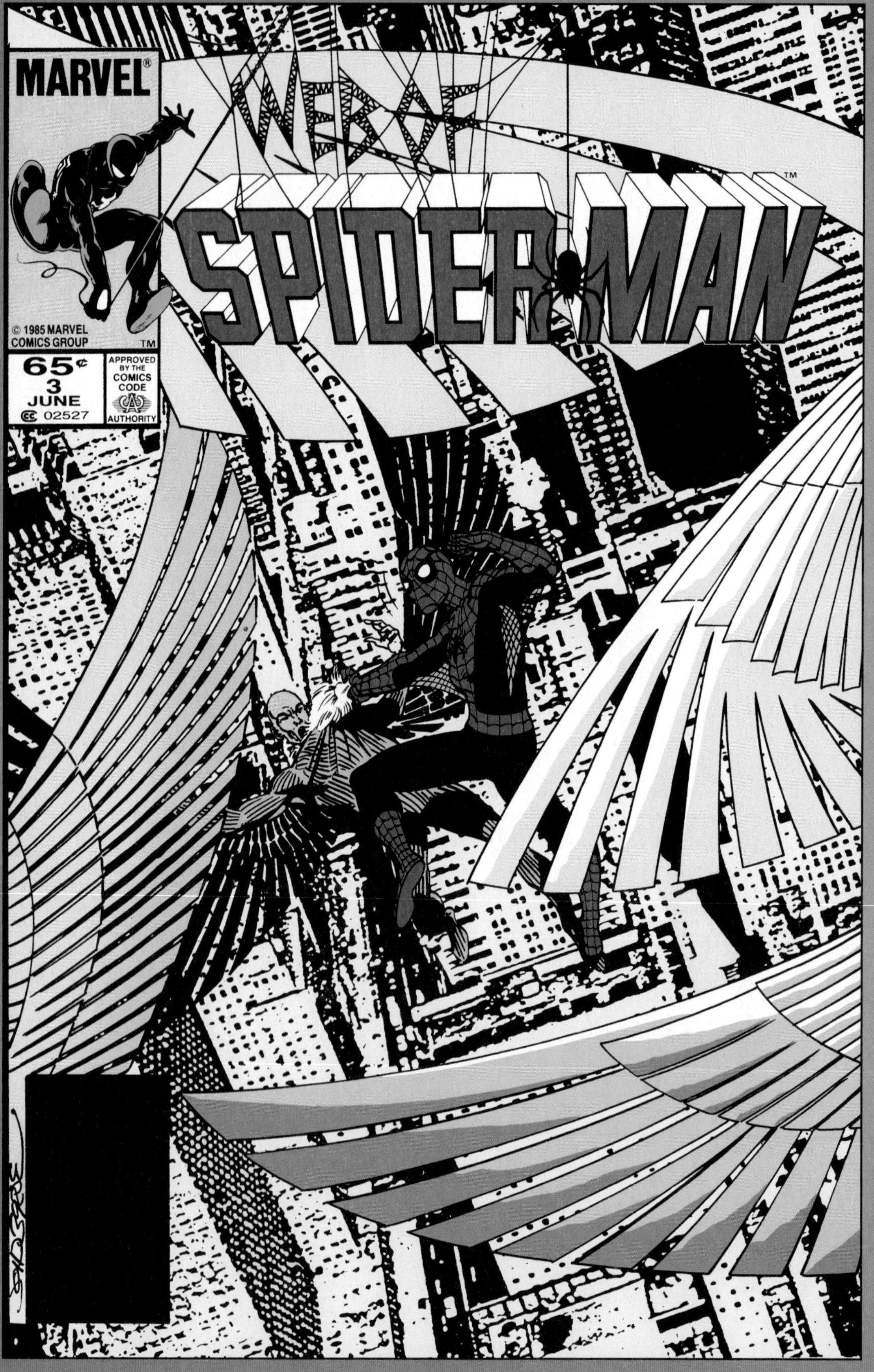
MARVEL
WEB OF
SPIDER-MAN
© 1985 MARVEL COMICS GROUP
65¢
3
JUNE
02527
APPROVED BY THE COMICS CODE AUTHORITY

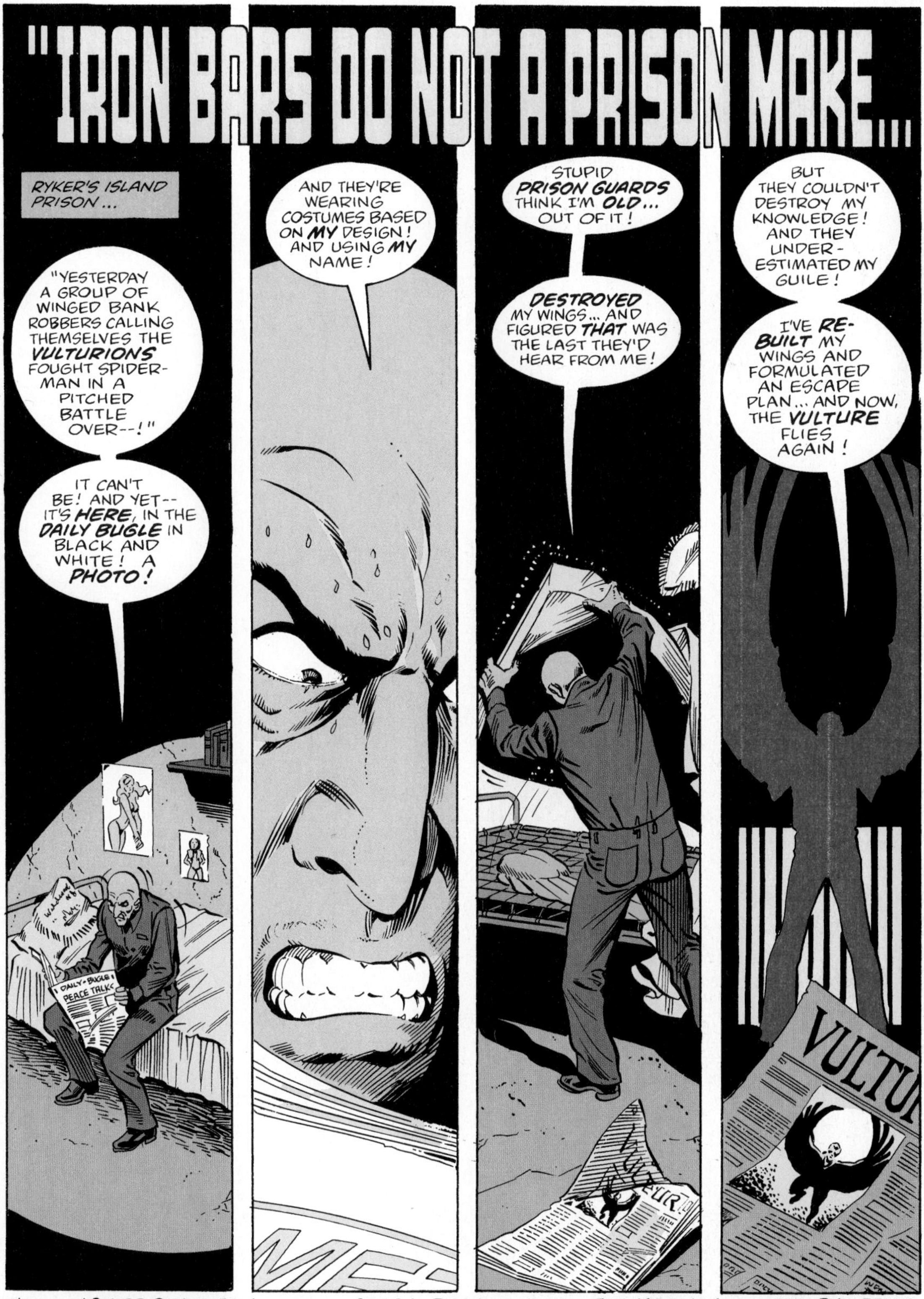
"IRON BARS DO NOT A PRISON MAKE...
RYKER'S ISLAND PRISON...
"YESTERDAY A GROUP OF WINGED BANK ROBBERS CALLING THEMSELVES THE VULTURIONS FOUGHT SPIDER-MAN IN A PITCHED BATTLE OVER--!"
IT CAN'T BE! AND YET-- IT'S HERE, IN THE DAILY BUGLE IN BLACK AND WHITE! A PHOTO!
DAILY BUGLE
PEACE TALKS
AND THEY'RE WEARING COSTUMES BASED ON MY DESIGN! AND USING MY NAME!
STUPID PRISON GUARDS THINK I'M OLD... OUT OF IT!
DESTROYED MY WINGS... AND FIGURED THAT WAS THE LAST THEY'D HEAR FROM ME!
BUT THEY COULDN'T DESTROY MY KNOWLEDGE! AND THEY UNDER-ESTIMATED MY GUILE!
I'VE RE-BUILT MY WINGS AND FORMULATED AN ESCAPE PLAN... AND NOW, THE VULTURE FLIES AGAIN!
VULTU

WRITER--LOUISE SIMONSON PENCILER--GREG LAROCQUE INKER--JIM MOONEY LETTERER--PHIL FELIX
COLORIST--GEORGE ROUSSOS EDITOR--JIM OWSLEY EDITOR-IN-CHIEF--JIM SHOOTER

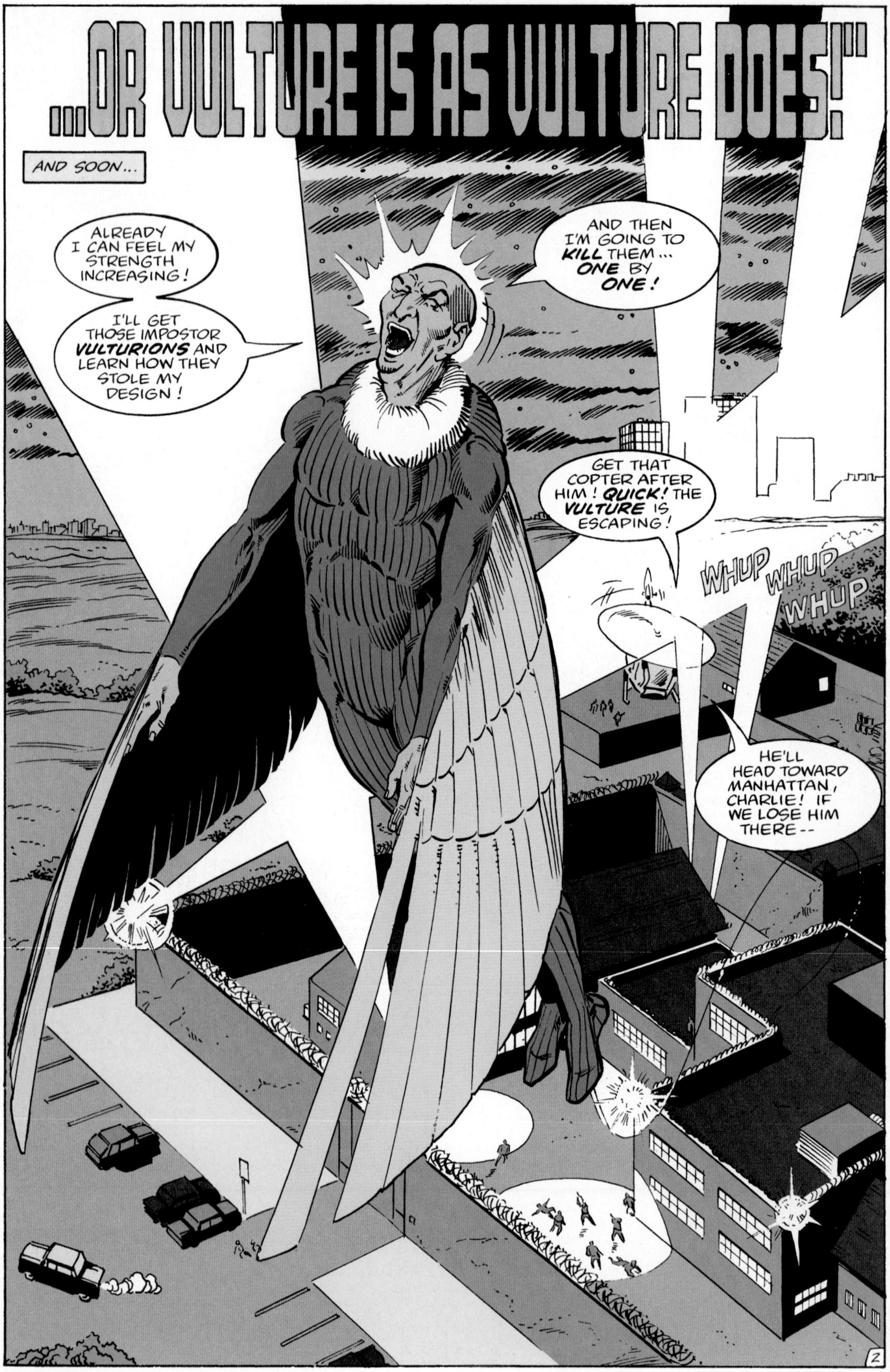
"...OR VULTURE IS AS VULTURE DOES!"
AND SOON...
ALREADY I CAN FEEL MY STRENGTH INCREASING!
I'LL GET THOSE IMPOSTOR VULTURIONS AND LEARN HOW THEY STOLE MY DESIGN!
AND THEN I'M GOING TO KILL THEM... ONE BY ONE!
GET THAT COPTER AFTER HIM! QUICK! THE VULTURE IS ESCAPING!
WHUP WHUP WHUP
HE'LL HEAD TOWARD MANHATTAN, CHARLIE! IF WE LOSE HIM THERE--
2

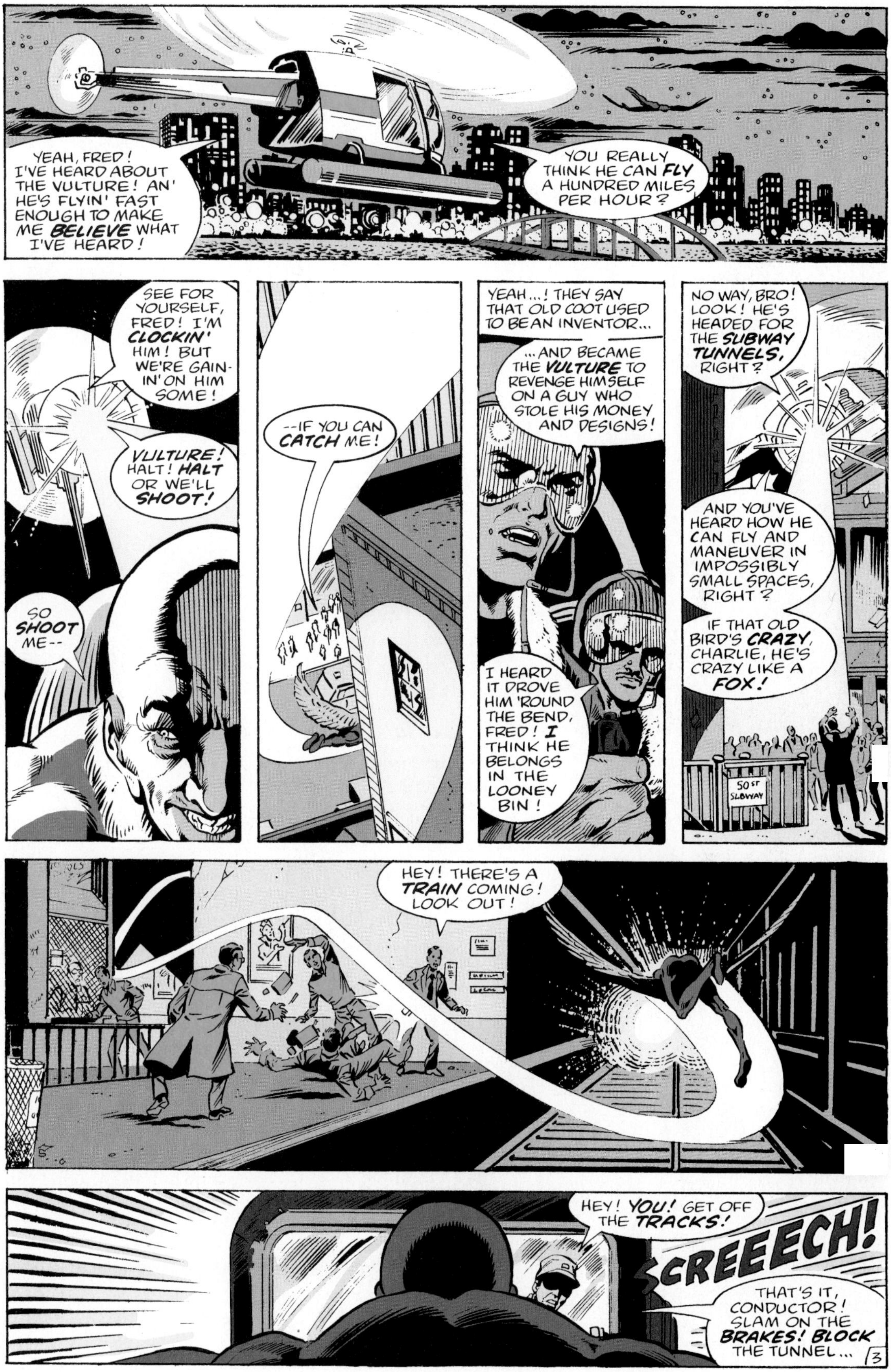
YEAH, FRED! I'VE HEARD ABOUT THE VULTURE! AN' HE'S FLYIN' FAST ENOUGH TO MAKE ME BELIEVE WHAT I'VE HEARD!
YOU REALLY THINK HE CAN FLY A HUNDRED MILES PER HOUR?
SEE FOR YOURSELF, FRED! I'M CLOCKIN' HIM! BUT WE'RE GAIN-IN' ON HIM SOME!
VULTURE! HALT! HALT OR WE'LL SHOOT!
SO SHOOT ME--
--IF YOU CAN CATCH ME!
YEAH...! THEY SAY THAT OLD COOT USED TO BE AN INVENTOR...
...AND BECAME THE VULTURE TO REVENGE HIMSELF ON A GUY WHO STOLE HIS MONEY AND DESIGNS!
I HEARD IT DROVE HIM 'ROUND THE BEND, FRED! I THINK HE BELONGS IN THE LOONEY BIN!
NO WAY, BRO! LOOK! HE'S HEADED FOR THE SUBWAY TUNNELS, RIGHT?
AND YOU'VE HEARD HOW HE CAN FLY AND MANEUVER IN IMPOSSIBLY SMALL SPACES, RIGHT?
IF THAT OLD BIRD'S CRAZY, CHARLIE, HE'S CRAZY LIKE A FOX!
50 ST SUBWAY
HEY! THERE'S A TRAIN COMING! LOOK OUT!
HEY! YOU! GET OFF THE TRACKS!
SCREEECH!
THAT'S IT, CONDUCTOR! SLAM ON THE BRAKES! BLOCK THE TUNNEL...
3

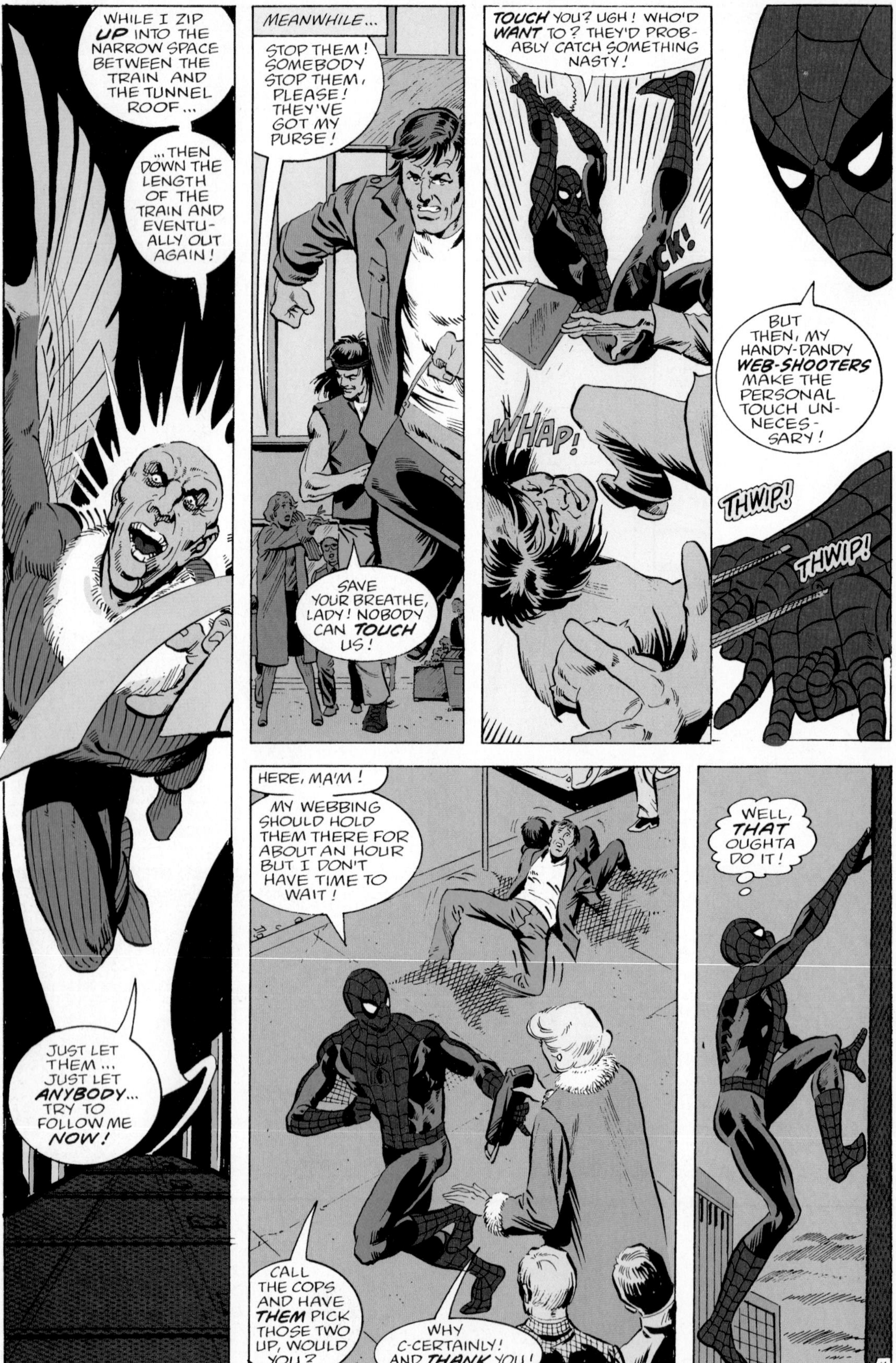
WHILE I ZIP UP INTO THE NARROW SPACE BETWEEN THE TRAIN AND THE TUNNEL ROOF...
...THEN DOWN THE LENGTH OF THE TRAIN AND EVENTUALLY OUT AGAIN!
JUST LET THEM... JUST LET ANYBODY... TRY TO FOLLOW ME NOW!
MEANWHILE...
STOP THEM! SOMEBODY STOP THEM, PLEASE! THEY'VE GOT MY PURSE!
SAVE YOUR BREATHE, LADY! NOBODY CAN TOUCH US!
TOUCH YOU? UGH! WHO'D WANT TO? THEY'D PROBABLY CATCH SOMETHING NASTY!
KICK!
WHAP!
BUT THEN, MY HANDY-DANDY WEB-SHOOTERS MAKE THE PERSONAL TOUCH UNNECESSARY!
THWIP!
THWIP!
HERE, MA'M!
MY WEBBING SHOULD HOLD THEM THERE FOR ABOUT AN HOUR BUT I DON'T HAVE TIME TO WAIT!
CALL THE COPS AND HAVE THEM PICK THOSE TWO UP, WOULD YOU?
WHY C-CERTAINLY! AND THANK YOU!
WELL, THAT OUGHTA DO IT!
4

THESE OUGHT TO BE **CLEARER** THAN MY SHOTS OF THE VULTURIONS ANYWAY!

ROBBIE SAID **THEY** LOOKED LIKE THEY WERE SHOT THROUGH GAUZE!

IF YE OLDE EDITOR-IN-CHIEF ONLY KNEW I SHOT THEM THROUGH MY **COSTUME** WITH MY CAMERA HOOKED TO MY UTILITY BELT AND RUNNING ON AUTOMATIC!

WONDER IF I SHOULD MAIL OFF AUNT MAY'S BIRTHDAY PRESENT **BEFORE** I STOP BY THE BUGLE!

IF I DON'T GET THIS HAT TO HER BY EXPRESS MAIL TO-**DAY**, IT'LL MISS HER BIRTHDAY **TOMORROW**!

SHE MAY STILL BE MAD AT ME FOR QUITTING GRAD SCHOOL, BUT IT'D BREAK HER HEART IF I DIDN'T SEND HER A PRESENT!

OH, HECK! THE BUGLE'S RIGHT ON THE WAY! I'LL STOP BY THERE AND DEVELOP THESE PICTURES FIRST!

AFTER ALL, THE POST OFFICE IS OPEN TILL **FIVE** AND MY BANK ACCOUNT'S PRETTY DEPLETED!

HEY, MAYBE I'LL TRY OUT THESE SHOTS ON JONAH!

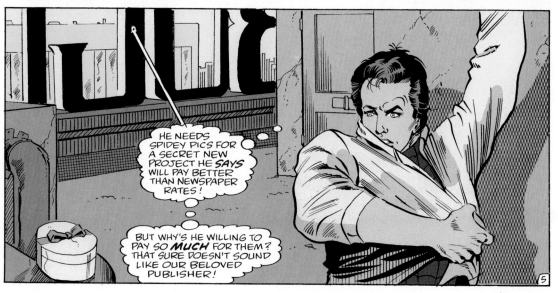

HE NEEDS SPIDEY PICS FOR A SECRET NEW PROJECT HE **SAYS** WILL PAY BETTER THAN NEWSPAPER RATES!

BUT WHY'S HE WILLING TO PAY SO **MUCH** FOR THEM? THAT SURE DOESN'T SOUND LIKE OUR BELOVED PUBLISHER!

5

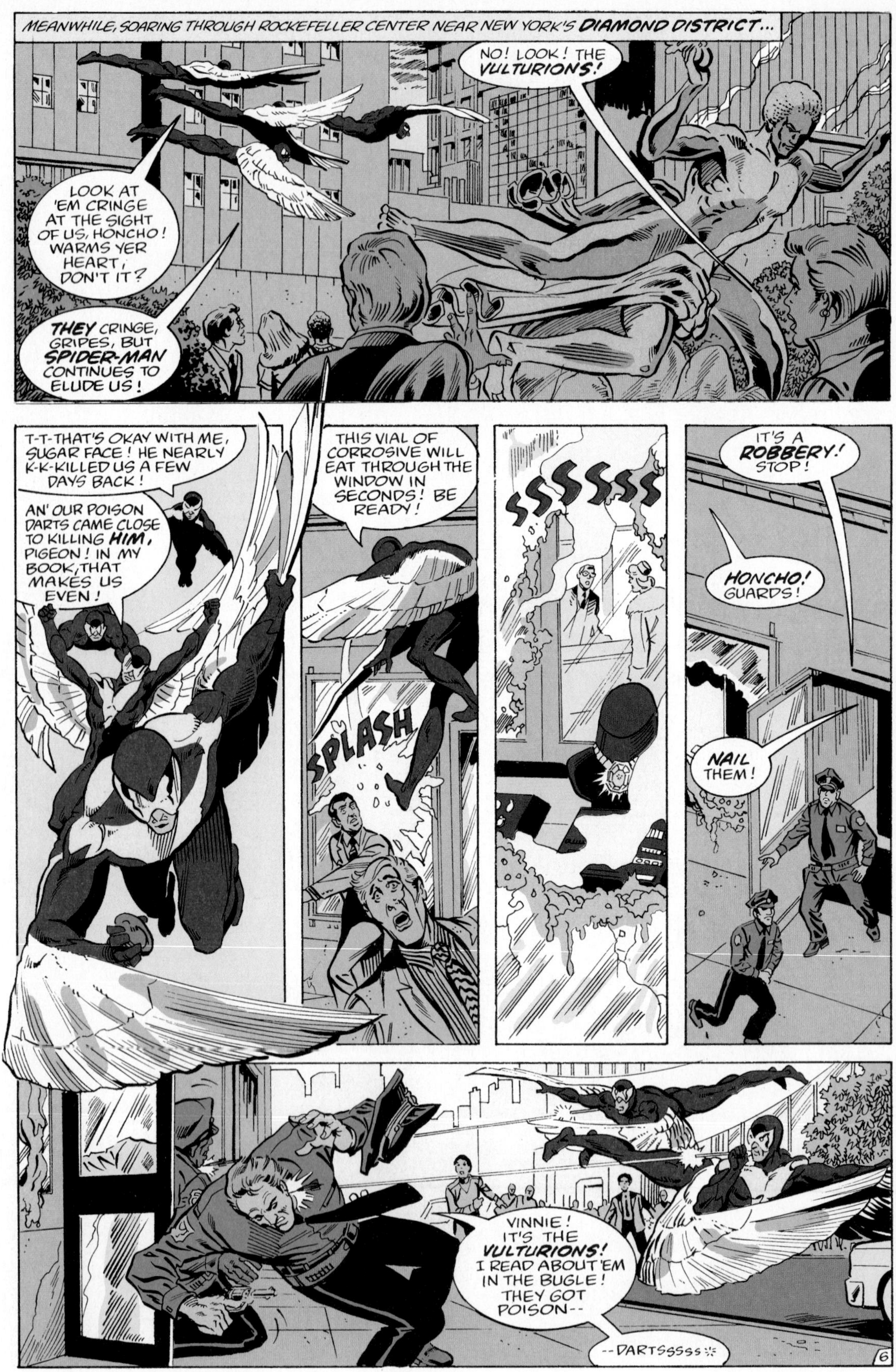

MEANWHILE, SOARING THROUGH ROCKEFELLER CENTER NEAR NEW YORK'S DIAMOND DISTRICT...
NO! LOOK! THE VULTURIONS!
LOOK AT 'EM CRINGE AT THE SIGHT OF US, HONCHO! WARMS YER HEART, DON'T IT?
THEY CRINGE, GRIPES, BUT SPIDER-MAN CONTINUES TO ELUDE US!
T-T-THAT'S OKAY WITH ME, SUGAR FACE! HE NEARLY K-K-KILLED US A FEW DAYS BACK!
AN' OUR POISON DARTS CAME CLOSE TO KILLING HIM, PIGEON! IN MY BOOK, THAT MAKES US EVEN!
THIS VIAL OF CORROSIVE WILL EAT THROUGH THE WINDOW IN SECONDS! BE READY!
SPLASH
SSSSSS
IT'S A ROBBERY! STOP!
HONCHO! GUARDS!
NAIL THEM!
VINNIE! IT'S THE VULTURIONS! I READ ABOUT 'EM IN THE BUGLE! THEY GOT POISON--
--DARTSSSSS
6

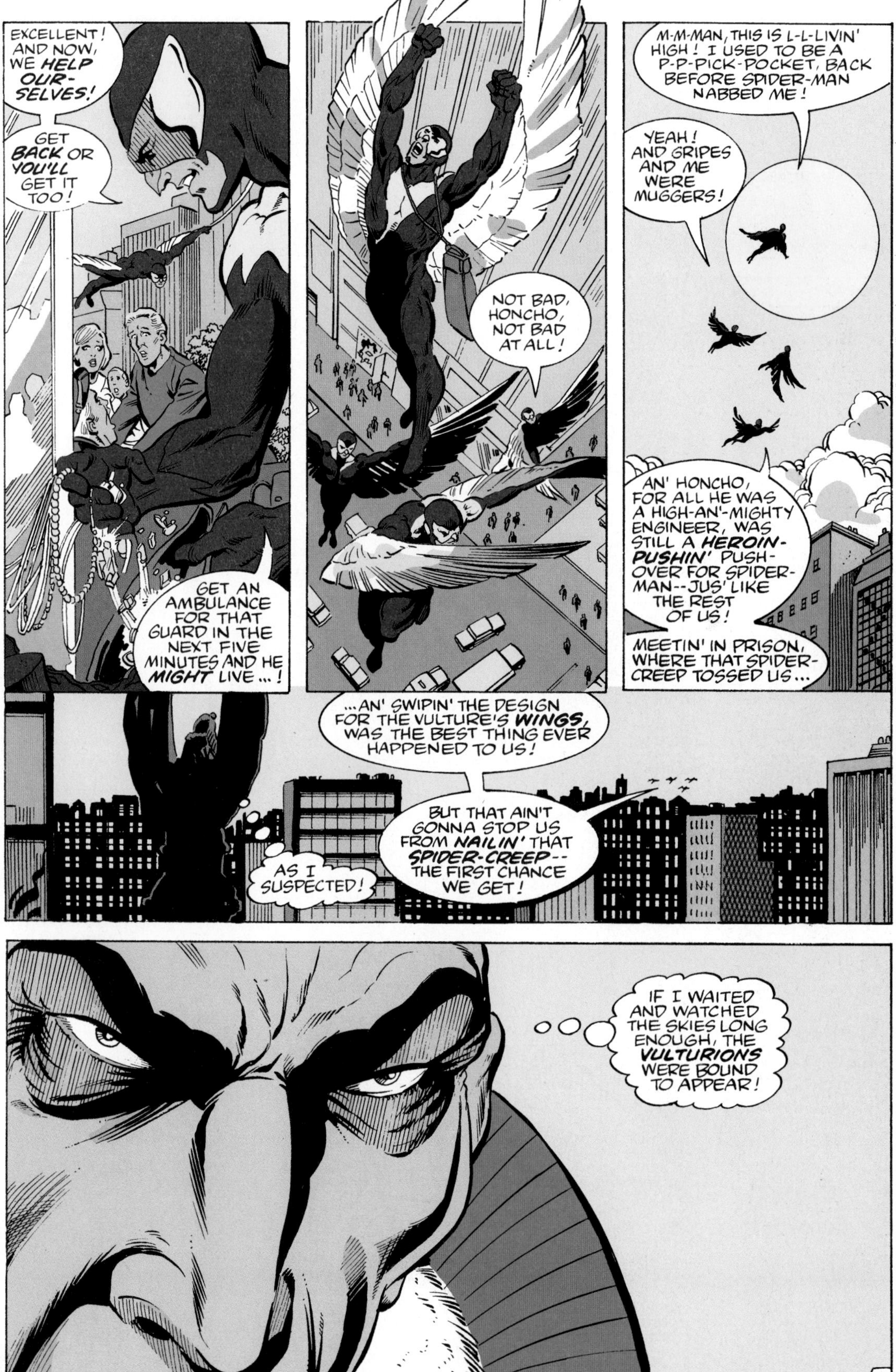

EXCELLENT! AND NOW, WE HELP OURSELVES!
GET BACK OR YOU'LL GET IT TOO!
GET AN AMBULANCE FOR THAT GUARD IN THE NEXT FIVE MINUTES AND HE MIGHT LIVE...!
NOT BAD, HONCHO, NOT BAD AT ALL!
M-M-MAN, THIS IS L-L-LIVIN' HIGH! I USED TO BE A P-P-PICK-POCKET, BACK BEFORE SPIDER-MAN NABBED ME!
YEAH! AND GRIPES AND ME WERE MUGGERS!
AN' HONCHO, FOR ALL HE WAS A HIGH-AN'-MIGHTY ENGINEER, WAS STILL A HEROIN-PUSHIN' PUSH-OVER FOR SPIDER-MAN--JUS' LIKE THE REST OF US!
MEETIN' IN PRISON, WHERE THAT SPIDER-CREEP TOSSED US...
...AN' SWIPIN' THE DESIGN FOR THE VULTURE'S WINGS, WAS THE BEST THING EVER HAPPENED TO US!
BUT THAT AIN'T GONNA STOP US FROM NAILIN' THAT SPIDER-CREEP-- THE FIRST CHANCE WE GET!
AS I SUSPECTED!
IF I WAITED AND WATCHED THE SKIES LONG ENOUGH, THE VULTURIONS WERE BOUND TO APPEAR!
7

I CAN FLY RINGS AROUND THOSE IMPOSTORS, AND WHEN I CATCH THEM, THEY'LL RUE THE DAY THEY STOLE MY PLANS!

OOOO

MEANWHILE...

RUBBISH, PETE! THEY'RE RUBBISH!

WHAT DO YOU MEAN "RUBBISH", JONAH? YOU SAID YOU WANTED SHOTS OF SPIDER-MAN!

WELL, JONAH, HERE THEY ARE! A WHOLE ROLL OF THEM!

YEAH, PARKER! BUT THOSE ARE SHOTS OF SPIDER-MAN BEING A HERO!

I WANT SHOTS OF SPIDER-MAN MAKING A FOOL OF HIMSELF OR BEING DESTRUCTIVE!

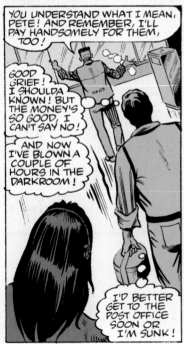
YOU UNDERSTAND WHAT I MEAN, PETE! AND REMEMBER, I'LL PAY HANDSOMELY FOR THEM, TOO!

GOOD GRIEF! I SHOULDA KNOWN! BUT THE MONEY'S SO GOOD, I CAN'T SAY NO!

AND NOW I'VE BLOWN A COUPLE OF HOURS IN THE DARKROOM!

I'D BETTER GET TO THE POST OFFICE SOON OR I'M SUNK!

PETE, I THOUGHT YOU'D FORGOTTEN OUR DATE FOR A LATE LUNCH!

BUT-- BUT, MARY JANE, I--

FORGET IT, PETER PARKER! I'M NOT TAKING NO FOR AN ANSWER! WE'VE GOT A LOT TO DISCUSS AND--

8

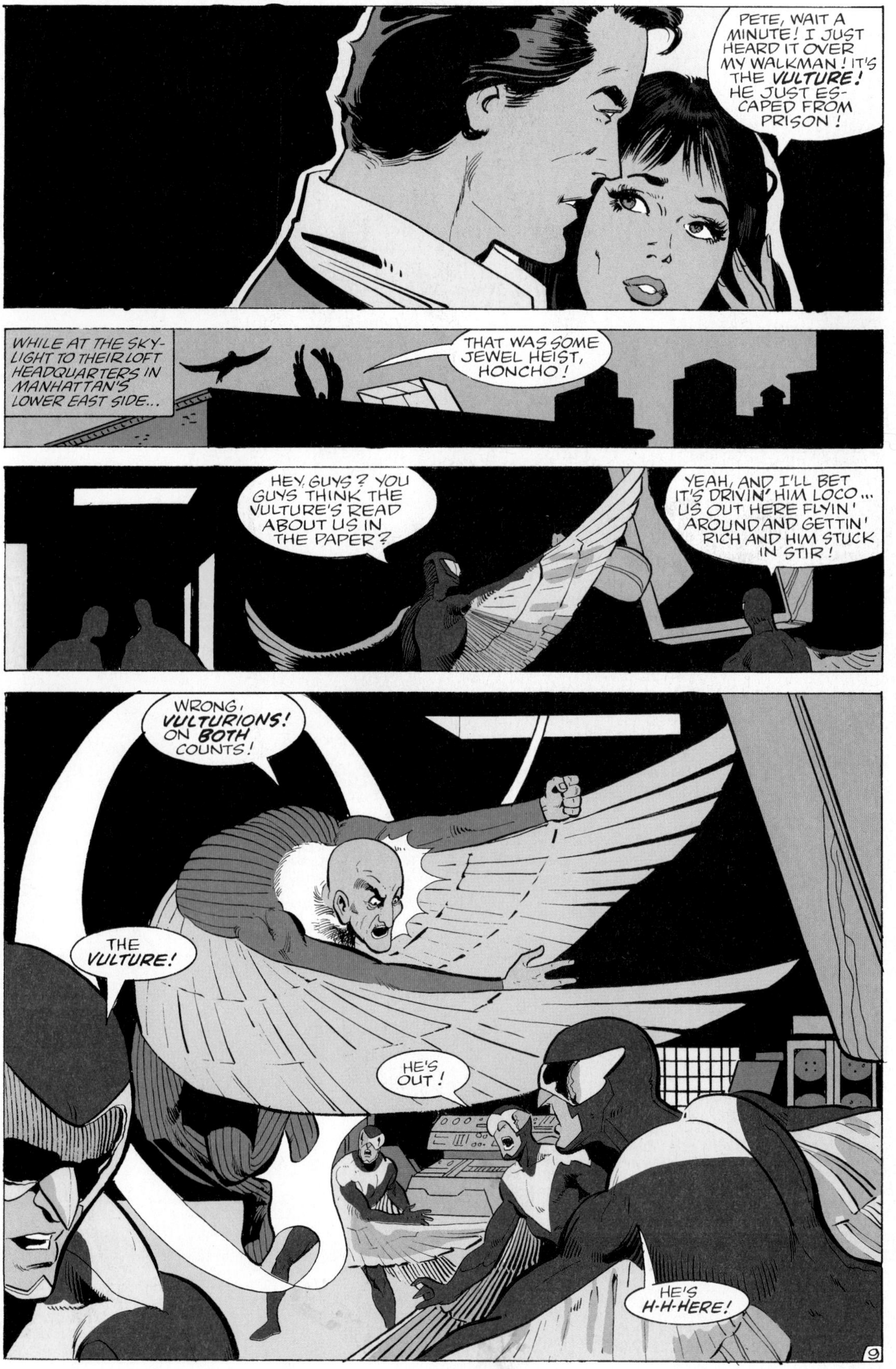
PETE, WAIT A MINUTE! I JUST HEARD IT OVER MY WALKMAN! IT'S THE VULTURE! HE JUST ESCAPED FROM PRISON!
WHILE AT THE SKYLIGHT TO THEIR LOFT HEADQUARTERS IN MANHATTAN'S LOWER EAST SIDE...
THAT WAS SOME JEWEL HEIST, HONCHO!
HEY, GUYS? YOU GUYS THINK THE VULTURE'S READ ABOUT US IN THE PAPER?
YEAH, AND I'LL BET IT'S DRIVIN' HIM LOCO... US OUT HERE FLYIN' AROUND AND GETTIN' RICH AND HIM STUCK IN STIR!
WRONG, VULTURIONS! ON BOTH COUNTS!
THE VULTURE!
HE'S OUT!
HE'S H-H-HERE!
9

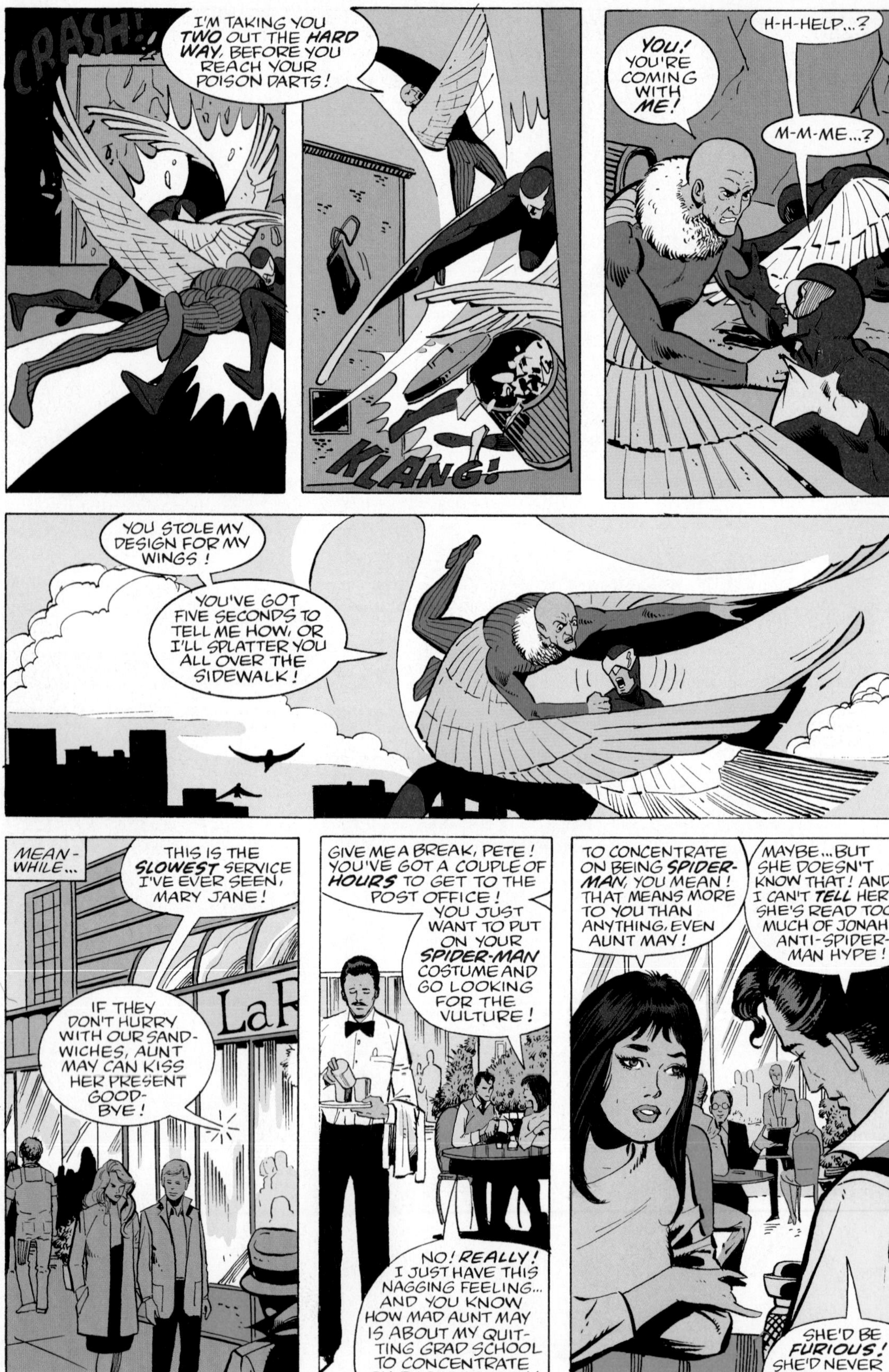
CRASH!
I'M TAKING YOU TWO OUT THE HARD WAY, BEFORE YOU REACH YOUR POISON DARTS!
KLANG!
YOU! YOU'RE COMING WITH ME!
H-H-HELP...?
M-M-ME...?
YOU STOLE MY DESIGN FOR MY WINGS!
YOU'VE GOT FIVE SECONDS TO TELL ME HOW, OR I'LL SPLATTER YOU ALL OVER THE SIDEWALK!
MEAN-WHILE...
THIS IS THE SLOWEST SERVICE I'VE EVER SEEN, MARY JANE!
IF THEY DON'T HURRY WITH OUR SAND-WICHES, AUNT MAY CAN KISS HER PRESENT GOOD-BYE!
GIVE ME A BREAK, PETE! YOU'VE GOT A COUPLE OF HOURS TO GET TO THE POST OFFICE!
YOU JUST WANT TO PUT ON YOUR SPIDER-MAN COSTUME AND GO LOOKING FOR THE VULTURE!
NO! REALLY! I JUST HAVE THIS NAGGING FEELING... AND YOU KNOW HOW MAD AUNT MAY IS ABOUT MY QUIT-TING GRAD SCHOOL TO CONCENTRATE ON PHOTOGRAPHY!
TO CONCENTRATE ON BEING SPIDER-MAN, YOU MEAN! THAT MEANS MORE TO YOU THAN ANYTHING, EVEN AUNT MAY!
MAYBE...BUT SHE DOESN'T KNOW THAT! AND I CAN'T TELL HER! SHE'S READ TOO MUCH OF JONAH'S ANTI-SPIDER-MAN HYPE!
SHE'D BE FURIOUS! SHE'D NEVER FORGIVE ME!
10

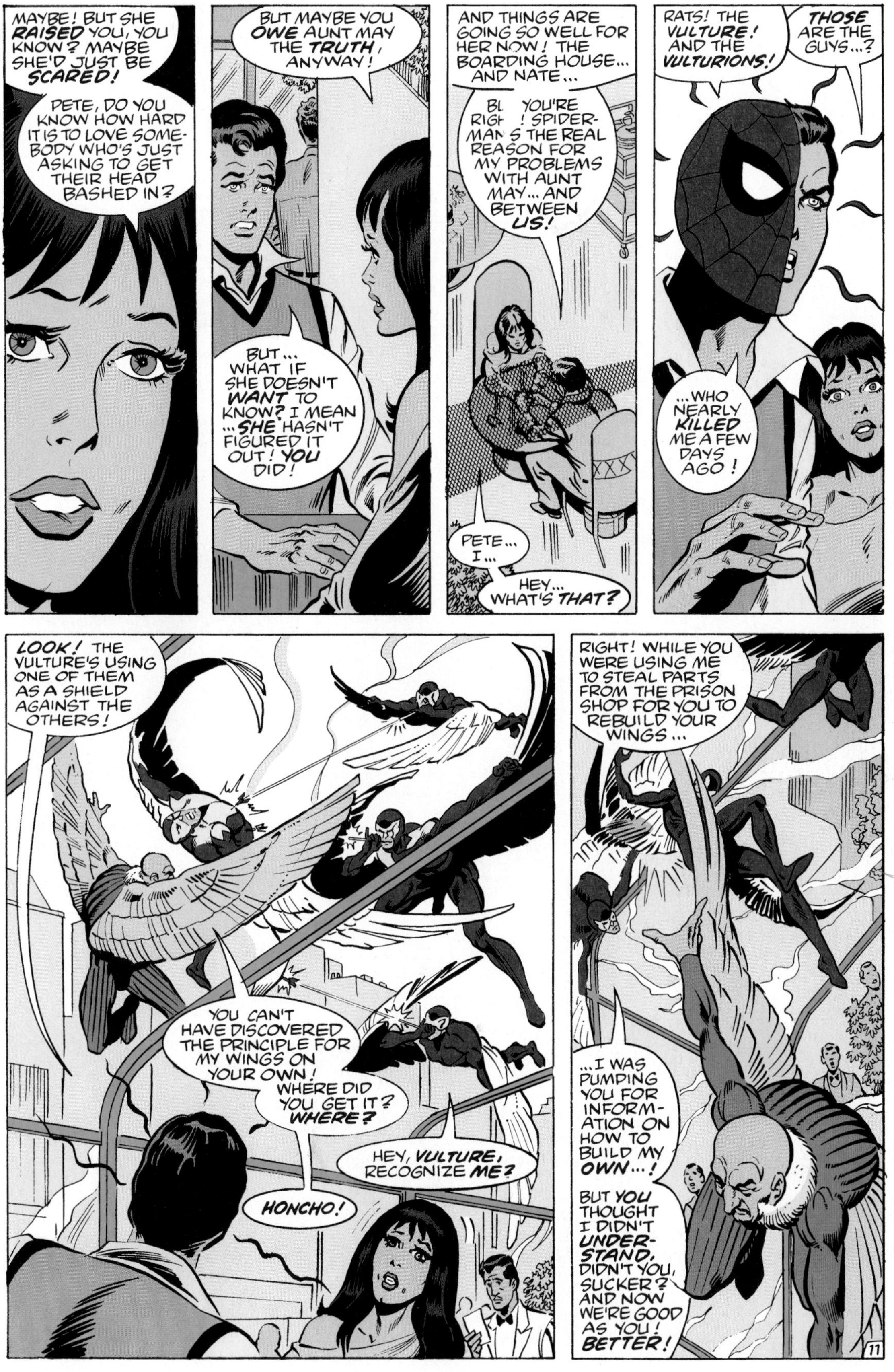
MAYBE! BUT SHE RAISED YOU, YOU KNOW? MAYBE SHE'D JUST BE SCARED!
PETE, DO YOU KNOW HOW HARD IT IS TO LOVE SOMEBODY WHO'S JUST ASKING TO GET THEIR HEAD BASHED IN?
BUT MAYBE YOU OWE AUNT MAY THE TRUTH, ANYWAY!
BUT... WHAT IF SHE DOESN'T WANT TO KNOW? I MEAN ...SHE HASN'T FIGURED IT OUT! YOU DID!
AND THINGS ARE GOING SO WELL FOR HER NOW! THE BOARDING HOUSE... AND NATE...
BL YOU'RE RIGH ! SPIDER-MAN S THE REAL REASON FOR MY PROBLEMS WITH AUNT MAY... AND BETWEEN US!
PETE... I...
HEY... WHAT'S THAT?
RATS! THE VULTURE! AND THE VULTURIONS!
THOSE ARE THE GUYS...?
...WHO NEARLY KILLED ME A FEW DAYS AGO!
LOOK! THE VULTURE'S USING ONE OF THEM AS A SHIELD AGAINST THE OTHERS!
YOU CAN'T HAVE DISCOVERED THE PRINCIPLE FOR MY WINGS ON YOUR OWN! WHERE DID YOU GET IT? WHERE?
HEY, VULTURE, RECOGNIZE ME?
HONCHO!
RIGHT! WHILE YOU WERE USING ME TO STEAL PARTS FROM THE PRISON SHOP FOR YOU TO REBUILD YOUR WINGS...
...I WAS PUMPING YOU FOR INFORMATION ON HOW TO BUILD MY OWN...!
BUT YOU THOUGHT I DIDN'T UNDERSTAND, DIDN'T YOU, SUCKER? AND NOW WE'RE GOOD AS YOU! BETTER!
11

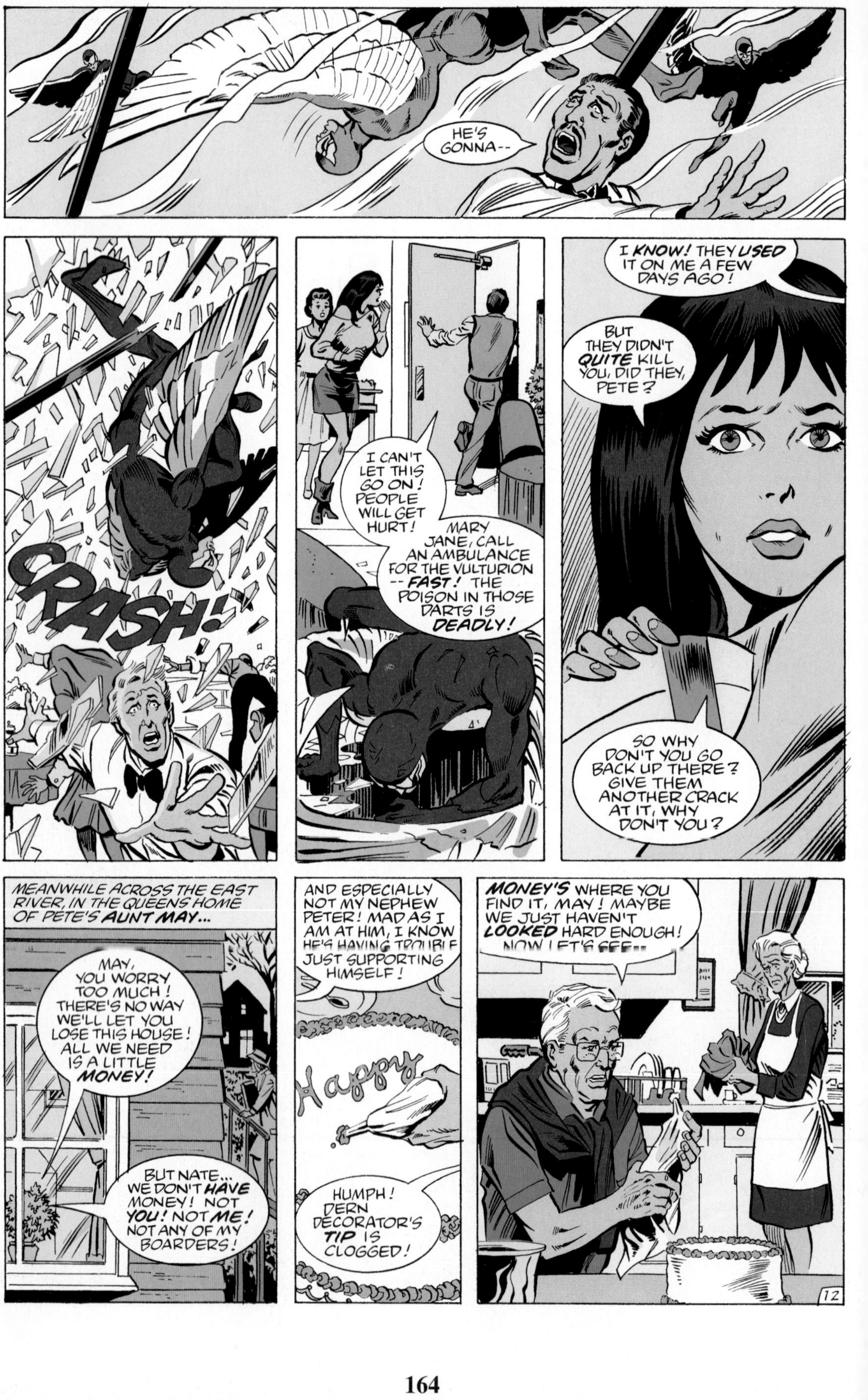
HE'S GONNA--
CRASH!
I CAN'T LET THIS GO ON! PEOPLE WILL GET HURT!
MARY JANE, CALL AN AMBULANCE FOR THE VULTURION --FAST! THE POISON IN THOSE DARTS IS DEADLY!
I KNOW! THEY USED IT ON ME A FEW DAYS AGO!
BUT THEY DIDN'T QUITE KILL YOU, DID THEY, PETE?
SO WHY DON'T YOU GO BACK UP THERE? GIVE THEM ANOTHER CRACK AT IT, WHY DON'T YOU?
MEANWHILE ACROSS THE EAST RIVER, IN THE QUEENS HOME OF PETE'S AUNT MAY...
MAY, YOU WORRY TOO MUCH! THERE'S NO WAY WE'LL LET YOU LOSE THIS HOUSE! ALL WE NEED IS A LITTLE MONEY!
BUT NATE... WE DON'T HAVE MONEY! NOT YOU! NOT ME! NOT ANY OF MY BOARDERS!
AND ESPECIALLY NOT MY NEPHEW PETER! MAD AS I AM AT HIM, I KNOW HE'S HAVING TROUBLE JUST SUPPORTING HIMSELF!
Happy
HUMPH! DERN DECORATOR'S TIP IS CLOGGED!
MONEY'S WHERE YOU FIND IT, MAY! MAYBE WE JUST HAVEN'T LOOKED HARD ENOUGH! NOW LET'S SEE--
12

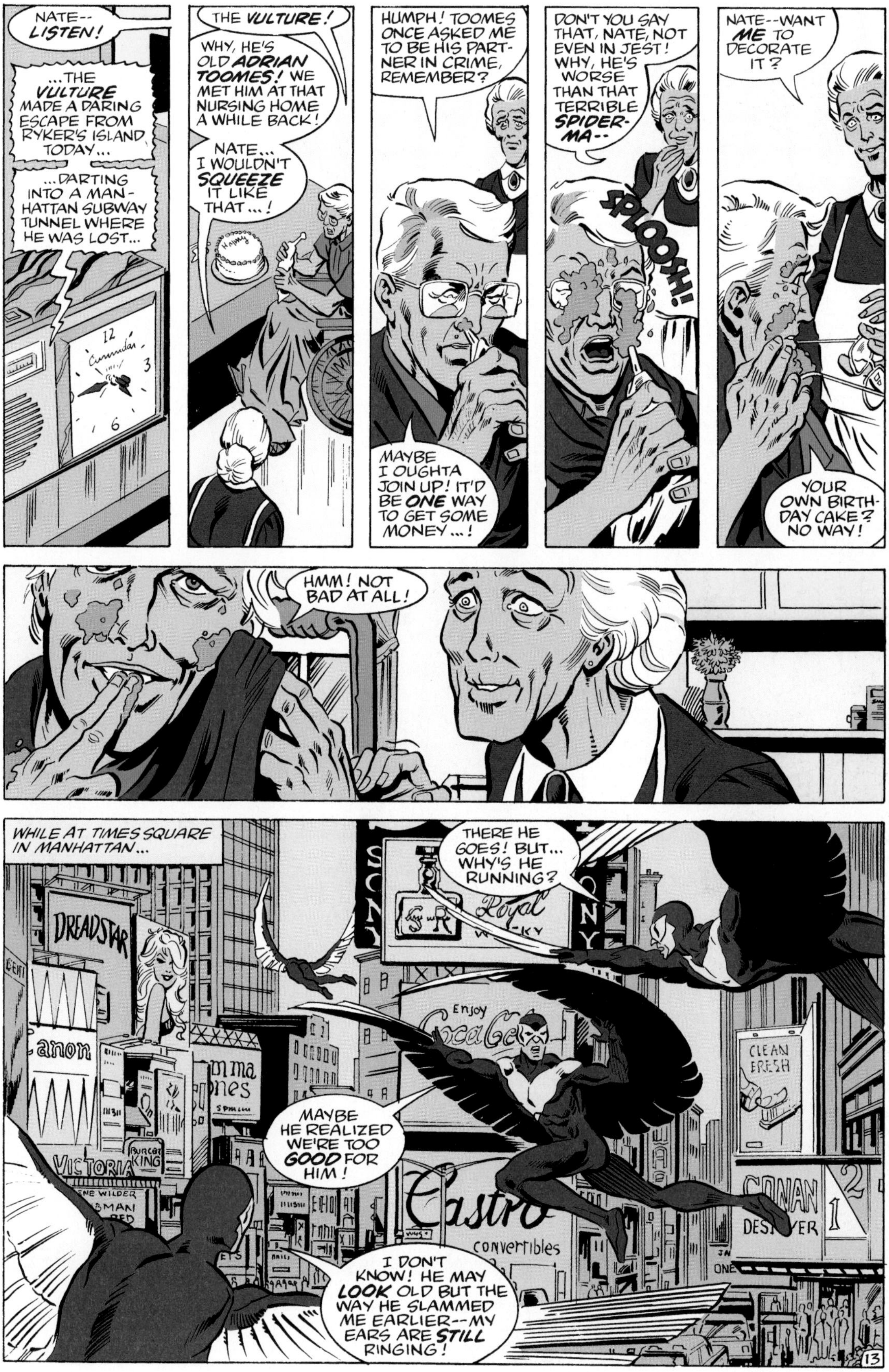
NATE-- LISTEN!
...THE VULTURE MADE A DARING ESCAPE FROM RYKER'S ISLAND TODAY...
...DARTING INTO A MANHATTAN SUBWAY TUNNEL WHERE HE WAS LOST...
THE VULTURE!
WHY, HE'S OLD ADRIAN TOOMES! WE MET HIM AT THAT NURSING HOME A WHILE BACK!
NATE... I WOULDN'T SQUEEZE IT LIKE THAT...!
HUMPH! TOOMES ONCE ASKED ME TO BE HIS PARTNER IN CRIME, REMEMBER?
MAYBE I OUGHTA JOIN UP! IT'D BE ONE WAY TO GET SOME MONEY...!
DON'T YOU SAY THAT, NATE, NOT EVEN IN JEST! WHY, HE'S WORSE THAN THAT TERRIBLE SPIDER-MA--
SPLOOSH!
NATE--WANT ME TO DECORATE IT?
YOUR OWN BIRTHDAY CAKE? NO WAY!
HMM! NOT BAD AT ALL!
WHILE AT TIMES SQUARE IN MANHATTAN...
THERE HE GOES! BUT... WHY'S HE RUNNING?
MAYBE HE REALIZED WE'RE TOO GOOD FOR HIM!
I DON'T KNOW! HE MAY LOOK OLD BUT THE WAY HE SLAMMED ME EARLIER--MY EARS ARE STILL RINGING!
DREADSTAR
Enjoy Coca-Cola
CLEAN FRESH
CONAN DESTROYER
Castro convertibles
VICTORIA
BURGER KING
13

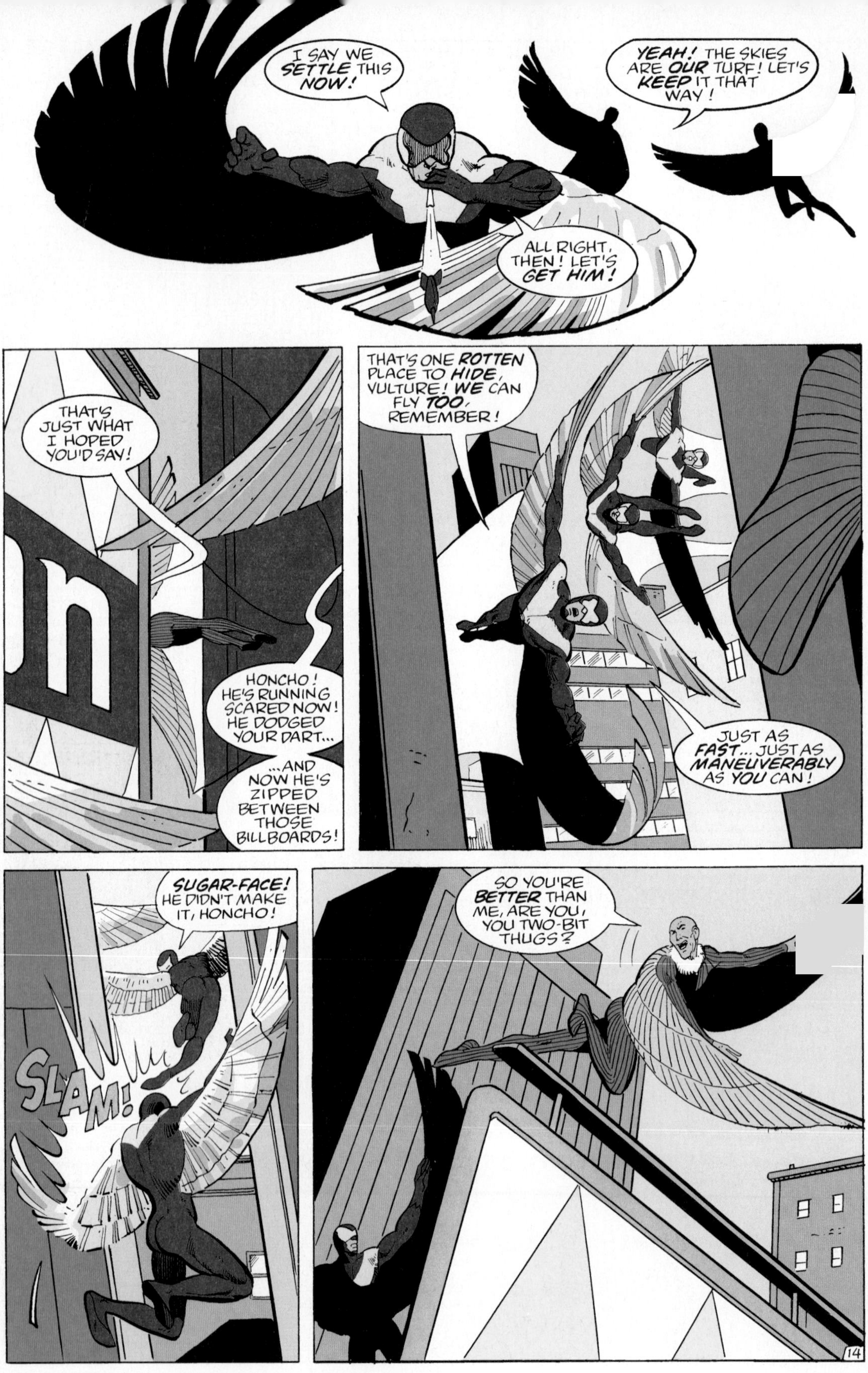

I SAY WE SETTLE THIS NOW!
YEAH! THE SKIES ARE OUR TURF! LET'S KEEP IT THAT WAY!
ALL RIGHT, THEN! LET'S GET HIM!
THAT'S JUST WHAT I HOPED YOU'D SAY!
HONCHO! HE'S RUNNING SCARED NOW! HE DODGED YOUR DART...
...AND NOW HE'S ZIPPED BETWEEN THOSE BILLBOARDS!
THAT'S ONE ROTTEN PLACE TO HIDE, VULTURE! WE CAN FLY TOO, REMEMBER!
JUST AS FAST... JUST AS MANEUVERABLY AS YOU CAN!
SUGAR-FACE! HE DIDN'T MAKE IT, HONCHO!
SLAM!
SO YOU'RE BETTER THAN ME, ARE YOU, YOU TWO-BIT THUGS?
14

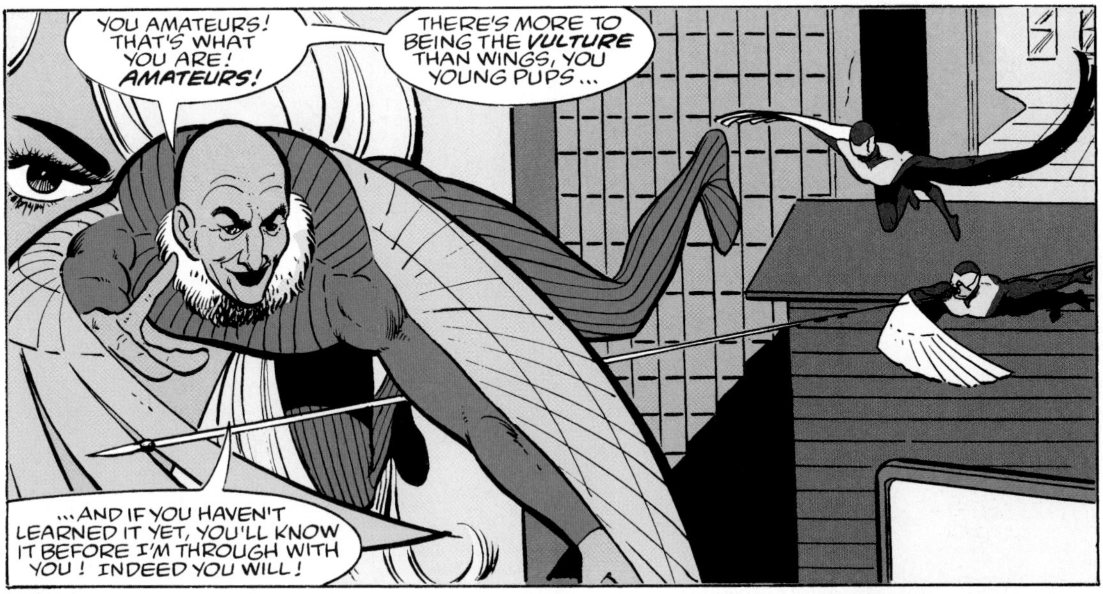
YOU AMATEURS! THAT'S WHAT YOU ARE! AMATEURS!
THERE'S MORE TO BEING THE VULTURE THAN WINGS, YOU YOUNG PUPS...
...AND IF YOU HAVEN'T LEARNED IT YET, YOU'LL KNOW IT BEFORE I'M THROUGH WITH YOU! INDEED YOU WILL!

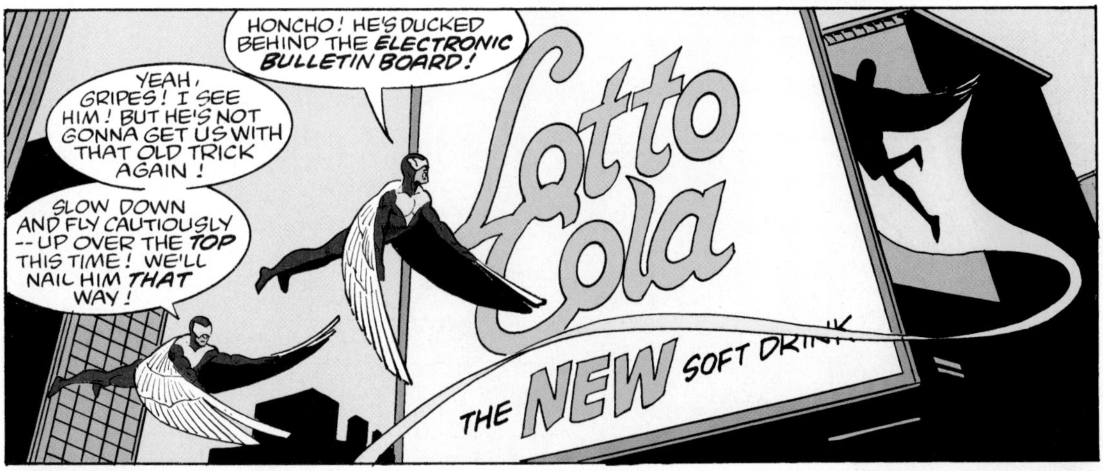
HONCHO! HE'S DUCKED BEHIND THE ELECTRONIC BULLETIN BOARD!
YEAH, GRIPES! I SEE HIM! BUT HE'S NOT GONNA GET US WITH THAT OLD TRICK AGAIN!
SLOW DOWN AND FLY CAUTIOUSLY -- UP OVER THE TOP THIS TIME! WE'LL NAIL HIM THAT WAY!
Lotto Cola
THE NEW SOFT DRINK

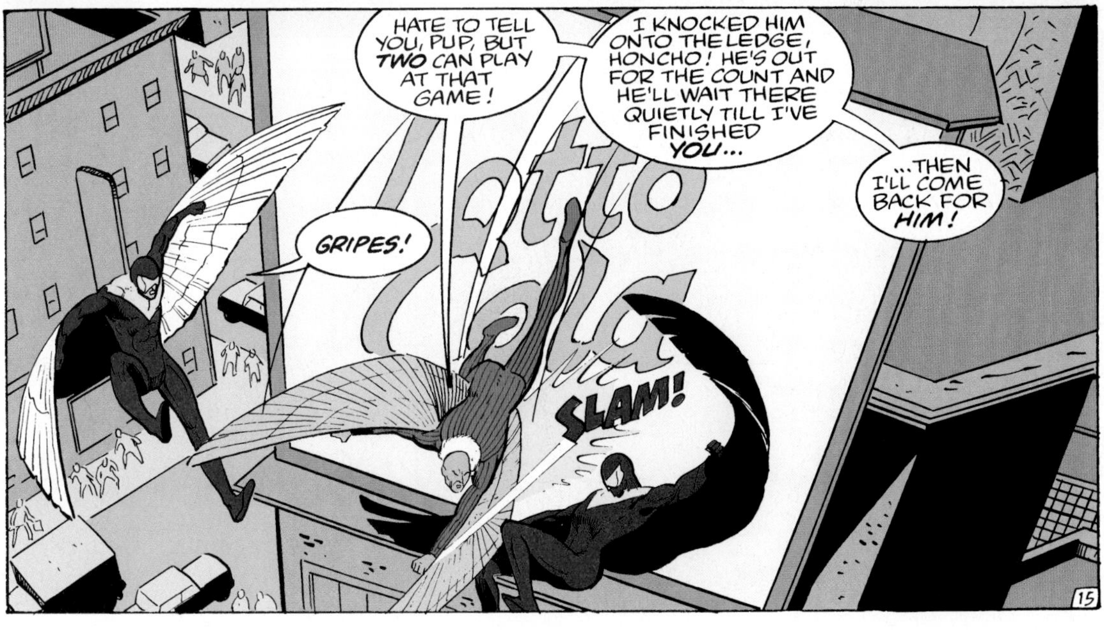
HATE TO TELL YOU, PUP, BUT TWO CAN PLAY AT THAT GAME!
I KNOCKED HIM ONTO THE LEDGE, HONCHO! HE'S OUT FOR THE COUNT AND HE'LL WAIT THERE QUIETLY TILL I'VE FINISHED YOU...
...THEN I'LL COME BACK FOR HIM!
GRIPES!
SLAM!
15

WHAT MARY JANE SAID ABOUT MY BEING SPIDER-MAN MADE A LOT OF SENSE... FOR US AS WELL AS AUNT MAY!
BUT... SHOULD I TELL AUNT MAY THE TRUTH? IT MIGHT MAKE THINGS WORSE!
MARY JANE SEEMS TO THINK I HAVE SORT OF A DEATH WISH!
COULD I BE SO GUILTY ABOUT NOT STOPPING THE CROOK WHO LATER KILLED MY UNCLE BEN THAT I'M TRYING TO ATONE FOR HIS DEATH WITH MY OWN?
OH NO! AUNT MAY'S HAT! I FORGOT IT! I GOTTA GO BACK!
Charlie
HATS
I CAN'T DISAPPOINT HER!
HOO BOY!
YOU THOUGHT I WAS OLD, DIDN'T YOU? THOUGHT YOU COULD STEAL MY DESIGN AND MAKE YOURSELVES RICH!
DID YOU THINK I'D SIT STILL FOR IT? THAT I WOULDN'T COME LOOKING FOR YOU?
KILLING YOU IS GOING TO BE A PIECE OF CAKE!
NO! IT ISN'T GUILT--BUT DARN IT, I DO FEEL RESPONSIBLE!
I WAS BITTEN BY A RADIO-ACTIVE SPIDER! GIVEN STRENGTH, AGILITY, THE ABILITY TO STICK TO ANY SURFACE! EVEN A SORT OF DANGER RADAR!
I HAVE TO USE THESE POWERS FOR RIGHT...
...THOUGH SAVING A GUY WHO TRIED TO KILL ME MIGHT BE CARRYING RESPONSIBILITY A BIT FAR!
16

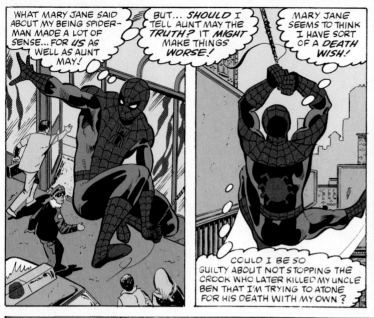

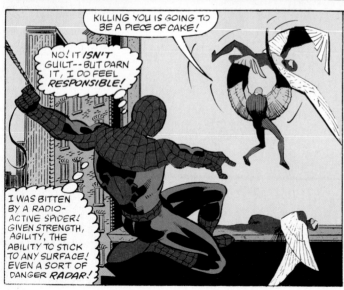

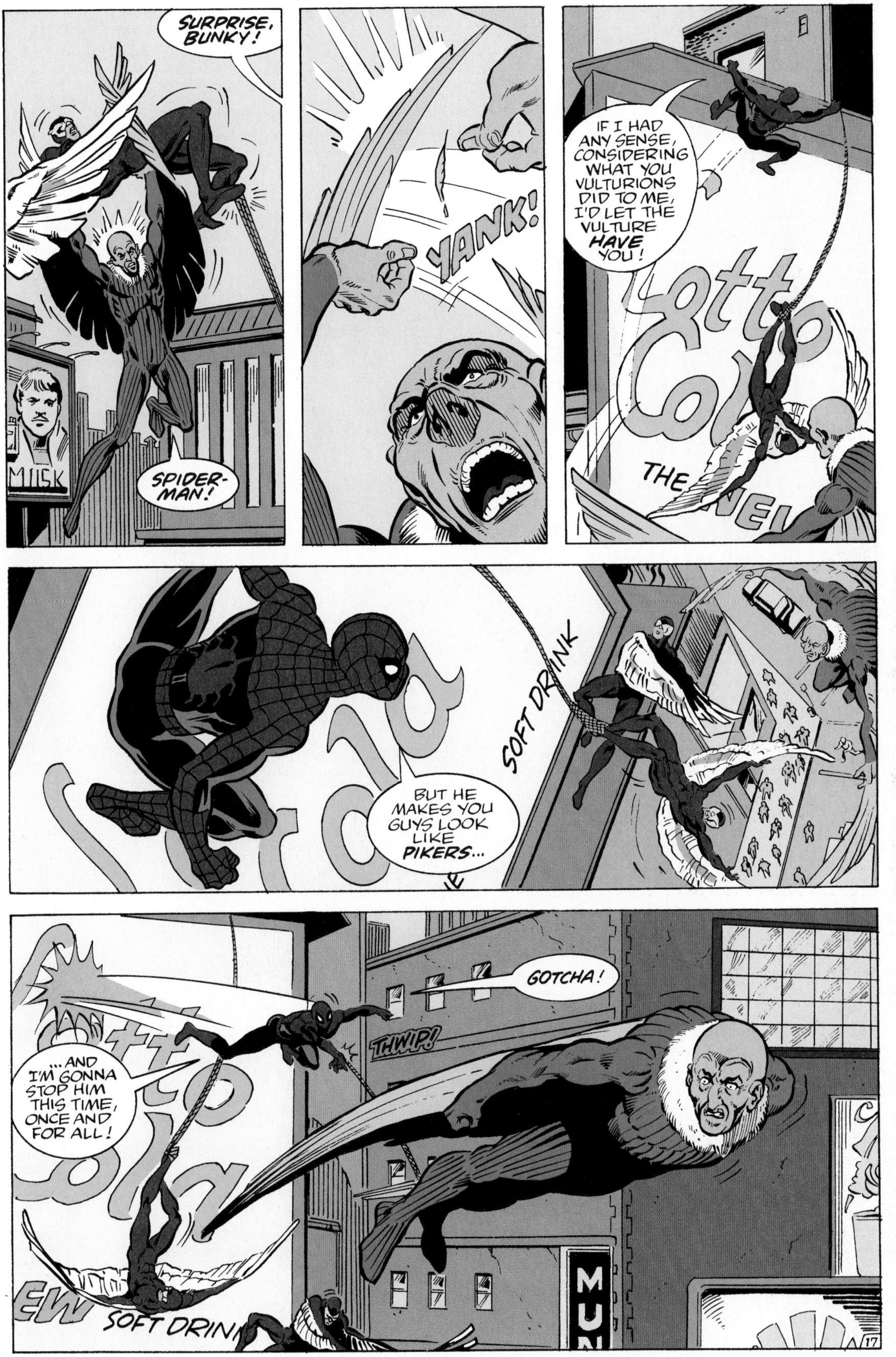
SURPRISE, BUNKY!
SPIDER-MAN!
YANK!
IF I HAD ANY SENSE, CONSIDERING WHAT YOU VULTURIONS DID TO ME, I'D LET THE VULTURE HAVE YOU!
BUT HE MAKES YOU GUYS LOOK LIKE PIKERS...
SOFT DRINK
GOTCHA!
THWIP!
...AND I'M GONNA STOP HIM THIS TIME, ONCE AND FOR ALL!
SOFT DRIN
17

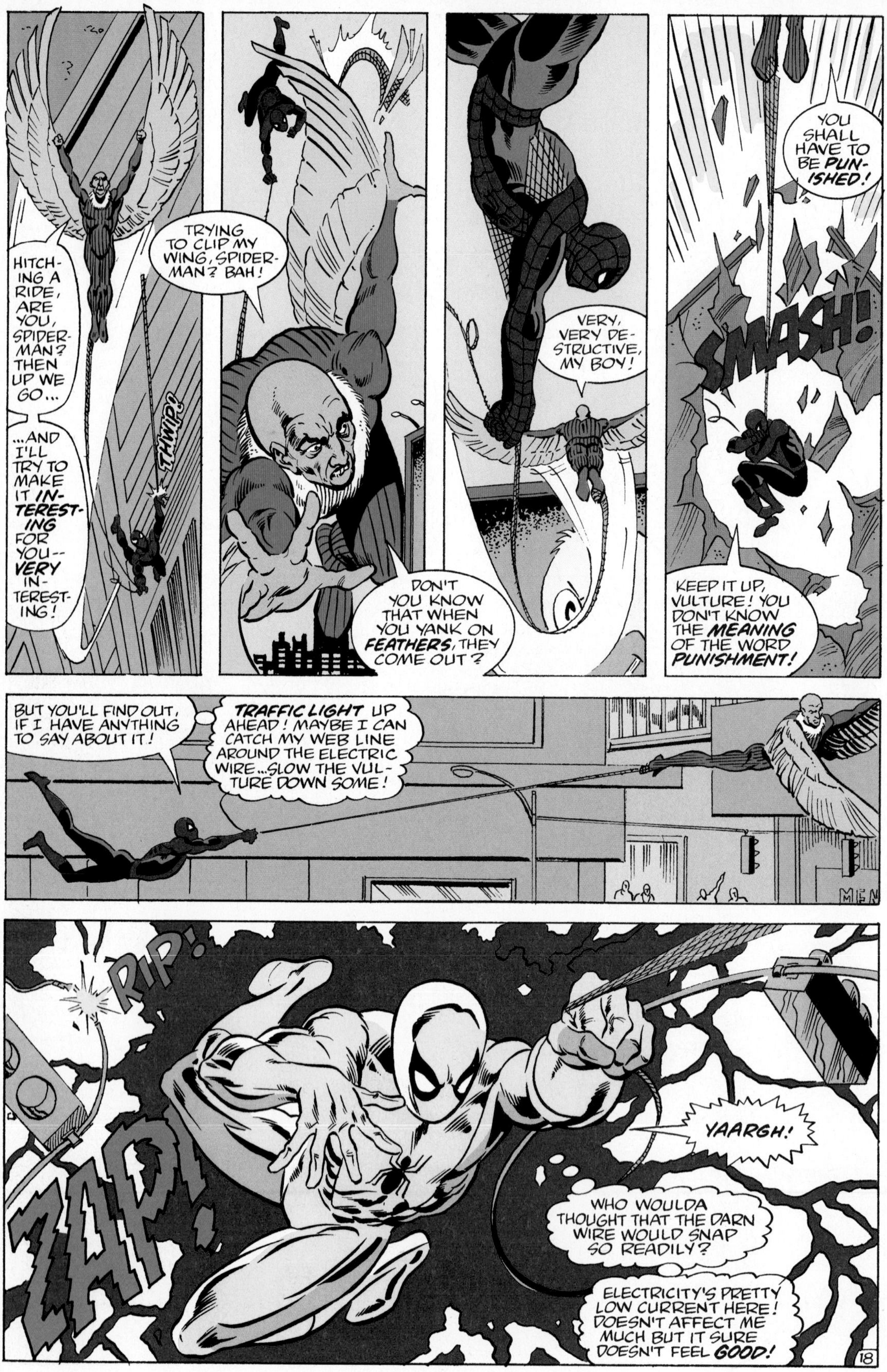
HITCHING A RIDE, ARE YOU, SPIDER-MAN? THEN UP WE GO...
...AND I'LL TRY TO MAKE IT INTERESTING FOR YOU-- VERY INTERESTING!
THWIP!
TRYING TO CLIP MY WING, SPIDER-MAN? BAH!
DON'T YOU KNOW THAT WHEN YOU YANK ON FEATHERS, THEY COME OUT?
VERY, VERY DESTRUCTIVE, MY BOY!
YOU SHALL HAVE TO BE PUNISHED!
SMASH!
KEEP IT UP, VULTURE! YOU DON'T KNOW THE MEANING OF THE WORD PUNISHMENT!
BUT YOU'LL FIND OUT, IF I HAVE ANYTHING TO SAY ABOUT IT!
TRAFFIC LIGHT UP AHEAD! MAYBE I CAN CATCH MY WEB LINE AROUND THE ELECTRIC WIRE...SLOW THE VULTURE DOWN SOME!
RIP!
ZAP!
YAARGH!
WHO WOULDA THOUGHT THAT THE DARN WIRE WOULD SNAP SO READILY?
ELECTRICITY'S PRETTY LOW CURRENT HERE! DOESN'T AFFECT ME MUCH BUT IT SURE DOESN'T FEEL GOOD!
18

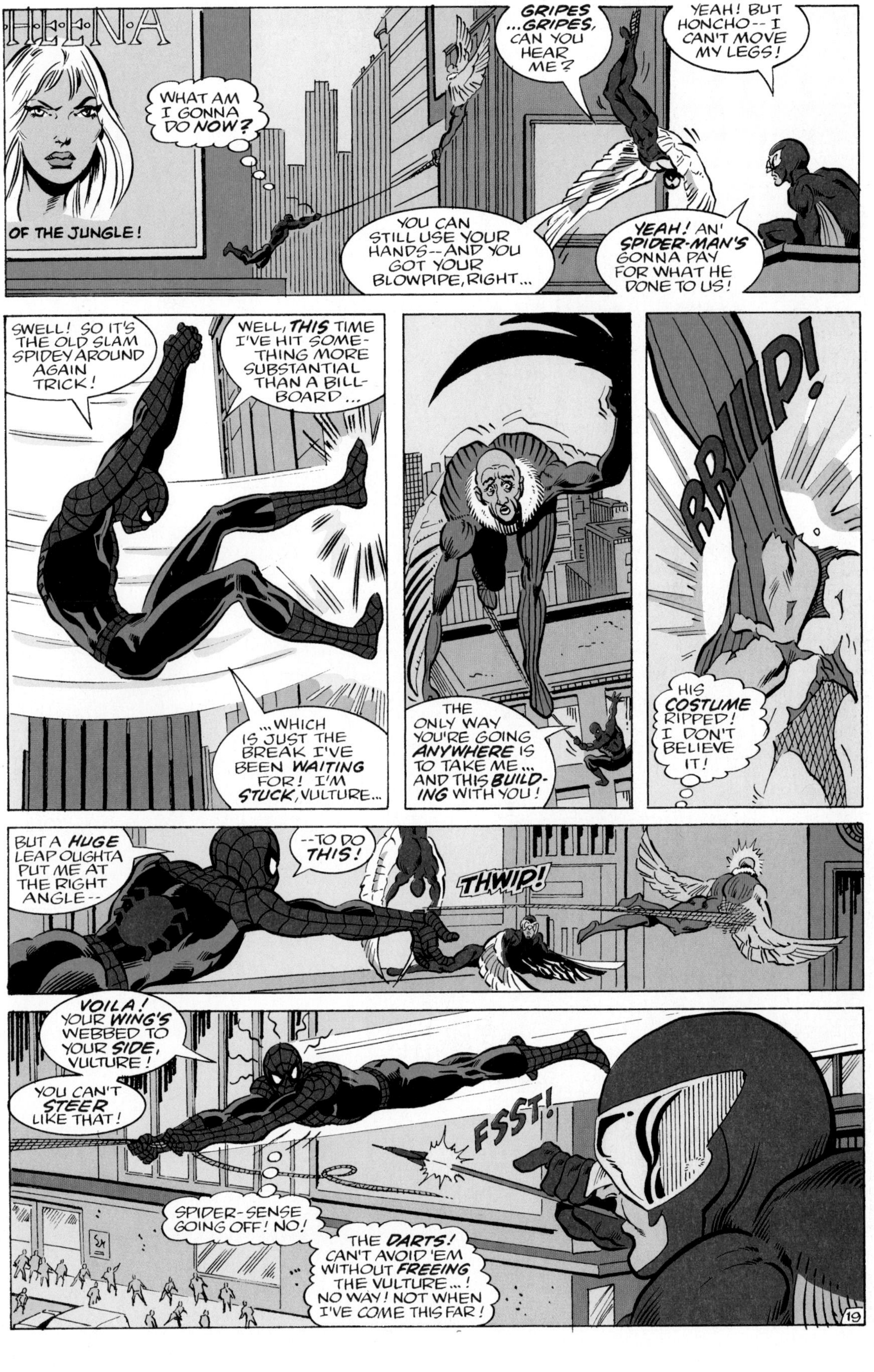
H·E·L·E·N·A
OF THE JUNGLE!
WHAT AM I GONNA DO NOW?
GRIPES ...GRIPES, CAN YOU HEAR ME?
YEAH! BUT HONCHO-- I CAN'T MOVE MY LEGS!
YOU CAN STILL USE YOUR HANDS--AND YOU GOT YOUR BLOWPIPE, RIGHT...
YEAH! AN' SPIDER-MAN'S GONNA PAY FOR WHAT HE DONE TO US!
SWELL! SO IT'S THE OLD SLAM SPIDEY AROUND AGAIN TRICK!
WELL, THIS TIME I'VE HIT SOMETHING MORE SUBSTANTIAL THAN A BILLBOARD...
...WHICH IS JUST THE BREAK I'VE BEEN WAITING FOR! I'M STUCK, VULTURE...
THE ONLY WAY YOU'RE GOING ANYWHERE IS TO TAKE ME... AND THIS BUILDING WITH YOU!
RRIIIP!
HIS COSTUME RIPPED! I DON'T BELIEVE IT!
BUT A HUGE LEAP OUGHTA PUT ME AT THE RIGHT ANGLE--
--TO DO THIS!
THWIP!
VOILA! YOUR WING'S WEBBED TO YOUR SIDE, VULTURE!
YOU CAN'T STEER LIKE THAT!
FSST!
SPIDER-SENSE GOING OFF! NO!
THE DARTS! CAN'T AVOID 'EM WITHOUT FREEING THE VULTURE...! NO WAY! NOT WHEN I'VE COME THIS FAR!
19

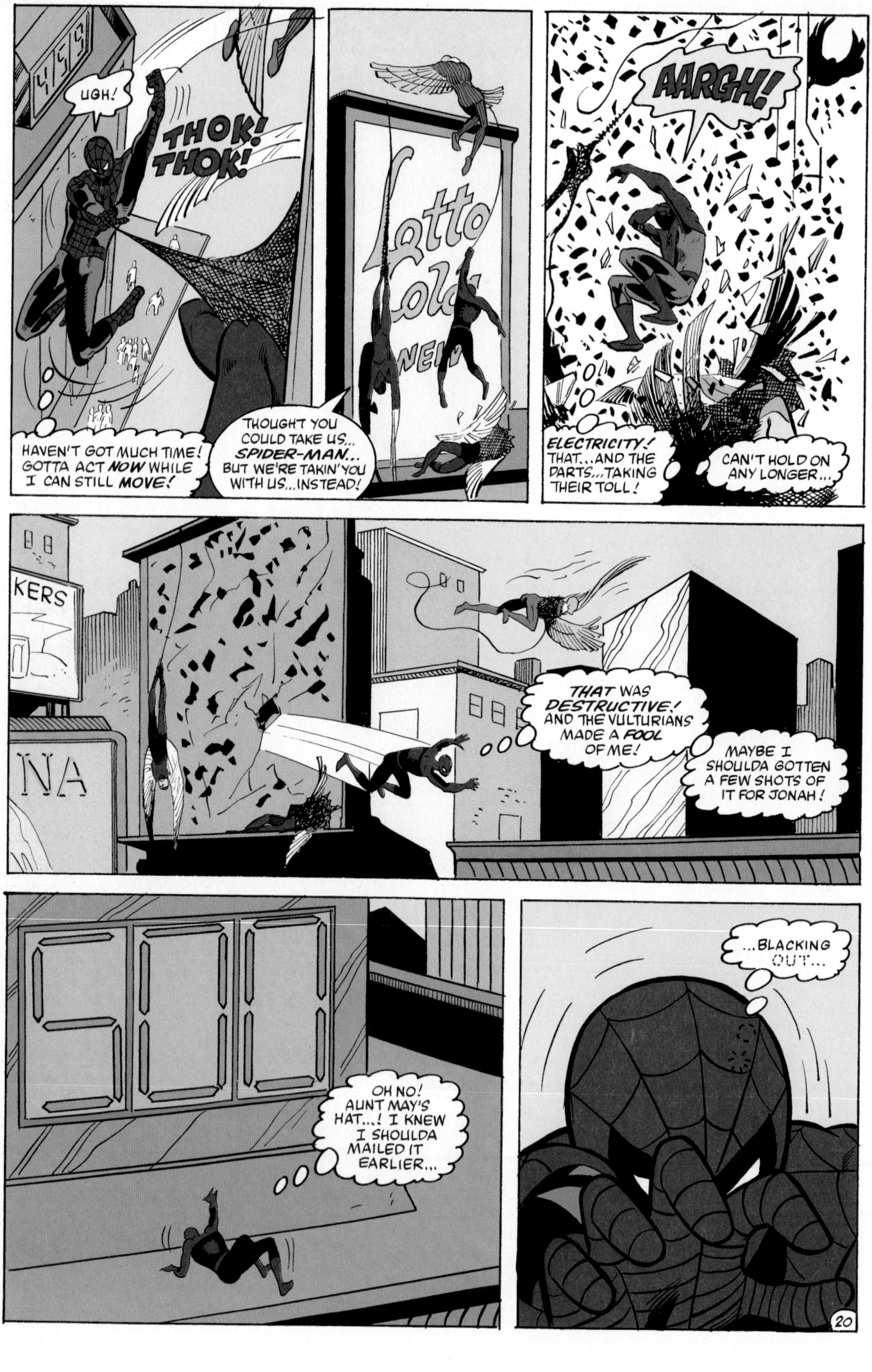
UGH!
THOK! THOK!
HAVEN'T GOT MUCH TIME! GOTTA ACT NOW WHILE I CAN STILL MOVE!
THOUGHT YOU COULD TAKE US... SPIDER-MAN... BUT WE'RE TAKIN' YOU WITH US... INSTEAD!
AARGH!
ELECTRICITY! THAT... AND THE DARTS... TAKING THEIR TOLL!
CAN'T HOLD ON ANY LONGER...
THAT WAS DESTRUCTIVE! AND THE VULTURIANS MADE A FOOL OF ME!
MAYBE I SHOULDA GOTTEN A FEW SHOTS OF IT FOR JONAH!
OH NO! AUNT MAY'S HAT...! I KNEW I SHOULDA MAILED IT EARLIER...
...BLACKING OUT...
20

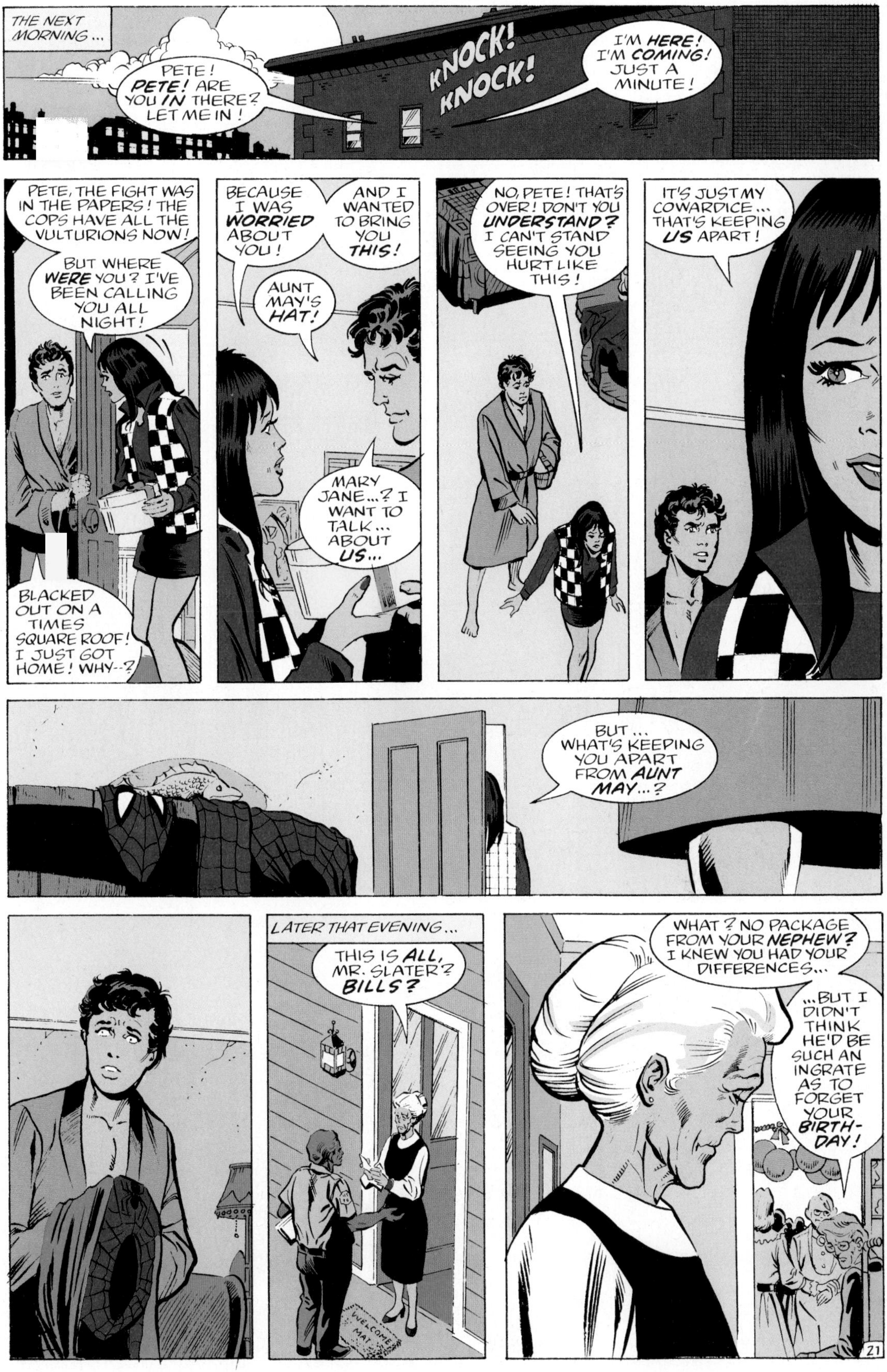
THE NEXT MORNING ...
PETE! PETE! ARE YOU IN THERE? LET ME IN!
KNOCK! KNOCK!
I'M HERE! I'M COMING! JUST A MINUTE!
PETE, THE FIGHT WAS IN THE PAPERS! THE COPS HAVE ALL THE VULTURIONS NOW!
BUT WHERE WERE YOU? I'VE BEEN CALLING YOU ALL NIGHT!
BLACKED OUT ON A TIMES SQUARE ROOF! I JUST GOT HOME! WHY--?
BECAUSE I WAS WORRIED ABOUT YOU!
AND I WANTED TO BRING YOU THIS!
AUNT MAY'S HAT!
MARY JANE...? I WANT TO TALK... ABOUT US...
NO, PETE! THAT'S OVER! DON'T YOU UNDERSTAND? I CAN'T STAND SEEING YOU HURT LIKE THIS!
IT'S JUST MY COWARDICE... THAT'S KEEPING US APART!
BUT... WHAT'S KEEPING YOU APART FROM AUNT MAY...?
LATER THAT EVENING...
THIS IS ALL, MR. SLATER? BILLS?
WELCOME MAT
WHAT? NO PACKAGE FROM YOUR NEPHEW? I KNEW YOU HAD YOUR DIFFERENCES...
...BUT I DIDN'T THINK HE'D BE SUCH AN INGRATE AS TO FORGET YOUR BIRTHDAY!
21

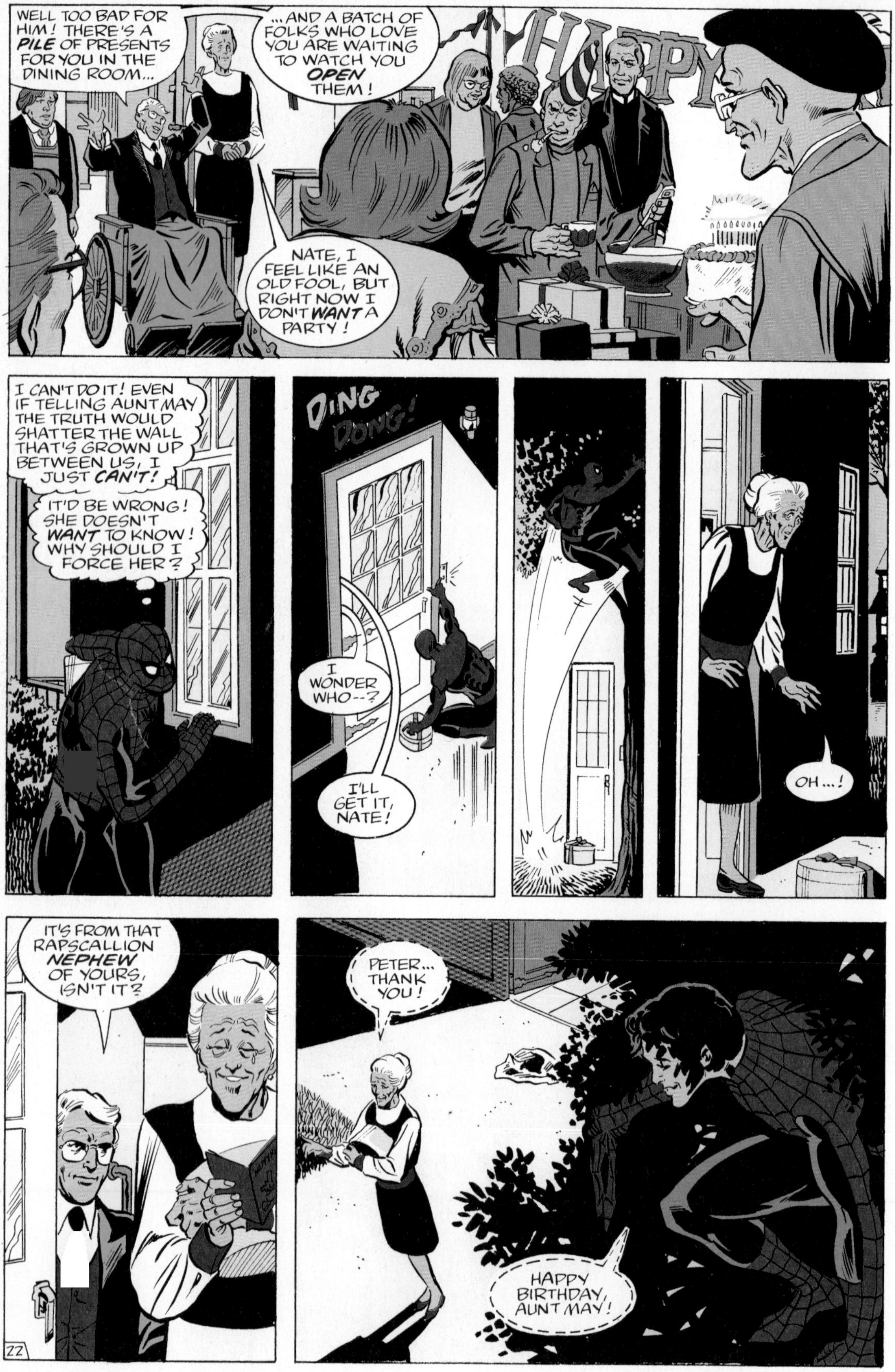
WELL TOO BAD FOR HIM! THERE'S A PILE OF PRESENTS FOR YOU IN THE DINING ROOM...
...AND A BATCH OF FOLKS WHO LOVE YOU ARE WAITING TO WATCH YOU OPEN THEM!
NATE, I FEEL LIKE AN OLD FOOL, BUT RIGHT NOW I DON'T WANT A PARTY!
I CAN'T DO IT! EVEN IF TELLING AUNT MAY THE TRUTH WOULD SHATTER THE WALL THAT'S GROWN UP BETWEEN US, I JUST CAN'T!
IT'D BE WRONG! SHE DOESN'T WANT TO KNOW! WHY SHOULD I FORCE HER?
DING DONG!
I WONDER WHO--?
I'LL GET IT, NATE!
OH...!
IT'S FROM THAT RAPSCALLION NEPHEW OF YOURS, ISN'T IT?
22
PETER... THANK YOU!
HAPPY BIRTHDAY, AUNT MAY!

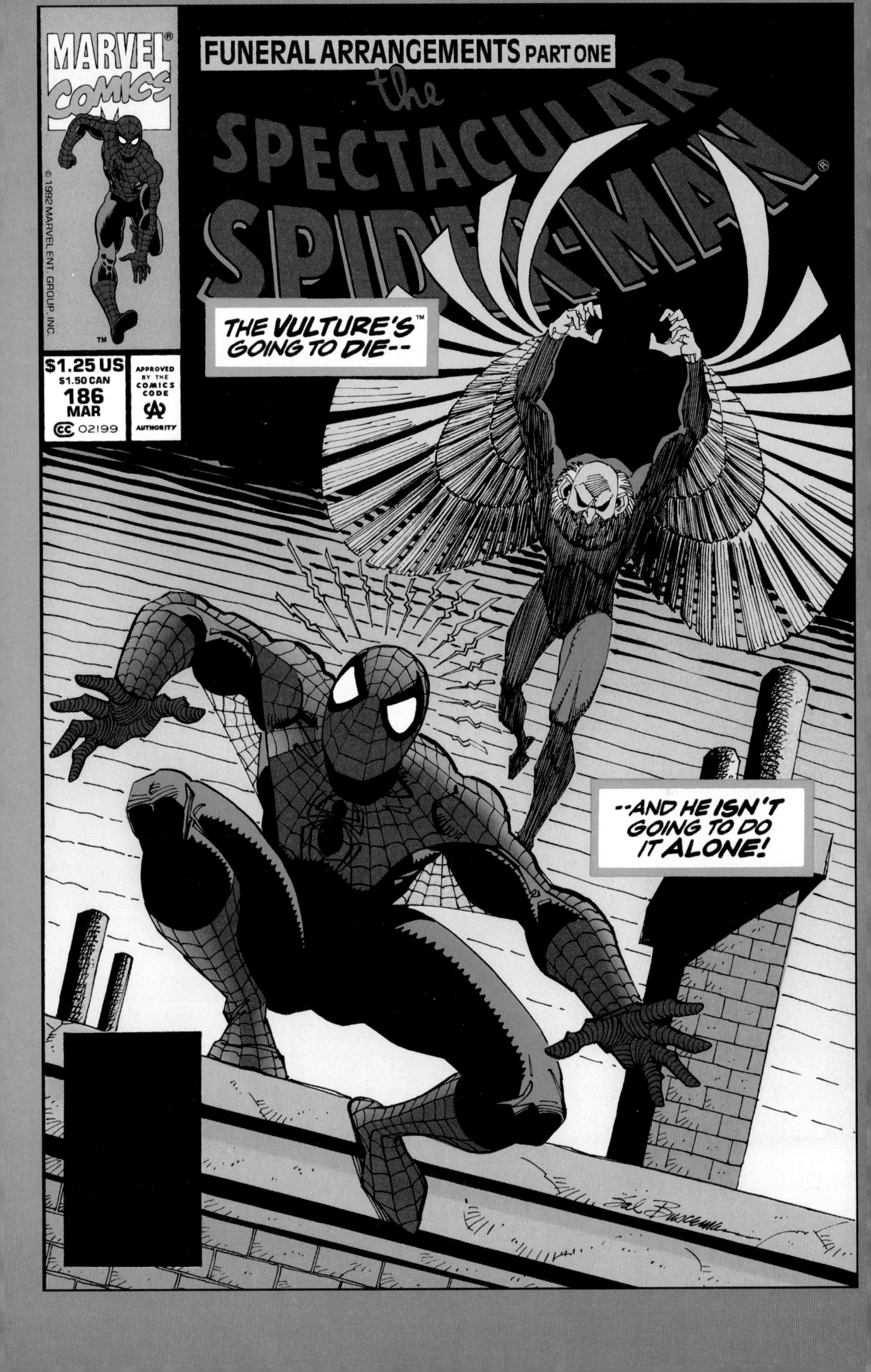
MARVEL® COMICS
FUNERAL ARRANGEMENTS PART ONE
the SPECTACULAR SPIDER-MAN®
© 1992 MARVEL ENT. GROUP, INC.
THE VULTURE'S™ GOING TO DIE--
$1.25 US
$1.50 CAN
186
MAR
02199
APPROVED BY THE COMICS CODE AUTHORITY
--AND HE ISN'T GOING TO DO IT ALONE!
Sal Buscema

BITTEN BY A RADIOACTIVE SPIDER, STUDENT **PETER PARKER** GAINED THE PROPORTIONATE STRENGTH AND AGILITY OF AN ARACHNID! ARMED WITH HIS WONDROUS WEB-SHOOTERS, THE RELUCTANT SUPER HERO STRUGGLES WITH SINISTER SUPER-VILLAINS, MAKING ENDS MEET, AND MAINTAINING SOME SEMBLANCE OF A NORMAL LIFE!

Stan Lee PRESENTS: **THE SPECTACULAR SPIDER-MAN!**™

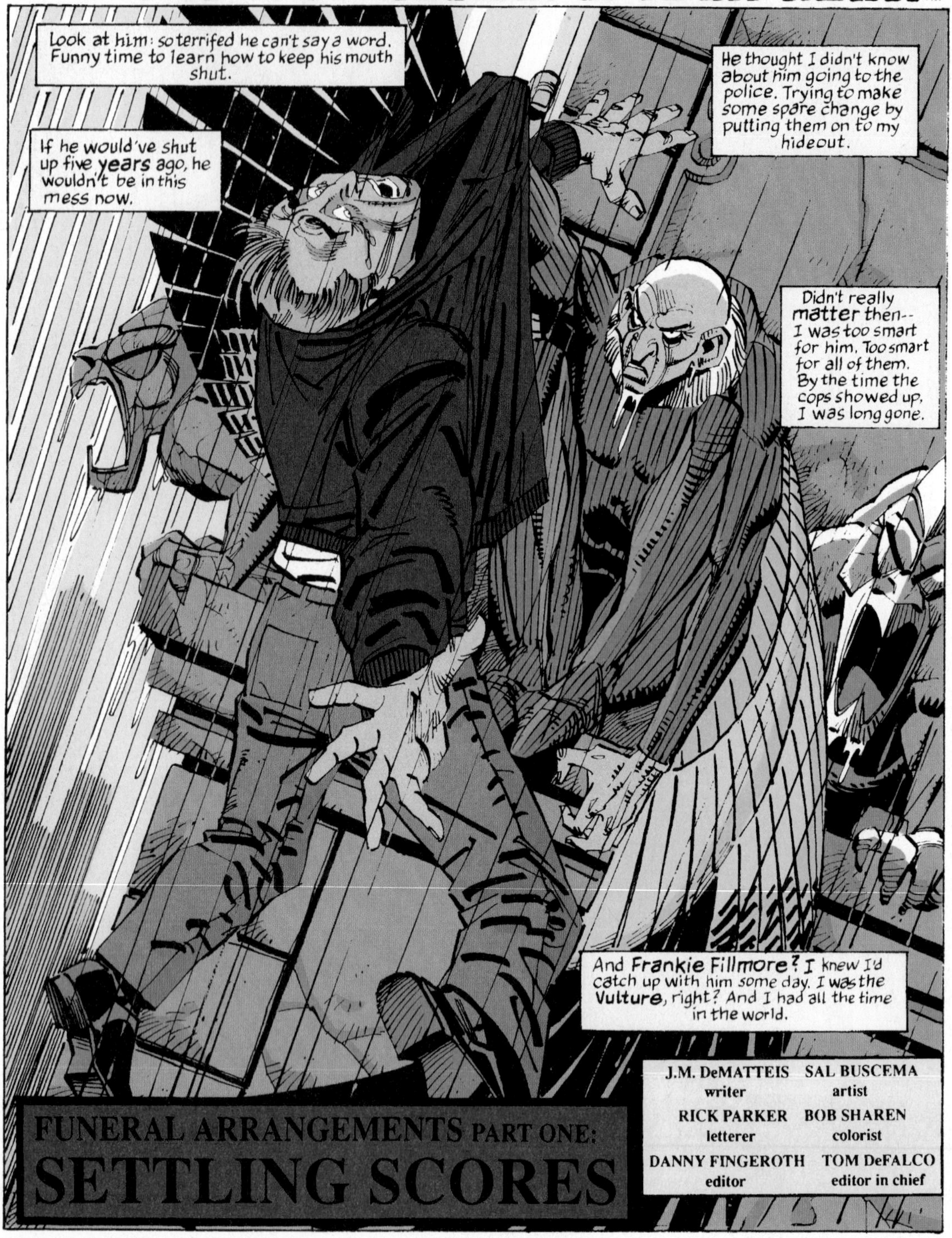
Look at him: so terrified he can't say a word. Funny time to learn how to keep his mouth shut.
If he would've shut up five years ago, he wouldn't be in this mess now.
He thought I didn't know about him going to the police. Trying to make some spare change by putting them on to my hideout.
Didn't really matter then-- I was too smart for him. Too smart for all of them. By the time the cops showed up, I was long gone.
And Frankie Fillmore? I knew I'd catch up with him some day. I was the Vulture, right? And I had all the time in the world.
FUNERAL ARRANGEMENTS PART ONE:
SETTLING SCORES
J.M. DeMATTEIS writer
SAL BUSCEMA artist
RICK PARKER letterer
BOB SHAREN colorist
DANNY FINGEROTH editor
TOM DeFALCO editor in chief

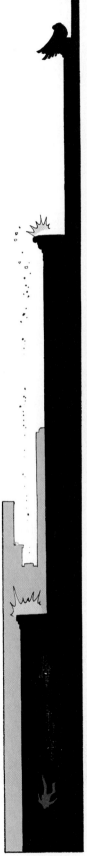

Not anymore.

177

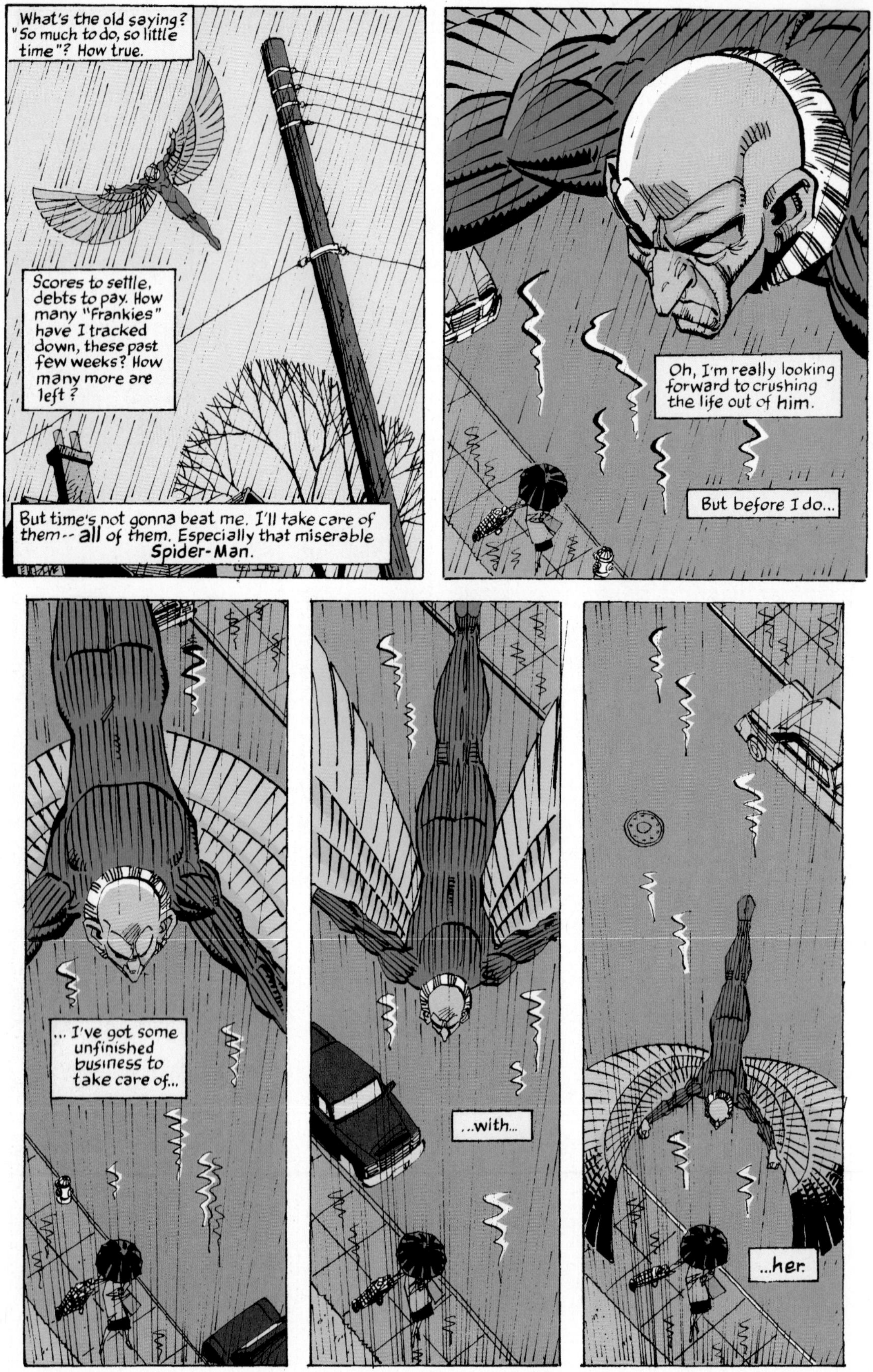
What's the old saying? "So much to do, so little time"? How true.
Scores to settle, debts to pay. How many "Frankies" have I tracked down, these past few weeks? How many more are left?
But time's not gonna beat me. I'll take care of them-- all of them. Especially that miserable Spider-Man.
Oh, I'm really looking forward to crushing the life out of him.
But before I do...
... I've got some unfinished business to take care of...
...with...
...her.

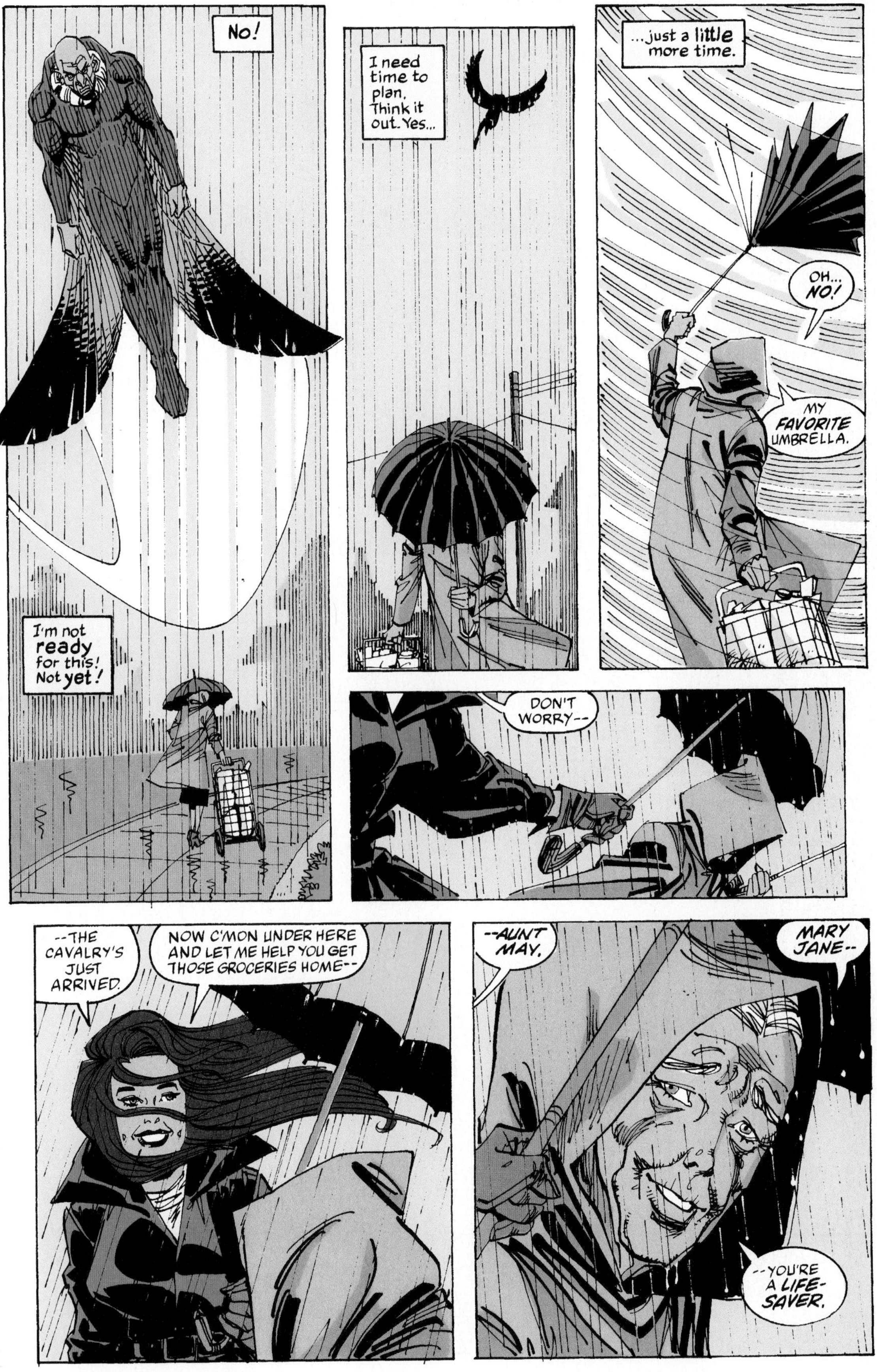
No!
I need time to plan. Think it out. Yes...
...just a little more time.
OH... NO!
MY FAVORITE UMBRELLA.
I'm not ready for this! Not yet!
DON'T WORRY--
--THE CAVALRY'S JUST ARRIVED.
NOW C'MON UNDER HERE AND LET ME HELP YOU GET THOSE GROCERIES HOME--
--AUNT MAY.
MARY JANE--
--YOU'RE A LIFE-SAVER.

KRASH
KLIK

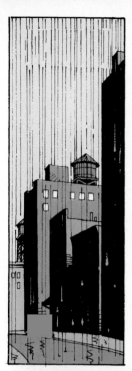

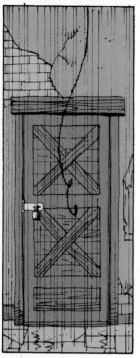

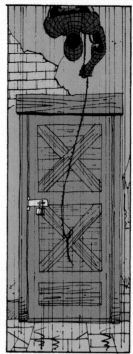

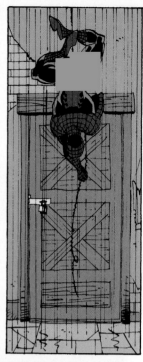

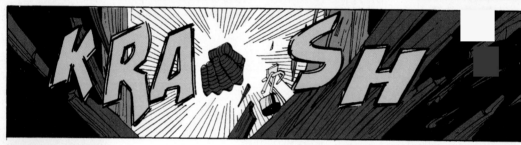

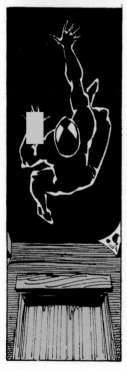

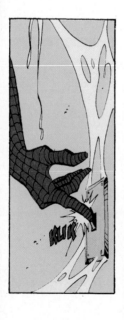

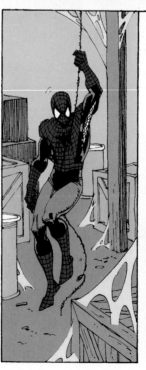

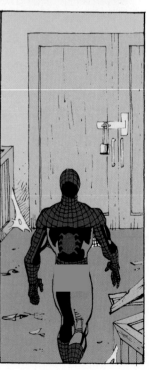

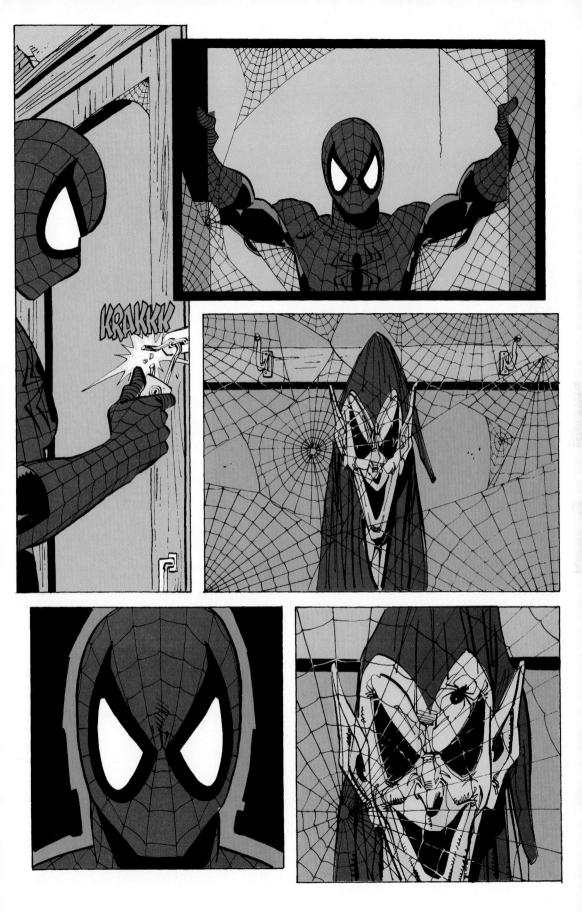

KRAKKK

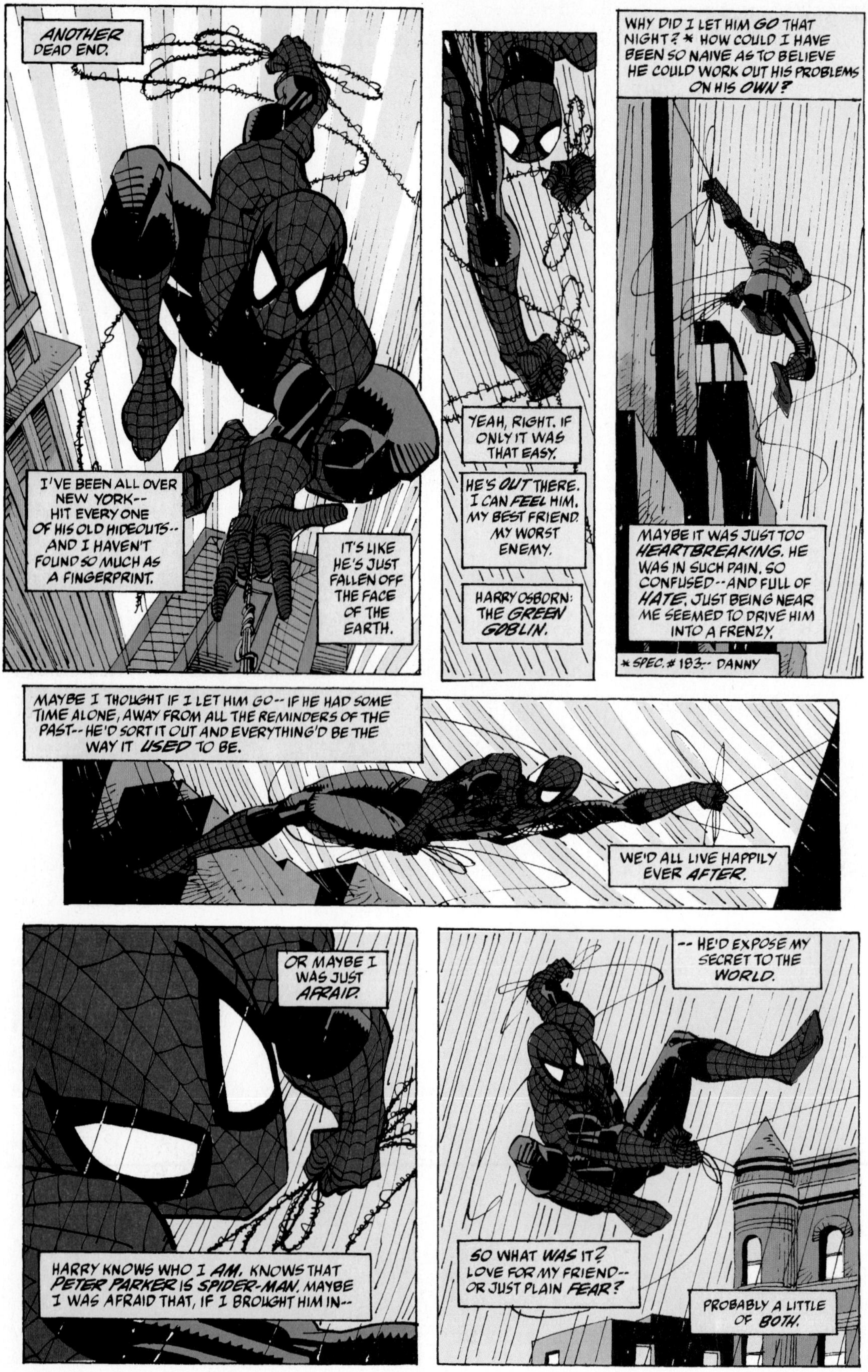
ANOTHER DEAD END.
I'VE BEEN ALL OVER NEW YORK-- HIT EVERY ONE OF HIS OLD HIDEOUTS-- AND I HAVEN'T FOUND SO MUCH AS A FINGERPRINT.
IT'S LIKE HE'S JUST FALLEN OFF THE FACE OF THE EARTH.
YEAH, RIGHT. IF ONLY IT WAS THAT EASY.
HE'S OUT THERE. I CAN FEEL HIM. MY BEST FRIEND. MY WORST ENEMY.
HARRY OSBORN: THE GREEN GOBLIN.
WHY DID I LET HIM GO THAT NIGHT? * HOW COULD I HAVE BEEN SO NAIVE AS TO BELIEVE HE COULD WORK OUT HIS PROBLEMS ON HIS OWN?
MAYBE IT WAS JUST TOO HEARTBREAKING. HE WAS IN SUCH PAIN. SO CONFUSED--AND FULL OF HATE. JUST BEING NEAR ME SEEMED TO DRIVE HIM INTO A FRENZY.
* SPEC. # 183.- DANNY
MAYBE I THOUGHT IF I LET HIM GO-- IF HE HAD SOME TIME ALONE, AWAY FROM ALL THE REMINDERS OF THE PAST-- HE'D SORT IT OUT AND EVERYTHING'D BE THE WAY IT USED TO BE.
WE'D ALL LIVE HAPPILY EVER AFTER.
OR MAYBE I WAS JUST AFRAID.
HARRY KNOWS WHO I AM. KNOWS THAT PETER PARKER IS SPIDER-MAN. MAYBE I WAS AFRAID THAT, IF I BROUGHT HIM IN--
-- HE'D EXPOSE MY SECRET TO THE WORLD.
SO WHAT WAS IT? LOVE FOR MY FRIEND-- OR JUST PLAIN FEAR?
PROBABLY A LITTLE OF BOTH.

BOTTOM LINE IS-- I MADE A *MISTAKE.*

HARRY'S MY FRIEND. HE NEEDS HELP. I'VE GOT TO FIND HIM. BRING HIM TO *DR. KAFKA.*

IF ANYONE CAN SORT THROUGH HARRY'S MADNESS, SHE'S THE *ONE.*

BUT LET'S BE *HONEST:* THERE ARE *OTHER* REASONS I HAVE TO BRING HIM IN.

AS LONG AS HE'S *OUT* THERE, HARRY'S A DANGER--TO *AUNT MAY, MARY JANE...* EVERYONE WHO'S *CLOSE* TO ME.

WHO KNOWS HOW FAR HE'LL GO... WHO HE'LL HURT... TO PAY ME BACK FOR EVERYTHING HE *BLAMES* ME FOR?

SO WE'RE BACK TO THE SAME *QUESTION:* AM I DOING THIS OUT OF LOVE -- OR FEAR?

AND WE'RE BACK TO THE SAME *ANSWER:*

PROBABLY A LITTLE OF *BOTH.*

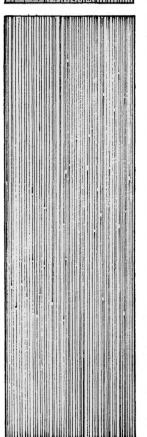

NO-- *ADRIAN--*

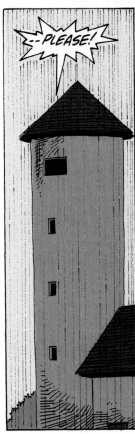

--*PLEASE!*

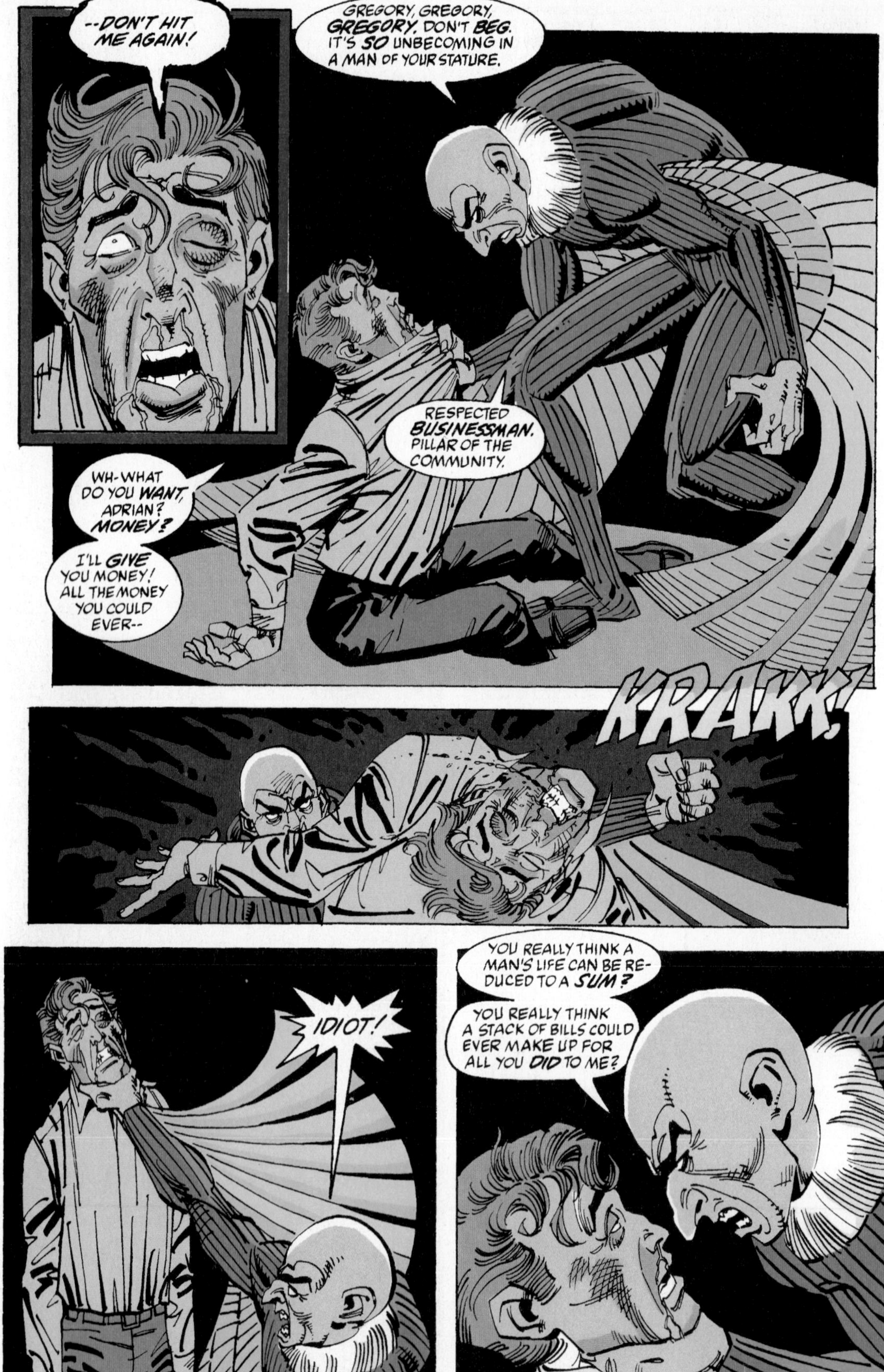
--DON'T HIT ME AGAIN!
GREGORY, GREGORY, GREGORY. DON'T BEG. IT'S SO UNBECOMING IN A MAN OF YOUR STATURE.
RESPECTED BUSINESSMAN. PILLAR OF THE COMMUNITY.
WH-WHAT DO YOU WANT, ADRIAN? MONEY?
I'LL GIVE YOU MONEY! ALL THE MONEY YOU COULD EVER--
KRAKK!
IDIOT!
YOU REALLY THINK A MAN'S LIFE CAN BE REDUCED TO A SUM?
YOU REALLY THINK A STACK OF BILLS COULD EVER MAKE UP FOR ALL YOU DID TO ME?

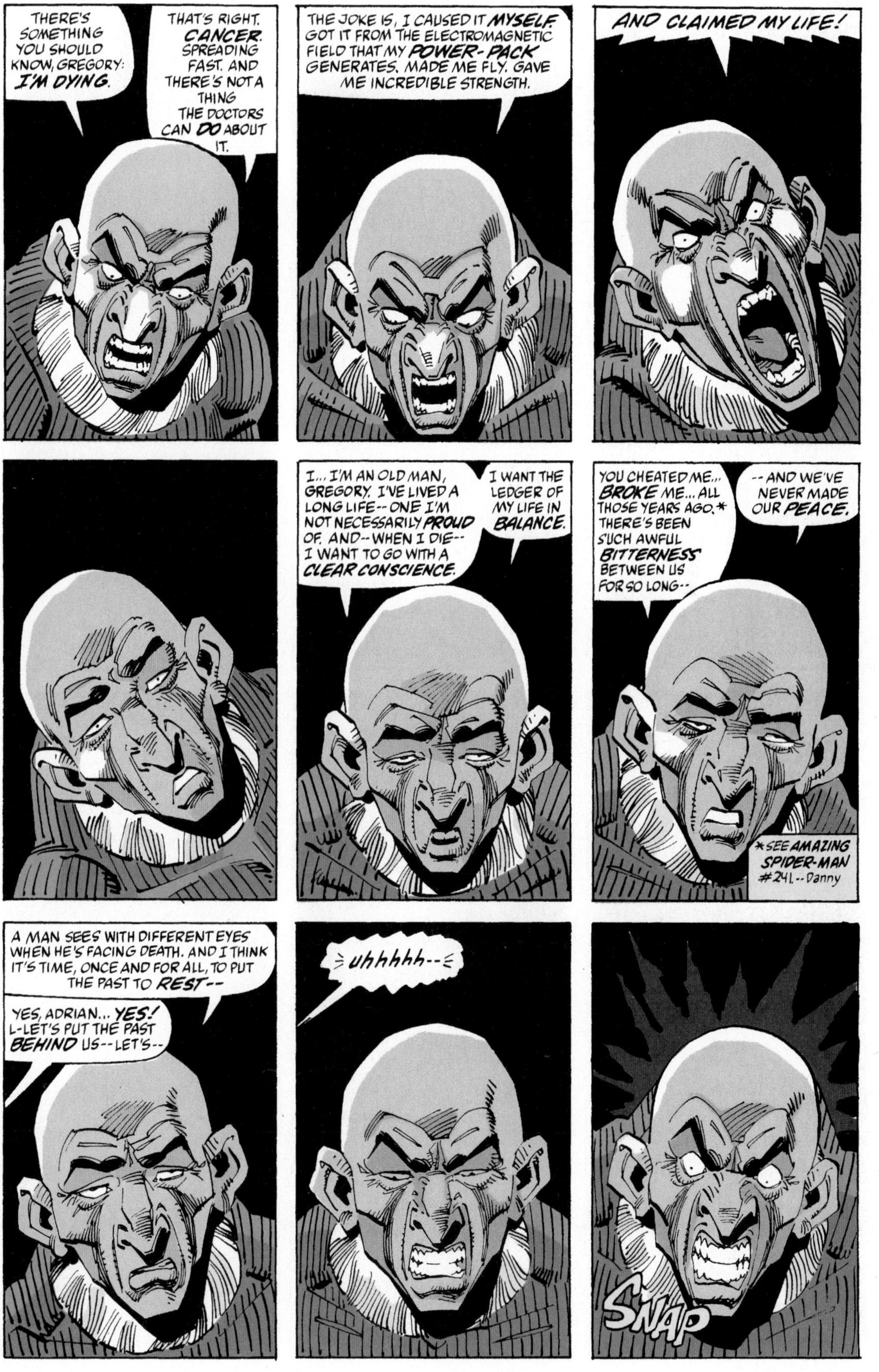
THERE'S SOMETHING YOU SHOULD KNOW, GREGORY: I'M DYING.
THAT'S RIGHT. CANCER. SPREADING FAST. AND THERE'S NOT A THING THE DOCTORS CAN DO ABOUT IT.
THE JOKE IS, I CAUSED IT MYSELF. GOT IT FROM THE ELECTROMAGNETIC FIELD THAT MY POWER-PACK GENERATES. MADE ME FLY. GAVE ME INCREDIBLE STRENGTH.
AND CLAIMED MY LIFE!
I... I'M AN OLD MAN, GREGORY. I'VE LIVED A LONG LIFE-- ONE I'M NOT NECESSARILY PROUD OF. AND-- WHEN I DIE-- I WANT TO GO WITH A CLEAR CONSCIENCE.
I WANT THE LEDGER OF MY LIFE IN BALANCE.
YOU CHEATED ME... BROKE ME... ALL THOSE YEARS AGO.* THERE'S BEEN SUCH AWFUL BITTERNESS BETWEEN US FOR SO LONG--
--AND WE'VE NEVER MADE OUR PEACE.
*SEE AMAZING SPIDER-MAN #241.--Danny
A MAN SEES WITH DIFFERENT EYES WHEN HE'S FACING DEATH. AND I THINK IT'S TIME, ONCE AND FOR ALL, TO PUT THE PAST TO REST--
YES, ADRIAN... YES! L-LET'S PUT THE PAST BEHIND US--LET'S--
uhhhhh--
SNAP

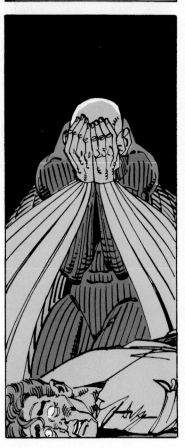

I FEEL SO MUCH *BETTER* NOW.

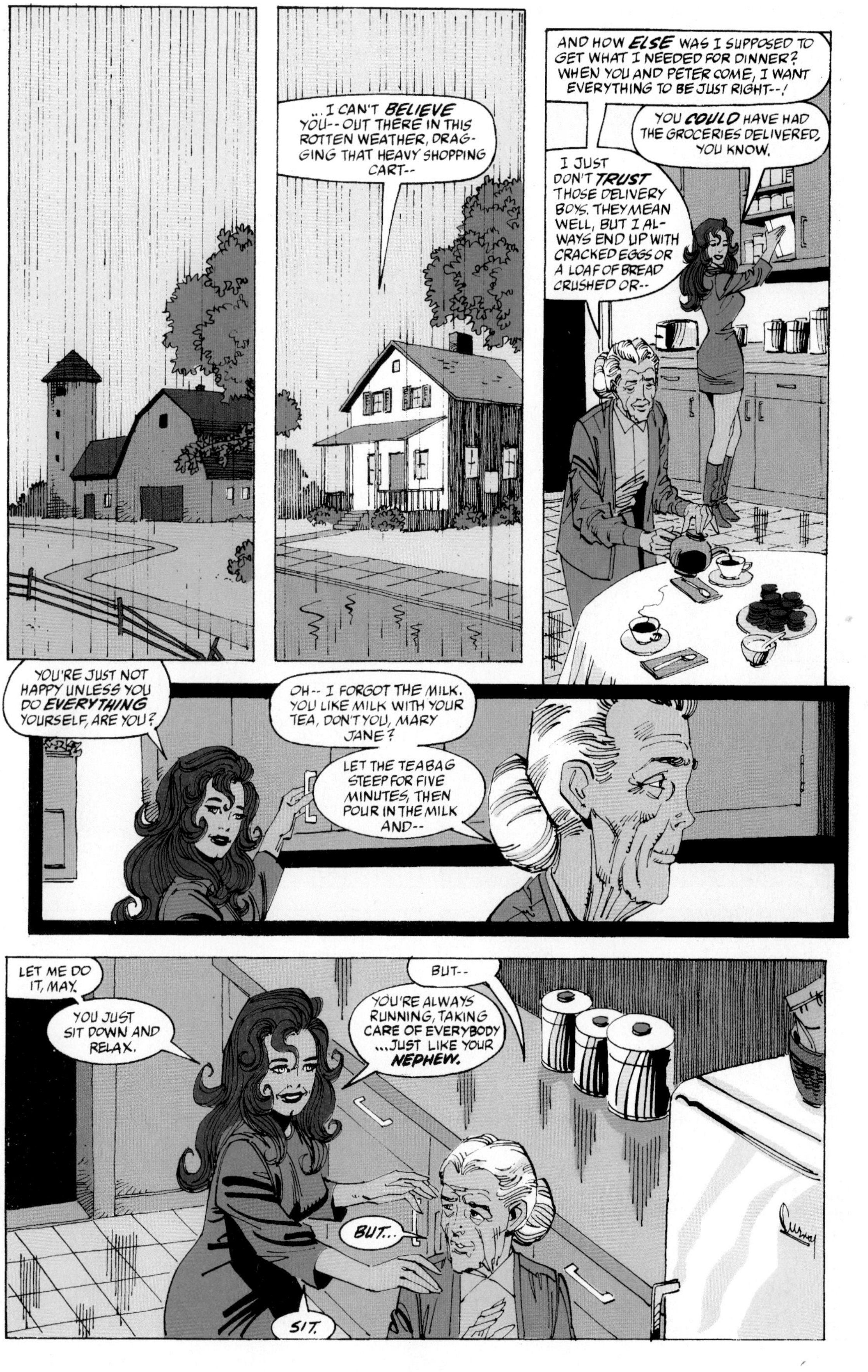
...I CAN'T **BELIEVE** YOU--OUT THERE IN THIS ROTTEN WEATHER, DRAGGING THAT HEAVY SHOPPING CART--
AND HOW **ELSE** WAS I SUPPOSED TO GET WHAT I NEEDED FOR DINNER? WHEN YOU AND PETER COME, I WANT EVERYTHING TO BE JUST RIGHT--!
YOU **COULD** HAVE HAD THE GROCERIES DELIVERED, YOU KNOW.
I JUST DON'T **TRUST** THOSE DELIVERY BOYS. THEY MEAN WELL, BUT I ALWAYS END UP WITH CRACKED EGGS OR A LOAF OF BREAD CRUSHED OR--
YOU'RE JUST NOT HAPPY UNLESS YOU DO **EVERYTHING** YOURSELF, ARE YOU?
OH-- I FORGOT THE MILK. YOU LIKE MILK WITH YOUR TEA, DON'T YOU, MARY JANE?
LET THE TEABAG STEEP FOR FIVE MINUTES, THEN POUR IN THE MILK AND--
LET ME DO IT, MAY.
YOU JUST SIT DOWN AND RELAX.
BUT--
YOU'RE ALWAYS RUNNING, TAKING CARE OF EVERYBODY ...JUST LIKE YOUR **NEPHEW.**
BUT...
SIT.

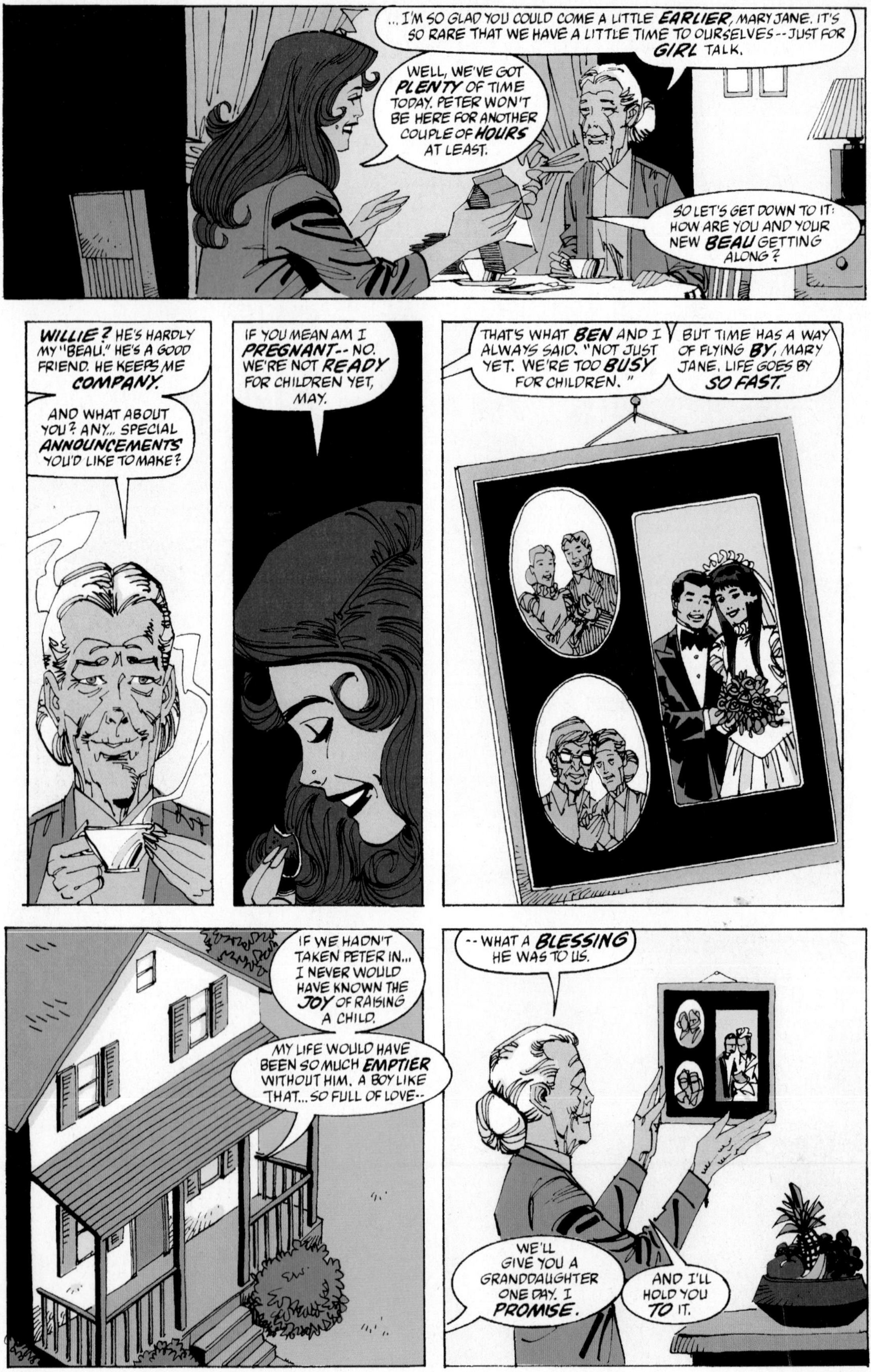
...I'M SO GLAD YOU COULD COME A LITTLE EARLIER, MARY JANE. IT'S SO RARE THAT WE HAVE A LITTLE TIME TO OURSELVES--JUST FOR GIRL TALK.
WELL, WE'VE GOT PLENTY OF TIME TODAY. PETER WON'T BE HERE FOR ANOTHER COUPLE OF HOURS AT LEAST.
SO LET'S GET DOWN TO IT: HOW ARE YOU AND YOUR NEW BEAU GETTING ALONG?
WILLIE? HE'S HARDLY MY "BEAU." HE'S A GOOD FRIEND. HE KEEPS ME COMPANY.
AND WHAT ABOUT YOU? ANY... SPECIAL ANNOUNCEMENTS YOU'D LIKE TO MAKE?
IF YOU MEAN AM I PREGNANT-- NO. WE'RE NOT READY FOR CHILDREN YET, MAY.
THAT'S WHAT BEN AND I ALWAYS SAID. "NOT JUST YET. WE'RE TOO BUSY FOR CHILDREN."
BUT TIME HAS A WAY OF FLYING BY, MARY JANE. LIFE GOES BY SO FAST.
IF WE HADN'T TAKEN PETER IN... I NEVER WOULD HAVE KNOWN THE JOY OF RAISING A CHILD.
MY LIFE WOULD HAVE BEEN SO MUCH EMPTIER WITHOUT HIM. A BOY LIKE THAT... SO FULL OF LOVE--
--WHAT A BLESSING HE WAS TO US.
WE'LL GIVE YOU A GRANDDAUGHTER ONE DAY. I PROMISE.
AND I'LL HOLD YOU TO IT.

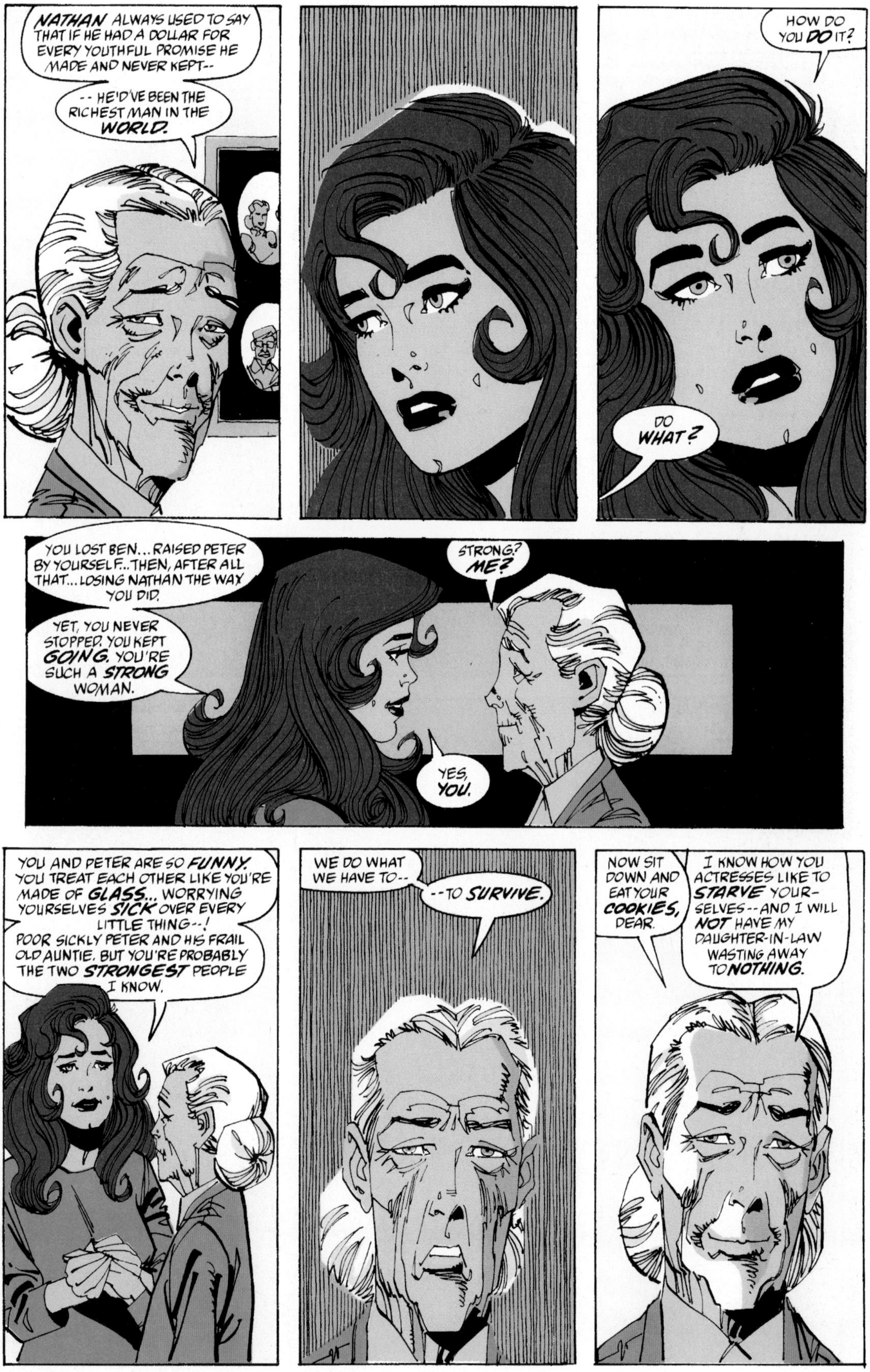
NATHAN ALWAYS USED TO SAY THAT IF HE HAD A DOLLAR FOR EVERY YOUTHFUL PROMISE HE MADE AND NEVER KEPT--
--HE'D'VE BEEN THE RICHEST MAN IN THE WORLD.
HOW DO YOU DO IT?
DO WHAT?
YOU LOST BEN... RAISED PETER BY YOURSELF... THEN, AFTER ALL THAT... LOSING NATHAN THE WAY YOU DID.
YET, YOU NEVER STOPPED. YOU KEPT GOING. YOU'RE SUCH A STRONG WOMAN.
STRONG? ME?
YES, YOU.
YOU AND PETER ARE SO FUNNY. YOU TREAT EACH OTHER LIKE YOU'RE MADE OF GLASS... WORRYING YOURSELVES SICK OVER EVERY LITTLE THING--! POOR SICKLY PETER AND HIS FRAIL OLD AUNTIE. BUT YOU'RE PROBABLY THE TWO STRONGEST PEOPLE I KNOW.
WE DO WHAT WE HAVE TO--
--TO SURVIVE.
NOW SIT DOWN AND EAT YOUR COOKIES, DEAR.
I KNOW HOW YOU ACTRESSES LIKE TO STARVE YOURSELVES--AND I WILL NOT HAVE MY DAUGHTER-IN-LAW WASTING AWAY TO NOTHING.

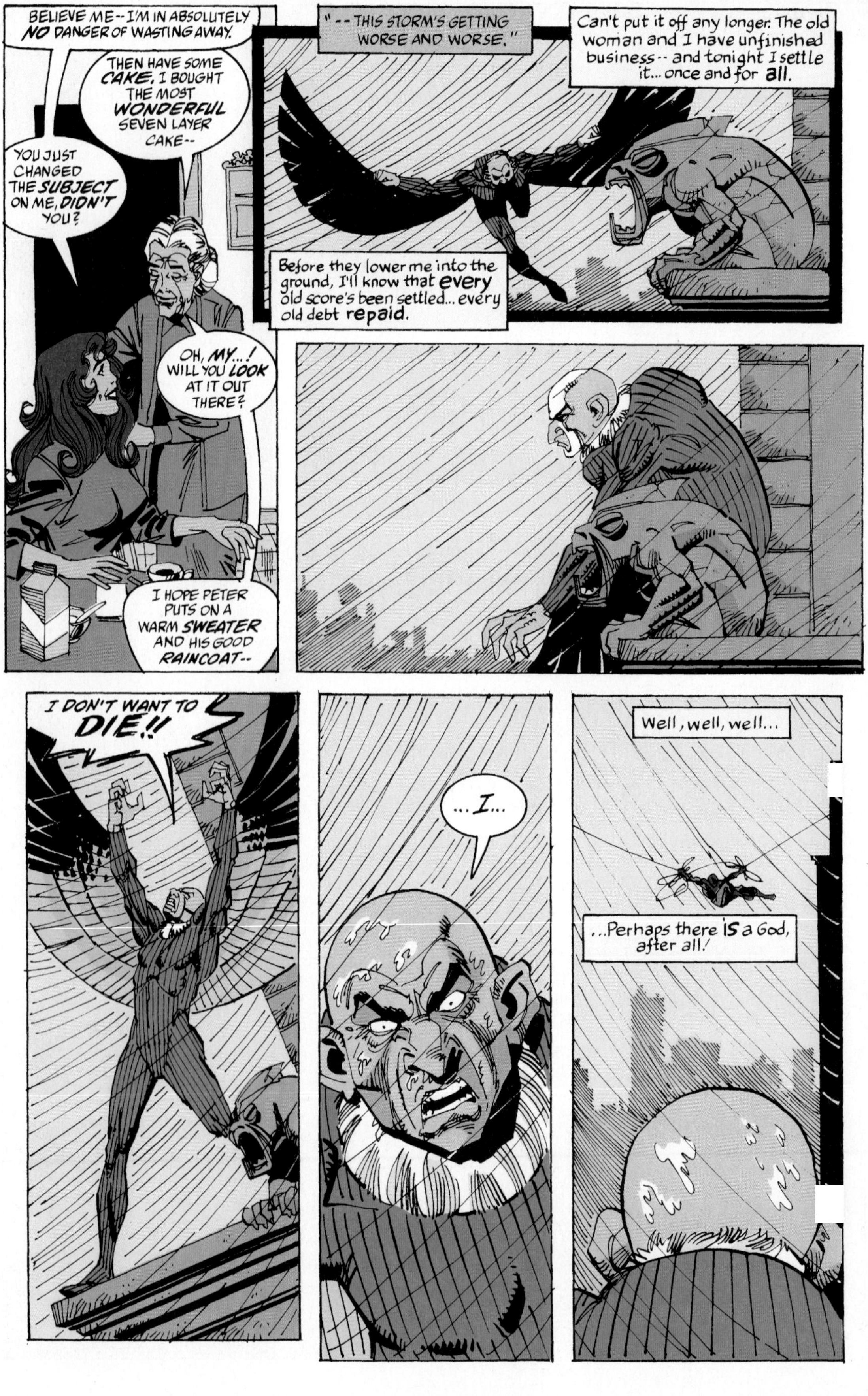
BELIEVE ME--I'M IN ABSOLUTELY NO DANGER OF WASTING AWAY.
THEN HAVE SOME CAKE. I BOUGHT THE MOST WONDERFUL SEVEN LAYER CAKE--
YOU JUST CHANGED THE SUBJECT ON ME, DIDN'T YOU?
OH, MY...! WILL YOU LOOK AT IT OUT THERE?
I HOPE PETER PUTS ON A WARM SWEATER AND HIS GOOD RAINCOAT--
"--THIS STORM'S GETTING WORSE AND WORSE."
Can't put it off any longer. The old woman and I have unfinished business--and tonight I settle it... once and for all.
Before they lower me into the ground, I'll know that every old score's been settled... every old debt repaid.
I DON'T WANT TO DIE!!
...I...
Well, well, well...
...Perhaps there IS a God, after all!

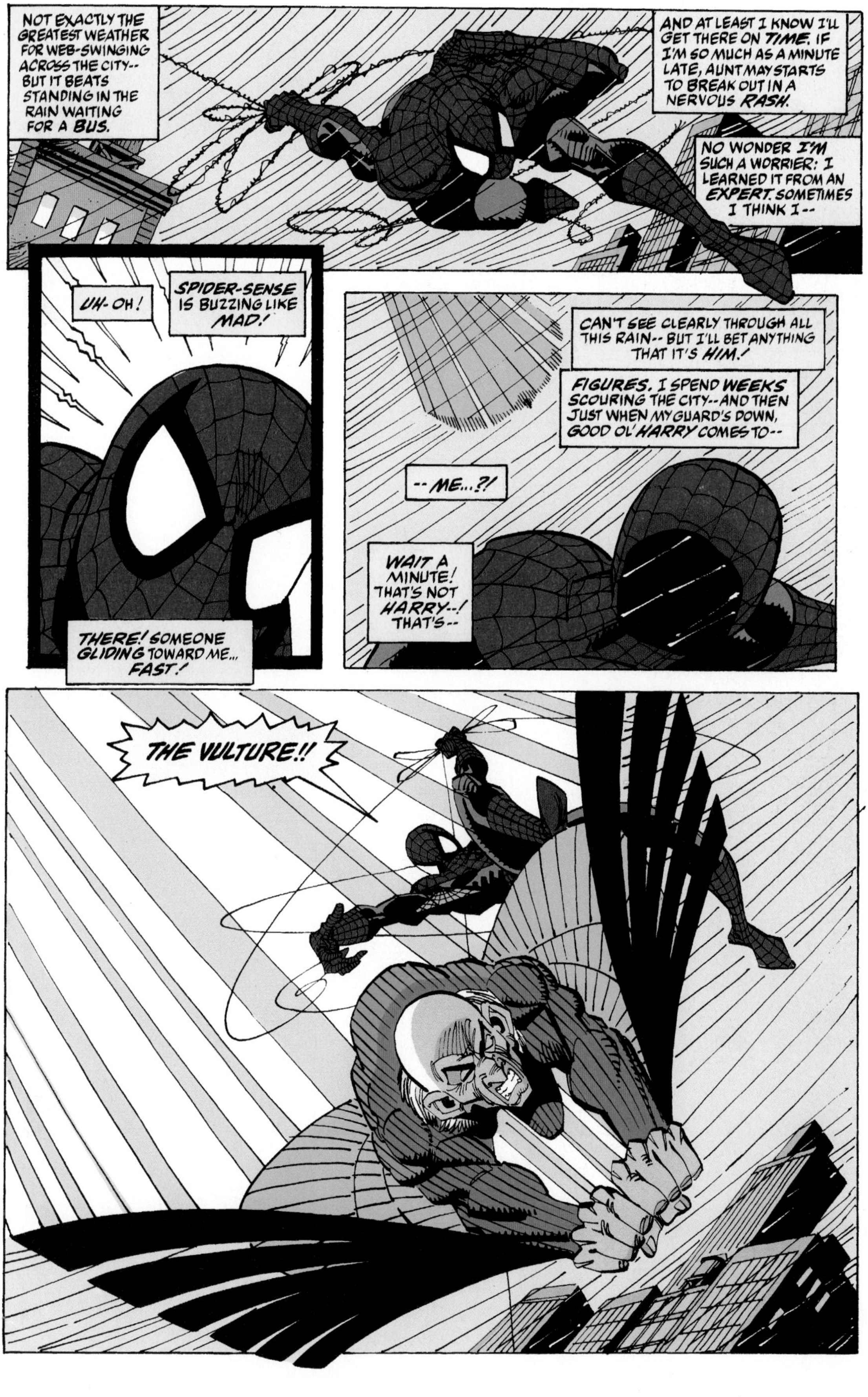

NOT EXACTLY THE GREATEST WEATHER FOR WEB-SWINGING ACROSS THE CITY-- BUT IT BEATS STANDING IN THE RAIN WAITING FOR A BUS.
AND AT LEAST I KNOW I'LL GET THERE ON TIME. IF I'M SO MUCH AS A MINUTE LATE, AUNT MAY STARTS TO BREAK OUT IN A NERVOUS RASH.
NO WONDER I'M SUCH A WORRIER: I LEARNED IT FROM AN EXPERT. SOMETIMES I THINK I--
UH-OH!
SPIDER-SENSE IS BUZZING LIKE MAD!
THERE! SOMEONE GLIDING TOWARD ME... FAST!
CAN'T SEE CLEARLY THROUGH ALL THIS RAIN-- BUT I'LL BET ANYTHING THAT IT'S HIM!
FIGURES. I SPEND WEEKS SCOURING THE CITY--AND THEN JUST WHEN MY GUARD'S DOWN, GOOD OL' HARRY COMES TO--
--ME...?!
WAIT A MINUTE! THAT'S NOT HARRY--! THAT'S--
THE VULTURE!!

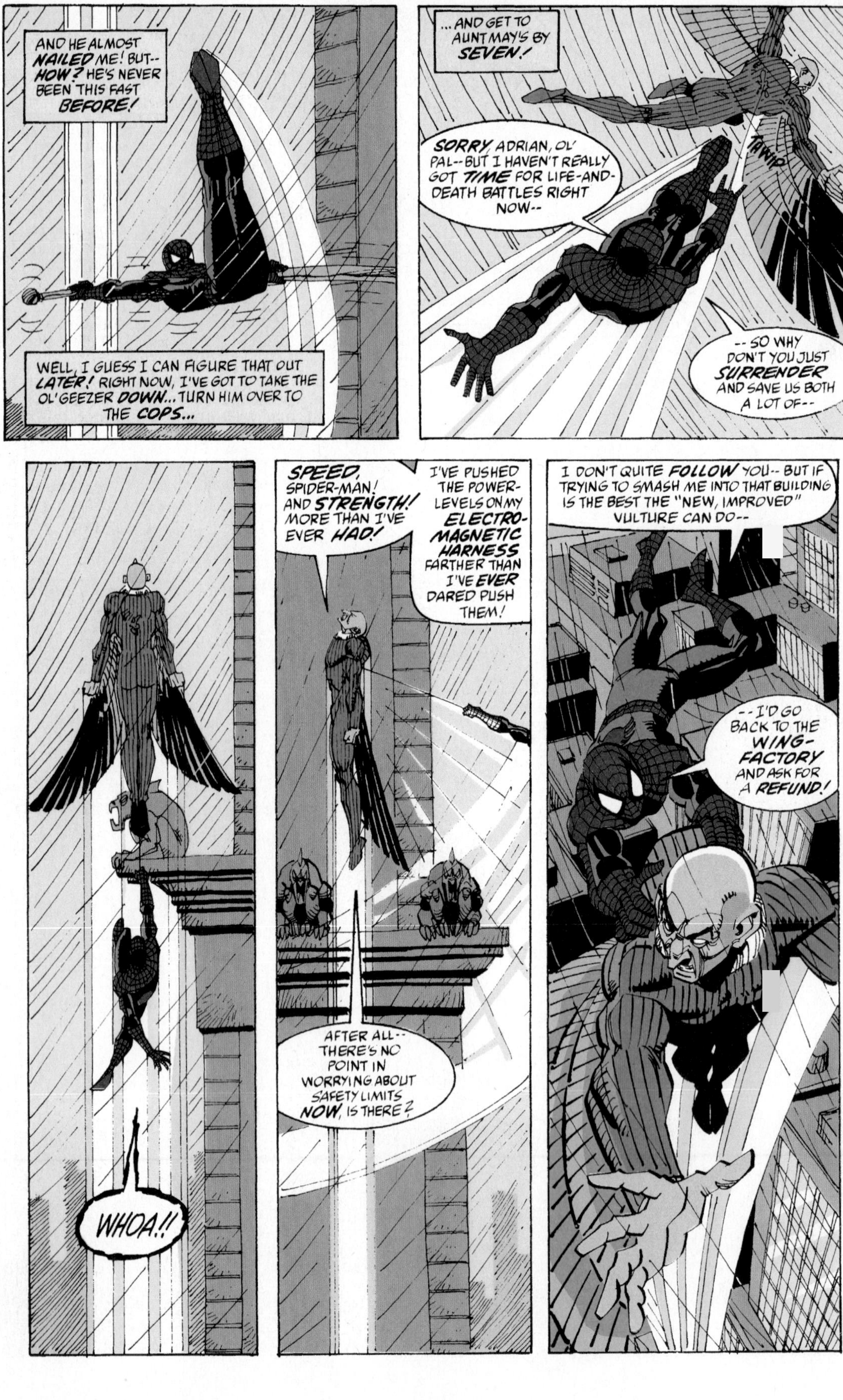

AND HE ALMOST NAILED ME! BUT-- HOW? HE'S NEVER BEEN THIS FAST BEFORE!
WELL, I GUESS I CAN FIGURE THAT OUT LATER! RIGHT NOW, I'VE GOT TO TAKE THE OL' GEEZER DOWN... TURN HIM OVER TO THE COPS...
...AND GET TO AUNT MAY'S BY SEVEN!
SORRY, ADRIAN, OL' PAL--BUT I HAVEN'T REALLY GOT TIME FOR LIFE-AND-DEATH BATTLES RIGHT NOW--
THWIP
--SO WHY DON'T YOU JUST SURRENDER AND SAVE US BOTH A LOT OF--
WHOA!!
SPEED, SPIDER-MAN! AND STRENGTH! MORE THAN I'VE EVER HAD!
I'VE PUSHED THE POWER-LEVELS ON MY ELECTRO-MAGNETIC HARNESS FARTHER THAN I'VE EVER DARED PUSH THEM!
AFTER ALL-- THERE'S NO POINT IN WORRYING ABOUT SAFETY LIMITS NOW, IS THERE?
I DON'T QUITE FOLLOW YOU-- BUT IF TRYING TO SMASH ME INTO THAT BUILDING IS THE BEST THE "NEW, IMPROVED" VULTURE CAN DO--
--I'D GO BACK TO THE WING-FACTORY AND ASK FOR A REFUND!

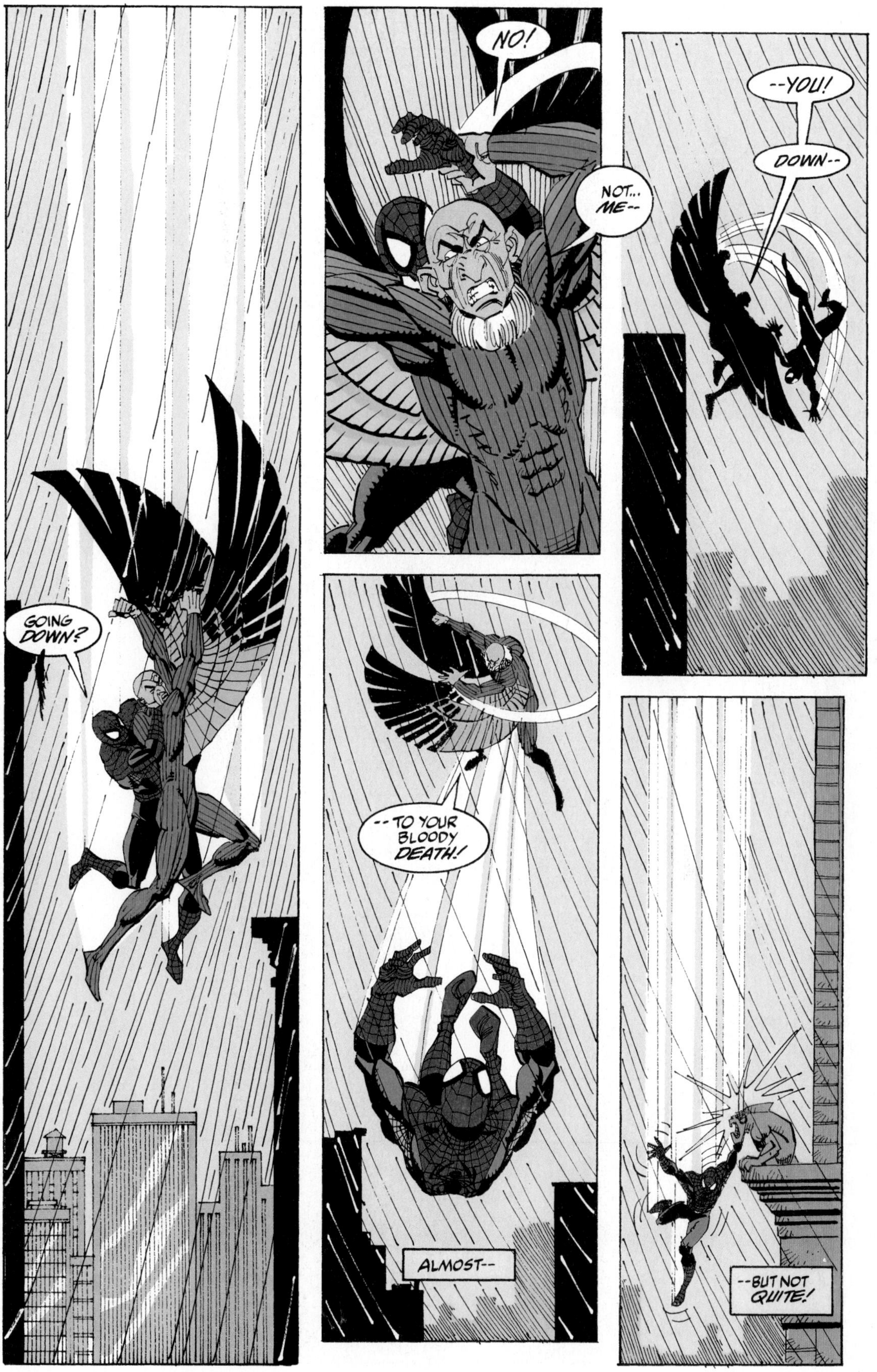
GOING DOWN?
NO!
NOT... ME--
--YOU!
DOWN--
--TO YOUR BLOODY DEATH!
ALMOST--
--BUT NOT QUITE!

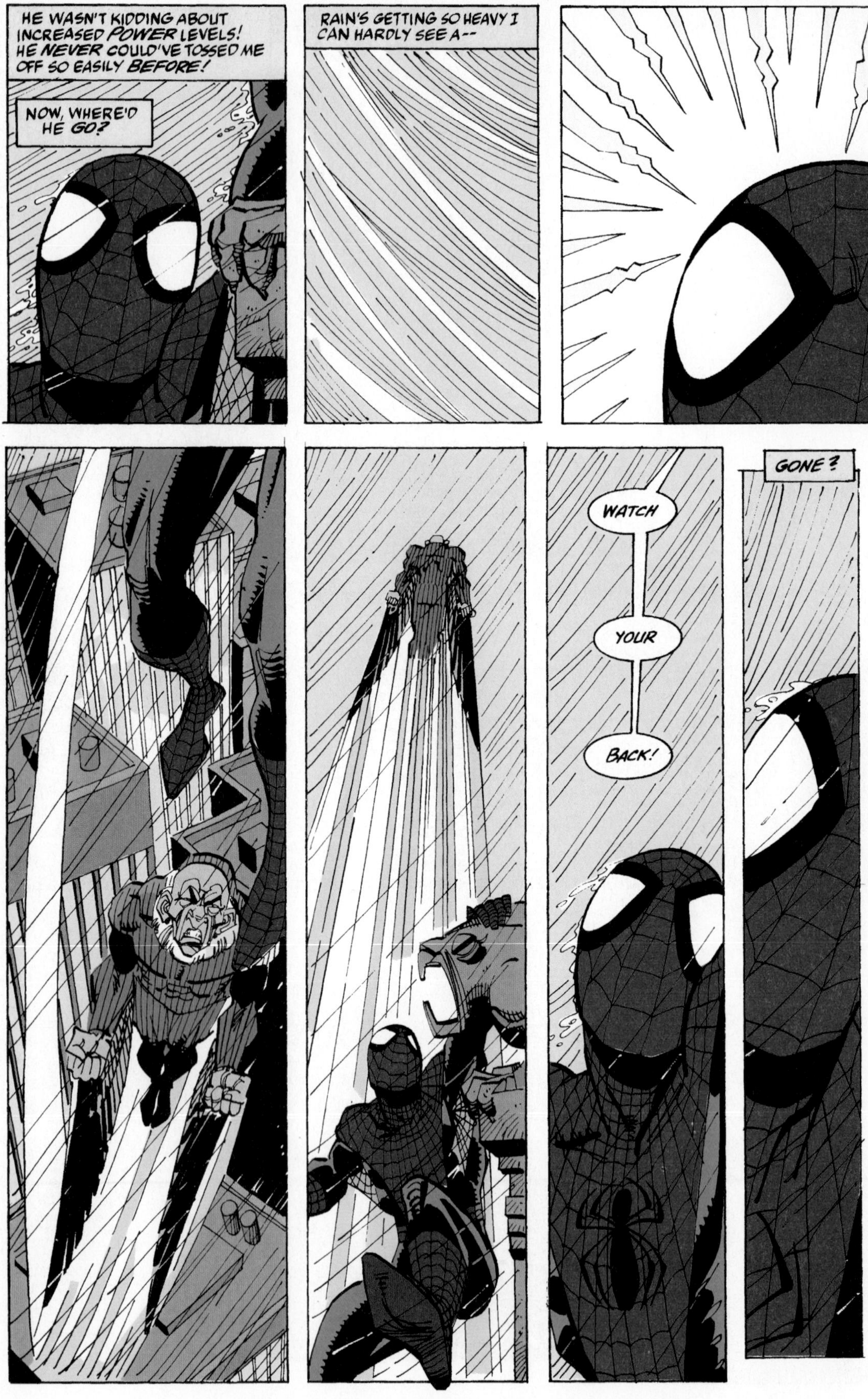

HE WASN'T KIDDING ABOUT INCREASED POWER LEVELS! HE NEVER COULD'VE TOSSED ME OFF SO EASILY BEFORE!
NOW, WHERE'D HE GO?
RAIN'S GETTING SO HEAVY I CAN HARDLY SEE A--
GONE?
WATCH
YOUR
BACK!

I COULD GO AFTER HIM -- BUT, GIVEN THE WEATHER CONDITIONS AND HOW *FAST* HE IS, IT'D BE A WASTE OF TIME.

AND I'VE GOT AUNT MAY TO THINK OF. IF I GET A MOVE ON, I SHOULDN'T BE MORE THAN A COUPLE OF MINUTES *LATE*.

ANYWAY, FROM THE SOUND OF THAT LITTLE *WARNING* THE VULTURE JUST GAVE ME--

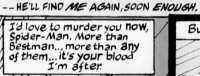

-- HE'LL FIND *ME* AGAIN, SOON *ENOUGH*.

I'd love to murder you now, Spider-Man. More than Bestman... more than any of them... it's your blood I'm after.

But I think I'll savor it... peck away at you, bit-by-bit-by-bit.

Besides, I've got more pressing business to attend to tonight. You can wait.

The old woman can't.

...YOU *SURE* YOU HAVE TO GO?

195

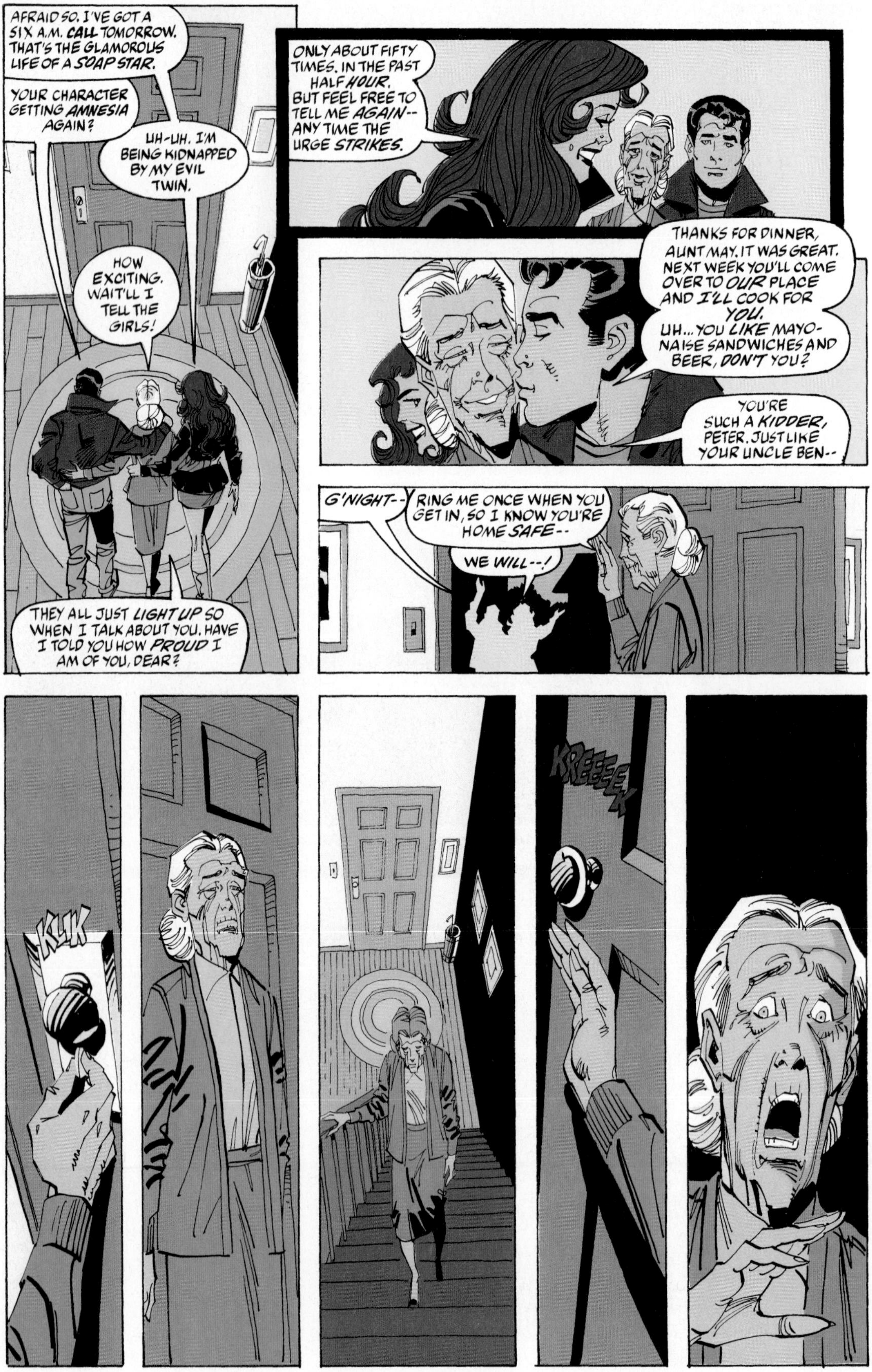
AFRAID SO. I'VE GOT A SIX A.M. CALL TOMORROW. THAT'S THE GLAMOROUS LIFE OF A SOAP STAR.
YOUR CHARACTER GETTING AMNESIA AGAIN?
UH-UH. I'M BEING KIDNAPPED BY MY EVIL TWIN.
HOW EXCITING. WAIT'LL I TELL THE GIRLS!
THEY ALL JUST LIGHT UP SO WHEN I TALK ABOUT YOU. HAVE I TOLD YOU HOW PROUD I AM OF YOU, DEAR?
ONLY ABOUT FIFTY TIMES. IN THE PAST HALF HOUR. BUT FEEL FREE TO TELL ME AGAIN-- ANY TIME THE URGE STRIKES.
THANKS FOR DINNER, AUNT MAY. IT WAS GREAT. NEXT WEEK YOU'LL COME OVER TO OUR PLACE AND I'LL COOK FOR YOU. UH... YOU LIKE MAYO-NAISE SANDWICHES AND BEER, DON'T YOU?
YOU'RE SUCH A KIDDER, PETER. JUST LIKE YOUR UNCLE BEN--
G'NIGHT--
RING ME ONCE WHEN YOU GET IN, SO I KNOW YOU'RE HOME SAFE--
WE WILL--!
KLIK
KREEEEK

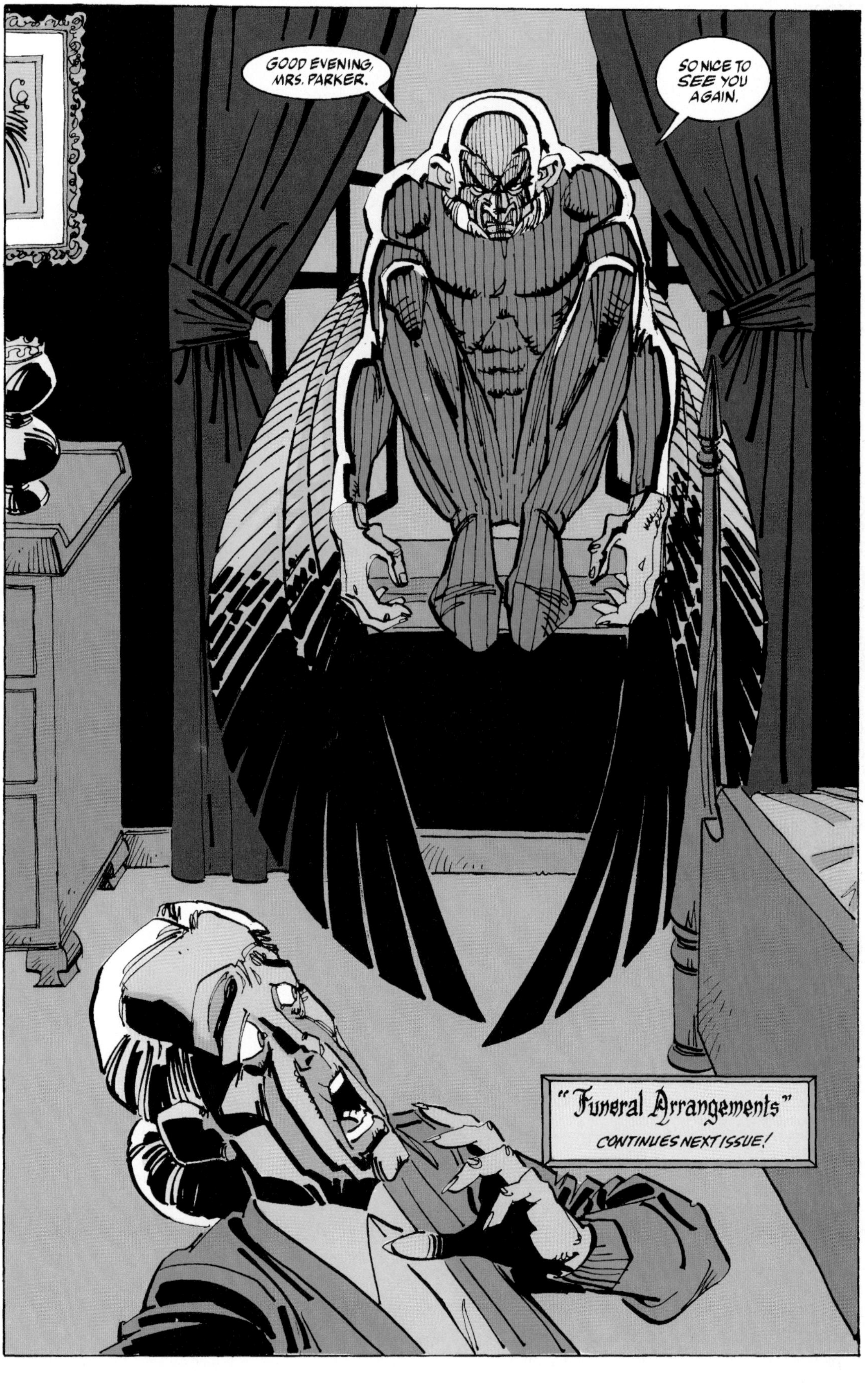
GOOD EVENING, MRS. PARKER.
SO NICE TO SEE YOU AGAIN.
"Funeral Arrangements" CONTINUES NEXT ISSUE!

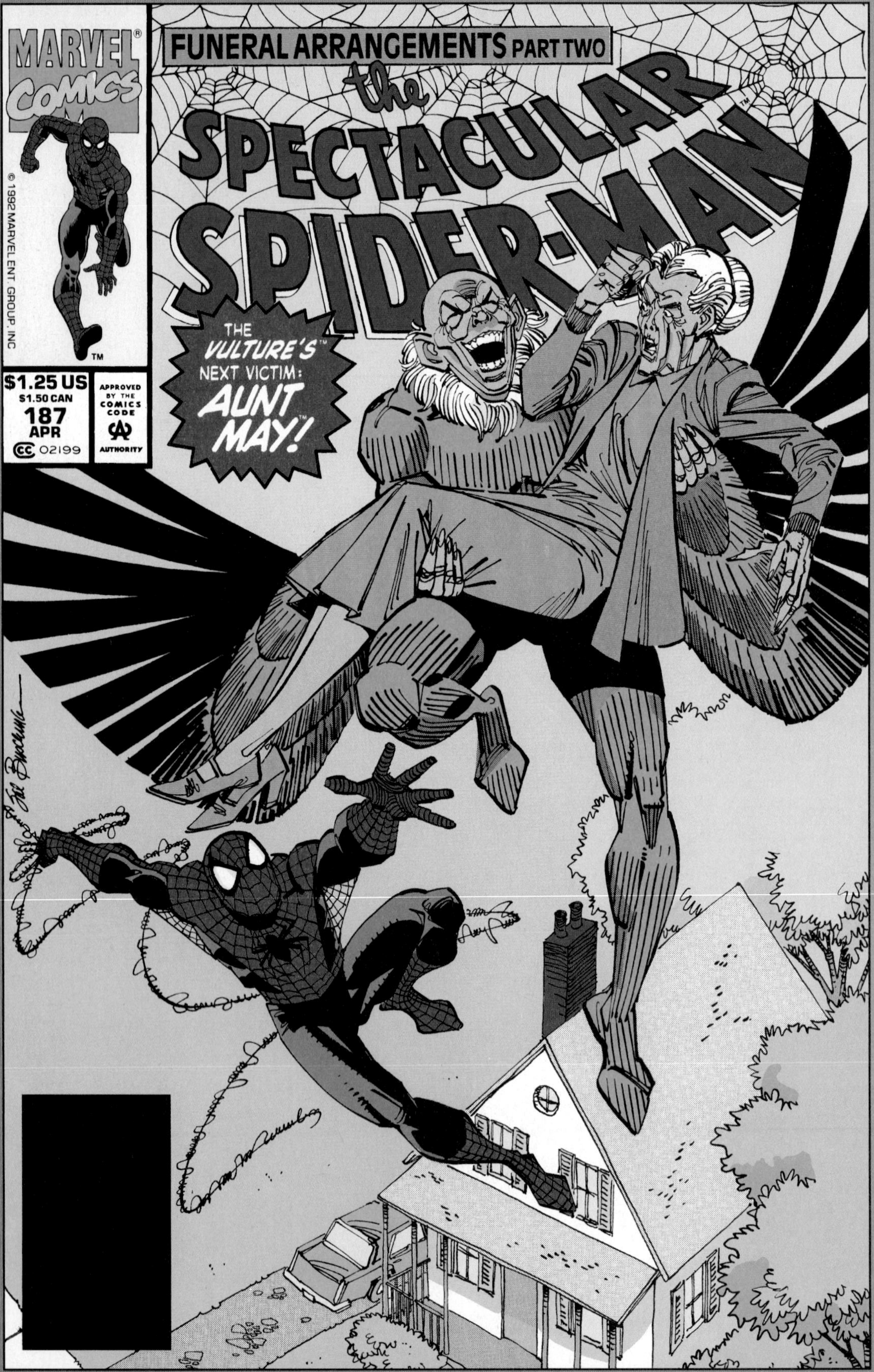
MARVEL COMICS
FUNERAL ARRANGEMENTS PART TWO
the SPECTACULAR SPIDER-MAN
THE VULTURE'S NEXT VICTIM: AUNT MAY!
$1.25 US
$1.50 CAN
187
APR
02199
APPROVED BY THE COMICS CODE AUTHORITY
© 1992 MARVEL ENT. GROUP, INC

BITTEN BY A RADIOACTIVE SPIDER, STUDENT PETER PARKER GAINED THE PROPORTIONATE STRENGTH AND AGILITY OF AN ARACHNID! ARMED WITH HIS WONDROUS WEB-SHOOTERS, THE RELUCTANT SUPER HERO STRUGGLES WITH SINISTER SUPER-VILLAINS, MAKING ENDS MEET, AND MAINTAINING SOME SEMBLANCE OF A NORMAL LIFE!

Stan Lee PRESENTS:

THE SPECTACULAR SPIDER-MAN!™

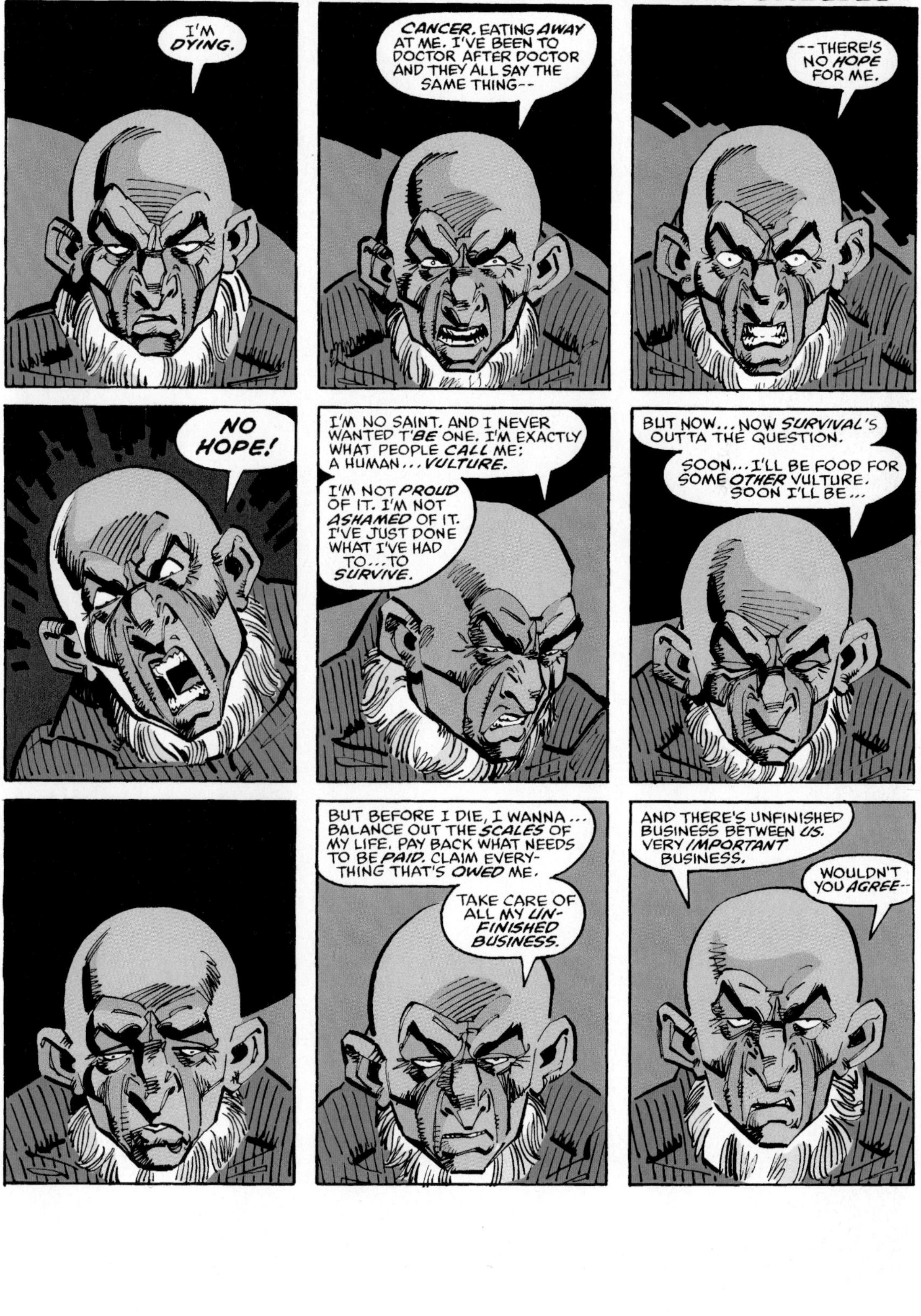

I'M DYING.
CANCER, EATING AWAY AT ME. I'VE BEEN TO DOCTOR AFTER DOCTOR AND THEY ALL SAY THE SAME THING--
--THERE'S NO HOPE FOR ME.
NO HOPE!
I'M NO SAINT. AND I NEVER WANTED T'BE ONE. I'M EXACTLY WHAT PEOPLE CALL ME: A HUMAN... VULTURE.
I'M NOT PROUD OF IT. I'M NOT ASHAMED OF IT. I'VE JUST DONE WHAT I'VE HAD TO... TO SURVIVE.
BUT NOW... NOW SURVIVAL'S OUTTA THE QUESTION.
SOON... I'LL BE FOOD FOR SOME OTHER VULTURE. SOON I'LL BE...
BUT BEFORE I DIE, I WANNA... BALANCE OUT THE SCALES OF MY LIFE. PAY BACK WHAT NEEDS TO BE PAID. CLAIM EVERY-THING THAT'S OWED ME.
TAKE CARE OF ALL MY UN-FINISHED BUSINESS.
AND THERE'S UNFINISHED BUSINESS BETWEEN US. VERY IMPORTANT BUSINESS.
WOULDN'T YOU AGREE--

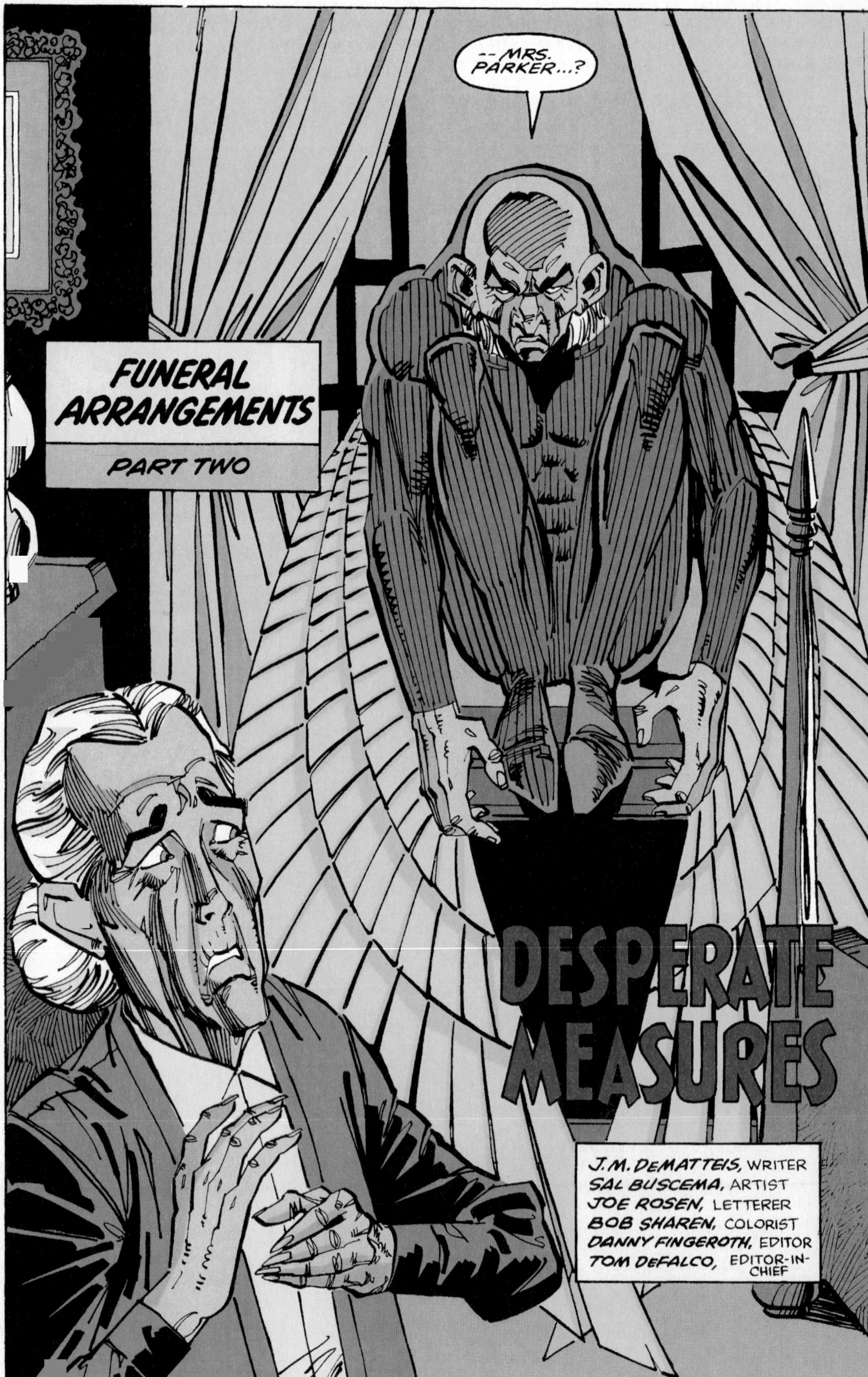

-- MRS. PARKER...?
FUNERAL ARRANGEMENTS
PART TWO
DESPERATE MEASURES
J.M. DEMATTEIS, WRITER
SAL BUSCEMA, ARTIST
JOE ROSEN, LETTERER
BOB SHAREN, COLORIST
DANNY FINGEROTH, EDITOR
TOM DEFALCO, EDITOR-IN-CHIEF

YOU AND I HAVE NO *BUSINESS.* YOU'RE A COMMON *CRIMINAL.* A *MURDERER.*

YOU *KILLED* MY *NATHAN!*

EXACTLY, MRS. PARKER. I'M RESPONSIBLE FOR NATHAN LUBENSKY'S DEATH*--

*IT HAPPENED IN *AMAZING SPIDER-MAN* #336. --DANNY

--AND I AM SO--

--SORRY.

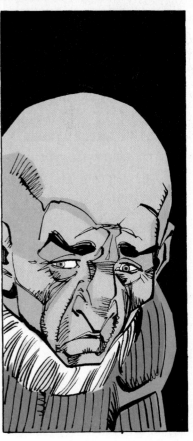

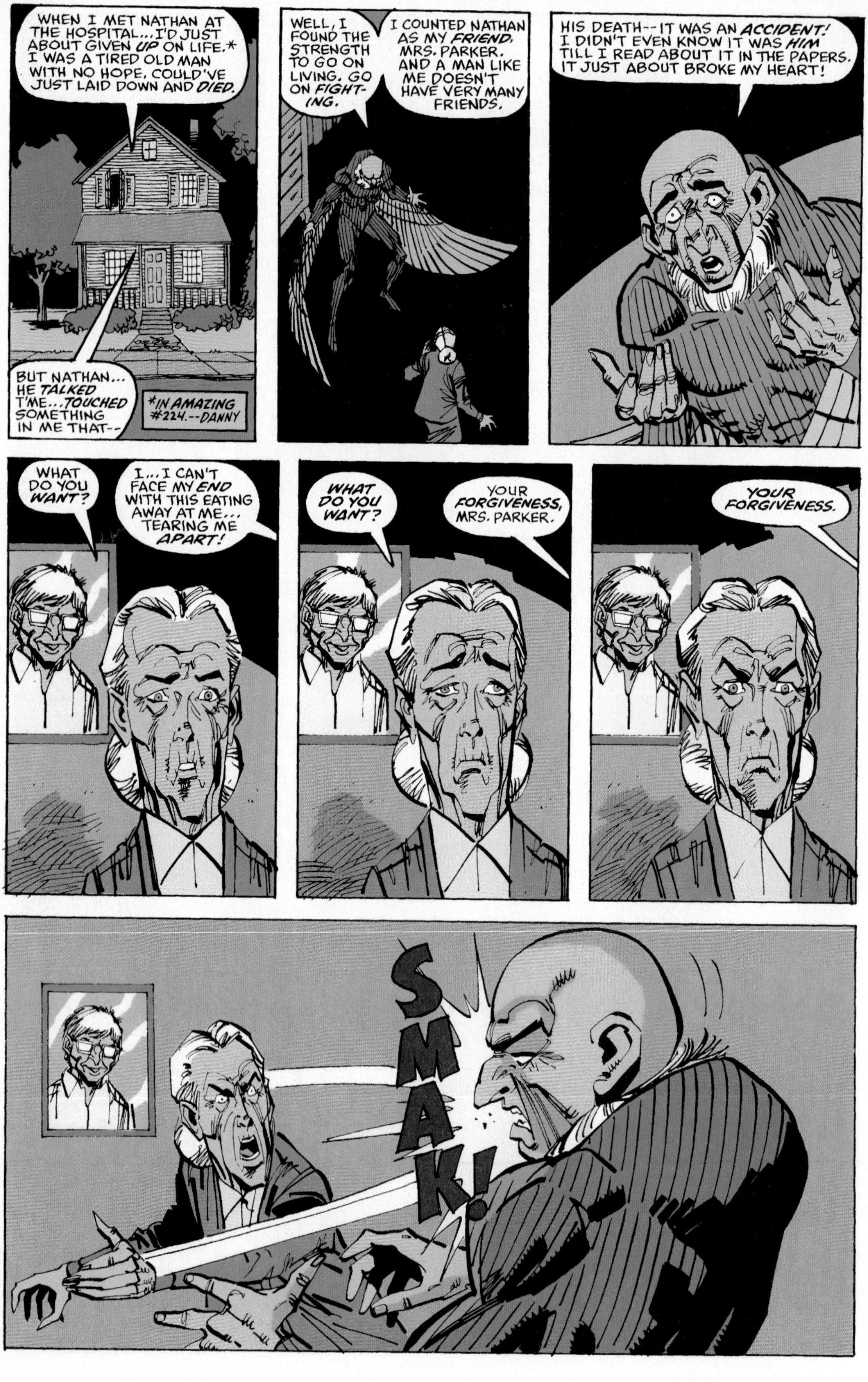
WHEN I MET NATHAN AT THE HOSPITAL... I'D JUST ABOUT GIVEN UP ON LIFE.* I WAS A TIRED OLD MAN WITH NO HOPE. COULD'VE JUST LAID DOWN AND DIED.
BUT NATHAN... HE TALKED T'ME... TOUCHED SOMETHING IN ME THAT--
*IN AMAZING #224.--DANNY
WELL, I FOUND THE STRENGTH TO GO ON LIVING. GO ON FIGHTING.
I COUNTED NATHAN AS MY FRIEND, MRS. PARKER. AND A MAN LIKE ME DOESN'T HAVE VERY MANY FRIENDS.
HIS DEATH--IT WAS AN ACCIDENT! I DIDN'T EVEN KNOW IT WAS HIM TILL I READ ABOUT IT IN THE PAPERS. IT JUST ABOUT BROKE MY HEART!
WHAT DO YOU WANT?
I... I CAN'T FACE MY END WITH THIS EATING AWAY AT ME... TEARING ME APART!
WHAT DO YOU WANT?
YOUR FORGIVENESS, MRS. PARKER.
YOUR FORGIVENESS.
SMAK!

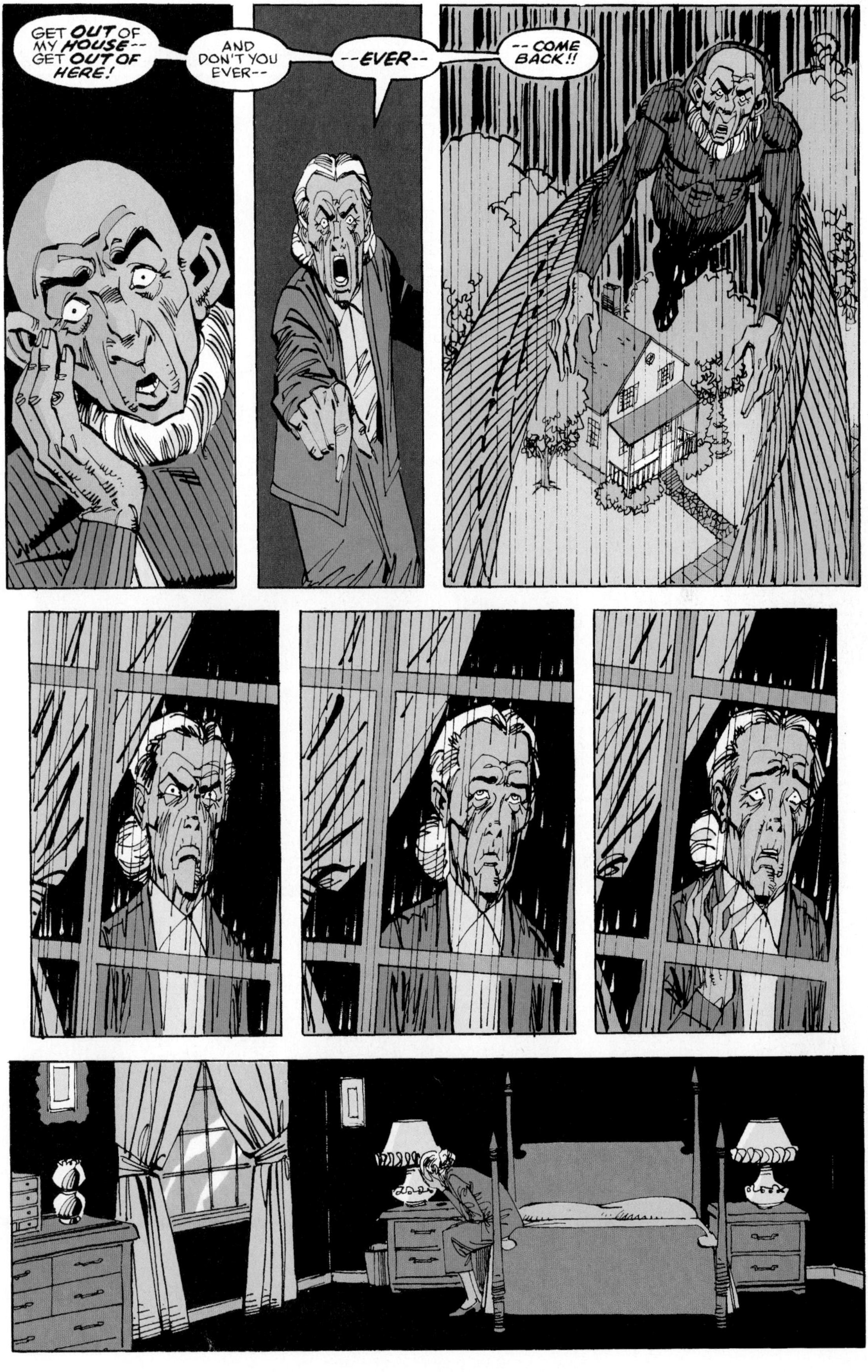
GET OUT OF MY HOUSE-- GET OUT OF HERE!
AND DON'T YOU EVER--
--EVER--
--COME BACK!!

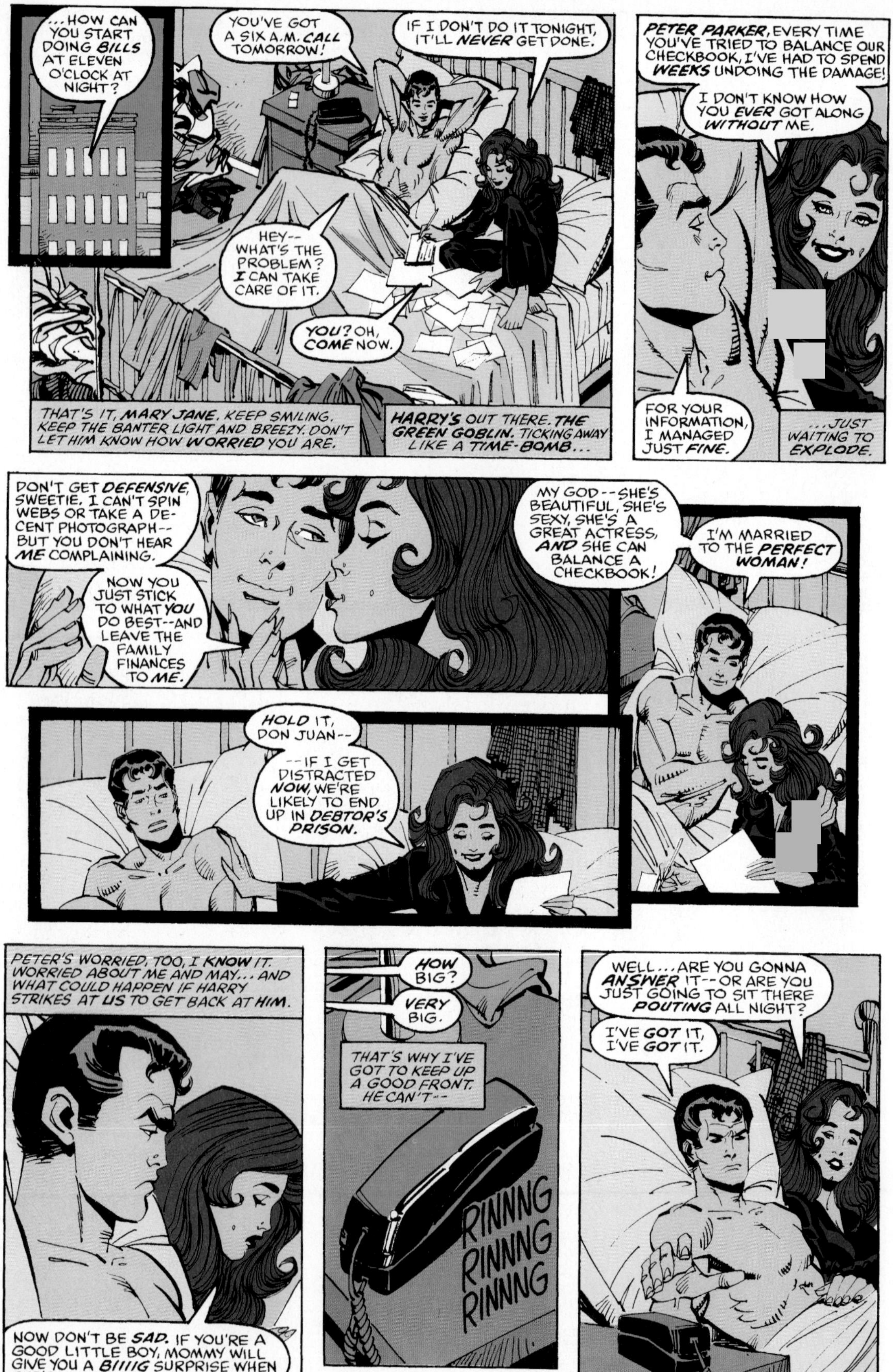
...HOW CAN YOU START DOING BILLS AT ELEVEN O'CLOCK AT NIGHT?
YOU'VE GOT A SIX A.M. CALL TOMORROW!
IF I DON'T DO IT TONIGHT, IT'LL NEVER GET DONE.
HEY-- WHAT'S THE PROBLEM? I CAN TAKE CARE OF IT.
YOU? OH, COME NOW.
THAT'S IT, MARY JANE. KEEP SMILING. KEEP THE BANTER LIGHT AND BREEZY. DON'T LET HIM KNOW HOW WORRIED YOU ARE.
HARRY'S OUT THERE. THE GREEN GOBLIN. TICKING AWAY LIKE A TIME-BOMB...
PETER PARKER, EVERY TIME YOU'VE TRIED TO BALANCE OUR CHECKBOOK, I'VE HAD TO SPEND WEEKS UNDOING THE DAMAGE!
I DON'T KNOW HOW YOU EVER GOT ALONG WITHOUT ME.
FOR YOUR INFORMATION, I MANAGED JUST FINE.
...JUST WAITING TO EXPLODE.
DON'T GET DEFENSIVE, SWEETIE. I CAN'T SPIN WEBS OR TAKE A DECENT PHOTOGRAPH-- BUT YOU DON'T HEAR ME COMPLAINING.
NOW YOU JUST STICK TO WHAT YOU DO BEST--AND LEAVE THE FAMILY FINANCES TO ME.
MY GOD--SHE'S BEAUTIFUL, SHE'S SEXY, SHE'S A GREAT ACTRESS, AND SHE CAN BALANCE A CHECKBOOK!
I'M MARRIED TO THE PERFECT WOMAN!
HOLD IT, DON JUAN--
--IF I GET DISTRACTED NOW, WE'RE LIKELY TO END UP IN DEBTOR'S PRISON.
PETER'S WORRIED, TOO, I KNOW IT. WORRIED ABOUT ME AND MAY... AND WHAT COULD HAPPEN IF HARRY STRIKES AT US TO GET BACK AT HIM.
NOW DON'T BE SAD. IF YOU'RE A GOOD LITTLE BOY, MOMMY WILL GIVE YOU A BIIIIG SURPRISE WHEN SHE'S ALL DONE WITH THE BILLS.
HOW BIG?
VERY BIG.
THAT'S WHY I'VE GOT TO KEEP UP A GOOD FRONT. HE CAN'T--
RINNNG
RINNNG
RINNNG
WELL...ARE YOU GONNA ANSWER IT--OR ARE YOU JUST GOING TO SIT THERE POUTING ALL NIGHT?
I'VE GOT IT, I'VE GOT IT.

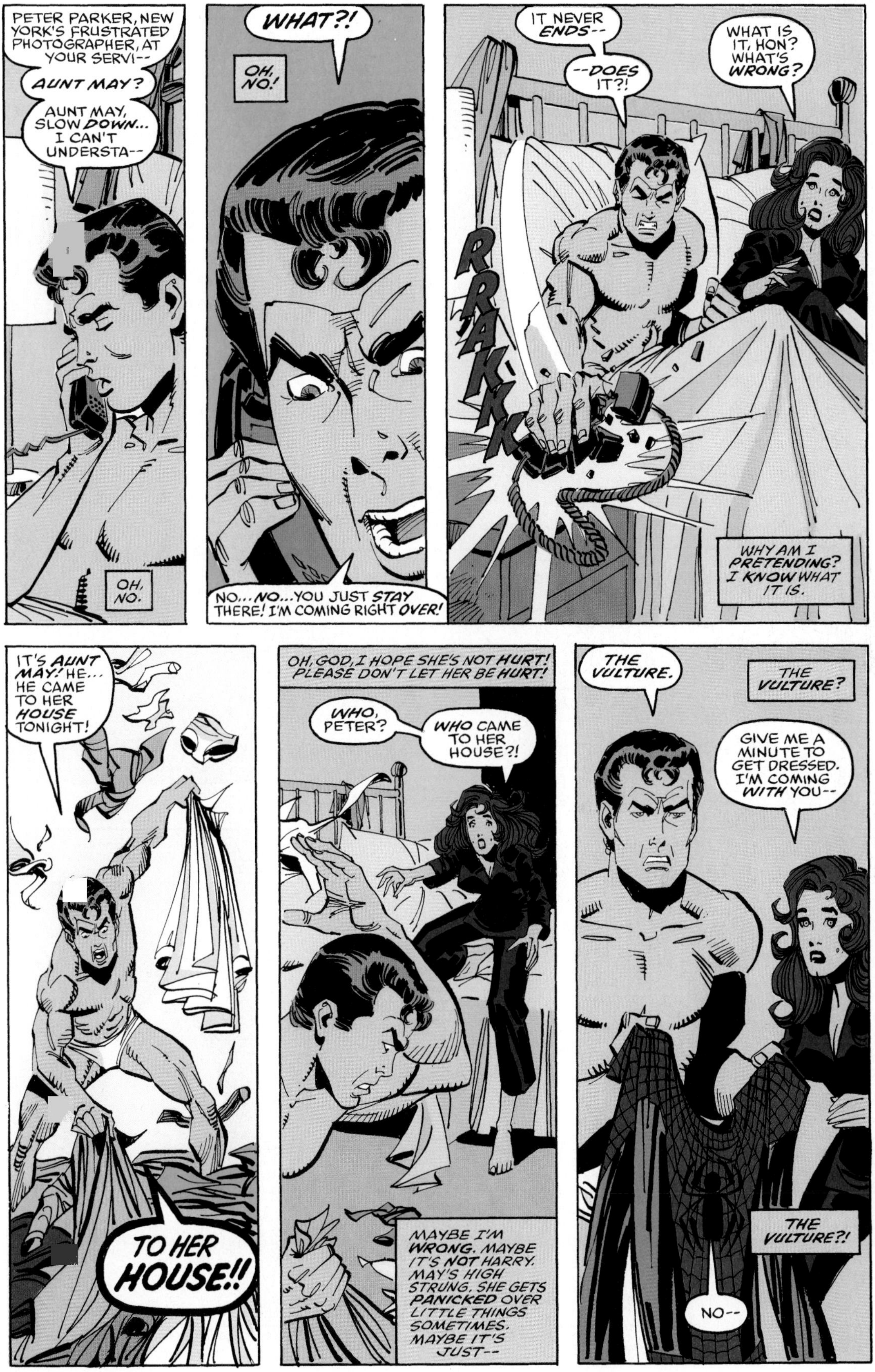
PETER PARKER, NEW YORK'S FRUSTRATED PHOTOGRAPHER, AT YOUR SERVI--
AUNT MAY?
AUNT MAY, SLOW DOWN... I CAN'T UNDERSTA--
OH, NO.
WHAT?!
OH, NO!
NO... NO... YOU JUST STAY THERE! I'M COMING RIGHT OVER!
IT NEVER ENDS--
--DOES IT?!
WHAT IS IT, HON? WHAT'S WRONG?
RRAKKK
WHY AM I PRETENDING? I KNOW WHAT IT IS.
IT'S AUNT MAY! HE... HE CAME TO HER HOUSE TONIGHT!
TO HER HOUSE!!
OH, GOD, I HOPE SHE'S NOT HURT! PLEASE DON'T LET HER BE HURT!
WHO, PETER?
WHO CAME TO HER HOUSE?!
MAYBE I'M WRONG. MAYBE IT'S NOT HARRY. MAY'S HIGH STRUNG. SHE GETS PANICKED OVER LITTLE THINGS SOMETIMES. MAYBE IT'S JUST--
THE VULTURE.
THE VULTURE?
GIVE ME A MINUTE TO GET DRESSED. I'M COMING WITH YOU--
THE VULTURE?!
NO--

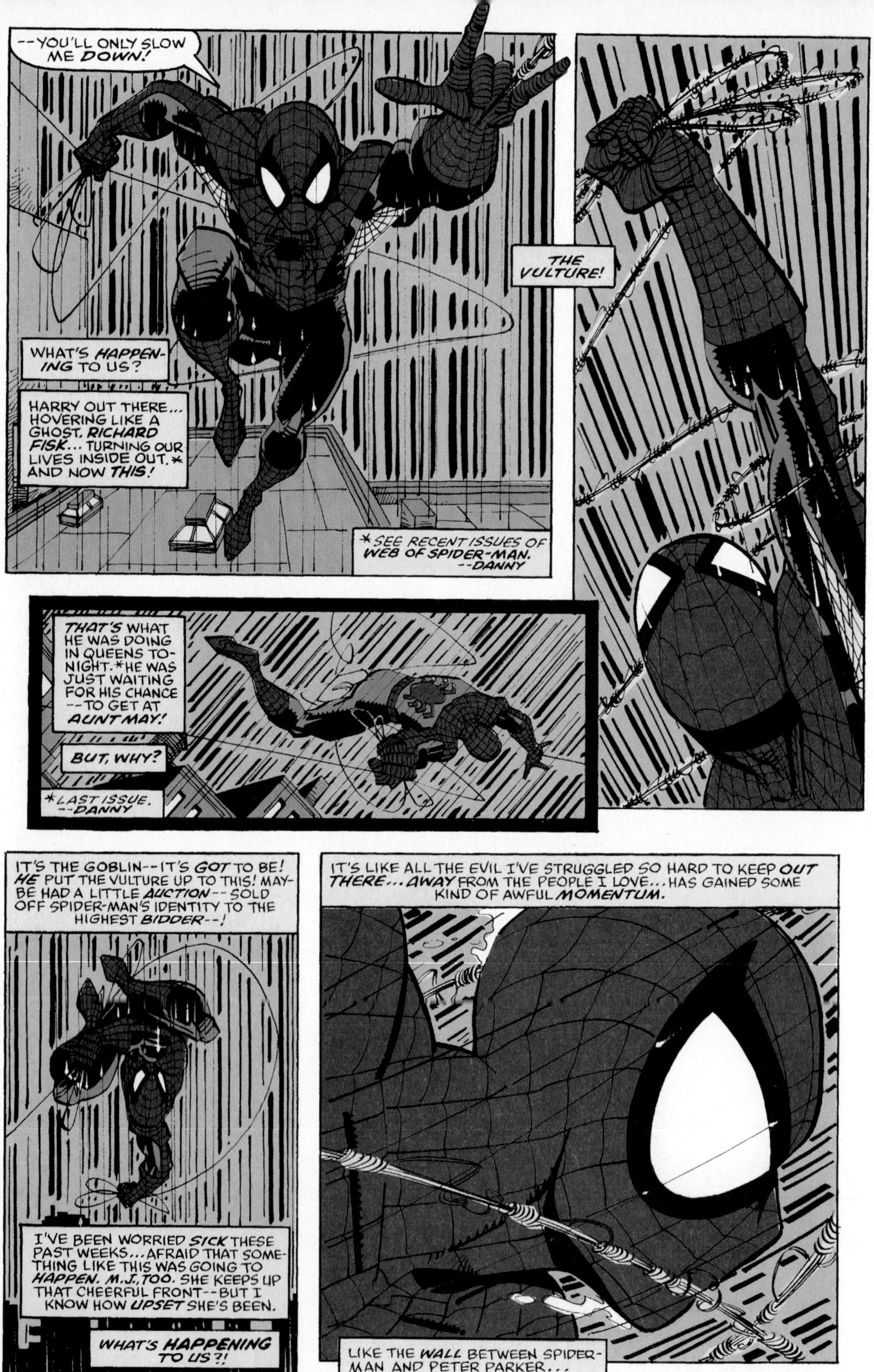
--YOU'LL ONLY SLOW ME DOWN!
WHAT'S HAPPENING TO US?
HARRY OUT THERE... HOVERING LIKE A GHOST. RICHARD FISK... TURNING OUR LIVES INSIDE OUT.* AND NOW THIS!
*SEE RECENT ISSUES OF WEB OF SPIDER-MAN. --DANNY
THE VULTURE!
THAT'S WHAT HE WAS DOING IN QUEENS TONIGHT.* HE WAS JUST WAITING FOR HIS CHANCE --TO GET AT AUNT MAY!
BUT, WHY?
*LAST ISSUE. --DANNY
IT'S THE GOBLIN--IT'S GOT TO BE! HE PUT THE VULTURE UP TO THIS! MAYBE HAD A LITTLE AUCTION--SOLD OFF SPIDER-MAN'S IDENTITY TO THE HIGHEST BIDDER--!
I'VE BEEN WORRIED SICK THESE PAST WEEKS... AFRAID THAT SOMETHING LIKE THIS WAS GOING TO HAPPEN. M.J., TOO. SHE KEEPS UP THAT CHEERFUL FRONT--BUT I KNOW HOW UPSET SHE'S BEEN.
WHAT'S HAPPENING TO US?!
IT'S LIKE ALL THE EVIL I'VE STRUGGLED SO HARD TO KEEP OUT THERE... AWAY FROM THE PEOPLE I LOVE... HAS GAINED SOME KIND OF AWFUL MOMENTUM.
LIKE THE WALL BETWEEN SPIDER-MAN AND PETER PARKER...

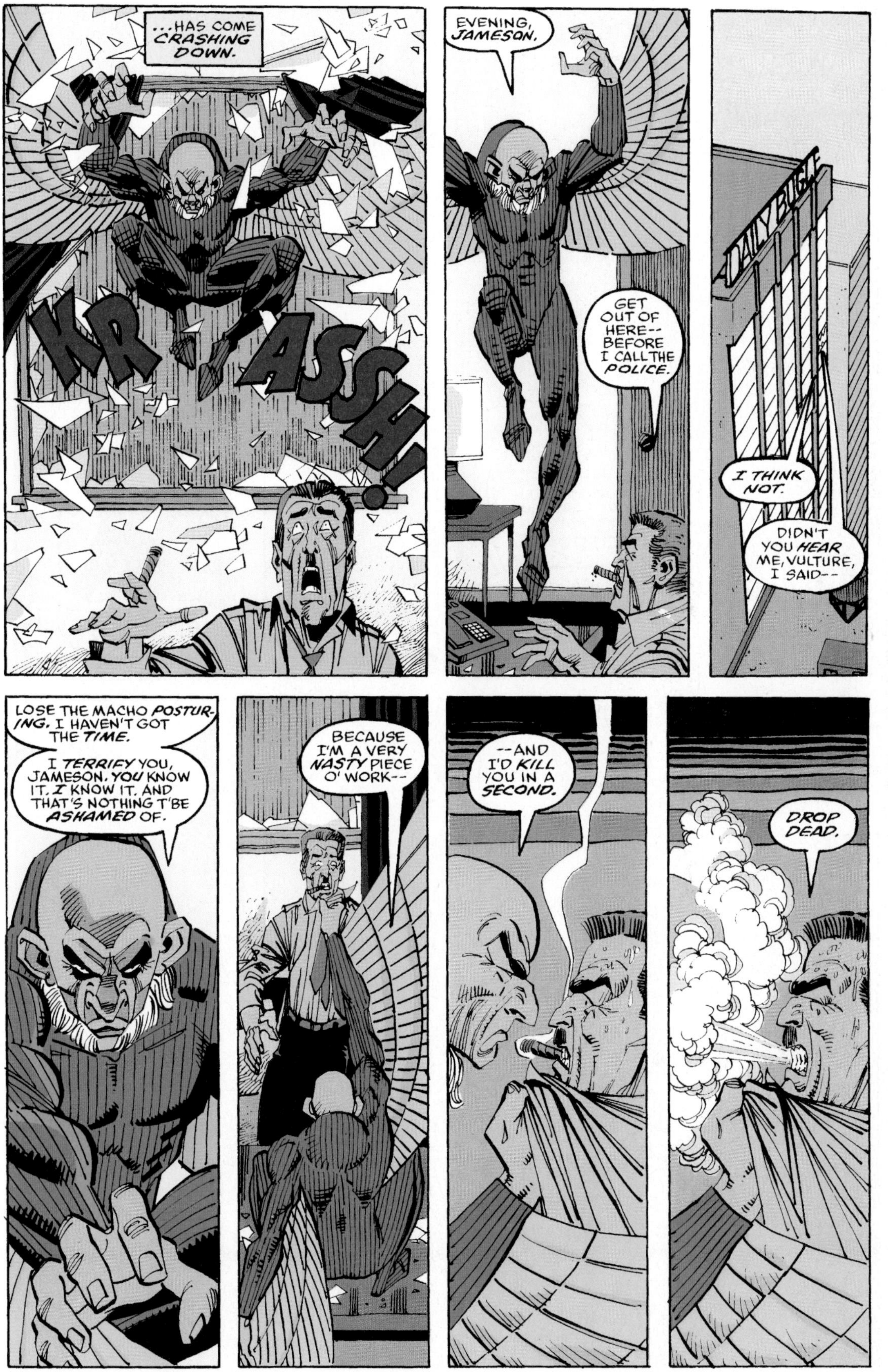

...HAS COME CRASHING DOWN.
KRASSH!
EVENING, JAMESON.
GET OUT OF HERE-- BEFORE I CALL THE POLICE.
I THINK NOT.
DIDN'T YOU HEAR ME, VULTURE, I SAID--
LOSE THE MACHO POSTURING. I HAVEN'T GOT THE TIME.
I TERRIFY YOU, JAMESON. YOU KNOW IT. I KNOW IT. AND THAT'S NOTHING T'BE ASHAMED OF.
BECAUSE I'M A VERY NASTY PIECE O' WORK--
--AND I'D KILL YOU IN A SECOND.
DROP DEAD.

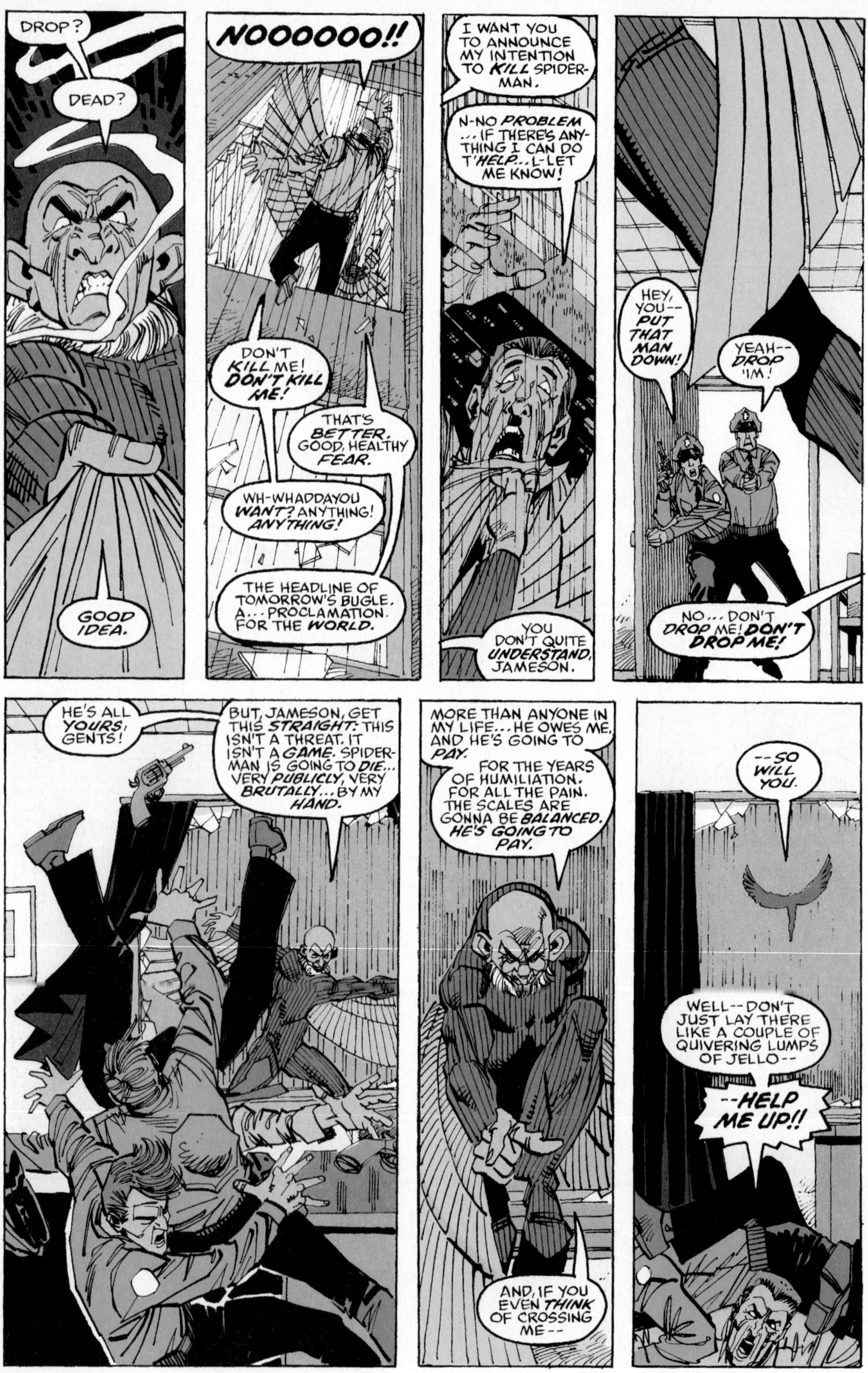
DROP?
DEAD?
GOOD IDEA.
NOOOOOO!!
DON'T KILL ME! DON'T KILL ME!
THAT'S BETTER. GOOD, HEALTHY FEAR.
WH-WHADDAYOU WANT? ANYTHING! ANYTHING!
THE HEADLINE OF TOMORROW'S BUGLE. A... PROCLAMATION. FOR THE WORLD.
I WANT YOU TO ANNOUNCE MY INTENTION TO KILL SPIDER-MAN.
N-NO PROBLEM ... IF THERE'S ANYTHING I CAN DO T'HELP... L-LET ME KNOW!
YOU DON'T QUITE UNDERSTAND, JAMESON.
HEY, YOU-- PUT THAT MAN DOWN!
YEAH-- DROP 'IM!
NO... DON'T DROP ME! DON'T DROP ME!
HE'S ALL YOURS, GENTS!
BUT, JAMESON, GET THIS STRAIGHT: THIS ISN'T A THREAT. IT ISN'T A GAME. SPIDER-MAN IS GOING TO DIE... VERY PUBLICLY, VERY BRUTALLY... BY MY HAND.
MORE THAN ANYONE IN MY LIFE... HE OWES ME, AND HE'S GOING TO PAY.
FOR THE YEARS OF HUMILIATION. FOR ALL THE PAIN. THE SCALES ARE GONNA BE BALANCED. HE'S GOING TO PAY.
AND, IF YOU EVEN THINK OF CROSSING ME--
--SO WILL YOU.
WELL-- DON'T JUST LAY THERE LIKE A COUPLE OF QUIVERING LUMPS OF JELLO--
--HELP ME UP!!

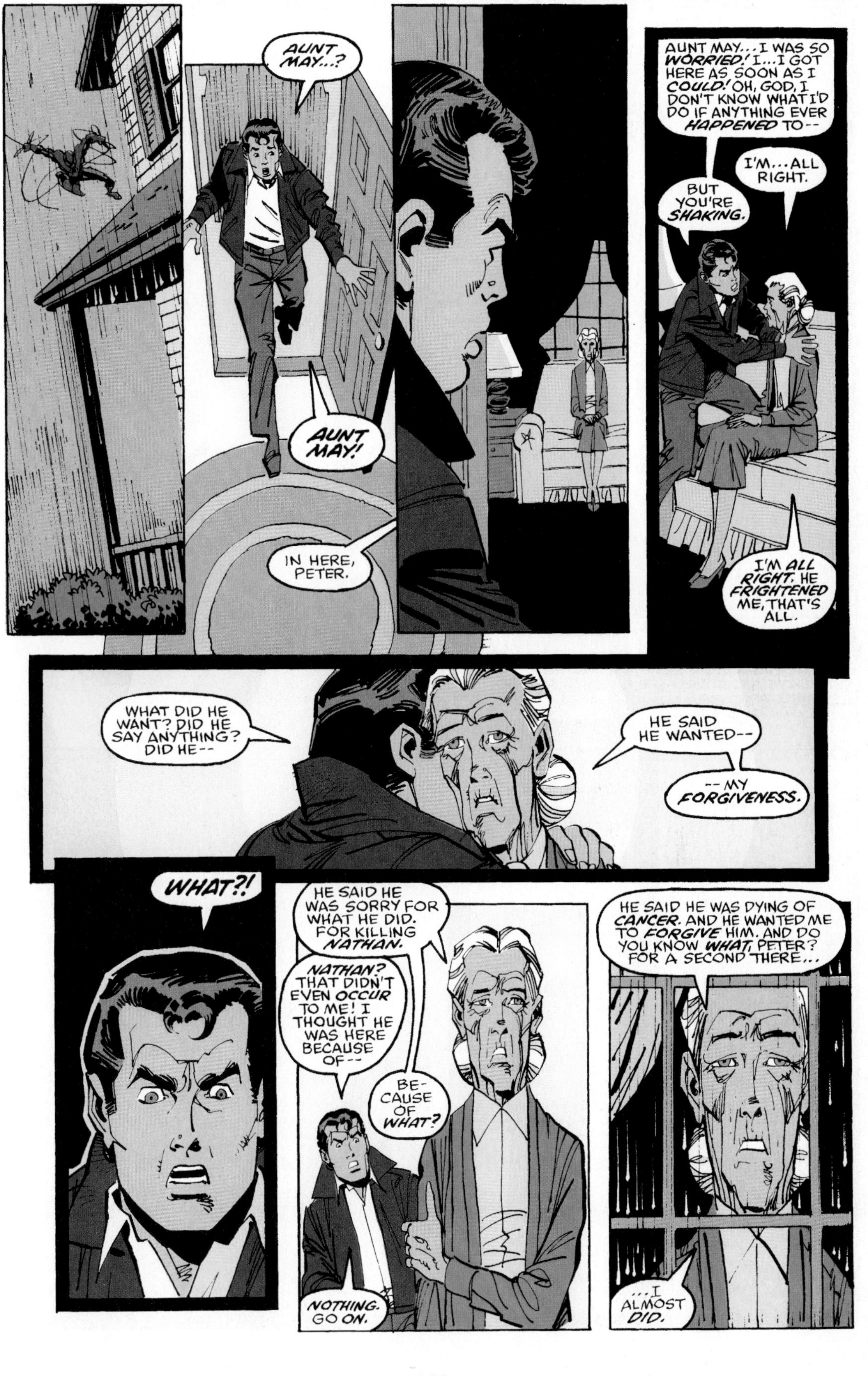

AUNT MAY...?
AUNT MAY!
IN HERE, PETER.
AUNT MAY... I WAS SO WORRIED! I... I GOT HERE AS SOON AS I COULD! OH, GOD, I DON'T KNOW WHAT I'D DO IF ANYTHING EVER HAPPENED TO--
I'M... ALL RIGHT.
BUT YOU'RE SHAKING.
I'M ALL RIGHT. HE FRIGHTENED ME, THAT'S ALL.
WHAT DID HE WANT? DID HE SAY ANYTHING? DID HE--
HE SAID HE WANTED--
-- MY FORGIVENESS.
WHAT?!
HE SAID HE WAS SORRY FOR WHAT HE DID. FOR KILLING NATHAN.
NATHAN? THAT DIDN'T EVEN OCCUR TO ME! I THOUGHT HE WAS HERE BECAUSE OF--
BE-CAUSE OF WHAT?
NOTHING. GO ON.
HE SAID HE WAS DYING OF CANCER. AND HE WANTED ME TO FORGIVE HIM. AND DO YOU KNOW WHAT, PETER? FOR A SECOND THERE...
...I ALMOST DID.

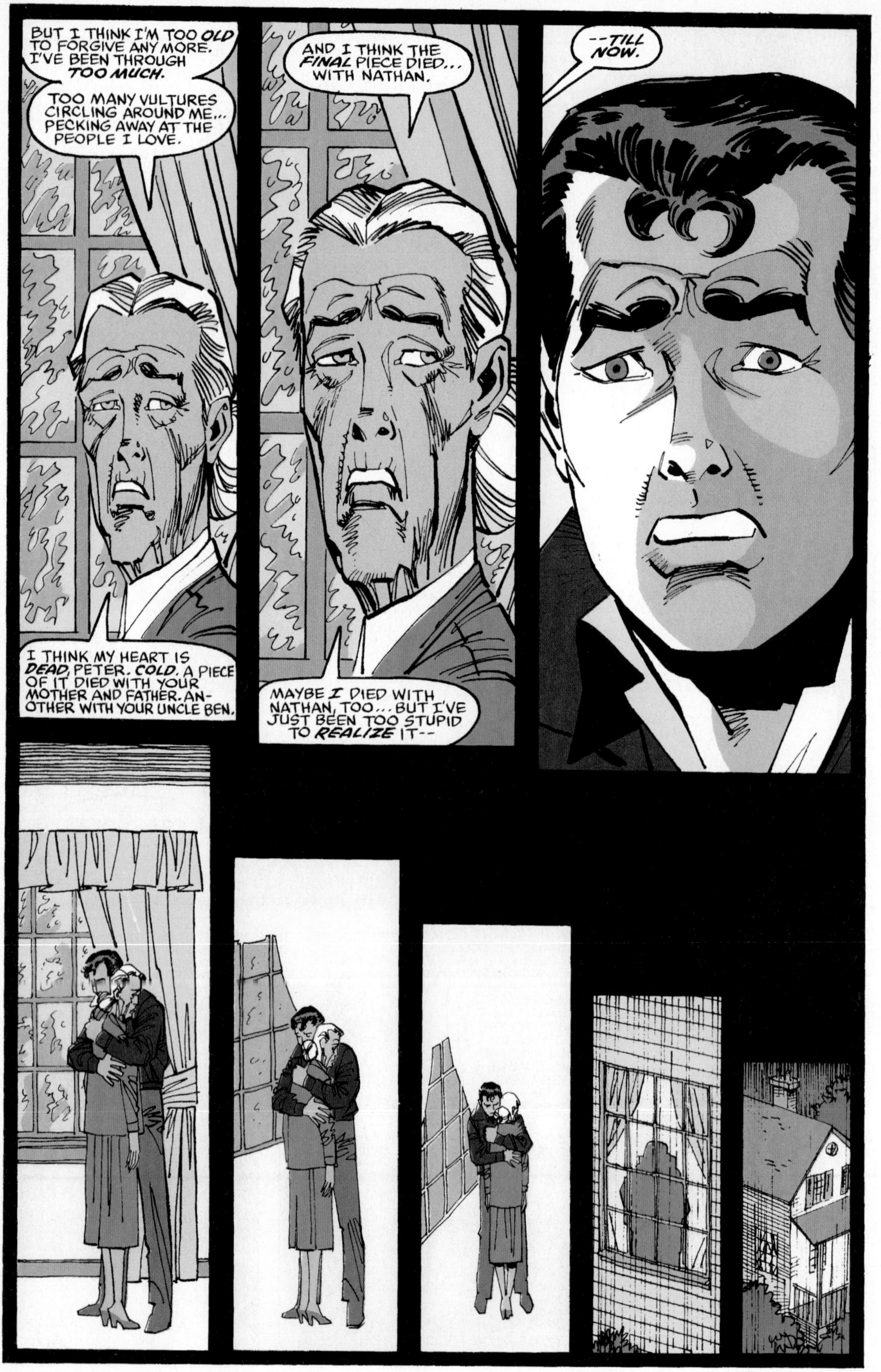
BUT I THINK I'M TOO OLD TO FORGIVE ANY MORE. I'VE BEEN THROUGH TOO MUCH.
TOO MANY VULTURES CIRCLING AROUND ME... PECKING AWAY AT THE PEOPLE I LOVE.
I THINK MY HEART IS DEAD, PETER. COLD. A PIECE OF IT DIED WITH YOUR MOTHER AND FATHER. ANOTHER WITH YOUR UNCLE BEN.
AND I THINK THE FINAL PIECE DIED... WITH NATHAN.
MAYBE I DIED WITH NATHAN, TOO... BUT I'VE JUST BEEN TOO STUPID TO REALIZE IT--
--TILL NOW.

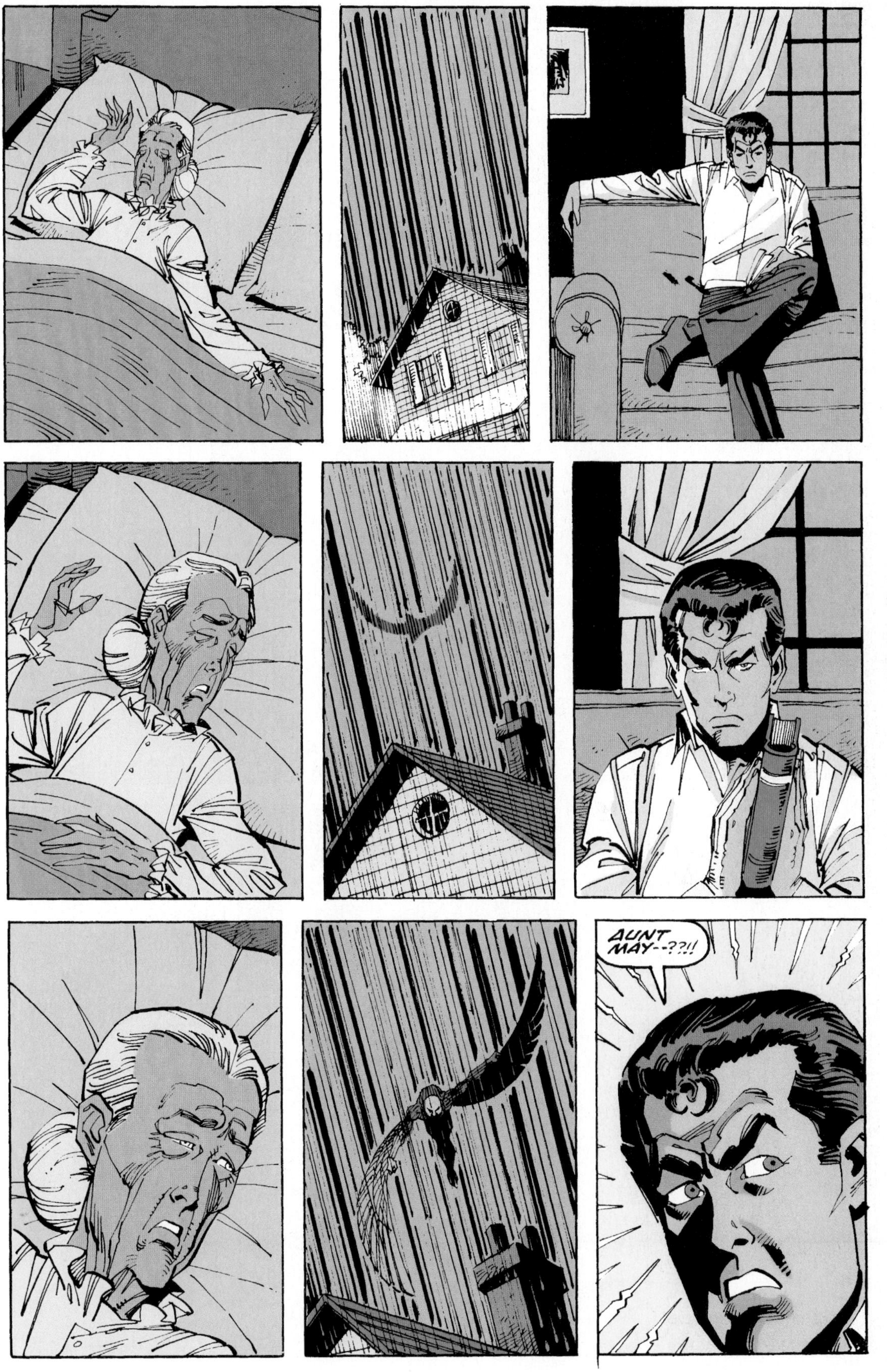
AUNT MAY--??!!

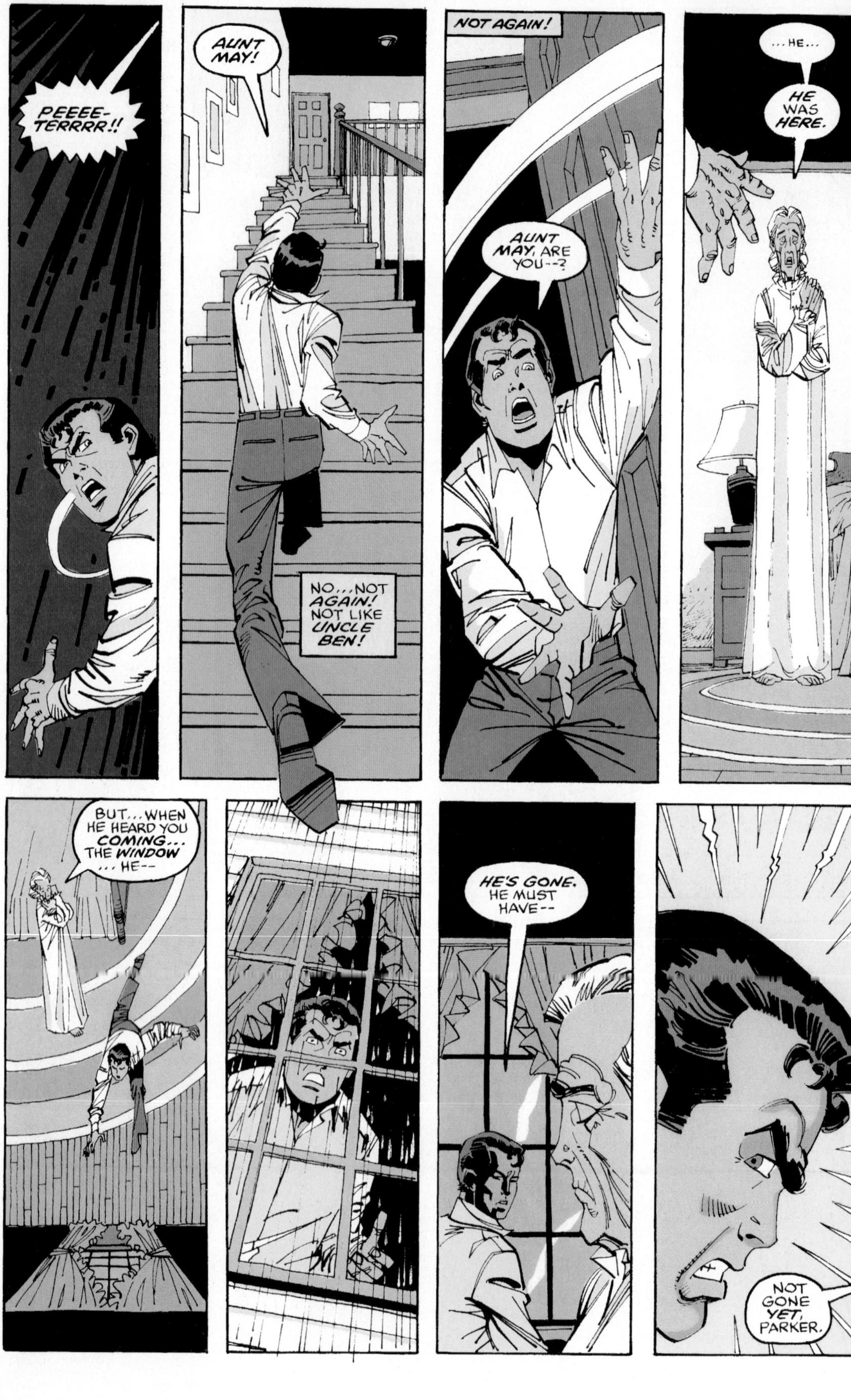

PEEEE-TERRRR!!
AUNT MAY!
NO... NOT AGAIN! NOT LIKE UNCLE BEN!
NOT AGAIN!
AUNT MAY, ARE YOU--?
...HE...
HE WAS HERE.
BUT... WHEN HE HEARD YOU COMING... THE WINDOW ... HE--
HE'S GONE. HE MUST HAVE--
NOT GONE YET, PARKER.

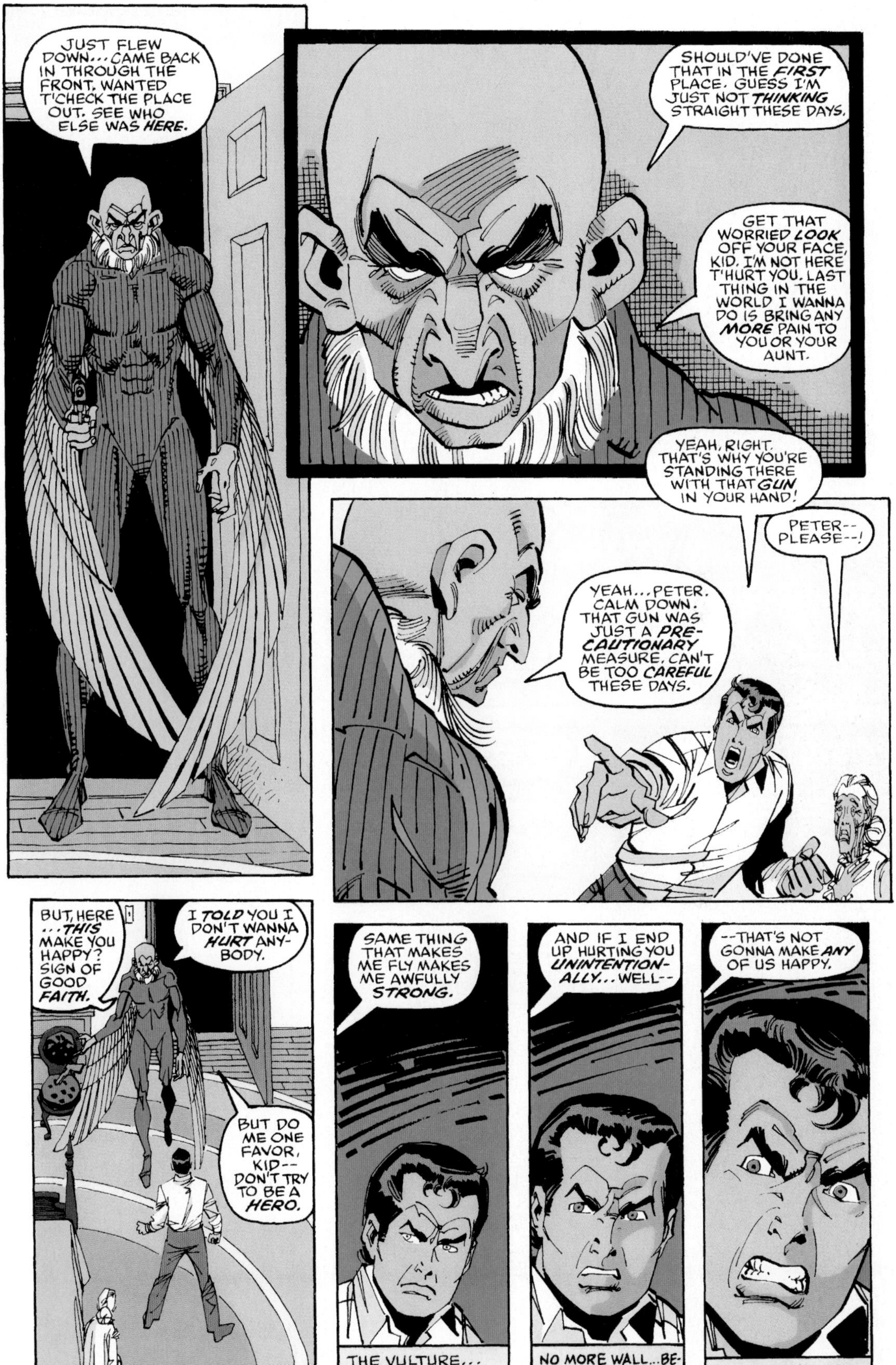

JUST FLEW DOWN... CAME BACK IN THROUGH THE FRONT. WANTED T'CHECK THE PLACE OUT. SEE WHO ELSE WAS HERE.
SHOULD'VE DONE THAT IN THE FIRST PLACE. GUESS I'M JUST NOT THINKING STRAIGHT THESE DAYS.
GET THAT WORRIED LOOK OFF YOUR FACE, KID. I'M NOT HERE T'HURT YOU. LAST THING IN THE WORLD I WANNA DO IS BRING ANY MORE PAIN TO YOU OR YOUR AUNT.
YEAH, RIGHT. THAT'S WHY YOU'RE STANDING THERE WITH THAT GUN IN YOUR HAND!
PETER-- PLEASE--!
YEAH... PETER. CALM DOWN. THAT GUN WAS JUST A PRE-CAUTIONARY MEASURE. CAN'T BE TOO CAREFUL THESE DAYS.
BUT, HERE ...THIS MAKE YOU HAPPY? SIGN OF GOOD FAITH.
I TOLD YOU I DON'T WANNA HURT ANY-BODY.
BUT DO ME ONE FAVOR, KID-- DON'T TRY TO BE A HERO.
SAME THING THAT MAKES ME FLY MAKES ME AWFULLY STRONG.
THE VULTURE... HERE... IN MY AUNT'S HOUSE.
AND IF I END UP HURTING YOU UNINTENTION-ALLY... WELL--
NO MORE WALL... BE-TWEEN SPIDER-MAN AND PETER PARKER.
--THAT'S NOT GONNA MAKE ANY OF US HAPPY.
BUT THERE'S GOT TO BE A WALL--

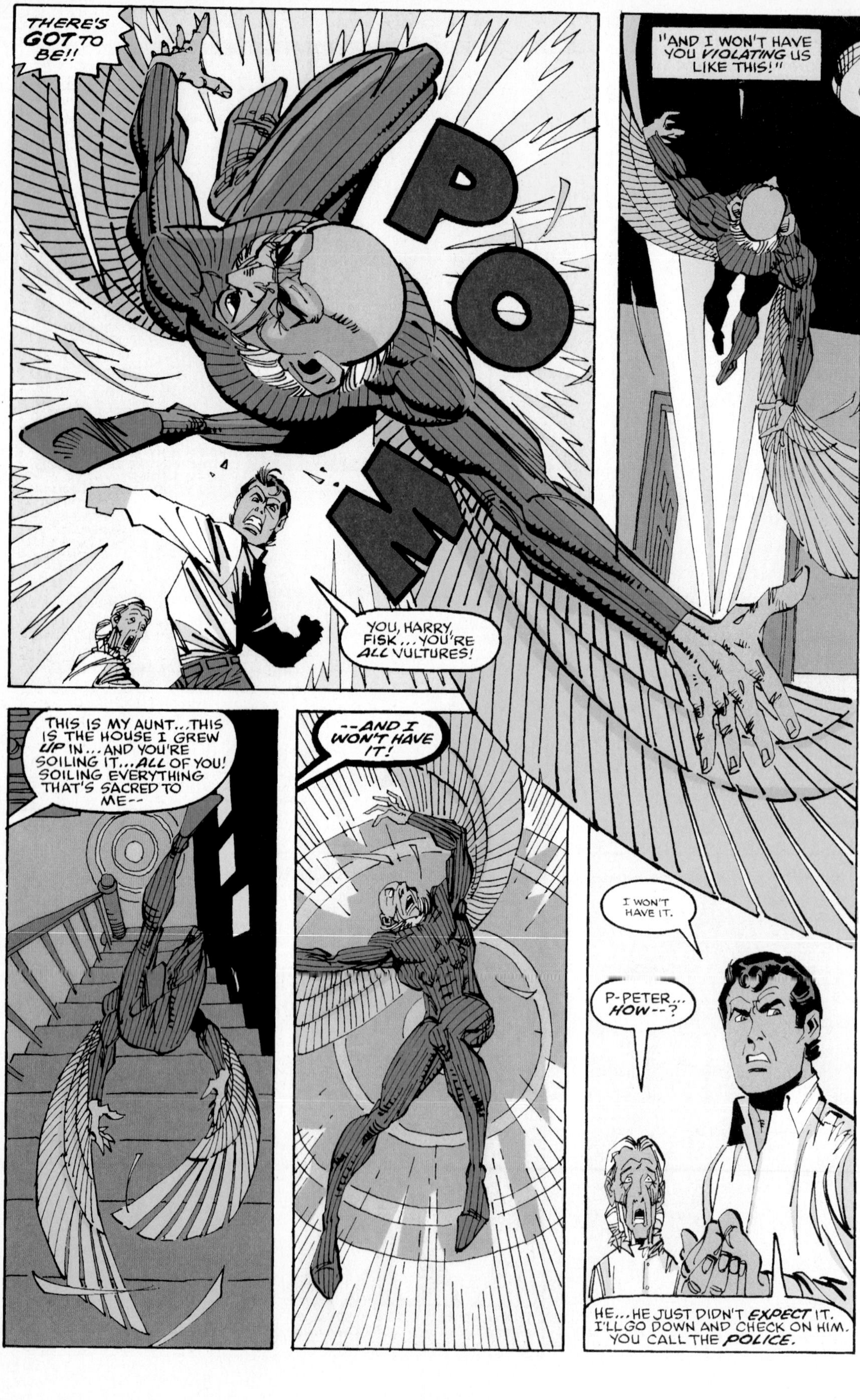

THERE'S GOT TO BE!!
POM
YOU, HARRY, FISK... YOU'RE ALL VULTURES!
"AND I WON'T HAVE YOU VIOLATING US LIKE THIS!"
THIS IS MY AUNT...THIS IS THE HOUSE I GREW UP IN...AND YOU'RE SOILING IT...ALL OF YOU! SOILING EVERYTHING THAT'S SACRED TO ME--
--AND I WON'T HAVE IT!
I WON'T HAVE IT.
P-PETER... HOW--?
HE...HE JUST DIDN'T EXPECT IT. I'LL GO DOWN AND CHECK ON HIM. YOU CALL THE POLICE.

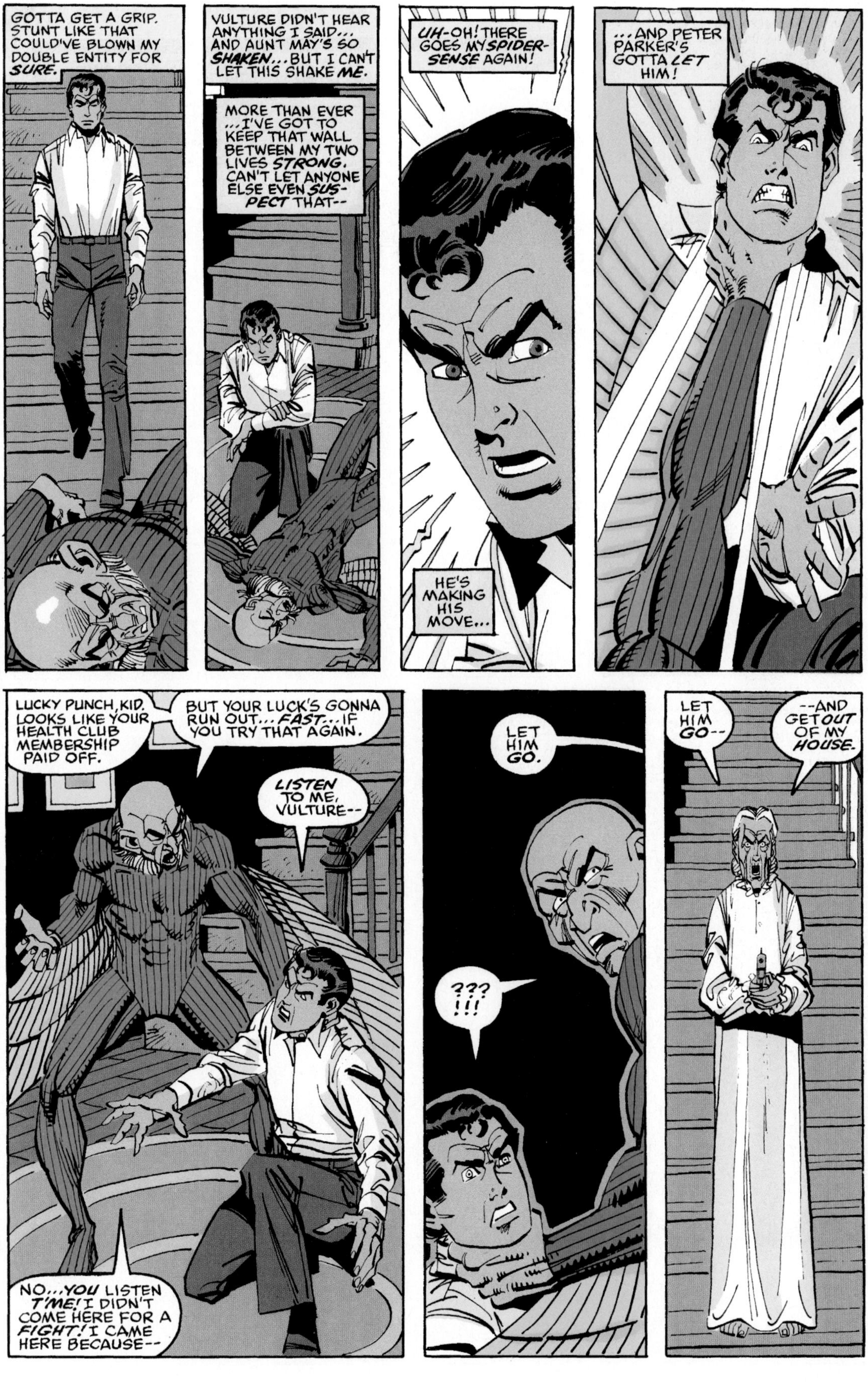
GOTTA GET A GRIP. STUNT LIKE THAT COULD'VE BLOWN MY DOUBLE ENTITY FOR SURE.
VULTURE DIDN'T HEAR ANYTHING I SAID... AND AUNT MAY'S SO SHAKEN... BUT I CAN'T LET THIS SHAKE ME.
MORE THAN EVER ...I'VE GOT TO KEEP THAT WALL BETWEEN MY TWO LIVES STRONG. CAN'T LET ANYONE ELSE EVEN SUS-PECT THAT--
UH-OH! THERE GOES MY SPIDER-SENSE AGAIN!
HE'S MAKING HIS MOVE...
...AND PETER PARKER'S GOTTA LET HIM!
LUCKY PUNCH, KID. LOOKS LIKE YOUR HEALTH CLUB MEMBERSHIP PAID OFF.
BUT YOUR LUCK'S GONNA RUN OUT... FAST... IF YOU TRY THAT AGAIN.
LISTEN TO ME, VULTURE--
NO... YOU LISTEN T'ME! I DIDN'T COME HERE FOR A FIGHT! I CAME HERE BECAUSE--
LET HIM GO.
???
!!!
LET HIM GO--
--AND GET OUT OF MY HOUSE.

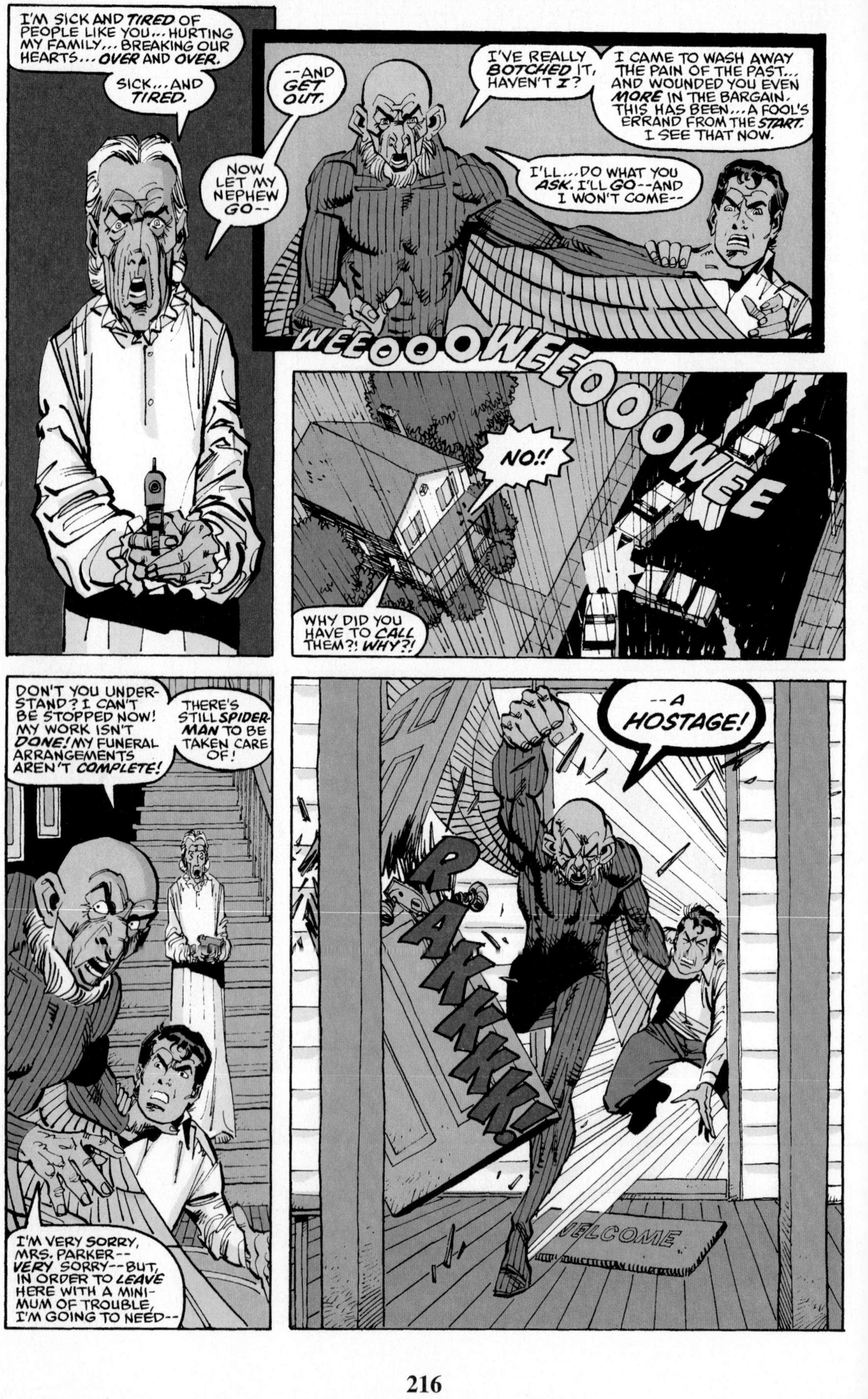
I'M SICK AND TIRED OF PEOPLE LIKE YOU... HURTING MY FAMILY... BREAKING OUR HEARTS... OVER AND OVER.
SICK... AND TIRED.
NOW LET MY NEPHEW GO--
--AND GET OUT.
I'VE REALLY BOTCHED IT, HAVEN'T I?
I CAME TO WASH AWAY THE PAIN OF THE PAST... AND WOUNDED YOU EVEN MORE IN THE BARGAIN. THIS HAS BEEN... A FOOL'S ERRAND FROM THE START. I SEE THAT NOW.
I'LL... DO WHAT YOU ASK. I'LL GO--AND I WON'T COME--
WEEOOOWEEOOOOWEE
NO!!
WHY DID YOU HAVE TO CALL THEM?! WHY?!
DON'T YOU UNDERSTAND? I CAN'T BE STOPPED NOW! MY WORK ISN'T DONE! MY FUNERAL ARRANGEMENTS AREN'T COMPLETE!
THERE'S STILL SPIDER-MAN TO BE TAKEN CARE OF!
I'M VERY SORRY, MRS. PARKER--VERY SORRY--BUT, IN ORDER TO LEAVE HERE WITH A MINIMUM OF TROUBLE, I'M GOING TO NEED--
--A HOSTAGE!
RAKKKK!
WELCOME

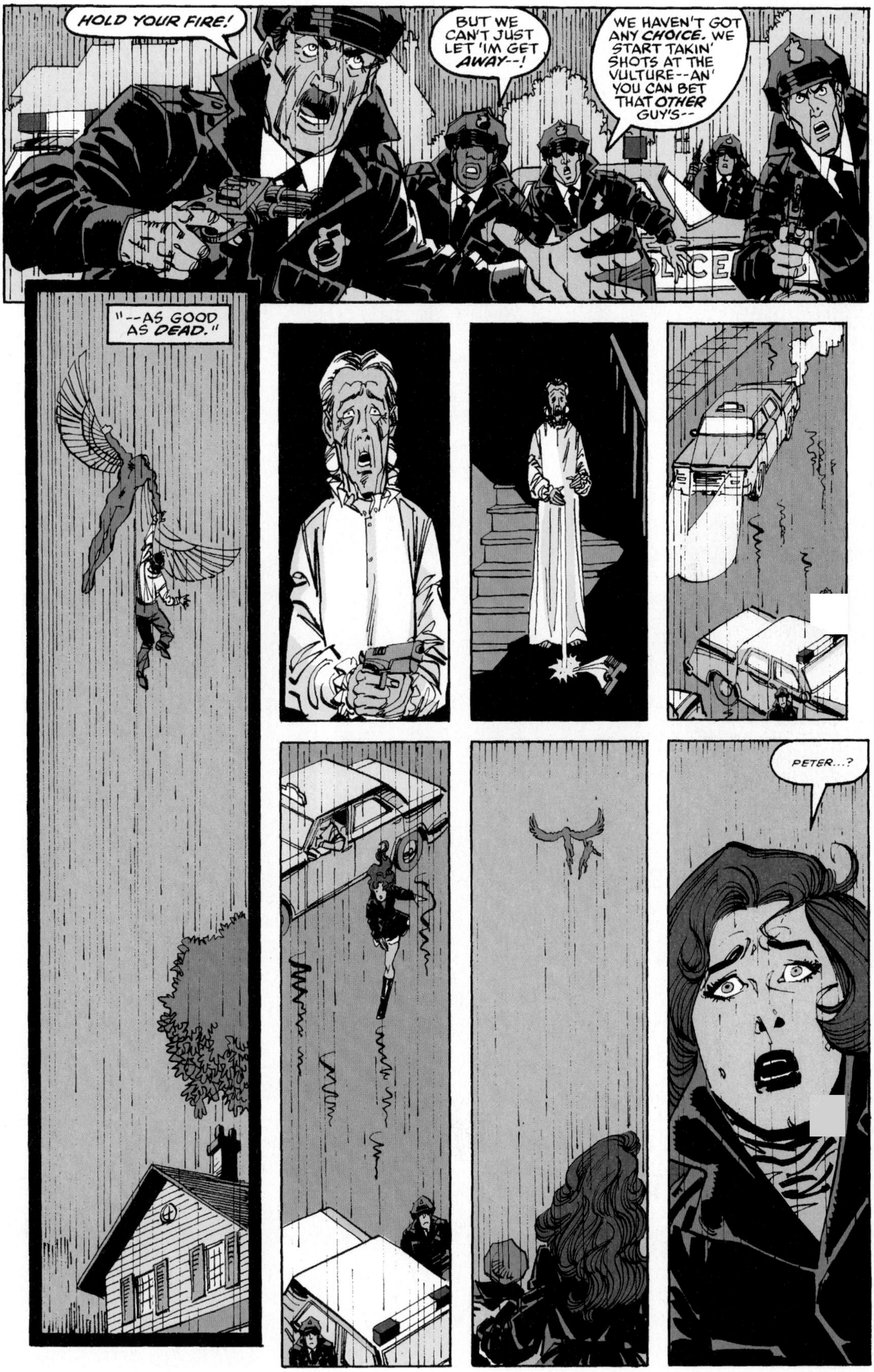
HOLD YOUR FIRE!
BUT WE CAN'T JUST LET 'IM GET AWAY--!
WE HAVEN'T GOT ANY CHOICE. WE START TAKIN' SHOTS AT THE VULTURE--AN' YOU CAN BET THAT OTHER GUY'S--
"--AS GOOD AS DEAD."
POLICE
PETER...?

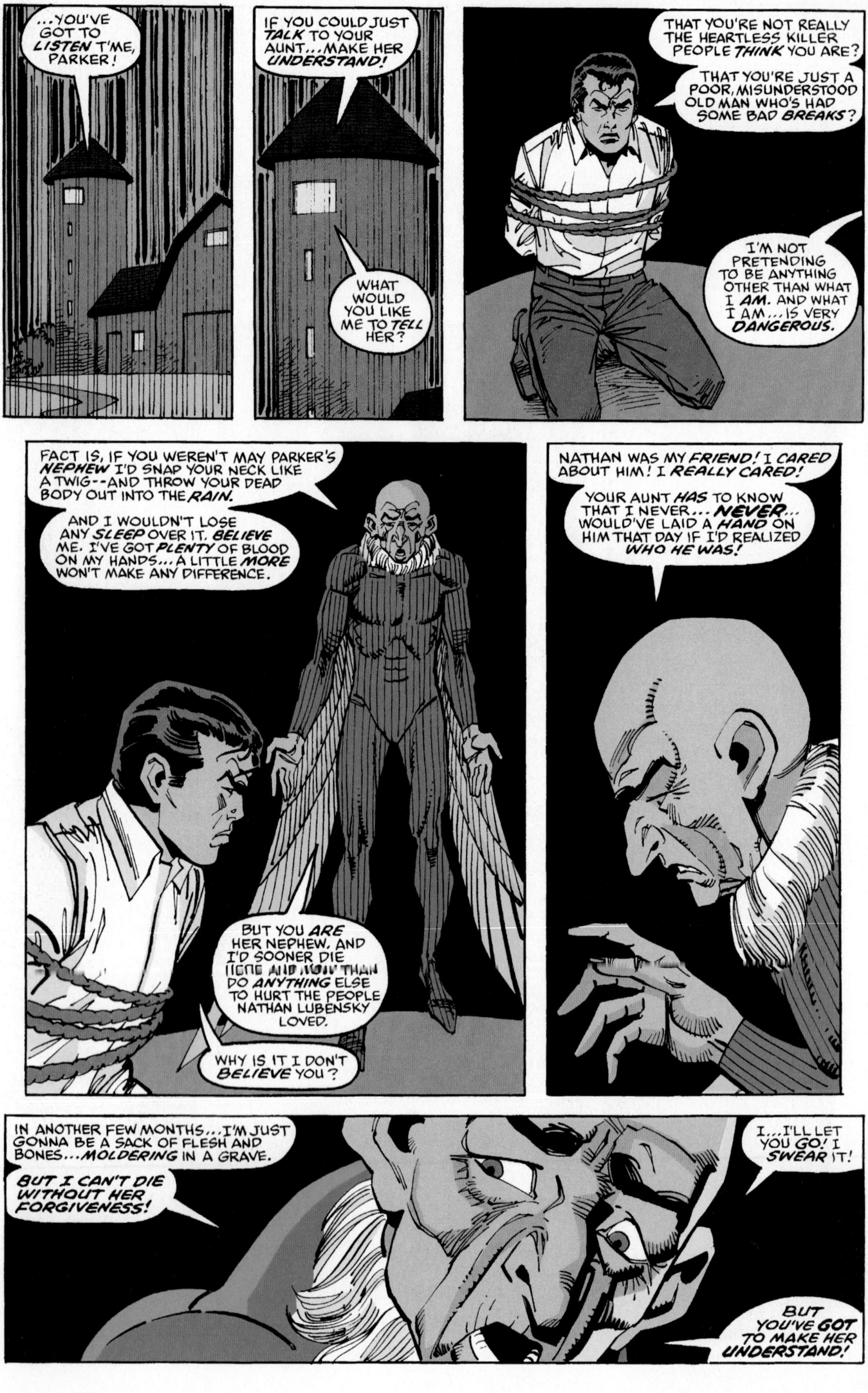
...YOU'VE GOT TO LISTEN T'ME, PARKER!
IF YOU COULD JUST TALK TO YOUR AUNT...MAKE HER UNDERSTAND!
WHAT WOULD YOU LIKE ME TO TELL HER?
THAT YOU'RE NOT REALLY THE HEARTLESS KILLER PEOPLE THINK YOU ARE?
THAT YOU'RE JUST A POOR, MISUNDERSTOOD OLD MAN WHO'S HAD SOME BAD BREAKS?
I'M NOT PRETENDING TO BE ANYTHING OTHER THAN WHAT I AM. AND WHAT I AM...IS VERY DANGEROUS.
FACT IS, IF YOU WEREN'T MAY PARKER'S NEPHEW I'D SNAP YOUR NECK LIKE A TWIG--AND THROW YOUR DEAD BODY OUT INTO THE RAIN.
AND I WOULDN'T LOSE ANY SLEEP OVER IT. BELIEVE ME. I'VE GOT PLENTY OF BLOOD ON MY HANDS...A LITTLE MORE WON'T MAKE ANY DIFFERENCE.
BUT YOU ARE HER NEPHEW. AND I'D SOONER DIE THAN DO ANYTHING ELSE TO HURT THE PEOPLE NATHAN LUBENSKY LOVED.
WHY IS IT I DON'T BELIEVE YOU?
NATHAN WAS MY FRIEND! I CARED ABOUT HIM! I REALLY CARED!
YOUR AUNT HAS TO KNOW THAT I NEVER...NEVER...WOULD'VE LAID A HAND ON HIM THAT DAY IF I'D REALIZED WHO HE WAS!
IN ANOTHER FEW MONTHS...I'M JUST GONNA BE A SACK OF FLESH AND BONES...MOLDERING IN A GRAVE.
BUT I CAN'T DIE WITHOUT HER FORGIVENESS!
I...I'LL LET YOU GO! I SWEAR IT!
BUT YOU'VE GOT TO MAKE HER UNDERSTAND!

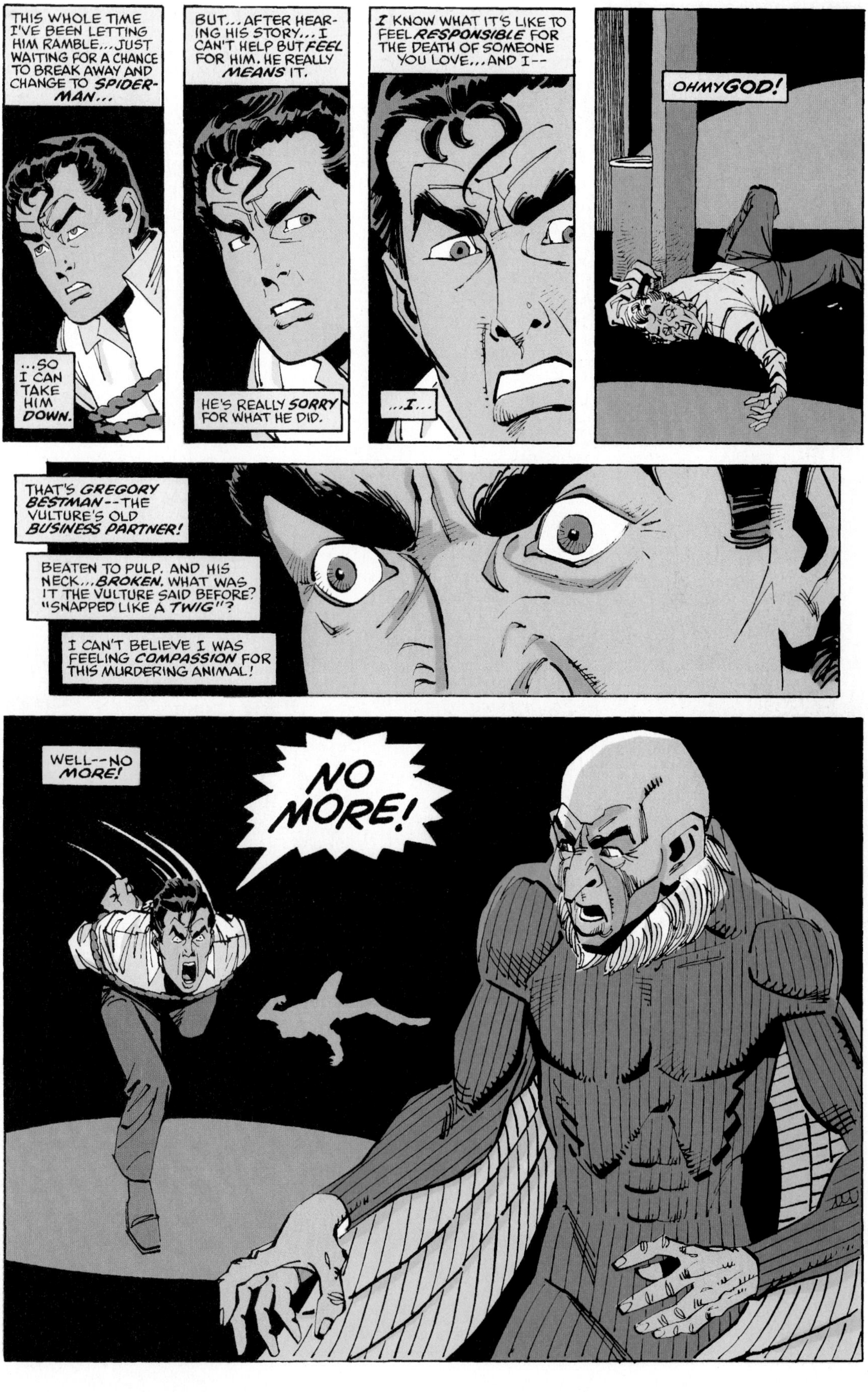
THIS WHOLE TIME I'VE BEEN LETTING HIM RAMBLE... JUST WAITING FOR A CHANCE TO BREAK AWAY AND CHANGE TO SPIDER-MAN...
...SO I CAN TAKE HIM DOWN.
BUT... AFTER HEARING HIS STORY... I CAN'T HELP BUT FEEL FOR HIM. HE REALLY MEANS IT.
HE'S REALLY SORRY FOR WHAT HE DID.
I KNOW WHAT IT'S LIKE TO FEEL RESPONSIBLE FOR THE DEATH OF SOMEONE YOU LOVE... AND I--
...I...
OHMYGOD!
THAT'S GREGORY BESTMAN--THE VULTURE'S OLD BUSINESS PARTNER!
BEATEN TO PULP. AND HIS NECK... BROKEN. WHAT WAS IT THE VULTURE SAID BEFORE? "SNAPPED LIKE A TWIG"?
I CAN'T BELIEVE I WAS FEELING COMPASSION FOR THIS MURDERING ANIMAL!
WELL--NO MORE!
NO MORE!

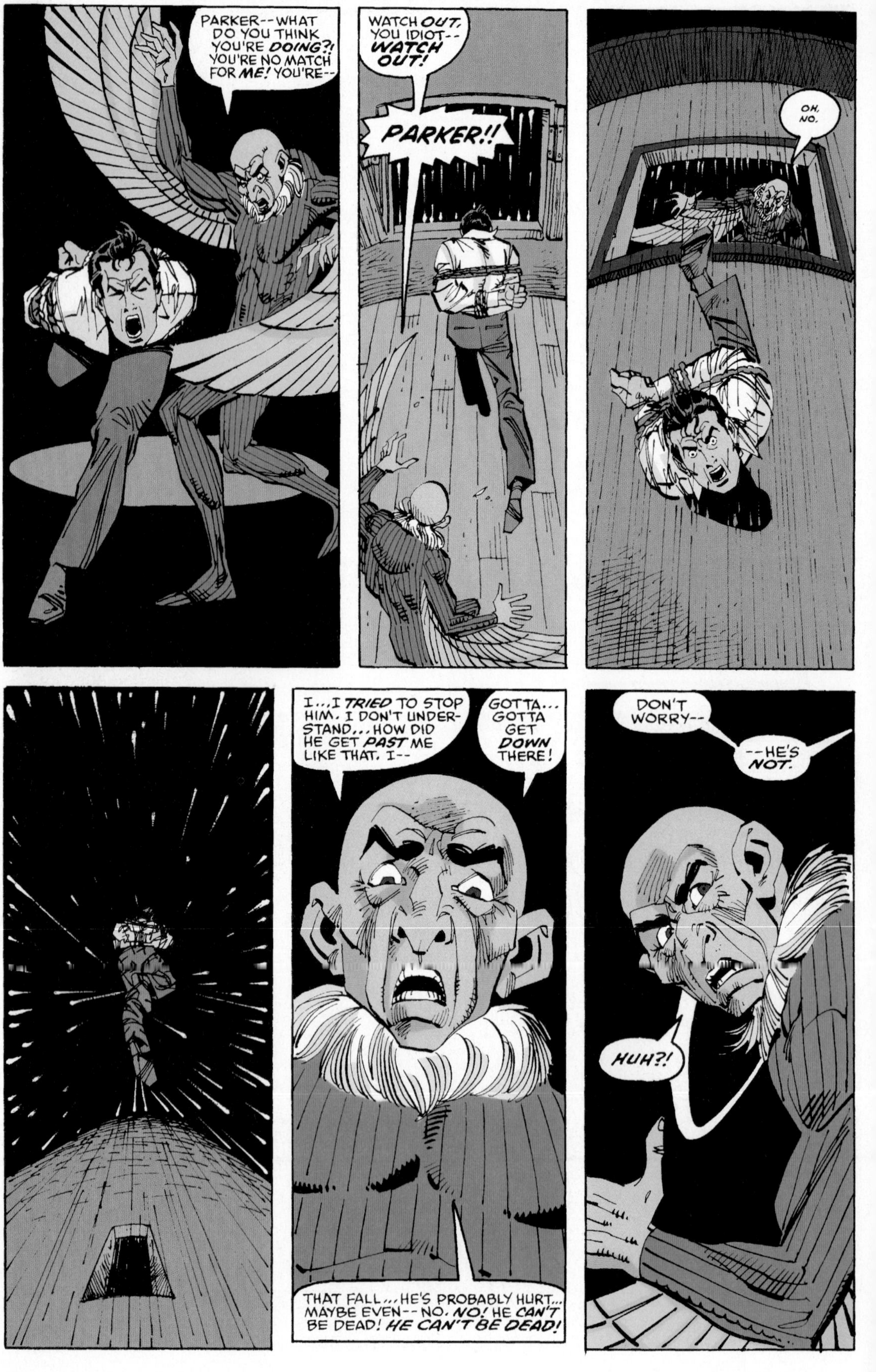
PARKER--WHAT DO YOU THINK YOU'RE DOING?! YOU'RE NO MATCH FOR ME! YOU'RE--
WATCH OUT, YOU IDIOT-- WATCH OUT!
PARKER!!
OH, NO.
I...I TRIED TO STOP HIM. I DON'T UNDERSTAND... HOW DID HE GET PAST ME LIKE THAT. I--
GOTTA... GOTTA GET DOWN THERE!
THAT FALL... HE'S PROBABLY HURT... MAYBE EVEN-- NO. NO! HE CAN'T BE DEAD! HE CAN'T BE DEAD!
DON'T WORRY--
--HE'S NOT.
HUH?!

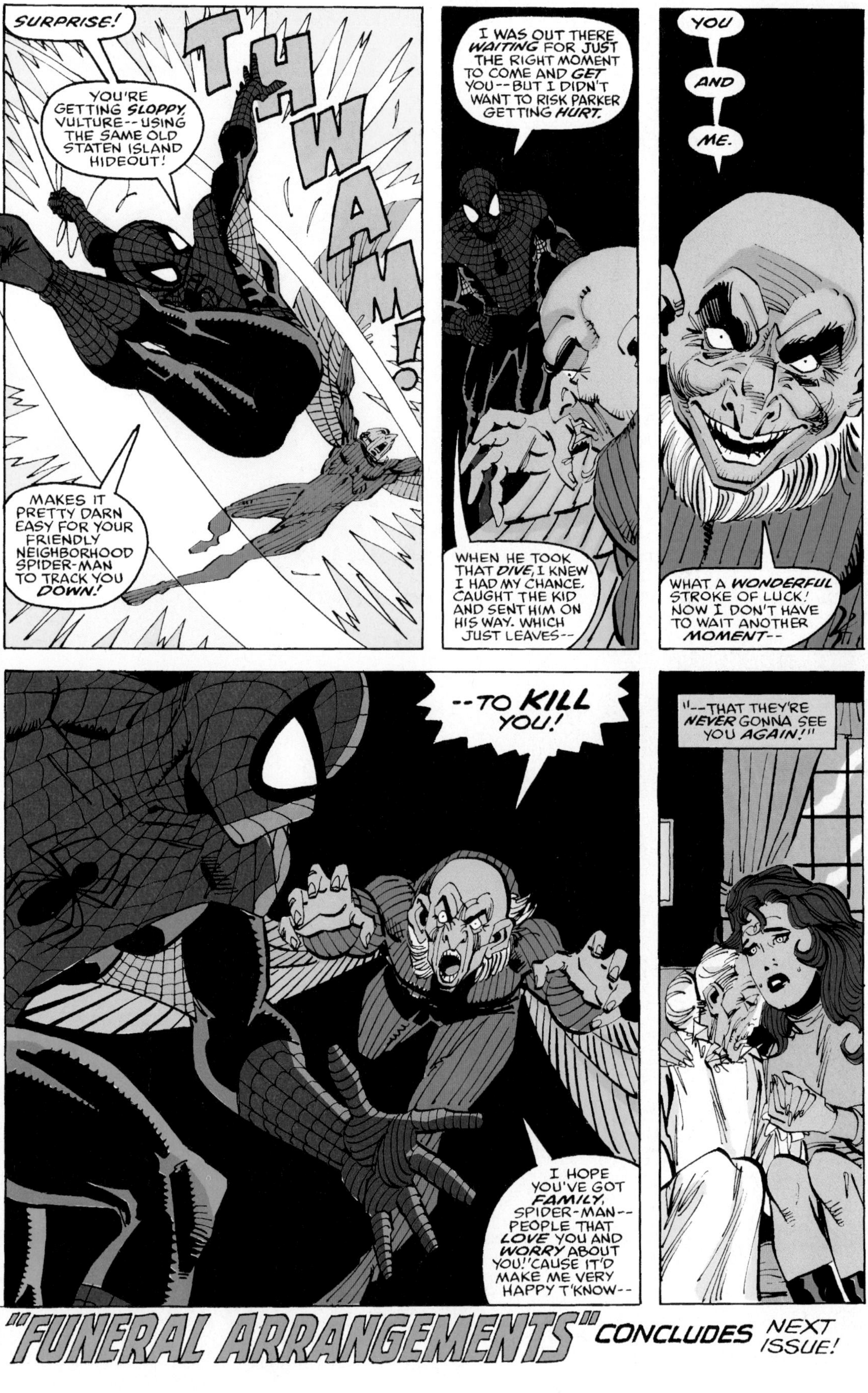
SURPRISE!
THWAM!
YOU'RE GETTING SLOPPY, VULTURE--USING THE SAME OLD STATEN ISLAND HIDEOUT!
MAKES IT PRETTY DARN EASY FOR YOUR FRIENDLY NEIGHBORHOOD SPIDER-MAN TO TRACK YOU DOWN!
I WAS OUT THERE WAITING FOR JUST THE RIGHT MOMENT TO COME AND GET YOU--BUT I DIDN'T WANT TO RISK PARKER GETTING HURT.
WHEN HE TOOK THAT DIVE, I KNEW I HAD MY CHANCE. CAUGHT THE KID AND SENT HIM ON HIS WAY. WHICH JUST LEAVES--
YOU
AND
ME.
WHAT A WONDERFUL STROKE OF LUCK! NOW I DON'T HAVE TO WAIT ANOTHER MOMENT--
--TO KILL YOU!
I HOPE YOU'VE GOT FAMILY, SPIDER-MAN--PEOPLE THAT LOVE YOU AND WORRY ABOUT YOU! 'CAUSE IT'D MAKE ME VERY HAPPY T'KNOW--
"--THAT THEY'RE NEVER GONNA SEE YOU AGAIN!"
"FUNERAL ARRANGEMENTS" CONCLUDES NEXT ISSUE!

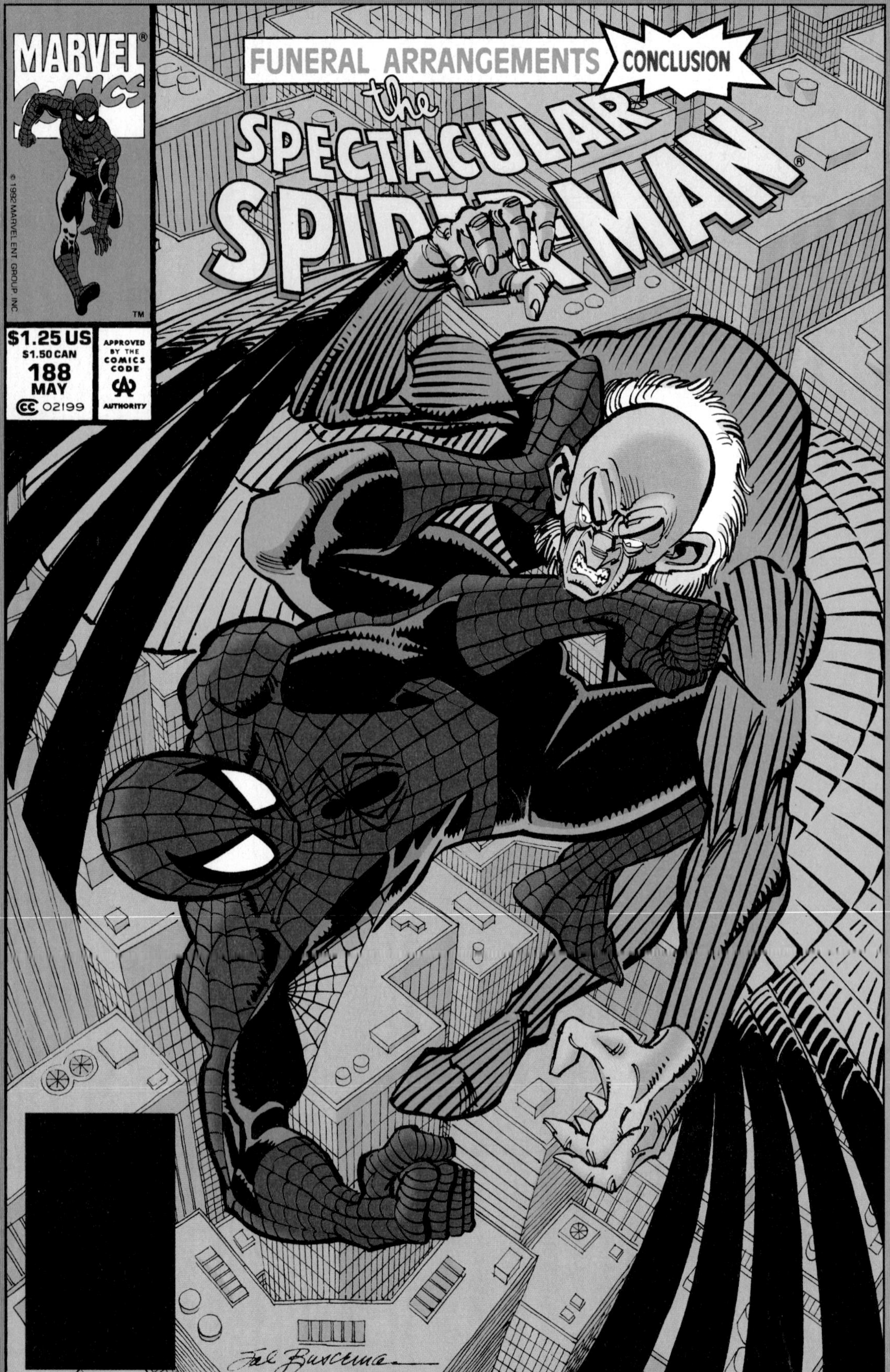
MARVEL COMICS
FUNERAL ARRANGEMENTS
CONCLUSION
the SPECTACULAR SPIDER-MAN
© 1992 MARVEL ENT GROUP INC
TM
$1.25 US
$1.50 CAN
188
MAY
02199
APPROVED BY THE COMICS CODE AUTHORITY
Sal Buscema

BITTEN BY A RADIOACTIVE SPIDER, STUDENT PETER PARKER GAINED THE PROPORTIONATE STRENGTH AND AGILITY OF AN ARACHNID! ARMED WITH HIS WONDROUS WEB-SHOOTERS, THE RELUCTANT SUPER HERO STRUGGLES WITH SINISTER SUPER-VILLAINS, MAKING ENDS MEET, AND MAINTAINING SOME SEMBLANCE OF A NORMAL LIFE!

Stan Lee PRESENTS: **THE SPECTACULAR SPIDER-MAN!** TM

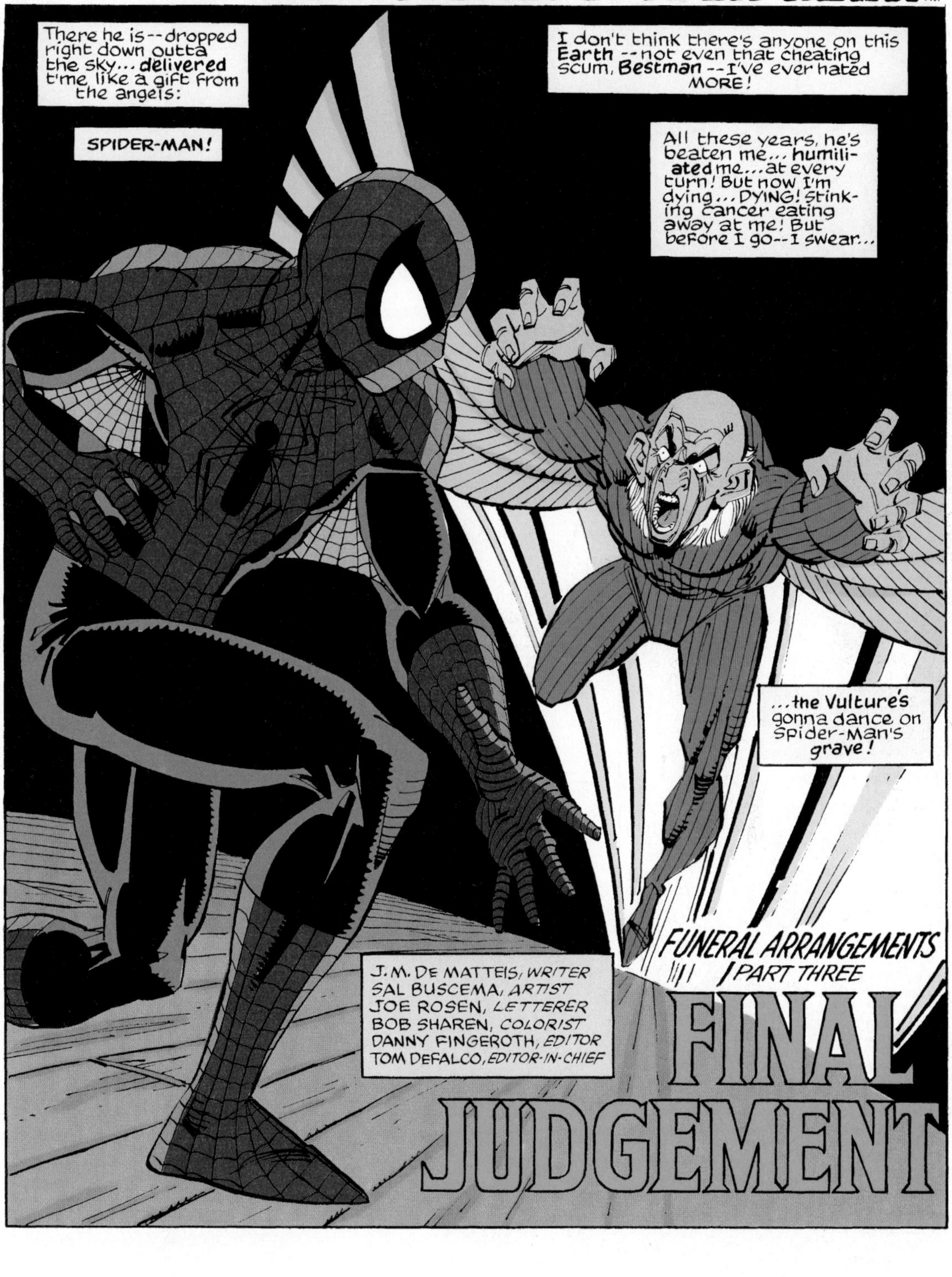

There he is--dropped right down outta the sky... delivered t'me like a gift from the angels:
SPIDER-MAN!
I don't think there's anyone on this Earth --not even that cheating scum, Bestman --I've ever hated MORE!
All these years, he's beaten me... humiliated me... at every turn! But now I'm dying... DYING! Stinking cancer eating away at me! But before I go--I swear...
...the Vulture's gonna dance on Spider-Man's grave!
FUNERAL ARRANGEMENTS /PART THREE
FINAL JUDGEMENT
J.M. DE MATTEIS, WRITER
SAL BUSCEMA, ARTIST
JOE ROSEN, LETTERER
BOB SHAREN, COLORIST
DANNY FINGEROTH, EDITOR
TOM DEFALCO, EDITOR-IN-CHIEF

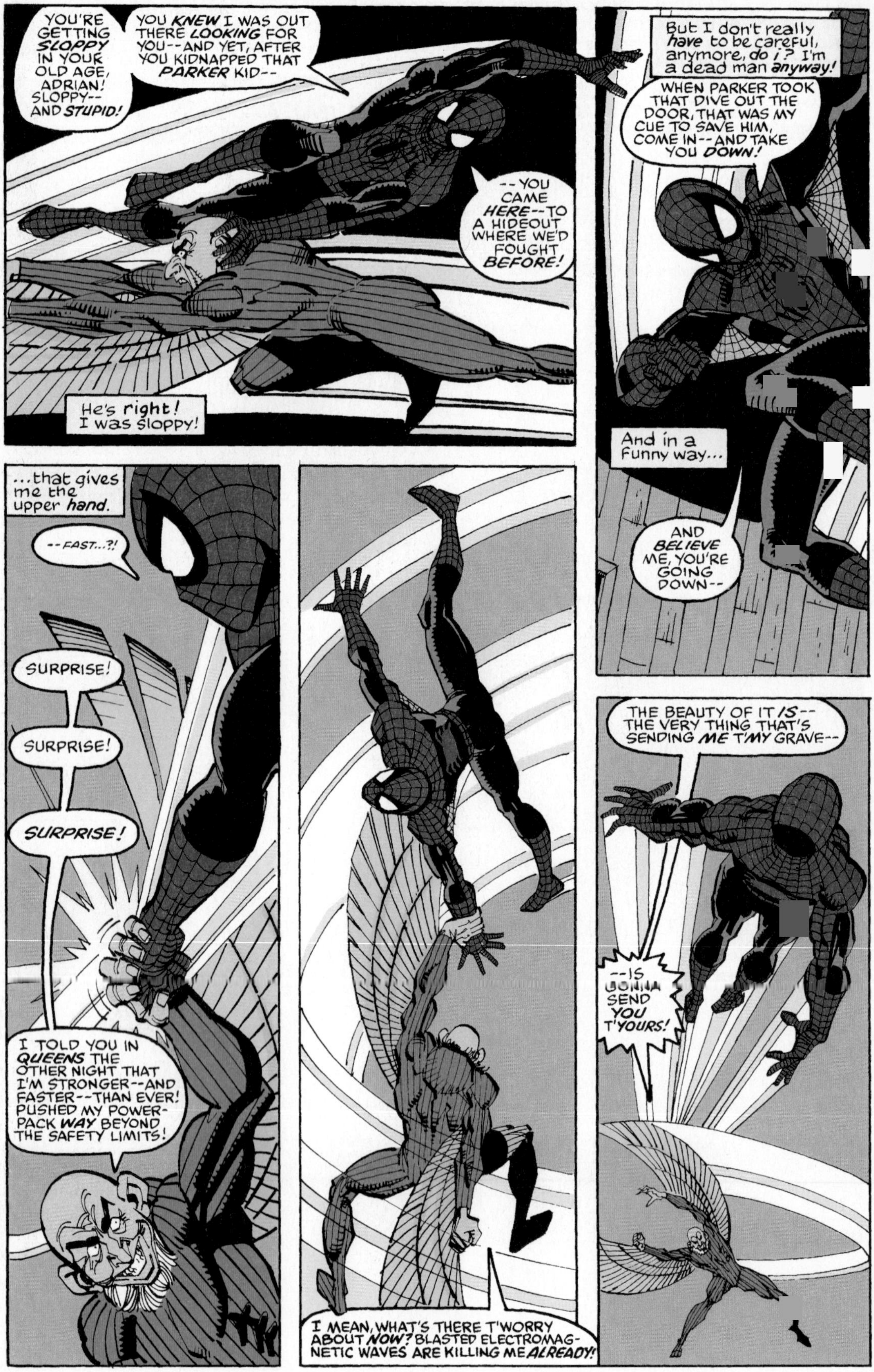

YOU'RE GETTING SLOPPY IN YOUR OLD AGE, ADRIAN! SLOPPY-- AND STUPID!
YOU KNEW I WAS OUT THERE LOOKING FOR YOU--AND YET, AFTER YOU KIDNAPPED THAT PARKER KID--
--YOU CAME HERE--TO A HIDEOUT WHERE WE'D FOUGHT BEFORE!
He's right! I was sloppy!
But I don't really have to be careful, anymore, do I? I'm a dead man anyway!
WHEN PARKER TOOK THAT DIVE OUT THE DOOR, THAT WAS MY CUE TO SAVE HIM, COME IN--AND TAKE YOU DOWN!
And in a funny way...
AND BELIEVE ME, YOU'RE GOING DOWN--
...that gives me the upper hand.
--FAST...?!
SURPRISE!
SURPRISE!
SURPRISE!
I TOLD YOU IN QUEENS THE OTHER NIGHT THAT I'M STRONGER--AND FASTER--THAN EVER! PUSHED MY POWER-PACK WAY BEYOND THE SAFETY LIMITS!
I MEAN, WHAT'S THERE T'WORRY ABOUT NOW? BLASTED ELECTROMAGNETIC WAVES ARE KILLING ME ALREADY!
THE BEAUTY OF IT IS--THE VERY THING THAT'S SENDING ME T'MY GRAVE--
--IS
SEND YOU T'YOURS!

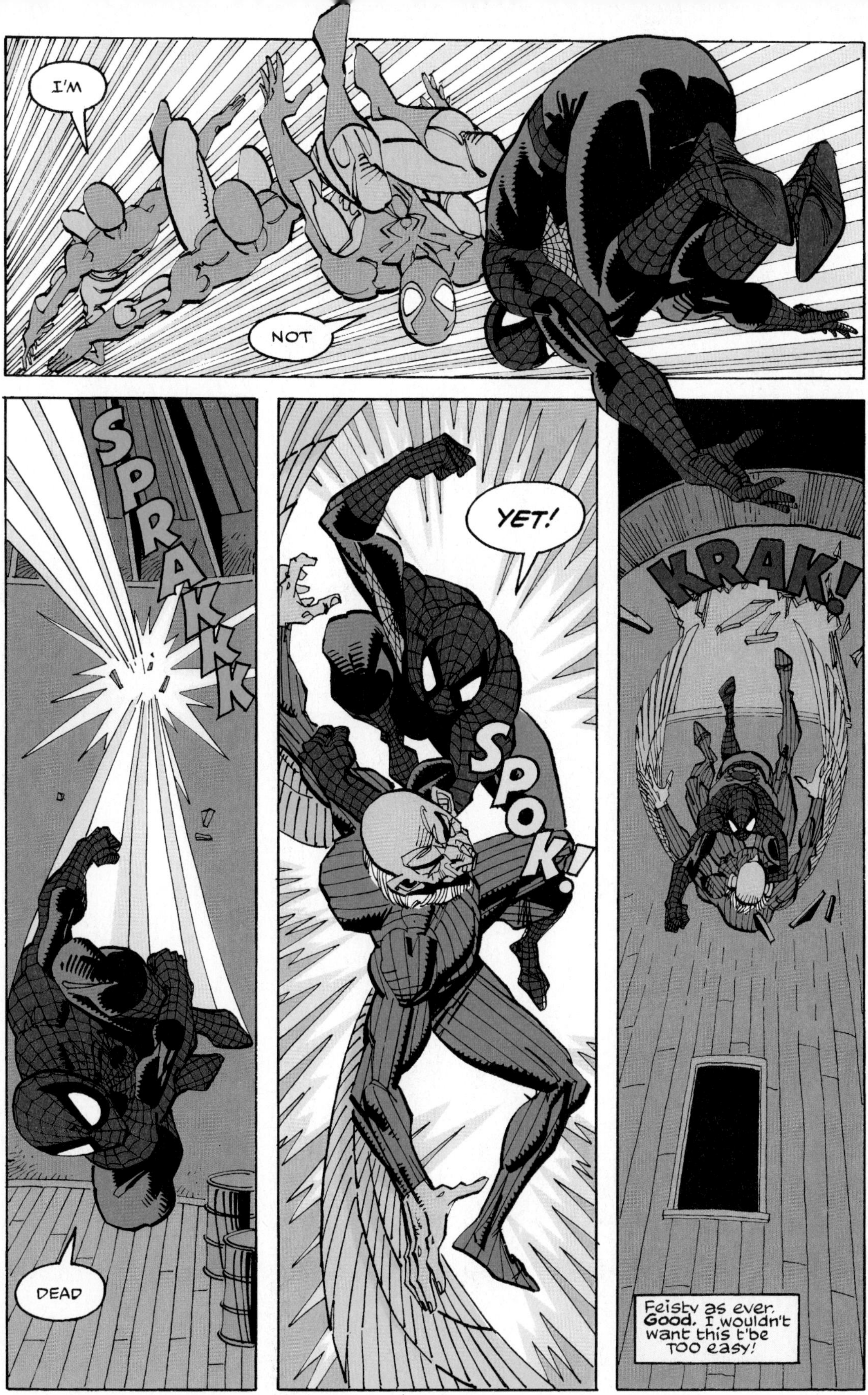
I'M
NOT
SPRAKKK
DEAD
YET!
SPOK!
KRAK!
Feisty as ever. Good. I wouldn't want this t'be TOO easy!

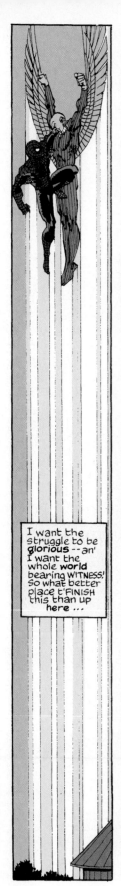

...at the **top** of the world?

WE'RE GOING **UP,** SPIDER-MAN! WAY, WAY UP!

THE TWO OF US ARE FLYING STRAIGHT TOWARD THE GATES OF **HEAVEN--**

I want the struggle to be **glorious**--an' I want the whole **world** bearing WITNESS! So what better place t'**FINISH** this than up here ...

--AND THEN **YOU'RE** MAKIN' THE LONG DROP DOWN TO THE PITS OF **HADES!**

VULTURE-- ARE YOU **CRAZY?** UP **THIS** HIGH-- THERE'S A GOOD CHANCE WE'RE **BOTH** GOING TO DIE!

I DON'T **THINK** SO!

THE SKY'S MY **ELEMENT!**

MY **home.** The rushing wind. Soaring so high above all the worthless **maggots** down below.

Sweet sky: Only place I've ever felt a little **peace.**

YOU'RE THE ONE WHO HASN'T GOT A **PRAYER!**

THIS DOESN'T MAKE ANY **SENSE!** IF WHAT YOU SAY IS **TRUE**-- IF YOU REALLY **ARE** DYING--

--THEN WHAT'S THE POINT IN SPENDING YOUR LAST DAYS INFLICTING MORE **PAIN** ON PEOPLE? HAVEN'T YOU DONE **ENOUGH** OF THAT?

FACE YOUR DEATH WITH **DIGNITY!** DON'T GO OUT LIKE SOME... **VULTURE--**

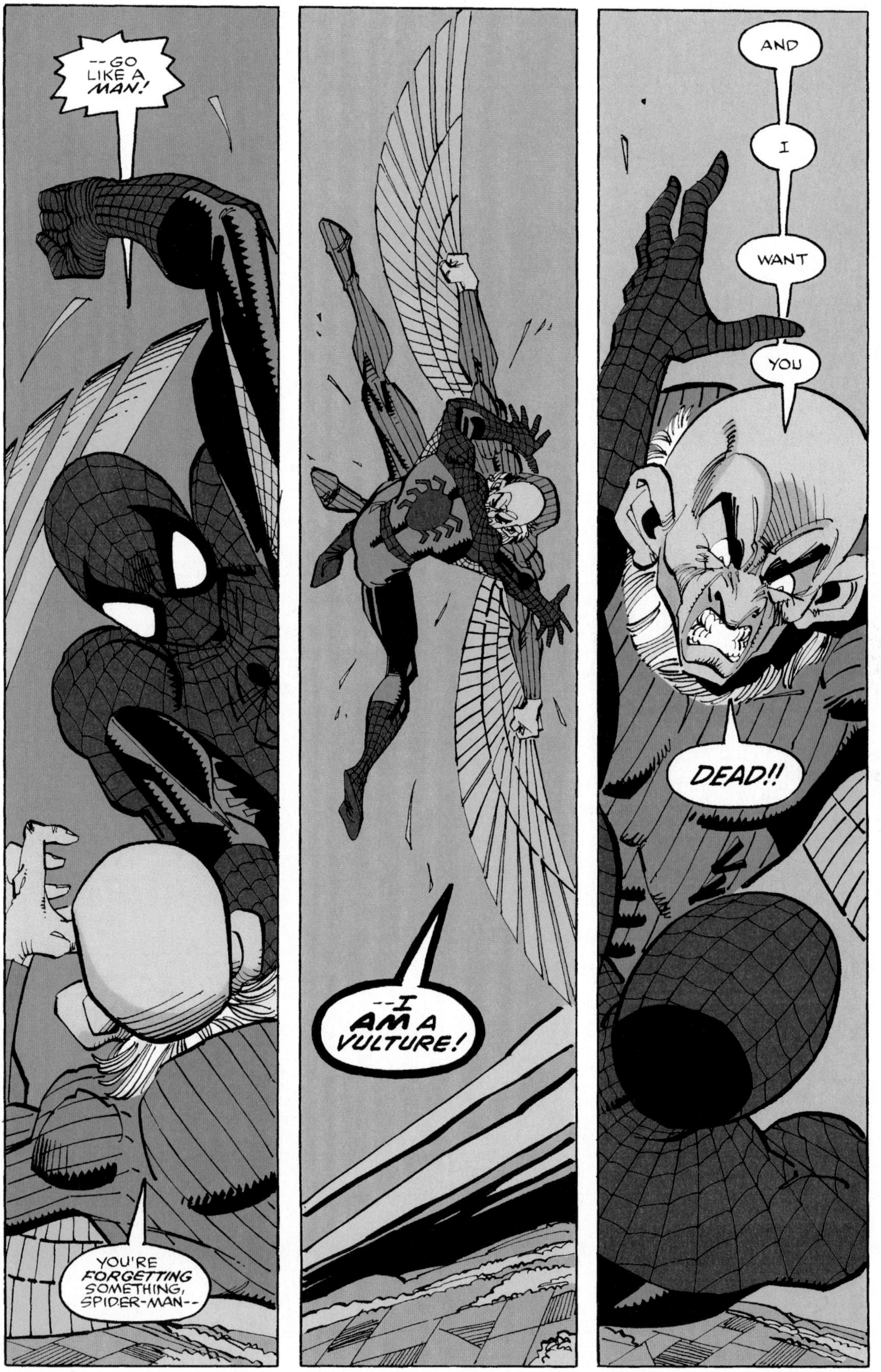
--GO LIKE A MAN!
YOU'RE FORGETTING SOMETHING, SPIDER-MAN--
--I AM A VULTURE!
AND
I
WANT
YOU
DEAD!!

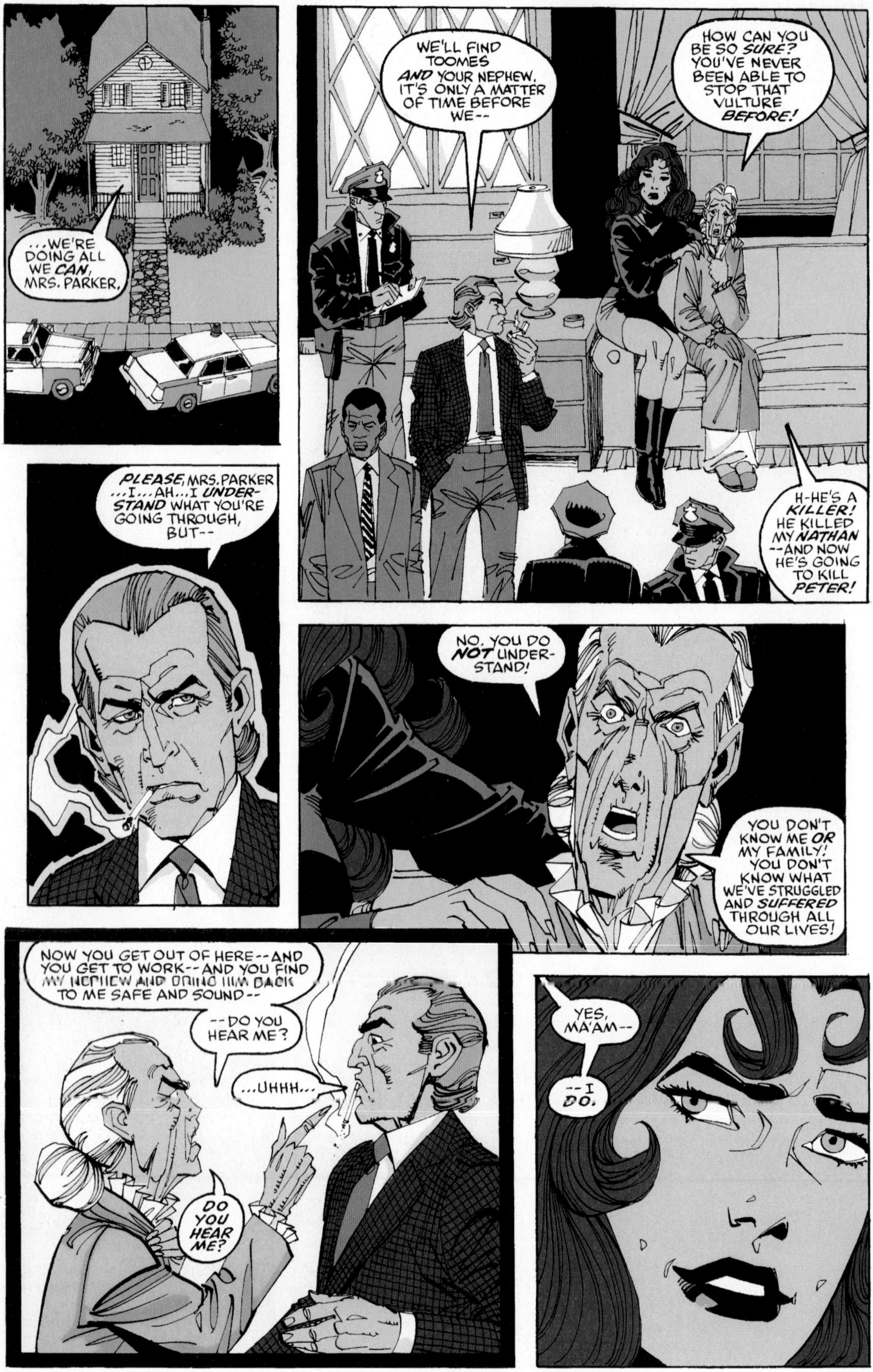
...WE'RE DOING ALL WE CAN, MRS. PARKER.
WE'LL FIND TOOMES AND YOUR NEPHEW. IT'S ONLY A MATTER OF TIME BEFORE WE--
HOW CAN YOU BE SO SURE? YOU'VE NEVER BEEN ABLE TO STOP THAT VULTURE BEFORE!
H-HE'S A KILLER! HE KILLED MY NATHAN --AND NOW HE'S GOING TO KILL PETER!
PLEASE, MRS. PARKER ...I...AH...I UNDERSTAND WHAT YOU'RE GOING THROUGH, BUT--
NO. YOU DO NOT UNDERSTAND!
YOU DON'T KNOW ME OR MY FAMILY! YOU DON'T KNOW WHAT WE'VE STRUGGLED AND SUFFERED THROUGH ALL OUR LIVES!
NOW YOU GET OUT OF HERE--AND YOU GET TO WORK--AND YOU FIND MY NEPHEW AND BRING HIM BACK TO ME SAFE AND SOUND--
--DO YOU HEAR ME?
...UHHH...
DO YOU HEAR ME?
YES, MA'AM--
--I DO.

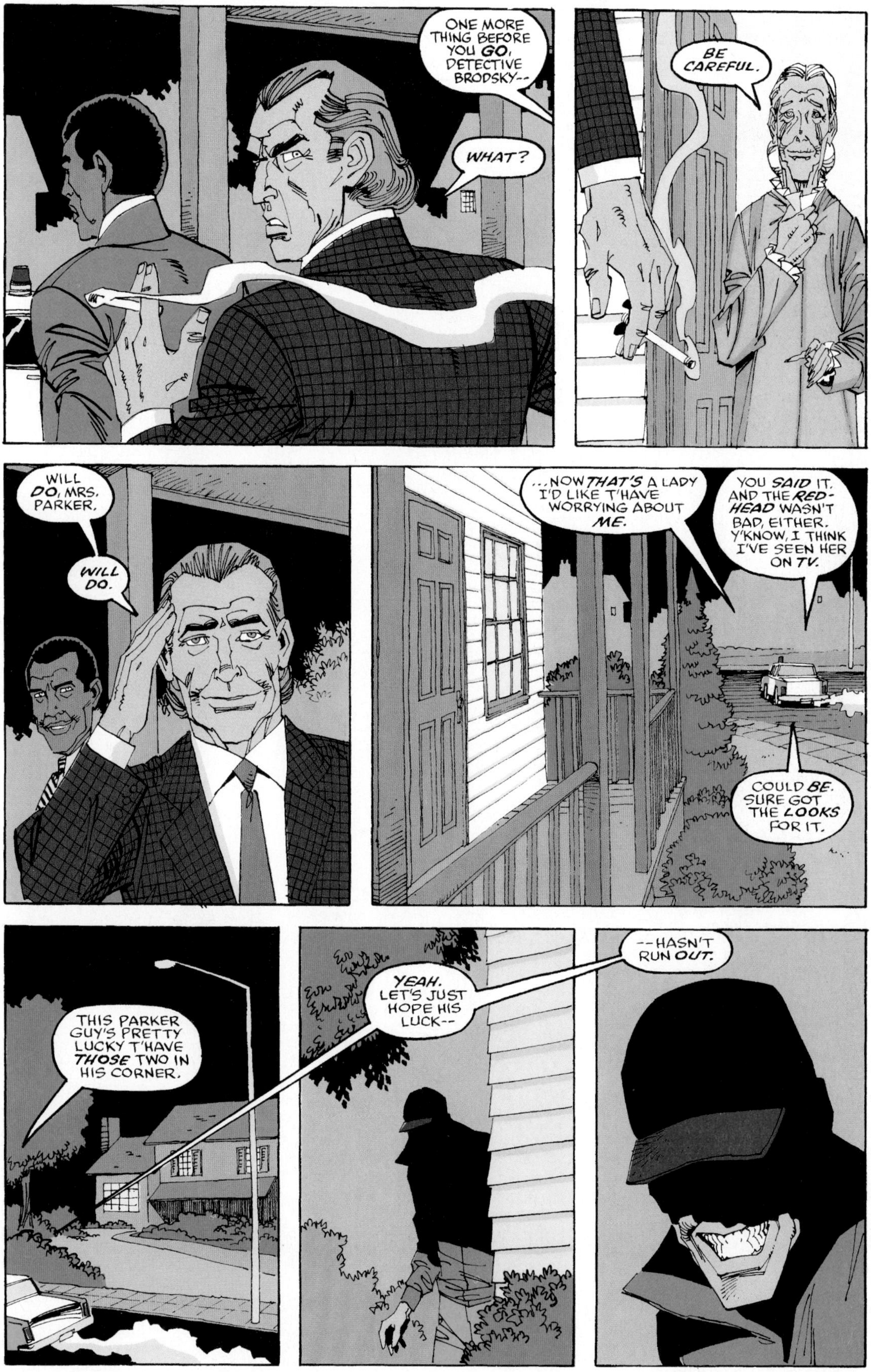
ONE MORE THING BEFORE YOU GO, DETECTIVE BRODSKY--
WHAT?
BE CAREFUL.
WILL DO, MRS. PARKER.
WILL DO.
...NOW THAT'S A LADY I'D LIKE T'HAVE WORRYING ABOUT ME.
YOU SAID IT. AND THE RED-HEAD WASN'T BAD, EITHER. Y'KNOW, I THINK I'VE SEEN HER ON TV.
COULD BE. SURE GOT THE LOOKS FOR IT.
THIS PARKER GUY'S PRETTY LUCKY T'HAVE THOSE TWO IN HIS CORNER.
YEAH. LET'S JUST HOPE HIS LUCK--
--HASN'T RUN OUT.

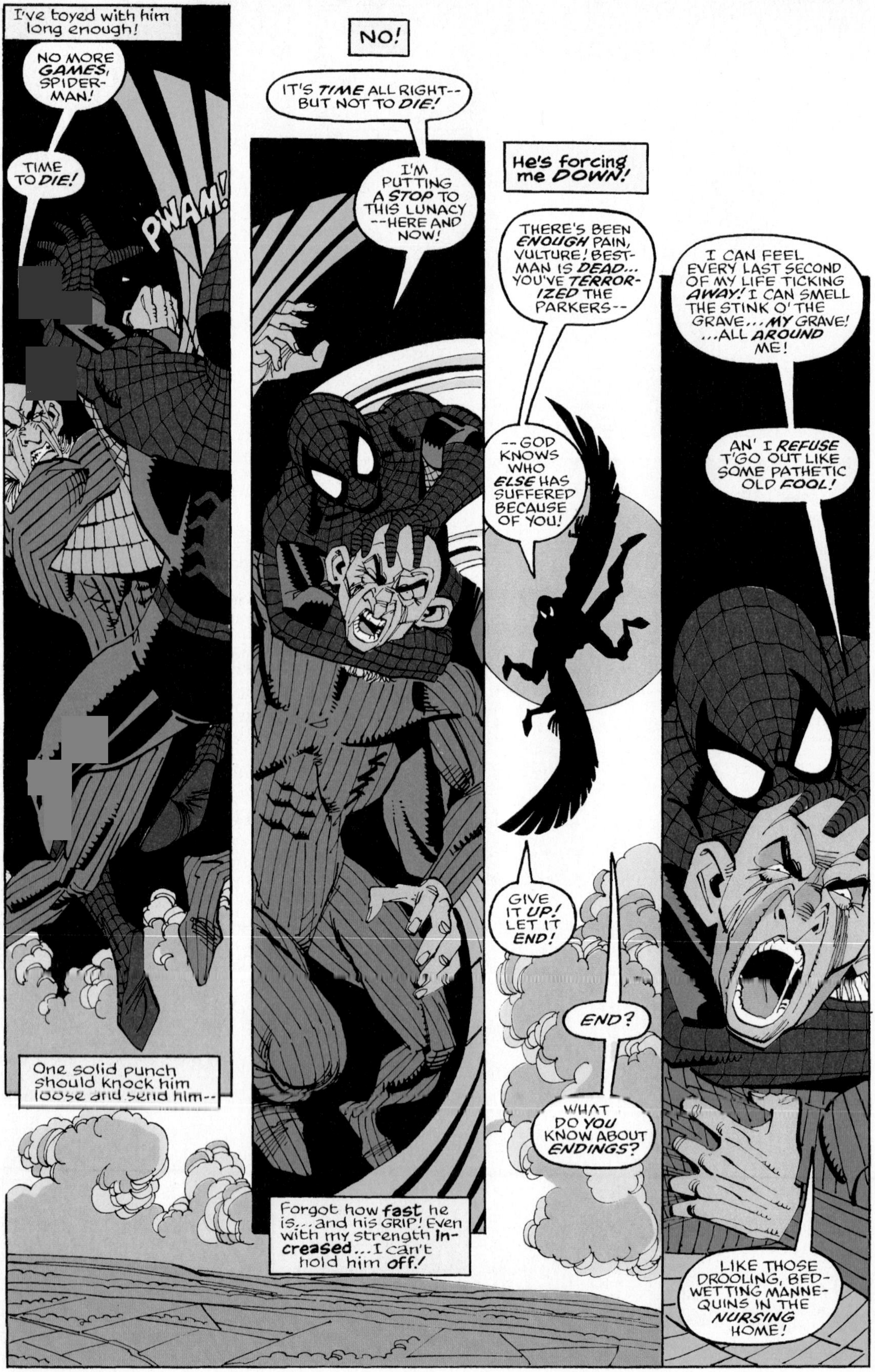
I've toyed with him long enough!
NO MORE GAMES, SPIDER-MAN!
TIME TO DIE!
PWAM!
One solid punch should knock him loose and send him--
NO!
IT'S TIME ALL RIGHT-- BUT NOT TO DIE!
I'M PUTTING A STOP TO THIS LUNACY --HERE AND NOW!
Forgot how fast he is...and his GRIP! Even with my strength increased...I can't hold him off!
He's forcing me DOWN!
THERE'S BEEN ENOUGH PAIN, VULTURE! BESTMAN IS DEAD... YOU'VE TERRORIZED THE PARKERS--
--GOD KNOWS WHO ELSE HAS SUFFERED BECAUSE OF YOU!
GIVE IT UP! LET IT END!
END?
WHAT DO YOU KNOW ABOUT ENDINGS?
I CAN FEEL EVERY LAST SECOND OF MY LIFE TICKING AWAY! I CAN SMELL THE STINK O' THE GRAVE... MY GRAVE! ...ALL AROUND ME!
AN' I REFUSE T'GO OUT LIKE SOME PATHETIC OLD FOOL!
LIKE THOSE DROOLING, BED-WETTING MANNEQUINS IN THE NURSING HOME!

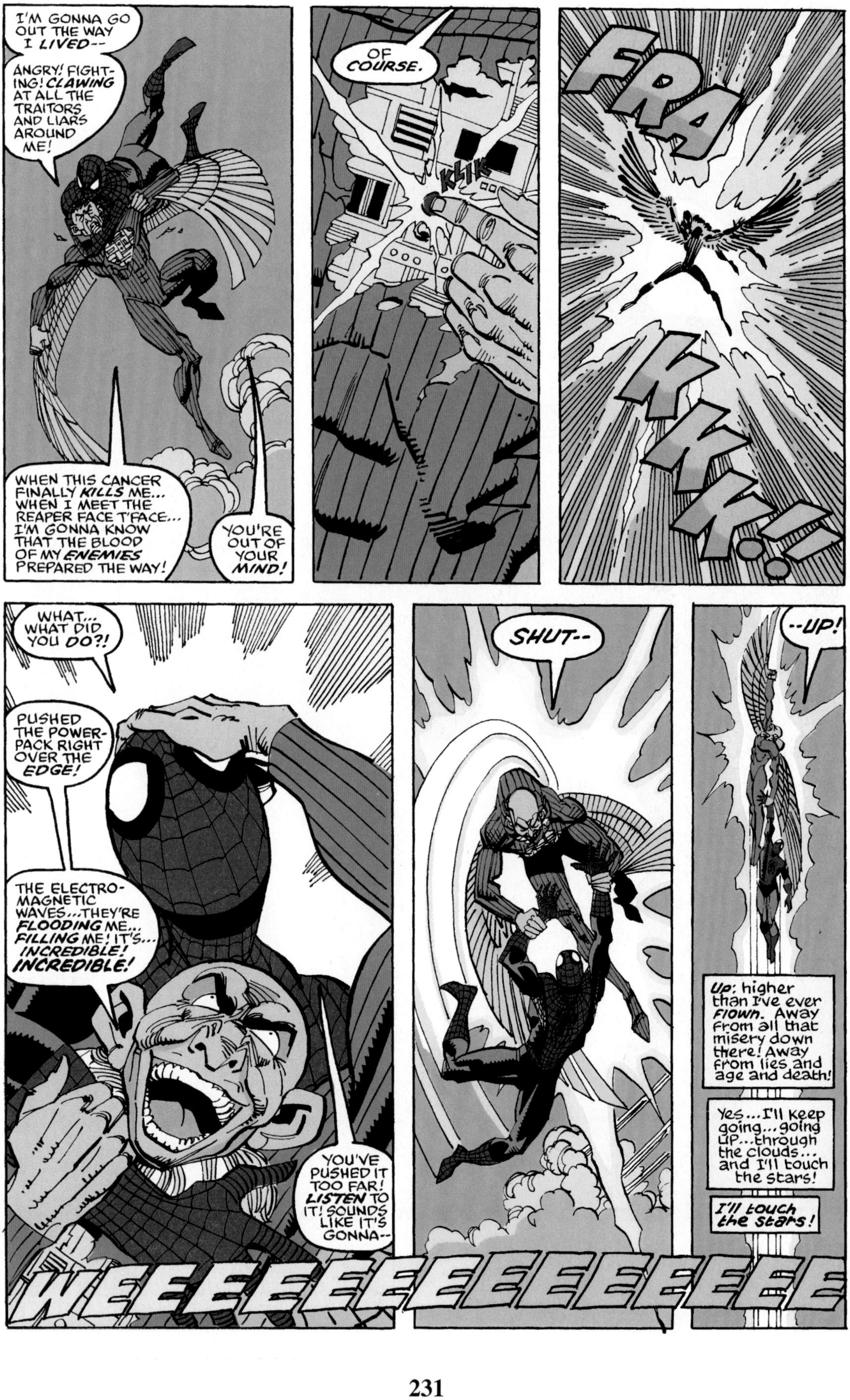

I'M GONNA GO OUT THE WAY I LIVED--
ANGRY! FIGHTING! CLAWING AT ALL THE TRAITORS AND LIARS AROUND ME!
WHEN THIS CANCER FINALLY KILLS ME... WHEN I MEET THE REAPER FACE T'FACE... I'M GONNA KNOW THAT THE BLOOD OF MY ENEMIES PREPARED THE WAY!
YOU'RE OUT OF YOUR MIND!
OF COURSE.
KLIK
FRAKKKK!!
WHAT... WHAT DID YOU DO?!
PUSHED THE POWER-PACK RIGHT OVER THE EDGE!
THE ELECTRO-MAGNETIC WAVES...THEY'RE FLOODING ME... FILLING ME! IT'S... INCREDIBLE! INCREDIBLE!
YOU'VE PUSHED IT TOO FAR! LISTEN TO IT! SOUNDS LIKE IT'S GONNA--
SHUT--
--UP!
Up: higher than I've ever flown. Away from all that misery down there! Away from lies and age and death!
Yes... I'll keep going... going up... through the clouds... and I'll touch the stars!
I'll touch the stars!
WEEEEEEEEEEEEEEE

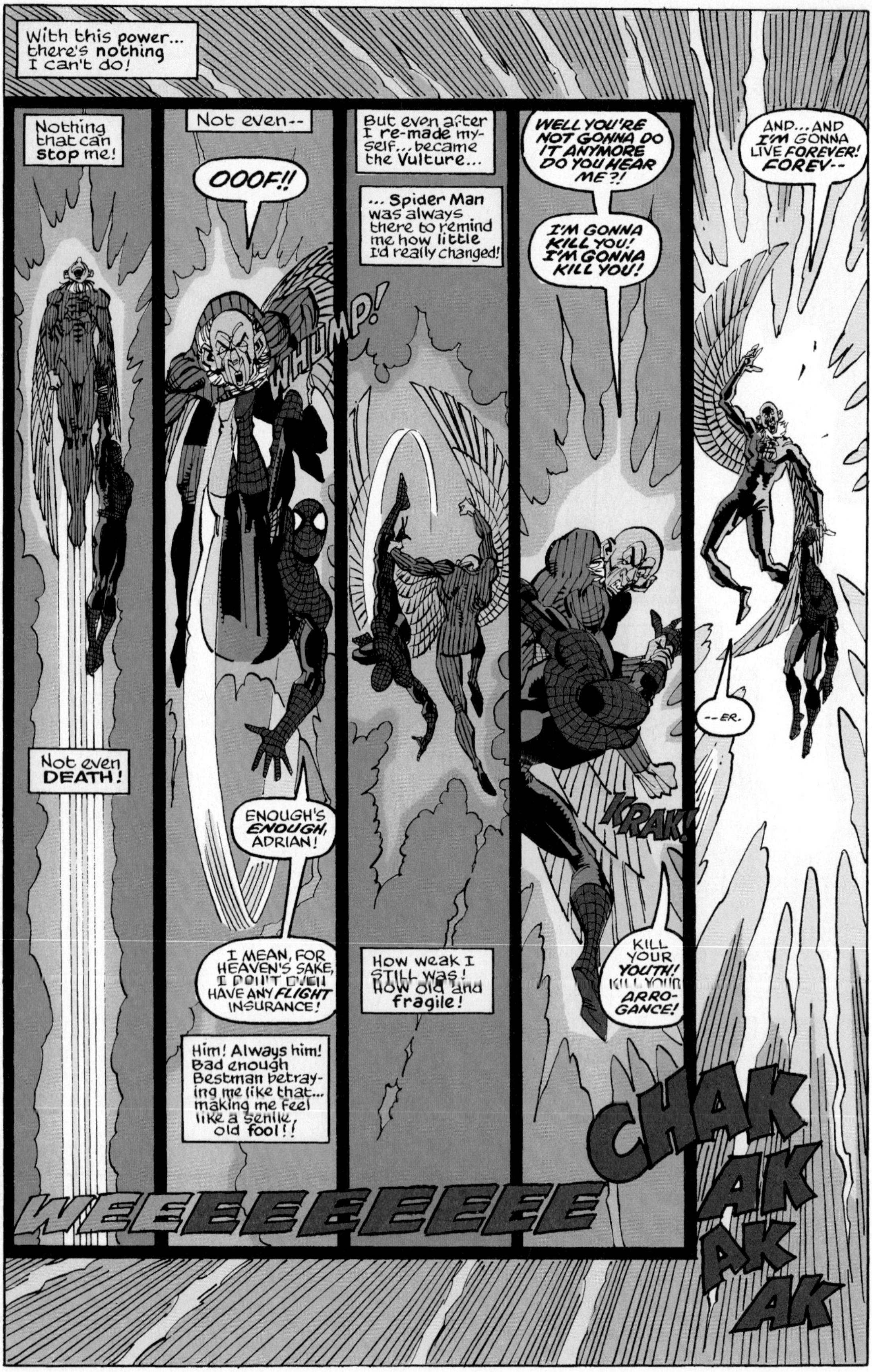
With this power... there's nothing I can't do!
Nothing that can stop me!
Not even DEATH!
Not even--
OOOF!!
WHUMP!
ENOUGH'S ENOUGH, ADRIAN!
I MEAN, FOR HEAVEN'S SAKE, I DON'T EVEN HAVE ANY FLIGHT INSURANCE!
Him! Always him! Bad enough Bestman betraying me like that... making me feel like a senile old fool!!
But even after I re-made myself... became the Vulture...
... Spider Man was always there to remind me how little I'd really changed!
How weak I still was! How old and fragile!
WELL YOU'RE NOT GONNA DO IT ANYMORE DO YOU HEAR ME?!
I'M GONNA KILL YOU! I'M GONNA KILL YOU!
KRAK!
KILL YOUR YOUTH! KILL YOUR ARROGANCE!
AND... AND I'M GONNA LIVE FOREVER! FOREV--
--ER.
WEEEEEEEEEEE
CHAK AK AK AK

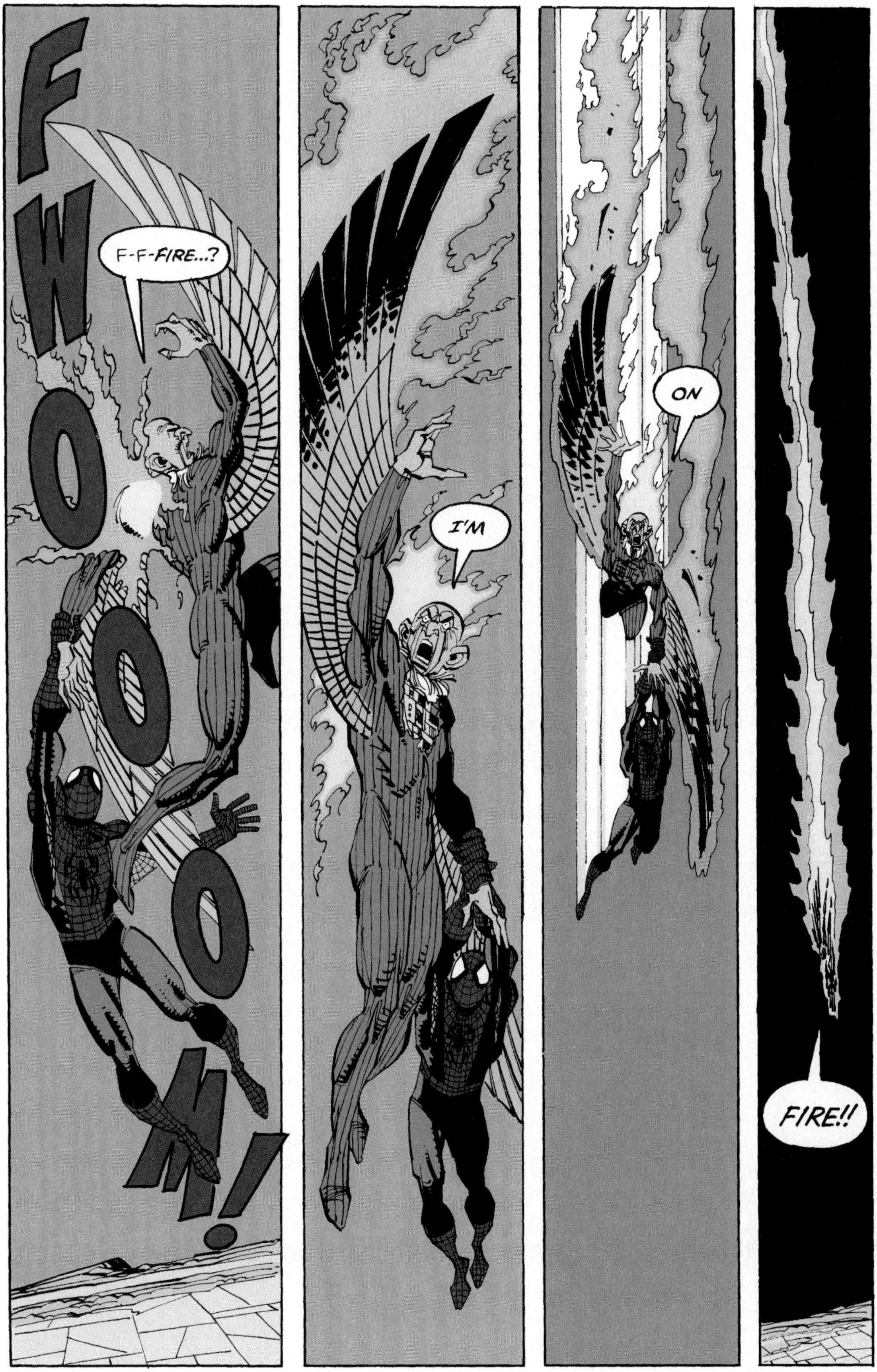
FWOOOOM!
F-F-FIRE...?
I'M
ON
FIRE!!

That's **it**, then: I die...even sooner than I **expected**.

VULTURE...**LISTEN** TO ME-- I THINK WE'VE...WE'VE GOT A **CHANCE**--!

What's wrong with him?

Battered half-conscious--and **still** he struggles back!

IF I CAN JUST GET THIS...POWER-PACK **OFF** YOU--

Doesn't he understand? It's **better** this way. Go down, fast, in a ball of **flame.**

My whole miserable life's been nothing but **one** failure after **another.**

THERE!

At least **this** way...it'll be over in the wink of an eye. No suffering. No pity.

Just a quick burn and crash into **oblivion.**

One less senile **idiot** in the world.

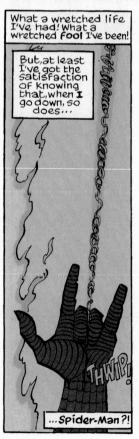

What a wretched life I've had! What a wretched **fool** I've been!

But, at least I've got the satisfaction of knowing that, when **I** go down, so does...

THWIP!

...Spider-Man?!

NO! WHAT ARE YOU **DOING?!**

WHAT ARE YOU **DOING?!**

SAVING OUR LIVES!

A WEB PARACHUTE TO SLOW OUR **DESCENT**--

THWIP!

--AND A LITTLE SOME-THING **EXTRA**--

--TO CUSHION THE--

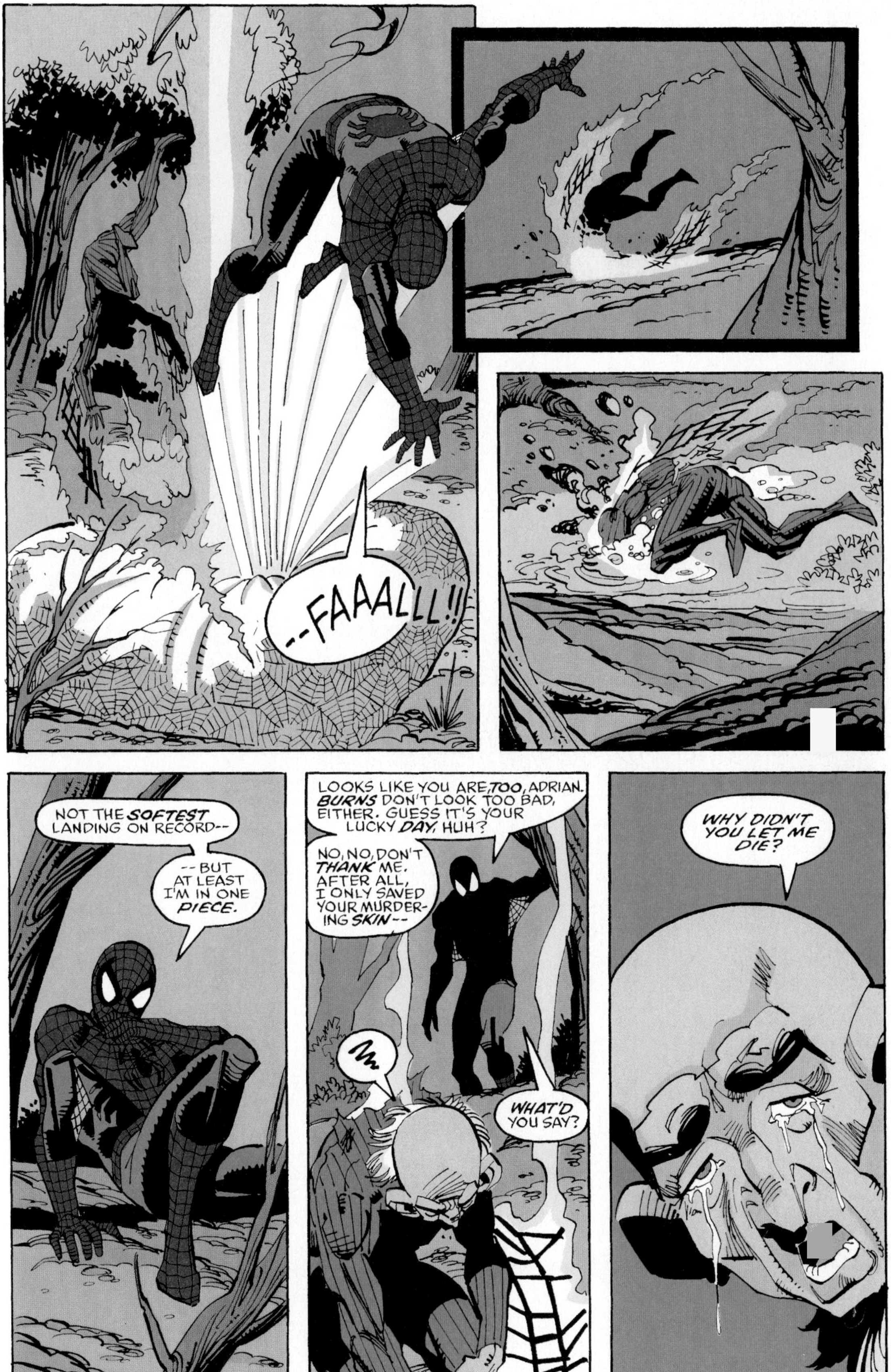
--FAAALLL!!
NOT THE SOFTEST LANDING ON RECORD--
-- BUT AT LEAST I'M IN ONE PIECE.
LOOKS LIKE YOU ARE TOO, ADRIAN. BURNS DON'T LOOK TOO BAD, EITHER. GUESS IT'S YOUR LUCKY DAY, HUH?
NO, NO, DON'T THANK ME. AFTER ALL, I ONLY SAVED YOUR MURDERING SKIN--
WHAT'D YOU SAY?
WHY DIDN'T YOU LET ME DIE?

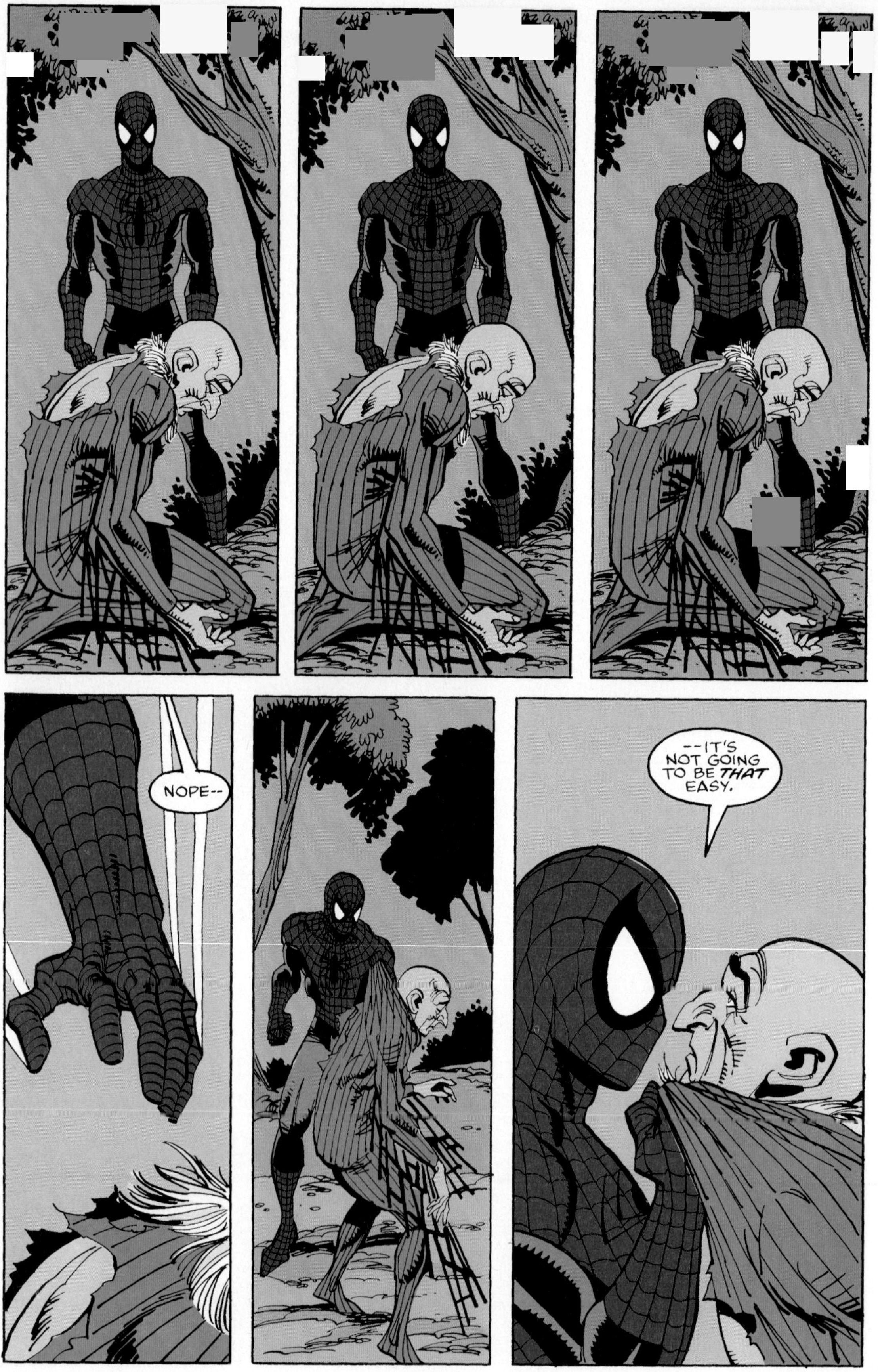
NOPE--
--IT'S NOT GOING TO BE *THAT* EASY.

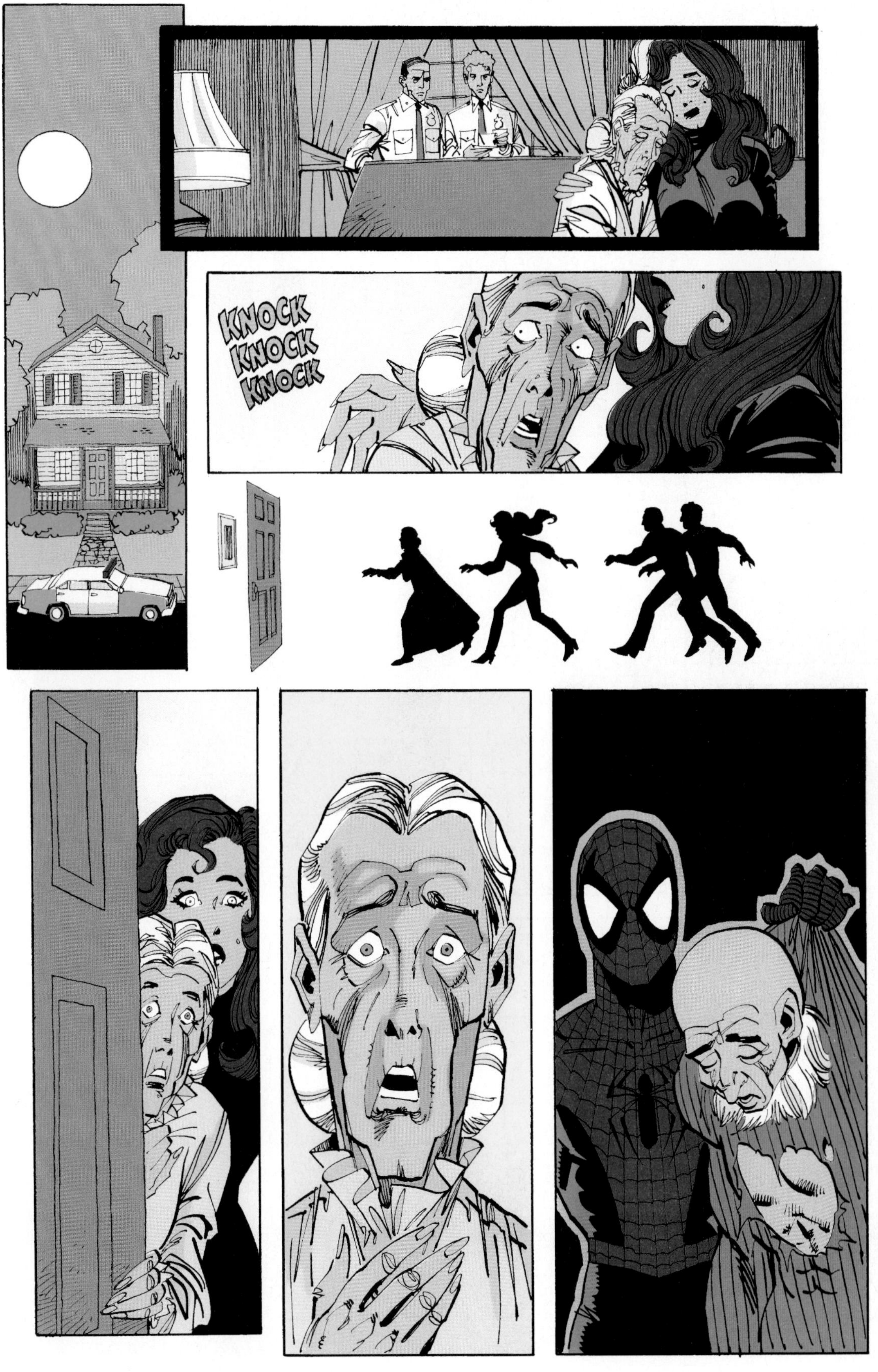
KNOCK
KNOCK
KNOCK

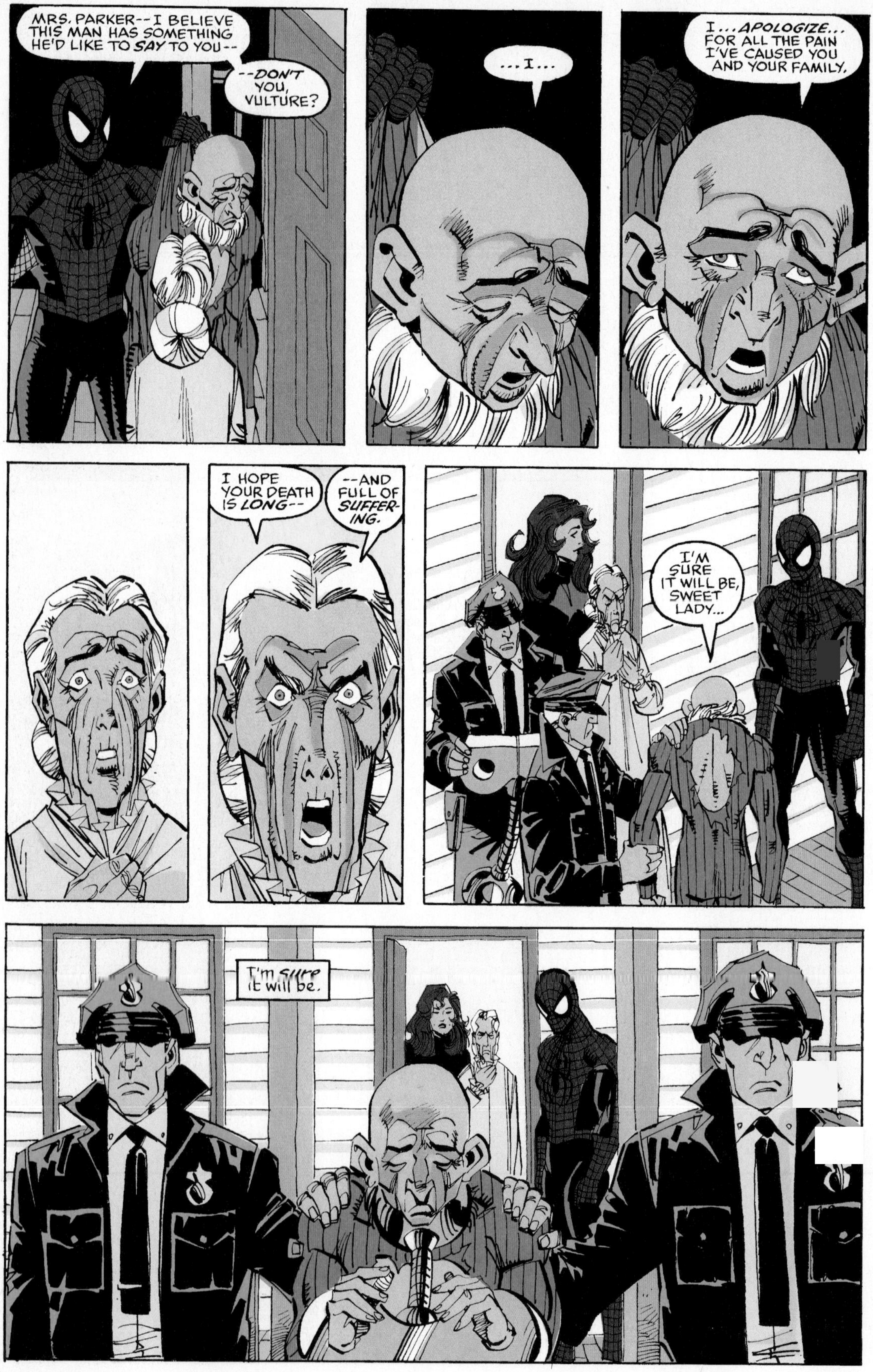
MRS. PARKER--I BELIEVE THIS MAN HAS SOMETHING HE'D LIKE TO SAY TO YOU--
--DON'T YOU, VULTURE?
...I...
I...APOLOGIZE... FOR ALL THE PAIN I'VE CAUSED YOU AND YOUR FAMILY.
I HOPE YOUR DEATH IS LONG--
--AND FULL OF SUFFER-ING.
I'M SURE IT WILL BE, SWEET LADY...
I'm sure it will be.

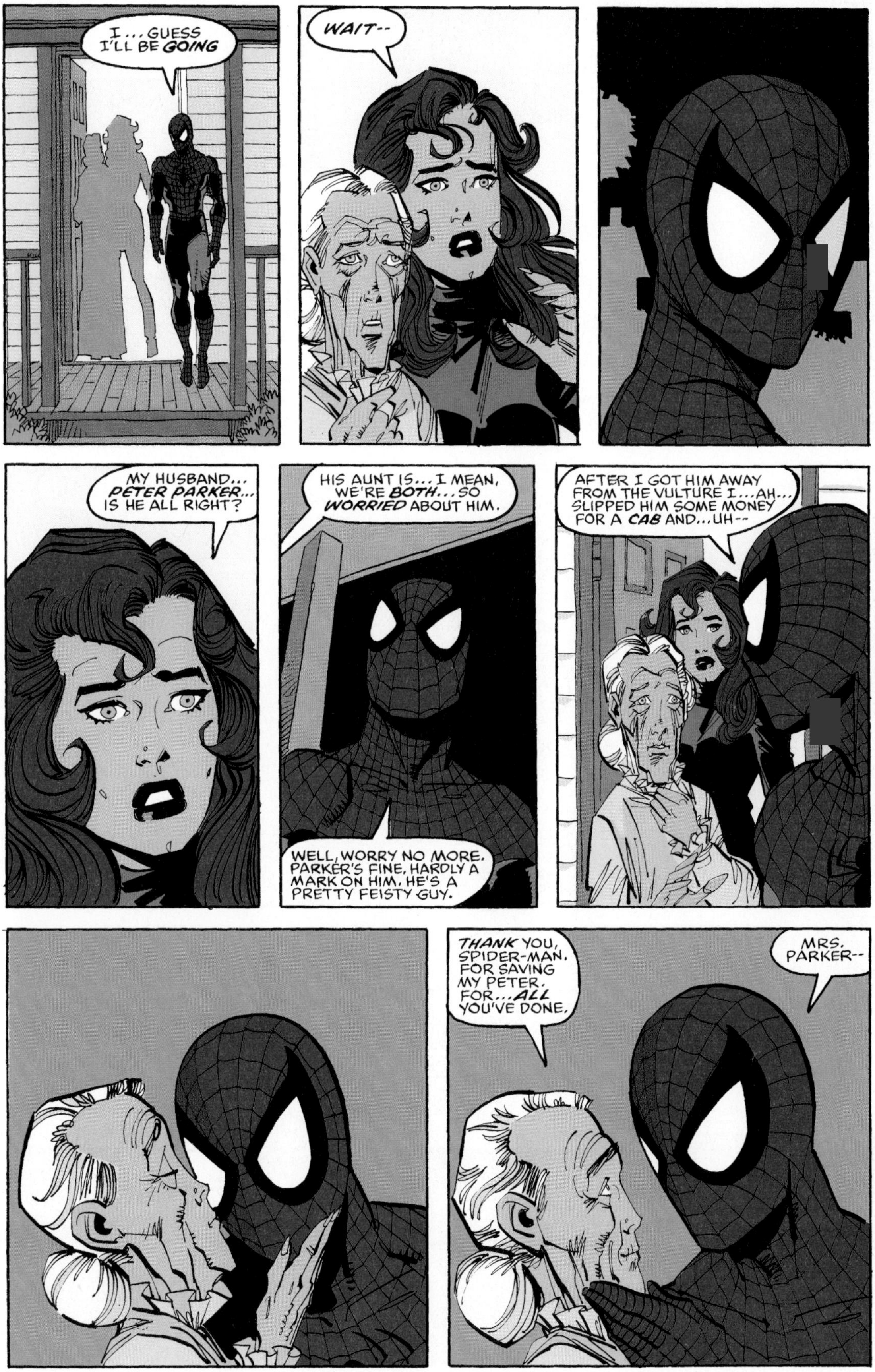
I... GUESS I'LL BE GOING
WAIT--
MY HUSBAND... PETER PARKER... IS HE ALL RIGHT?
HIS AUNT IS... I MEAN, WE'RE BOTH... SO WORRIED ABOUT HIM.
WELL, WORRY NO MORE. PARKER'S FINE, HARDLY A MARK ON HIM. HE'S A PRETTY FEISTY GUY.
AFTER I GOT HIM AWAY FROM THE VULTURE I...AH... SLIPPED HIM SOME MONEY FOR A CAB AND...UH--
THANK YOU, SPIDER-MAN. FOR SAVING MY PETER. FOR...ALL YOU'VE DONE.
MRS. PARKER--

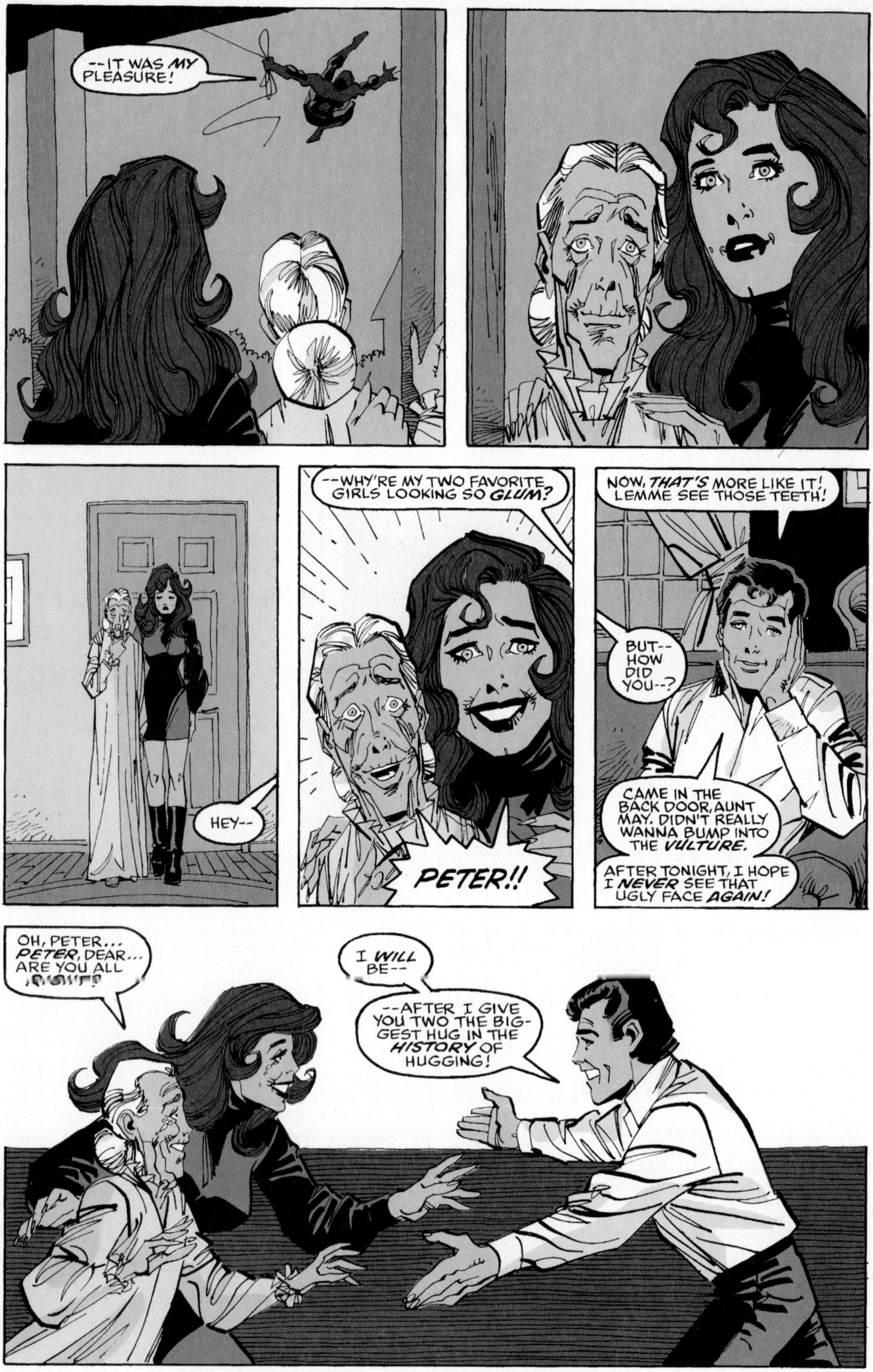
--IT WAS MY PLEASURE!
HEY--
--WHY'RE MY TWO FAVORITE GIRLS LOOKING SO GLUM?
PETER!!
NOW, THAT'S MORE LIKE IT! LEMME SEE THOSE TEETH!
BUT--HOW DID YOU--?
CAME IN THE BACK DOOR, AUNT MAY. DIDN'T REALLY WANNA BUMP INTO THE VULTURE.
AFTER TONIGHT, I HOPE I NEVER SEE THAT UGLY FACE AGAIN!
OH, PETER... PETER, DEAR... ARE YOU ALL
I WILL BE--
--AFTER I GIVE YOU TWO THE BIGGEST HUG IN THE HISTORY OF HUGGING!

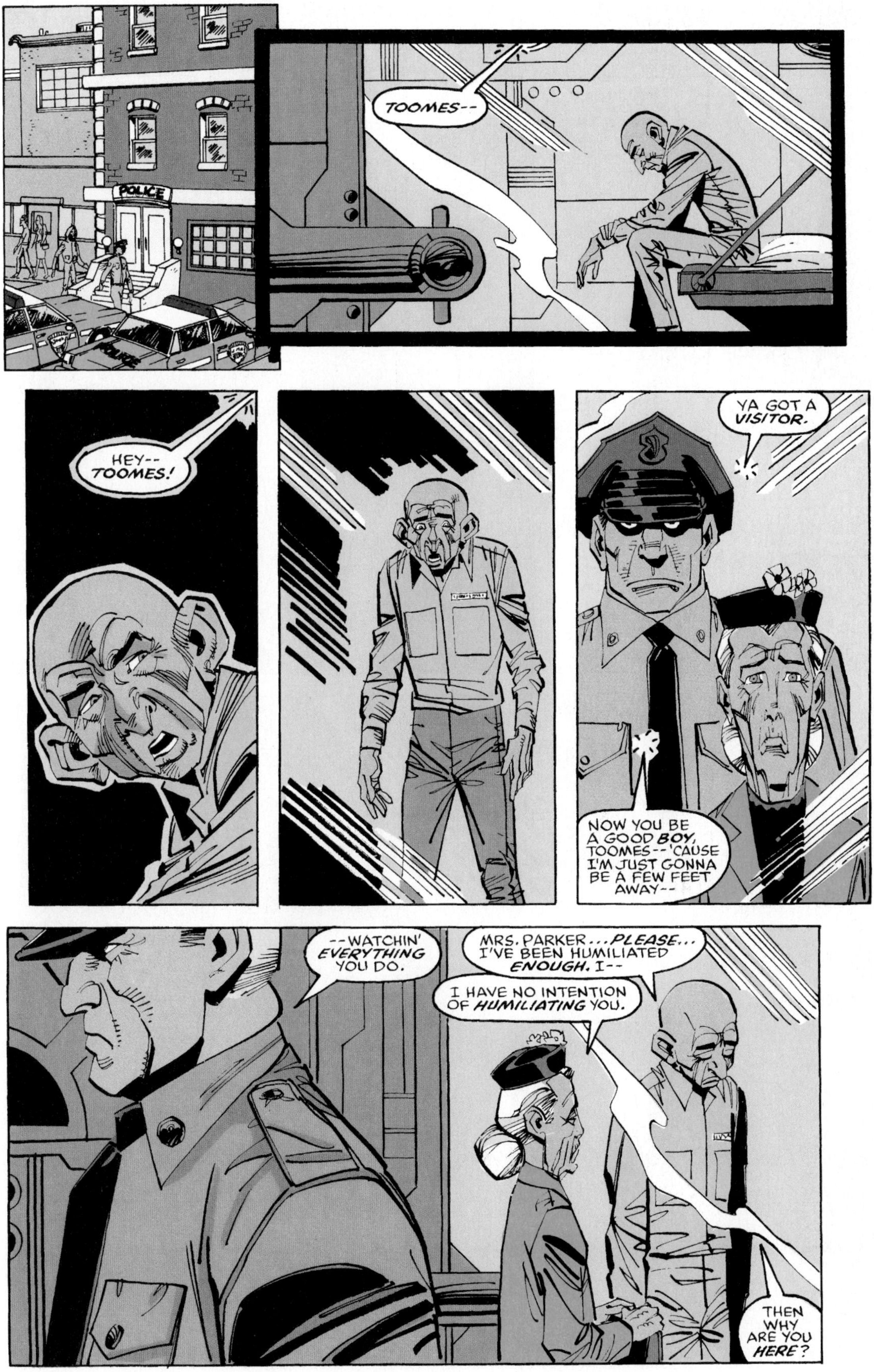
POLICE
TOOMES--
HEY-- TOOMES!
YA GOT A VISITOR.
NOW YOU BE A GOOD BOY, TOOMES--'CAUSE I'M JUST GONNA BE A FEW FEET AWAY--
--WATCHIN' EVERYTHING YOU DO.
MRS. PARKER...PLEASE... I'VE BEEN HUMILIATED ENOUGH. I--
I HAVE NO INTENTION OF HUMILIATING YOU.
THEN WHY ARE YOU HERE?

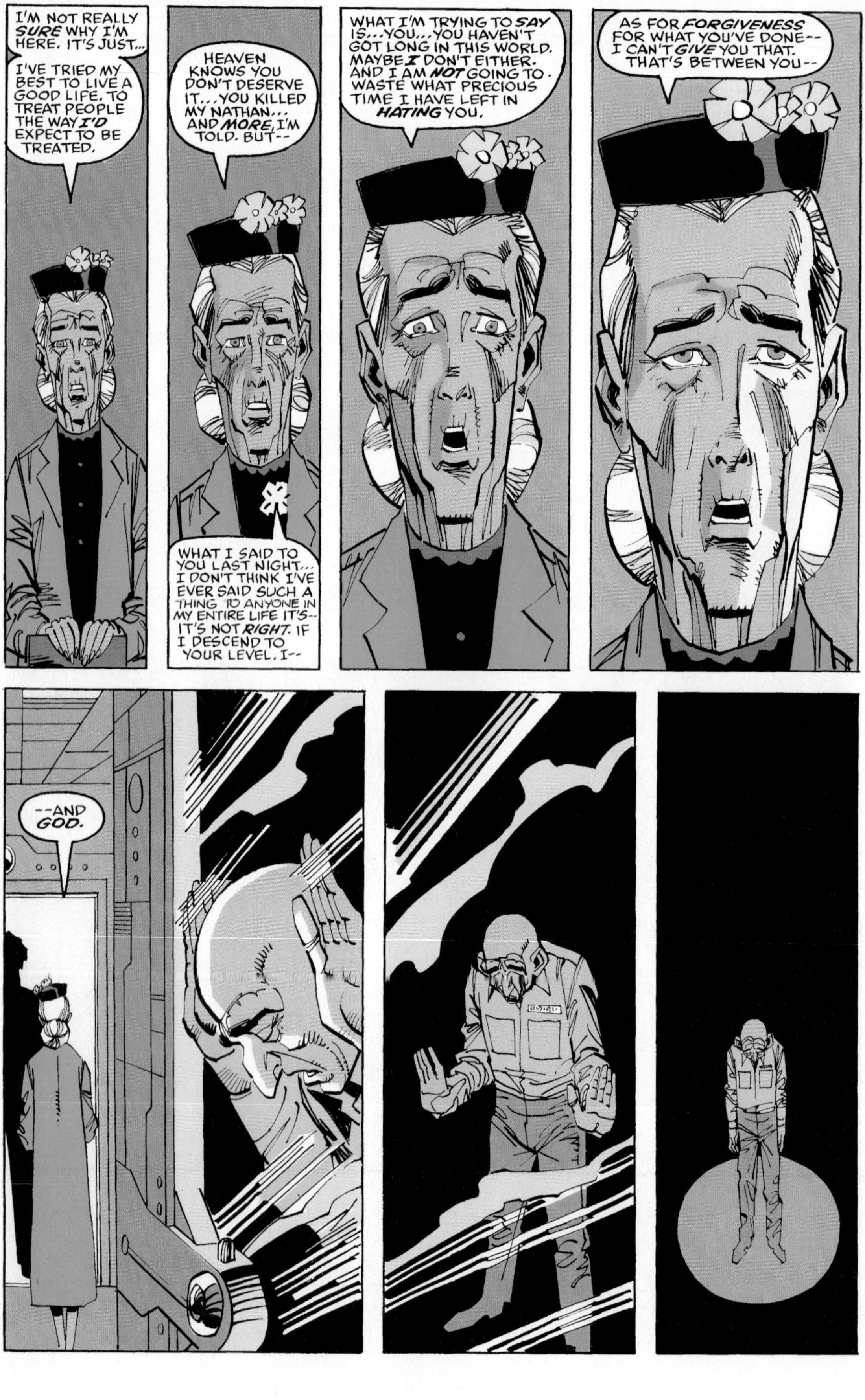
I'M NOT REALLY SURE WHY I'M HERE. IT'S JUST...
I'VE TRIED MY BEST TO LIVE A GOOD LIFE. TO TREAT PEOPLE THE WAY I'D EXPECT TO BE TREATED.
HEAVEN KNOWS YOU DON'T DESERVE IT... YOU KILLED MY NATHAN... AND MORE, I'M TOLD. BUT--
WHAT I SAID TO YOU LAST NIGHT... I DON'T THINK I'VE EVER SAID SUCH A THING TO ANYONE IN MY ENTIRE LIFE IT'S-- IT'S NOT RIGHT. IF I DESCEND TO YOUR LEVEL. I--
WHAT I'M TRYING TO SAY IS... YOU... YOU HAVEN'T GOT LONG IN THIS WORLD. MAYBE I DON'T EITHER. AND I AM NOT GOING TO WASTE WHAT PRECIOUS TIME I HAVE LEFT IN HATING YOU.
AS FOR FORGIVENESS FOR WHAT YOU'VE DONE-- I CAN'T GIVE YOU THAT. THAT'S BETWEEN YOU--
--AND GOD.

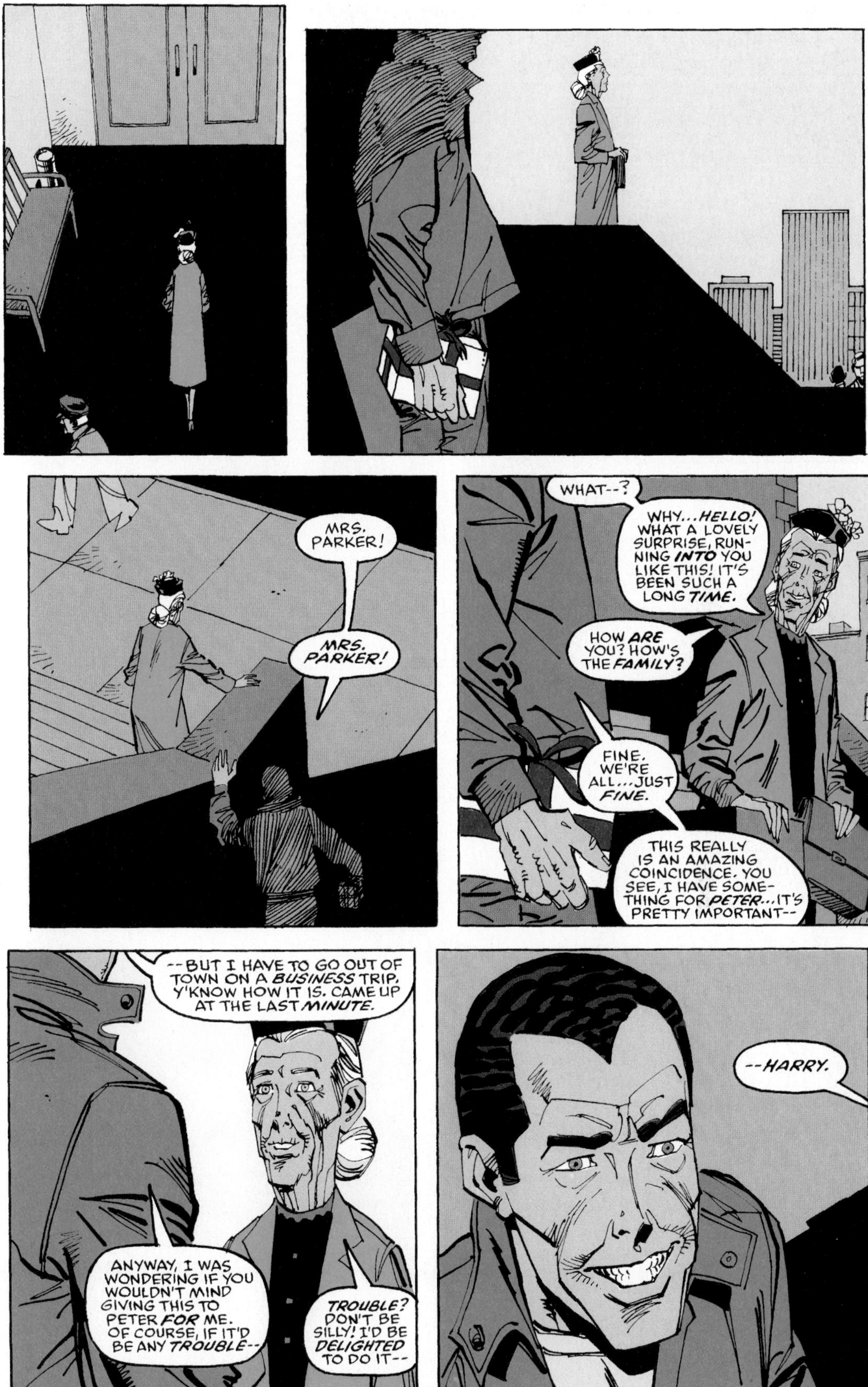
MRS. PARKER!
MRS. PARKER!
WHAT--?
WHY... HELLO! WHAT A LOVELY SURPRISE, RUNNING INTO YOU LIKE THIS! IT'S BEEN SUCH A LONG TIME.
HOW ARE YOU? HOW'S THE FAMILY?
FINE. WE'RE ALL... JUST FINE.
THIS REALLY IS AN AMAZING COINCIDENCE. YOU SEE, I HAVE SOMETHING FOR PETER... IT'S PRETTY IMPORTANT--
--BUT I HAVE TO GO OUT OF TOWN ON A BUSINESS TRIP, Y'KNOW HOW IT IS. CAME UP AT THE LAST MINUTE.
ANYWAY, I WAS WONDERING IF YOU WOULDN'T MIND GIVING THIS TO PETER FOR ME. OF COURSE, IF IT'D BE ANY TROUBLE--
TROUBLE? DON'T BE SILLY! I'D BE DELIGHTED TO DO IT--
--HARRY.

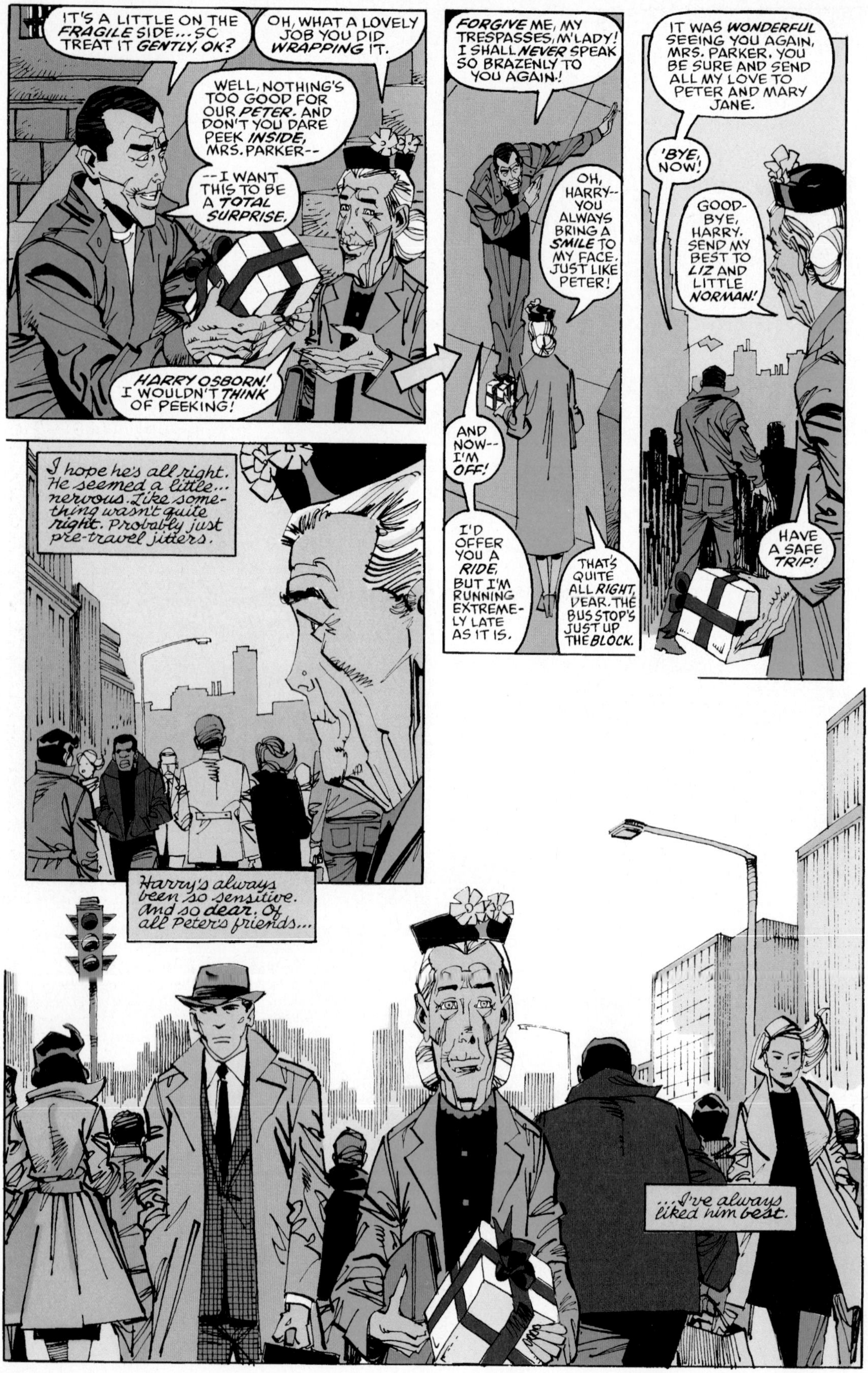
IT'S A LITTLE ON THE FRAGILE SIDE... SO TREAT IT GENTLY, OK?
OH, WHAT A LOVELY JOB YOU DID WRAPPING IT.
WELL, NOTHING'S TOO GOOD FOR OUR PETER. AND DON'T YOU DARE PEEK INSIDE, MRS. PARKER--
--I WANT THIS TO BE A TOTAL SURPRISE.
HARRY OSBORN! I WOULDN'T THINK OF PEEKING!
FORGIVE ME, MY TRESPASSES, M'LADY! I SHALL NEVER SPEAK SO BRAZENLY TO YOU AGAIN!
OH, HARRY-- YOU ALWAYS BRING A SMILE TO MY FACE. JUST LIKE PETER!
AND NOW-- I'M OFF!
I'D OFFER YOU A RIDE, BUT I'M RUNNING EXTREMELY LATE AS IT IS.
THAT'S QUITE ALL RIGHT, DEAR. THE BUS STOP'S JUST UP THE BLOCK.
IT WAS WONDERFUL SEEING YOU AGAIN, MRS. PARKER. YOU BE SURE AND SEND ALL MY LOVE TO PETER AND MARY JANE.
'BYE, NOW!
GOOD-BYE, HARRY. SEND MY BEST TO LIZ AND LITTLE NORMAN!
HAVE A SAFE TRIP!
I hope he's all right. He seemed a little... nervous. Like something wasn't quite right. Probably just pre-travel jitters.
Harry's always been so sensitive. And so dear. Of all Peter's friends...
...I've always liked him best.

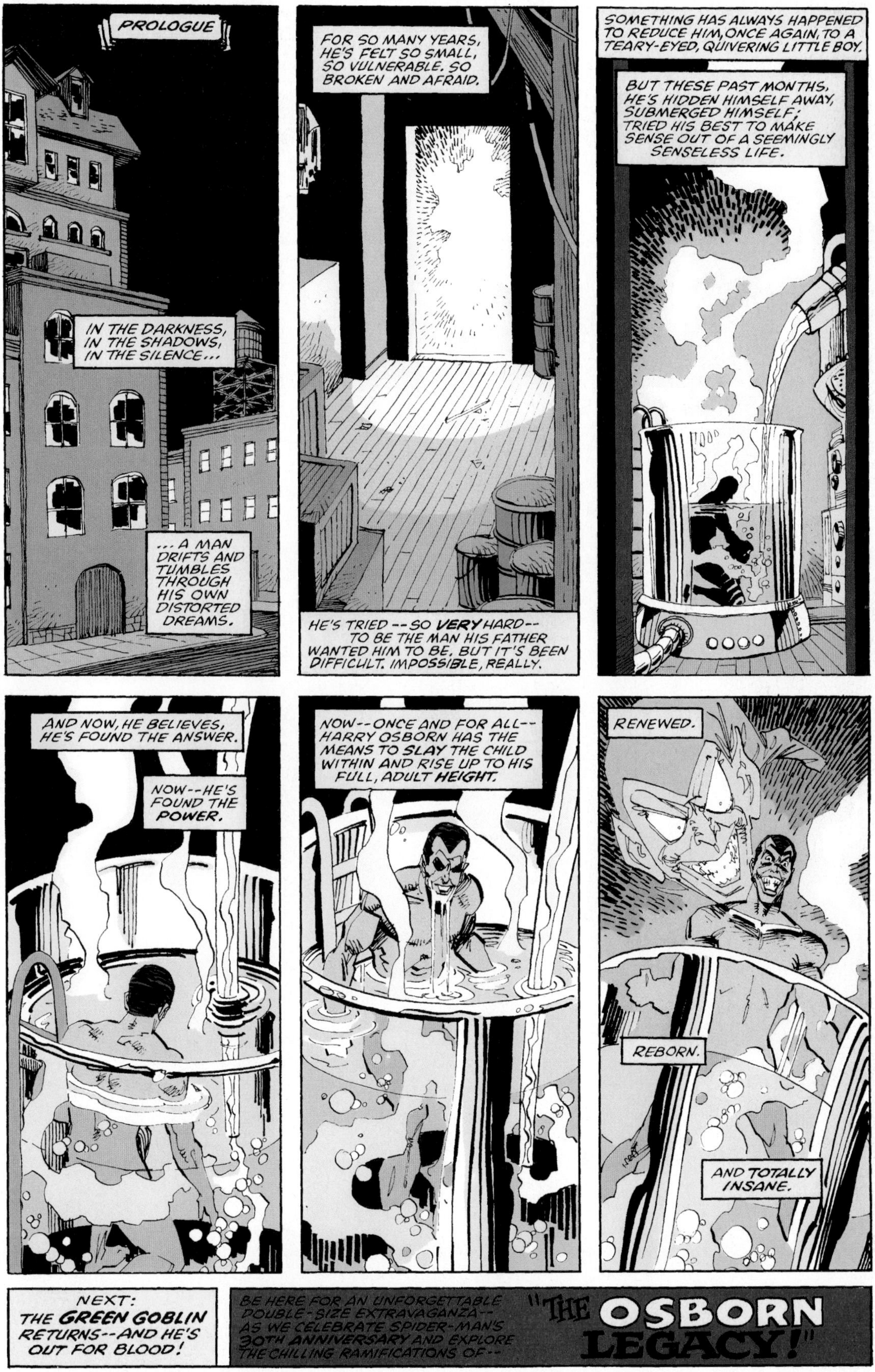
PROLOGUE
IN THE DARKNESS, IN THE SHADOWS, IN THE SILENCE...
...A MAN DRIFTS AND TUMBLES THROUGH HIS OWN DISTORTED DREAMS.
FOR SO MANY YEARS, HE'S FELT SO SMALL, SO VULNERABLE. SO BROKEN AND AFRAID.
HE'S TRIED --SO VERY HARD-- TO BE THE MAN HIS FATHER WANTED HIM TO BE. BUT IT'S BEEN DIFFICULT. IMPOSSIBLE, REALLY.
SOMETHING HAS ALWAYS HAPPENED TO REDUCE HIM, ONCE AGAIN, TO A TEARY-EYED, QUIVERING LITTLE BOY.
BUT THESE PAST MONTHS, HE'S HIDDEN HIMSELF AWAY, SUBMERGED HIMSELF; TRIED HIS BEST TO MAKE SENSE OUT OF A SEEMINGLY SENSELESS LIFE.
AND NOW, HE BELIEVES, HE'S FOUND THE ANSWER.
NOW--HE'S FOUND THE POWER.
NOW--ONCE AND FOR ALL-- HARRY OSBORN HAS THE MEANS TO SLAY THE CHILD WITHIN AND RISE UP TO HIS FULL, ADULT HEIGHT.
RENEWED.
REBORN.
AND TOTALLY INSANE.
NEXT: THE GREEN GOBLIN RETURNS--AND HE'S OUT FOR BLOOD!
BE HERE FOR AN UNFORGETTABLE DOUBLE-SIZE EXTRAVAGANZA-- AS WE CELEBRATE SPIDER-MAN'S 30TH ANNIVERSARY AND EXPLORE THE CHILLING RAMIFICATIONS OF--
"THE OSBORN LEGACY!"

WHEN THE SUPERHUMAN REGISTRATION ACT PASSED, IRON MAN CONVINCED SPIDER-MAN TO PUBLICLY UNMASK — REVEALING HIS IDENTITY TO THE WORLD. BUT SPIDER-MAN SOON TURNED AGAINST IRON MAN, JOINING CAPTAIN AMERICA'S UNDERGROUND REBELLION AGAINST THE ACT. NOW, PETER IS A FUGITIVE...AND THOSE HE CARES ABOUT ARE TARGETS FOR SPIDER-MAN'S ENEMIES.

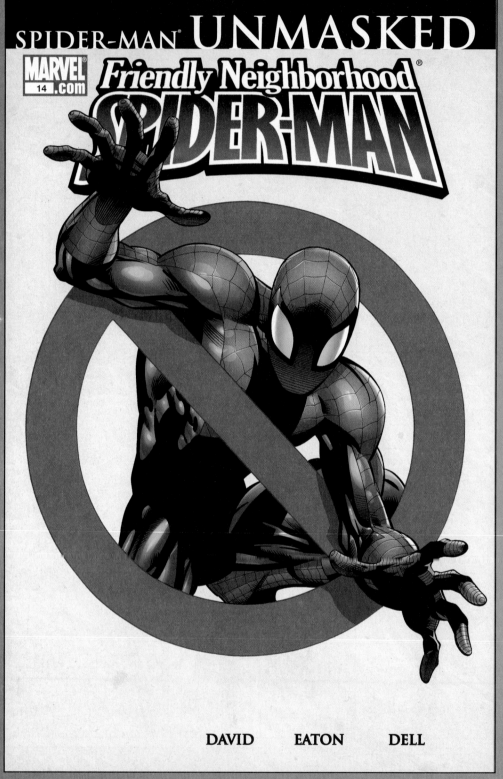

SPIDER-MAN® UNMASKED

MARVEL® 14 .com

Friendly Neighborhood® SPIDER-MAN®

DAVID   EATON   DELL

"TAKING WING, PART 1"

WRITER *Peter David* · PENCILER *Scot Eaton* · INKER *John Dell* · COLORIST *Matt Milla*
LETTERER *VC's Cory Petit* · PRODUCTION *Brad Johansen* · ASSISTANT EDITOR *Michael O'Connor*
EDITOR *Axel Alonso* · EDITOR IN CHIEF *Joe Quesada* · PUBLISHER *Dan Buckley*

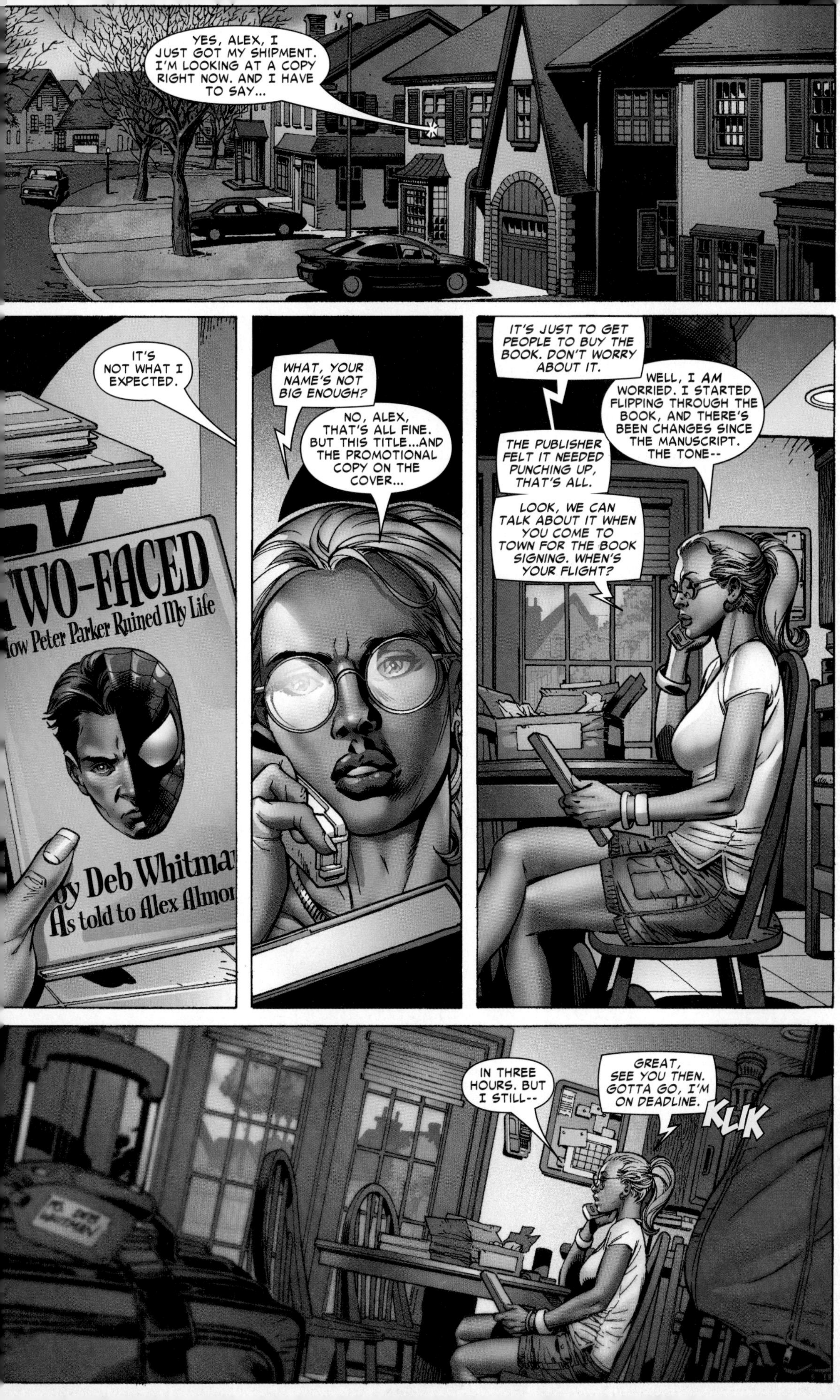
YES, ALEX, I JUST GOT MY SHIPMENT. I'M LOOKING AT A COPY RIGHT NOW. AND I HAVE TO SAY...
IT'S NOT WHAT I EXPECTED.
TWO-FACED
How Peter Parker Ruined My Life
by Deb Whitman
As told to Alex Almon
WHAT, YOUR NAME'S NOT BIG ENOUGH?
NO, ALEX, THAT'S ALL FINE. BUT THIS TITLE...AND THE PROMOTIONAL COPY ON THE COVER...
IT'S JUST TO GET PEOPLE TO BUY THE BOOK. DON'T WORRY ABOUT IT.
WELL, I AM WORRIED. I STARTED FLIPPING THROUGH THE BOOK, AND THERE'S BEEN CHANGES SINCE THE MANUSCRIPT. THE TONE--
THE PUBLISHER FELT IT NEEDED PUNCHING UP, THAT'S ALL.
LOOK, WE CAN TALK ABOUT IT WHEN YOU COME TO TOWN FOR THE BOOK SIGNING. WHEN'S YOUR FLIGHT?
IN THREE HOURS. BUT I STILL--
GREAT, SEE YOU THEN. GOTTA GO, I'M ON DEADLINE.
KLIK

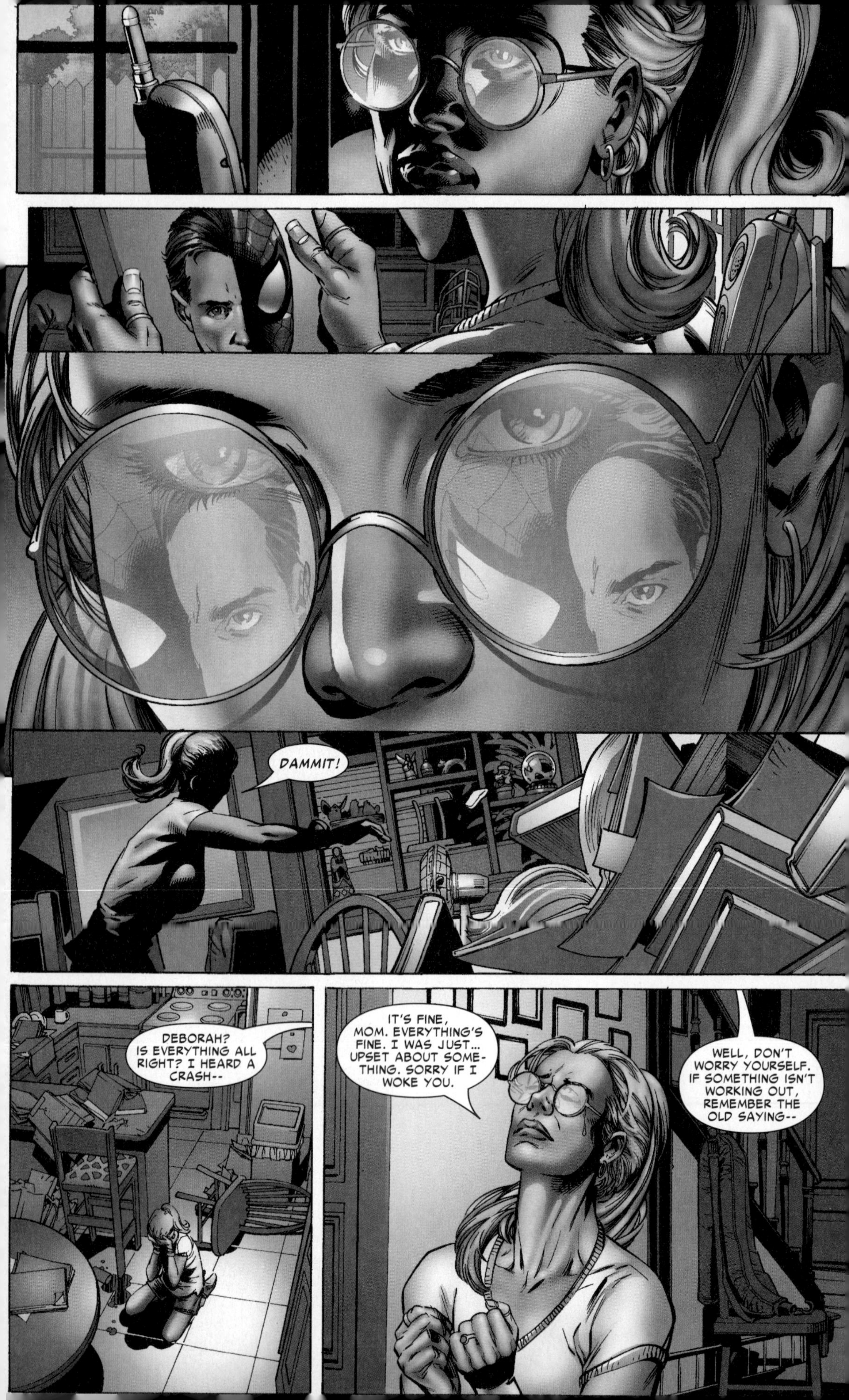
DAMMIT!
DEBORAH? IS EVERYTHING ALL RIGHT? I HEARD A CRASH--
IT'S FINE, MOM. EVERYTHING'S FINE. I WAS JUST... UPSET ABOUT SOME-THING. SORRY IF I WOKE YOU.
WELL, DON'T WORRY YOURSELF. IF SOMETHING ISN'T WORKING OUT, REMEMBER THE OLD SAYING--

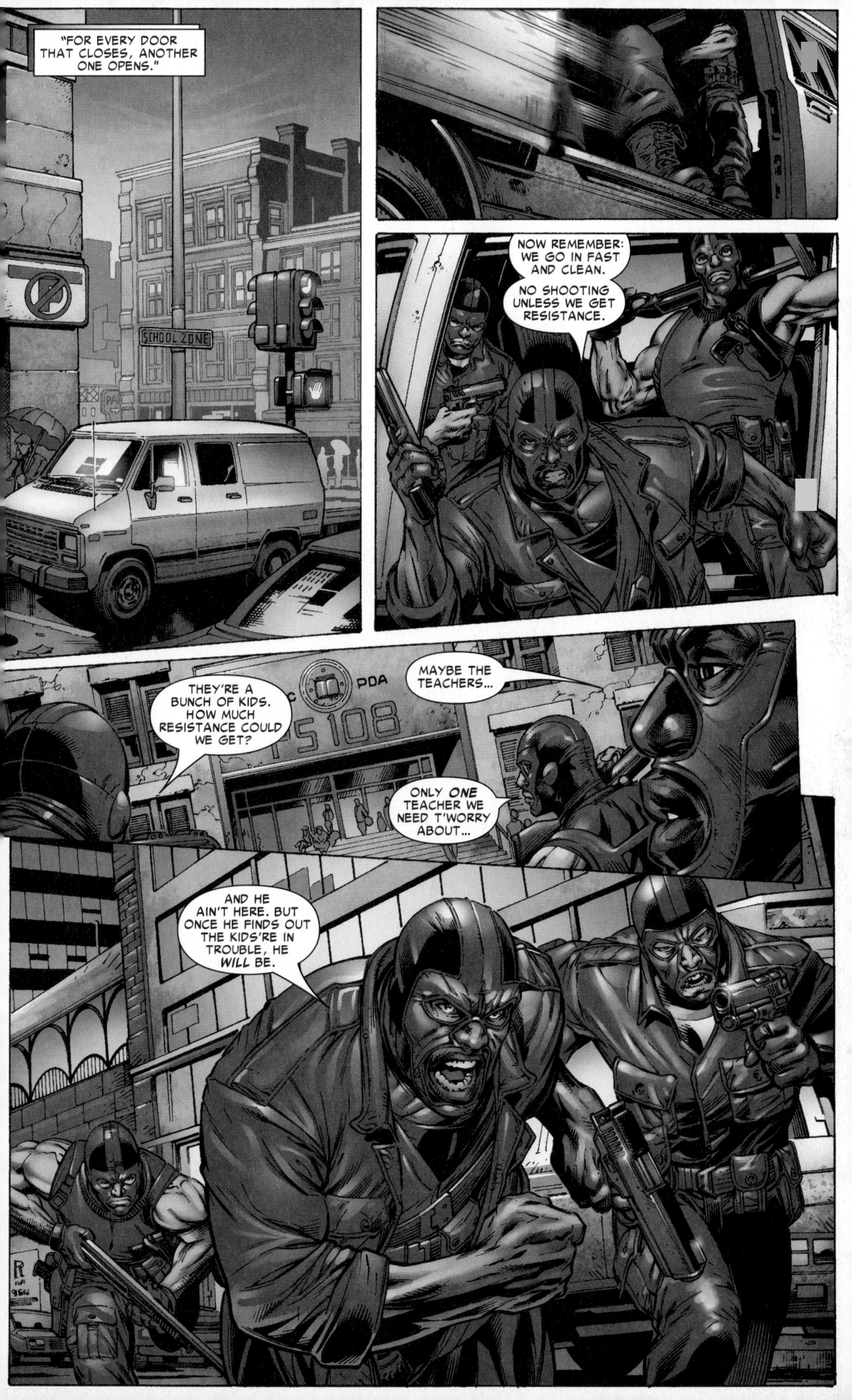
"FOR EVERY DOOR THAT CLOSES, ANOTHER ONE OPENS."
SCHOOL ZONE
NOW REMEMBER: WE GO IN FAST AND CLEAN.
NO SHOOTING UNLESS WE GET RESISTANCE.
THEY'RE A BUNCH OF KIDS. HOW MUCH RESISTANCE COULD WE GET?
MAYBE THE TEACHERS...
PS 108
ONLY ONE TEACHER WE NEED T'WORRY ABOUT...
AND HE AIN'T HERE. BUT ONCE HE FINDS OUT THE KIDS'RE IN TROUBLE, HE WILL BE.

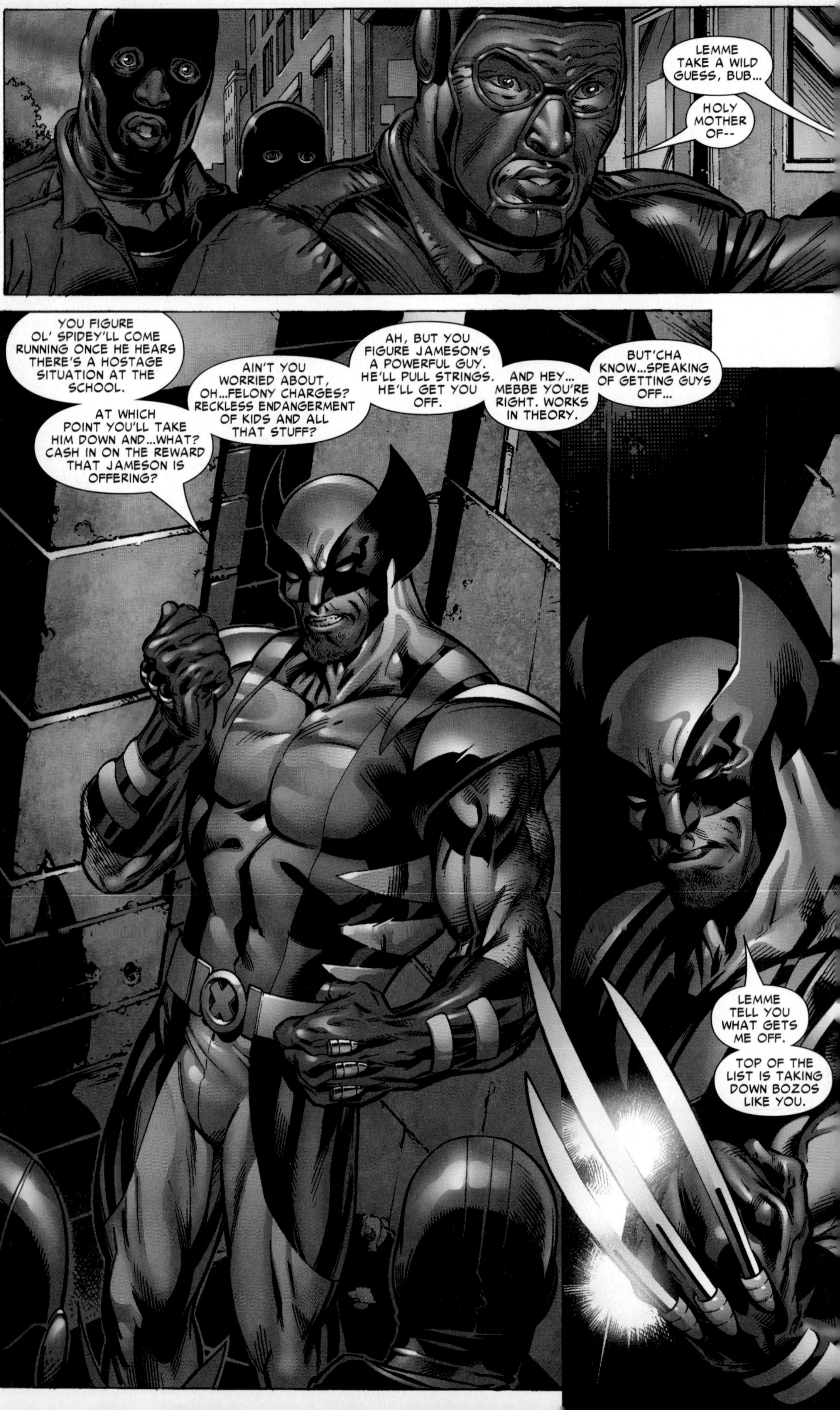
LEMME TAKE A WILD GUESS, BUB...
HOLY MOTHER OF--
YOU FIGURE OL' SPIDEY'LL COME RUNNING ONCE HE HEARS THERE'S A HOSTAGE SITUATION AT THE SCHOOL.
AT WHICH POINT YOU'LL TAKE HIM DOWN AND...WHAT? CASH IN ON THE REWARD THAT JAMESON IS OFFERING?
AIN'T YOU WORRIED ABOUT, OH...FELONY CHARGES? RECKLESS ENDANGERMENT OF KIDS AND ALL THAT STUFF?
AH, BUT YOU FIGURE JAMESON'S A POWERFUL GUY. HE'LL PULL STRINGS. HE'LL GET YOU OFF.
AND HEY... MEBBE YOU'RE RIGHT. WORKS IN THEORY.
BUT'CHA KNOW...SPEAKING OF GETTING GUYS OFF...
LEMME TELL YOU WHAT GETS ME OFF.
TOP OF THE LIST IS TAKING DOWN BOZOS LIKE YOU.

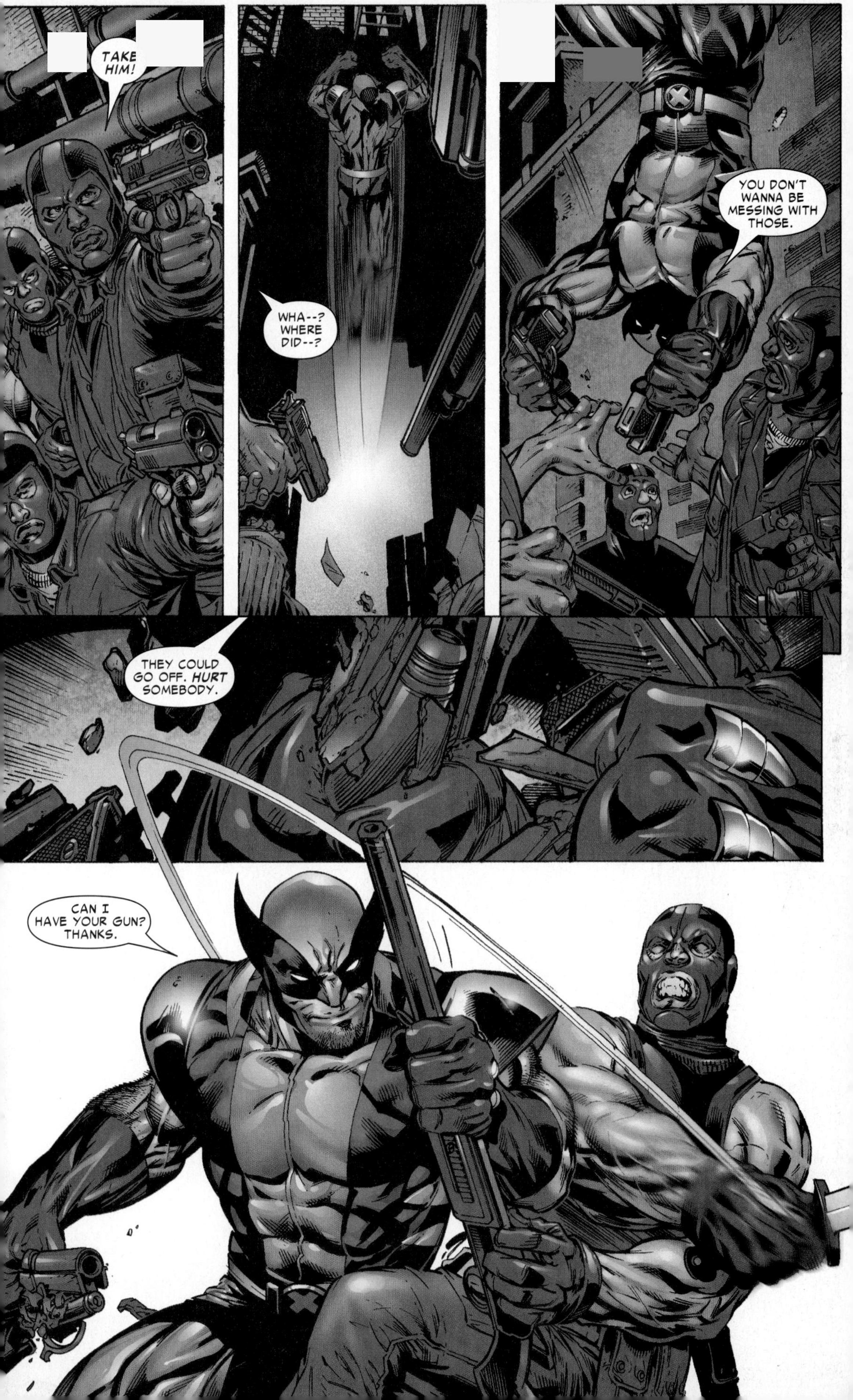
TAKE HIM!
WHA--? WHERE DID--?
YOU DON'T WANNA BE MESSING WITH THOSE.
THEY COULD GO OFF. HURT SOMEBODY.
CAN I HAVE YOUR GUN? THANKS.

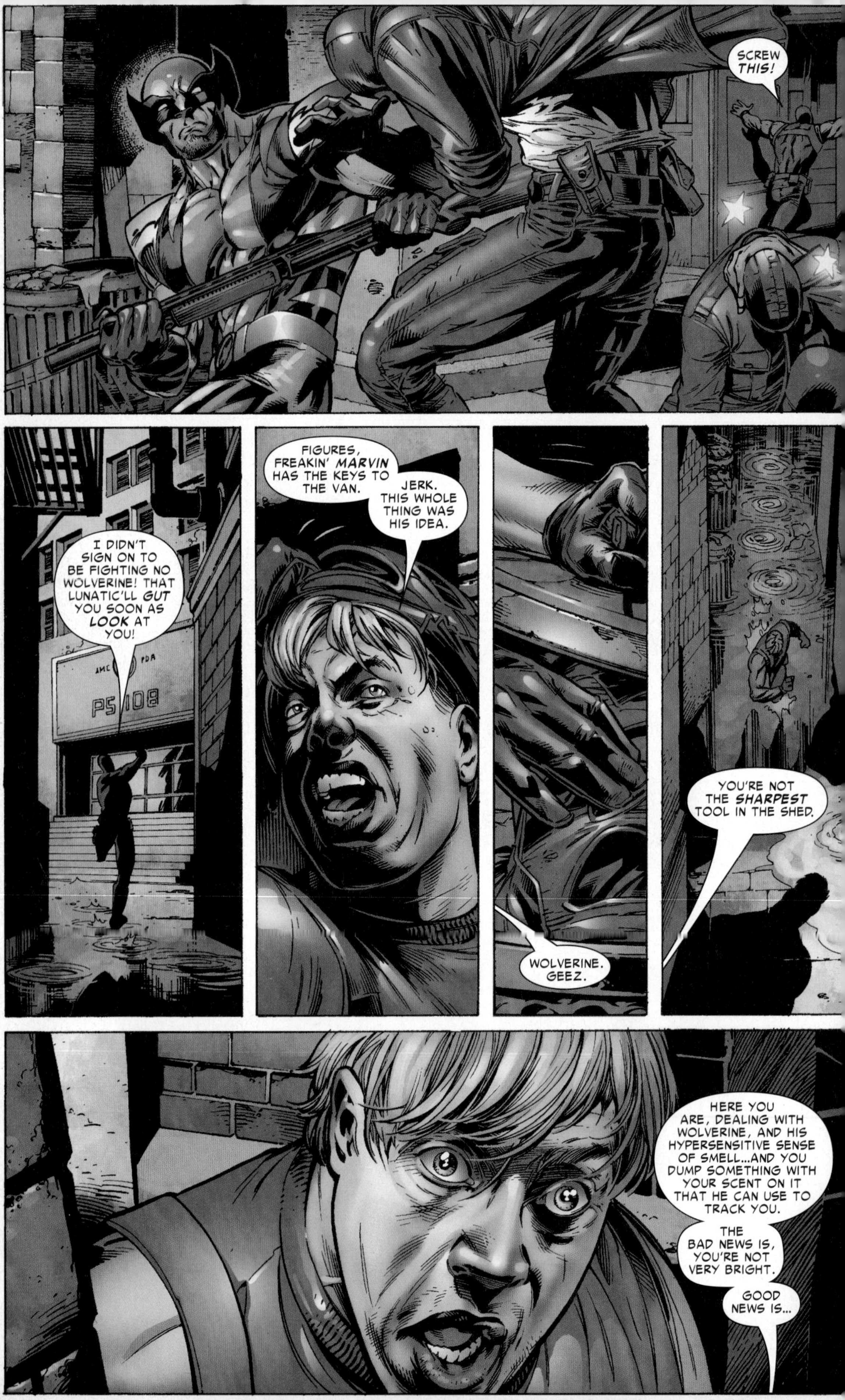
SCREW THIS!
I DIDN'T SIGN ON TO BE FIGHTING NO WOLVERINE! THAT LUNATIC'LL GUT YOU SOON AS LOOK AT YOU!
PS 108
FIGURES, FREAKIN' MARVIN HAS THE KEYS TO THE VAN.
JERK. THIS WHOLE THING WAS HIS IDEA.
WOLVERINE. GEEZ.
YOU'RE NOT THE SHARPEST TOOL IN THE SHED.
HERE YOU ARE, DEALING WITH WOLVERINE, AND HIS HYPERSENSITIVE SENSE OF SMELL...AND YOU DUMP SOMETHING WITH YOUR SCENT ON IT THAT HE CAN USE TO TRACK YOU.
THE BAD NEWS IS, YOU'RE NOT VERY BRIGHT.
GOOD NEWS IS...

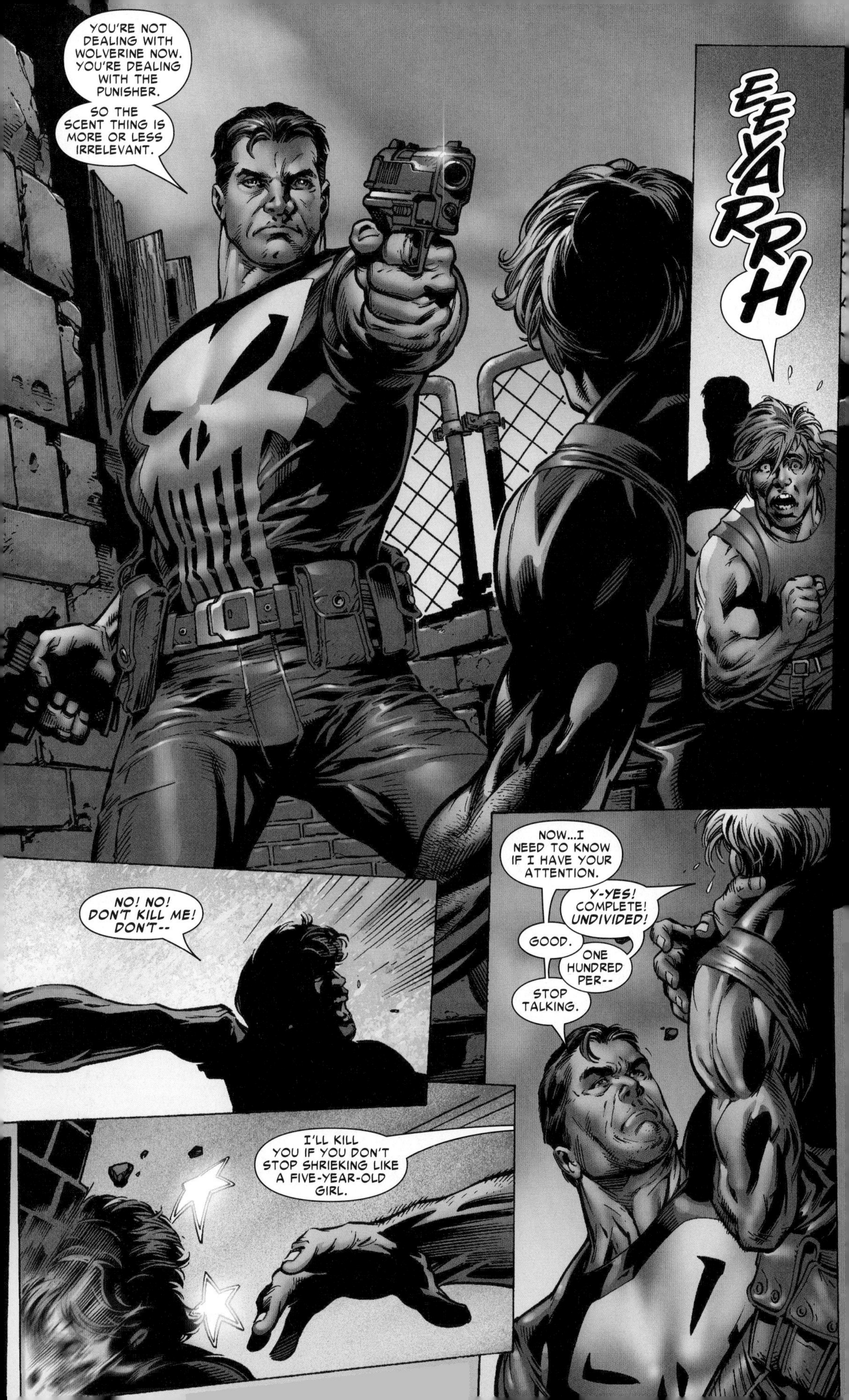
YOU'RE NOT DEALING WITH WOLVERINE NOW. YOU'RE DEALING WITH THE PUNISHER.
SO THE SCENT THING IS MORE OR LESS IRRELEVANT.
EEYARRH
NO! NO! DON'T KILL ME! DON'T--
I'LL KILL YOU IF YOU DON'T STOP SHRIEKING LIKE A FIVE-YEAR-OLD GIRL.
NOW...I NEED TO KNOW IF I HAVE YOUR ATTENTION.
Y-YES! COMPLETE! UNDIVIDED!
GOOD.
ONE HUNDRED PER--
STOP TALKING.

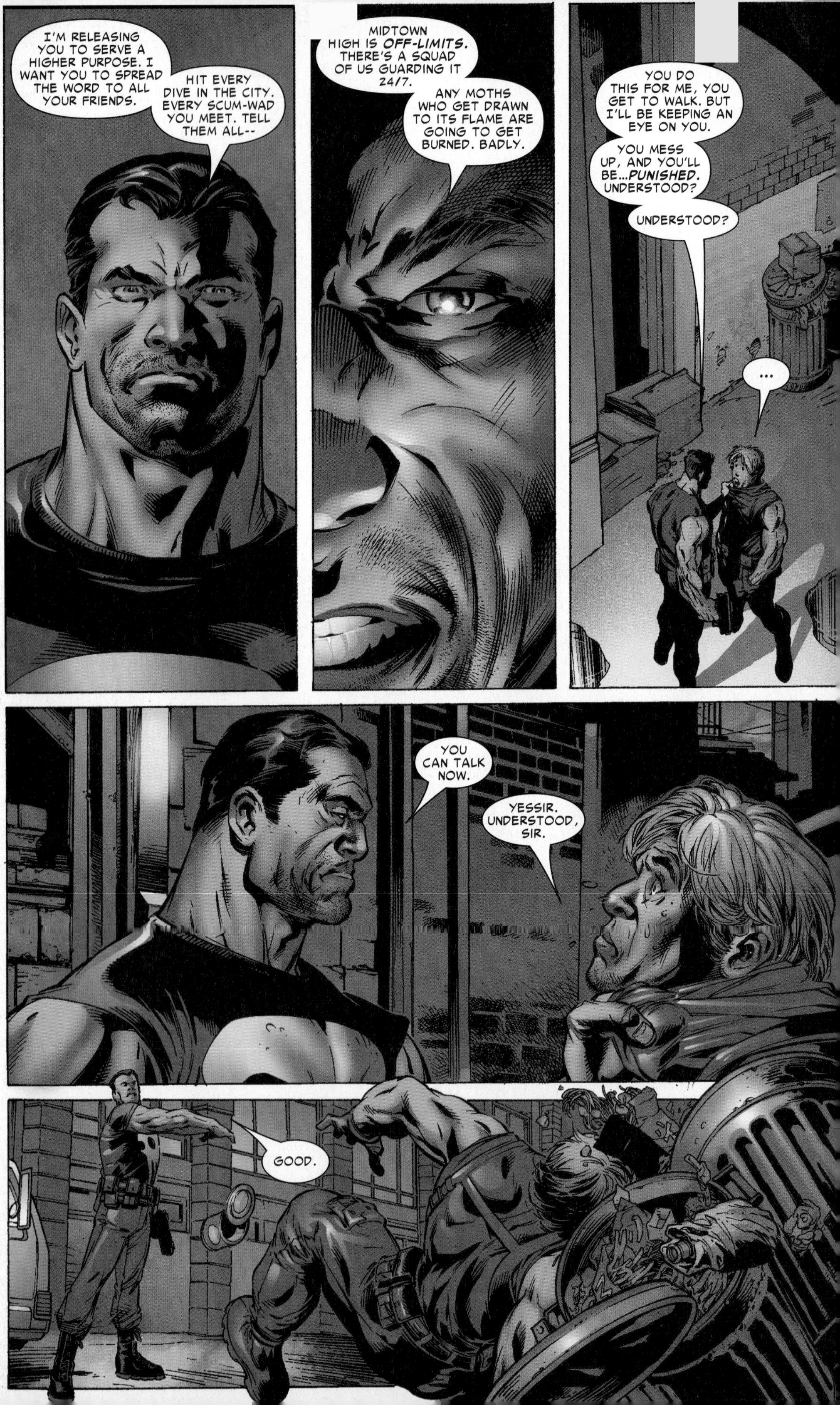
I'M RELEASING YOU TO SERVE A HIGHER PURPOSE. I WANT YOU TO SPREAD THE WORD TO ALL YOUR FRIENDS.
HIT EVERY DIVE IN THE CITY. EVERY SCUM-WAD YOU MEET. TELL THEM ALL--
MIDTOWN HIGH IS OFF-LIMITS. THERE'S A SQUAD OF US GUARDING IT 24/7.
ANY MOTHS WHO GET DRAWN TO ITS FLAME ARE GOING TO GET BURNED. BADLY.
YOU DO THIS FOR ME, YOU GET TO WALK. BUT I'LL BE KEEPING AN EYE ON YOU.
YOU MESS UP, AND YOU'LL BE...PUNISHED. UNDERSTOOD?
UNDERSTOOD?
...
YOU CAN TALK NOW.
YESSIR. UNDERSTOOD, SIR.
GOOD.

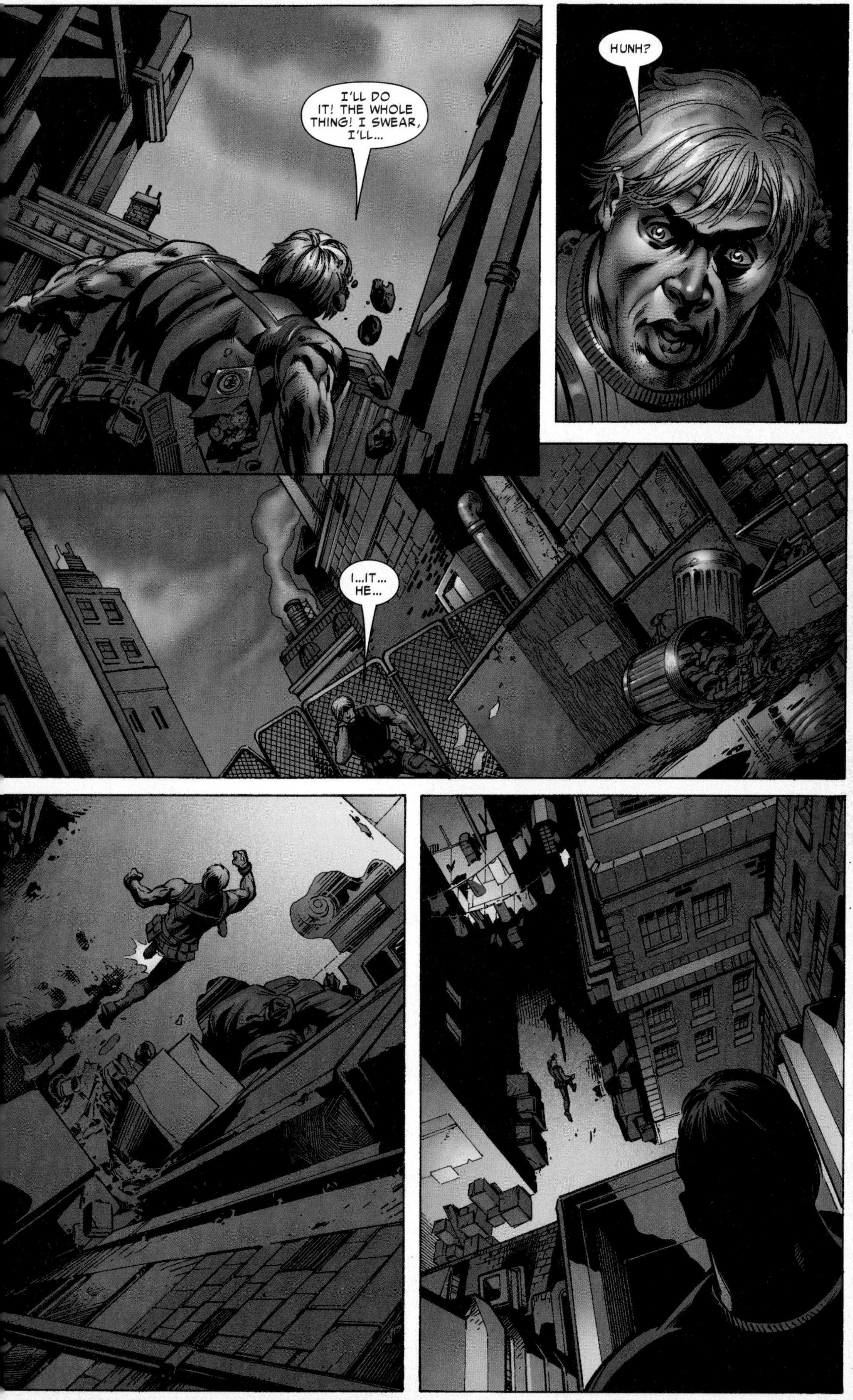
I'LL DO IT! THE WHOLE THING! I SWEAR, I'LL...
HUNH?
I...IT... HE...

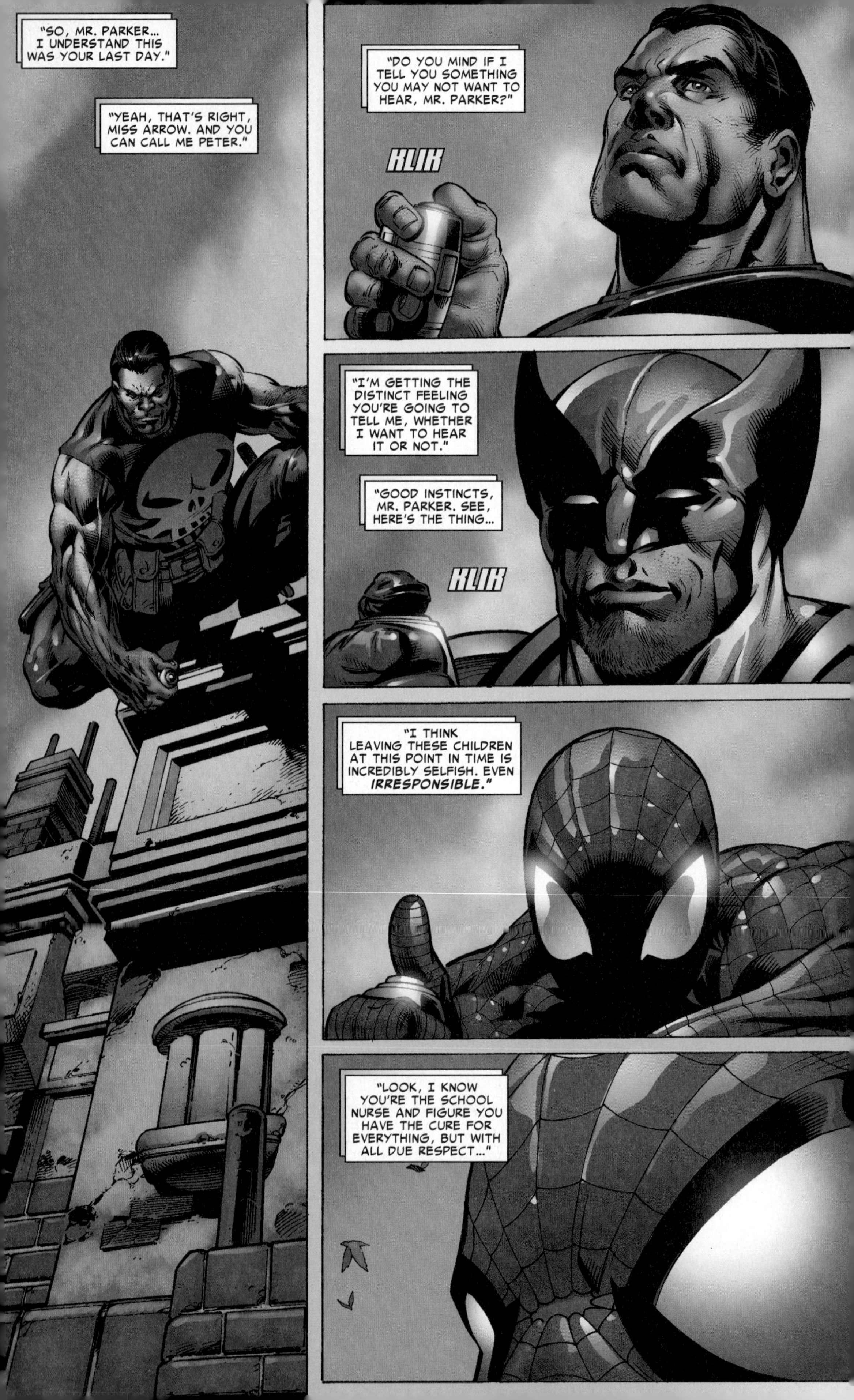
"SO, MR. PARKER... I UNDERSTAND THIS WAS YOUR LAST DAY."
"YEAH, THAT'S RIGHT, MISS ARROW. AND YOU CAN CALL ME PETER."
"DO YOU MIND IF I TELL YOU SOMETHING YOU MAY NOT WANT TO HEAR, MR. PARKER?"
KLIK
"I'M GETTING THE DISTINCT FEELING YOU'RE GOING TO TELL ME, WHETHER I WANT TO HEAR IT OR NOT."
"GOOD INSTINCTS, MR. PARKER. SEE, HERE'S THE THING...
KLIK
"I THINK LEAVING THESE CHILDREN AT THIS POINT IN TIME IS INCREDIBLY SELFISH. EVEN *IRRESPONSIBLE*."
"LOOK, I KNOW YOU'RE THE SCHOOL NURSE AND FIGURE YOU HAVE THE CURE FOR EVERYTHING, BUT WITH ALL DUE RESPECT..."

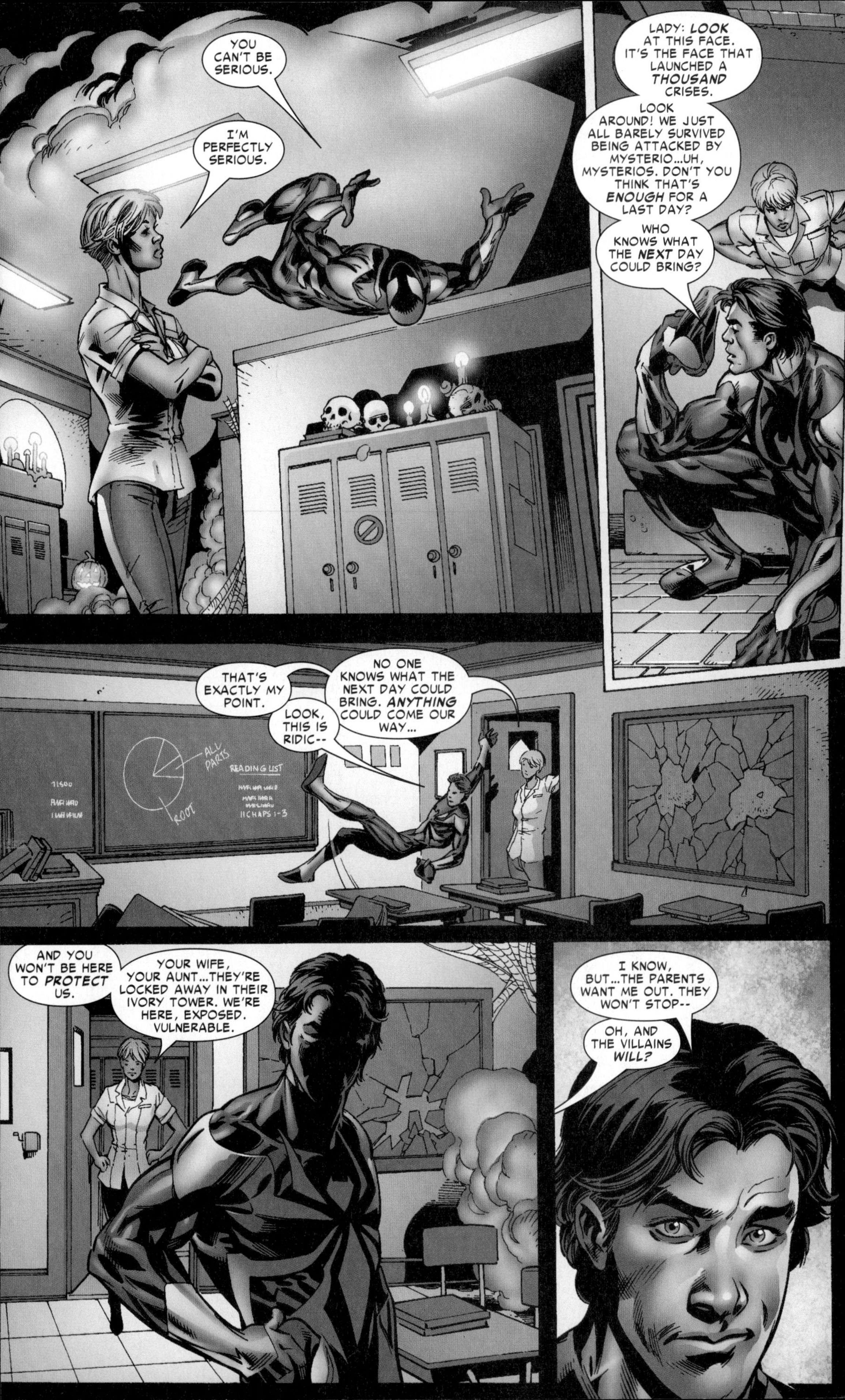

YOU CAN'T BE SERIOUS.
I'M PERFECTLY SERIOUS.
LADY: LOOK AT THIS FACE. IT'S THE FACE THAT LAUNCHED A THOUSAND CRISES.
LOOK AROUND! WE JUST ALL BARELY SURVIVED BEING ATTACKED BY MYSTERIO...UH, MYSTERIOS. DON'T YOU THINK THAT'S ENOUGH FOR A LAST DAY?
WHO KNOWS WHAT THE NEXT DAY COULD BRING?
THAT'S EXACTLY MY POINT.
NO ONE KNOWS WHAT THE NEXT DAY COULD BRING. ANYTHING COULD COME OUR WAY...
LOOK, THIS IS RIDIC--
ALL PARTS
READING LIST
ROOT
II CHAPS 1-3
AND YOU WON'T BE HERE TO PROTECT US.
YOUR WIFE, YOUR AUNT...THEY'RE LOCKED AWAY IN THEIR IVORY TOWER. WE'RE HERE, EXPOSED. VULNERABLE.
I KNOW, BUT...THE PARENTS WANT ME OUT. THEY WON'T STOP--
OH, AND THE VILLAINS WILL?

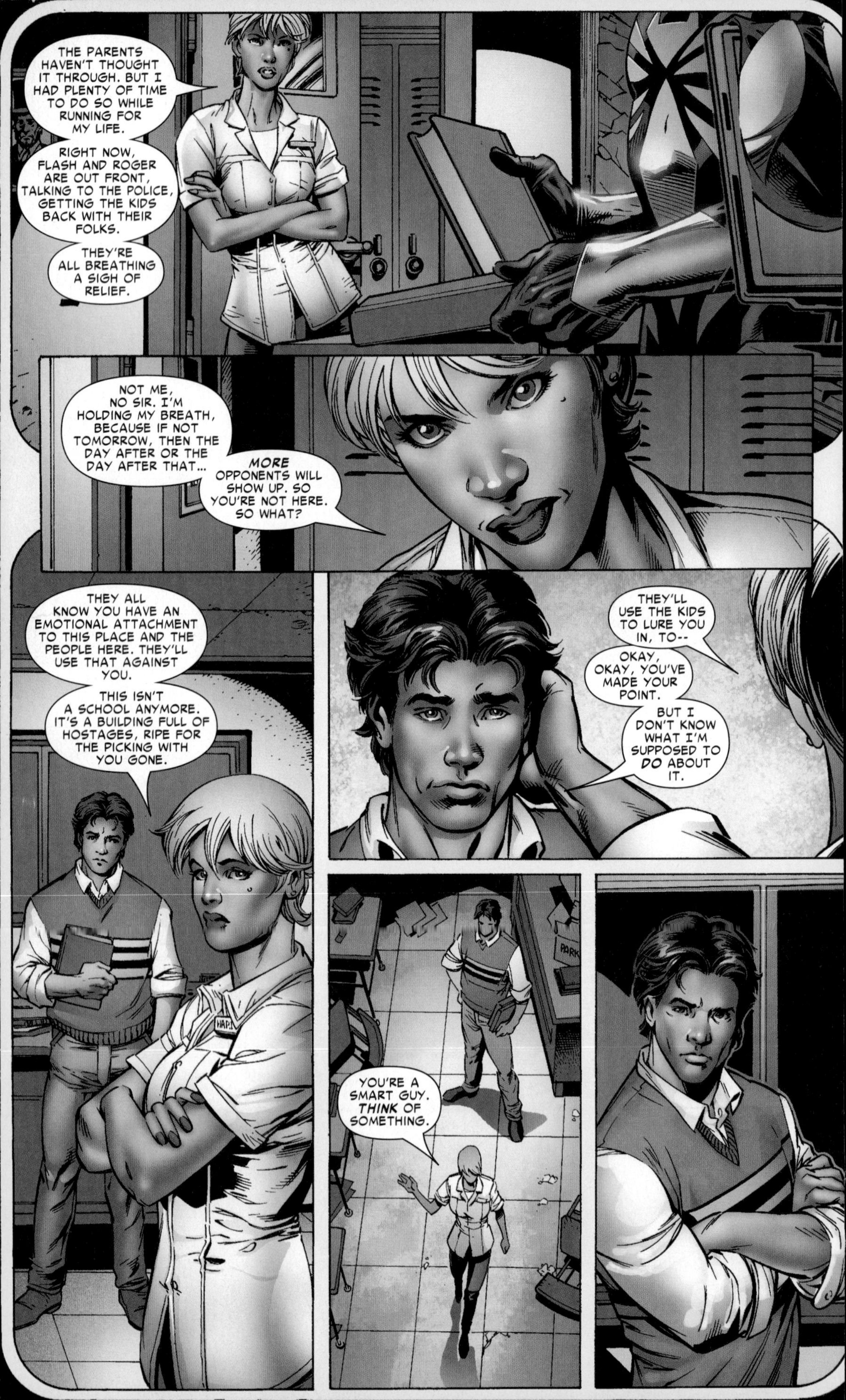
THE PARENTS HAVEN'T THOUGHT IT THROUGH. BUT I HAD PLENTY OF TIME TO DO SO WHILE RUNNING FOR MY LIFE.
RIGHT NOW, FLASH AND ROGER ARE OUT FRONT, TALKING TO THE POLICE, GETTING THE KIDS BACK WITH THEIR FOLKS.
THEY'RE ALL BREATHING A SIGH OF RELIEF.
NOT ME, NO SIR. I'M HOLDING MY BREATH, BECAUSE IF NOT TOMORROW, THEN THE DAY AFTER OR THE DAY AFTER THAT...
MORE OPPONENTS WILL SHOW UP. SO YOU'RE NOT HERE. SO WHAT?
THEY ALL KNOW YOU HAVE AN EMOTIONAL ATTACHMENT TO THIS PLACE AND THE PEOPLE HERE. THEY'LL USE THAT AGAINST YOU.
THIS ISN'T A SCHOOL ANYMORE. IT'S A BUILDING FULL OF HOSTAGES, RIPE FOR THE PICKING WITH YOU GONE.
THEY'LL USE THE KIDS TO LURE YOU IN, TO--
OKAY, OKAY, YOU'VE MADE YOUR POINT.
BUT I DON'T KNOW WHAT I'M SUPPOSED TO *DO* ABOUT IT.
YOU'RE A SMART GUY. *THINK* OF SOMETHING.

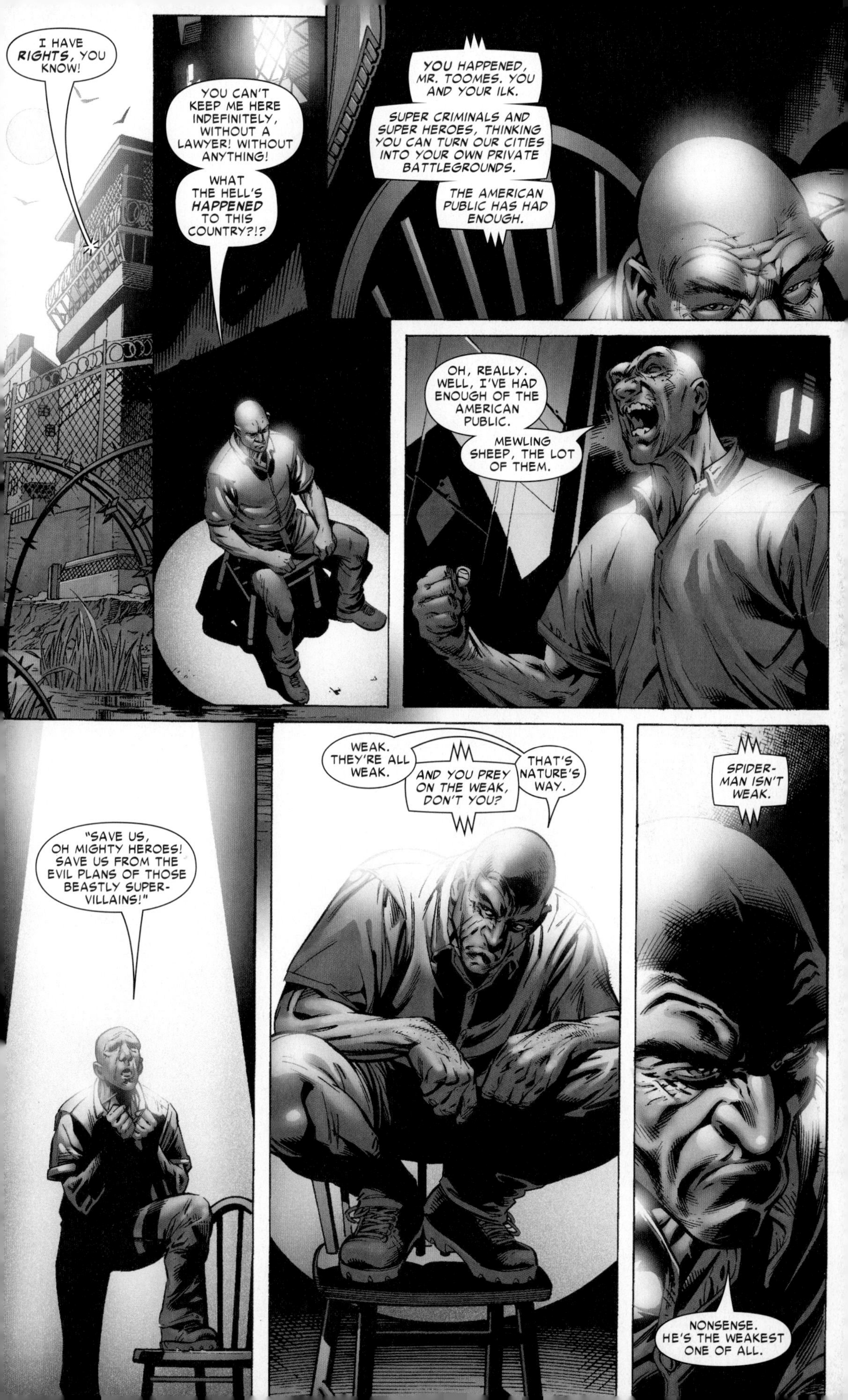
I HAVE RIGHTS, YOU KNOW!
YOU CAN'T KEEP ME HERE INDEFINITELY, WITHOUT A LAWYER! WITHOUT ANYTHING!
WHAT THE HELL'S HAPPENED TO THIS COUNTRY?!?
YOU HAPPENED, MR. TOOMES. YOU AND YOUR ILK.
SUPER CRIMINALS AND SUPER HEROES, THINKING YOU CAN TURN OUR CITIES INTO YOUR OWN PRIVATE BATTLEGROUNDS.
THE AMERICAN PUBLIC HAS HAD ENOUGH.
OH, REALLY. WELL, I'VE HAD ENOUGH OF THE AMERICAN PUBLIC.
MEWLING SHEEP, THE LOT OF THEM.
"SAVE US, OH MIGHTY HEROES! SAVE US FROM THE EVIL PLANS OF THOSE BEASTLY SUPER-VILLAINS!"
WEAK. THEY'RE ALL WEAK.
AND YOU PREY ON THE WEAK, DON'T YOU?
THAT'S NATURE'S WAY.
SPIDER-MAN ISN'T WEAK.
NONSENSE. HE'S THE WEAKEST ONE OF ALL.

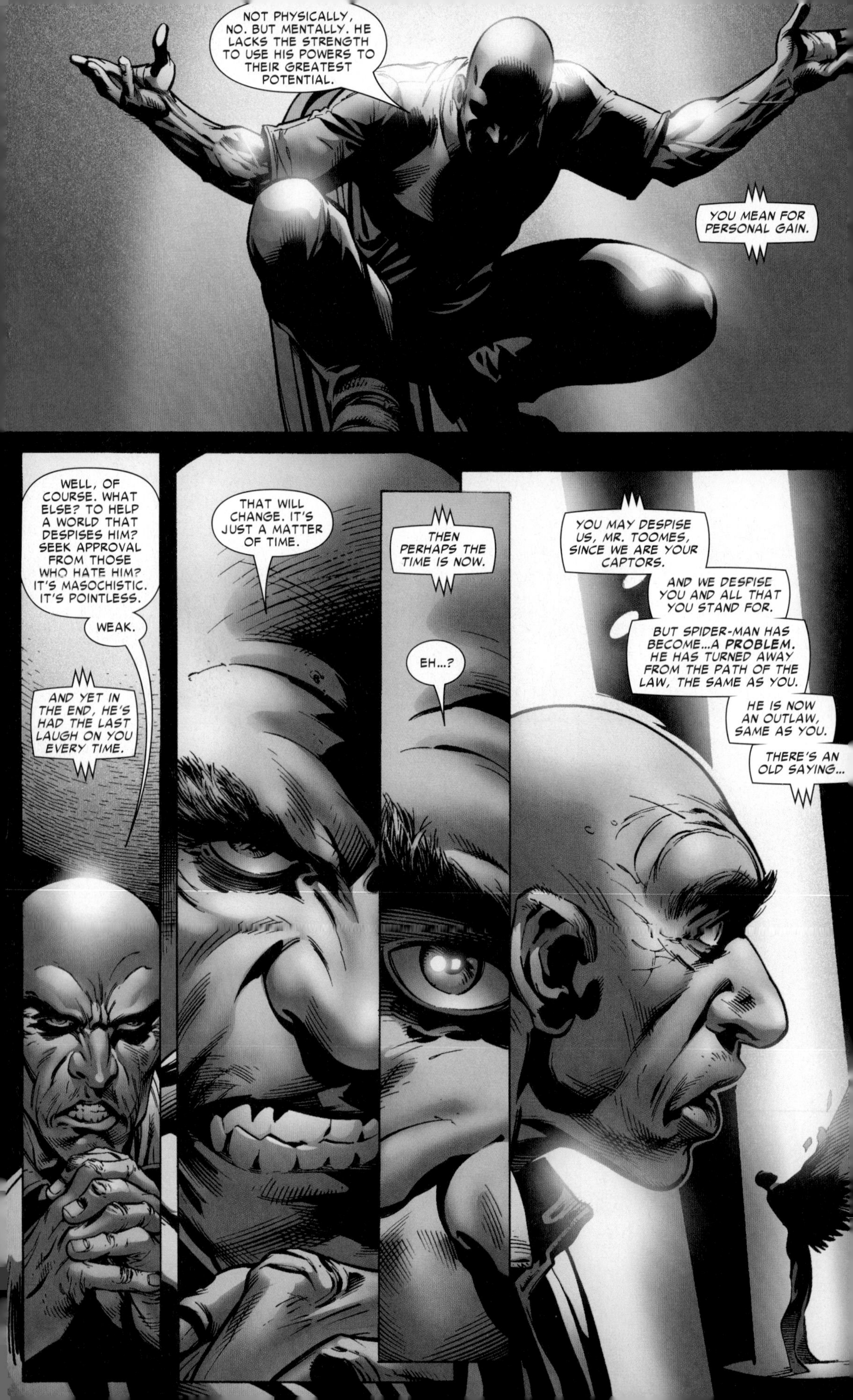
NOT PHYSICALLY, NO. BUT MENTALLY. HE LACKS THE STRENGTH TO USE HIS POWERS TO THEIR GREATEST POTENTIAL.
YOU MEAN FOR PERSONAL GAIN.
WELL, OF COURSE. WHAT ELSE? TO HELP A WORLD THAT DESPISES HIM? SEEK APPROVAL FROM THOSE WHO HATE HIM? IT'S MASOCHISTIC. IT'S POINTLESS.
WEAK.
AND YET IN THE END, HE'S HAD THE LAST LAUGH ON YOU EVERY TIME.
THAT WILL CHANGE. IT'S JUST A MATTER OF TIME.
THEN PERHAPS THE TIME IS NOW.
EH...?
YOU MAY DESPISE US, MR. TOOMES, SINCE WE ARE YOUR CAPTORS.
AND WE DESPISE YOU AND ALL THAT YOU STAND FOR.
BUT SPIDER-MAN HAS BECOME...A **PROBLEM**. HE HAS TURNED AWAY FROM THE PATH OF THE LAW, THE SAME AS YOU.
HE IS NOW AN OUTLAW, SAME AS YOU.
THERE'S AN OLD SAYING...

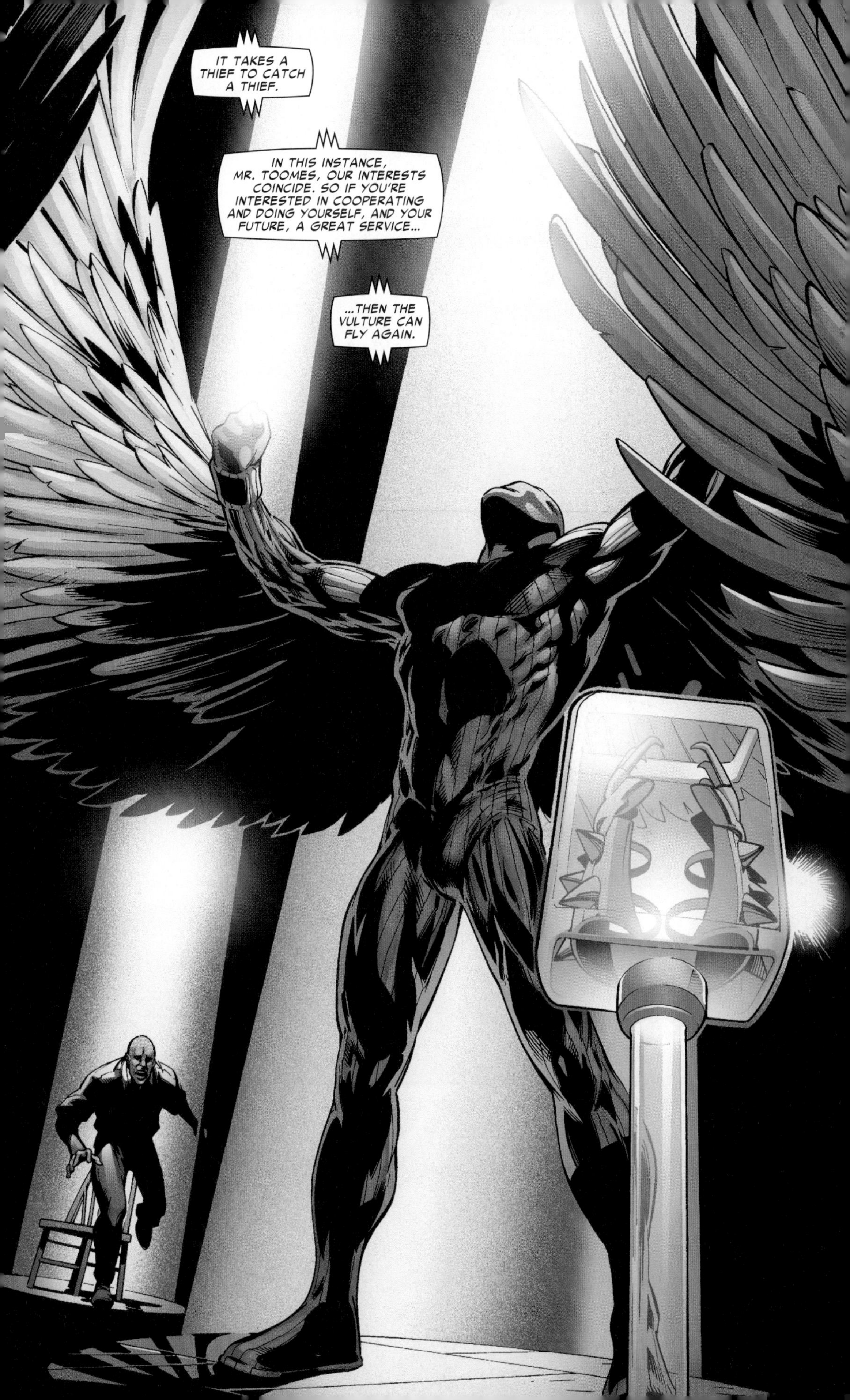
IT TAKES A THIEF TO CATCH A THIEF.
IN THIS INSTANCE, MR. TOOMES, OUR INTERESTS COINCIDE. SO IF YOU'RE INTERESTED IN COOPERATING AND DOING YOURSELF, AND YOUR FUTURE, A GREAT SERVICE...
...THEN THE VULTURE CAN FLY AGAIN.

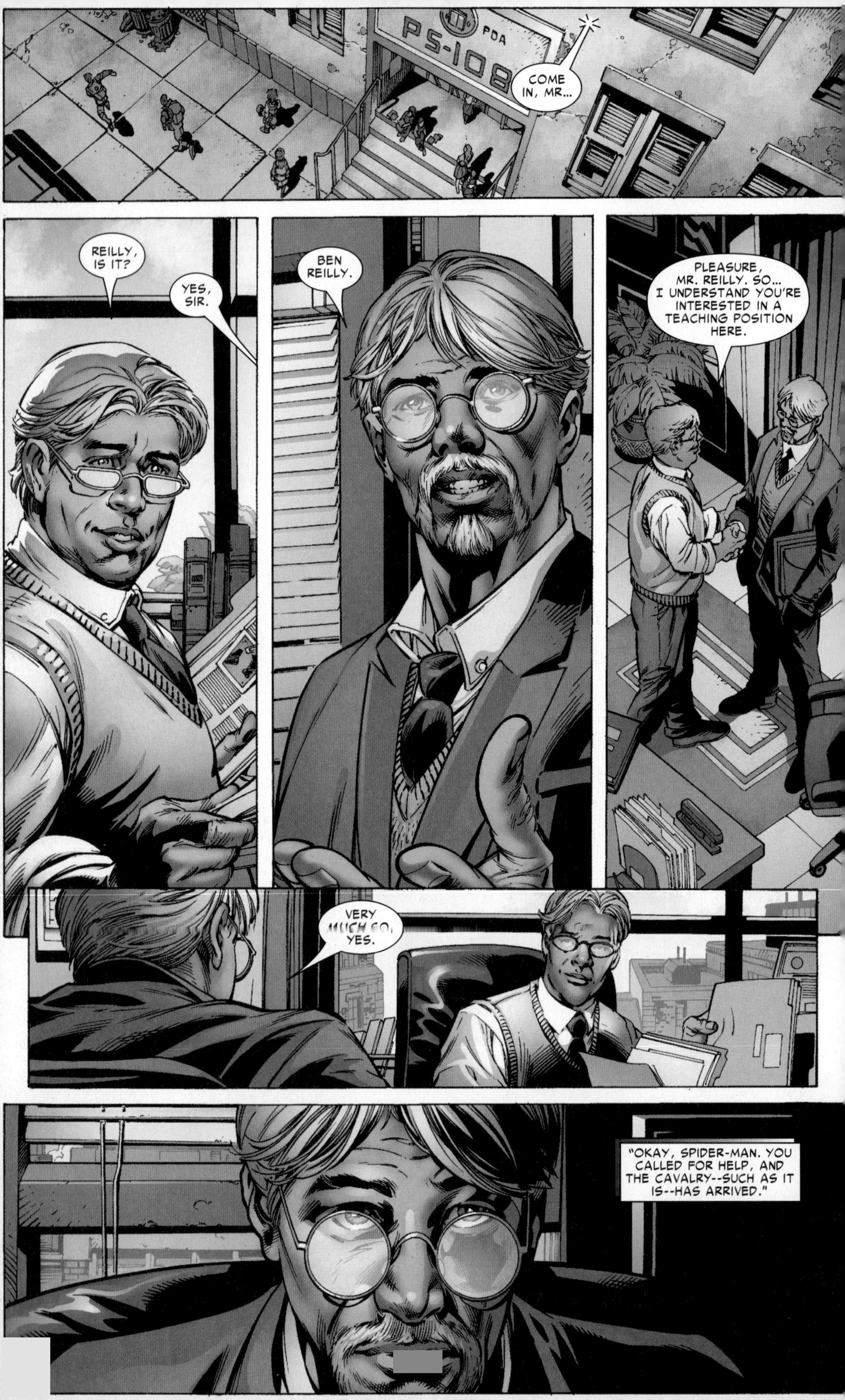
PS-108
PDA
COME IN, MR...
REILLY, IS IT?
YES, SIR.
BEN REILLY.
PLEASURE, MR. REILLY. SO... I UNDERSTAND YOU'RE INTERESTED IN A TEACHING POSITION HERE.
VERY MUCH SO, YES.
"OKAY, SPIDER-MAN. YOU CALLED FOR HELP, AND THE CAVALRY--SUCH AS IT IS--HAS ARRIVED."

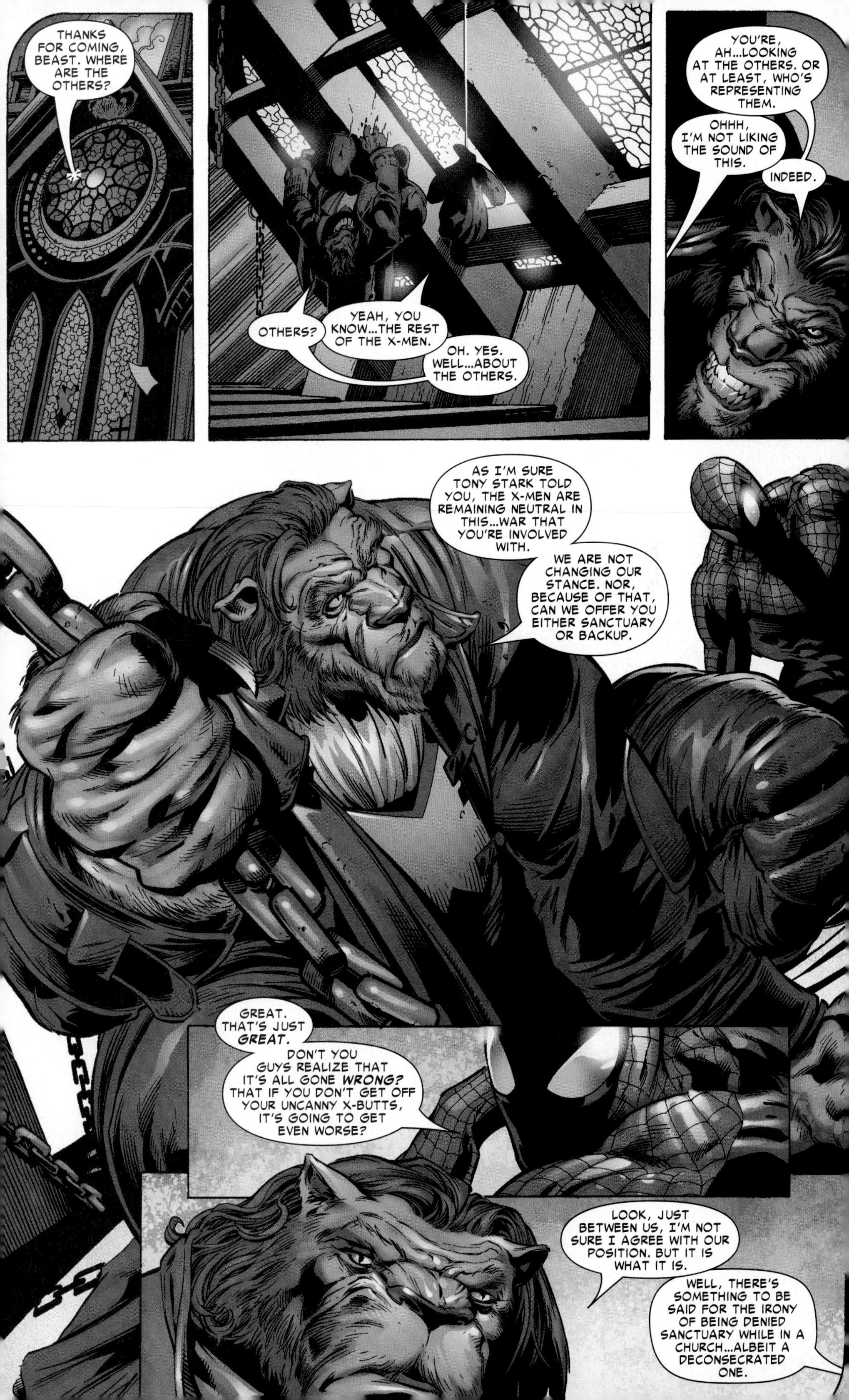

THANKS FOR COMING, BEAST. WHERE ARE THE OTHERS?
OTHERS?
YEAH, YOU KNOW...THE REST OF THE X-MEN.
OH. YES. WELL...ABOUT THE OTHERS.
YOU'RE, AH...LOOKING AT THE OTHERS. OR AT LEAST, WHO'S REPRESENTING THEM.
OHHH, I'M NOT LIKING THE SOUND OF THIS.
INDEED.
AS I'M SURE TONY STARK TOLD YOU, THE X-MEN ARE REMAINING NEUTRAL IN THIS...WAR THAT YOU'RE INVOLVED WITH.
WE ARE NOT CHANGING OUR STANCE. NOR, BECAUSE OF THAT, CAN WE OFFER YOU EITHER SANCTUARY OR BACKUP.
GREAT. THAT'S JUST GREAT.
DON'T YOU GUYS REALIZE THAT IT'S ALL GONE WRONG? THAT IF YOU DON'T GET OFF YOUR UNCANNY X-BUTTS, IT'S GOING TO GET EVEN WORSE?
LOOK, JUST BETWEEN US, I'M NOT SURE I AGREE WITH OUR POSITION. BUT IT IS WHAT IT IS.
WELL, THERE'S SOMETHING TO BE SAID FOR THE IRONY OF BEING DENIED SANCTUARY WHILE IN A CHURCH...ALBEIT A DECONSECRATED ONE.

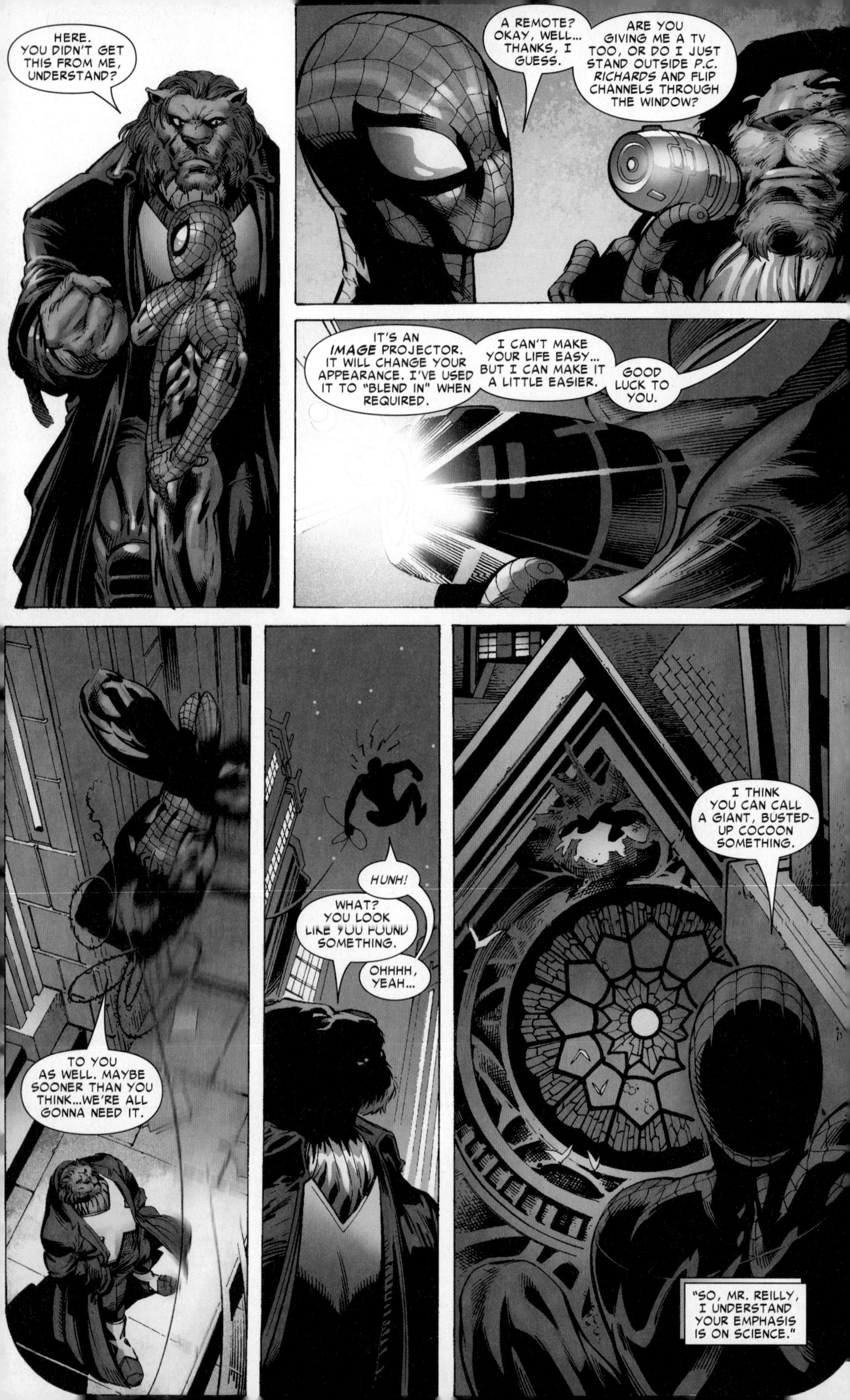
HERE. YOU DIDN'T GET THIS FROM ME, UNDERSTAND?
A REMOTE? OKAY, WELL... THANKS, I GUESS.
ARE YOU GIVING ME A TV TOO, OR DO I JUST STAND OUTSIDE P.C. RICHARDS AND FLIP CHANNELS THROUGH THE WINDOW?
IT'S AN IMAGE PROJECTOR. IT WILL CHANGE YOUR APPEARANCE. I'VE USED IT TO "BLEND IN" WHEN REQUIRED.
I CAN'T MAKE YOUR LIFE EASY... BUT I CAN MAKE IT A LITTLE EASIER.
GOOD LUCK TO YOU.
TO YOU AS WELL. MAYBE SOONER THAN YOU THINK...WE'RE ALL GONNA NEED IT.
HUNH!
WHAT? YOU LOOK LIKE YOU FOUND SOMETHING.
OHHHH, YEAH...
I THINK YOU CAN CALL A GIANT, BUSTED-UP COCOON SOMETHING.
"SO, MR. REILLY, I UNDERSTAND YOUR EMPHASIS IS ON SCIENCE."

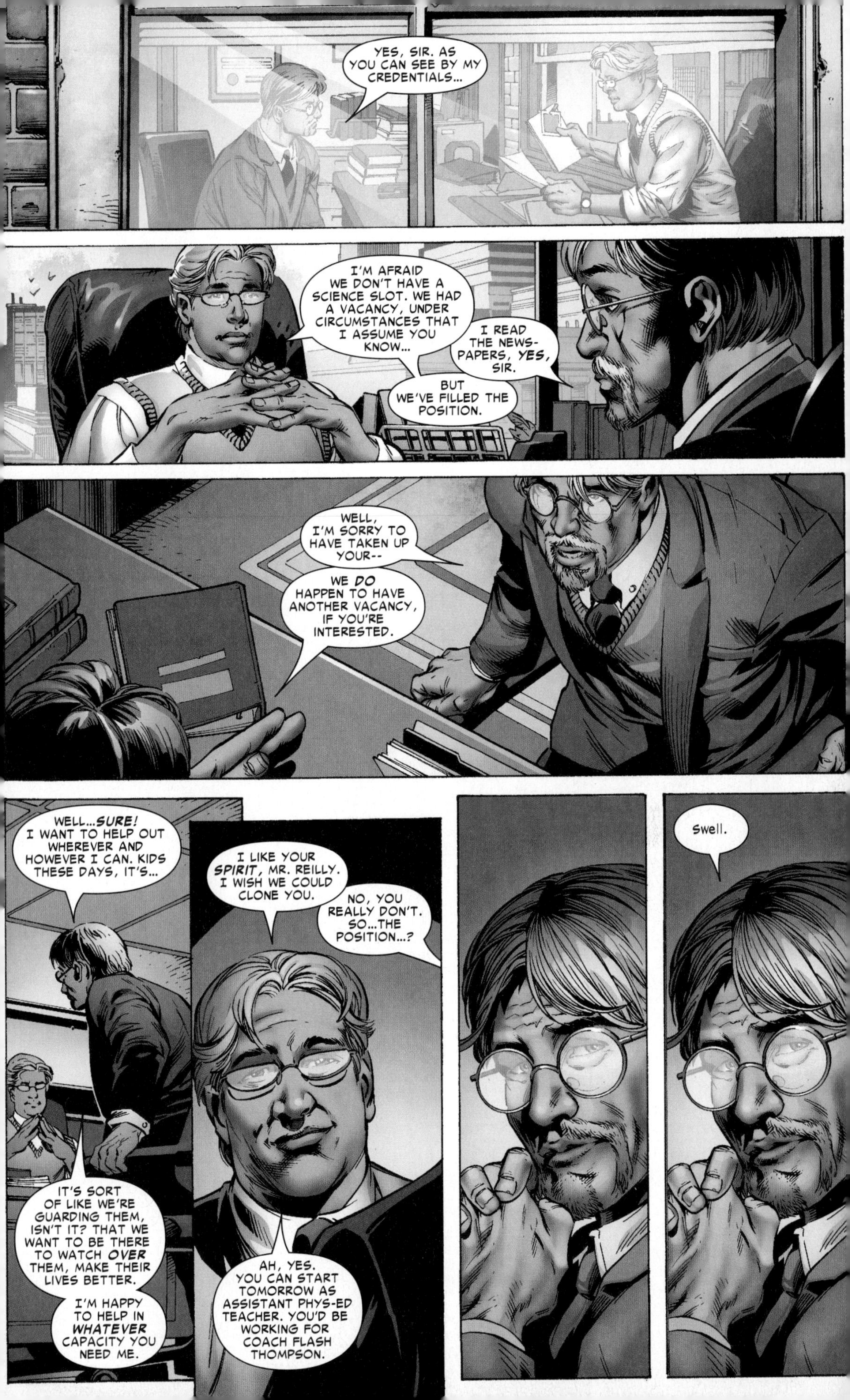
YES, SIR. AS YOU CAN SEE BY MY CREDENTIALS...
I'M AFRAID WE DON'T HAVE A SCIENCE SLOT. WE HAD A VACANCY, UNDER CIRCUMSTANCES THAT I ASSUME YOU KNOW...
I READ THE NEWS-PAPERS, YES, SIR.
BUT WE'VE FILLED THE POSITION.
WELL, I'M SORRY TO HAVE TAKEN UP YOUR--
WE DO HAPPEN TO HAVE ANOTHER VACANCY, IF YOU'RE INTERESTED.
WELL...SURE! I WANT TO HELP OUT WHEREVER AND HOWEVER I CAN. KIDS THESE DAYS, IT'S...
IT'S SORT OF LIKE WE'RE GUARDING THEM, ISN'T IT? THAT WE WANT TO BE THERE TO WATCH OVER THEM, MAKE THEIR LIVES BETTER.
I'M HAPPY TO HELP IN WHATEVER CAPACITY YOU NEED ME.
I LIKE YOUR SPIRIT, MR. REILLY. I WISH WE COULD CLONE YOU.
NO, YOU REALLY DON'T. SO...THE POSITION...?
AH, YES. YOU CAN START TOMORROW AS ASSISTANT PHYS-ED TEACHER. YOU'D BE WORKING FOR COACH FLASH THOMPSON.
Swell.

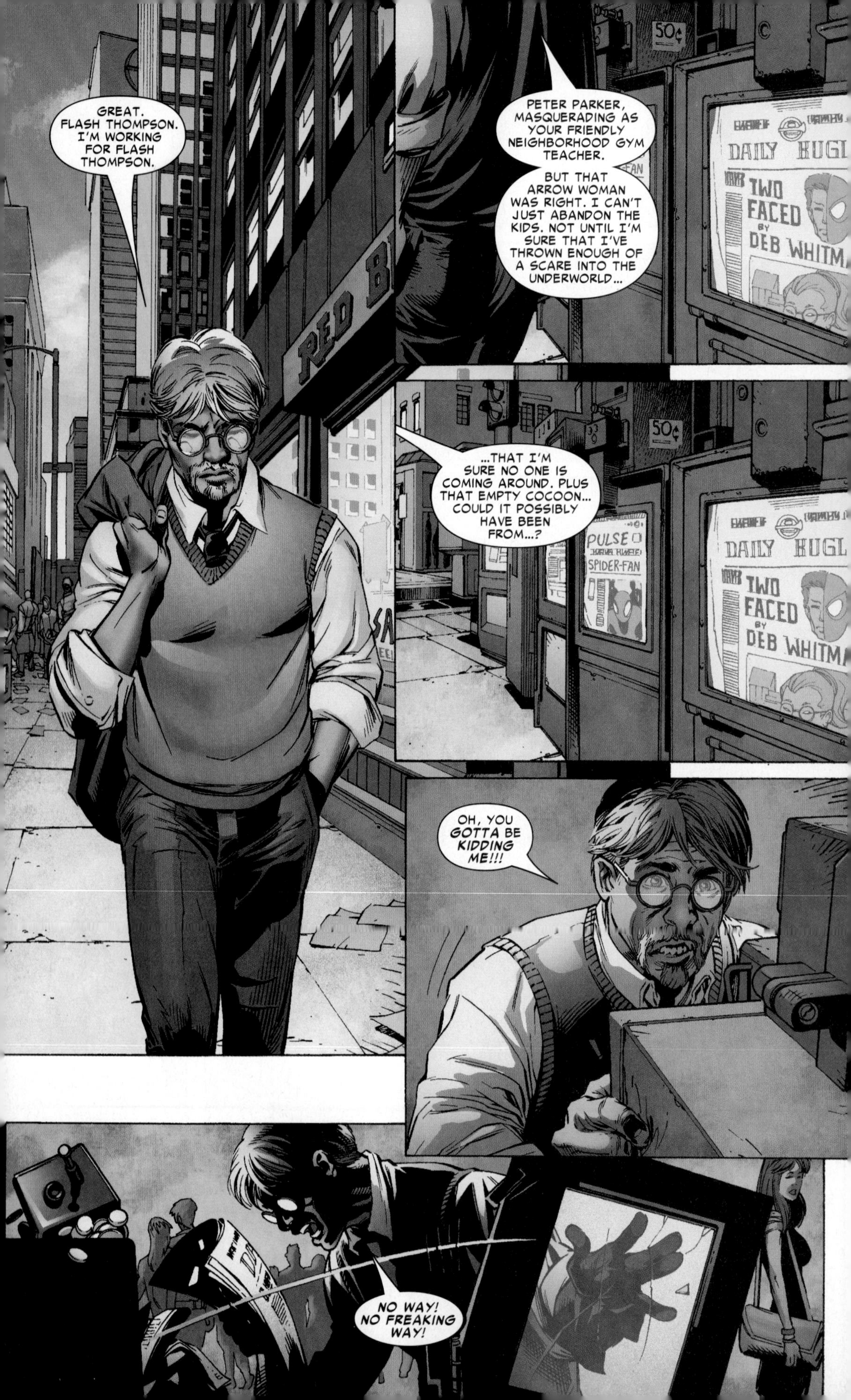
GREAT. FLASH THOMPSON. I'M WORKING FOR FLASH THOMPSON.
PETER PARKER, MASQUERADING AS YOUR FRIENDLY NEIGHBORHOOD GYM TEACHER.
BUT THAT ARROW WOMAN WAS RIGHT. I CAN'T JUST ABANDON THE KIDS. NOT UNTIL I'M SURE THAT I'VE THROWN ENOUGH OF A SCARE INTO THE UNDERWORLD...
50¢
DAILY BUGL
TWO FACED
BY DEB WHITM
RED B
...THAT I'M SURE NO ONE IS COMING AROUND. PLUS THAT EMPTY COCOON... COULD IT POSSIBLY HAVE BEEN FROM...?
50¢
PULSE
SPIDER-FAN
DAILY BUGL
TWO FACED
BY DEB WHITM
OH, YOU GOTTA BE KIDDING ME!!!
NO WAY! NO FREAKING WAY!

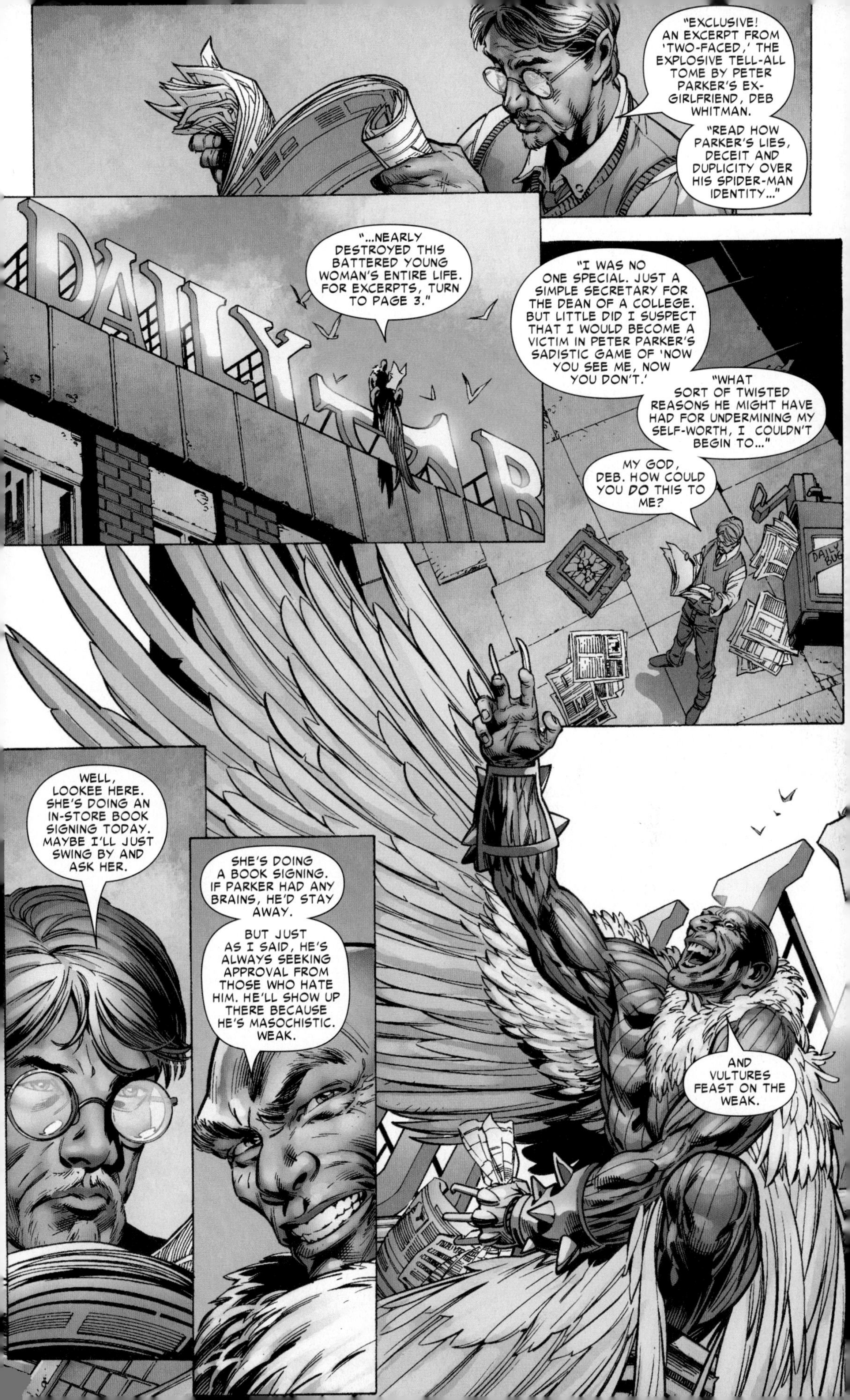
"EXCLUSIVE! AN EXCERPT FROM 'TWO-FACED,' THE EXPLOSIVE TELL-ALL TOME BY PETER PARKER'S EX-GIRLFRIEND, DEB WHITMAN.
"READ HOW PARKER'S LIES, DECEIT AND DUPLICITY OVER HIS SPIDER-MAN IDENTITY..."
"...NEARLY DESTROYED THIS BATTERED YOUNG WOMAN'S ENTIRE LIFE. FOR EXCERPTS, TURN TO PAGE 3."
DAILY
"I WAS NO ONE SPECIAL. JUST A SIMPLE SECRETARY FOR THE DEAN OF A COLLEGE. BUT LITTLE DID I SUSPECT THAT I WOULD BECOME A VICTIM IN PETER PARKER'S SADISTIC GAME OF 'NOW YOU SEE ME, NOW YOU DON'T.'
"WHAT SORT OF TWISTED REASONS HE MIGHT HAVE HAD FOR UNDERMINING MY SELF-WORTH, I COULDN'T BEGIN TO..."
MY GOD, DEB. HOW COULD YOU DO THIS TO ME?
WELL, LOOKEE HERE. SHE'S DOING AN IN-STORE BOOK SIGNING TODAY. MAYBE I'LL JUST SWING BY AND ASK HER.
SHE'S DOING A BOOK SIGNING. IF PARKER HAD ANY BRAINS, HE'D STAY AWAY.
BUT JUST AS I SAID, HE'S ALWAYS SEEKING APPROVAL FROM THOSE WHO HATE HIM. HE'LL SHOW UP THERE BECAUSE HE'S MASOCHISTIC. WEAK.
AND VULTURES FEAST ON THE WEAK.

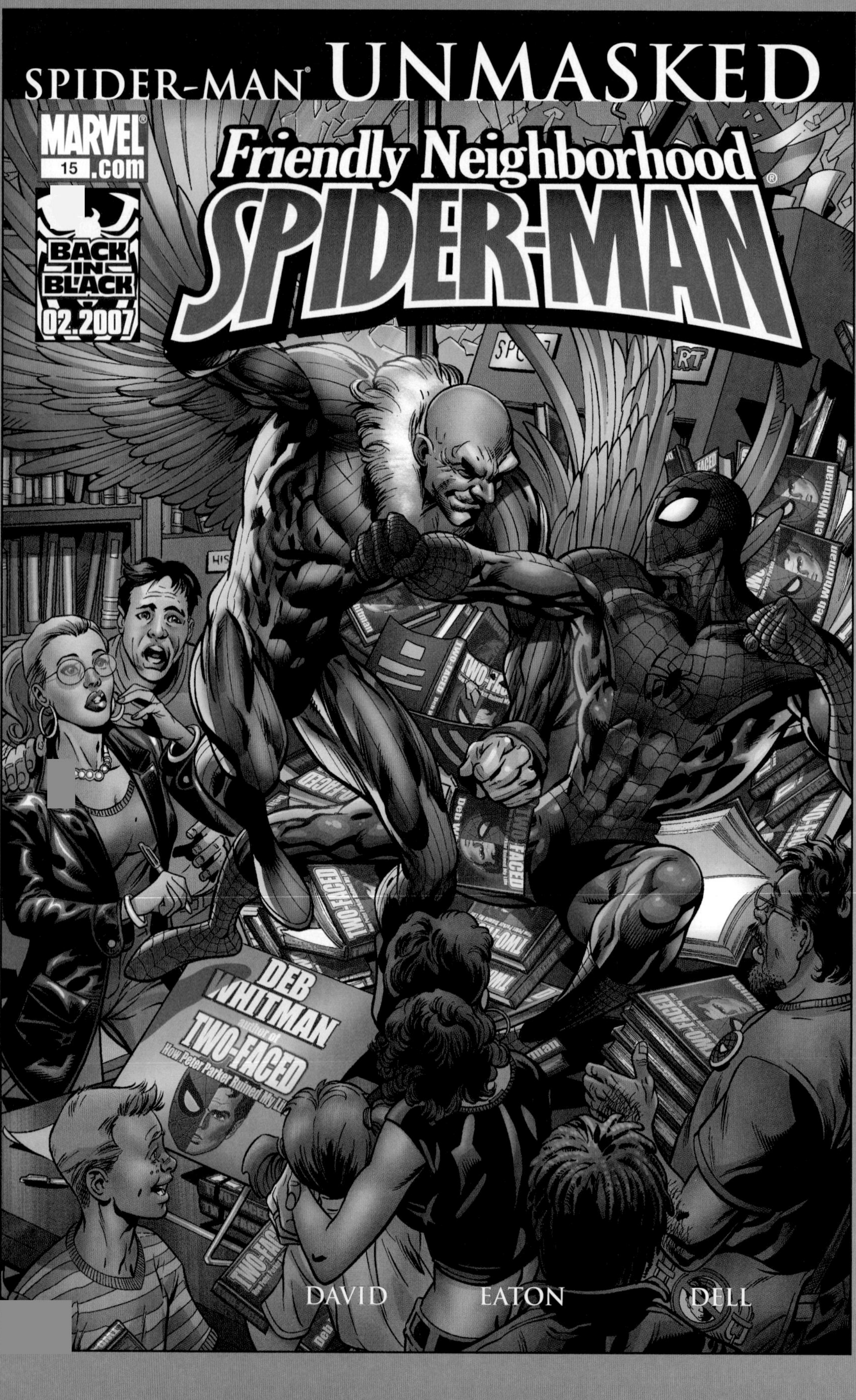
SPIDER-MAN® UNMASKED
MARVEL®
15 .com
Friendly Neighborhood
SPIDER-MAN®
BACK IN BLACK
02.2007
DEB WHITMAN
author of
TWO-FACED
How Peter Parker Ruined My
DAVID
EATON
DELL

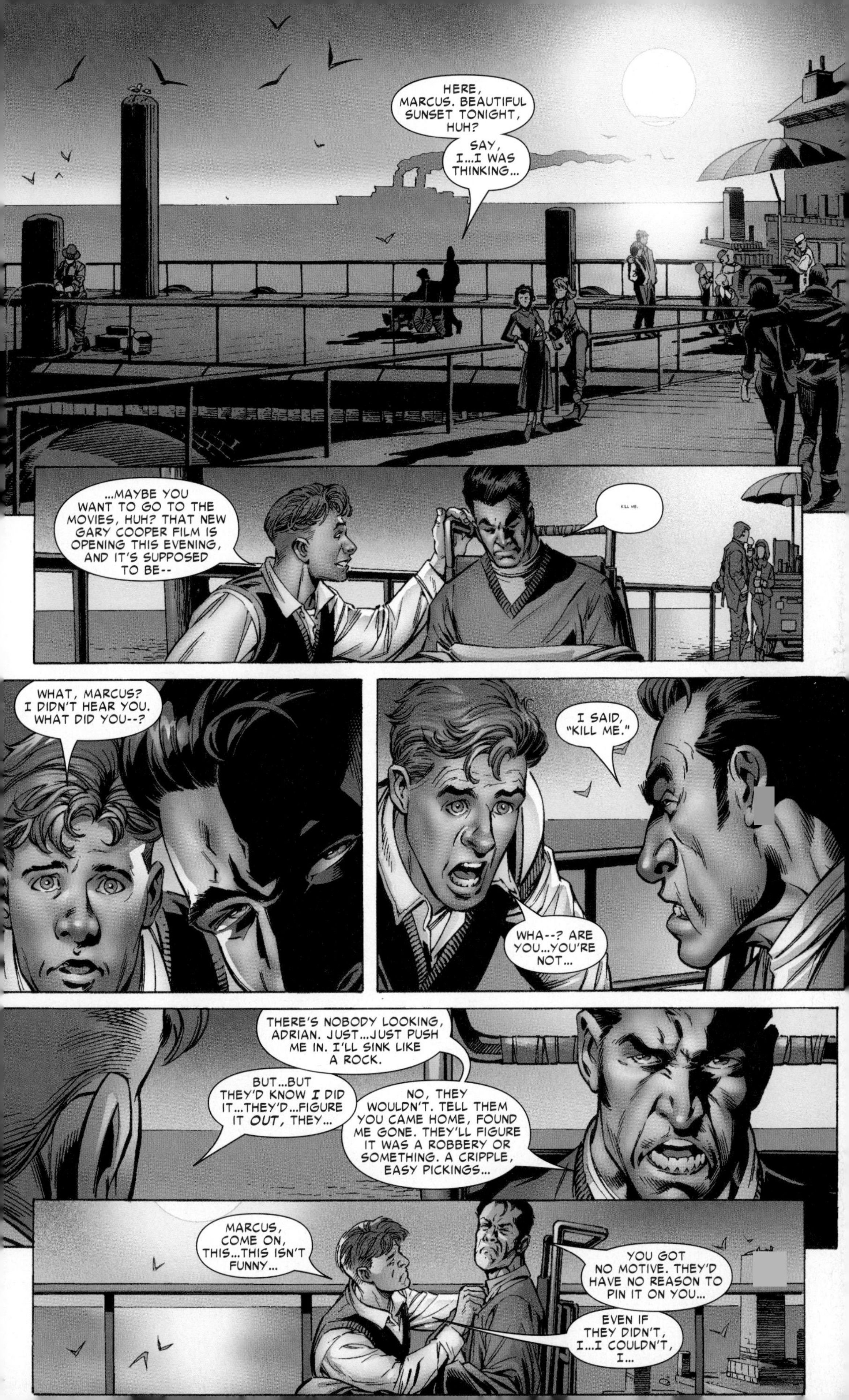
HERE, MARCUS. BEAUTIFUL SUNSET TONIGHT, HUH?
SAY, I...I WAS THINKING...
...MAYBE YOU WANT TO GO TO THE MOVIES, HUH? THAT NEW GARY COOPER FILM IS OPENING THIS EVENING, AND IT'S SUPPOSED TO BE--
KILL ME.
WHAT, MARCUS? I DIDN'T HEAR YOU. WHAT DID YOU--?
I SAID, "KILL ME."
WHA--? ARE YOU...YOU'RE NOT...
THERE'S NOBODY LOOKING, ADRIAN. JUST...JUST PUSH ME IN. I'LL SINK LIKE A ROCK.
BUT...BUT THEY'D KNOW *I* DID IT...THEY'D...FIGURE IT *OUT*, THEY...
NO, THEY WOULDN'T. TELL THEM YOU CAME HOME, FOUND ME GONE. THEY'LL FIGURE IT WAS A ROBBERY OR SOMETHING. A CRIPPLE, EASY PICKINGS...
MARCUS, COME ON, THIS...THIS ISN'T FUNNY...
YOU GOT NO MOTIVE. THEY'D HAVE NO REASON TO PIN IT ON YOU...
EVEN IF THEY DIDN'T, I...I COULDN'T, I...

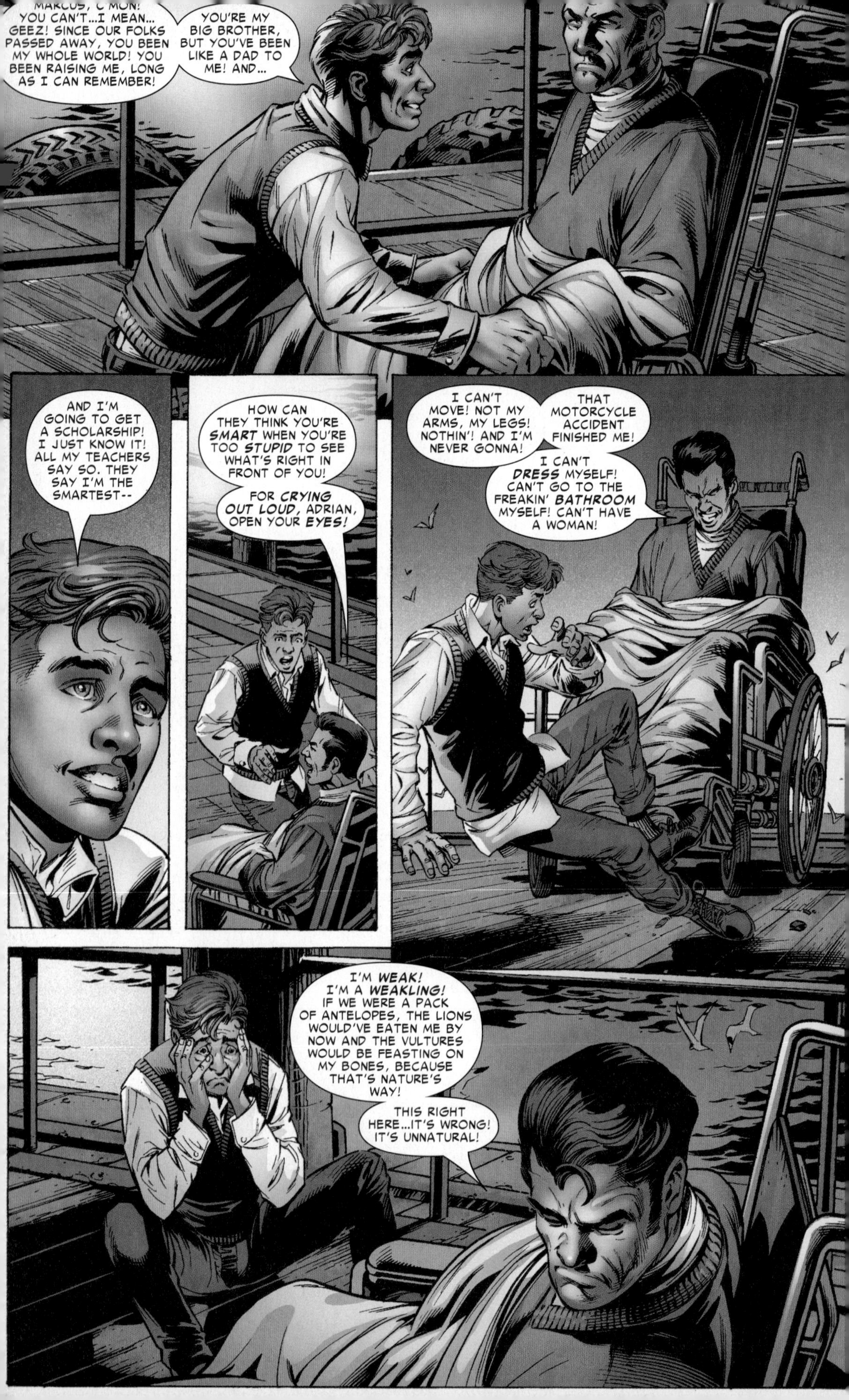
MARCUS, C'MON! YOU CAN'T...I MEAN... GEEZ! SINCE OUR FOLKS PASSED AWAY, YOU BEEN MY WHOLE WORLD! YOU BEEN RAISING ME, LONG AS I CAN REMEMBER!
YOU'RE MY BIG BROTHER, BUT YOU'VE BEEN LIKE A DAD TO ME! AND...
AND I'M GOING TO GET A SCHOLARSHIP! I JUST KNOW IT! ALL MY TEACHERS SAY SO. THEY SAY I'M THE SMARTEST--
HOW CAN THEY THINK YOU'RE SMART WHEN YOU'RE TOO STUPID TO SEE WHAT'S RIGHT IN FRONT OF YOU!
FOR CRYING OUT LOUD, ADRIAN, OPEN YOUR EYES!
I CAN'T MOVE! NOT MY ARMS, MY LEGS! NOTHIN'! AND I'M NEVER GONNA!
THAT MOTORCYCLE ACCIDENT FINISHED ME!
I CAN'T DRESS MYSELF! CAN'T GO TO THE FREAKIN' BATHROOM MYSELF! CAN'T HAVE A WOMAN!
I'M WEAK! I'M A WEAKLING! IF WE WERE A PACK OF ANTELOPES, THE LIONS WOULD'VE EATEN ME BY NOW AND THE VULTURES WOULD BE FEASTING ON MY BONES, BECAUSE THAT'S NATURE'S WAY!
THIS RIGHT HERE...IT'S WRONG! IT'S UNNATURAL!

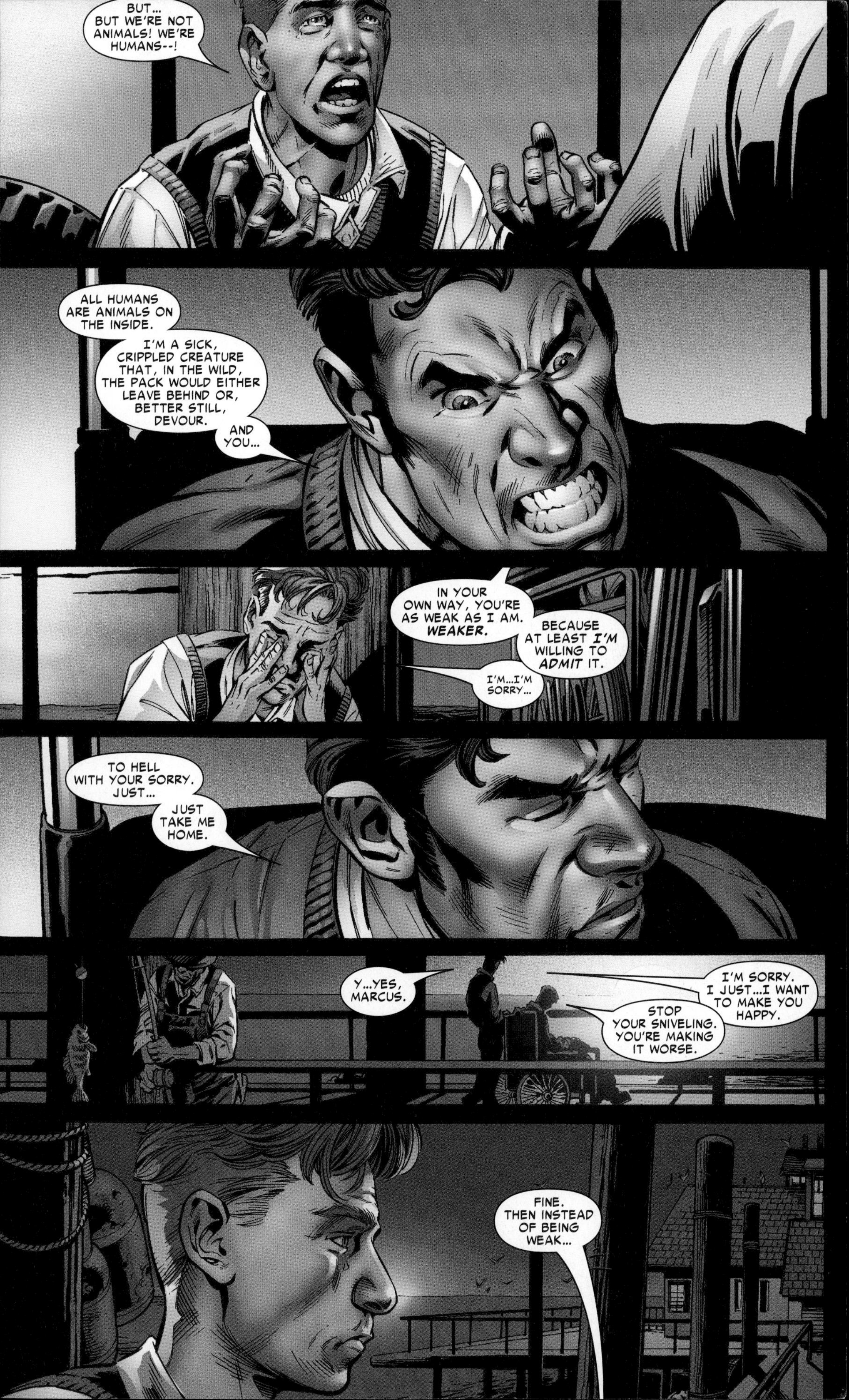
BUT... BUT WE'RE NOT ANIMALS! WE'RE HUMANS--!
ALL HUMANS ARE ANIMALS ON THE INSIDE.
I'M A SICK, CRIPPLED CREATURE THAT, IN THE WILD, THE PACK WOULD EITHER LEAVE BEHIND OR, BETTER STILL, DEVOUR.
AND YOU...
IN YOUR OWN WAY, YOU'RE AS WEAK AS I AM. WEAKER.
BECAUSE AT LEAST I'M WILLING TO ADMIT IT.
I'M...I'M SORRY...
TO HELL WITH YOUR SORRY. JUST...
JUST TAKE ME HOME.
Y...YES, MARCUS.
I'M SORRY. I JUST...I WANT TO MAKE YOU HAPPY.
STOP YOUR SNIVELING. YOU'RE MAKING IT WORSE.
FINE. THEN INSTEAD OF BEING WEAK...

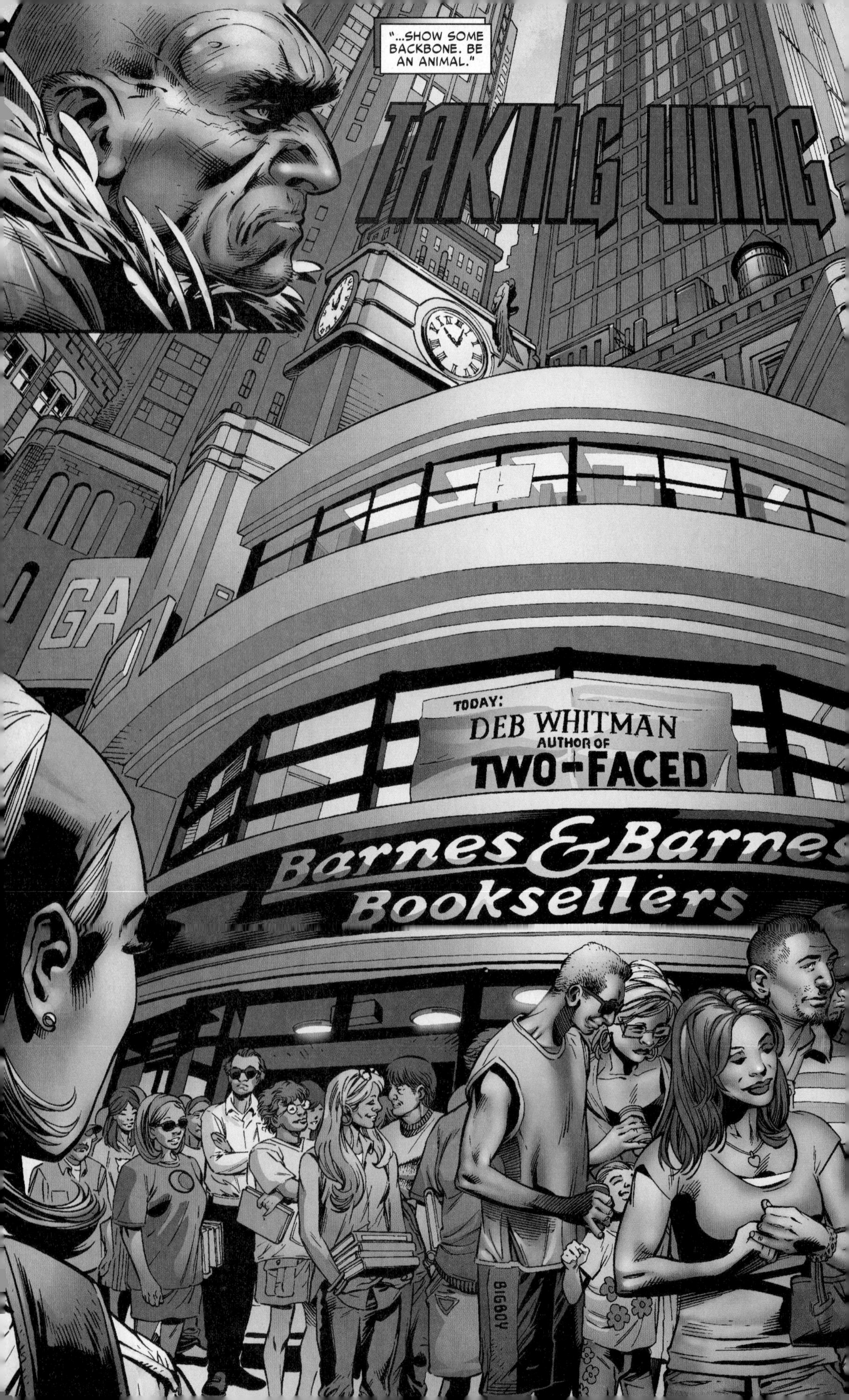
"...SHOW SOME BACKBONE. BE AN ANIMAL."
TAKING WING
GA
TODAY:
DEB WHITMAN
AUTHOR OF
TWO-FACED
Barnes & Barnes
Booksellers
BIGBOY

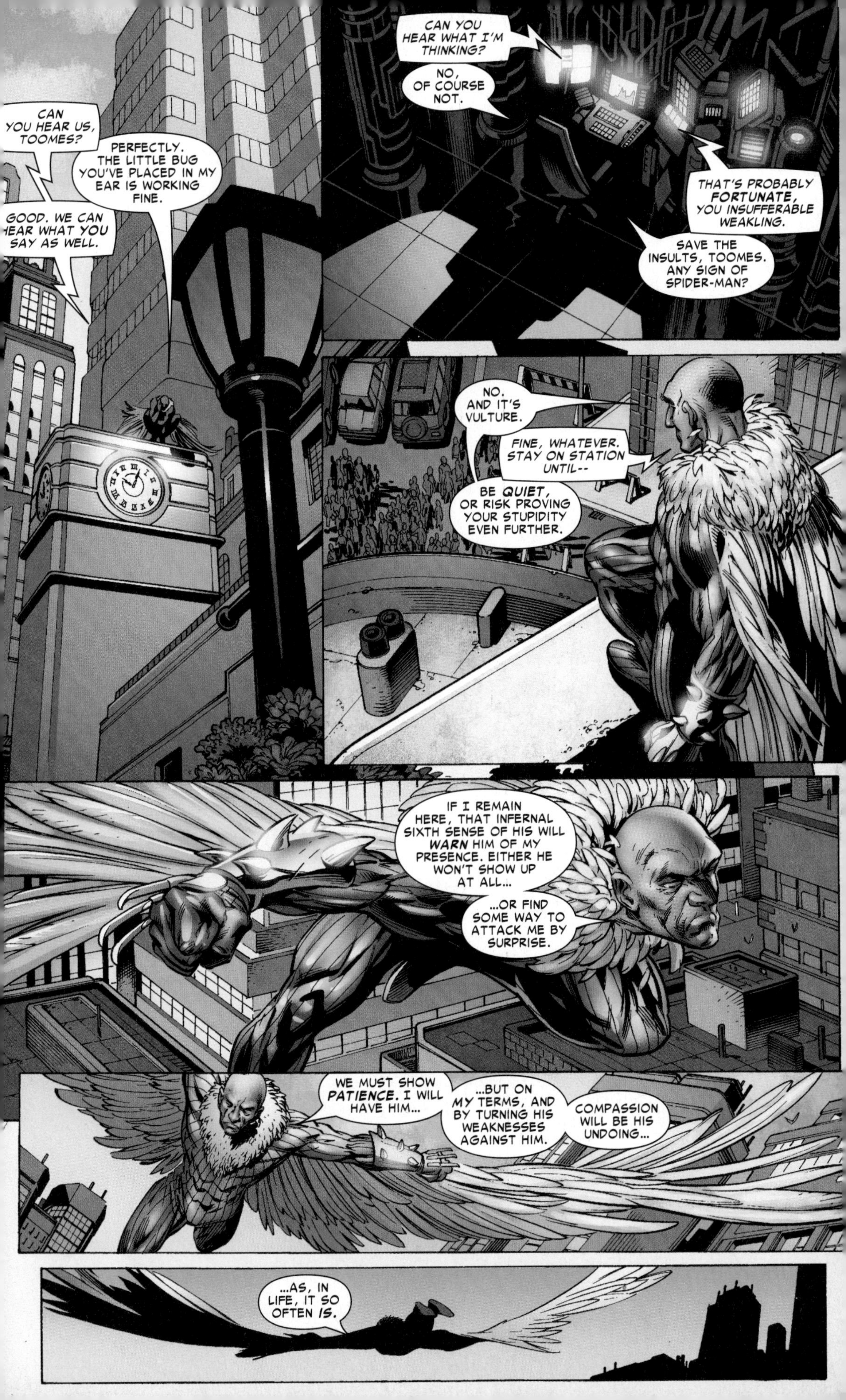
CAN YOU HEAR US, TOOMES?
PERFECTLY. THE LITTLE BUG YOU'VE PLACED IN MY EAR IS WORKING FINE.
GOOD. WE CAN HEAR WHAT YOU SAY AS WELL.
CAN YOU HEAR WHAT I'M THINKING?
NO, OF COURSE NOT.
THAT'S PROBABLY FORTUNATE, YOU INSUFFERABLE WEAKLING.
SAVE THE INSULTS, TOOMES. ANY SIGN OF SPIDER-MAN?
NO. AND IT'S VULTURE.
FINE, WHATEVER. STAY ON STATION UNTIL--
BE QUIET, OR RISK PROVING YOUR STUPIDITY EVEN FURTHER.
IF I REMAIN HERE, THAT INFERNAL SIXTH SENSE OF HIS WILL WARN HIM OF MY PRESENCE. EITHER HE WON'T SHOW UP AT ALL...
...OR FIND SOME WAY TO ATTACK ME BY SURPRISE.
WE MUST SHOW PATIENCE. I WILL HAVE HIM...
...BUT ON MY TERMS, AND BY TURNING HIS WEAKNESSES AGAINST HIM.
COMPASSION WILL BE HIS UNDOING...
...AS, IN LIFE, IT SO OFTEN IS.

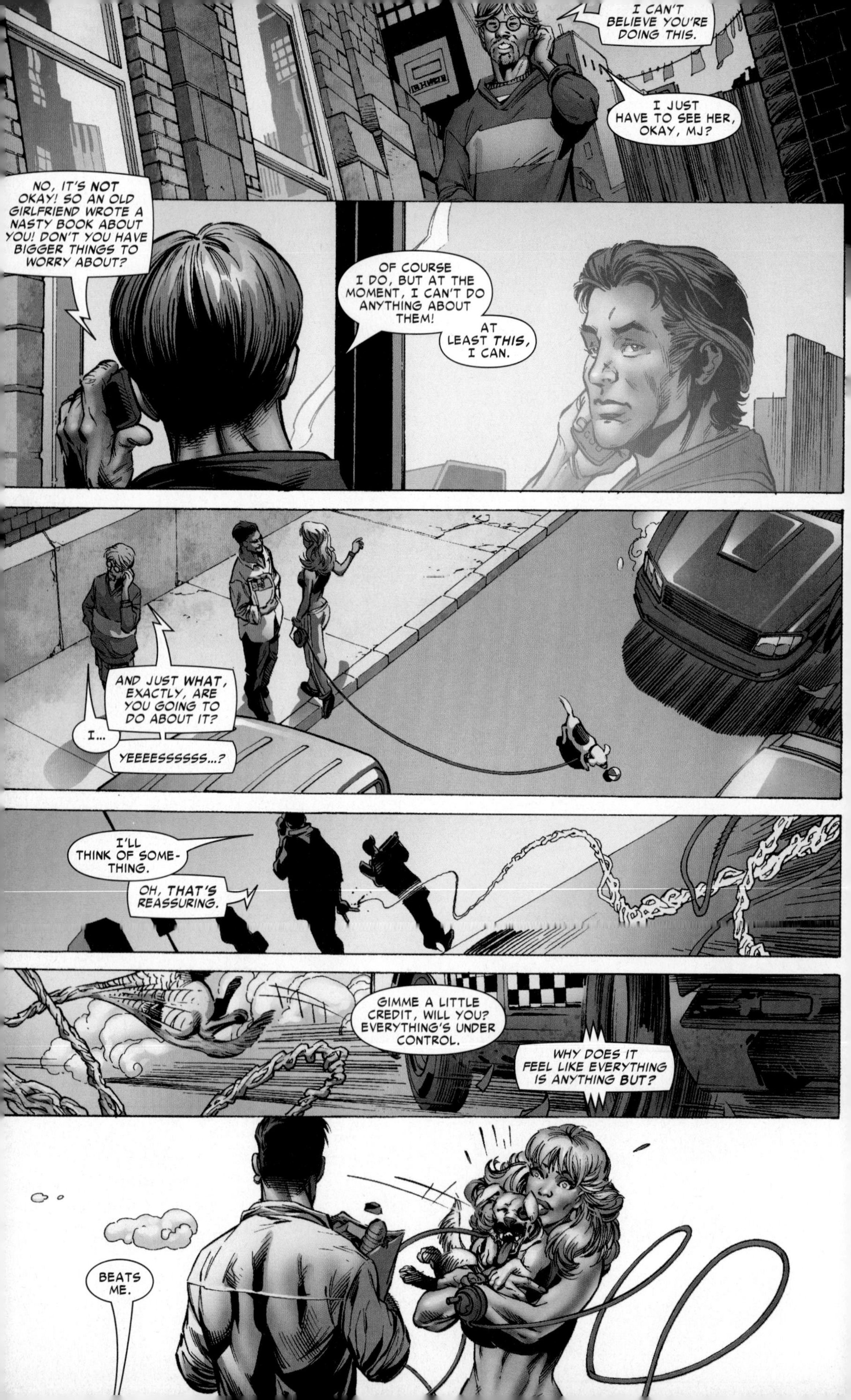
I CAN'T BELIEVE YOU'RE DOING THIS.
I JUST HAVE TO SEE HER, OKAY, MJ?
NO, IT'S NOT OKAY! SO AN OLD GIRLFRIEND WROTE A NASTY BOOK ABOUT YOU! DON'T YOU HAVE BIGGER THINGS TO WORRY ABOUT?
OF COURSE I DO, BUT AT THE MOMENT, I CAN'T DO ANYTHING ABOUT THEM!
AT LEAST THIS, I CAN.
AND JUST WHAT, EXACTLY, ARE YOU GOING TO DO ABOUT IT?
I...
YEEEESSSSSS...?
I'LL THINK OF SOME-THING.
OH, THAT'S REASSURING.
GIMME A LITTLE CREDIT, WILL YOU? EVERYTHING'S UNDER CONTROL.
WHY DOES IT FEEL LIKE EVERYTHING IS ANYTHING BUT?
BEATS ME.

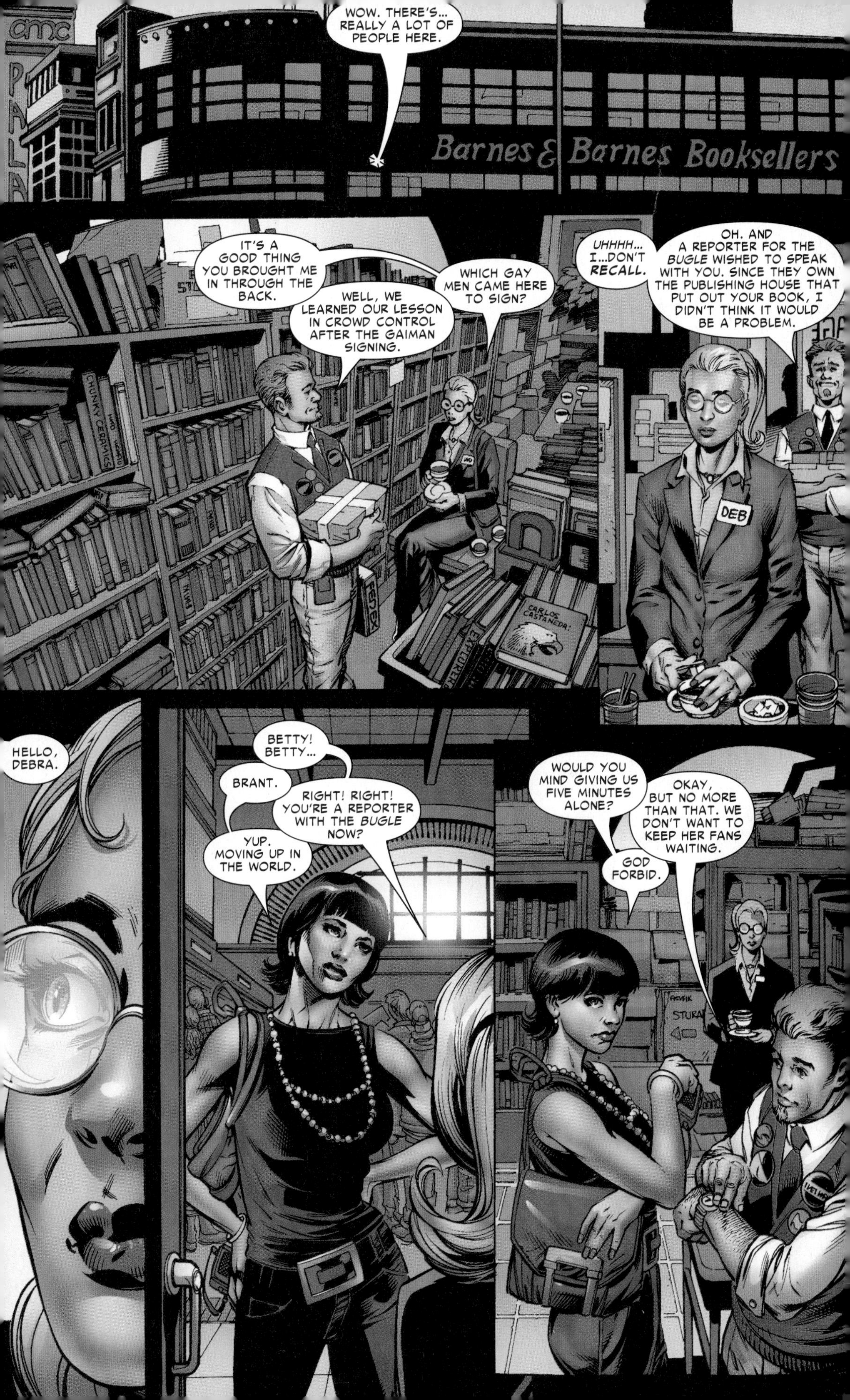
WOW. THERE'S... REALLY A LOT OF PEOPLE HERE.
Barnes & Barnes Booksellers
IT'S A GOOD THING YOU BROUGHT ME IN THROUGH THE BACK.
WELL, WE LEARNED OUR LESSON IN CROWD CONTROL AFTER THE GAIMAN SIGNING.
WHICH GAY MEN CAME HERE TO SIGN?
CHUNKY CERAMICS
CARLOS CASTANEDA:
UHHHH... I...DON'T RECALL.
OH. AND A REPORTER FOR THE BUGLE WISHED TO SPEAK WITH YOU. SINCE THEY OWN THE PUBLISHING HOUSE THAT PUT OUT YOUR BOOK, I DIDN'T THINK IT WOULD BE A PROBLEM.
DEB
HELLO, DEBRA.
BETTY! BETTY...
BRANT.
RIGHT! RIGHT! YOU'RE A REPORTER WITH THE BUGLE NOW?
YUP. MOVING UP IN THE WORLD.
WOULD YOU MIND GIVING US FIVE MINUTES ALONE?
OKAY, BUT NO MORE THAN THAT. WE DON'T WANT TO KEEP HER FANS WAITING.
GOD FORBID.

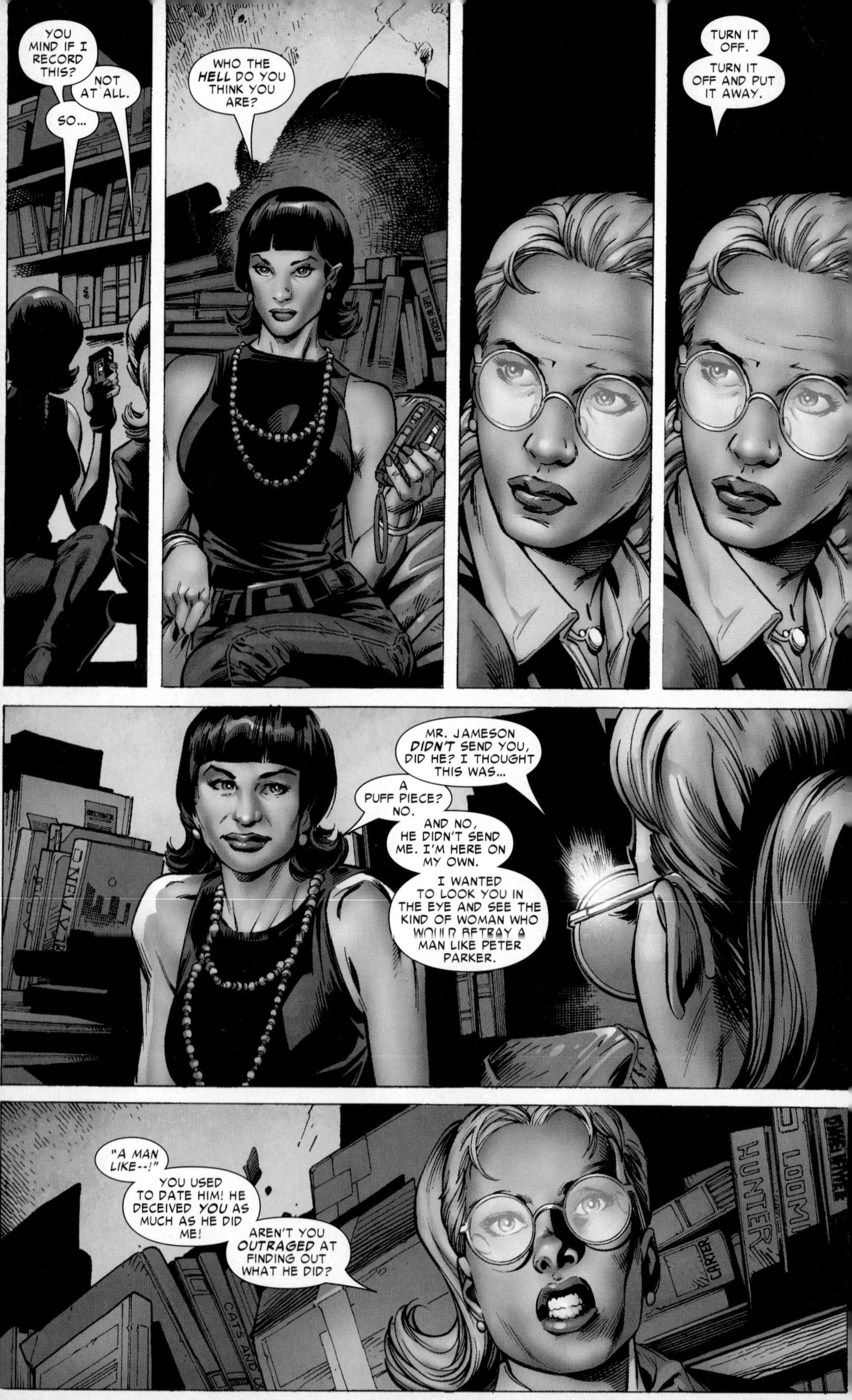
YOU MIND IF I RECORD THIS?
NOT AT ALL.
SO...
WHO THE HELL DO YOU THINK YOU ARE?
TURN IT OFF.
TURN IT OFF AND PUT IT AWAY.
MR. JAMESON DIDN'T SEND YOU, DID HE? I THOUGHT THIS WAS...
A PUFF PIECE? NO.
AND NO, HE DIDN'T SEND ME. I'M HERE ON MY OWN.
I WANTED TO LOOK YOU IN THE EYE AND SEE THE KIND OF WOMAN WHO WOULD BETRAY A MAN LIKE PETER PARKER.
"A MAN LIKE--!"
YOU USED TO DATE HIM! HE DECEIVED YOU AS MUCH AS HE DID ME!
AREN'T YOU OUTRAGED AT FINDING OUT WHAT HE DID?

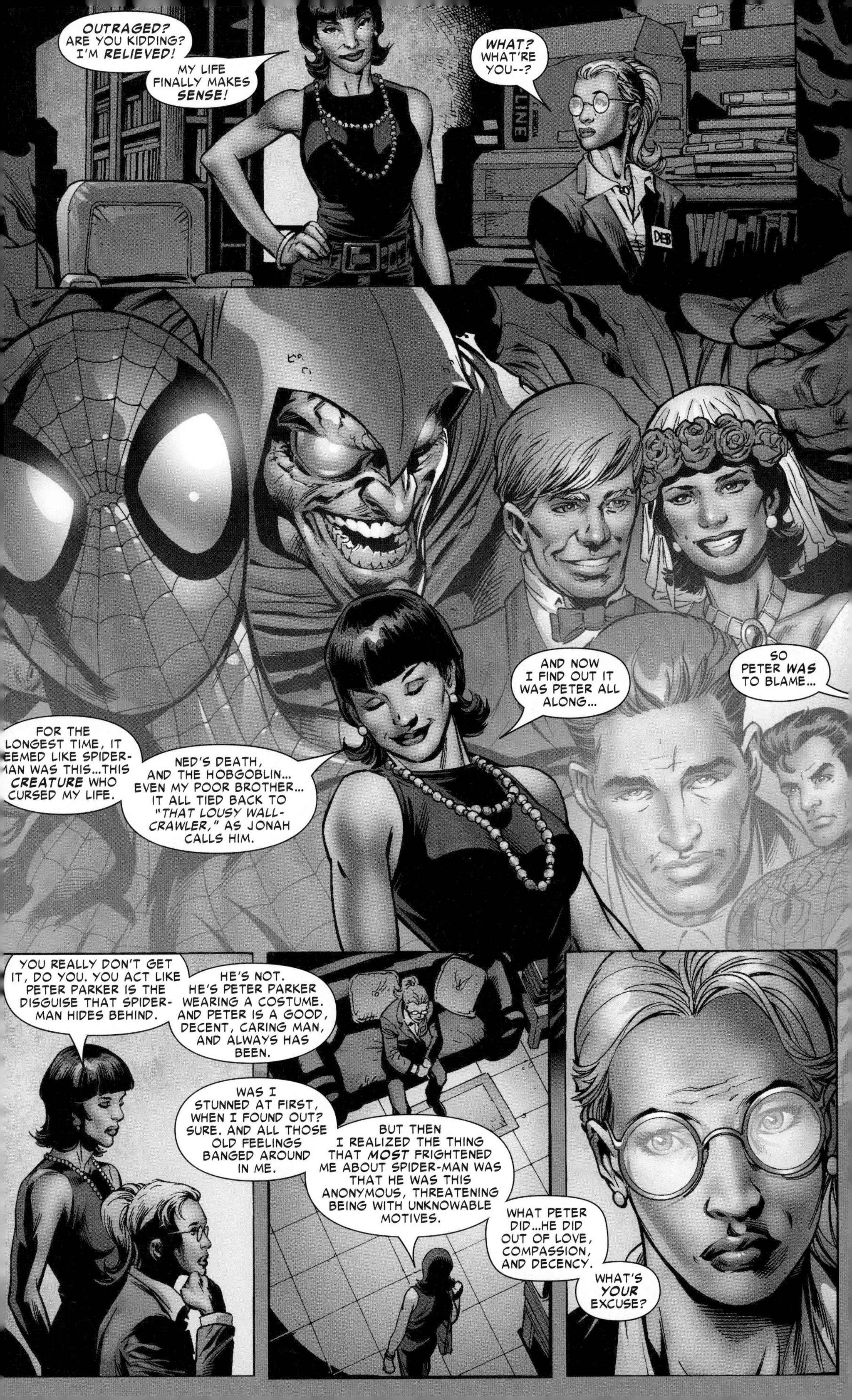
OUTRAGED? ARE YOU KIDDING? I'M RELIEVED!
MY LIFE FINALLY MAKES SENSE!
WHAT? WHAT'RE YOU--?
DEB
FOR THE LONGEST TIME, IT EEMED LIKE SPIDER-AN WAS THIS...THIS CREATURE WHO CURSED MY LIFE.
NED'S DEATH, AND THE HOBGOBLIN... EVEN MY POOR BROTHER... IT ALL TIED BACK TO "THAT LOUSY WALL-CRAWLER," AS JONAH CALLS HIM.
AND NOW I FIND OUT IT WAS PETER ALL ALONG...
SO PETER WAS TO BLAME...
YOU REALLY DON'T GET IT, DO YOU. YOU ACT LIKE PETER PARKER IS THE DISGUISE THAT SPIDER-MAN HIDES BEHIND.
HE'S NOT. HE'S PETER PARKER WEARING A COSTUME. AND PETER IS A GOOD, DECENT, CARING MAN, AND ALWAYS HAS BEEN.
WAS I STUNNED AT FIRST, WHEN I FOUND OUT? SURE. AND ALL THOSE OLD FEELINGS BANGED AROUND IN ME.
BUT THEN I REALIZED THE THING THAT MOST FRIGHTENED ME ABOUT SPIDER-MAN WAS THAT HE WAS THIS ANONYMOUS, THREATENING BEING WITH UNKNOWABLE MOTIVES.
WHAT PETER DID...HE DID OUT OF LOVE, COMPASSION, AND DECENCY.
WHAT'S YOUR EXCUSE?

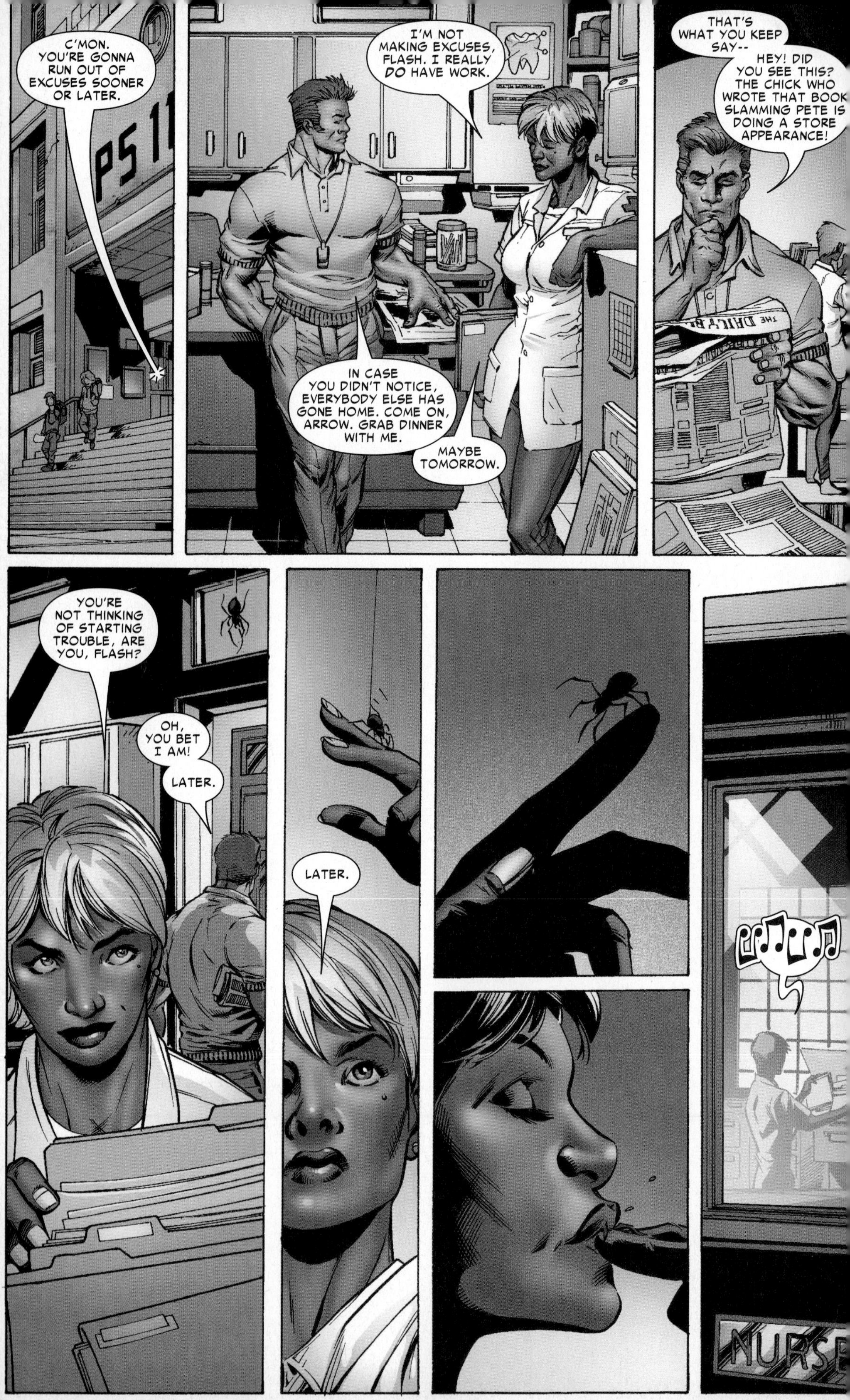
C'MON. YOU'RE GONNA RUN OUT OF EXCUSES SOONER OR LATER.
PS 11
I'M NOT MAKING EXCUSES, FLASH. I REALLY DO HAVE WORK.
IN CASE YOU DIDN'T NOTICE, EVERYBODY ELSE HAS GONE HOME. COME ON, ARROW. GRAB DINNER WITH ME.
MAYBE TOMORROW.
THAT'S WHAT YOU KEEP SAY--
HEY! DID YOU SEE THIS? THE CHICK WHO WROTE THAT BOOK SLAMMING PETE IS DOING A STORE APPEARANCE!
THE DAILY B
YOU'RE NOT THINKING OF STARTING TROUBLE, ARE YOU, FLASH?
OH, YOU BET I AM!
LATER.
LATER.
NURSE

ONE BOOK TO A CUSTOMER, PLEASE! MS. WHITMAN ONLY HAS TWO HOURS!

YOUR BOOK HAS MADE A HUGE DIFFERENCE IN MY LIFE!

WELL, I'M PLEASED TO HEAR THAT.

I'M STARTING TO THINK MY BOYFRIEND MIGHT ACTUALLY BE A SUPER-VILLAIN. IT WOULD EXPLAIN SO MUCH.

WHAT DO *YOU* THINK?

WELL...THESE DAYS THERE ARE PEOPLE YOU CAN CALL. THEY CAN CHECK HIM OUT, I SUPPOSE. I THINK S.H.I.E.L.D. HAS A HOTLINE NOW.

HOLY COW. IT'S LIKE NAZI GERMANY. CALL THE AUTHORITIES AND RAT OUT YOUR LOVED ONES.

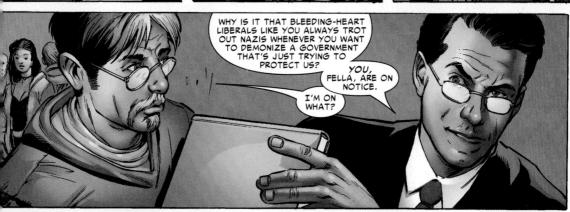

WHY IS IT THAT BLEEDING-HEART LIBERALS LIKE YOU ALWAYS TROT OUT NAZIS WHENEVER YOU WANT TO DEMONIZE A GOVERNMENT THAT'S JUST TRYING TO PROTECT US?

YOU, FELLA, ARE ON NOTICE.

I'M ON *WHAT?*

WAAAIIT A MINUTE. AREN'T YOU--?

NOPE.

BECAUSE YOU SURE *LOOK* LIKE...

NOT HIM. MOVIN' ON.

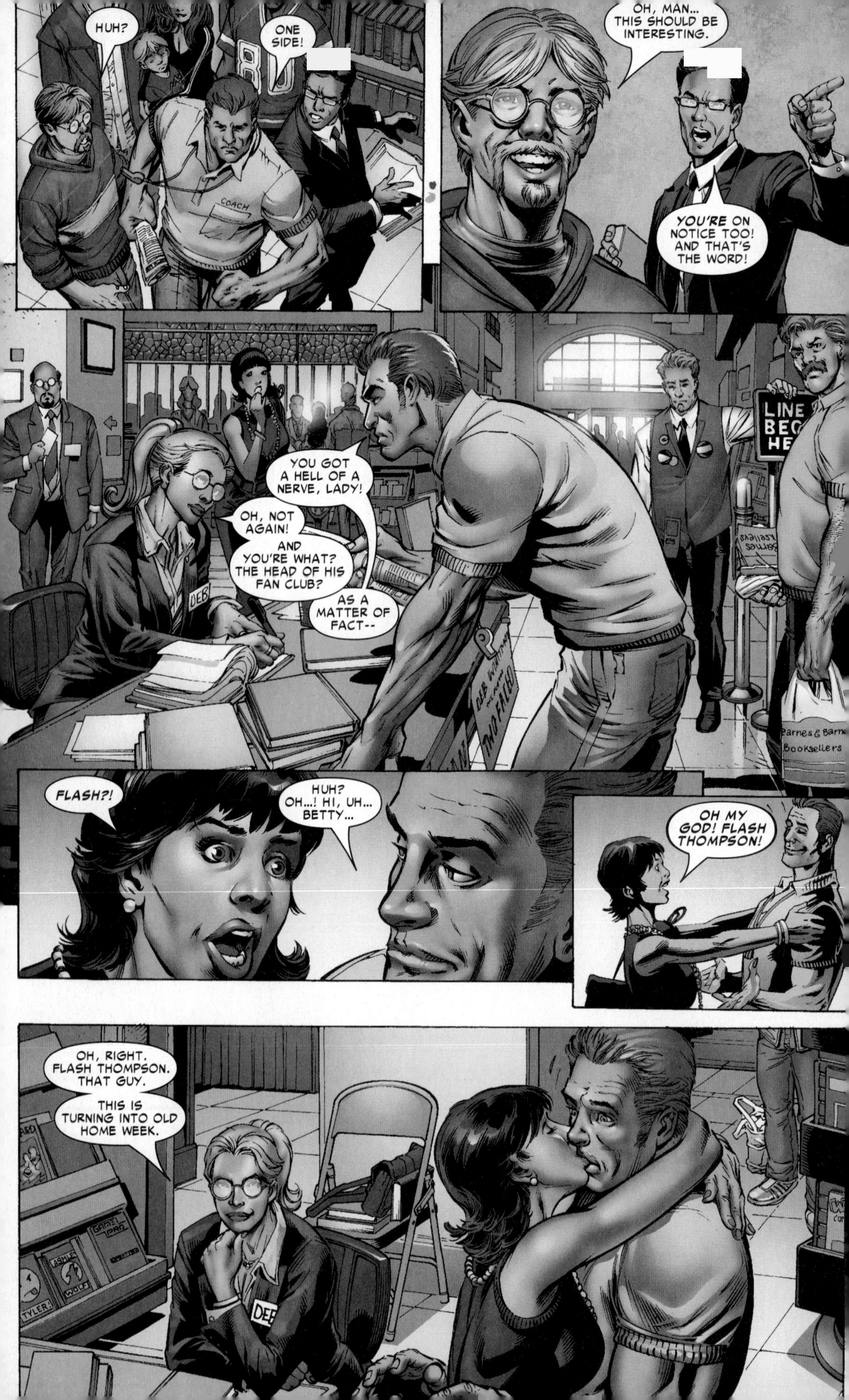
HUH?
ONE SIDE!
OH, MAN... THIS SHOULD BE INTERESTING.
YOU'RE ON NOTICE TOO! AND THAT'S THE WORD!
YOU GOT A HELL OF A NERVE, LADY!
OH, NOT AGAIN!
AND YOU'RE WHAT? THE HEAD OF HIS FAN CLUB?
AS A MATTER OF FACT--
FLASH?!
HUH? OH...! HI, UH... BETTY...
OH MY GOD! FLASH THOMPSON!
OH, RIGHT. FLASH THOMPSON. THAT GUY.
THIS IS TURNING INTO OLD HOME WEEK.

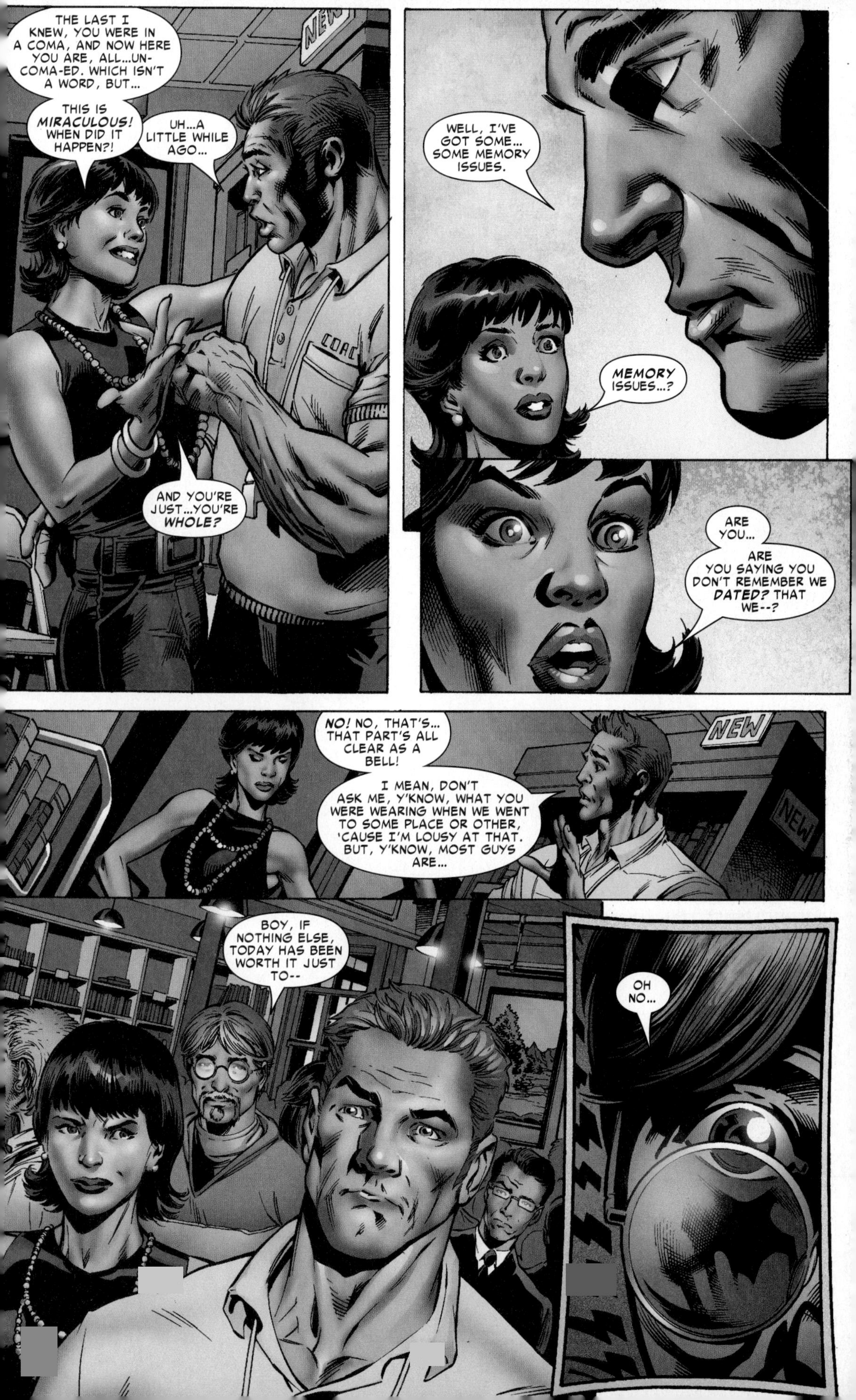
THE LAST I KNEW, YOU WERE IN A COMA, AND NOW HERE YOU ARE, ALL...UN-COMA-ED. WHICH ISN'T A WORD, BUT...
THIS IS MIRACULOUS! WHEN DID IT HAPPEN?!
UH...A LITTLE WHILE AGO...
AND YOU'RE JUST...YOU'RE WHOLE?
WELL, I'VE GOT SOME... SOME MEMORY ISSUES.
MEMORY ISSUES...?
ARE YOU...
ARE YOU SAYING YOU DON'T REMEMBER WE DATED? THAT WE--?
NO! NO, THAT'S... THAT PART'S ALL CLEAR AS A BELL!
I MEAN, DON'T ASK ME, Y'KNOW, WHAT YOU WERE WEARING WHEN WE WENT TO SOME PLACE OR OTHER, 'CAUSE I'M LOUSY AT THAT. BUT, Y'KNOW, MOST GUYS ARE...
BOY, IF NOTHING ELSE, TODAY HAS BEEN WORTH IT JUST TO--
OH NO...

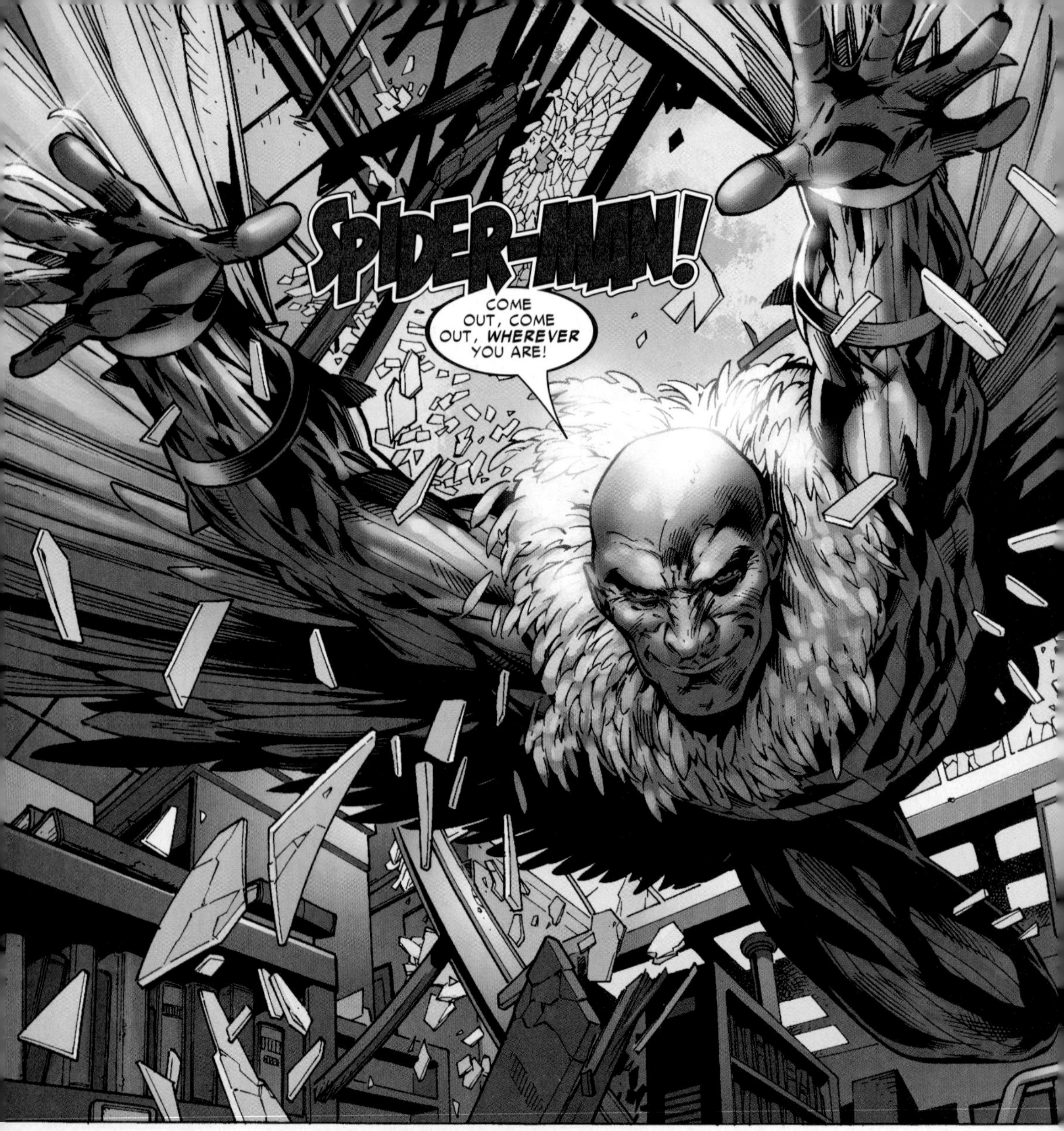
SPIDER-MAN!
COME OUT, COME OUT, WHEREVER YOU ARE!

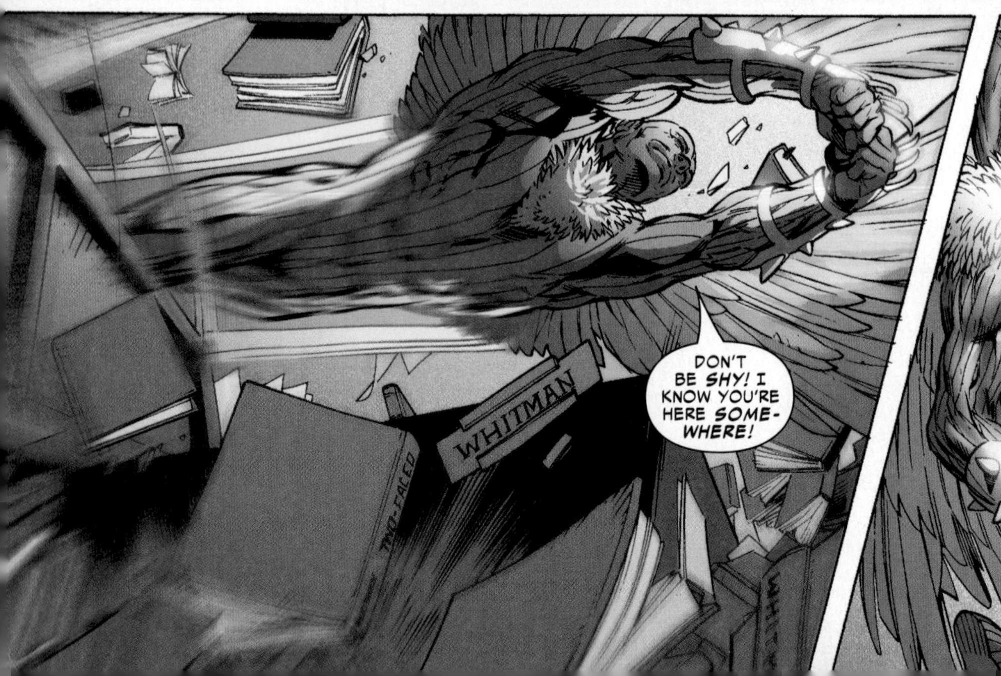
DON'T BE SHY! I KNOW YOU'RE HERE SOME-WHERE!
WHITMAN

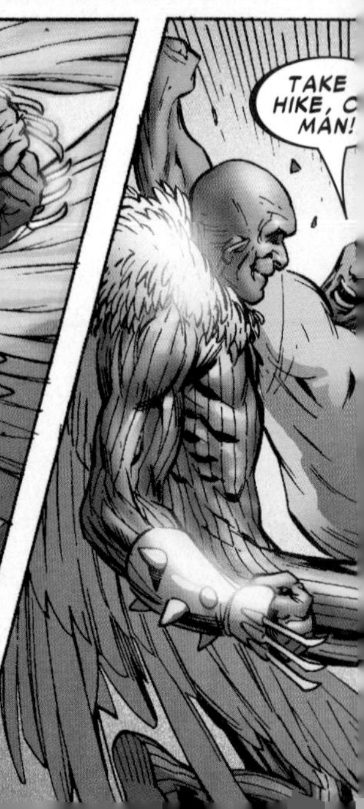
TAKE HIKE, C MAN!

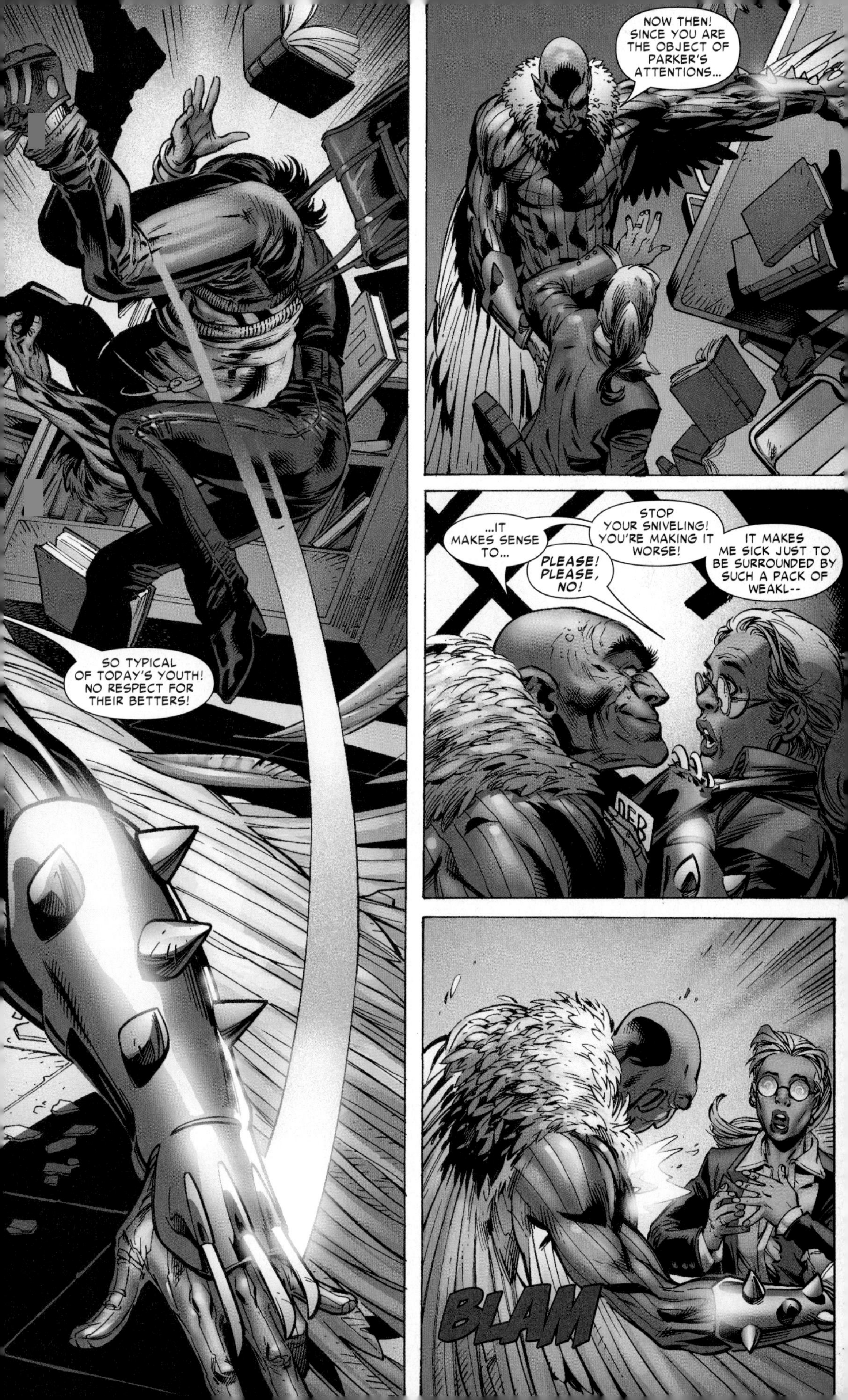
SO TYPICAL OF TODAY'S YOUTH! NO RESPECT FOR THEIR BETTERS!
NOW THEN! SINCE YOU ARE THE OBJECT OF PARKER'S ATTENTIONS...
...IT MAKES SENSE TO...
STOP YOUR SNIVELING! YOU'RE MAKING IT WORSE!
PLEASE! PLEASE, NO!
IT MAKES ME SICK JUST TO BE SURROUNDED BY SUCH A PACK OF WEAKL--
BLAM

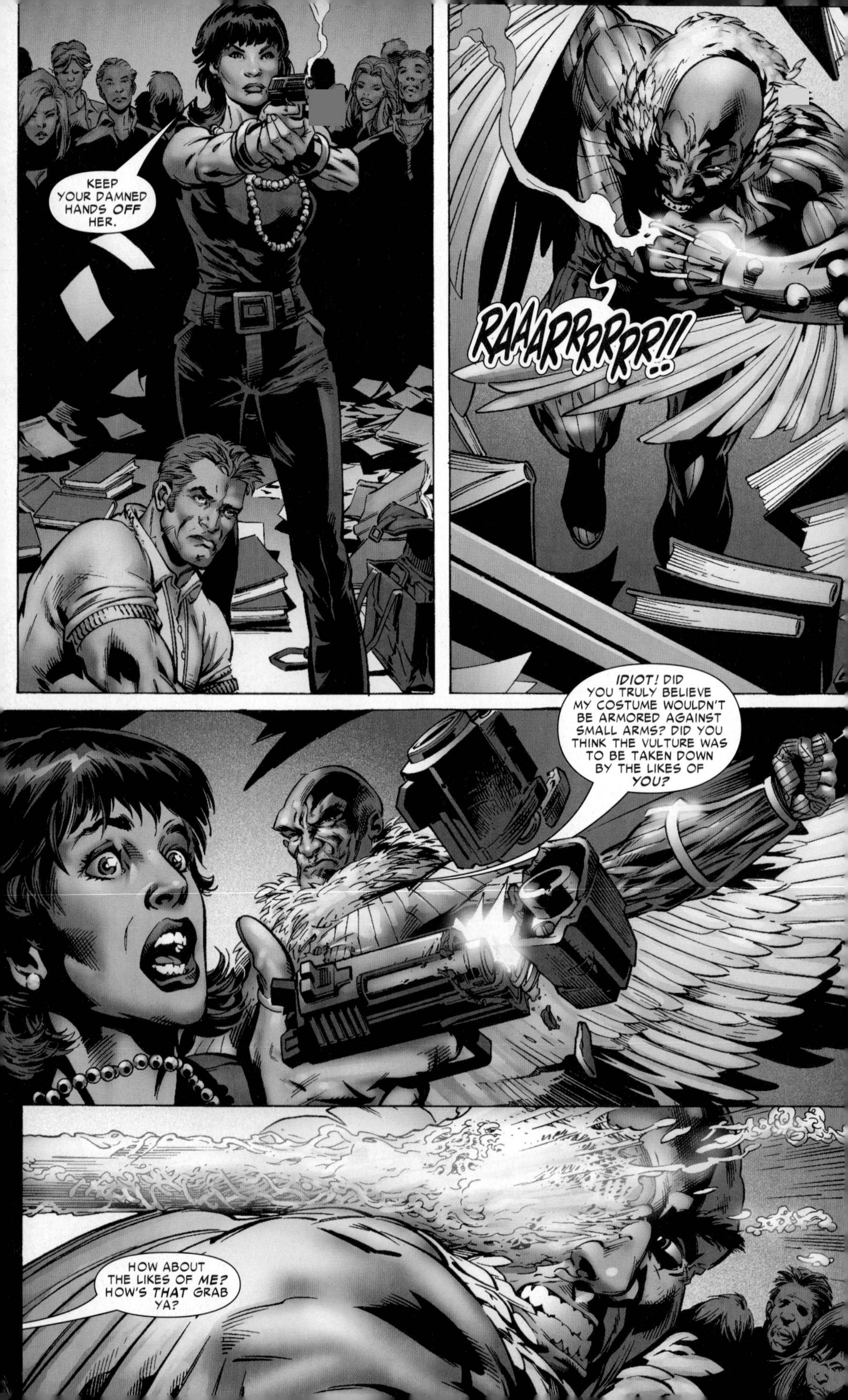
KEEP YOUR DAMNED HANDS OFF HER.
RAAARRRRRR!!
IDIOT! DID YOU TRULY BELIEVE MY COSTUME WOULDN'T BE ARMORED AGAINST SMALL ARMS? DID YOU THINK THE VULTURE WAS TO BE TAKEN DOWN BY THE LIKES OF YOU?
HOW ABOUT THE LIKES OF ME? HOW'S THAT GRAB YA?

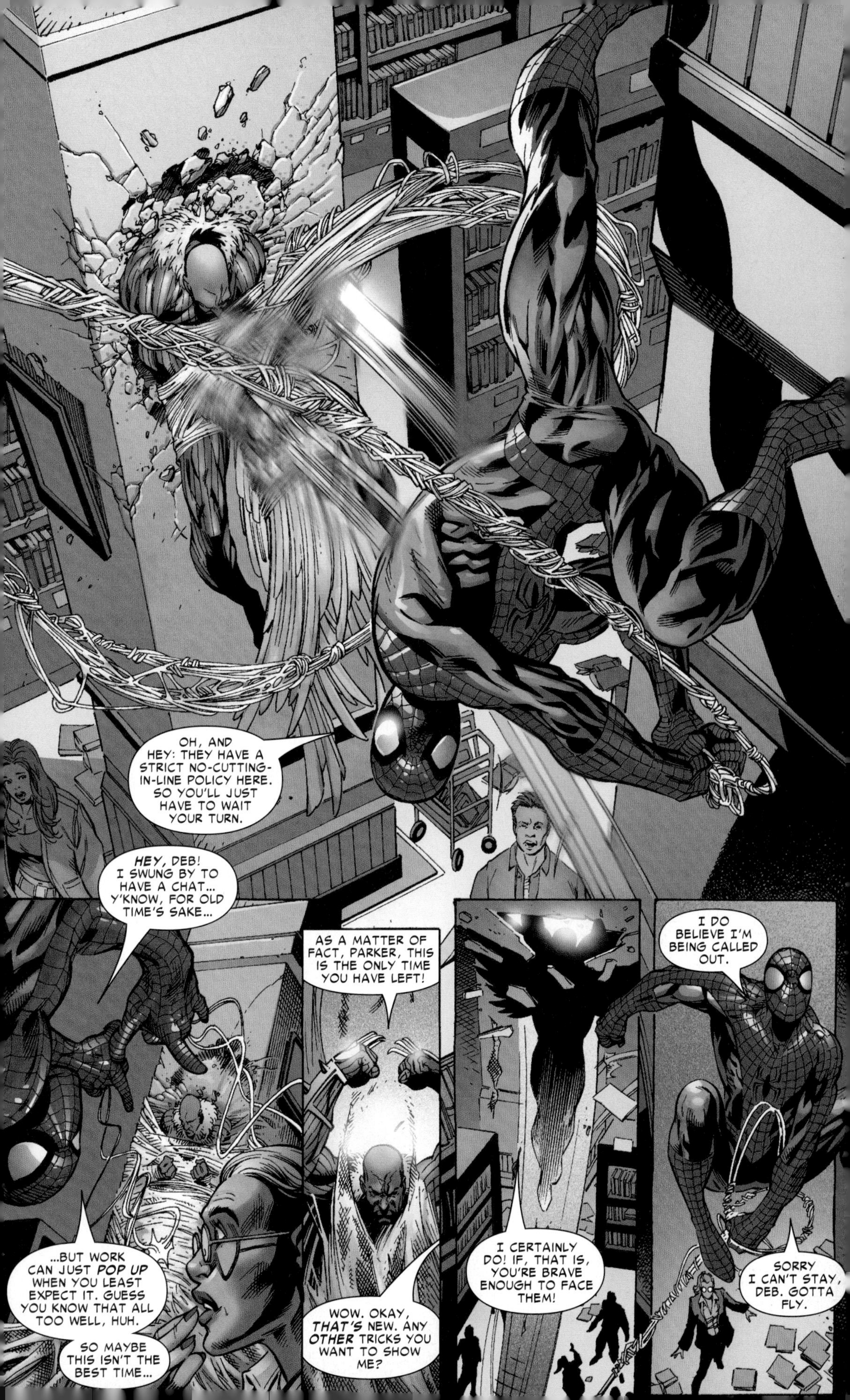
OH, AND HEY: THEY HAVE A STRICT NO-CUTTING-IN-LINE POLICY HERE. SO YOU'LL JUST HAVE TO WAIT YOUR TURN.
HEY, DEB! I SWUNG BY TO HAVE A CHAT... Y'KNOW, FOR OLD TIME'S SAKE...
...BUT WORK CAN JUST POP UP WHEN YOU LEAST EXPECT IT. GUESS YOU KNOW THAT ALL TOO WELL, HUH.
SO MAYBE THIS ISN'T THE BEST TIME...
AS A MATTER OF FACT, PARKER, THIS IS THE ONLY TIME YOU HAVE LEFT!
WOW. OKAY, THAT'S NEW. ANY OTHER TRICKS YOU WANT TO SHOW ME?
I CERTAINLY DO! IF, THAT IS, YOU'RE BRAVE ENOUGH TO FACE THEM!
I DO BELIEVE I'M BEING CALLED OUT.
SORRY I CAN'T STAY, DEB. GOTTA FLY.

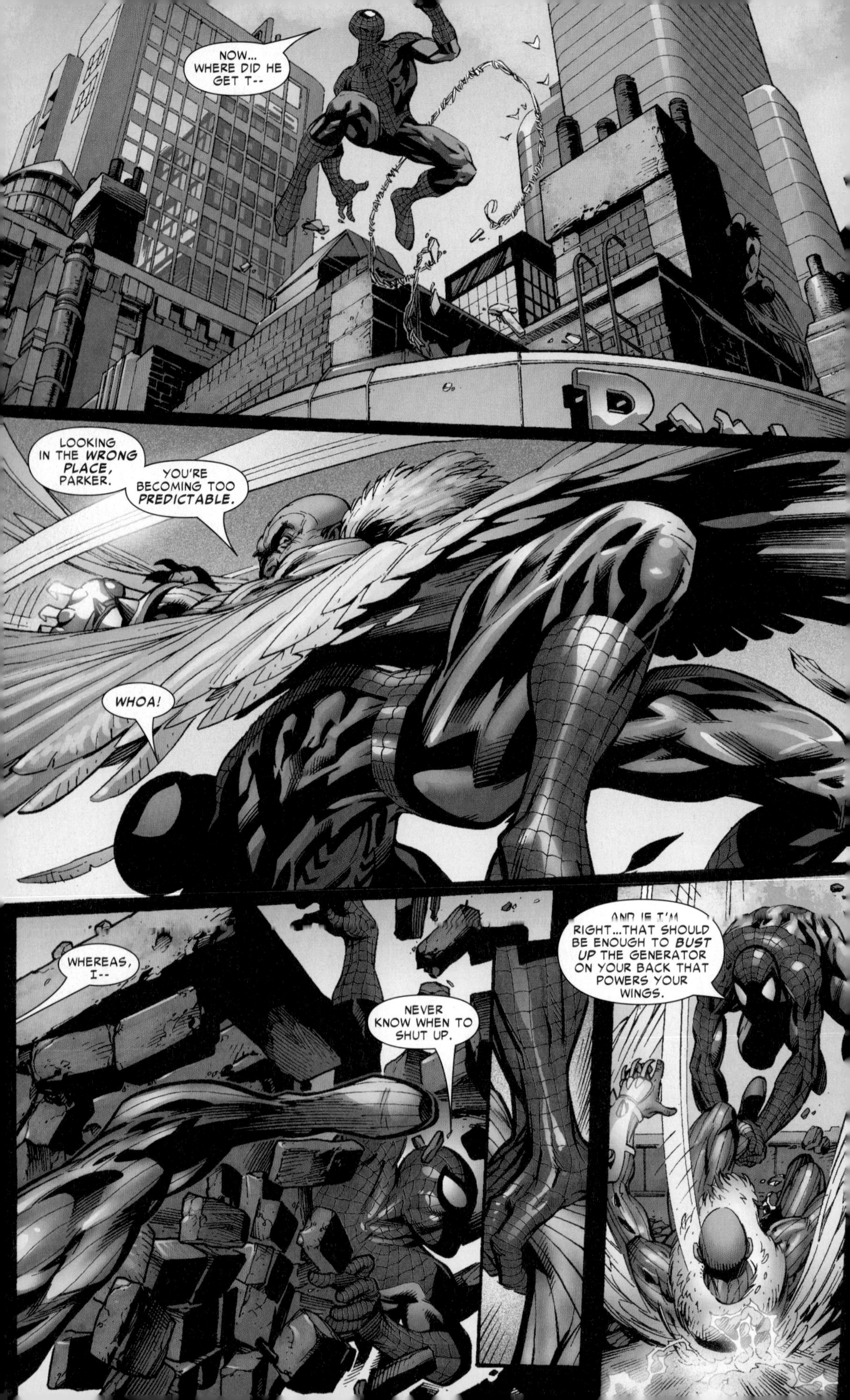
NOW... WHERE DID HE GET T--
LOOKING IN THE WRONG PLACE, PARKER.
YOU'RE BECOMING TOO PREDICTABLE.
WHOA!
WHEREAS, I--
NEVER KNOW WHEN TO SHUT UP.
AND IF I'M RIGHT...THAT SHOULD BE ENOUGH TO BUST UP THE GENERATOR ON YOUR BACK THAT POWERS YOUR WINGS.

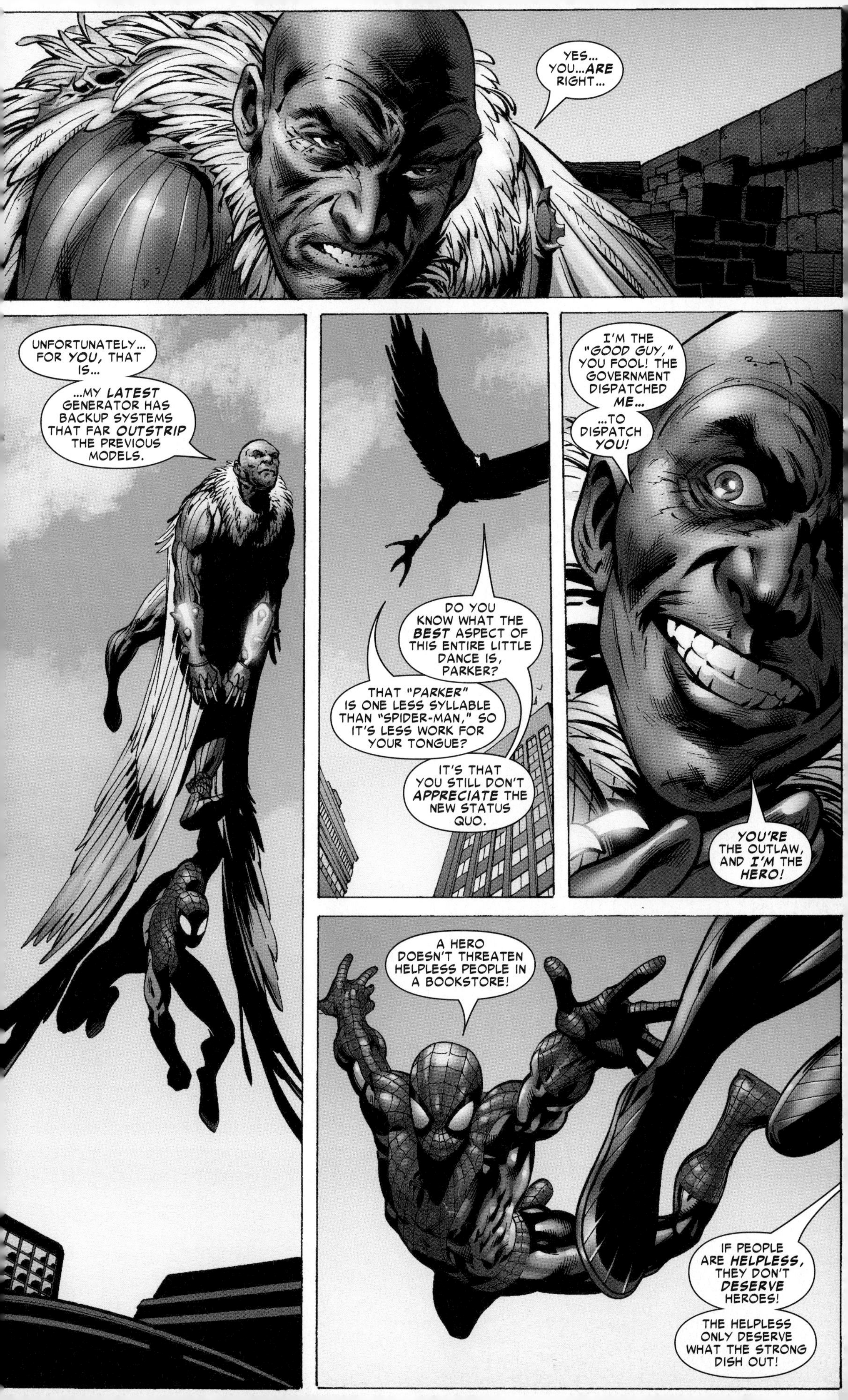
YES... YOU...ARE RIGHT...
UNFORTUNATELY... FOR YOU, THAT IS...
...MY LATEST GENERATOR HAS BACKUP SYSTEMS THAT FAR OUTSTRIP THE PREVIOUS MODELS.
DO YOU KNOW WHAT THE BEST ASPECT OF THIS ENTIRE LITTLE DANCE IS, PARKER?
THAT "PARKER" IS ONE LESS SYLLABLE THAN "SPIDER-MAN," SO IT'S LESS WORK FOR YOUR TONGUE?
IT'S THAT YOU STILL DON'T APPRECIATE THE NEW STATUS QUO.
I'M THE "GOOD GUY," YOU FOOL! THE GOVERNMENT DISPATCHED ME...
...TO DISPATCH YOU!
YOU'RE THE OUTLAW, AND I'M THE HERO!
A HERO DOESN'T THREATEN HELPLESS PEOPLE IN A BOOKSTORE!
IF PEOPLE ARE HELPLESS, THEY DON'T DESERVE HEROES!
THE HELPLESS ONLY DESERVE WHAT THE STRONG DISH OUT!

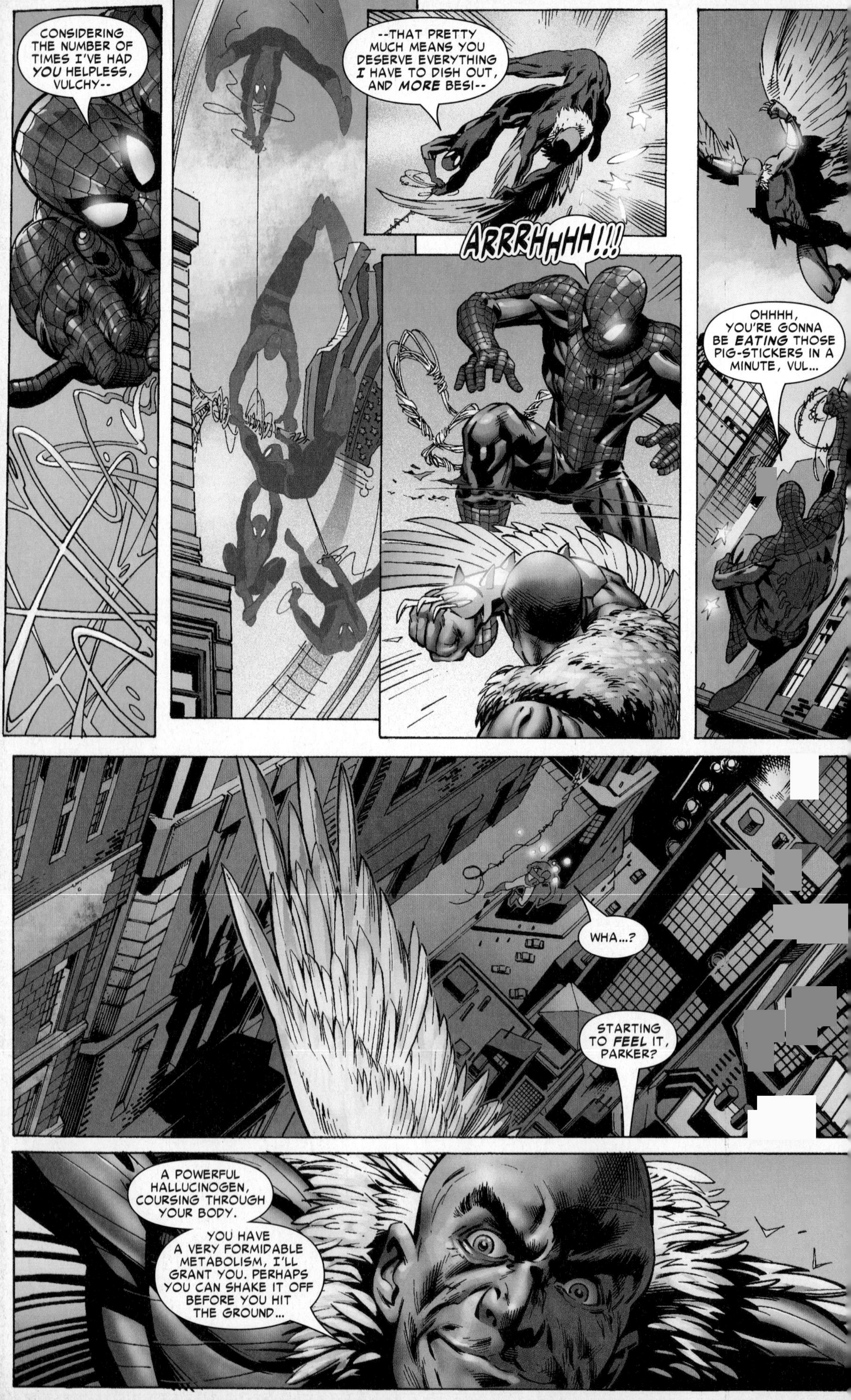
CONSIDERING THE NUMBER OF TIMES I'VE HAD YOU HELPLESS, VULCHY--
--THAT PRETTY MUCH MEANS YOU DESERVE EVERYTHING I HAVE TO DISH OUT, AND MORE BESI--
ARRRHHHH!!!
OHHHH, YOU'RE GONNA BE EATING THOSE PIG-STICKERS IN A MINUTE, VUL...
WHA...?
STARTING TO FEEL IT, PARKER?
A POWERFUL HALLUCINOGEN, COURSING THROUGH YOUR BODY.
YOU HAVE A VERY FORMIDABLE METABOLISM, I'LL GRANT YOU. PERHAPS YOU CAN SHAKE IT OFF BEFORE YOU HIT THE GROUND...

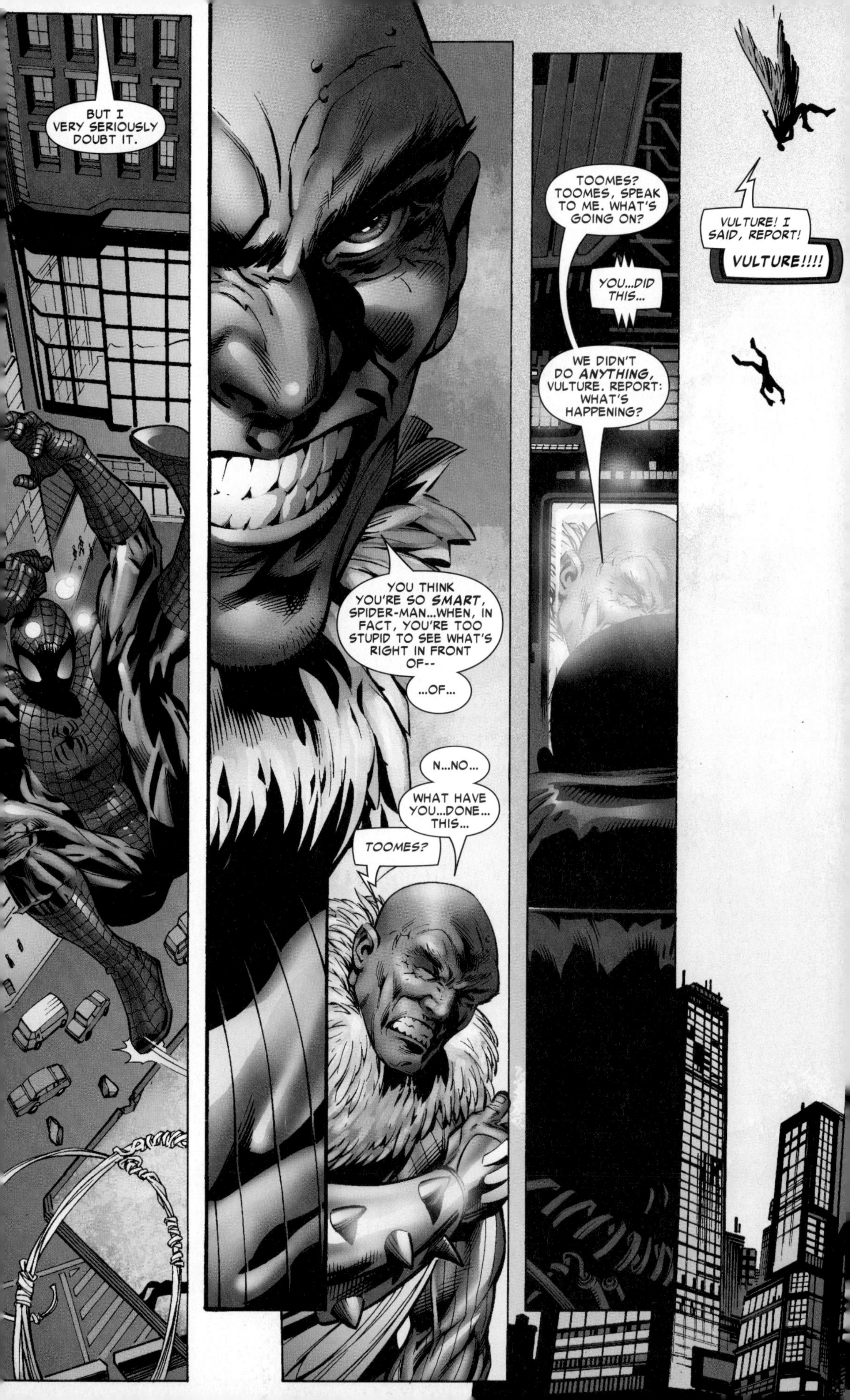

BUT I VERY SERIOUSLY DOUBT IT.
YOU THINK YOU'RE SO SMART, SPIDER-MAN...WHEN, IN FACT, YOU'RE TOO STUPID TO SEE WHAT'S RIGHT IN FRONT OF--
...OF...
N...NO...
WHAT HAVE YOU...DONE... THIS...
TOOMES?
TOOMES? TOOMES, SPEAK TO ME. WHAT'S GOING ON?
YOU...DID THIS...
WE DIDN'T DO ANYTHING, VULTURE. REPORT: WHAT'S HAPPENING?
VULTURE! I SAID, REPORT!
VULTURE!!!!

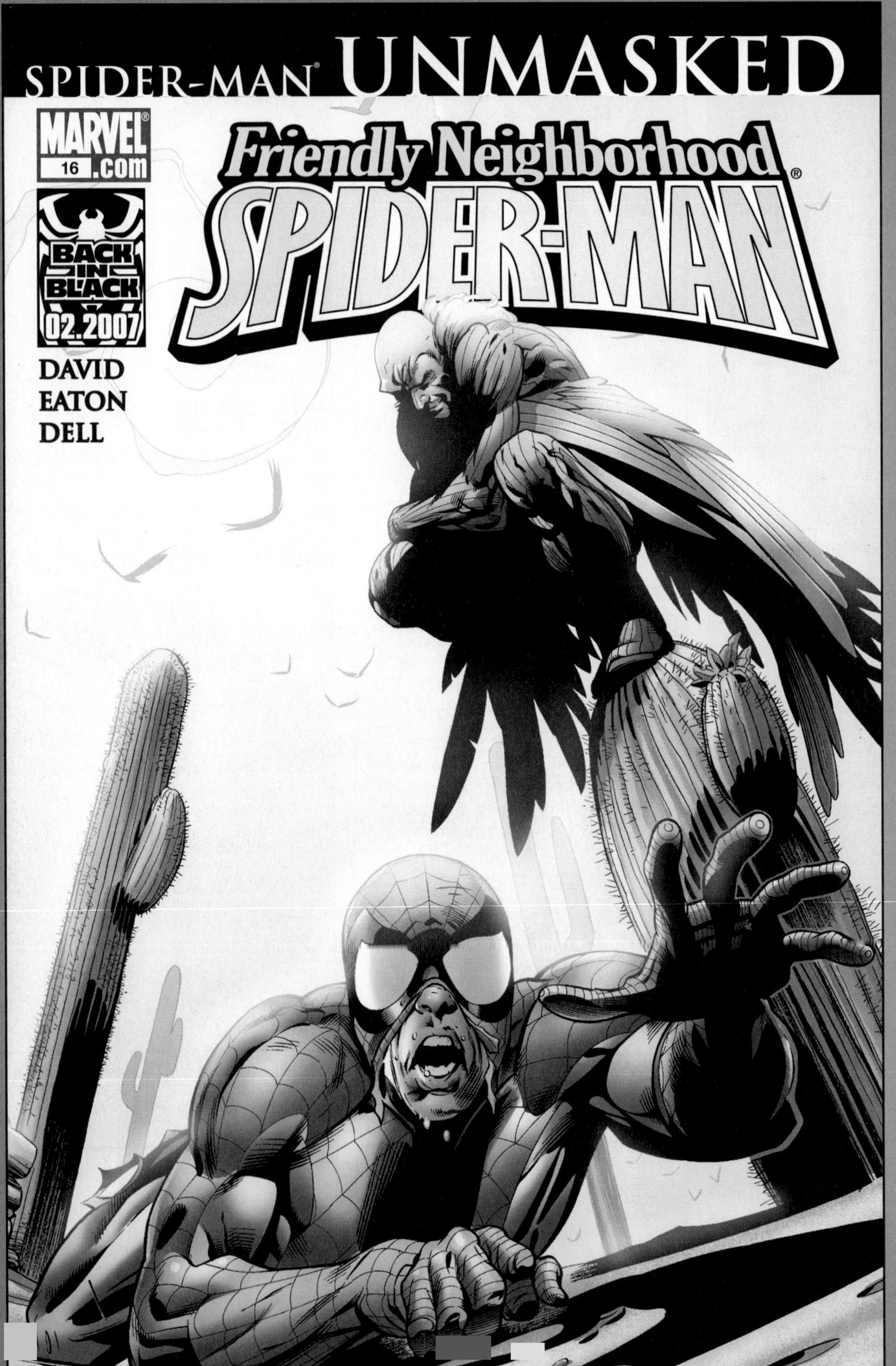
SPIDER-MAN® UNMASKED
MARVEL®
16 .com
Friendly Neighborhood
SPIDER-MAN®
BACK IN BLACK
02.2007
DAVID
EATON
DELL

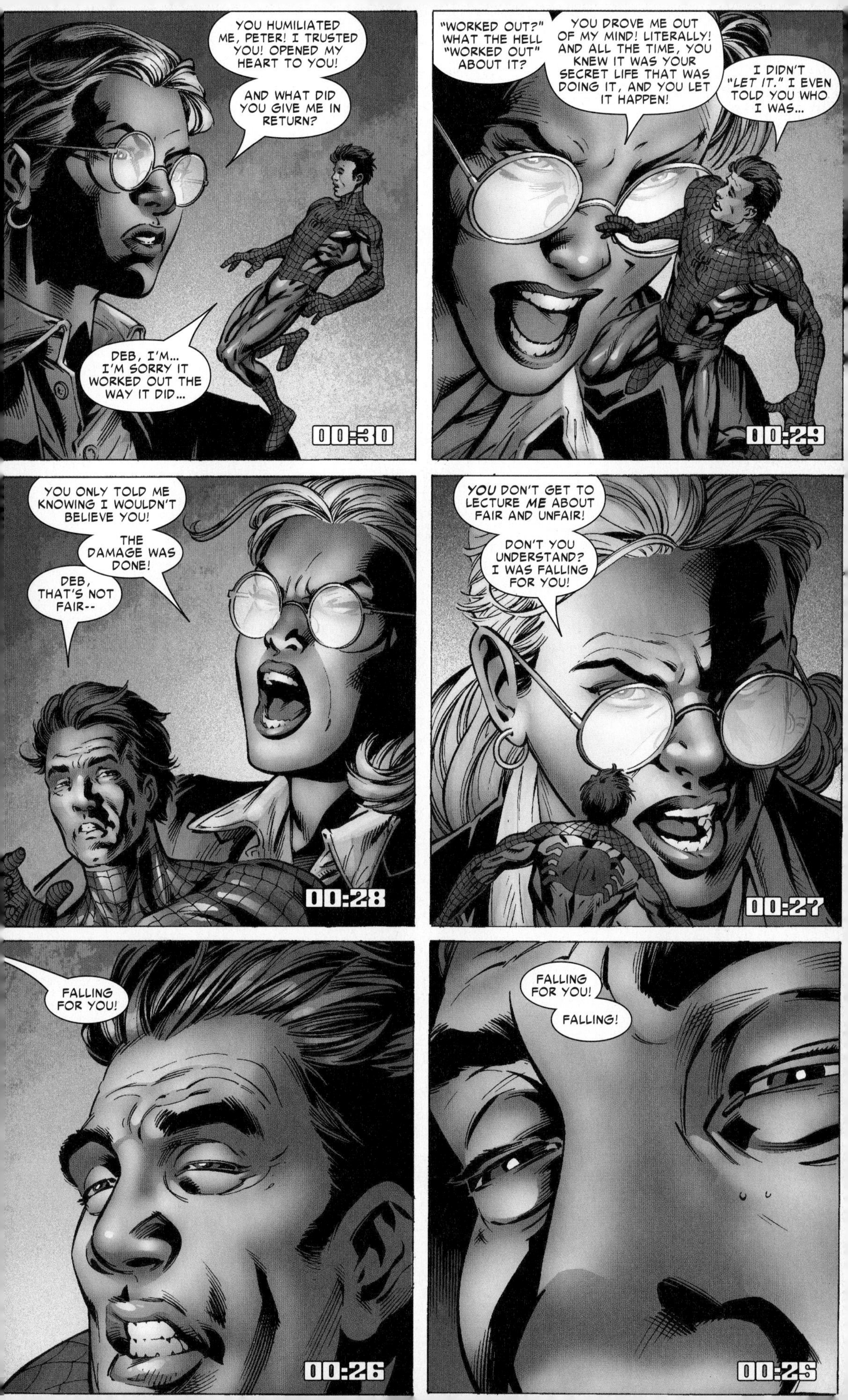
YOU HUMILIATED ME, PETER! I TRUSTED YOU! OPENED MY HEART TO YOU!
AND WHAT DID YOU GIVE ME IN RETURN?
DEB, I'M... I'M SORRY IT WORKED OUT THE WAY IT DID...
00:30
"WORKED OUT?" WHAT THE HELL "WORKED OUT" ABOUT IT?
YOU DROVE ME OUT OF MY MIND! LITERALLY! AND ALL THE TIME, YOU KNEW IT WAS YOUR SECRET LIFE THAT WAS DOING IT, AND YOU LET IT HAPPEN!
I DIDN'T "LET IT." I EVEN TOLD YOU WHO I WAS...
00:29
YOU ONLY TOLD ME KNOWING I WOULDN'T BELIEVE YOU!
THE DAMAGE WAS DONE!
DEB, THAT'S NOT FAIR--
00:28
YOU DON'T GET TO LECTURE ME ABOUT FAIR AND UNFAIR!
DON'T YOU UNDERSTAND? I WAS FALLING FOR YOU!
00:27
FALLING FOR YOU!
00:26
FALLING FOR YOU!
FALLING!
00:25

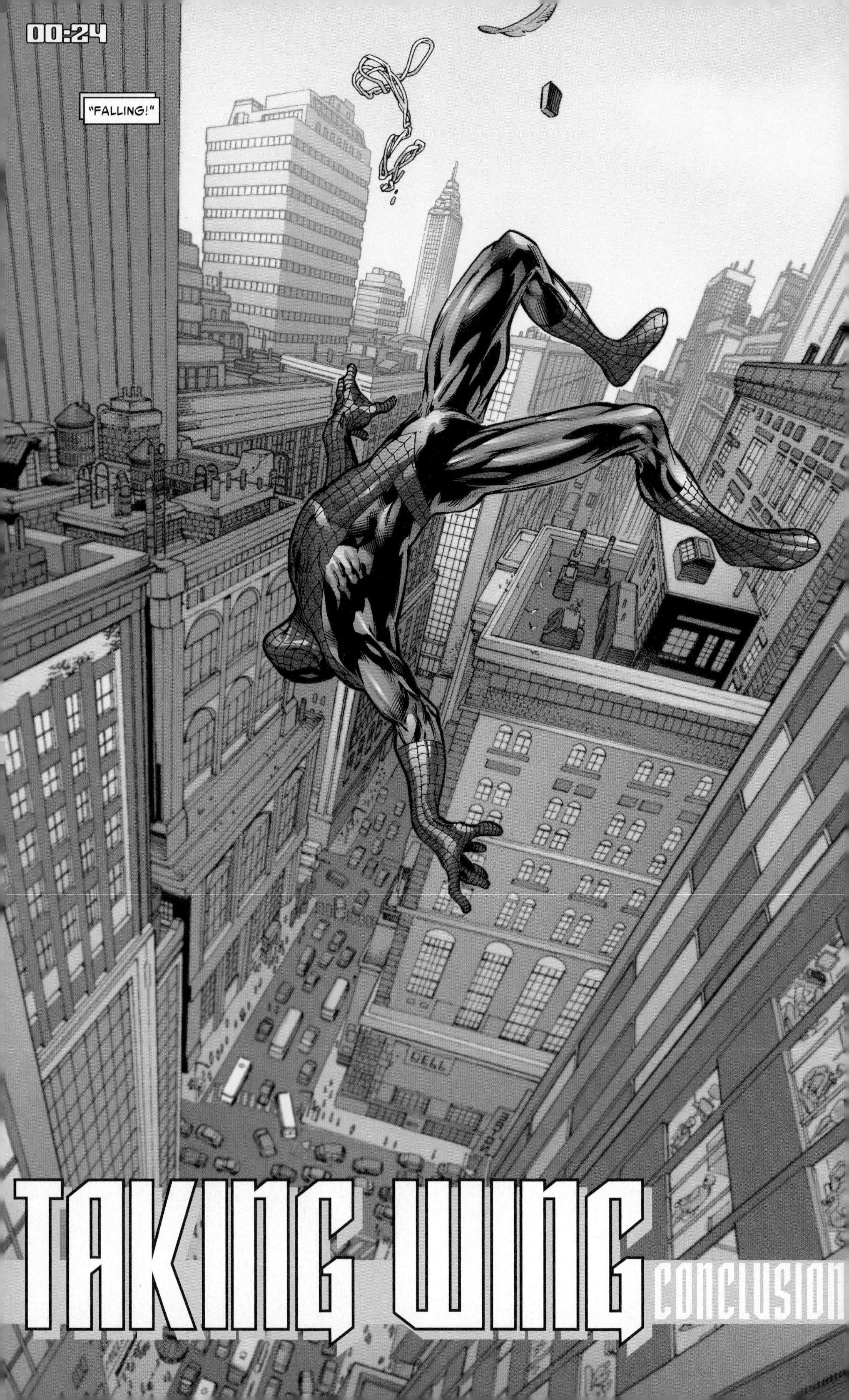

00:24
"FALLING!"
DELL
TAKING WING
CONCLUSION

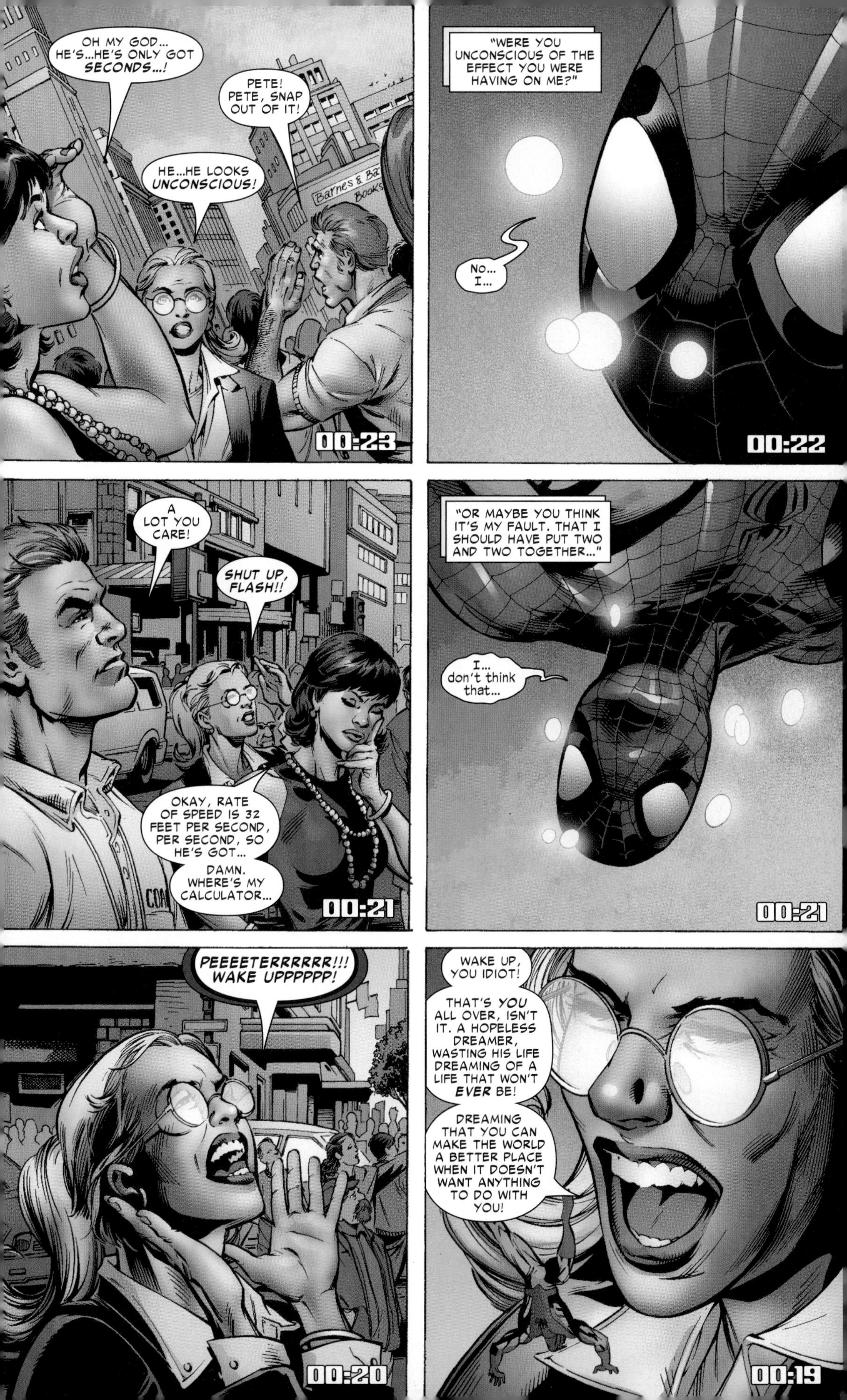
OH MY GOD... HE'S...HE'S ONLY GOT SECONDS...!
PETE! PETE, SNAP OUT OF IT!
HE...HE LOOKS UNCONSCIOUS!
Barnes & Ba Books
00:23
"WERE YOU UNCONSCIOUS OF THE EFFECT YOU WERE HAVING ON ME?"
No... I...
00:22
A LOT YOU CARE!
SHUT UP, FLASH!!
OKAY, RATE OF SPEED IS 32 FEET PER SECOND, PER SECOND, SO HE'S GOT...
DAMN. WHERE'S MY CALCULATOR...
00:21
"OR MAYBE YOU THINK IT'S MY FAULT. THAT I SHOULD HAVE PUT TWO AND TWO TOGETHER..."
I... don't think that...
00:21
PEEEETERRRRRR!!! WAKE UPPPPPP!
00:20
WAKE UP, YOU IDIOT!
THAT'S YOU ALL OVER, ISN'T IT. A HOPELESS DREAMER, WASTING HIS LIFE DREAMING OF A LIFE THAT WON'T EVER BE!
DREAMING THAT YOU CAN MAKE THE WORLD A BETTER PLACE WHEN IT DOESN'T WANT ANYTHING TO DO WITH YOU!
00:19

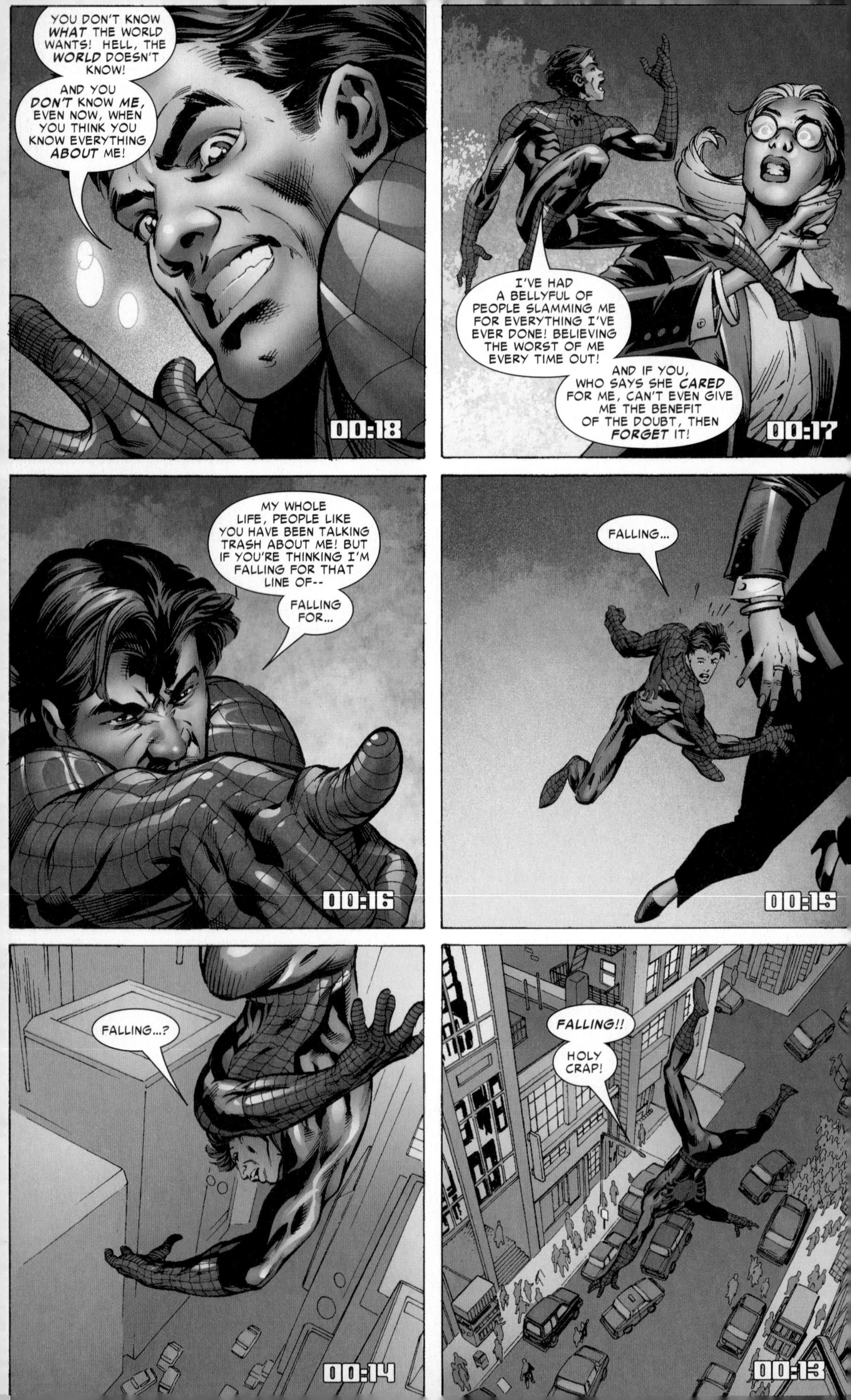
YOU DON'T KNOW WHAT THE WORLD WANTS! HELL, THE WORLD DOESN'T KNOW!
AND YOU DON'T KNOW ME, EVEN NOW, WHEN YOU THINK YOU KNOW EVERYTHING ABOUT ME!
00:18
I'VE HAD A BELLYFUL OF PEOPLE SLAMMING ME FOR EVERYTHING I'VE EVER DONE! BELIEVING THE WORST OF ME EVERY TIME OUT!
AND IF YOU, WHO SAYS SHE CARED FOR ME, CAN'T EVEN GIVE ME THE BENEFIT OF THE DOUBT, THEN FORGET IT!
00:17
MY WHOLE LIFE, PEOPLE LIKE YOU HAVE BEEN TALKING TRASH ABOUT ME! BUT IF YOU'RE THINKING I'M FALLING FOR THAT LINE OF--
FALLING FOR...
00:16
FALLING...
00:15
FALLING...?
00:14
FALLING!!
HOLY CRAP!
00:13

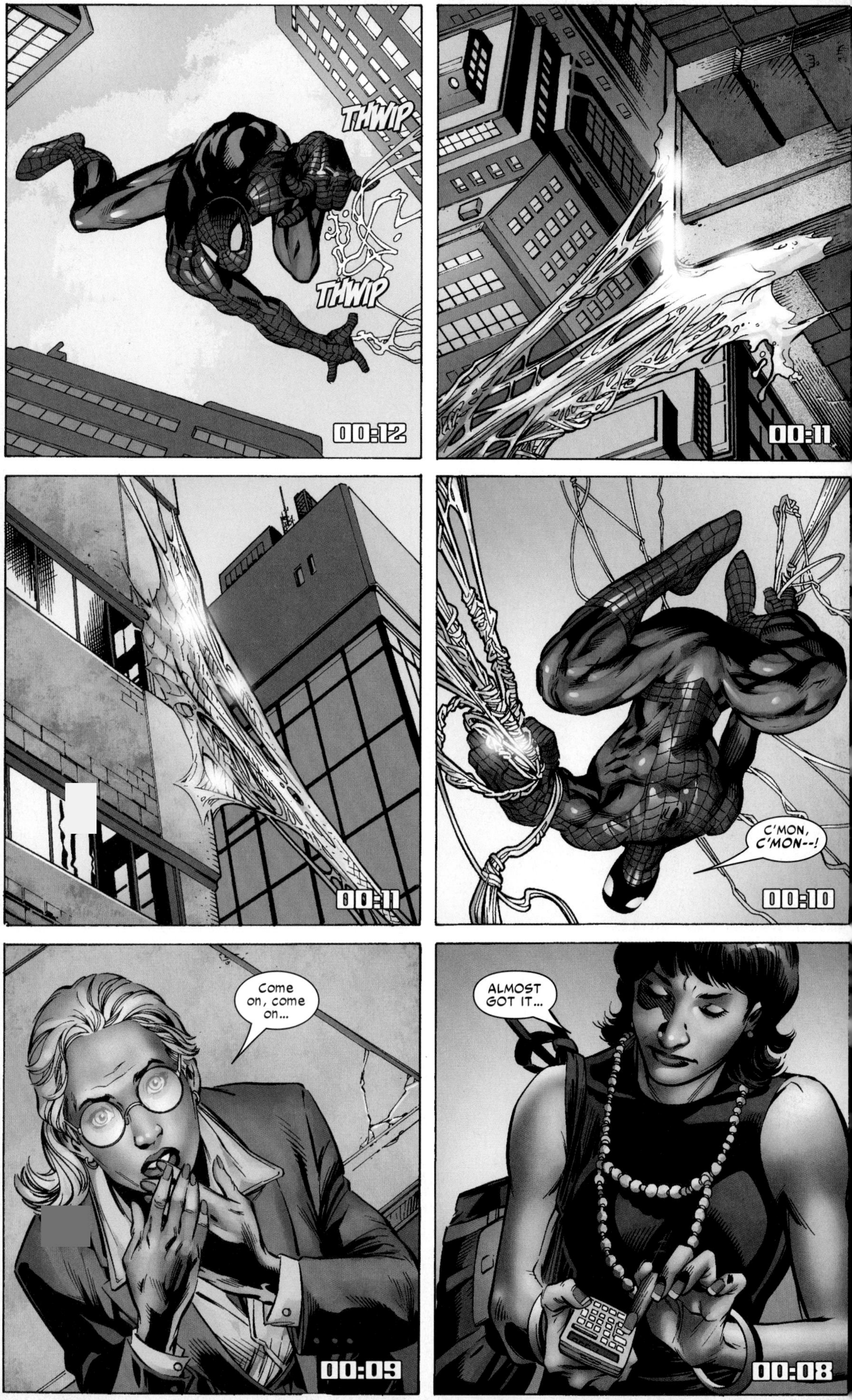
THWIP
THWIP
00:12
00:11
00:11
C'MON, C'MON--!
00:10
Come on, come on...
00:09
ALMOST GOT IT...
00:08

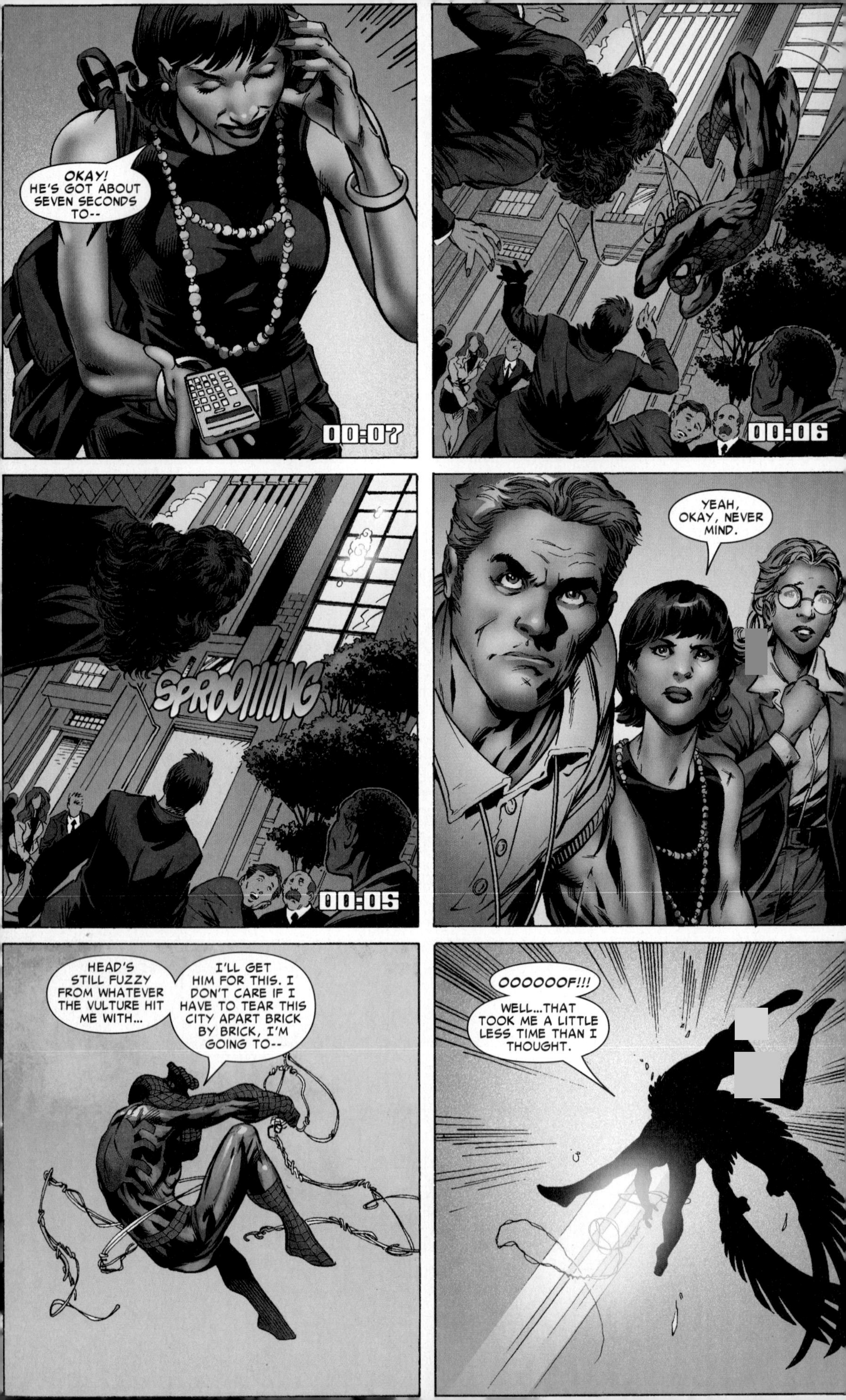

OKAY! HE'S GOT ABOUT SEVEN SECONDS TO--
00:07
00:06
SPROOIIIING
00:05
YEAH, OKAY, NEVER MIND.
HEAD'S STILL FUZZY FROM WHATEVER THE VULTURE HIT ME WITH...
I'LL GET HIM FOR THIS. I DON'T CARE IF I HAVE TO TEAR THIS CITY APART BRICK BY BRICK, I'M GOING TO--
OOOOOOF!!!
WELL...THAT TOOK ME A LITTLE LESS TIME THAN I THOUGHT.

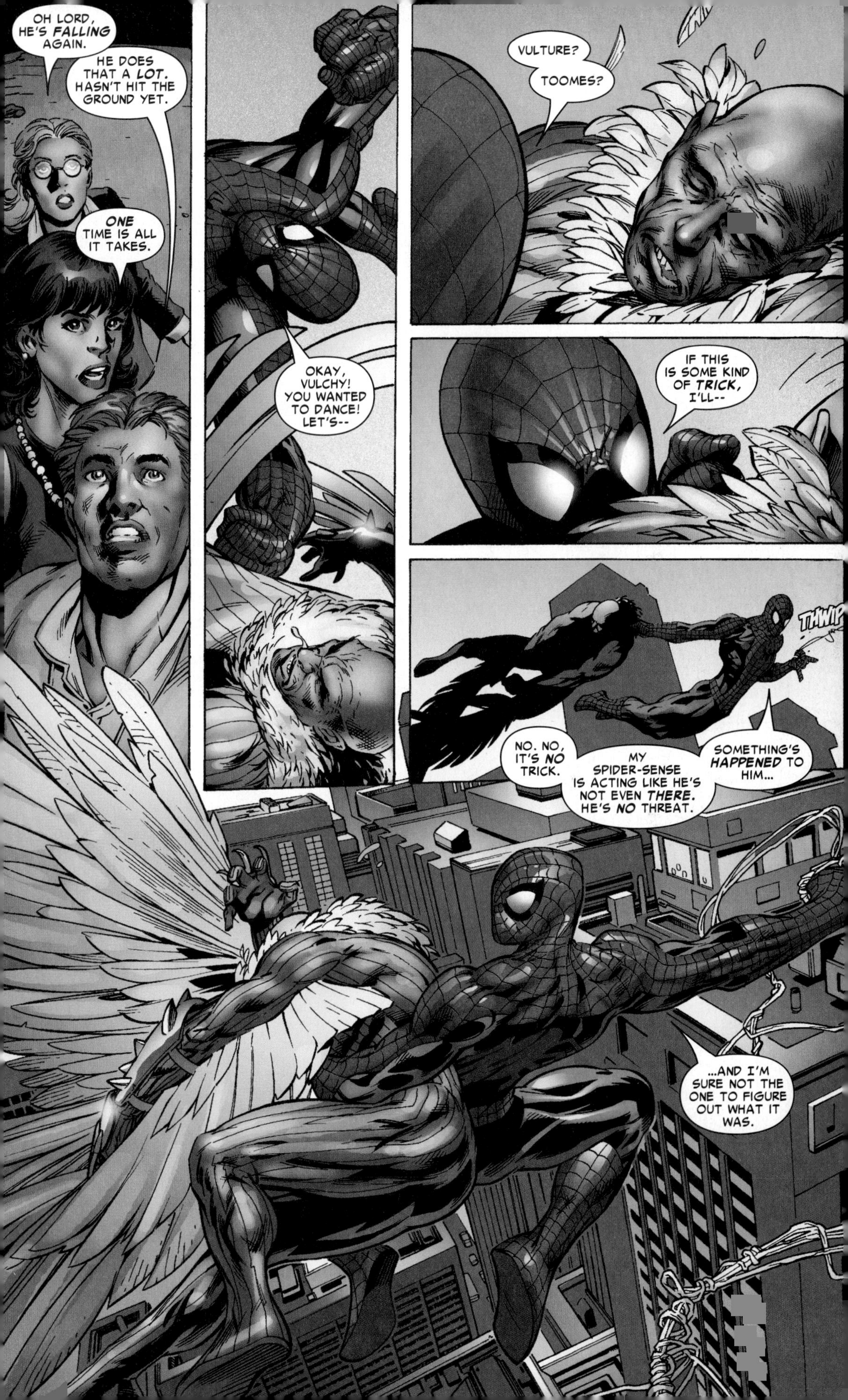
OH LORD, HE'S FALLING AGAIN.
HE DOES THAT A LOT. HASN'T HIT THE GROUND YET.
ONE TIME IS ALL IT TAKES.
OKAY, VULCHY! YOU WANTED TO DANCE! LET'S--
VULTURE?
TOOMES?
IF THIS IS SOME KIND OF TRICK, I'LL--
THWIP
NO. NO, IT'S NO TRICK.
MY SPIDER-SENSE IS ACTING LIKE HE'S NOT EVEN THERE. HE'S NO THREAT.
SOMETHING'S HAPPENED TO HIM...
...AND I'M SURE NOT THE ONE TO FIGURE OUT WHAT IT WAS.

WOW. A LOT OF PEOPLE CERTAINLY TURNED OUT FOR THIS SIGNING.

OH! AND THERE'S *FLASH--*!

I THOUGHT HE WAS DEAD. GOD AS MY WITNESS, I THOUGHT HE WAS GOING TO DIE, RIGHT HERE, IN FRONT OF US...

OH, AND YOU'D HAVE *LIKED* THAT, WOULDN'T YOU. WOULD'VE MADE EVERYTHING SQUARE BETWEEN--

WAAAP

YOU DON'T KNOW *ANYTHING*! NOT A *THING*, YOU--!

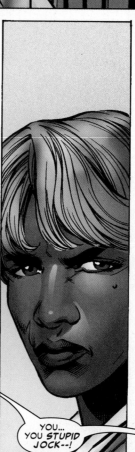

YOU... YOU *STUPID JOCK--*!

HOW *DARE* YOU! YOU DON'T...

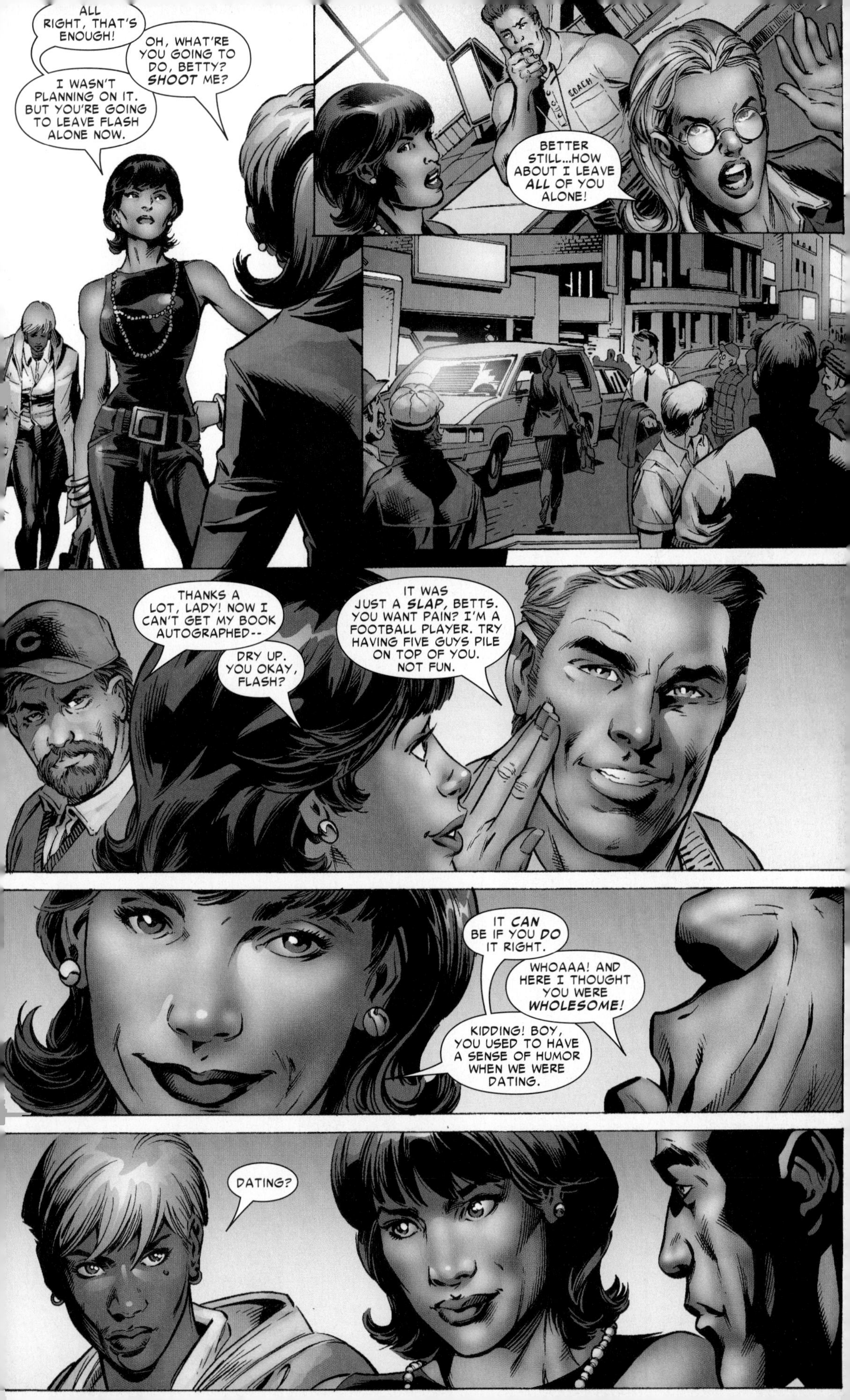
ALL RIGHT, THAT'S ENOUGH!
OH, WHAT'RE YOU GOING TO DO, BETTY? SHOOT ME?
I WASN'T PLANNING ON IT. BUT YOU'RE GOING TO LEAVE FLASH ALONE NOW.
BETTER STILL...HOW ABOUT I LEAVE ALL OF YOU ALONE!
THANKS A LOT, LADY! NOW I CAN'T GET MY BOOK AUTOGRAPHED--
DRY UP. YOU OKAY, FLASH?
IT WAS JUST A SLAP, BETTS. YOU WANT PAIN? I'M A FOOTBALL PLAYER. TRY HAVING FIVE GUYS PILE ON TOP OF YOU. NOT FUN.
IT CAN BE IF YOU DO IT RIGHT.
WHOAAA! AND HERE I THOUGHT YOU WERE WHOLESOME!
KIDDING! BOY, YOU USED TO HAVE A SENSE OF HUMOR WHEN WE WERE DATING.
DATING?

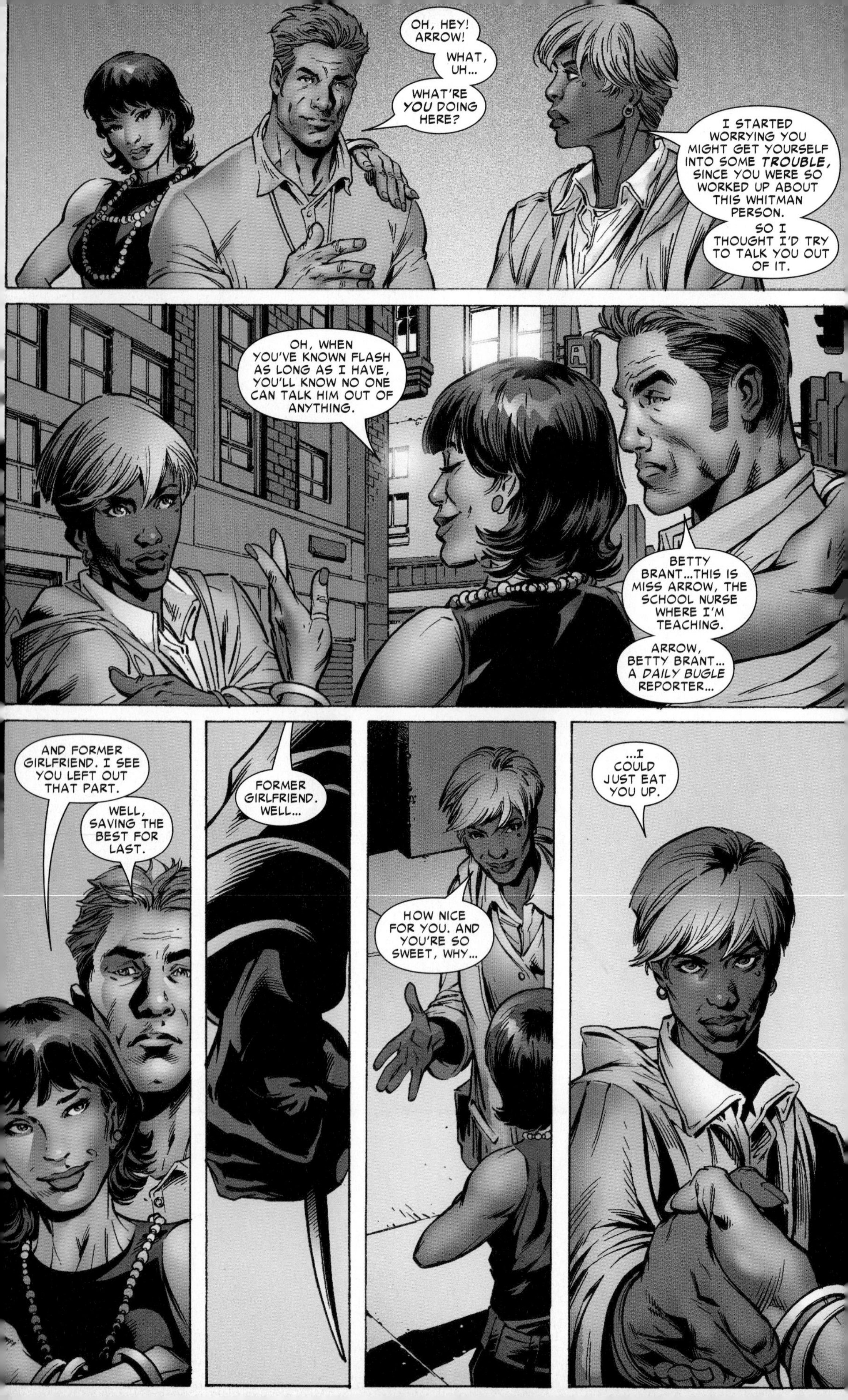
OH, HEY! ARROW!
WHAT, UH...
WHAT'RE *YOU* DOING HERE?
I STARTED WORRYING YOU MIGHT GET YOURSELF INTO SOME *TROUBLE*, SINCE YOU WERE SO WORKED UP ABOUT THIS WHITMAN PERSON.
SO I THOUGHT I'D TRY TO TALK YOU OUT OF IT.
OH, WHEN YOU'VE KNOWN FLASH AS LONG AS I HAVE, YOU'LL KNOW NO ONE CAN TALK HIM OUT OF ANYTHING.
BETTY BRANT...THIS IS MISS ARROW, THE SCHOOL NURSE WHERE I'M TEACHING.
ARROW, BETTY BRANT... A *DAILY BUGLE* REPORTER...
AND FORMER GIRLFRIEND. I SEE YOU LEFT OUT THAT PART.
WELL, SAVING THE BEST FOR LAST.
FORMER GIRLFRIEND. WELL...
HOW NICE FOR YOU. AND YOU'RE SO SWEET, WHY...
...I COULD JUST EAT YOU UP.

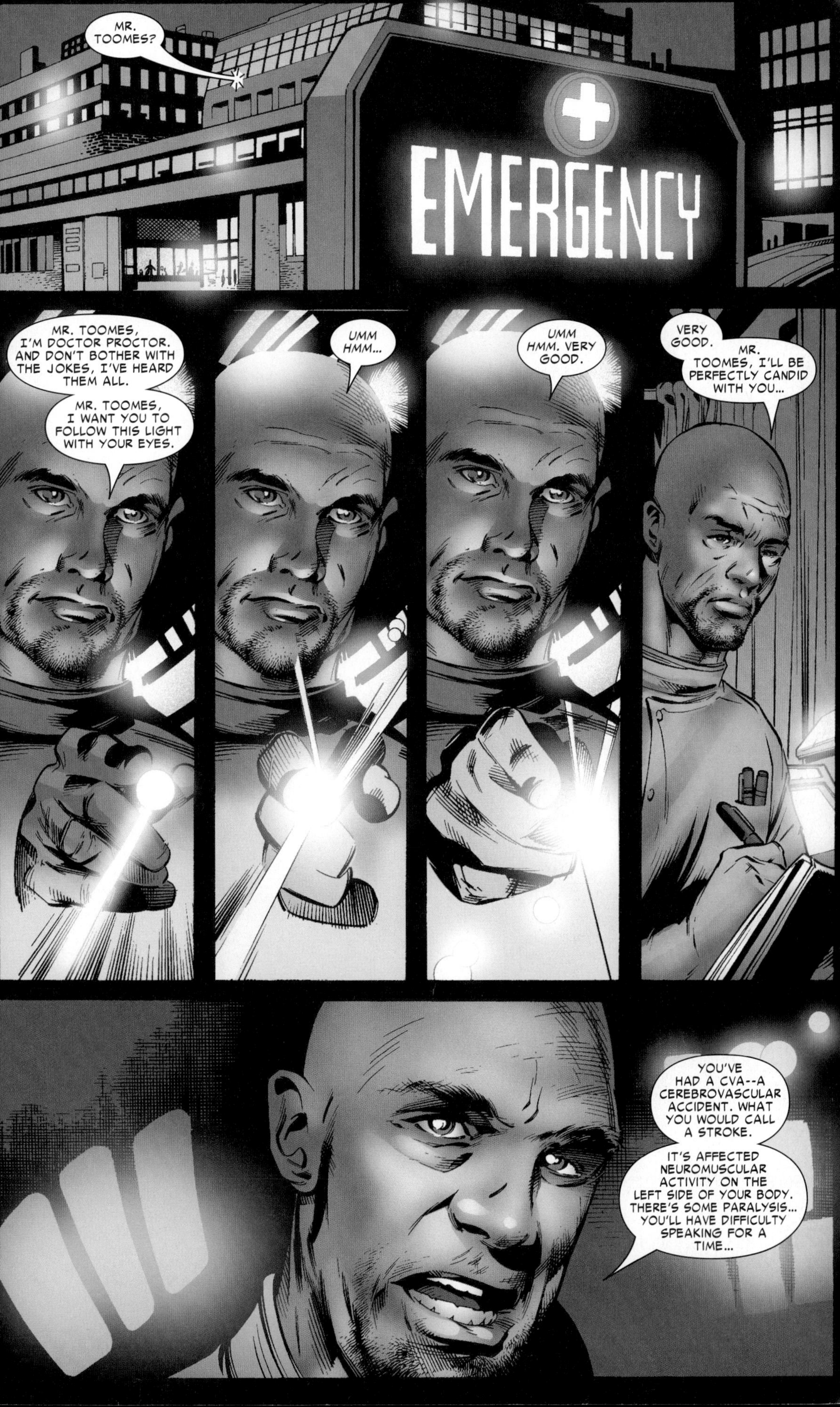
MR. TOOMES?
EMERGENCY
MR. TOOMES, I'M DOCTOR PROCTOR. AND DON'T BOTHER WITH THE JOKES, I'VE HEARD THEM ALL.
MR. TOOMES, I WANT YOU TO FOLLOW THIS LIGHT WITH YOUR EYES.
UMM HMM...
UMM HMM. VERY GOOD.
VERY GOOD.
MR. TOOMES, I'LL BE PERFECTLY CANDID WITH YOU...
YOU'VE HAD A CVA--A CEREBROVASCULAR ACCIDENT. WHAT YOU WOULD CALL A STROKE.
IT'S AFFECTED NEUROMUSCULAR ACTIVITY ON THE LEFT SIDE OF YOUR BODY. THERE'S SOME PARALYSIS... YOU'LL HAVE DIFFICULTY SPEAKING FOR A TIME...

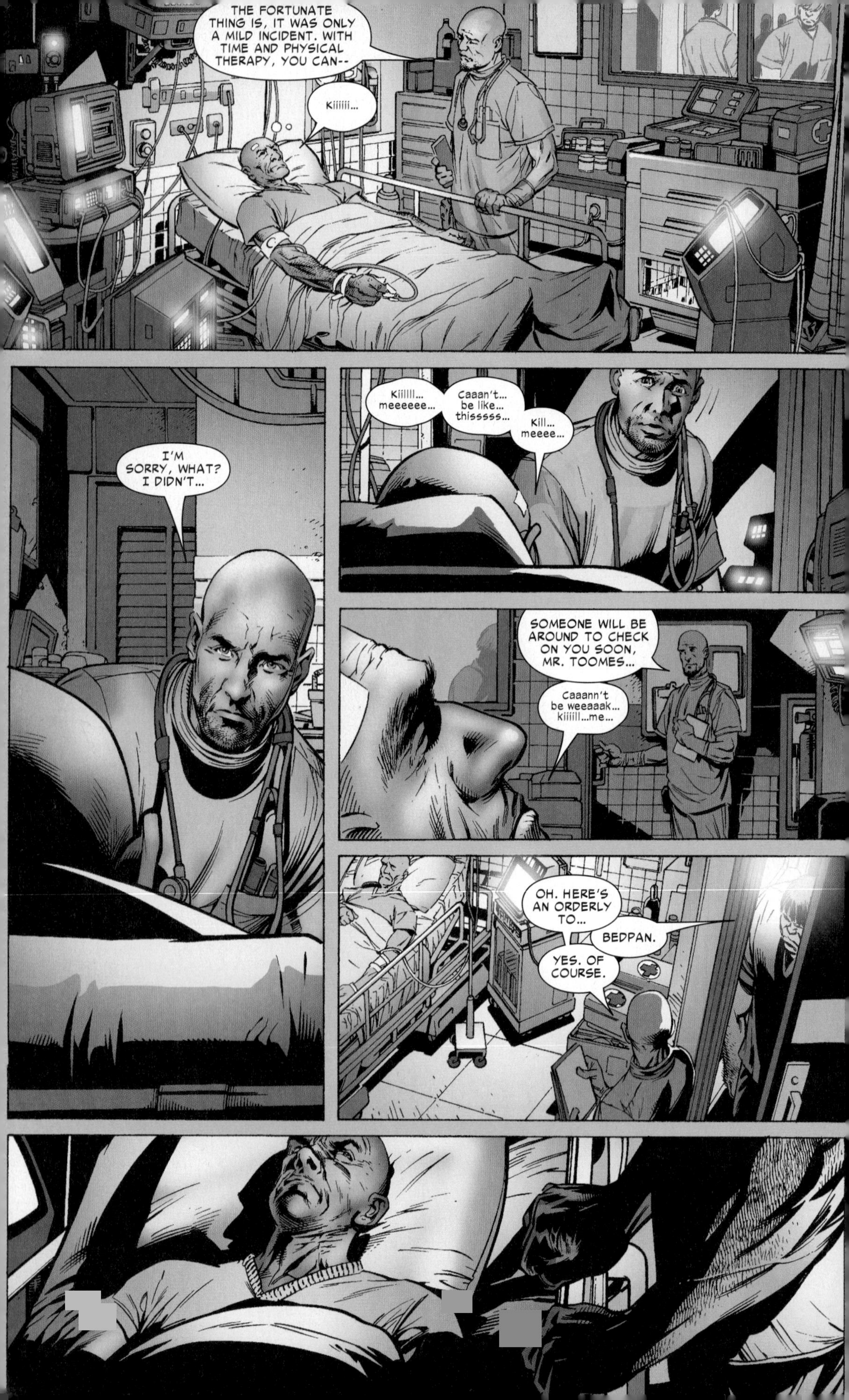
THE FORTUNATE THING IS, IT WAS ONLY A MILD INCIDENT. WITH TIME AND PHYSICAL THERAPY, YOU CAN--
Kiiiiii...
I'M SORRY, WHAT? I DIDN'T...
Kiiilll... meeeeee...
Caaan't... be like... thissssss...
Kill... meeee...
SOMEONE WILL BE AROUND TO CHECK ON YOU SOON, MR. TOOMES...
Caaann't be weeaaak... kiiiiil...me...
OH. HERE'S AN ORDERLY TO...
BEDPAN.
YES. OF COURSE.

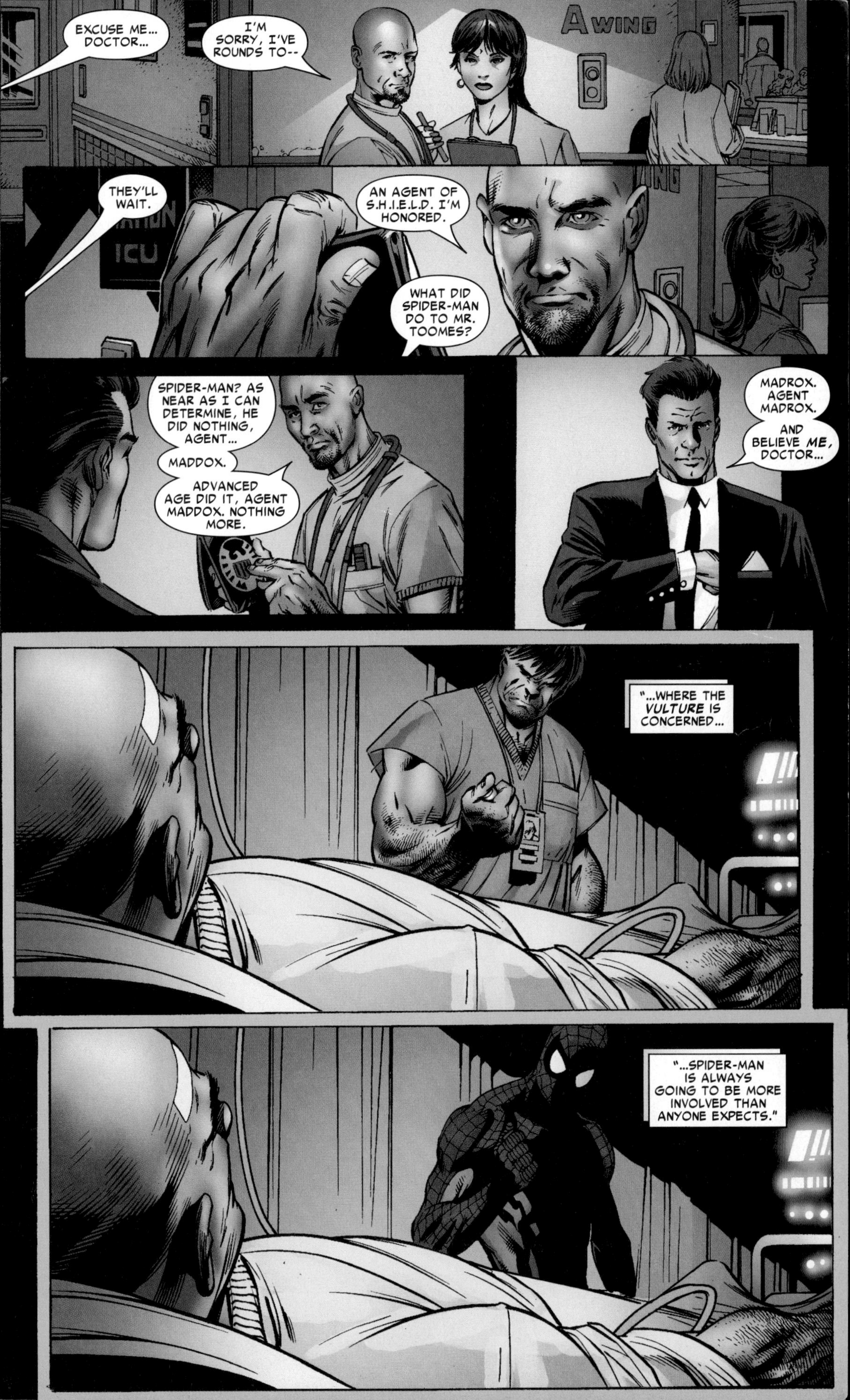
EXCUSE ME... DOCTOR...
I'M SORRY, I'VE ROUNDS TO--
A WING
THEY'LL WAIT.
ICU
AN AGENT OF S.H.I.E.L.D. I'M HONORED.
WHAT DID SPIDER-MAN DO TO MR. TOOMES?
SPIDER-MAN? AS NEAR AS I CAN DETERMINE, HE DID NOTHING, AGENT...
MADDOX.
ADVANCED AGE DID IT, AGENT MADDOX. NOTHING MORE.
MADROX. AGENT MADROX.
AND BELIEVE *ME*, DOCTOR...
"...WHERE THE *VULTURE* IS CONCERNED...
"...SPIDER-MAN IS ALWAYS GOING TO BE MORE INVOLVED THAN ANYONE EXPECTS."

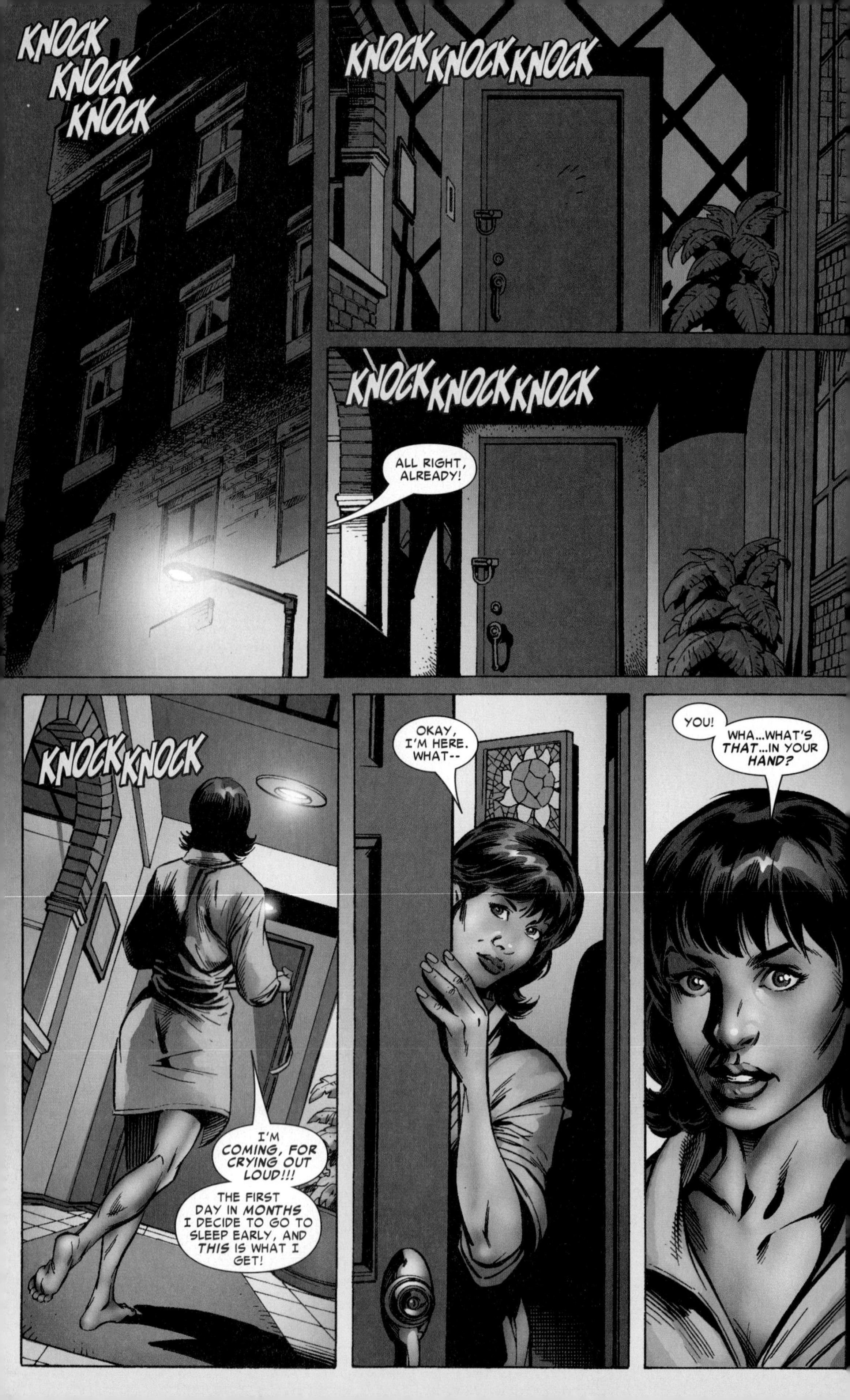
KNOCK KNOCK KNOCK
KNOCK KNOCK KNOCK
KNOCK KNOCK KNOCK
ALL RIGHT, ALREADY!
KNOCK KNOCK
I'M COMING, FOR CRYING OUT LOUD!!!
THE FIRST DAY IN MONTHS I DECIDE TO GO TO SLEEP EARLY, AND THIS IS WHAT I GET!
OKAY, I'M HERE. WHAT--
YOU!
WHA...WHAT'S THAT...IN YOUR HAND?

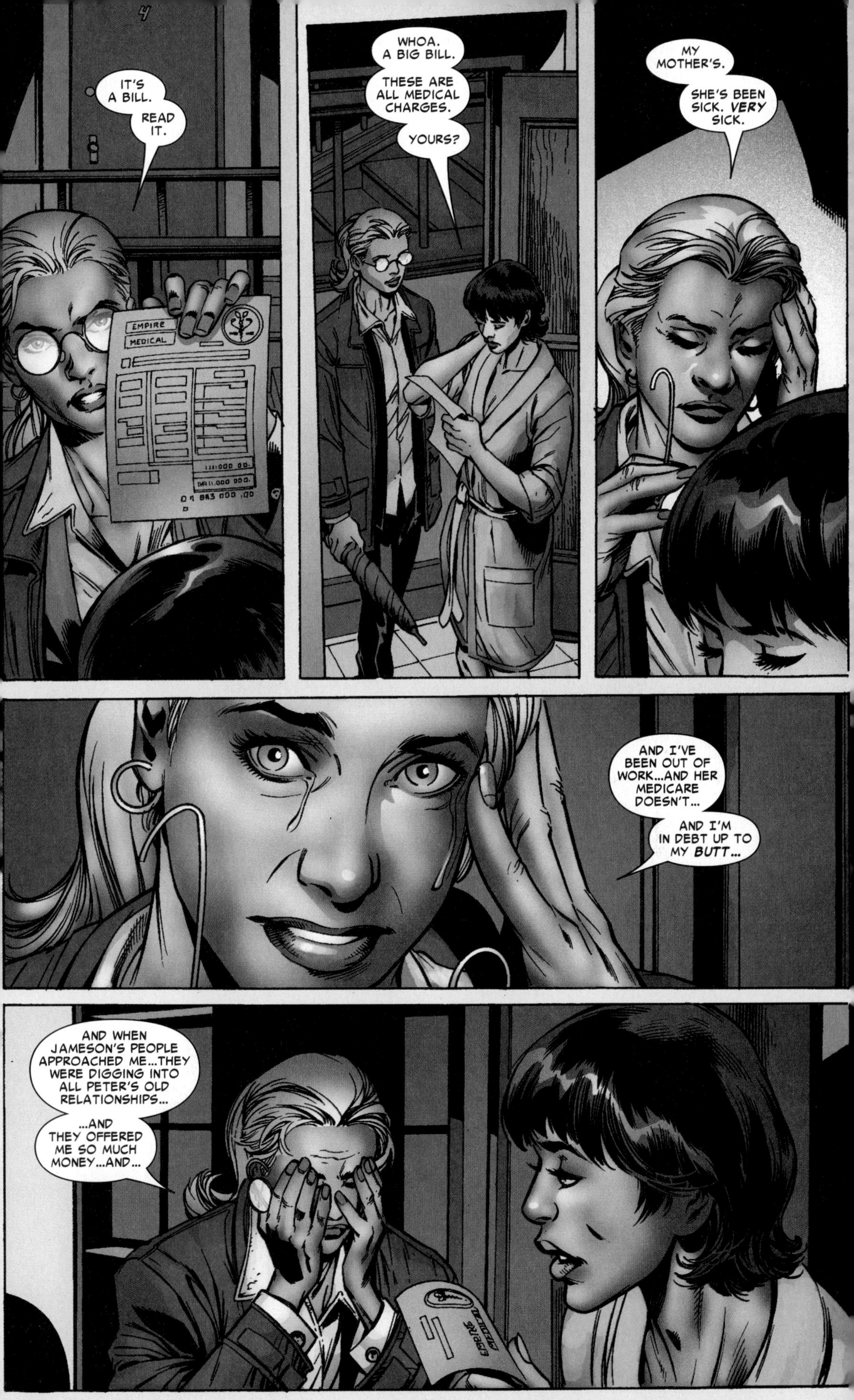
IT'S A BILL.
READ IT.
EMPIRE MEDICAL
WHOA. A BIG BILL.
THESE ARE ALL MEDICAL CHARGES.
YOURS?
MY MOTHER'S.
SHE'S BEEN SICK. VERY SICK.
AND I'VE BEEN OUT OF WORK...AND HER MEDICARE DOESN'T...
AND I'M IN DEBT UP TO MY BUTT...
AND WHEN JAMESON'S PEOPLE APPROACHED ME...THEY WERE DIGGING INTO ALL PETER'S OLD RELATIONSHIPS...
...AND THEY OFFERED ME SO MUCH MONEY...AND...

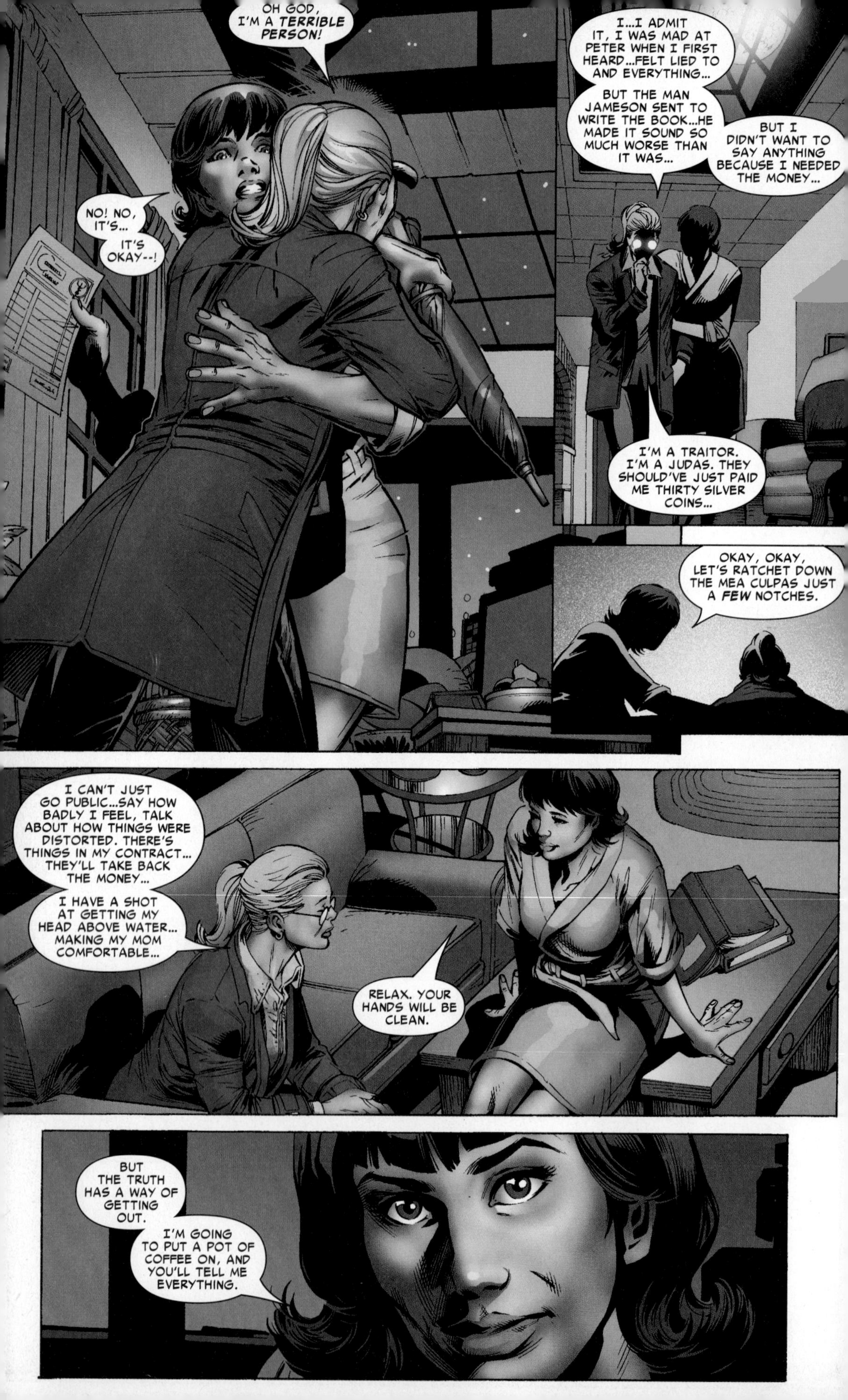
OH GOD, I'M A *TERRIBLE PERSON!*
NO! NO, IT'S...
IT'S OKAY--!
I...I ADMIT IT, I WAS MAD AT PETER WHEN I FIRST HEARD...FELT LIED TO AND EVERYTHING...
BUT THE MAN JAMESON SENT TO WRITE THE BOOK...HE MADE IT SOUND SO MUCH WORSE THAN IT WAS...
BUT I DIDN'T WANT TO SAY ANYTHING BECAUSE I NEEDED THE MONEY...
I'M A TRAITOR. I'M A JUDAS. THEY SHOULD'VE JUST PAID ME THIRTY SILVER COINS...
OKAY, OKAY, LET'S RATCHET DOWN THE MEA CULPAS JUST A *FEW* NOTCHES.
I CAN'T JUST GO PUBLIC...SAY HOW BADLY I FEEL, TALK ABOUT HOW THINGS WERE DISTORTED. THERE'S THINGS IN MY CONTRACT... THEY'LL TAKE BACK THE MONEY...
I HAVE A SHOT AT GETTING MY HEAD ABOVE WATER... MAKING MY MOM COMFORTABLE...
RELAX. YOUR HANDS WILL BE CLEAN.
BUT THE TRUTH HAS A WAY OF GETTING OUT.
I'M GOING TO PUT A POT OF COFFEE ON, AND YOU'LL TELL ME EVERYTHING.

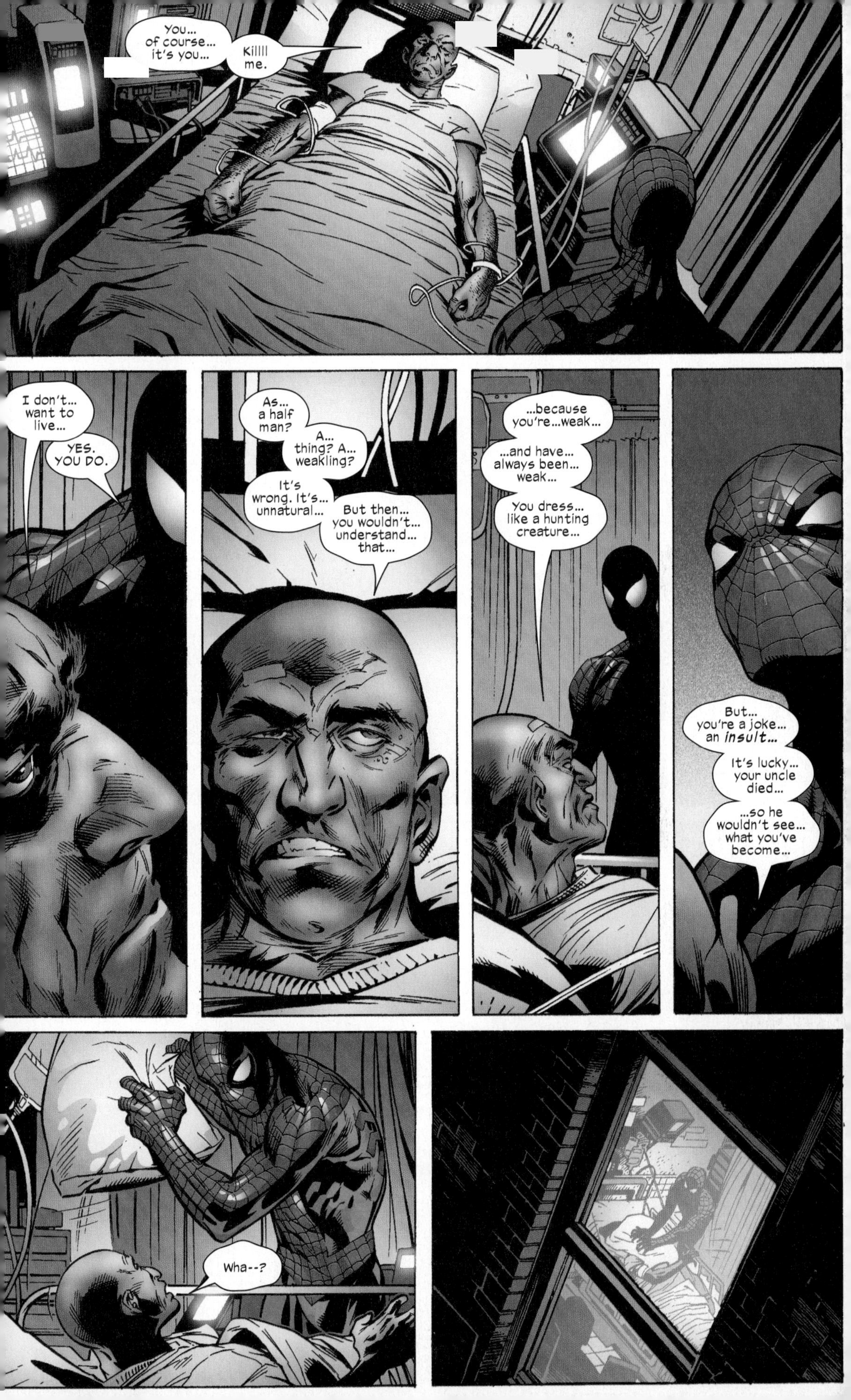

You... of course... it's you...
Killll me.
I don't... want to live...
YES. YOU DO.
As... a half man?
A... thing? A... weakling?
It's wrong. It's... unnatural...
But then... you wouldn't... understand... that...
...because you're...weak...
...and have... always been... weak...
You dress... like a hunting creature...
But... you're a joke... an *insult...*
It's lucky... your uncle died...
...so he wouldn't see... what you've become...
Wha--?

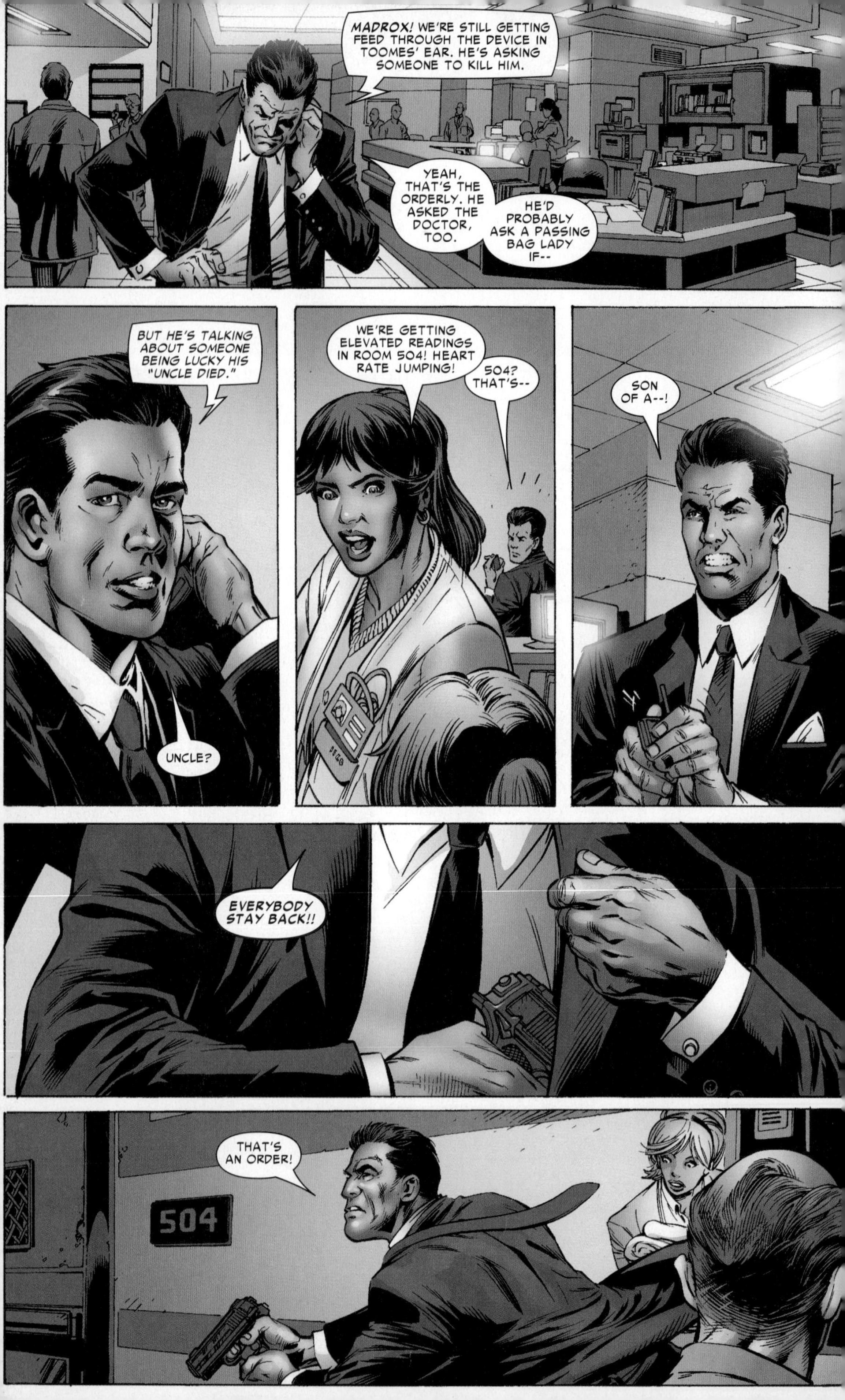
MADROX! WE'RE STILL GETTING FEED THROUGH THE DEVICE IN TOOMES' EAR. HE'S ASKING SOMEONE TO KILL HIM.
YEAH, THAT'S THE ORDERLY. HE ASKED THE DOCTOR, TOO.
HE'D PROBABLY ASK A PASSING BAG LADY IF--
BUT HE'S TALKING ABOUT SOMEONE BEING LUCKY HIS "UNCLE DIED."
UNCLE?
WE'RE GETTING ELEVATED READINGS IN ROOM 504! HEART RATE JUMPING!
504? THAT'S--
SON OF A--!
EVERYBODY STAY BACK!!
THAT'S AN ORDER!
504

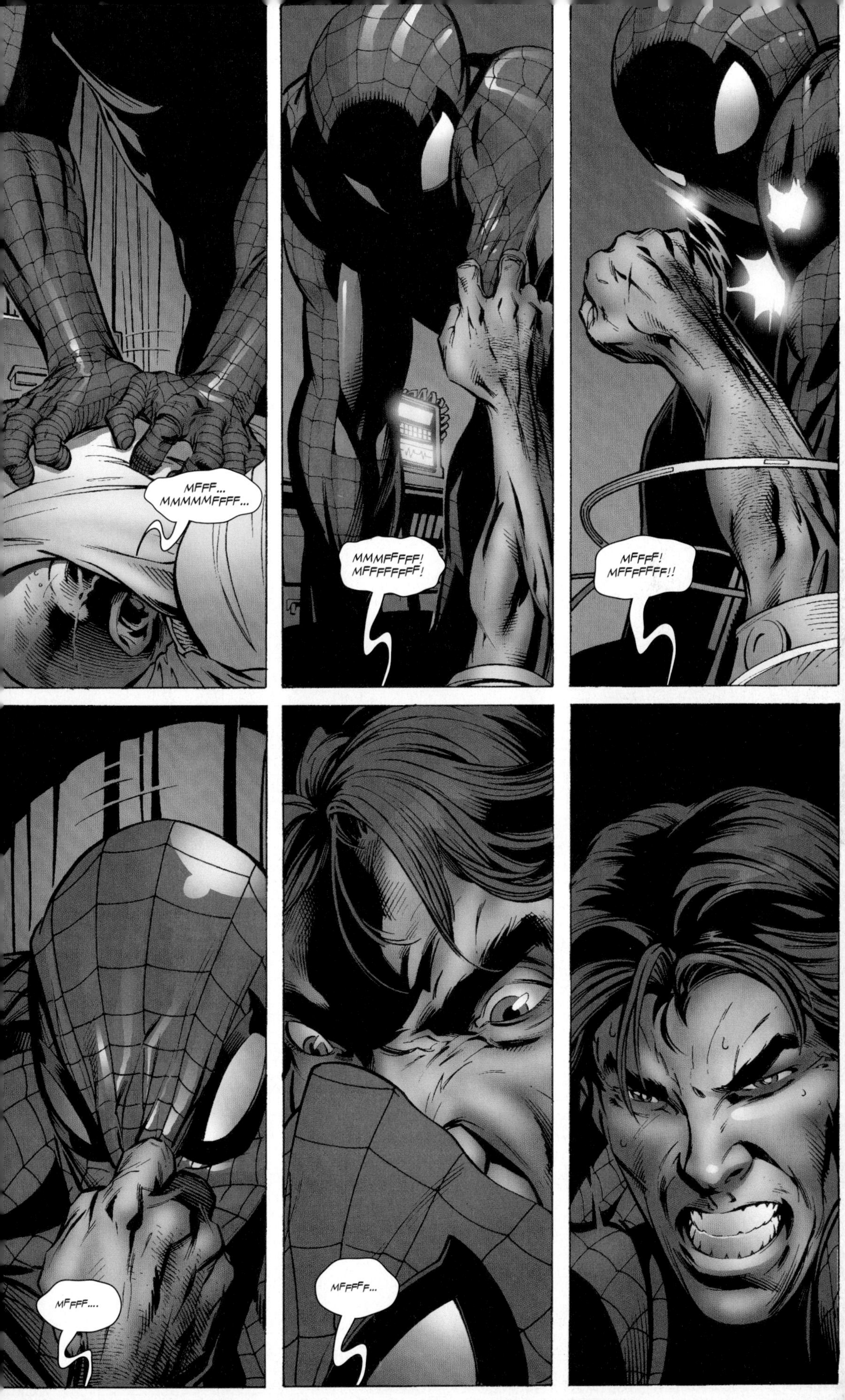
MFFF... MMMMMFFFF...
MMMFFFFF! MFFFFFFFF!
MFFFF! MFFFFFFF!!
MFFFF....
MFFFFF...

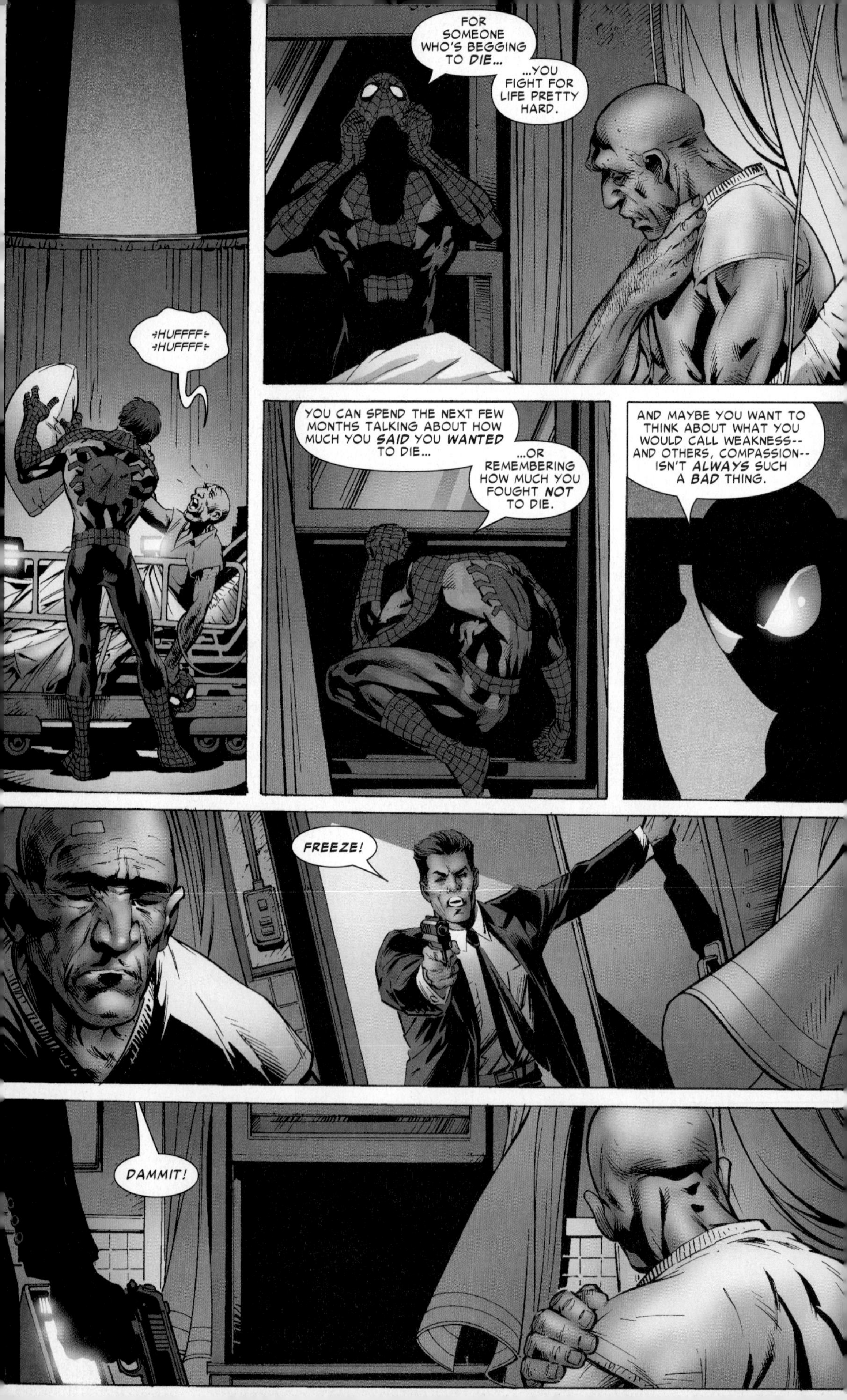

FOR SOMEONE WHO'S BEGGING TO DIE...
...YOU FIGHT FOR LIFE PRETTY HARD.
≠HUFFFF≠ ≠HUFFFF≠
YOU CAN SPEND THE NEXT FEW MONTHS TALKING ABOUT HOW MUCH YOU SAID YOU WANTED TO DIE...
...OR REMEMBERING HOW MUCH YOU FOUGHT NOT TO DIE.
AND MAYBE YOU WANT TO THINK ABOUT WHAT YOU WOULD CALL WEAKNESS-- AND OTHERS, COMPASSION-- ISN'T ALWAYS SUCH A BAD THING.
FREEZE!
DAMMIT!

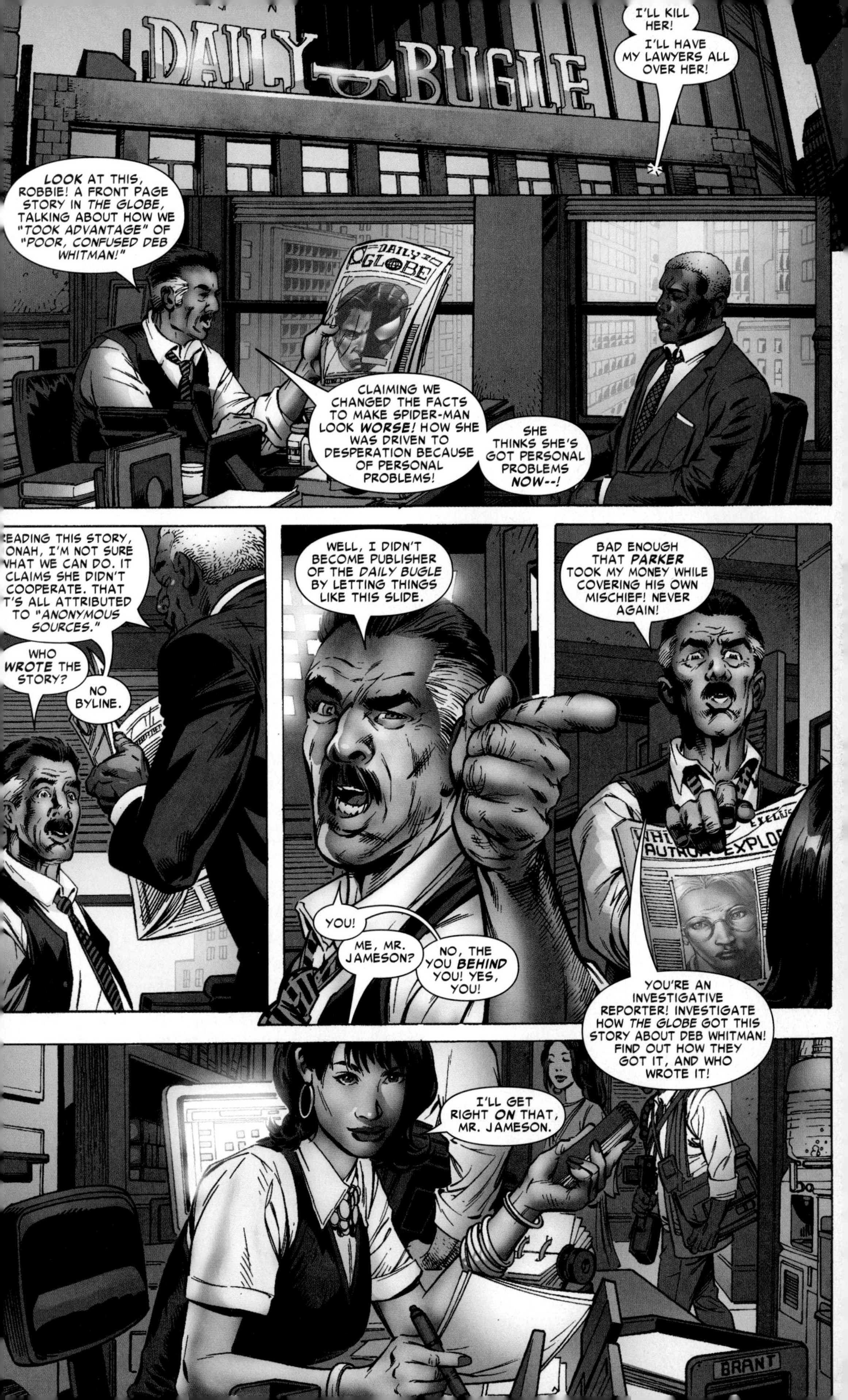
DAILY BUGLE
I'LL KILL HER!
I'LL HAVE MY LAWYERS ALL OVER HER!
LOOK AT THIS, ROBBIE! A FRONT PAGE STORY IN THE GLOBE, TALKING ABOUT HOW WE "TOOK ADVANTAGE" OF "POOR, CONFUSED DEB WHITMAN!"
DAILY GLOBE
CLAIMING WE CHANGED THE FACTS TO MAKE SPIDER-MAN LOOK WORSE! HOW SHE WAS DRIVEN TO DESPERATION BECAUSE OF PERSONAL PROBLEMS!
SHE THINKS SHE'S GOT PERSONAL PROBLEMS NOW--!
READING THIS STORY, JONAH, I'M NOT SURE WHAT WE CAN DO. IT CLAIMS SHE DIDN'T COOPERATE. THAT IT'S ALL ATTRIBUTED TO "ANONYMOUS SOURCES."
WHO WROTE THE STORY?
NO BYLINE.
WELL, I DIDN'T BECOME PUBLISHER OF THE DAILY BUGLE BY LETTING THINGS LIKE THIS SLIDE.
YOU!
ME, MR. JAMESON?
NO, THE YOU BEHIND YOU! YES, YOU!
BAD ENOUGH THAT PARKER TOOK MY MONEY WHILE COVERING HIS OWN MISCHIEF! NEVER AGAIN!
YOU'RE AN INVESTIGATIVE REPORTER! INVESTIGATE HOW THE GLOBE GOT THIS STORY ABOUT DEB WHITMAN! FIND OUT HOW THEY GOT IT, AND WHO WROTE IT!
I'LL GET RIGHT ON THAT, MR. JAMESON.
BRANT

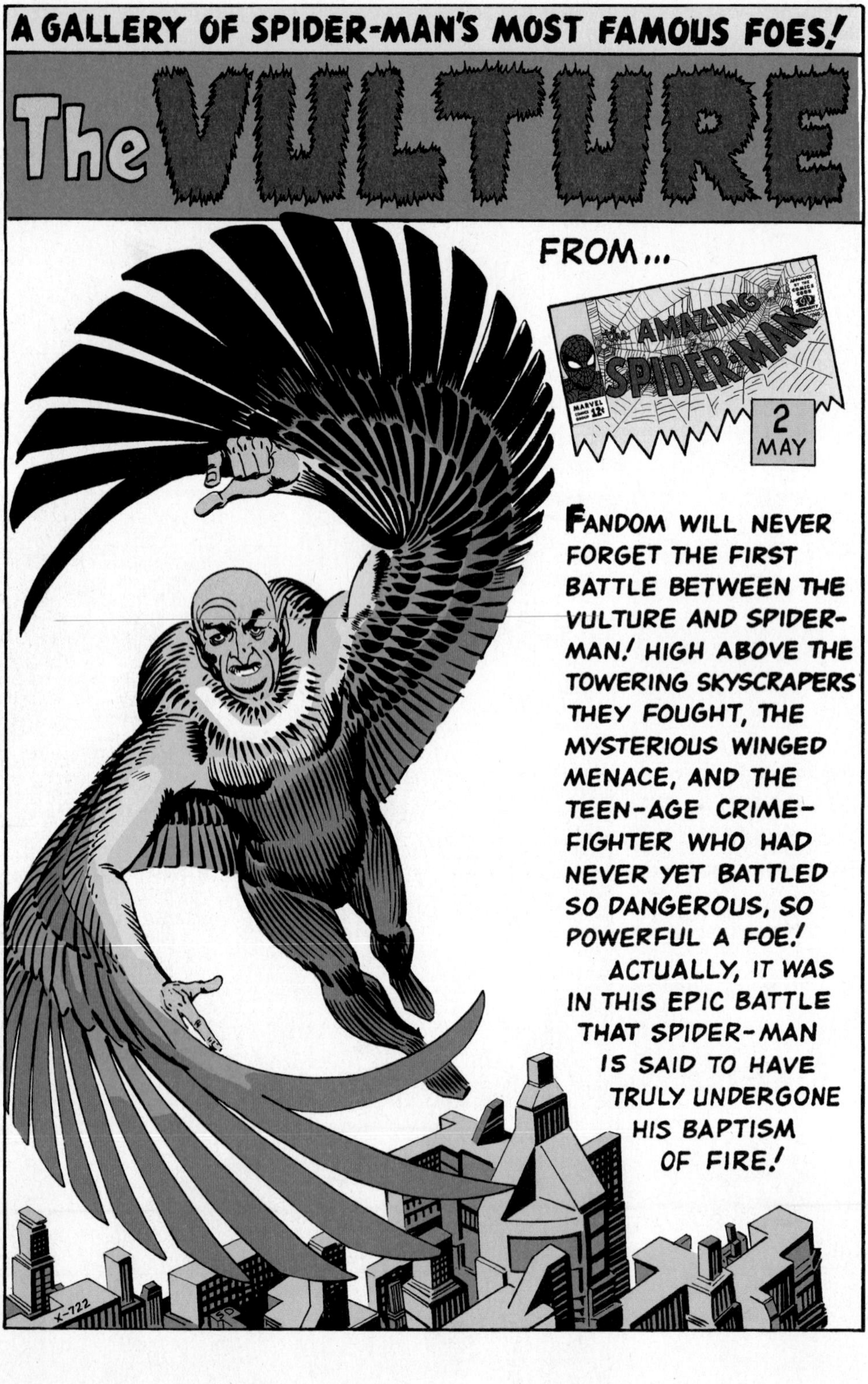
A GALLERY OF SPIDER-MAN'S MOST FAMOUS FOES!
The VULTURE
FROM...
THE AMAZING SPIDER-MAN
MARVEL COMICS GROUP 12¢
2
MAY
FANDOM WILL NEVER FORGET THE FIRST BATTLE BETWEEN THE VULTURE AND SPIDER-MAN! HIGH ABOVE THE TOWERING SKYSCRAPERS THEY FOUGHT, THE MYSTERIOUS WINGED MENACE, AND THE TEEN-AGE CRIME-FIGHTER WHO HAD NEVER YET BATTLED SO DANGEROUS, SO POWERFUL A FOE!
ACTUALLY, IT WAS IN THIS EPIC BATTLE THAT SPIDER-MAN IS SAID TO HAVE TRULY UNDERGONE HIS BAPTISM OF FIRE!
X-722

AMAZING SPIDER-MAN ANNUAL #1 PINUP BY Steve Ditko

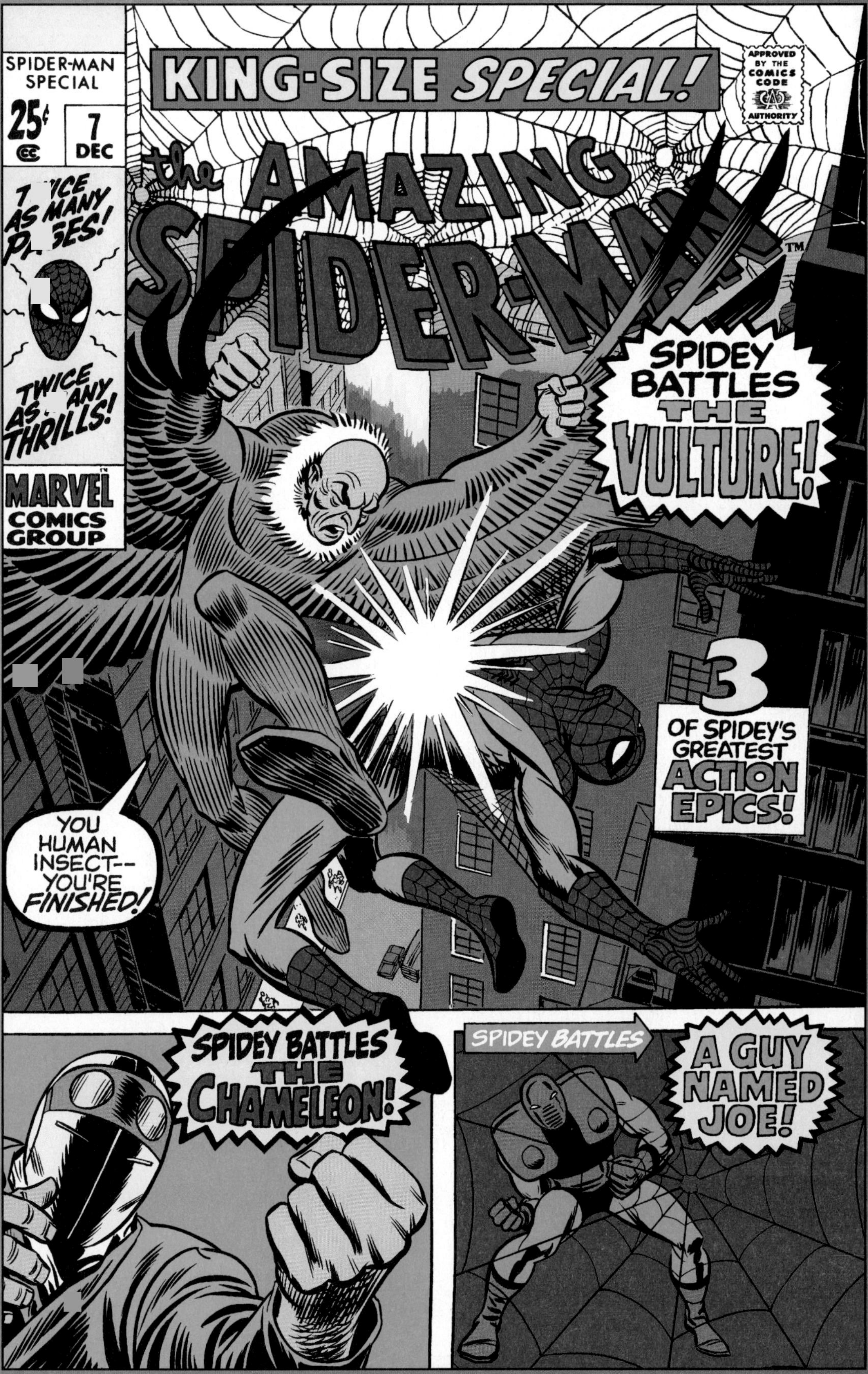
SPIDER-MAN SPECIAL
25¢
7 DEC
KING-SIZE SPECIAL!
APPROVED BY THE COMICS CODE AUTHORITY
the AMAZING SPIDER-MAN™
MARVEL™ COMICS GROUP
SPIDEY BATTLES THE VULTURE!
3 OF SPIDEY'S GREATEST ACTION EPICS!
YOU HUMAN INSECT-- YOU'RE FINISHED!
SPIDEY BATTLES THE CHAMELEON!
SPIDEY BATTLES
A GUY NAMED JOE!

AMAZING SPIDER-MAN ANNUAL #7 REPRINTED *AMAZING SPIDER-MAN #2*. COVER ART BY John Romita Sr.

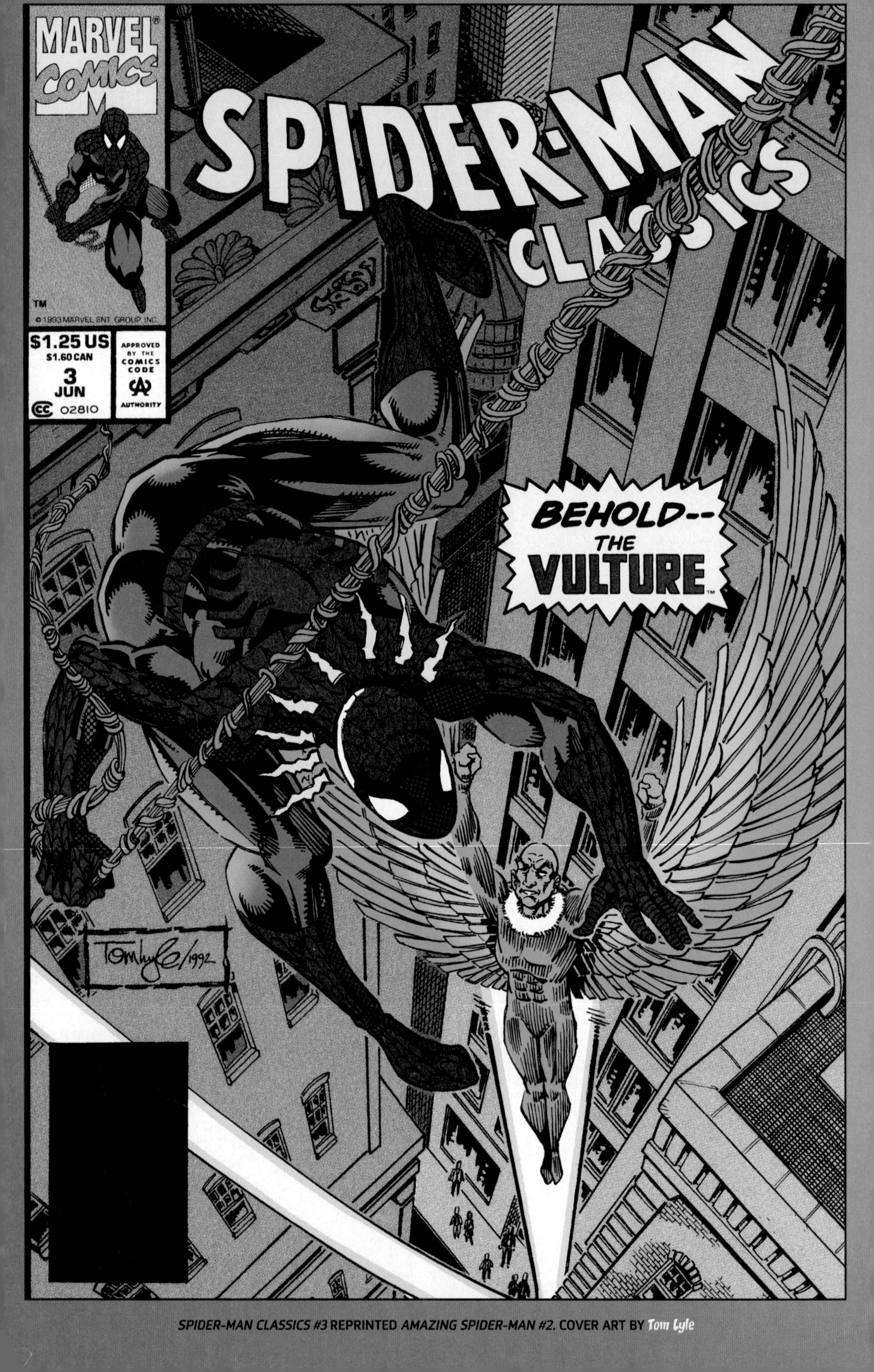
MARVEL COMICS
SPIDER-MAN CLASSICS
TM
© 1993 MARVEL ENT. GROUP, INC.
$1.25 US
$1.60 CAN
3
JUN
02810
APPROVED BY THE COMICS CODE AUTHORITY
BEHOLD-- THE VULTURE
TM

SPIDER-MAN CLASSICS #3 REPRINTED *AMAZING SPIDER-MAN #2*. COVER ART BY Tom Lyle

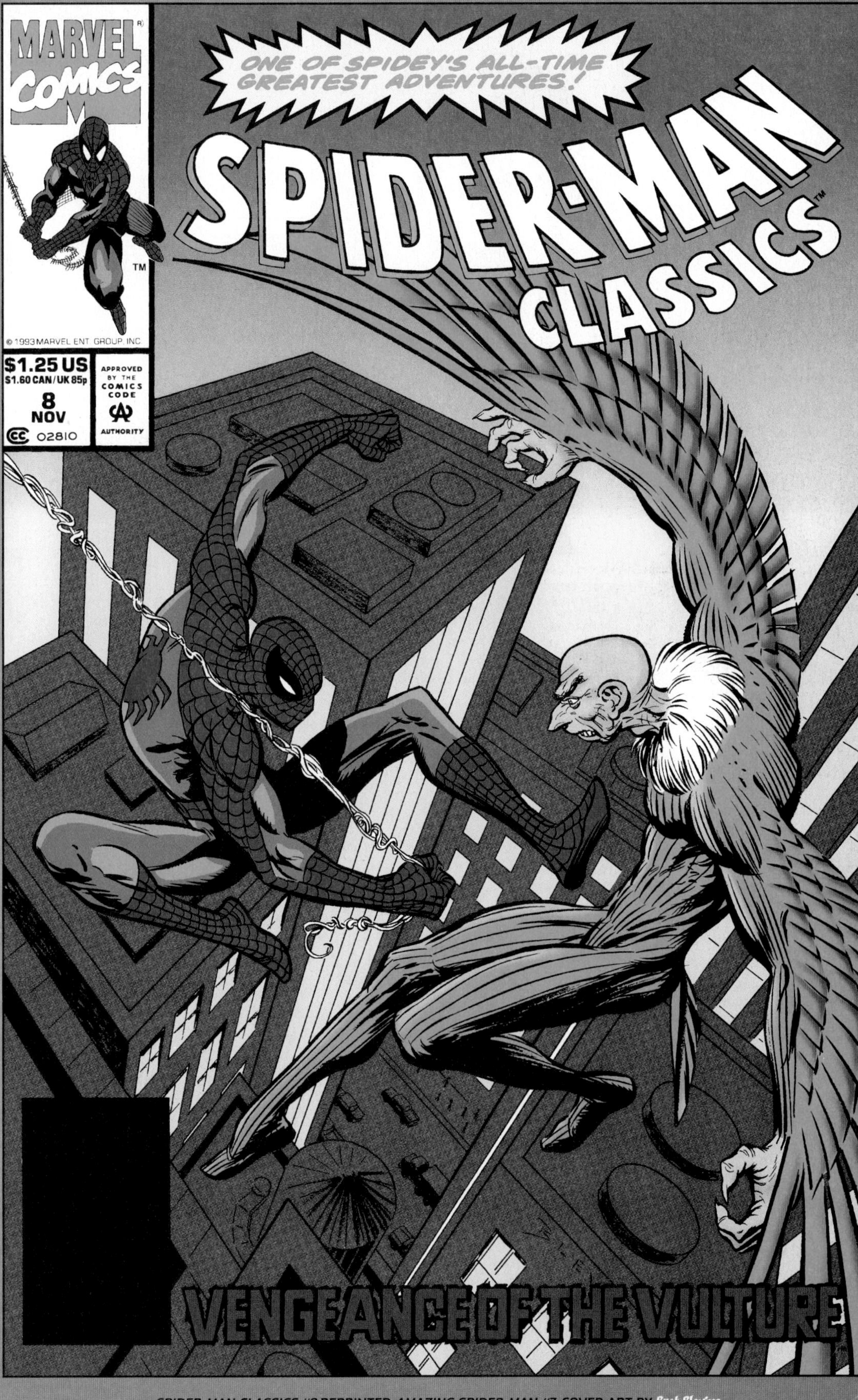

MARVEL COMICS
ONE OF SPIDEY'S ALL-TIME GREATEST ADVENTURES!
SPIDER-MAN CLASSICS
© 1993 MARVEL ENT. GROUP, INC.
$1.25 US
$1.60 CAN/UK 85p
8
NOV
02810
APPROVED BY THE COMICS CODE AUTHORITY
VENGEANCE OF THE VULTURE

SPIDER-MAN CLASSICS #8 REPRINTED *AMAZING SPIDER-MAN #7*. COVER ART BY Bret Blevins

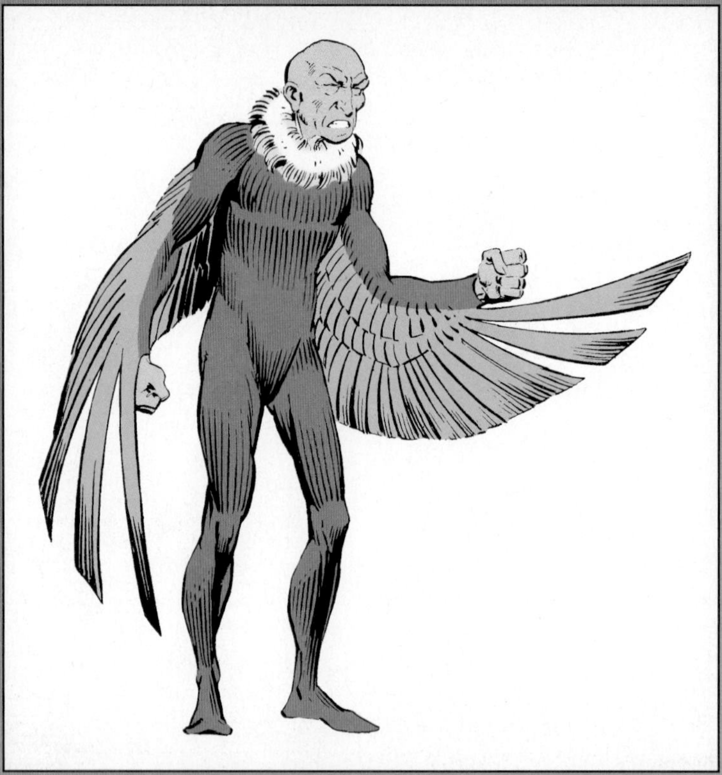

OFFICIAL HANDBOOK OF THE MARVEL UNIVERSE (1983) PROFILE ART BY Bret Blevins, Josef Rubinstein & Andy Yanchus

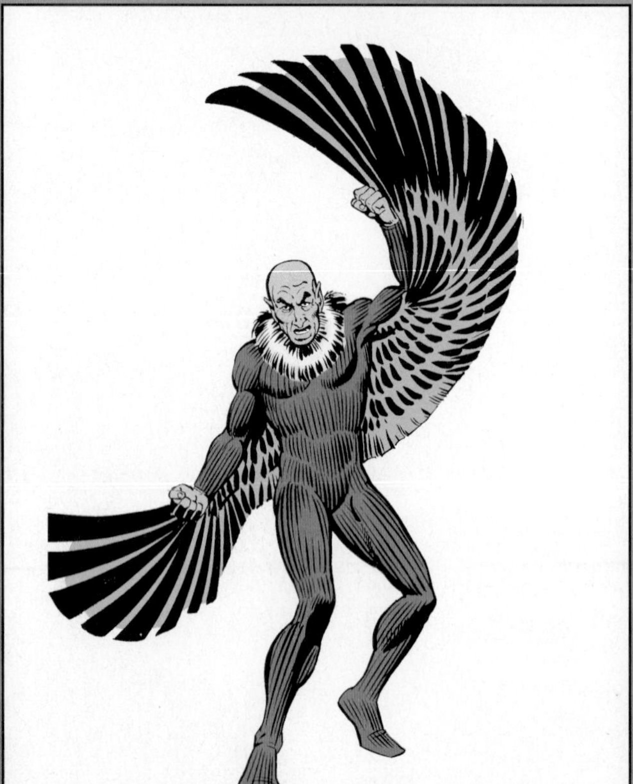

OFFICIAL HANDBOOK OF THE MARVEL UNIVERSE: DELUXE EDITION (1985) PROFILE ART BY Ron Frenz, Josef Rubinstein & Andy Yanchus

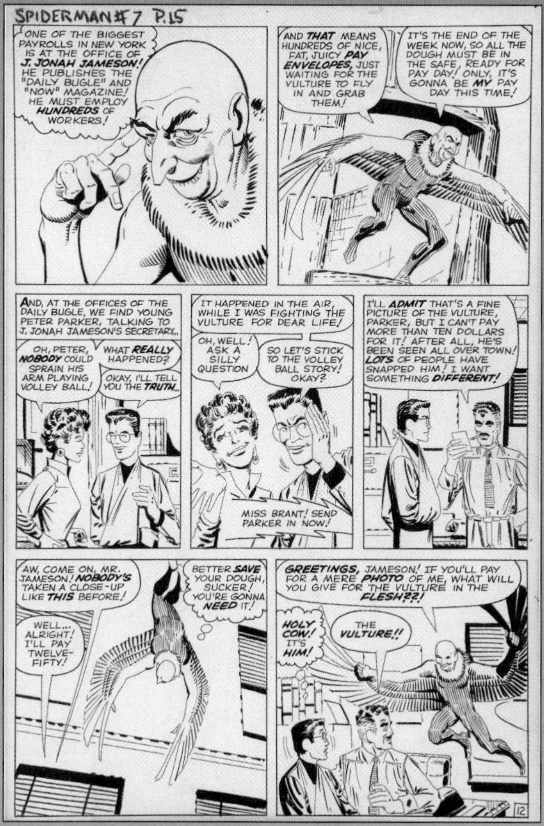

SPIDERMAN #7 P.15
ONE OF THE BIGGEST PAYROLLS IN NEW YORK IS AT THE OFFICE OF J. JONAH JAMESON! HE PUBLISHES THE "DAILY BUGLE" AND "NOW" MAGAZINE! HE MUST EMPLOY HUNDREDS OF WORKERS!
AND THAT MEANS HUNDREDS OF NICE, FAT, JUICY PAY ENVELOPES, JUST WAITING FOR THE VULTURE TO FLY IN AND GRAB THEM!
IT'S THE END OF THE WEEK NOW, SO ALL THE DOUGH MUST BE IN THE SAFE, READY FOR PAY DAY! ONLY, IT'S GONNA BE MY PAY DAY THIS TIME!
AND, AT THE OFFICES OF THE DAILY BUGLE, WE FIND YOUNG PETER PARKER, TALKING TO J. JONAH JAMESON'S SECRETARY...
OH, PETER, NOBODY COULD SPRAIN HIS ARM PLAYING VOLLEY BALL!
WHAT REALLY HAPPENED?
OKAY, I'LL TELL YOU THE TRUTH...
IT HAPPENED IN THE AIR, WHILE I WAS FIGHTING THE VULTURE FOR DEAR LIFE!
OH, WELL! ASK A SILLY QUESTION
SO LET'S STICK TO THE VOLLEY BALL STORY! OKAY?
MISS BRANT! SEND PARKER IN NOW!
I'LL ADMIT THAT'S A FINE PICTURE OF THE VULTURE, PARKER, BUT I CAN'T PAY MORE THAN TEN DOLLARS FOR IT! AFTER ALL, HE'S BEEN SEEN ALL OVER TOWN! LOTS OF PEOPLE HAVE SNAPPED HIM! I WANT SOMETHING DIFFERENT!
AW, COME ON, MR. JAMESON! NOBODY'S TAKEN A CLOSE-UP LIKE THIS BEFORE!
BETTER SAVE YOUR DOUGH, SUCKER! YOU'RE GONNA NEED IT!
WELL... ALRIGHT! I'LL PAY TWELVE-FIFTY!
GREETINGS, JAMESON! IF YOU'LL PAY FOR A MERE PHOTO OF ME, WHAT WILL YOU GIVE FOR THE VULTURE IN THE FLESH??!
HOLY COW! IT'S HIM!
THE VULTURE!!
12

AMAZING SPIDER-MAN #7, PAGE 12 ART
BY Steve Ditko

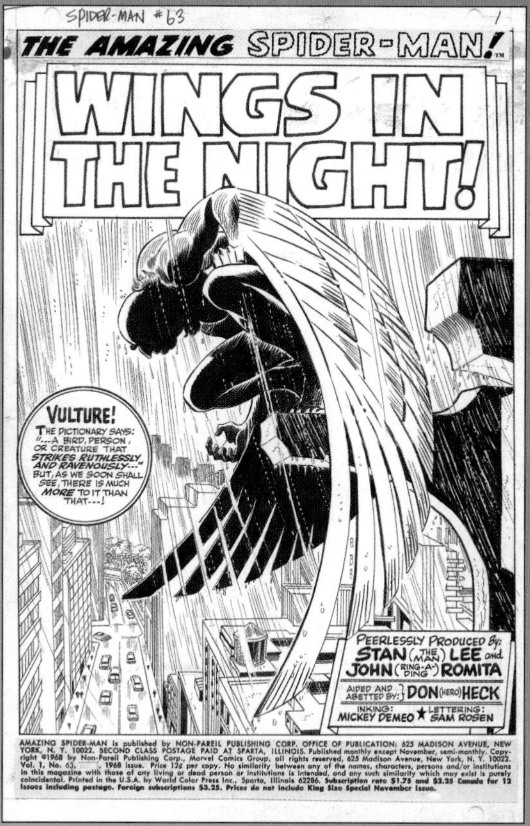

SPIDER-MAN #63
1
THE AMAZING SPIDER-MAN!
WINGS IN THE NIGHT!
VULTURE! THE DICTIONARY SAYS: "...A BIRD, PERSON, OR CREATURE THAT STRIKES RUTHLESSLY, AND RAVENOUSLY--" BUT, AS WE SOON SHALL SEE, THERE IS MUCH MORE TO IT THAN THAT---!
PEERLESSLY PRODUCED BY: STAN (THE MAN) LEE and JOHN (RING-A-DING) ROMITA
AIDED AND ABETTED BY: DON (HERO) HECK
INKING: MICKEY DEMEO ★ LETTERING: SAM ROSEN
AMAZING SPIDER-MAN is published by NON-PAREIL PUBLISHING CORP. OFFICE OF PUBLICATION: 625 MADISON AVENUE, NEW YORK, N. Y. 10022. SECOND CLASS POSTAGE PAID AT SPARTA, ILLINOIS. Published monthly except November, semi-monthly. Copyright ©1968 by Non-Pareil Publishing Corp., Marvel Comics Group, all rights reserved, 625 Madison Avenue, New York, N. Y. 10022. Vol. 1, No. 63, , 1968 issue. Price 12¢ per copy. No similarity between any of the names, characters, persons and/or institutions in this magazine with those of any living or dead person or institutions is intended, and any such similarity which may exist is purely coincidental. Printed in the U.S.A. by World Color Press Inc., Sparta, Illinois 62286. Subscription rate $1.75 and $2.25 Canada for 12 issues including postage. Foreign subscriptions $3.25. Prices do not include King Size Special November issue.

AMAZING SPIDER-MAN #63, PAGE 1 ART
BY John Romita Sr., Don Heck & Mike Esposito

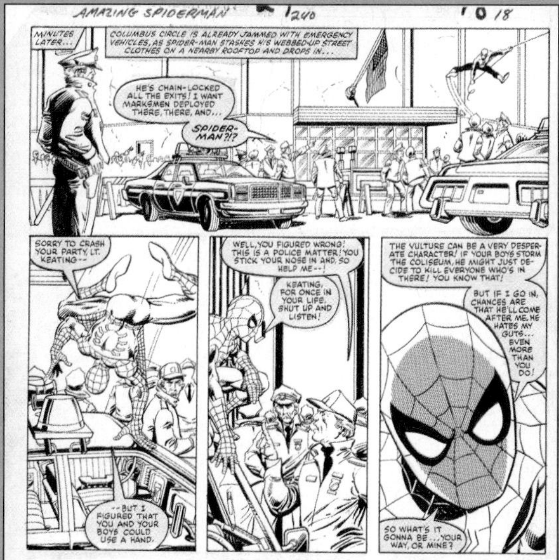

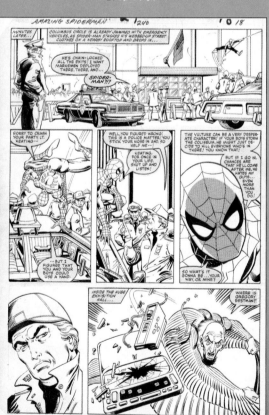

AMAZING SPIDERMAN 240
18
MINUTES LATER...
COLUMBUS CIRCLE IS ALREADY JAMMED WITH EMERGENCY VEHICLES, AS SPIDER-MAN STASHES HIS WEBBED-UP STREET CLOTHES ON A NEARBY ROOFTOP AND DROPS IN...
HE'S CHAIN-LOCKED ALL THE EXITS! I WANT MARKSMEN DEPLOYED THERE, THERE, AND...
SPIDER-MAN?!?
SORRY TO CRASH YOUR PARTY, LT. KEATING...
WELL, YOU FIGURED WRONG! THIS IS A POLICE MATTER! YOU STICK YOUR NOSE IN AND, SO HELP ME--!
KEATING, FOR ONCE IN YOUR LIFE, SHUT UP AND LISTEN!
--BUT I FIGURED THAT YOU AND YOUR BOYS COULD USE A HAND.
THE VULTURE CAN BE A VERY DESPERATE CHARACTER! IF YOUR BOYS STORM THE COLISEUM, HE MIGHT JUST DECIDE TO KILL EVERYONE WHO'S IN THERE! YOU KNOW THAT!
BUT IF I GO IN, CHANCES ARE THAT HE'LL COME AFTER ME. HE SPILLS MY GUTS... EVEN MORE THAN YOU DO!
SO WHAT'S IT GONNA BE... YOUR WAY, OR MINE?
INSIDE THE HUGE EXHIBITION HALL...
WHERE IS GREGORY BESTMAN?

AMAZING SPIDER-MAN #240, PAGE 14 ART
BY John Romita Jr. & Bob Layton

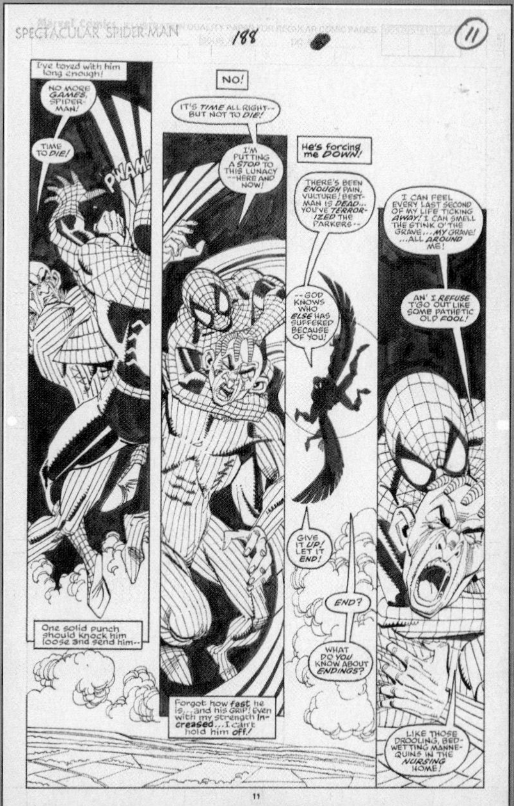

SPECTACULAR SPIDER-MAN 188
11
I've toyed with him long enough!
NO MORE GAMES, SPIDER-MAN!
TIME TO DIE!
PWAM!
NO!
IT'S TIME ALL RIGHT-- BUT NOT TO DIE!
I'M PUTTING A STOP TO THIS LUNACY --HERE AND NOW!
He's forcing me DOWN!
THERE'S BEEN ENOUGH PAIN, VULTURE! BESTMAN IS DEAD... YOU'VE TERRORIZED THE PARKERS--
--GOD KNOWS WHO ELSE HAS SUFFERED BECAUSE OF YOU!
I CAN FEEL EVERY LAST SECOND OF MY LIFE TICKING AWAY! I CAN SMELL THE STINK O' THE GRAVE... MY GRAVE! ...ALL AROUND ME!
AN' I REFUSE T'GO OUT LIKE SOME PATHETIC OLD FOOL!
GIVE IT UP! LET IT END!
END?
WHAT DO YOU KNOW ABOUT ENDINGS?
One solid punch should knock him loose and send him--
Forgot how fast he is... and his GRIP! Even with me, my strength increased... I can't hold him off!
LIKE THOSE DROOLING, BED-WETTING MANNEQUINS IN THE NURSING HOME!
11

SPECTACULAR SPIDER-MAN #188, PAGE 8 ART
BY Sal Buscema

COURTESY OF HERITAGEAUCTIONS.COM

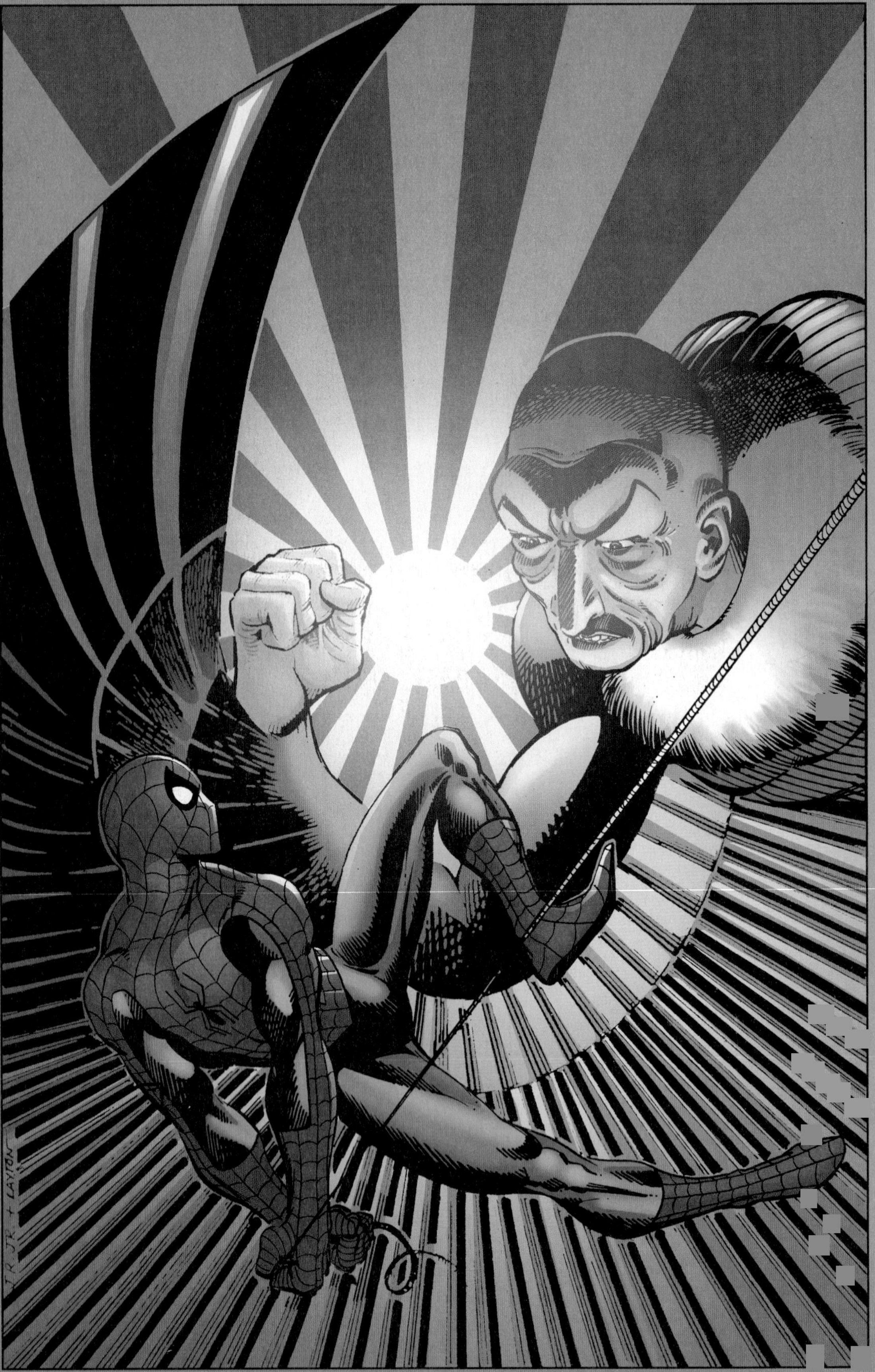

ESSENTIAL SPIDER-MAN VOL. 11 TPB COVER ART BY John Romita Jr., Bob Layton & John Kalisz

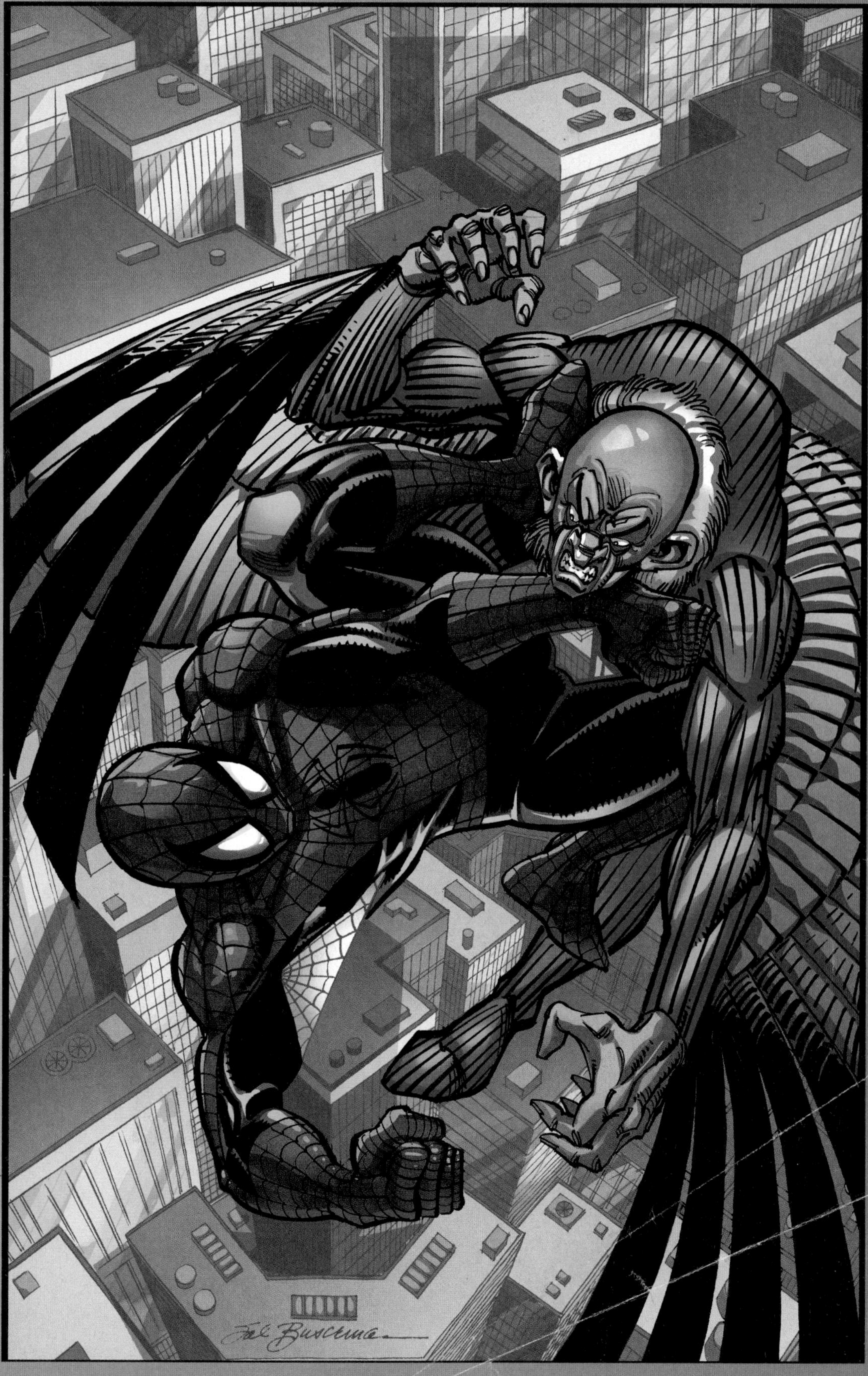
Sal Buscema

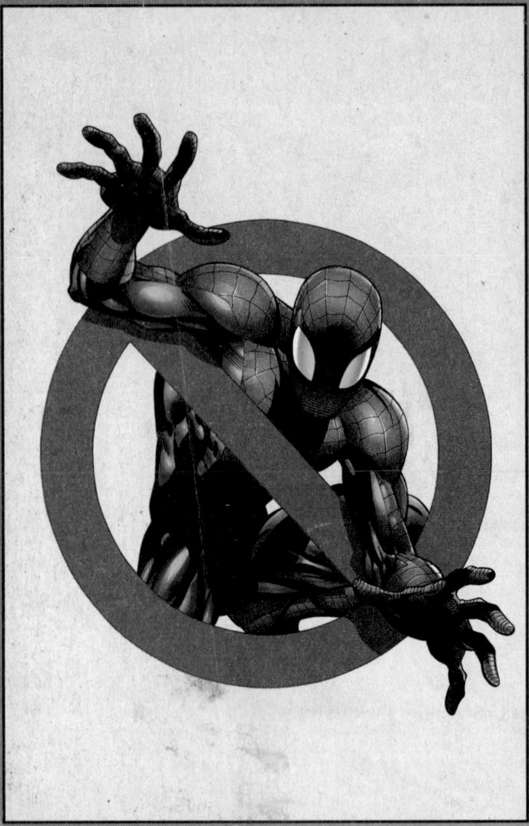

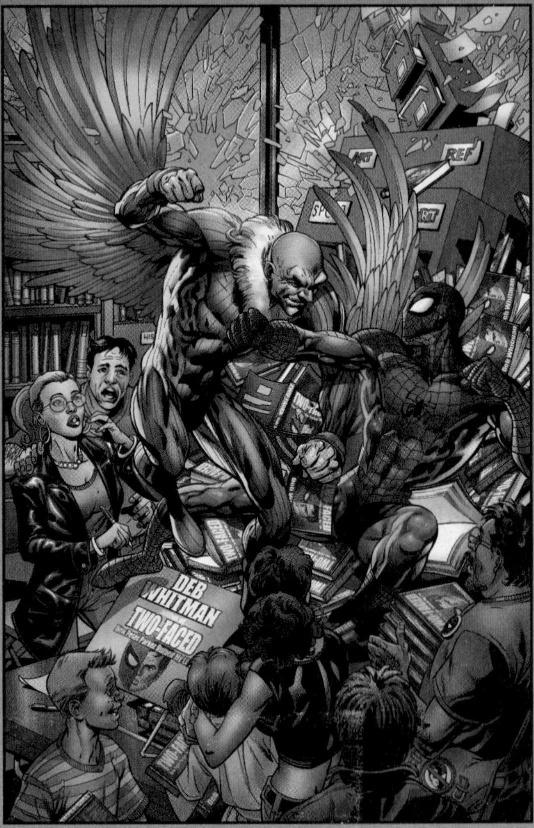
DEB
WHITMAN
TWO-FACED

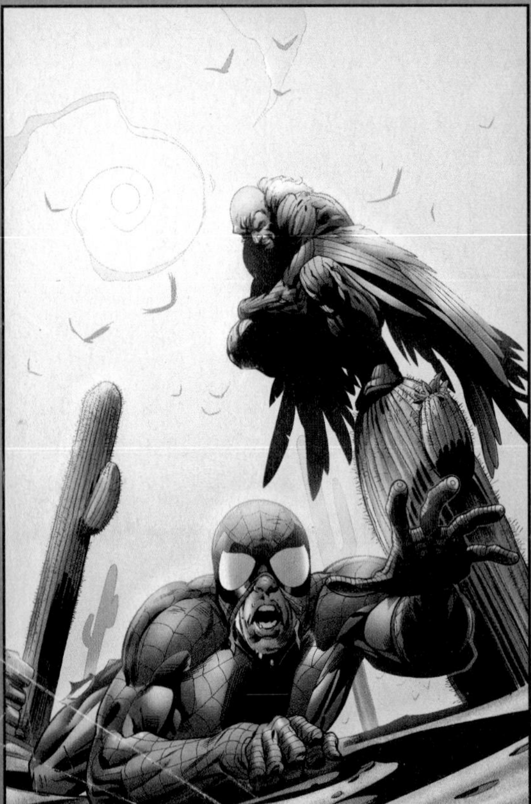